CONTENTS

	Page
Index to questions and answers	P.5
Analysis of past exams	P.10
Exam technique	P.11
AFM specific information	P.13
Kaplan's recommended revision approach	P.14
Kaplan's detailed revision plan	P.16
Mathematical tables and formulae sheet	P.22

Section

1	Practice questions – Section A	1
2	Practice questions – Section B	55
3	Answers to practice questions – Section A	131
4	Answers to practice questions – Section B	253

Key features in this edition

In addition to providing a wide ranging bank of real past exam questions, we have also included in this edition:

- An analysis of all of the recent examinations.

- AFM specific information and advice on exam technique.

- Our recommended approach to make your revision for this particular subject as effective as possible.

  This includes step by step guidance on how best to use our Kaplan material (Study Text, Pocket Notes and Exam Kit) at this stage in your studies.

- Enhanced tutorial answers packed with specific key answer tips, technical tutorial notes and exam technique tips from our experienced tutors.

- Complementary online resources including full tutor debriefs and question assistance to point you in the right direction when you get stuck.

You will find a wealth of other resources to help you with your studies on the following sites:

www.mykaplan.co.uk

http://future.accaglobal.com/changes-to-the-qualification/the-qualification-journey/strategic-professional/advanced-financial-management

Quality and accuracy are of the utmost importance to us so if you spot an error in any of our products, please send an email to mykaplanreporting@kaplan.com with full details.

Our Quality Co-ordinator will work with our technical team to verify the error and take action to ensure it is corrected in future editions.

INDEX TO QUESTIONS AND ANSWERS

INTRODUCTION

The majority of the questions within this kit are past ACCA exam questions. The index identifies which sitting the questions were from. An 'A' next to the question in the index means that the past exam question has been adapted in some way, for example some of the past exam questions have been modified to reflect the current format of the exam.

KEY TO THE INDEX

ENHANCEMENTS

We have added the following enhancements to the answers in this exam kit:

Key answer tips

All answers include key answer tips to help your understanding of each question.

Tutorial note

All answers include more tutorial notes to explain some of the technical points in more detail.

Top tutor tips

For selected questions, we 'walk through the answer' giving guidance on how to approach the questions with helpful 'tips from a top tutor', together with technical tutor notes.

These answers are indicated with the 'footsteps' icon in the index.

ONLINE ENHANCEMENTS

 Question debrief

For selected questions, we recommend that they are to be completed in full exam conditions (i.e. properly timed in a closed book environment).

In addition to the examiner's technical answer, enhanced with key answer tips and tutorial notes in this exam kit, online you can find an answer debrief by a top tutor that:

- works through the question in full

- points out how to approach the question

- how to ensure that the easy marks are obtained as quickly as possible, and

- emphasises how to tackle exam questions and exam technique.

These questions are indicated with the 'clock' icon in the index.

 Online question assistance

Have you ever looked at a question and not known where to start, or got stuck part way through?

For selected questions, we have produced 'Online question assistance' offering different levels of guidance, such as:

- ensuring that you understand the question requirements fully, highlighting key terms and the meaning of the verbs used

- how to read the question proactively, with knowledge of the requirements, to identify the topic areas covered

- assessing the detail content of the question body, pointing out key information and explaining why it is important

- help in devising a plan of attack

With this assistance, you should then be able to attempt your answer confident that you know what is expected of you.

These questions are indicated with the 'signpost' icon in the index.

Online question enhancements and answer debriefs will be available on MyKaplan at:

www.mykaplan.co.uk

Kaplan Publishing are constantly finding new ways to make a difference to your studies and our exciting online resources really do offer something different to students looking for exam success.

This book comes with free MyKaplan online resources so that you can study anytime, anywhere. This free online resource is not sold separately and is included in the price of the book.

Having purchased this book, you have access to the following online study materials:

CONTENT	ACCA (including FFA,FAB,FMA)		FIA (excluding FFA,FAB,FMA)	
	Text	Kit	Text	Kit
Eletronic version of the book	✓	✓	✓	✓
Check Your Understanding Test with instant answers	✓			
Material updates	✓	✓	✓	✓
Latest official ACCA exam questions*		✓		
Extra question assistance using the signpost icon**		✓		
Question debriefs using clock icon***		✓		
Consolidation Test including questions and answers	✓			

* Excludes AB, MA, FA, LW, FAB, FMA and FFA; for all other subjects includes a selection of questions, as released by ACCA

** For ACCA SBR, AFM, APM, AAA only

*** Excludes AB, MA, FA, LW, FAB, FMA and FFA

How to access your online resources

Kaplan Financial students will already have a MyKaplan account and these extra resources will be available to you online. You do not need to register again, as this process was completed when you enrolled. If you are having problems accessing online materials, please ask your course administrator.

If you are not studying with Kaplan and did not purchase your book via a Kaplan website, to unlock your extra online resources please go to www.mykaplan.co.uk/addabook (even if you have set up an account and registered books previously). You will then need to enter the ISBN number (on the title page and back cover) and the unique pass key number contained in the scratch panel below to gain access.

You will also be required to enter additional information during this process to set up or confirm your account details.

If you purchased through Kaplan Flexible Learning or via the Kaplan Publishing website you will automatically receive an e-mail invitation to MyKaplan. Please register your details using this email to gain access to your content. If you do not receive the e-mail or book content, please contact Kaplan Publishing.

Your Code and Information

This code can only be used once for the registration of one book online. This registration and your online content will expire when the final sittings for the examinations covered by this book have taken place. Please allow one hour from the time you submit your book details for us to process your request.

Please scratch the film to access your MyKaplan code.

Please be aware that this code is case-sensitive and you will need to include the dashes within the passcode, but not when entering the ISBN. For further technical support, please visit www.MyKaplan.co.uk

ACC

Strategic Professio – Options

Advanced Financial Management (AFM)

EXAM KIT

KAPLAN

PUBLISHING

British Library Cataloguing-in-Publication Data

A catalogue record for this book is available from the British Library.

Published by:

Kaplan Publishing UK
Unit 2 The Business Centre
Molly Millar's Lane
Wokingham
Berkshire
RG41 2QZ

ISBN: 978-1-78740-110-5

Printed and bound in Great Britain

Acknowledgements

These materials are reviewed by the ACCA examining team. The objective of the review is to ensure that the material properly covers the syllabus and study guide outcomes, used by the examining team in setting the exams, in the appropriate breadth and depth. The review does not ensure that every eventuality, combination or application of examinable topics is addressed by the ACCA Approved Content. Nor does the review comprise a detailed technical check of the content as the Approved Content Provider has its own quality assurance processes in place in this respect.

The past ACCA examination questions are the copyright of the Association of Chartered Certified Accountants. The original answers to the questions from June 1994 onwards were produced by the examiners themselves and have been adapted by Kaplan Publishing.

We are grateful to the Chartered Institute of Management Accountants and the Institute of Chartered Accountants in England and Wales for permission to reproduce past examination questions. The answers have been prepared by Kaplan Publishing.

SECTION A-TYPE QUESTIONS

			Question	Answer	Past exam
			Page number		

Page number

			Question	Answer	Past exam

Role of senior financial adviser in the multinational organisation

1	Vadener plc		1	131	*Jun 06(A)*

Advanced investment appraisal

2	Wurrall Inc		3	134	*Jun 04 (A)*
3	Daron		6	138	*Dec 95 (A)*
4	Sleepon Hotels Inc		8	145	*Dec 05 (A)*
5	Blipton International		10	150	*Dec 08 (A)*
6	Tramont Co		12	155	*Pilot 12*
7	Chmura Co		14	160	*Dec 13*
8	Yilandwe		16	166	*Jun 15*

Acquisitions and mergers

9	Stanzial Inc		19	171	*Dec 06 (A)*
10	Burcolene		21	176	*Dec 07 (A)*
11	Pursuit Co		23	181	*Jun 11 (A)*
12	Nente Co		25	185	*Jun 12 (A)*
13	Mlima Co		27	189	*Jun 13*
14	Nahara Co and Fugae Co		30	195	*Dec 14*

Corporate reconstruction and reorganisation

15	BBS Stores		32	200	*Jun 09 (A)*
16	Cigno Co		35	206	*Sep/Dec 15*
17	Morada Co		38	212	*Sep/Dec 16*
18	Chrysos Co		40	218	*Mar/Jun 17*
19	Conejo Co		43	223	*Sep/Dec 17*

Treasury and advanced risk management techniques

20	Lammer plc		46	230	*Jun 06 (A)*
21	Casasophia Co		47	234	*Jun 11 (A)*
22	CMC Co		49	239	*Specimen 18*
23	Lirio Co		51	245	*Mar/Jun 16*

SECTION B-TYPE QUESTIONS

			Page number		
			Question	*Answer*	*Past exam*

Role of senior financial adviser in the multinational organisation

24	Moose Co		55	253	*Dec 09 (A)*
25	Lamri Co		56	255	*Dec 10 (A)*
26	Strom Co		57	258	*Dec 12 (A)*
27	Ennea Co		58	261	*Jun 12*
28	Limni Co		60	264	*Jun 13*
29	Chawan Co		61	267	*Jun 15*
30	Chithurst Co		63	270	*Sep/Dec 16*
31	Bournelorth Co		64	274	*Mar/Jun 17*
32	High K Co		65	277	*Sep/Dec 17*

Advanced investment appraisal

33	Strayer Inc		68	281	*Jun 02 (A)*
34	Digunder		68	284	*Dec 07 (A)*
35	Kenand Co		69	287	–
36	Fubuki Co		70	291	*Dec 10*
37	Investment project review		72	295	*Jun 09 (A)*
38	MMC		73	299	*Jun 11 (A)*
39	Tisa Co		73	301	*Jun 12 (A)*
40	Coeden Co		75	303	*Dec 12 (A)*
41	Arbore Co		76	305	*Dec 12 (A)*
42	Burung Co		78	307	*Specimen 18*
43	Riviere Co		79	310	*Dec 14*
44	Furlion Co		80	314	*Mar/Jun 16*
45	Fernhurst Co		81	317	*Sep/Dec 16*
46	Moonstar Co		83	320	*Sep/Dec 15*
47	GNT Co		84	323	*Pilot 12*
48	Toltuck Co		85	326	*Mar/Jun 17*

			Page number		
			Question	Answer	Past exam

Acquisitions and mergers

49	Kodiak Company		86	329	Dec 09 (A)
50	Kilenc Co		88	332	Jun 12 (A)
51	Sigra Co		89	335	Dec 12 (A)
52	Makonis Co		90	337	Dec 13
53	Vogel Co		91	340	Jun 14
54	Louieed Co		93	343	Mar/Jun 16
55	Hav Co		94	347	Specimen 18

Corporate reconstruction and reorganisation

56	Alaska Salvage		96	350	Dec 09 (A)
57	Proteus Co		97	353	Dec 11 (A)
58	Doric Co	🕐	98	356	Pilot 12
59	Nubo Co		100	358	Dec 13
60	Bento Co		101	361	Jun 15
61	Flufftort Co		103	364	Sep/Dec 15
62	Staple Group		105	369	Mar/Jun 16
63	Eview Cinemas Co		107	372	Sep/Dec 17

Treasury and advanced risk management techniques

64	Faoilean Co		110	375	Jun 14
65	Levante Co		110	378	Dec 11 (A)
66	Sembilan Co		111	381	Jun 12 (A)
67	Pault Co		112	384	Sep/Dec 16
68	Interest Rate Hedges	▨	113	387	Jun 05 (A)
69	Arnbrook plc		114	389	Jun 06 (A)
70	Pondhills		115	391	Jun 01 (A)
71	Currency Swaps		116	394	Dec 04 (A)
72	FNDC plc		117	396	Dec 06 (A)
73	Lignum Co		118	399	Dec 12 (A)
74	Alecto Co		120	402	Pilot 12
75	Kenduri Co		121	405	Jun 13
76	Awan Co	◪	122	408	Dec 13
77	Keshi Co		123	411	Dec 14
78	Daikon Co		124	414	Jun 15
79	The Armstrong Group		126	417	Sep/Dec 15
80	Buryecs Co		127	421	Mar/Jun 17
81	Wardegul Co		128	424	Sep/Dec 17

ANALYSIS OF PAST EXAMS

The table below summarises the key topics that have been tested in recent Advanced Financial Management examinations. The list of topics matches the chapter titles in the Kaplan Study Text.

Note that the references are to the number of the question in this edition of the Exam Kit.

Topic	Dec 14	Jun 15	Sep/Dec 15	Mar/Jun 16	Sep/Dec 16	Mar/Jun 17	Sep/Dec 17
The role and responsibility of the financial manager	Q77	Q8		Q62			Q81
Investment appraisal	Q14, Q43				Q45		
International operations and international investment appraisal	Q14, Q43	Q8	Q46	Q44			
The financing decision	Q77	Q29	Q46	Q23		Q31	Q32
The dividend decision				Q23	Q30		
WACC					Q17	Q48	Q19, Q63
Risk adjusted WACC and APV			Q16		Q17		
Option pricing				Q44			
An introduction to risk management	Q14, Q43	Q78			Q17, Q45	Q31	
Hedging foreign exchange risk			Q79	Q23		Q80	
Hedging interest rate risk	Q77	Q78	Q79		Q67		Q81
Strategic aspects of acquisitions	Q14		Q16	Q54		Q18	
Business valuation	Q14	Q60	Q16	Q23, Q54	Q30	Q18, Q48	Q19, Q63
Corporate failure/ reconstruction		Q29, Q60	Q16, Q61	Q62		Q18	Q19, Q32, Q63

EXAM TECHNIQUE

GENERAL COMMENTS

- We recommend that you spend **15 minutes reading the paper** at the beginning of the exam:

    - read the questions and examination requirements carefully, and

    - begin planning your answers.

    See the AFM Specific Information for advice on how to use this time for this paper.

- If 15 minutes are spent reading the examination paper, this leaves three hours to attempt the questions.

- **Divide the time** you spend on questions in proportion to the marks on offer:

    - one suggestion for this examination is to allocate 1.8 minutes to each mark available (180 minutes/100 marks), so a 25 mark question should be completed in approximately 45 minutes. If you plan to spend more or less time than 15 minutes reading the paper, your time allocation per mark will be different.

    - within that, try to allow time at the end of each question to review your answer and address any obvious issues

    Whatever happens, always keep your eye on the clock and **do not over run on any part of any question!**

- If you **get completely stuck** with a question:

    - leave space in your answer book, and

    - **return to it later.**

- Stick to the question and **tailor your answer** to what you are asked.

    - Pay particular attention to the verbs in the question.

    - Try to apply your comments to the scenario where possible.

- If you do not understand what a question is asking, **state your assumptions**.

    Even if you do not answer in precisely the way the examiner hoped, you should be given some credit, if your assumptions are reasonable.

- You should do everything you can to make things easy for the marker.

    The marker will find it easier to identify the points you have made if your **answers are legible**.

WRITTEN TEST QUESTIONS

- **Written elements**:

  Your answer should have:

  - a clear structure

  - a brief introduction, a main section and a conclusion.

  Be concise.

  It is better to write a little about a lot of different points than a great deal about one or two points.

  Where possible, try to relate comments to the specific context given rather than your answer looking like it was simply copied out of the textbook.

- **Computations**:

  It is essential to include all your workings in your answers.

  Many computational questions require the use of a standard format:

  e.g. net present value

  Be sure you know these formats thoroughly before the exam and use the layouts that you see in the answers given in this book and in model answers.

AFM SPECIFIC INFORMATION

THE EXAM

FORMAT OF THE EXAM

		Number of marks
Section A:	1 compulsory question worth 50 marks	50
Section B:	2 compulsory questions worth 25 marks each	50
		———
		100
Total time allowed: 3 hours and 15 minutes		———

AIM

To apply relevant knowledge, skills and exercise professional judgement as expected of a senior financial executive or advisor, in taking or recommending decisions relating to the financial management of an organisation.

OBJECTIVES

On successful completion of this exam, candidates should be able to:

- Explain and evaluate the role and responsibility of the senior financial executive or advisor in meeting conflicting needs of stakeholders and recognise the role of international financial institutions in the financial management of multinationals

- Evaluate potential investment decisions and assessing their financial and strategic consequences, both domestically and internationally

- Assess and plan acquisitions and mergers as an alternative growth strategy

- Evaluate and advise on alternative corporate re-organisation strategies

- Apply and evaluate alternative advanced treasury and risk management techniques

PASS MARK

The pass mark is 50%.

DETAILED SYLLABUS

The detailed syllabus and study guide written by the ACCA can be found at:

http://future.accaglobal.com/changes-to-the-qualification/the-qualification-journey/strategic-professional/advanced-financial-management

KAPLAN'S RECOMMENDED REVISION APPROACH

QUESTION PRACTICE IS THE KEY TO SUCCESS

Success in professional examinations relies upon you acquiring a firm grasp of the required knowledge at the tuition phase. In order to be able to do the questions, knowledge is essential.

However, the difference between success and failure often hinges on your exam technique on the day and making the most of the revision phase of your studies.

The **Kaplan Study Text** is the starting point, designed to provide the underpinning knowledge to tackle all questions. However, in the revision phase, pouring over text books is not the answer.

Kaplan Online fixed tests help you consolidate your knowledge and understanding and are a useful tool to check whether you can remember key topic areas.

Kaplan Pocket Notes are designed to help you quickly revise a topic area; however you then need to practise questions. There is a need to progress to full exam standard questions as soon as possible, and to tie your exam technique and technical knowledge together.

The importance of question practice cannot be over-emphasised.

The recommended approach below is designed by expert tutors in the field, in conjunction with their knowledge of the examiner and their recent real exams.

The approach taken for the Applied Knowledge and Applied Skills exams is to revise by topic area. However, with the Strategic Professional exams, a multi topic approach is required to answer the scenario based questions.

You need to practise as many questions as possible in the time you have left.

OUR AIM

Our aim is to get you to the stage where you can attempt exam standard questions confidently, to time, in a closed book environment, with no supplementary help (i.e. to simulate the real examination experience).

Practising your exam technique on real past examination questions, in timed conditions, is also vitally important for you to assess your progress and identify areas of weakness that may need more attention in the final run up to the examination.

In order to achieve this we recognise that initially you may feel the need to practise some questions with open book help and exceed the required time.

The approach below shows you which questions you should use to build up to coping with exam standard question practice, and references to the sources of information available should you need to revisit a topic area in more detail.

KAPLAN PUBLISHING

Remember that in the real examination, all you have to do is:

- attempt all questions required by the exam
- only spend the allotted time on each question, and
- get them at least 50% right!

Try to practise this approach on every question you attempt from now to the real exam.

EXAMINER'S COMMENTS

We have included many of the examiner's comments to the examination questions in this kit for you to see the main pitfalls that students fall into with regard to technical content.

However, too many times in the general section of the report, the examiner comments that students had failed due to:

- 'misallocation of time'
- 'running out of time' and
- showing signs of 'spending too much time on an earlier question and clearly rushing the answer to a subsequent question'.

Good exam technique is vital.

THE KAPLAN AFM REVISION PLAN

Stage 1: Assess areas of strengths and weaknesses

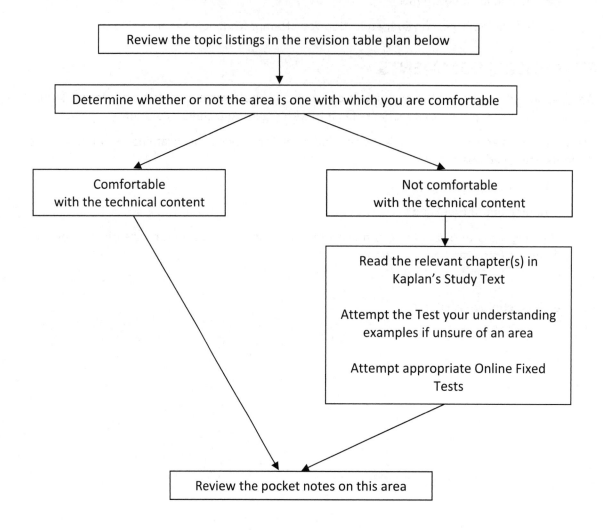

Stage 2: Practise questions

Follow the order of revision of topics as recommended in the revision table plan below and attempt the questions in the order suggested.

Try to avoid referring to text books and notes and the model answer until you have completed your attempt.

Try to answer the question in the allotted time.

Review your attempt with the model answer and assess how much of the answer you achieved in the allocated exam time.

Fill in the self-assessment box below and decide on your best course of action.

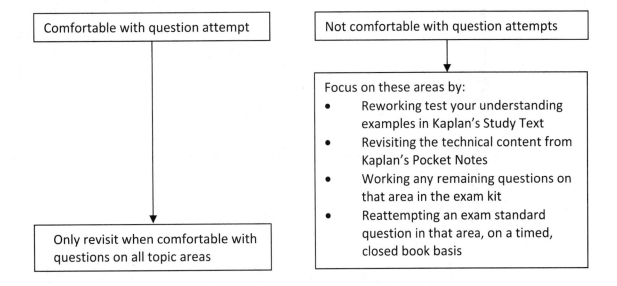

Comfortable with question attempt	Not comfortable with question attempts

Focus on these areas by:

- Reworking test your understanding examples in Kaplan's Study Text
- Revisiting the technical content from Kaplan's Pocket Notes
- Working any remaining questions on that area in the exam kit
- Reattempting an exam standard question in that area, on a timed, closed book basis

Only revisit when comfortable with questions on all topic areas

Note that:

 The 'signpost questions' offer online question assistance to help you to attempt your question confidently and know what is expected of you.

 The 'clock questions' have an online debrief where a tutor talks you through the exam technique and approach to that question and works the question in full.

Stage 3: Final pre-exam revision

We recommend that you **attempt at least one three hour and fifteen minutes mock examination** containing a set of previously unseen exam standard questions.

It is important that you get a feel for the breadth of coverage of a real exam without advanced knowledge of the topic areas covered – just as you will expect to see on the real exam day.

Ideally this mock should be sat in timed, closed book, real exam conditions and could be a mock examination offered by your tuition provider.

KAPLAN'S DETAILED REVISION PLAN

Module 1: Investment appraisal and WACC

Topic	Study Text Chapter	Pocket notes Chapter	Questions to attempt	Tutor guidance	Date attempted	Self-assessment
WACC	6	6	–	Before you can start appraising projects, it is vital to understand how the WACC can be calculated. Notice that several formulae used to derive WACC appear on the formula sheet. Make sure you identify which need to be learned and which are given.		
Investment appraisal	2	2	45	Investment appraisal is very commonly tested. Make sure you understand NPV and MIRR in particular.		
Foreign investment appraisal	3	3	5, 8	Foreign NPV is very similar to 'normal' NPV. The parity theories are frequently tested, so learn how to apply the formulae.		
Risk adjusted WACC	7	7	39	Degearing and regearing betas is one of the examiner's favourite topics. The formula is given in the exam, but learn how to apply it.		
APV	7	7	36	APV questions are very common. The key is to remember to discount the investment cash flows at an ungeared cost of equity and the financing cash flows using the risk free rate.		
Module 1 Revision Test			**4, 6, 17, 41, 42**	**Attempt these questions to check your understanding of Module 1 topics.**		

KAPLAN PUBLISHING

Module 2: Acquisitions and business valuation

Topic	Study Text Chapter	Pocket notes Chapter	Questions to attempt	Tutor guidance	Date attempted	Self-assessment
Strategic aspects of acquisitions	12	12	50	Valuation questions tend to contain calculations and discussion. This chapter covers the key discursive aspects.		
Free cash flow analysis	13	13	11, 12	The examiner's favourite method of business valuation is the discounted free cash flow approach, so revise the method from Chapter 13.		
Business valuation	13	13	9	Now cover the other valuation methods. Questions will tend to mix discursive and computational elements, so focus on both aspects.		
Module 2 Revision Test			*14, 48, 52, 54, 63*	*Attempt these questions to check your understanding of Module 1 and 2 topics.*		

Module 3: Option pricing, corporate failure and roles/responsibilities of the financial manager

Topic	Study Text Chapter	Pocket notes Chapter	Questions to attempt	Tutor guidance	Date attempted	Self-assessment
Option pricing	8	8	34, 38, 56	The Black Scholes formulae are given on the formula sheet, but make sure you can apply them in various circumstances.		
Corporate failure/ reconstruction	14	14	32, 58	This is a very topical area, so highly examinable. Learn the indicators of financial distress and the calculation of ratios.		
Roles/responsibilities of the financial manager	1	1	26			
Module 3 Revision Test			*7, 16, 18, 44, 62, 64*	*Attempt these questions to check your understanding of Module 1, 2 and 3 topics.*		

Module 4: Risk management and hedging

Topic	Study Text Chapter	Pocket notes Chapter	Questions to attempt	Tutor guidance	Date attempted	Self-assessment
Risk management	9	9	43	Chapter 9 gives a good introduction to risk management topics.		
Hedging – currency risk	10	10	20, 21	Learn the different methods of hedging. The key here is to adapt a systematic approach, laying out your workings carefully so that you don't get muddled.		
Hedging – interest rate risk	11	11	68, 74	As with currency hedging, learn all the methods, and the advantages and disadvantages of using each of them.		
Swaps	10, 11	10, 11	69, 80	Swaps are often overlooked by some students who focus mainly on futures and options. However, they are quite frequently tested.		
Module 4 Revision Test			**22, 23, 76, 79, 81**	**Attempt these questions to check your understanding of Module 1, 2, 3 and 4 topics.**		

Note that not all of the questions are referred to in the programme above. The remaining questions are available in the kit for extra practice for those who require more questions on some areas.

MATHEMATICAL TABLES AND FORMULAE SHEET

Modigliani and Miller Proposition 2 (with tax)

$$k_e = k_e^i + (1 - T)(k_e^i - k_d)\frac{V_d}{V_e}$$

The Capital Asset Pricing Model

$$E(r_i) = R_f + \beta_i(E(r_m) - R_f)$$

The asset beta formula

$$\beta_a = \left[\frac{V_e}{(V_e + V_d(1-T))}\beta_e\right] + \left[\frac{V_d(1-T)}{(V_e + V_d(1-T))}\beta_d\right]$$

The Growth Model

$$P_0 = \frac{D_0(1+g)}{(r_e - g)}$$

Gordon's growth approximation

$$g = br_e$$

The weighted average cost of capital

$$WACC = \left[\frac{V_e}{V_e + V_d}\right]k_e + \left[\frac{V_d}{V_e + V_d}\right]k_d(1-T)$$

The Fisher formula

$$(1+i) = (1+r)(1+h)$$

Purchasing power parity and interest rate parity

$$S_1 = S_0 \times \frac{(1+h_c)}{(1+h_b)} \qquad F_0 = S_0 \times \frac{(1+i_c)}{(1+i_b)}$$

Modified Internal Rate of Return

$$MIRR = \left[\frac{PV_R}{PV_I}\right]^{\frac{1}{n}}(1+r_e)-1$$

The Black-Scholes option pricing model

$$c = P_aN(d_1) - P_eN(d_2)e^{-rt}$$

Where:

$$d_1 = \frac{\ln(P_a/P_e)+(r+0.5s^2)t}{s\sqrt{t}}$$

$$d_2 = d_1 - s\sqrt{t}$$

The Put Call Parity relationship

$$p = c - P_a + P_ee^{-rt}$$

MATHEMATICAL TABLES

Standard normal distribution table

	0.00	0.01	0.02	0.03	0.04	0.05	0.06	0.07	0.08	0.09
0.0	.0000	.0040	.0080	.0120	.0159	.0199	.0239	.0279	.0319	.0359
0.1	.0398	.0438	.0478	.0517	.0557	.0596	.0636	.0675	.0714	.0753
0.2	.0793	.0832	.0871	.0910	.0948	.0987	.1026	.1064	.1103	.1141
0.3	.1179	.1217	.1255	.1293	.1331	.1368	.1406	.1443	.1480	.1517
0.4	.1554	.1591	.1628	.1664	.1700	.1736	.1772	.1808	.1844	.1879
0.5	.1915	.1950	.1985	.2019	.2054	.2088	.2123	.2157	.2190	.2224
0.6	.2257	.2291	.2324	.2357	.2389	.2422	.2454	.2486	.2518	.2549
0.7	.2580	.2611	.2642	.2673	.2704	.2734	.2764	.2794	.2823	.2852
0.8	.2881	.2910	.2939	.2967	.2995	.3023	.3051	.3078	.3106	.3133
0.9	.3159	.3186	.3212	.3238	.3264	.3289	.3315	.3340	.3365	.3389
1.0	.3413	.3438	.3461	.3485	.3508	.3531	.3554	.3577	.3599	.3621
1.1	.3643	.3665	.3686	.3708	.3729	.3749	.3770	.3790	.3810	.3830
1.2	.3849	.3869	.3888	.3907	.3925	.3944	.3962	.3980	.3997	.4015
1.3	.4032	.4049	.4066	.4082	.4099	.4115	.4131	.4147	.4162	.4177
1.4	.4192	.4207	.4222	.4236	.4251	.4265	.4279	.4292	.4306	.4319
1.5	.4332	.4345	.4357	.4370	.4382	.4394	.4406	.4418	.4430	.4441
1.6	.4452	.4463	.4474	.4485	.4495	.4505	.4515	.4525	.4535	.4545
1.7	.4554	.4564	.4573	.4582	.4591	.4599	.4608	.4616	.4625	.4633
1.8	.4641	.4649	.4656	.4664	.4671	.4678	.4686	.4693	.4699	.4706
1.9	.4713	.4719	.4726	.4732	.4738	.4744	.4750	.4756	.4762	.4767
2.0	.4772	.4778	.4783	.4788	.4793	.4798	.4803	.4808	.4812	.4817
2.1	.4821	.4826	.4830	.4834	.4838	.4842	.4846	.4850	.4854	.4857
2.2	.4861	.4865	.4868	.4871	.4875	.4878	.4881	.4884	.4887	.4890
2.3	.4893	.4896	.4898	.4901	.4904	.4906	.4909	.4911	.4913	.4916
2.4	.4918	.4920	.4922	.4925	.4927	.4929	.4931	.4932	.4934	.4936
2.5	.4938	.4940	.4941	.4943	.4945	.4946	.4948	.4949	.4951	.4952
2.6	.4953	.4955	.4956	.4957	.4959	.4960	.4961	.4962	.4963	.4964
2.7	.4965	.4966	.4967	.4968	.4969	.4970	.4971	.4972	.4973	.4974
2.8	.4974	.4975	.4976	.4977	.4977	.4978	.4979	.4980	.4980	.4981
2.9	.4981	.4982	.4983	.4983	.4984	.4984	.4985	.4985	.4986	.4986
3.0	.4987	.4987	.4987	.4988	.4988	.4989	.4989	.4989	.4990	.4990

This table can be used to calculate $N(d_1)$, the cumulative normal distribution function needed for the Black-Scholes model of option pricing. If $d_1 > 0$, add 0.5 to the relevant number above. If $d_1 < 0$, subtract the relevant number above from 0.5.

Present value table

Present value of 1, i.e. $(1 + r)^{-n}$

where   r = discount rate

n = number of periods until payment

Periods (n)	1%	2%	3%	4%	5%	6%	7%	8%	9%	10%
1	0.990	0.980	0.971	0.962	0.952	0.943	0.935	0.926	0.917	0.909
2	0.980	0.961	0.943	0.925	0.907	0.890	0.873	0.857	0.842	0.826
3	0.971	0.942	0.915	0.889	0.864	0.840	0.816	0.794	0.772	0.751
4	0.961	0.924	0.888	0.855	0.823	0.792	0.763	0.735	0.708	0.683
5	0.951	0.906	0.863	0.822	0.784	0.747	0.713	0.681	0.650	0.621
6	0.942	0.888	0.837	0.790	0.746	0.705	0.666	0.630	0.596	0.564
7	0.933	0.871	0.813	0.760	0.711	0.665	0.623	0.583	0.547	0.513
8	0.923	0.853	0.789	0.731	0.677	0.627	0.582	0.540	0.502	0.467
9	0.914	0.837	0.766	0.703	0.645	0.592	0.544	0.500	0.460	0.424
10	0.905	0.820	0.744	0.676	0.614	0.558	0.508	0.463	0.422	0.386
11	0.896	0.804	0.722	0.650	0.585	0.527	0.475	0.429	0.388	0.350
12	0.887	0.788	0.701	0.625	0.557	0.497	0.444	0.397	0.356	0.319
13	0.879	0.773	0.681	0.601	0.530	0.469	0.415	0.368	0.326	0.290
14	0.870	0.758	0.661	0.577	0.505	0.442	0.388	0.340	0.299	0.263
15	0.861	0.743	0.642	0.555	0.481	0.417	0.362	0.315	0.275	0.239

Periods (n)	11%	12%	13%	14%	15%	16%	17%	18%	19%	20%
1	0.901	0.893	0.885	0.877	0.870	0.862	0.855	0.847	0.840	0.833
2	0.812	0.797	0.783	0.769	0.756	0.743	0.731	0.718	0.706	0.694
3	0.731	0.712	0.693	0.675	0.658	0.641	0.624	0.609	0.593	0.579
4	0.659	0.636	0.613	0.592	0.572	0.552	0.534	0.516	0.499	0.482
5	0.593	0.567	0.543	0.519	0.497	0.476	0.456	0.437	0.419	0.402
6	0.535	0.507	0.480	0.456	0.432	0.410	0.390	0.370	0.352	0.335
7	0.482	0.452	0.425	0.400	0.376	0.354	0.333	0.314	0.296	0.279
8	0.434	0.404	0.376	0.351	0.327	0.305	0.285	0.266	0.249	0.233
9	0.391	0.361	0.333	0.308	0.284	0.263	0.243	0.225	0.206	0.194
10	0.352	0.322	0.295	0.270	0.247	0.227	0.208	0.191	0.176	0.162
11	0.317	0.287	0.261	0.237	0.215	0.195	0.178	0.162	0.148	0.135
12	0.286	0.257	0.231	0.208	0.187	0.168	0.152	0.137	0.124	0.112
13	0.258	0.229	0.204	0.182	0.163	0.145	0.130	0.116	0.104	0.933
14	0.232	0.205	0.181	0.160	0.141	0.125	0.111	0.099	0.088	0.078
15	0.209	0.183	0.160	0.140	0.123	0.108	0.095	0.084	0.074	0.065

Annuity table

Present value of an annuity of 1, i.e. $\dfrac{1-(1+r)^{-n}}{r}$

where   r = interest rate

              n = number of periods

Periods (n)	1%	2%	3%	4%	5%	6%	7%	8%	9%	10%
1	0.990	0.980	0.971	0.962	0.952	0.943	0.935	0.926	0.917	0.909
2	1.970	1.942	1.913	1.886	1.859	1.833	1.808	.1783	1.759	1.736
3	2.941	2.884	2.829	2.775	2.723	2.673	2.624	2.577	2.531	2.487
4	3.902	3.808	3.717	3.630	3.546	3.465	3.387	3.312	3.240	3.170
5	4.853	4.713	4.580	4.452	4.329	4.212	4.100	3.993	3.890	3.791
6	5.795	5.601	5.417	5.242	5.076	4.917	4.767	4.623	4.486	4.355
7	6.728	6.472	6.230	6.002	5.786	5.582	5.389	5.206	5.033	4.868
8	7.652	7.325	7.020	6.733	6.463	6.210	5.971	5.747	5.535	5.335
9	8.566	8.162	7.786	7.435	7.108	6.802	6.515	6.247	5.995	5.759
10	9.471	8.893	8.530	8.111	7.722	7.360	7.024	6.710	6.418	6.145
11	10.37	9.787	9.253	8.760	8.306	7.887	7.499	7.139	6.805	6.495
12	11.26	10.58	9.954	9.385	8.863	8.384	7.943	7.536	7.161	6.814
13	12.13	11.35	10.63	9.986	9.394	8.853	8.358	7.904	7.487	7.103
14	13.00	12.11	11.30	10.56	9.899	9.295	8.745	8.244	7.786	7.367
15	13.87	12.85	11.94	11.12	10.38	9.712	9.108	8.559	8.061	7.606

Periods (n)	11%	12%	13%	14%	15%	16%	17%	18%	19%	20%
1	0.901	0.893	0.885	0.877	0.870	0.862	0.855	0.847	0.840	0.833
2	1.713	1.690	1.668	1.647	1.626	1.605	1.585	1.566	1.547	1.528
3	2.444	2.402	2.361	2.322	2.283	2.246	2.210	2.174	2.140	2.106
4	3.102	3.037	2.974	2.914	2.855	2.798	2.743	2.690	2.639	2.589
5	3.696	3.605	3.517	3.433	3.352	3.274	3.199	3.127	3.058	2.991
6	4.231	4.111	3.998	3.889	3.784	3.685	3.589	3.496	3.410	3.326
7	4.712	4.564	4.423	4.288	4.160	4.039	3.922	3.812	3.706	3.605
8	5.146	4.968	4.799	4.639	4.487	4.344	4.207	4.078	3.954	3.837
9	5.537	5.328	5.132	4.946	4.772	4.607	4.451	4.303	4.163	4.031
10	5.889	5.650	5.426	5.216	5.019	4.833	4.659	4.494	4.339	4.192
11	6.207	5.938	5.687	5.453	5.234	5.029	4.836	4.656	4.586	4.327
12	6.492	6.194	5.918	5.660	5.421	5.197	4.988	4.793	4.611	4.439
13	6.750	6.424	6.122	5.842	5.583	5.342	5.118	4.910	4.715	4.533
14	6.982	6.628	6.302	6.002	5.724	5.468	5.229	5.008	4.802	4.611
15	7.191	6.811	6.462	6.142	5.847	5.575	5.324	5.092	4.876	4.675

KAPLAN PUBLISHING

Section 1

PRACTICE QUESTIONS – SECTION A

ROLE OF SENIOR FINANCIAL ADVISER IN THE MULTINATIONAL ORGANISATION

1 VADENER PLC (JUN 06 ADAPTED)

Vadener plc, a UK company, has instigated a review of the group's recent performance and potential future strategy. The Board of Directors has publicly stated that it is pleased with the group's performance and proposes to devote resources equally to its three operating divisions. Two of the divisions are in the UK, and focus on construction and leisure respectively, and one is in the USA and manufactures pharmaceuticals.

Recent summarised accounts for the group and data for the individual divisions are shown below:

Statements of profit or loss:

	Group data £ million		
	20X3	*20X4*	*20X5*
Revenue	1,210	1,410	1,490
Operating costs	800	870	930
Operating profit	410	540	560
Net interest	40	56	65
Profit before tax	370	484	495
Tax (30%)	111	145	149
Profit after tax	259	339	346
Equity dividends	146	170	185
Retained earnings	113	169	161

Statements of financial position:

Non-current assets:	20X3	20X4	20X5
Tangible assets	1,223	1,280	1,410
Intangible assets	100	250	250
Current assets:			
Inventory	340	410	490
Receivables	378	438	510
Cash	10	15	15
Total assets	2,051	2,393	2,675
Shareholders' equity	1,086	1,255	1,406
Long term liabilities	400	410	470
Payables falling due within one year:			
Trade payables	302	401	430
Short term loans	135	170	201
Taxation	55	72	75
Dividends	73	85	93
	2,051	2,393	2,675

Note: The 20X5 amount for shareholders' equity includes a £10 million loss on translation from the US division due to the recent weakness of the $US.

Other group data at year end:	20X3	20X4	20X5
Share price (pence)	1,220	1,417	1,542
Number of issued shares (million)	300	300	300
Equity beta			1.10

The company's share price has increased by an average of 12% per year over the last five years.

Other data at year end:	20X3	20X4	20X5
FT 100 index	3,700	4,600	4,960
PE ratio of similar companies	15:1	14:1	15:1
Risk free rate (%)			5
Market return (%)			12

Divisional data 20X5:	*Construction*	*Leisure*	*Pharmaceuticals*
Revenue (£m)	480	560	450
Operating profit	160	220	180
Estimated after tax return (%)	13	16	14
Data for the sector:	*Construction*	*Leisure*	*Pharmaceuticals*
Average asset beta 20X5	0.75	1.10	1.40

Required:

(a) Evaluate and comment on the performance of Vadener plc and each of its divisions. Highlight performance that appears favourable, and any areas of potential concern for the managers of Vadener. Comment upon the likely validity of the company's strategy to devote resources equally to the operating divisions.

All relevant calculations must be shown. Approximately 19 marks are available for calculations, and 9 for discussion. **(28 marks)**

Professional marks for format, structure and presentation of the report for part (a). **(4 marks)**

(b) Discuss what additional information would be useful in order to more accurately assess the performance of Vadener plc and its divisions. **(7 marks)**

(c) Discuss the possible implications for Vadener plc of the £10 million loss on translation, and recommend what action, if any, the company should take as a result of this loss. **(7 marks)**

(d) The company has been advised that it can increase income by writing (selling) options. Discuss whether or not this is correct, and provide a reasoned recommendation as to whether or not Vadener plc should adopt this strategy. **(4 marks)**

(Total: 50 marks)

ADVANCED INVESTMENT APPRAISAL

2 WURRALL INC (JUN 04 ADAPTED)

The board of directors of Wurrall Inc has requested the production of a four-year financial plan. The key assumptions behind the plan are:

(i) Historically, sales growth has been 9% per year. Uncertainty about future economic prospects over the next four years from 20X5–8, however, implies that this growth rate will reduce by 1% per year after the financial year 20X5 (e.g. to 8% in 20X6). After four years, growth is expected to remain constant at the 20X8 rate.

(ii) Cash operating costs are estimated to be approximately 68% of sales.

(iii) Tax allowable depreciation for the past few years has been approximately 15% of the net book value of plant and machinery at year end. This is expected to continue for the next few years.

(iv) Inventories, receivables, cash in hand and 'other payables' are assumed to increase in proportion to the increase in sales.

(v) Investment in, and net book value of, plant and machinery is expected to increase in line with sales. No investment is planned in other non-current assets other than a refurbishment of buildings at an estimated cost of $40 million in late 20X7.

(vi) Any change in interest paid as a result of changes in borrowing may be assumed to be effective in the next year. Wurrall plans to meet any changes in financing needs, with the exception of the repayment of the fixed-rate loan, by adjusting its overdraft.

(vii) Wurrall currently pays 7% per annum interest on its short-term borrowing.

(viii) Corporation tax is expected to continue at its present rate over the next four years.

(ix)   For the last few years, the company's dividend policy has been to pay a constant percentage of earnings after tax. No changes in this policy are planned.

(x)   Wurrall has borrowed extensively from the banking system, and covenants exist that prevent the company's gearing (book value of total loans to book value of total loans plus equity) exceeding 40% for a period of more than one year.

(xi)   The company's managing director has publicly stated that both profits before tax and Wurrall's share price should increase by at least 100% during the next four years.

Summarised financial accounts of Wurrall Inc:

Statement of profit or loss for the year ended March 20X4

	$ (million)
Sales revenue	1,639
Operating costs before depreciation	(1,225)
EBITDA	414
Tax allowable depreciation	(152)
EBIT	262
Net interest payable	(57)
Profit on ordinary activities before tax	205
Tax on ordinary activities (30%)	(62)
Profit after tax	143
Note: Dividends	80

Statement of financial position as at 31 March 20X4

	$ (million)	$ (million)
Non-current assets		
Land and buildings		310
Plant and machinery (net)		1,012
Investments (i)		32
		1,354
Current assets		
Inventory	448	
Receivables	564	
Cash in hand and short-term deposits	20	
		1,032
Total assets		2,386

	$ (million)	$ (million)
Equity and liabilities		
Called-up share capital (10 cents par)		240
Reserves		864
		———
		1,104
Non-current liabilities		
Borrowings (8% fixed rate) (ii)		580
Current liabilities		
Short-term loans and overdrafts	230	
Other payables	472	
	———	
		702
		———
Total equity and liabilities		2,386
		———

(i)   The investments yield negligible interest.

(ii) Borrowings are scheduled to be repaid at the end of 20X6 and will be refinanced with a similar type of loan in 20X6.

The company's current share price is 210 cents, and its weighted average cost of capital is 11%.

Required:

Prepare a report for the Board of Directors in which you:

(a)   **Produce proforma statements of financial position and statements of profit or loss for each of the next four years. Clearly state any assumptions that you make.**

(16 marks)

(b)   **Critically discuss any problems or implications of the assumptions that are made in each of points (i) to (iv) and point (ix) in the question.   (8 marks)**

(c)   **Using free cash flow analysis, evaluate and discuss whether or not the managing director's claims for the future share price are likely to be achievable. (The operating cash flow element of free cash flow may be estimated by: EBIT(1–T) plus depreciation.)   (10 marks)**

(d)   **Using financial ratios or other forms of analysis, highlight any potential financial problems for the company during this period. Discuss what actions might be taken with respect to these problems.   (12 marks)**

Professional marks for format, structure and presentation of the report.   (4 marks)

(Total: 50 marks)

3   DARON (DEC 95 ADAPTED)

Assume that 'now' is December 20X3.

The senior managers of Daron, a company located in a European country, are reviewing the company's medium-term prospects. The company is in a declining industry, and is heavily dependent on a single product. Sales volume is likely to fall for the next few years. A general election will take place in the near future and the managers believe that the future level of inflation will depend upon the result of the election. Inflation is expected to remain at approximately 5% per year if political party A wins the election, or will quickly move to approximately 10% per year if party B wins the election. Opinion polls suggest that there is a 40% chance of party B winning. An increase in the level of inflation is likely to reduce the volume of sales of Daron.

Projected financial data for the next five years, including expected inflation where relevant, are shown below.

Political party A wins, inflation 5% per year

	20X4	20X5	20X6	20X7	20X8
Operating cash flows ($m):					
Sales	28	29	26	22	19
Variable costs	17	18	16	14	12
Fixed costs	3	3	3	3	3
Other financial data:					
Incremental working capital*	–	(1)	(2)	(3)	(3)
Tax allowable depreciation	4	3	3	2	1

Political party B wins, inflation 10% per year

	20X4	20X5	20X6	20X7	20X8
Operating cash flows ($m):					
Sales	30	26	24	20	16
Variable costs	18	16	15	12	11
Fixed costs	3	3	4	4	4
Other financial data:					
Incremental working capital*	1	(2)	(2)	(3)	(3)
Tax allowable depreciation	4	3	3	2	1

*A bracket signifies a decrease in working capital.

Tax allowable depreciation will be negligible after 20X8 in both cases.

Cash flows after year 20X8, excluding tax savings from tax allowable depreciation, are expected to be similar to year 20X8 cash flows for a period of five years, after which substantial new fixed investment would be necessary in order to continue operations.

Working capital will remain approximately constant after the year 20X8.

Corporate taxation is at a rate of 30% per year, and is expected to continue at this rate. Tax may be assumed to be payable in the year that the income arises.

Daron's current ordinary share price is 92 centos (100 centos = $1).

Summarised statement of financial position of Daron Inc as at 31 March 20X3

	$ (million)
Tangible non-current assets	24
Net current assets	12
Total assets less current liabilities	36
Loans and other non-current liabilities	14
Capital and reserves:	
Called-up share capital (25 centos par value)	5
Reserves	17
	36

The company can currently borrow long term from its bank at an interest rate of 10% per year. This is likely to quickly rise to 15.5% per year if the political party B wins the election.

The real risk-free rate (i.e. excluding inflation) is 4% and the real market return is 10%.

Daron's equity beta is estimated to be 1.25. This is not expected to significantly change if inflation increases.

Three alternatives are available to the managers of Daron:

(i)   Recommend the sale of the company now. An informal, unpublicised offer of $20 million for the company's shares has been received from a competitor.

(ii)   Continue existing operations, with negligible capital investment for the foreseeable future.

(iii)   If the political party A wins the election, diversify operations by buying a going concern in the hotel industry at a cost of $9 million. The purchase would be financed by the issue of 10% convertible debentures. Issue costs are 2% of the gross sum raised. Daron has no previous experience of the hotel industry.

Financial projections of the hotel purchase

	$ (million)				
	20X4	20X5	20X6	20X7	20X8
Revenue	9	10	11	12	13
Variable costs	6	6	7	7	8
Fixed costs	2	2	2	2	2
Other financial data:					
Incremental working capital	1	–	–	1	–

Tax allowable depreciation is negligible for the hotel purchase. The after-tax realisable value of the hotel at the end of year 20X8 is expected to be $10 million, including working capital. The systematic risk of operating the hotels is believed to be similar to that of the company's existing operations.

Required:

(a) Using the above data, prepare a report advising the managers of Daron which, if any, of the three alternatives to adopt. Include in your report comment on any weaknesses/limitations of your data analysis. Relevant calculations, including:

(i) estimates of the present values of future cash flows from existing operations, and

(ii) the estimated adjusted present value of diversifying into the hotel industry should form appendices to your report.

The book value and market value of debt may be assumed to be the same. State clearly any other assumptions that you make. **(32 marks)**

Approximately 20 marks are available for calculations and 12 for discussion.

Professional marks for format, structure and presentation of the report for part (a).
(4 marks)

(b) Details of the possible convertible debenture issue for the purchase of the hotel are shown below:

10% $100 convertible debentures 20Y7 (i.e. 14 years from now), issued and redeemable at par. The debentures are convertible into 60 ordinary shares at any date between 1 January 20X9 and 31 December 20Y1. The debentures are callable for conversion by the company subject to the company's ordinary share price exceeding 200 centos between 1 January 20X9 and 31 December 20Y1, and puttable for redemption by the debenture holders if the share price falls below 100 centos between the same dates.

Required:

Discuss the implications for Daron if the diversification is financed with convertible debentures with these terms. **(8 marks)**

(c) The regulation of takeovers varies from country to country. Outline the typical factors that such regulation includes. **(6 marks)**

(Total: 50 marks)

4   SLEEPON HOTELS INC (DEC 05 ADAPTED) *Walk in the footsteps of a top tutor*

Sleepon Hotels Inc owns a successful chain of hotels. The company is considering diversifying its activities through the construction of a theme park near its capital city. The theme park would have a mixture of family activities and adventure rides. Sleepon has just spent $230,000 on market research into the theme park, and is encouraged by the findings.

The theme park is expected to attract an average of 15,000 visitors per day for at least four years, after which major new investment would be required in order to maintain demand. The price of admission to the theme park is expected to be $18 per adult and $10 per child; 60% of visitors are forecast to be children. In addition to admission revenues, it is expected that the average visitor will spend $8 on food and drinks (of which 30% is profit), and $5 on gifts and souvenirs (of which 40% is profit). The park would open for 360 days per year.

All costs and receipts (excluding maintenance and construction costs and the realisable value) are shown at current prices; the company expects all costs and receipts to rise by 3% per year from current values.

The theme park would cost a total of $400 million and could be constructed and working in one year's time. Half of the $400 million would be payable immediately, and half in one year's time. In addition, working capital of $50 million will be required from the end of year one. The after-tax realisable value of non-current assets is expected to be between $250 million and $300 million after four years of operation.

Maintenance costs (excluding labour) are expected to be $15 million in the first year of operation, increasing by $4 million per year thereafter. Annual insurance costs are $2 million, and the company would apportion $2.5 million per year to the theme park from existing overheads. The theme park would require 1,500 staff costing a total of $40 million per annum (at current prices). Sleepon will use the existing advertising campaigns for its hotels to also advertise the theme park. This will save approximately $2 million per year in advertising expenses.

As Sleepon has no previous experience of theme park management, it has investigated the current risk and financial structure of the closest domestic theme park competitor, Thrillall Inc. Details are summarised below.

Thrillall Inc, summarised statement of financial position

	$ (million)
Non-current assets (net)	1,440
Current assets	570
	2,010
Equity and liabilities	
$1 ordinary shares	400
Reserves	530
	930
Medium- and long-term debt	460
Current liabilities	620
	2,010

Other information:

(i)   Sleepon has access to a $450 million Eurodollar loan at 7.5% fixed rate to provide the necessary finance for the theme park.

(ii) $250 million of the investment will attract 25% per year tax allowable depreciation allowances on a reducing balance basis.

(iii)   Corporate tax is at a rate of 30%.

(iv)   The average stock market return is 10% and the risk-free rate 3.5%.

(v)   Sleepon's current weighted average cost of capital is 9%.

(vi)   Sleepon's market weighted gearing if the theme park project is undertaken is estimated to be 61.4% equity, 38.6% debt.

(vii)   Sleepon's equity beta is 0.70.

(viii) The current share price of Sleepon is 148 cents, and of Thrillall 386 cents.

(ix)   Thrillall's medium- and long-term debt comprises long-term bonds with a par value of $100 and current market price of $93.

(x)   Thrillall's equity beta is 1.45.

Required:

(a)   **Prepare a report analysing whether or not Sleepon should undertake the investment in the theme park. Your report should include a discussion of what other information would be useful to Sleepon in making the investment decision. All relevant calculations must be included in the report or as an appendix to it. State clearly any assumptions that you make.**

Approximately 26 marks are available for calculations and 10 for discussion.

(36 marks)

Professional marks for format, structure and presentation of the report for part (a).

(4 marks)

(b)   **Prepare briefing notes for the board of directors discussing issues that might influence the company's capital structure strategy.**   **(10 marks)**

(Total: 50 marks)

5   BLIPTON INTERNATIONAL (DEC 08 ADAPTED)

It is now 1 December 20X8. You have been hired as a financial consultant to the Blipton International Entertainment Group which is evaluating a proposal from its hotel division to build a 400 bedroom hotel in the East End of London. This area has developed rapidly over the last 15 years and the prospects have been further enhanced by the announcement that London is to host the 20Y2 Olympics. Blipton is based in Dubai and both reports and accounts for all its transactions in dollars. The current dollar/sterling spot rate is $1.4925/£. The operating costs for the hotel are expected to be £30 per occupied room per day (variable) and a fixed cost of £1.7 million per annum expressed in current prices.

The proportion of bedrooms occupied, on the basis of opening for 365 days a year, is expected to be as follows:

Year ended	Occupancy
31 December 20X9	construction
31 December 20Y0	40%
31 December 20Y1	50%
31 December 20Y2	90%
31 December 20Y3	60%
31 December 20Y4	60%

UK inflation is currently projected by the Bank of England as 2.5% per annum and inflation in the United States is 4.8% per annum. These rates are expected to be constant over the term of the project. Blipton's real cost of capital is 4.2%. UK hotel property values within the London area are expected to rise in real terms by 8% per annum.

The construction cost for this hotel is estimated to be £6.2 million and it will be built over the 12 months to 31 December 20X9. As part of the UK's Olympic Development Plan, a 50% first year capital allowance is available for tax purposes on building projects related to the Games. The balance of the capital expenditure can be claimed in equal instalments over the following three years. UK profit tax is 30% and is levied and paid on profits in the year they arise. There is no additional tax liability on remittance to or from Dubai. The company has sufficient UK profits on its other activities to absorb the tax allowable depreciation on this project.

In making investment decisions of this type the company operates the following procedure:

1   All cash flows including construction costs are assumed to arise at the end of the year concerned and are to be projected in nominal (money) terms over the six year period.

2   The residual value of the investment at the end of six years is assumed to be the open market value of the property less a charge for repairs and renewals.

3   The charge for repairs and renewals is expected to be £1.2 million in current prices payable on disposal.

4   The net present value of the project should be based upon a 100% remittance of net cash flows to Dubai and should be calculated in dollars.

5   Average room rates are set at the level required to recover variable cost plus 100%.

Required:

Prepare a report for management to include the following:

(a)   **A six year nominal dollar projection of the after tax cash flow for this project distinguishing between cash flows arising from its investment phase and those arising from its return phase.**   **(12 marks)**

(b)   **An estimate of the project's dollar net present value and the modified internal rate of return.**   **(8 marks)**

(c)   **An assessment of the viability of the project with a summary of the relative advantages and disadvantages of the net present value and modified internal rate of return methods in investment appraisal.**   **(8 marks)**

Professional marks for format, structure and presentation of the report.   **(4 marks)**

(d)   Blipton's board of directors is considering the introduction of an executive share option scheme.

The scheme would be offered to all middle managers of the company. It would replace the existing scheme of performance bonuses linked to the post-tax earnings per share of the company. Such bonuses in the last year ranged between $5,000 and $7,000. If the option scheme is introduced, new options are expected to be offered to the managers each year.

It is proposed for the first year that all middle managers are offered options to purchase 5,000 shares at a price of 500 cents per share, after the options have been held for one year. Assume that the tax authorities allow the exercise of such options after they have been held for one year. If the options are not exercised at that time they will lapse.

The company's shares have just come ex-div and have a current market price of 610 cents. The dividend paid was 25 cents per share, a level that has remained constant for the last three years. Assume that dividends are only paid annually.

The company's share price has experienced a standard deviation of 38% during the last year. The short-term risk-free interest rate is 6% annum.

Required:

Evaluate whether or not the proposed share option scheme is likely to be attractive to middle managers of Blipton. **(11 marks)**

(e)   When told of the scheme one manager stated that he would rather receive put options than call options, as they would be more valuable to him.

Required:

(i)   **Discuss whether or not Blipton should agree to offer him put options.**

(3 marks)

(ii)   **Calculate whether or not he is correct in his statement that put options would be more valuable to him.** **(4 marks)**

(Total: 50 marks)

6   TRAMONT CO (PILOT 12)

Tramont Co is a listed company that is based in the USA and manufactures electronic devices. One of its devices, the X-IT, is produced exclusively for the American market. Tramont Co is considering ceasing the production of the X-IT gradually over a period of four years because it needs the manufacturing facilities used to make the X-IT for other products.

The government of Gamala, a country based in south-east Asia, is keen to develop its manufacturing industry and has offered Tramont Co first rights to produce the X-IT in Gamala and sell it to the USA market for a period of four years. At the end of the four-year period, the full production rights will be sold to a government backed company for Gamalan Rupiahs (GR) 450 million after tax (this amount is not subject to inflationary increases). Tramont Co has to decide whether to continue production of the X-IT in the USA for the next four years or to move the production to Gamala immediately.

Currently each X-IT unit sold makes a unit contribution of $20. This unit contribution is not expected to be subject to any inflationary increase in the next four years. Next year's production and sales estimated at 40,000 units will fall by 20% each year for the following three years. It is anticipated that after four years the production of X-IT will stop. It is expected that the financial impact of the gradual closure over the four years will be cost neutral (the revenue from sale of assets will equal the closure costs). If production is stopped immediately, the excess assets would be sold for $2.3 million and the costs of closure, including redundancy costs of excess labour, would be $1.7 million.

The following information relates to the production of the X-IT moving to Gamala. The Gamalan project will require an initial investment of GR 230 million, to pay for the cost of land and buildings (GR 150 million) and machinery (GR 80 million). The cost of machinery is tax allowable and will be depreciated on a straight line basis over the next four years, at the end of which it will have a negligible value.

Tramont Co will also need GR 40 million for working capital immediately. It is expected that the working capital requirement will increase in line with the annual inflation rate in Gamala. When the project is sold, the working capital will not form part of the sale price and will be released back to Tramont Co.

Production and sales of the device are expected to be 12,000 units in the first year, rising to 22,000 units, 47,000 units and 60,000 units in the next three years respectively.

The following revenues and costs apply to the first year of operation:

- Each unit will be sold for $70

- The variable cost per unit comprising of locally sourced materials and labour will be GR 1,350, and

- In addition to the variable cost above, each unit will require a component bought from Tramont Co for $7, on which Tramont Co makes $4 contribution per unit

- Total fixed costs for the first year will be GR 30 million.

The costs are expected to increase by their countries' respective rates of inflation, but the selling price will remain fixed at $70 per unit for the four-year period.

The annual corporation tax rate in Gamala is 20% and Tramont Co currently pays corporation tax at a rate of 30% per year. Both countries' corporation taxes are payable in the year that the tax liability arises. A bi-lateral tax treaty exists between the USA and Gamala, which permits offset of overseas tax against any US tax liability on overseas earnings. The USA and Gamalan tax authorities allow losses to be carried forward and written off against future profits for taxation purposes.

Tramont Co has decided to finance the project by borrowing the funds required in Gamala. The commercial borrowing rate is 13% but the Gamalan government has offered Tramont Co a 6% subsidised loan for the entire amount of the initial funds required. The Gamalan government has agreed that it will not ask for the loan to be repaid as long as Tramont Co fulfils its contract to undertake the project for the four years. Tramont Co can borrow dollar funds at an interest rate of 5%.

Tramont Co's financing consists of 25 million shares currently trading at $2.40 each and $40 million 7% bonds trading at $1,428 per $1,000. Tramont Co's quoted beta is 1.17. The current risk free rate of return is estimated at 3% and the market risk premium is 6%. Due to the nature of the project, it is estimated that the beta applicable to the project if it is all-equity financed will be 0.4 more than the current all-equity financed beta of Tramont Co. If the Gamalan project is undertaken, the cost of capital applicable to the cash flows in the USA is expected to be 7%.

The spot exchange rate between the dollar and the Gamalan Rupiah is GR 55 per $1. The annual inflation rates are currently 3% in the USA and 9% in Gamala. It can be assumed that these inflation rates will not change for the foreseeable future. All net cash flows arising from the project will be remitted back to Tramont Co at the end of each year.

There are two main political parties in Gamala: the Gamala Liberal (GL) Party and the Gamala Republican (GR) Party. Gamala is currently governed by the GL Party but general elections are due to be held soon. If the GR Party wins the election, it promises to increase taxes of international companies operating in Gamala and review any commercial benefits given to these businesses by the previous government.

Required:

(a) Prepare a report for the Board of Directors (BoD) of Tramont Co that

    (i) Evaluates whether or not Tramont Co should undertake the project to produce the X-IT in Gamala and cease its production in the USA immediately. In the evaluation, include all relevant calculations in the form of a financial assessment and explain any assumptions made.

    It is suggested that the financial assessment should be based on present value of the operating cash flows from the Gamalan project, discounted by an appropriate all-equity rate, and adjusted by the present value of all other relevant cash flows. **(27 marks)**

    (ii) Discusses the potential change in government and other business factors that Tramont Co should consider before making a final decision. **(8 marks)**

Professional marks for format, structure and presentation of the report for part (a).
(4 marks)

(b) Although not mandatory for external reporting purposes, one of the members of the BoD suggested that adopting a triple bottom line approach when monitoring the X-IT investment after its implementation, would provide a better assessment of how successful it has been.

Discuss how adopting aspects of triple bottom line reporting may provide a better assessment of the success of the X-IT. **(6 marks)**

(c) Another member of the BoD felt that, despite Tramont Co having a wide range of shareholders holding well- diversified portfolios of investments, moving the production of the X-IT to Gamala would result in further risk diversification benefits.

Discuss whether moving the production of the X-IT to Gamala may result in further risk diversification for the shareholders already holding well diversified portfolios.
(5 marks)

(Total: 50 marks)

7 CHMURA CO (DEC 13)

 Online question assistance

Since becoming independent just over 20 years ago, the country of Mehgam has adopted protectionist measures which have made it difficult for multinational companies to trade there. However, recently, after discussions with the World Trade Organisation (WTO), it seems likely that Mehgam will reduce its protectionist measures significantly.

Encouraged by these discussions, Chmura Co, a company producing packaged foods, is considering a project to set up a manufacturing base in Mehgam to sell its goods there and in other regional countries nearby. An initial investigation costing $500,000 established that Mehgam had appropriate manufacturing facilities, adequate transport links and a reasonably skilled but cheap work force. The investigation concluded that, if the protectionist measures were reduced, then the demand potential for Chmura Co's products looked promising. It is also felt that an early entry into Mehgam would give Chmura Co an advantage over its competitors for a period of five years, after which the current project will cease, due to the development of new advanced manufacturing processes.

Mehgam's currency, the Peso (MP), is currently trading at MP72 per $1. Setting up the manufacturing base in Mehgam will require an initial investment of MP2,500 million immediately, to cover the cost of land and buildings (MP1,250 million) and machinery (MP1,250 million). Tax allowable depreciation is available on the machinery at an annual rate of 10% on cost on a straight-line basis. A balancing adjustment will be required at the end of year five, when it is expected that the machinery will be sold for MP500 million (after inflation). The market value of the land and buildings in five years' time is estimated to be 80% of the current value. These amounts are inclusive of any tax impact.

Chmura Co will require MP200 million for working capital immediately. It is not expected that any further injections of working capital will be required for the five years. When the project ceases at the end of the fifth year, the working capital will be released back to Chmura Co.

Production of the packaged foods will take place in batches of product mixes. These batches will then be sold to supermarket chains, wholesalers and distributors in Mehgam and its neighbouring countries, who will repackage them to their individual requirements. All sales will be in MP. The estimated average number of batches produced and sold each year is given below:

Year	1	2	3	4	5
Batches produced and sold	10,000	15,000	30,000	26,000	15,000

The current selling price for each batch is estimated to be MP115,200. The costs related to producing and selling each batch are currently estimated to be MP46,500. In addition to these costs, a number of products will need a special packaging material which Chmura Co will send to Mehgam. Currently the cost of the special packaging material is $200 per batch. Training and development costs, related to the production of the batches, are estimated to be 80% of the production and selling costs (excluding the cost of the special packaging) in the first year, before falling to 20% of these costs (excluding the cost of the special packaging) in the second year, and then nil for the remaining years. It is expected that the costs relating to the production and sale of each batch will increase annually by 10% but the selling price and the special packaging costs will only increase by 5% every year.

The current annual corporation tax rate in Mehgam is 25% and Chmura Co pays annual corporation tax at a rate of 20% in the country where it is based. Both countries' taxes are payable in the year that the tax liability arises. A bi-lateral tax treaty exists between the two countries which permits offset of overseas tax against any tax liabilities Chmura Co incurs on overseas earnings.

The risk-adjusted cost of capital applicable to the project on $-based cash flows is 12%, which is considerably higher than the return on short-dated $ treasury bills of 4%. The current rate of inflation in Mehgam is 8%, and in the country where Chmura Co is based, it is 2%. It can be assumed that these inflation rates will not change for the foreseeable future. All net cash flows from the project will be remitted back to Chmura Co at the end of each year.

Chmura Co's finance director is of the opinion that there are many uncertainties surrounding the project and has assessed that the cash flows can vary by a standard deviation of as much as 35% because of these uncertainties.

Recently Bulud Co offered Chmura Co the option to sell the entire project to Bulud Co for $28 million at the start of year three. Chmura Co will make the decision of whether or not to sell the project at the end of year two.

Required:

(a) Discuss the role of the World Trade Organisation (WTO) and the possible benefits and drawbacks to Mehgam of reducing protectionist measures. **(9 marks)**

(b) Prepare an evaluative report for the Board of Directors of Chmura Co which addresses the following parts and recommends an appropriate course of action:

(i) An estimate of the value of the project before considering Bulud Co's offer. Show all relevant calculations **(14 marks)**

(ii) An estimate of the value of the project taking into account Bulud Co's offer. Show all relevant calculations **(9 marks)**

(iii) A discussion of the assumptions made in parts (i) and (ii) above and the additional business risks which Chmura Co should consider before it makes the final decision whether or not to undertake the project. **(14 marks)**

Professional marks will be awarded in part (b) for the format, structure and presentation of the report. **(4 marks)**

(Total: 50 marks)

8 YILANDWE (JUN 15)

 Question debrief

Yilandwe, whose currency is the Yilandwe Rand (YR), has faced extremely difficult economic challenges in the past 25 years because of some questionable economic policies and political decisions made by its previous governments. Although Yilandwe's population is generally poor, its people are nevertheless well-educated and ambitious. Just over three years ago, a new government took office and since then it has imposed a number of strict monetary and fiscal controls, including an annual corporation tax rate of 40%, in an attempt to bring Yilandwe out of its difficulties. As a result, the annual rate of inflation has fallen rapidly from a high of 65% to its current level of 33%. These strict monetary and fiscal controls have made Yilandwe's government popular in the larger cities and towns, but less popular in the rural areas which seem to have suffered disproportionately from the strict monetary and fiscal controls.

It is expected that Yilandwe's annual inflation rate will continue to fall in the coming few years as follows:

Year	Inflation rate
1	22.0%
2	14.7%
3 onwards	9.8%

Yilandwe's government has decided to continue the progress made so far, by encouraging foreign direct investment into the country. Recently, government representatives held trade shows internationally and offered businesses a number of concessions, including:

(i) zero corporation tax payable in the first two years of operation; and

(ii) an opportunity to carry forward tax losses and write them off against future profits made after the first two years.

The government representatives also promised international companies investing in Yilandwe prime locations in towns and cities with good transport links.

Imoni Co

Imoni Co, a large listed company based in the USA with the US dollar ($) as its currency, manufactures high tech diagnostic components for machinery, which it exports worldwide. After attending one of the trade shows, Imoni Co is considering setting up an assembly plant in Yilandwe where parts would be sent and assembled into a specific type of component, which is currently being assembled in the USA. Once assembled, the component will be exported directly to companies based in the European Union (EU). These exports will be invoiced in Euro (€).

Assembly plant in Yilandwe: financial and other data projections

It is initially assumed that the project will last for four years. The four-year project will require investments of YR21,000 million for land and buildings, YR18,000 million for machinery and YR9,600 million for working capital to be made immediately. The working capital will need to be increased annually at the start of each of the next three years by Yilandwe's inflation rate and it is assumed that this will be released at the end of the project's life.

It can be assumed that the assembly plant can be built very quickly and production started almost immediately. This is because the basic facilities and infrastructure are already in place as the plant will be built on the premises and grounds of a school. The school is ideally located, near the main highway and railway lines. As a result, the school will close and the children currently studying there will be relocated to other schools in the city. The government has kindly agreed to provide free buses to take the children to these schools for a period of six months to give parents time to arrange appropriate transport in the future for their children.

The current selling price of each component is €700 and this price is likely to increase by the average EU rate of inflation from year 1 onwards.

The number of components expected to be sold every year are as follows:

Year	1	2	3	4
Sales component units (000s)	150	480	730	360

The parts needed to assemble into the components in Yilandwe will be sent from the USA by Imoni Co at a cost of $200 per component unit, from which Imoni Co would currently earn a pre-tax contribution of $40 for each component unit. However, Imoni Co feels that it can negotiate with Yilandwe's government and increase the transfer price to $280 per component unit. The variable costs related to assembling the components in Yilandwe are currently

YR15,960 per component unit. The current annual fixed costs of the assembly plant are YR4,600 million. All these costs, wherever incurred, are expected to increase by that country's annual inflation every year from year 1 onwards.

Imoni Co pays corporation tax on profits at an annual rate of 20% in the USA. The tax in both the USA and Yilandwe is payable in the year that the tax liability arises. A bilateral tax treaty exists between Yilandwe and the USA. Tax allowable depreciation is available at 25% per year on the machinery on a straight-line basis.

Imoni Co will expect annual royalties from the assembly plant to be made every year. The normal annual royalty fee is currently $20 million, but Imoni Co feels that it can negotiate this with Yilandwe's government and increase the royalty fee by 80%. Once agreed, this fee will not be subject to any inflationary increase in the project's four-year period.

If Imoni Co does decide to invest in an assembly plant in Yilandwe, its exports from the USA to the EU will fall and it will incur redundancy costs. As a result, Imoni Co's after-tax cash flows will reduce by the following amounts:

Year	1	2	3	4
Redundancy and lost contribution	20,000	55,697	57,368	59,089

Imoni Co normally uses its cost of capital of 9% to assess new projects. However, the finance director suggests that Imoni Co should use a project specific discount rate of 12% instead.

Other financial information

Current spot rates

Euro per Dollar	€0.714/$1
YR per Euro	YR142/€1
YR per Dollar	YR101.4/$1

Forecast future rates based on expected inflation rate differentials

Year	1	2	3	4
YR/$1	120.1	133.7	142.5	151.9
Year	1	2	3	4
YR/€1	165.0	180.2	190.2	200.8

Expected inflation rates

EU expected inflation rate: Next two years	5%
EU expected inflation rate: Year 3 onwards	4%
USA expected inflation rate: Year 1 onwards	3%

Required:

(a) Discuss the possible benefits and drawbacks to Imoni Co of setting up its own assembly plant in Yilandwe, compared to licensing a company based in Yilandwe to undertake the assembly on its behalf. **(5 marks)**

(b) Prepare a report which:

(i) Evaluates the financial acceptability of the investment in the assembly plant in Yilandwe **(21 marks)**

(ii) Discusses the assumptions made in producing the estimates, and the other risks and issues which Imoni Co should consider before making the final decision; **(17 marks)**

(iii) Provides a reasoned recommendation on whether or not Imoni Co should invest in the assembly plant in Yilandwe. **(3 marks)**

Professional marks will be awarded in part (b) for the format, structure and presentation of the report. **(4 marks)**

(Total: 50 marks)

 Calculate your allowed time and allocate the time to the separate parts

ACQUISITIONS AND MERGERS

9   STANZIAL INC (DEC 06 ADAPTED)

Stanzial Inc is a listed telecommunications company. The company is considering the purchase of Besserlot Co, an unlisted company that has developed, patented and marketed a secure, medium-range, wireless link to broadband. The wireless link is expected to increase Besserlot's revenue by 25% per year for three years, and by 10% per year thereafter. Besserlot is currently owned 35% by its senior managers, 30% by a venture capital company, 25% by a single shareholder on the board of directors, and 10% by about 100 other private investors.

Summarised accounts for Besserlot for the last two years are shown below:

Statements of profit or loss for the years ended 31 March ($000)

	20X6	20X5
Sales revenue	22,480	20,218
Operating profit before exceptional items	1,302	820
Exceptional items	(2,005)	–
Interest paid (net)	(280)	(228)
Profit before taxation	(983)	592
Taxation	(210)	(178)
Profit after taxation	(1,193)	414
Note: Dividend	200	100

Statements of financial position as at 31 March ($000)

	20X6	20X5
Non-current assets (net)		
Tangible assets	5,430	5,048
Goodwill	170	200
Current assets		
Inventory	3,400	2,780
Receivables falling due within one year	2,658	2,462
Receivables falling due after one year	100	50
Cash at bank and in hand	48	48
Total assets	11,806	10,588

	20X6	20X5
Equity and liabilities		
Called-up share capital (25 cents par)	2,000	1,000
Retained profits	3,037	4,430
Other reserves	1,249	335
Total equity	6,286	5,765
Current liabilities – payables	5,520	4,823
	11,806	10,588

Other information relating to Besserlot:

(i)   Non-cash expenses, including depreciation, were $820,000 in 20X5–6.

(ii)   Corporate taxation is at the rate of 30% per year.

(iii)   Capital investment was $1 million in 20X5–6, and is expected to grow at approximately the same rate as revenue.

(iv)   Working capital, interest payments and non-cash expenses are expected to increase at the same rate as revenue.

(v)   The estimated value of the patent if sold now is $10 million. This has not been included in non-current assets.

(vi)   Operating profit is expected to be approximately 8% of revenue in 20X6–7, and to remain at the same percentage in future years.

(vii)   Dividends are expected to grow at the same rate as revenue.

(viii) The realisable value of existing inventory is expected to be 70% of its book value.

(ix)   The estimated cost of equity of Besserlot is 14%.

Information regarding the industry sector of Besserlot:

(i)   The average PE ratio of listed companies of similar size to Besserlot is 30:1.

(ii)   Average earnings growth in the industry is 6% per year.

Required:

(a)   **Prepare a report that:**

   (i)   **Estimates the value of Besserlot Co using:**

   - **Asset based valuation**

   - **PE ratios**

   - **Dividend based valuation**

   - **The present value of expected future cash flows.**

   State clearly any assumptions that you make.   **(16 marks)**

   (ii)   **Discusses the potential accuracy of each of the methods used and recommends, with reasons, a value, or range of values that Stanzial might bid for Besserlot.**   **(11 marks)**

   Professional marks will be awarded in part (a) for the format, structure and presentation of the report.   **(4 marks)**

(b)   **Discuss how the shareholder mix of Besserlot and type of payment used might influence the success or failure of the bid.**   **(8 marks)**

(c) Assuming that the bid was successful, discuss other factors that might influence the medium-term financial success of the acquisition. **(5 marks)**

(d) The directors of Stanzial Inc are also considering whether to dispose of one of the company's business units.

Required:

Explain the potential advantages for Stanzial of undertaking the divestment by means of

(i) a sell-off and

(ii) a demerger **(6 marks)**

(Total: 50 marks)

10 BURCOLENE (DEC 07 ADAPTED) *Walk in the footsteps of a top tutor*

Burcolene is a large European-based petrochemical manufacturer, with a wide range of basic bulk chemicals in its product range and with strong markets in Europe and the Pacific region. In recent years, margins have fallen as a result of competition from China and, more importantly, Eastern European countries that have favourable access to the Russian petrochemical industry. However, the company has managed to sustain a 5% growth rate in earnings through aggressive management of its cost base, the management of its risk and careful attention to its value base.

As part of its strategic development, Burcolene is considering a leveraged (debt-financed) acquisition of PetroFrancais, a large petrochemical business that has engaged in a number of high quality alliances with oil drilling and extraction companies in the newly opened Russian Arctic fields. However, the growth of the company has not been particularly strong in recent years, although Burcolene believes that an expected long term growth of 4% per annum is realistic under its current management.

Preliminary discussions with its banks have led Burcolene to the conclusion that an acquisition of 100% of the equity of PetroFrancais, financed via a bond issue, would not have a significant impact upon the company's existing credit rating. The key issues, according to the company's advisors, are the terms of the deal and the likely effect of the acquisition on the company's value and its financial leverage.

Both companies are quoted on an international stock exchange and below are relevant data relating to each company:

Financial data as at 30 November 20X7

	Burcolene	PetroFrancais
Market value of debt in issue ($bn)	3.30	5.80
Market value of equity in issue ($bn)	9.90	6.70
Number of shares in issue (million)	340.00	440.00
Share options outstanding (million)	25.40	–
Exercise price of options ($ per share)	22.00	–
Company tax rate (%)	30.00	25.00
Equity beta	1.85	0.95
Default risk premium	1.6%	3.0%
Net operating profit after tax and net reinvestment ($ million)	450.00	205.00
Current EPS ($ per share)	1.19	0.44

The global equity risk premium is 4.0% and the most appropriate risk free rate derived from the returns on government stock is 3.0%.

Burcolene has a share option scheme as part of its executive remuneration package. In accordance with the accounting standards, the company has expensed its share options at fair value. The share options held by the employees of Burcolene were granted on 1 January 20X4. The vesting date is 30 November 20X9 and the exercise date is 30 November 20Y0. Currently, the company has a 5% attrition rate as members leave the company and, of those remaining at the vesting date, 20% are expected not to have achieved the standard of performance required. Your estimate is that the options have a time value of $7.31.

PetroFrancais operates a defined benefits pension scheme which, at its current actuarial valuation, shows a deficit of $430 million.

You have been appointed to advise the senior management team of Burcolene on the validity of the free cash flow to equity model as a basis for valuing both firms and on the financial implications of this acquisition for Burcolene. Following your initial discussions with management, you decide that the following points are relevant:

1   The free cash flow to all classes of capital invested can be reliably approximated as net operating profit after tax (NOPAT) less net reinvestment.

2   Given the rumours in the market concerning a potential acquisition, the existing market valuations may not fully reflect each company's value.

3   The acquisition would be financed by a new debt issue by Burcolene.

Required:

(a)   **Estimate the weighted average cost of capital and the current entity value for each business, taking into account the impact of the share option scheme and the pension fund deficit on the value of each company.**   **(16 marks)**

(b)   **Write a report for management, advising them on:**

(i)   **The validity of the free cash flow model, given the growth rate assumptions made by management for both firms**

(ii)   **The most appropriate method of deriving a bid price; and**

(iii)   **The implications of an acquisition such as this for Burcolene's gearing and cost of capital.**   **(16 marks)**

Professional marks for format, structure and presentation of the report for part (b)
(4 marks)

(c)   The managers of Burcolene are also discussing whether or not to set up a foreign subsidiary in a South American country. The government of the country has recently changed, and the country's new leaders have stated that they intend to introduce economic policies to improve the balance of payments. Burcolene is concerned that one of these measures could be to block the remittance of dividends from the South American country to Europe. Burcolene expects to remit about 180 million pesos per year to Europe if the government does not intervene. Blocked funds may be invested internally within the South American country, but the government is likely to control domestic interest rates.

The investment in the South American subsidiary has an expected NPV of $2 million. The peso is expected to devalue by approximately 10% per year relative to the $. Burcolene used a discount rate of 20% per year in the appraisal of its South American capital investment. The current spot exchange rate is 20 pesos/$1.

Required:

(i) Assuming that the government blocks the remittance of dividends for a period of three years, estimate the approximate interest rate that would have to exist in the South American country for the proposed investment to remain financially viable. Taxation may be ignored. **(8 marks)**

(ii) Briefly discuss methods by which Burcolene might try to avoid the block on the remittance of dividends. **(6 marks)**

(Total: 50 marks)

11 PURSUIT CO (JUN 11 ADAPTED)

Pursuit Co, a listed company which manufactures electronic components, is interested in acquiring Fodder Co, an unlisted company involved in the development of sophisticated but high risk electronic products. The owners of Fodder Co are a consortium of private equity investors who have been looking for a suitable buyer for their company for some time. Pursuit Co estimates that a payment of the equity value plus a 25% premium would be sufficient to secure the purchase of Fodder Co. Pursuit Co would also pay off any outstanding debt that Fodder Co owed. Pursuit Co wishes to acquire Fodder Co using a combination of debt finance (borrowed from either the domestic banking system or from the Euromarkets) and its cash reserves of $20 million, such that the capital structure of the combined company remains at Pursuit Co's current capital structure level.

Information on Pursuit Co and Fodder Co

Pursuit Co

Pursuit Co has a market debt to equity ratio of 50:50 and an equity beta of 1.18. Currently Pursuit Co has a total firm value (market value of debt and equity combined) of $140 million.

Fodder Co, Statement of profit or loss extracts

Year Ended	31 May 20Y1	31 May 20Y0	31 May 20X9	31 May 20X8
All amounts are in $000				
Sales revenue	16,146	15,229	14,491	13,559
Operating profit (after operating costs and tax allowable depreciation)	5,169	5,074	4,243	4,530
Net interest costs	489	473	462	458
Profit before tax	4,680	4,601	3,781	4,072
Taxation (28%)	1,310	1,288	1,059	1,140
After tax profit	3,370	3,313	2,722	2,932
Dividends	123	115	108	101
Retained earnings	3,247	3,198	2,614	2,831

Fodder Co has a market debt to equity ratio of 10:90 and an estimated equity beta of 1.53. It can be assumed that its tax allowable depreciation is equivalent to the amount of investment needed to maintain current operational levels. However, Fodder Co will require an additional investment in assets of 22c per $1 increase in sales revenue, for the next four years. It is anticipated that Fodder Co will pay interest at 9% on its future borrowings.

For the next four years, Fodder Co's sales revenue will grow at the same average rate as the previous years. After the forecasted four-year period, the growth rate of its free cash flows will be half the initial forecast sales revenue growth rate for the foreseeable future.

Information about the combined company

Following the acquisition, it is expected that the combined company's sales revenue will be $51,952,000 in the first year, and its profit margin on sales will be 30% for the foreseeable future. After the first year the growth rate in sales revenue will be 5.8% per year for the following three years. Following the acquisition, it is expected that the combined company will pay annual interest at 6.4% on future borrowings.

The combined company will require additional investment in assets of $513,000 in the first year and then 18c per $1 increase in sales revenue for the next three years. It is anticipated that after the forecasted four-year period, its free cash flow growth rate will be half the sales revenue growth rate.

It can be assumed that the asset beta of the combined company is the weighted average of the individual companies' asset betas, weighted in proportion of the individual companies' market value.

Other information

The current annual government base rate is 4.5% and the market risk premium is estimated at 6% per year. The relevant annual tax rate applicable to all the companies is 28%.

SGF Co's interest in Pursuit Co

There have been rumours of a potential bid by SGF Co to acquire Pursuit Co. Some financial press reports have suggested that this is because Pursuit Co's share price has fallen recently. SGF Co is in a similar line of business as Pursuit Co and until a couple of years ago, SGF Co was the smaller company. However, a successful performance has resulted in its share price rising, and SGF Co is now the larger company.

The rumours of SGF Co's interest have raised doubts about Pursuit Co's ability to acquire Fodder Co. Although SGF Co has made no formal bid yet, Pursuit Co's board is keen to reduce the possibility of such a bid. The Chief Financial Officer has suggested that the most effective way to reduce the possibility of a takeover would be to distribute the $20 million in its cash reserves to its shareholders in the form of a special dividend. Fodder Co would then be purchased using debt finance. He conceded that this would increase Pursuit Co's gearing level but suggested it may increase the company's share price and make Pursuit Co less appealing to SGF Co.

Required:

(a) Discuss the advantages and disadvantages of organic growth and growth by acquisition. (8 marks)

(b) Discuss the advantages and disadvantages of borrowing funds from the domestic banking system compared to the Euromarkets. (6 marks)

(c)   **Prepare a report to the Board of Directors of Pursuit Co that**

(i)   Evaluates whether the acquisition of Fodder Co would be beneficial to Pursuit Co and its shareholders. The free cash flow to firm method should be used to estimate the values of Fodder Co and the combined company assuming that the combined company's capital structure stays the same as that of Pursuit Co's current capital structure. Include all relevant calculations.

(16 marks)

(ii)   Discusses the limitations of the estimated valuations in part (i) above.

(4 marks)

(iii)   Estimates the amount of debt finance needed, in addition to the cash reserves, to acquire Fodder Co and concludes whether Pursuit Co's current capital structure can be maintained. **(3 marks)**

(iv)   Explains the implications of a change in the capital structure of the combined company, to the valuation method used in part (i) and how the issue can be resolved. **(4 marks)**

(v)   Assesses whether the Chief Financial Officer's recommendation would provide a suitable defence against a bid from SGF Co and would be a viable option for Pursuit Co. **(5 marks)**

Professional marks will be awarded in this question for the format, structure and presentation of the report in part (c). **(4 marks)**

(Total: 50 marks)

12   NENTE CO (JUN 12 ADAPTED)

Nente Co, an unlisted company, designs and develops tools and parts for specialist machinery. The company was formed four years ago by three friends, who own 20% of the equity capital in total, and a consortium of five business angel organisations, who own the remaining 80%, in roughly equal proportions. Nente Co also has a large amount of debt finance in the form of variable rate loans. Initially the amount of annual interest payable on these loans was low and allowed Nente Co to invest internally generated funds to expand its business. Recently though, due to a rapid increase in interest rates, there has been limited scope for future expansion and no new product development.

The Board of Directors, consisting of the three friends and a representative from each business angel organisation, met recently to discuss how to secure the company's future prospects. Two proposals were put forward, as follows:

Proposal 1

To accept a takeover offer from Mije Co, a listed company, which develops and manufactures specialist machinery tools and parts. The takeover offer is for $2.95 cash per share or a share-for-share exchange where two Mije Co shares would be offered for three Nente Co shares. Mije Co would need to get the final approval from its shareholders if either offer is accepted:

Proposal 2

To pursue an opportunity to develop a small prototype product that just breaks even financially, but gives the company exclusive rights to produce a follow-on product within two years.

The meeting concluded without agreement on which proposal to pursue.

After the meeting, Mije Co was consulted about the exclusive rights. Mije Co's directors indicated that they had not considered the rights in their computations and were willing to continue with the takeover offer on the same terms without them.

Currently, Mije Co has 10 million shares in issue and these are trading for $4.80 each. Mije Co's price to earnings (P/E) ratio is 15. It has sufficient cash to pay for Nente Co's equity and a substantial proportion of its debt, and believes that this will enable Nente Co to operate on a P/E level of 15 as well. In addition to this, Mije Co believes that it can find cost-based synergies of $150,000 after tax per year for the foreseeable future. Mije Co's current profit after tax is $3,200,000.

The following financial information relates to Nente Co and to the development of the new product.

Nente Co financial information

Extract from the most recent statement of profit or loss

	$000
Sales revenue	8,780
Profit before interest and tax	1,230
Interest	(455)
Tax	(155)
Profit after tax	620
Dividends	Nil

Extract from the most recent statement of financial position

	$000
Net non-current assets	10,060
Current assets	690
Total Assets	10,750
Share capital (40c per share par value)	960
Reserves	1,400
Non-current liabilities: Variable rate loans	6,500
Current liabilities	1,890
Total liabilities and capital	10,750

In arriving at the profit after tax amount, Nente Co deducted tax allowable depreciation and other non-cash expenses totalling $1,206,000. It requires an annual cash investment of $1,010,000 in non-current assets and working capital to continue its operations.

Nente Co's profits before interest and tax in its first year of operation were $970,000 and have been growing steadily in each of the following three years, to their current level. Nente Co's cash flows grew at the same rate as well, but it is likely that this growth rate will reduce to 25% of the original rate for the foreseeable future.

Nente Co currently pays interest of 7% per year on its loans, which is 380 basis points over the government base rate, and corporation tax of 20% on profits after interest. It is estimated that an overall cost of capital of 11% is reasonable compensation for the risk undertaken on an investment of this nature.

New product development (Proposal 2)

Developing the new follow-on product will require an investment of $2,500,000 initially. The total expected cash flows and present values of the product over its five-year life, with a volatility of 42% standard deviation, are as follows:

Year(s)	Now	1	2	3 to 7 (in total)
Cash flows ($000)	–	–	(2,500)	3,950
Present values ($000)	–	–	(2,029)	2,434

Required:

(a) Explain why synergy might exist when one company merges with or takes over another company. **(7 marks)**

(b) Prepare a report for the Board of Directors of Nente Co that:

 (i) Estimates the current value of a Nente Co share, using the free cash flow to firm methodology. **(7 marks)**

 (ii) Estimates the percentage gain in value to a Nente Co share and a Mije Co share under each payment offer. **(8 marks)**

 (iii) Estimates the percentage gain in the value of the follow-on product to a Nente Co share, based on its cash flows and on the assumption that the production can be delayed following acquisition of the exclusive rights of production. **(8 marks)**

 (iv) Discusses the likely reaction of Nente Co and Mije Co shareholders to the takeover offer, including the assumptions made in the estimates above and how the follow-on product's value can be utilised by Nente Co. **(8 marks)**

 Professional marks will be awarded in part (b) for the presentation, structure and clarity of the answer. **(4 marks)**

(c) Explain the circumstances in which the Black-Scholes option pricing (BSOP) model could be used to assess the value of a company, including the data required for the variables used in the model. **(8 marks)**

(Total: 50 marks)

13 MLIMA CO (JUN 13)

Mlima Co is a private company involved in aluminium mining. About eight years ago, the company was bought out by its management and employees through a leveraged buyout (LBO). Due to high metal prices worldwide, the company has been growing successfully since the LBO. However, because the company has significant debt borrowings with strict restrictive covenants and high interest levels, it has had to reject a number of profitable projects. The company has currently two bonds in issue, as follows:

• A 16% secured bond with a nominal value of $80m, which is redeemable at par in five years. An early redemption option is available on this bond, giving Mlima Co the option to redeem the bond at par immediately if it wants to; and

• A 13% unsecured bond with a nominal value of $40m, which is redeemable at par in ten years.

Mlima Co's Board of Directors (BoD) has been exploring the idea of redeeming both bonds to provide it with more flexibility when making future investment decisions. To do so, the BoD has decided to consider a public listing of the company on a major stock exchange. It is intended that a total of 100 million shares will be issued in the newly-listed company. From the total shares, 20% will be sold to the public, 10% will be offered to the holders of the unsecured bond in exchange for redeeming the bond through an equity-for-debt swap, and the remaining 70% of the equity will remain in the hands of the current owners. The secured bond would be paid out of the funds raised from the listing.

The details of the possible listing and the distribution of equity were published in national newspapers recently. As a result, potential investors suggested that due to the small proportion of shares offered to the public and for other reasons, the shares should be offered at a substantial discount of as much as 20% below the expected share price on the day of the listing.

Mlima Co, financial information

It is expected that after the listing, deployment of new strategies and greater financial flexibility will boost Mlima Co's future sales revenue and, for the next four years, the annual growth rate will be 120% of the previous two years' average growth rate. After the four years, the annual growth rate of the free cash flows to the company will be 3.5%, for the foreseeable future. Operating profit margins are expected to be maintained in the future. Although it can be assumed that the current tax-allowable depreciation is equivalent to the amount of investment needed to maintain the current level of operations, the company will require an additional investment in assets of 30c per $1 increase in sales revenue for the next four years.

Extracts from Mlima Co's past three years' Statement of Profit or Loss

Year ended	31 May 20X3 $ million	31 May 20X2 $ million	31 May 20X1 $ million
Sales revenue	389.1	366.3	344.7
Operating profit	58.4	54.9	51.7
Net interest costs	17.5	17.7	18.0
Profit before tax	40.9	37.2	33.7
Taxation	10.2	9.3	8.4
Profit after tax	30.7	27.9	25.3

Once listed, Mlima Co will be able to borrow future debt at an interest rate of 7%, which is only 3% higher than the risk-free rate of return. It has no plans to raise any new debt after listing, but any future debt will carry considerably fewer restrictive covenants. However, these plans do not take into consideration the Bahari project (see below).

Bahari Project

Bahari is a small country with agriculture as its main economic activity. A recent geological survey concluded that there may be a rich deposit of copper available to be mined in the north-east of the country. This area is currently occupied by subsistence farmers, who would have to be relocated to other parts of the country. When the results of the survey were announced, some farmers protested that the proposed new farmland where they would be moved to was less fertile and that their communities were being broken up.

However, the protesters were intimidated and violently put down by the government, and the state-controlled media stopped reporting about them. Soon afterwards, their protests were ignored and forgotten.

In a meeting between the Bahari government and Mlima Co's BoD, the Bahari government offered Mlima Co exclusive rights to mine the copper. It is expected that there are enough deposits to last at least 15 years. Initial estimates suggest that the project will generate free cash flows of $4 million in the first year, rising by 100% per year in each of the next two years, and then by 15% in each of the two years after that. The free cash flows are then expected to stabilise at the year-five level for the remaining 10 years.

The cost of the project, payable at the start, is expected to be $150 million, comprising machinery, working capital and the mining rights fee payable to the Bahari government. None of these costs is expected to be recoverable at the end of the project's 15-year life.

The Bahari government has offered Mlima Co a subsidised loan over 15 years for the full $150 million at an interest rate of 3% instead of Mlima Co's normal borrowing rate of 7%. The interest payable is allowable for taxation purposes. It can be assumed that Mlima Co's business risk is not expected to change as a result of undertaking the Bahari project.

At the conclusion of the meeting between the Bahari government and Mlima Co's BoD, the president of Bahari commented that working together would be like old times when he and Mlima Co's chief executive officer (CEO) used to run a business together.

Other Information

Mlima Co's closest competitor is Ziwa Co, a listed company which mines metals worldwide. Mlima Co's directors are of the opinion that after listing Mlima Co's cost of capital should be based on Ziwa Co's ungeared cost of equity. Ziwa Co's cost of capital is estimated at 9.4%, its geared cost of equity is estimated at 16.83% and its pre-tax cost of debt is estimated at 4.76%. These costs are based on a capital structure comprising of 200 million shares, trading at $7 each, and $1,700 million 5% irredeemable bonds, trading at $105 per $100. Both Ziwa Co and Mlima Co pay tax at an annual rate of 25% on their taxable profits.

It can be assumed that all cash flows will be in $ instead of the Bahari currency and therefore Mlima Co does not have to take account of any foreign exchange exposure from this venture.

Required:

(a)   **Prepare a report for the Board of Directors (BoD) of Mlima Co that:**

   (i)   **Explains why Mlima Co's directors are of the opinion that Mlima Co's cost of capital should be based on Ziwa Co's ungeared cost of equity and, showing relevant calculations, estimate an appropriate cost of capital for Mlima Co.**

   (7 marks)

   (ii)   **Estimates Mlima Co's value without undertaking the Bahari project and then with the Bahari project. The valuations should use the free cash flow methodology and the cost of capital calculated in part (i). Include relevant calculations.**   **(14 marks)**

   (iii)   **Advises the BoD whether or not the unsecured bond holders are likely to accept the equity-for-debt swap offer. Include relevant calculations.**

   (5 marks)

     (iv)   Advises the BoD on the listing and the possible share price range, if a total of 100 million shares are issued. The advice should also include:

- A discussion of the assumptions made in estimating the share price range

- In addition to the reasons mentioned in the scenario above, a brief explanation of other possible reasons for changing its status from a private company to a listed one; and

- An assessment of the possible reasons for issuing the share price at a discount for the initial listing   **(12 marks)**

Professional marks will be awarded in part (a) for the format, structure and presentation of the report.   **(4 marks)**

(b)   Discuss the possible impact on, and response of, Mlima Co to the following ethical issues, with respect to the Bahari project:

    (i)   The relocation of the farmers; and

    (ii)   The relationship between the Bahari president and Mlima Co's chief executive officer.

Note: The total marks will be split equally between each part.   **(8 marks)**

(Total: 50 marks)

14 NAHARA CO AND FUGAE CO (DEC 14)

 Online question assistance

Nahara Co is a private holding company owned by the government of a wealthy oil-rich country to invest its sovereign funds. Nahara Co has followed a strategy of risk diversification for a number of years by acquiring companies from around the world in many different sectors.

One of Nahara Co's acquisition strategies is to identify and purchase undervalued companies in the airline industry in Europe. A recent acquisition was Fugae Co, a company based in a country which is part of the European Union (EU). Fugae Co repairs and maintains aircraft engines.

A few weeks ago, Nahara Co stated its intention to pursue the acquisition of an airline company based in the same country as Fugae Co. The EU, concerned about this, asked Nahara Co to sell Fugae Co before pursuing any further acquisitions in the airline industry.

Avem Co's acquisition interest in Fugae Co

Avem Co, a UK-based company specialising in producing and servicing business jets, has approached Nahara Co with a proposal to acquire Fugae Co for $1,200 million. Nahara Co expects to receive a premium of at least 30% on the estimated equity value of Fugae Co, if it is sold.

Given below are extracts from the most recent statements of financial position of both Avem Co and Fugae Co.

	Avem Co	Fugae Co
	$ million	$ million
Share capital (50c/share)	800	100
Reserves	3,550	160
Non-current liabilities	2,200	380
Current liabilities	130	30
Total capital and liabilities	6,680	670

Each Avem Co share is currently trading at $7.50, which is a multiple of 7.2 of its free cash flow to equity. Avem Co expects that the total free cash flows to equity of the combined company will increase by $40 million due to synergy benefits. After adding the synergy benefits of $40 million, Avem Co then expects the multiple of the total free cash flow of the combined company to increase to 7.5.

Fugae Co's free cash flow to equity is currently estimated at $76.5 million and it is expected to generate a return on equity of 11%. Over the past few years, Fugae Co has returned 77.3% of its annual free cash flow to equity back to Nahara Co, while retaining the balance for new investments.

Fugae Co's non-current liabilities consist entirely of $100 nominal value bonds which are redeemable in four years at the nominal value, on which the company pays a coupon of 5.4%. The debt is rated at B+ and the credit spread on B+ rated debt is 80 basis points above the risk-free rate of return.

Proposed luxury transport investment project by Fugae Co

In recent years, the country in which Fugae Co is based has been expanding its tourism industry and hopes that this industry will grow significantly in the near future. At present tourists normally travel using public transport and taxis, but there is a growing market for luxury travel. If the tourist industry does expand, then the demand for luxury travel is expected to grow rapidly. Fugae Co is considering entering this market through a four-year project. The project will cease after four years because of increasing competition.

The initial cost of the project is expected to be $42,000,000 and it is expected to generate the following after-tax cash flows over its four-year life:

Year	1	2	3	4
Cash flows ($000s)	3,277.6	16,134.3	36,504.7	35,683.6

The above figures are based on the tourism industry expanding as expected. However, it is estimated that there is a 25% probability that the tourism industry will not grow as expected in the first year. If this happens, then the present value of the project's cash flows will be 50% of the original estimates over its four-year life.

It is also estimated that if the tourism industry grows as expected in the first year, there is still a 20% probability that the expected growth will slow down in the second and subsequent years, and the present value of the project's cash flows would then be 40% of the original estimates in each of these years.

Lumi Co, a leisure travel company, has offered $50 million to buy the project from Fugae Co at the start of the second year. Fugae Co is considering whether having this choice would add to the value of the project.

If Fugae Co is bought by Avem Co after the project has begun, it is thought that the project will not result in any additional synergy benefits and will not generate any additional value for the combined company, above any value the project has already generated for Fugae Co.

Although there is no beta for companies offering luxury forms of travel in the tourist industry, Reka Co, a listed company, offers passenger transportation services on coaches, trains and luxury vehicles. About 15% of its business is in the luxury transport market and Reka Co's equity beta is 1.6. It is estimated that the asset beta of the non-luxury transport industry is 0.80. Reka Co's shares are currently trading at $4.50 per share and its debt is currently trading at $105 per $100. It has 80 million shares in issue and the book value of its debt is $340 million. The debt beta is estimated to be zero.

General information

The corporation tax rate applicable to all companies is 20%. The risk-free rate is estimated to be 4% and the market risk premium is estimated to be 6%.

Required:

(a)   Discuss whether or not Nahara Co's acquisition strategies, of pursuing risk diversification and of purchasing undervalued companies, can be valid.   **(7 marks)**

(b)   Discuss why the European Union (EU) may be concerned about Nahara Co's stated intention and how selling Fugae Co could reduce this concern.   **(4 marks)**

(c)   Prepare a report for the Board of Directors of Avem Co, which:

   (i)   Estimates the additional value created for Avem Co, if it acquires Fugae Co without considering the luxury transport project   **(10 marks)**

   (ii)   Estimates the additional value of the luxury transport project to Fugae Co, both with and without the offer from Lumi Co   **(18 marks)**

   (iii)   Evaluates the benefit attributable to Avem Co and Fugae Co from combining the two companies with and without the project, and concludes whether or not the acquisition is beneficial. The evaluation should include any assumptions made.   **(7 marks)**

   Professional marks will be awarded in part (c) for the format, structure and presentation of the report.   **(4 marks)**

   (Total: 50 marks)

CORPORATE RECONSTRUCTION AND REORGANISATION

15   BBS STORES (JUN 09 ADAPTED)

BBS Stores, a publicly quoted limited company, is considering unbundling a section of its property portfolio. The company believes that it should use the proceeds to reduce the company's medium-term borrowing and to reinvest the balance in the business (option 1). However, the company's investors have argued strongly that a sale and rental scheme would release substantial cash to investors (option 2). You are a financial consultant and have been given the task of assessing the likely impact of these alternative proposals on the company's financial performance, cost of capital and market value. The company owns all its stores.

BBS Stores' statement of financial position

	As at year end 20X8	As at year end 20X7
ASSETS	$m	$m
Non-current assets		
Intangible assets	190	160
Property, plant and equipment	4,050	3,600
Other assets	500	530
	4,740	4,290
Current assets	840	1,160
Total assets	5,580	5,450
EQUITY		
Called up share capital – equity	425	420
Retained earnings	1,535	980
Total equity	1,960	1,400
LIABILITIES		
Current liabilities	1,600	2,020
Non-current liabilities		
Medium-term loan notes	1,130	1,130
Other non-financial liabilities	890	900
	2,020	2,030
Total liabilities	3,620	4,050
Total equity and liabilities	5,580	5,450

The company's profitability has improved significantly in recent years and earnings for 20X8 were $670 million (20X7: $540 million).

The company's property, plant and equipment within non-current assets for 20X8 are as follows:

	Land and buildings $m	Fixtures, fittings and equipment $m	Assets under construction $m	Total $m
Year end 20X8				
At revaluation	2,297	4,038	165	6,500
Accumulated depreciation		(2,450)		(2,450)
Net book value	2,297	1,588	165	4,050

The property portfolio was revalued at the year end 20X8. The assets under construction are valued at a market value of $165 million and relate to new building.

In recent years commercial property values have risen in real terms by 4% per annum. Current inflation is 2.5% per annum. Property rentals currently earn an 8% return.

The proposal is that 50% of the property portfolio (land and buildings) and 50% of the assets under construction would be sold to a newly established property holding company called RPH that would issue bonds backed by the assured rental income stream from BBS Stores. BBS Stores would not hold any equity interest in the newly formed company nor would they take any part in its management.

BBS Stores is currently financed by equity in the form of 25c fully paid ordinary shares with a current market value of 400c per share. The capital debt for the company consists of medium-term loan notes of which $360 million are repayable at the end of two years and $770 million are repayable at the end of six years. Both issues of medium term notes carry a floating rate of LIBOR plus 70 basis points.

The interest liability on the six year notes has been swapped at a fixed rate of 5.5% in exchange for LIBOR which is also currently 5.5%. The reduction in the firm's gearing implied by option 1 would improve the firm's credit rating and reduce its current credit spread by 30 basis points. The change in gearing resulting from the second option is not expected to have any impact upon the firm's credit rating. There has been no alteration in the rating of the company since the earliest debt was issued.

The BBS Stores equity beta is currently 1.824. A representative portfolio of commercial property companies has an equity beta of 1.25 and an average market gearing (adjusted for tax) of 50%. The risk free rate of return is 5% and the equity risk premium is 3%. The company's current accounting rate of return on new investment is 13% before tax. You may assume that debt betas are zero throughout.

The effective rate of company tax is 35%.

Required:

(a) **On the assumption that the property unbundling proceeds, prepare a report for consideration by senior management which should include the following:**

    (i) **A comparative statement showing the impact upon the statement of financial position and on the earnings per share on the assumption that the cash proceeds of the property sale are used:**

        • **To repay the debt, repayable in two years, in full and for reinvestment in non-current assets**

        • **To repay the debt, repayable in two years, in full and to finance a share repurchase at the current share price with the balance of the proceeds.**

                                                        (13 marks)

    (ii) **An estimate of the weighted average cost of capital for the remaining business under both options on the assumption that the share price remains unchanged.** **(10 marks)**

    (iii) **An evaluation of the potential impact of each alternative on the market value of the firm (you are not required to calculate a revised market value for the firm).** **(6 marks)**

Professional marks will be awarded in part (a) for the format, structure and presentation of the report. **(4 marks)**

(b) **Discuss whether or not an increase in dividends is likely to benefit the shareholders of a publicly quoted company.** **(7 marks)**

(c) 'Behavioural finance' seeks to combine behavioural and cognitive psychological theory with conventional economics and finance to provide explanations for why people make irrational financial decisions.

Required:

Explain the key factors, identified by researchers in the field of behavioural finance, that contribute to irrational and potentially detrimental financial decision making.

(10 marks)

(Total: 50 marks)

16 CIGNO CO (SEP/DEC 15)

 Question debrief

Cigno Co is a large pharmaceutical company, involved in the research and development (R&D) of medicines and other healthcare products. Over the past few years, Cigno Co has been finding it increasingly difficult to develop new medical products. In response to this, it has followed a strategy of acquiring smaller pharmaceutical companies which already have successful products in the market and/or have products in development which look very promising for the future. It has mainly done this without having to resort to major cost-cutting and has therefore avoided large-scale redundancies. This has meant that not only has Cigno Co performed reasonably well in the stock market, but it has also maintained a high level of corporate reputation.

Anatra Co is involved in two business areas: the first area involves the R&D of medical products, and the second area involves the manufacture of medical and dental equipment. Until recently, Anatra Co's financial performance was falling, but about three years ago a new chief executive officer (CEO) was appointed and she started to turn the company around. Recently, the company has developed and marketed a range of new medical products, and is in the process of developing a range of cancer-fighting medicines. This has resulted in a good performance in the stock market, but many analysts believe that its shares are still trading below their true value. Anatra Co's CEO is of the opinion that the turnaround in the company's fortunes makes it particularly vulnerable to a takeover threat, and she is thinking of defence strategies that the company could undertake to prevent such a threat. In particular, she was thinking of disposing some of the company's assets and focussing on its core business.

Cigno Co is of the opinion that Anatra Co is being held back from achieving its true potential by its equipment manufacturing business and that by separating the two business areas, corporate value can be increased. As a result, it is considering the possibility of acquiring Anatra Co, unbundling the manufacturing business, and then absorbing Anatra Co's R&D of medical products business. Cigno Co estimates that it would need to pay a premium of 35% to Anatra Co's shareholders to buy the company.

Financial information: Anatra Co

Given below are extracts from Anatra Co's latest statement of profit or loss and statement of financial position for the year ended 30 November 20X5.

	20X5
	$ million
Sales revenue	21,400
Profit before interest and tax (PBIT)	3,210
Interest	720
Pre-tax profit	2,490
Non-current liabilities	9,000
Share capital (50c/share)	3,500
Reserves	4,520

Anatra Co's share of revenue and profits between the two business areas are as follows:

	Medical products R&D	Equipment manufacturing
Share of revenue and profit	70%	30%

Post-acquisition benefits from acquiring Anatra Co

Cigno Co estimates that following the acquisition and unbundling of the manufacturing business, Anatra Co's future sales revenue and profitability of the medical R&D business will be boosted. The annual sales growth rate is expected to be 5% and the profit margin before interest and tax is expected to be 17.25% of sales revenue, for the next four years. It can be assumed that the current tax allowable depreciation will remain equivalent to the amount of investment needed to maintain the current level of operations, but that the company will require an additional investment in assets of 40c for every $1 increase in sales revenue.

After the four years, the annual growth rate of the company's free cash flows is expected to be 3% for the foreseeable future.

Anatra Co's unbundled equipment manufacturing business is expected to be divested through a sell-off, although other options such as a management buy-in were also considered. The value of the sell-off will be based on the medical and dental equipment manufacturing industry. Cigno Co has estimated that Anatra Co's manufacturing business should be valued at a factor of 1.2 times higher than the industry's average price-to-earnings ratio. Currently the industry's average earnings-per-share is 30c and the average share price is $2.40.

Possible additional post-acquisition benefits

Cigno Co estimates that it could achieve further cash flow benefits following the acquisition of Anatra Co, if it undertakes a limited business re-organisation. There is some duplication of the R&D work conducted by Cigno Co and Anatra Co, and the costs related to this duplication could be saved if Cigno Co closes some of its own operations. However, it would mean that many redundancies would have to be made including employees who have worked in Cigno Co for many years. Anatra Co's employees are considered to be better qualified and more able in these areas of duplication, and would therefore not be made redundant.

Cigno Co could also move its headquarters to the country where Anatra Co is based and thereby potentially save a significant amount of tax, other than corporation tax. However, this would mean a loss of revenue for the government where Cigno Co is based.

The company is concerned about how the government and the people of the country where it is based might react to these issues. It has had a long and beneficial relationship with the country and with the country's people.

Cigno Co has estimated that it would save $1,600 million after-tax free cash flows to the firm at the end of the first year as a result of these post-acquisition benefits. These cash flows would increase by 4% every year for the next three years.

Estimating the combined company's weighted average cost of capital

Cigno Co is of the opinion that as a result of acquiring Anatra Co, the cost of capital will be based on the equity beta and the cost of debt of the combined company. The asset beta of the combined company is the individual companies' asset betas weighted in proportion of the individual companies' market value of equity. Cigno Co has a market debt to equity ratio of 40:60 and an equity beta of 1.10.

It can be assumed that the proportion of market value of debt to market value of equity will be maintained after the two companies combine.

Currently, Cigno Co's total firm value (market values of debt and equity combined) is $60,000 million and Anatra Co's asset beta is 0.68.

Additional information

- The estimate of the risk free rate of return is 4.3% and of the market risk premium is 7%.

- The corporation tax rate applicable to all companies is 22%.

- Anatra Co's current share price is $3 per share, and it can be assumed that the book value and the market value of its debt are equivalent.

- The pre-tax cost of debt of the combined company is expected to be 6.0%.

Important note:

Cigno Co's board of directors (BoD) does not require any discussion or computations of currency movements or exposure in this report. All calculations are to be presented in $ millions. Currency movements and their management will be considered in a separate report. The BoD also does not expect any discussion or computations relating to the financing of acquisition in this report, other than the information provided above on the estimation of the cost of capital.

Required:

(a) Distinguish between a divestment through a sell-off and a management buy-in as forms of unbundling. **(4 marks)**

(b) Prepare a report for the board of directors (BoD) of Cigno Co which:

(i) Estimates the value attributable to Cigno Co's shareholders from the acquisition of Anatra Co before taking into account the cash benefits of potential tax savings and redundancies, and then after taking these into account; **(18 marks)**

(ii) Assesses the value created from (b)(i) above, including a discussion of the estimations made and methods used; **(8 marks)**

(iii) Advises the BoD on the key factors it should consider in relation to the redundancies and potential tax savings. **(4 marks)**

Professional marks will be awarded in part (b) for the format, structure and presentation of the report. **(4 marks)**

(c) Discuss whether the defence strategy suggested by Anatra Co's CEO of disposing assets is feasible. **(6 marks)**

(d) Takeover regulation, where Anatra Co is based, offers the following conditions aimed at protecting shareholders: the mandatory-bid condition through sell out rights, the principle of equal treatment, and squeeze-out rights.

Required:

Explain the main purpose of each of the three conditions. **(6 marks)**

(Total: 50 marks)

 Calculate your allowed time and allocate the time to the separate parts

---

17 MORADA CO (SEP/DEC 16)

Morada Co is involved in offering bespoke travel services and maintenance services. In addition to owning a few hotels, it has built strong relationships with companies in the hospitality industry all over the world. It has a good reputation of offering unique, high quality holiday packages at reasonable costs for its clients. The strong relationships have also enabled it to offer repair and maintenance services to a number of hotel chains and cruise ship companies.

Following a long discussion at a meeting of the board of directors (BoD) about the future strategic direction which Morada Co should follow, three directors continued to discuss one particular issue over dinner. In the meeting, the BoD had expressed concern that Morada Co was exposed to excessive risk and therefore its cost of capital was too high. The BoD feared that several good projects had been rejected over the previous two years, because they did not meet Morada Co's high cost of capital threshold. Each director put forward a proposal, which they then discussed in turn. At the conclusion of the dinner, the directors decided to ask for a written report on the proposals put forward by the first director and the second director, before taking all three proposals to the BoD for further discussion.

First director's proposal

The first director is of the opinion that Morada Co should reduce its debt in order to mitigate its risk and therefore reduce its cost of capital. He proposes that the company should sell its repair and maintenance services business unit and focus just on offering bespoke travel services and hotel accommodation. In the sale, the book value of non-current assets will reduce by 30% and the book value of current liabilities will reduce by 10%. It is thought that the non-current assets can be sold for an after-tax profit of 15%.

The first director suggests that the funds arising from the sale of the repair and maintenance services business unit and cash resources should be used to pay off 80% of the long-term debt. It is estimated that as a result of this, Morada Co's credit rating will improve from Baa2 to A2.

Second director's proposal

The second director is of the opinion that risk diversification is the best way to reduce Morada Co's risk and therefore reduce its cost of capital. He proposes that the company raise additional funds using debt finance and then create a new strategic business unit. This business unit will focus on construction of new commercial properties.

The second director suggests that $70 million should be borrowed and used to invest in purchasing non-current assets for the construction business unit. The new debt will be issued in the form of four-year redeemable bonds paying an annual coupon of 6.2%. It is estimated that if this amount of debt is raised, then Morada Co's credit rating will worsen to Ca3 from Baa2. Current liabilities are estimated to increase to $28 million.

Third director's proposal

The third director is of the opinion that Morada Co does not need to undertake the proposals suggested by the first director and the second director just to reduce the company's risk profile. She feels that the above proposals require a fundamental change in corporate strategy and should be considered in terms of more than just tools to manage risk. Instead, she proposes that a risk management system should be set up to appraise Morada Co's current risk profile, considering each type of business risk and financial risk within the company, and taking appropriate action to manage the risk where it is deemed necessary.

Morada Co, extracts from the forecast financial position for the coming year

	$000
Non-current assets	280,000
Current assets	48,000
Total assets	328,000
Equity and liabilities	
Share capital (40c/share)	50,000
Retained earnings	137,000
Total equity	187,000
Non-current liabilities (6.2% redeemable bonds)	120,000
Current liabilities	21,000
Total liabilities	141,000
Total liabilities and equity capital	328,000

Other financial information

Morada Co's forecast after-tax earnings for the coming year are expected to be $28 million. It is estimated that the company will make a 9% return after-tax on any new investment in non-current assets, and will suffer a 9% decrease in after-tax earnings on any reduction in investment in non-current assets.

Morada Co's current share price is $2.88 per share. According to the company's finance division, it is very difficult to predict how the share price will react to either the proposal made by the first director or the proposal made by the second director. Therefore it has been assumed that the share price will not change following either proposal.

The finance division has further assumed that the proportion of the book value of non-current assets invested in each business unit gives a fair representation of the size of each business unit within Morada Co.

Morada Co's equity beta is estimated at 1.2, while the asset beta of the repairs and maintenance services business unit is estimated to be 0.65. The relevant equity beta for the new, larger company including the construction unit relevant to the second director's proposals has been estimated as 1.21.

The bonds are redeemable in four years' time at face value. For the purposes of estimating the cost of capital, it can be assumed that debt beta is zero. However, the four-year credit spread over the risk free rate of return is 60 basis points for A2 rated bonds, 90 basis points for Baa2 rated bonds and 240 basis points for Ca3 rated bonds.

A tax rate of 20% is applicable to all companies. The current risk free rate of return is estimated to be 3.8% and the market risk premium is estimated to be 7%.

Required:

(a) **Explain how business risk and financial risk are related; and how risk mitigation and risk diversification can form part of a company's risk management strategy.**

(6 marks)

(b) **Prepare a report for the board of directors of Morada Co which:**

(i) **Estimates Morada Co's cost of equity and cost of capital, based on market value of equity and debt, before any changes and then after implementing the proposals put forward by the first and by the second directors.**

(17 marks)

(ii) **Estimates the impact of the first and second directors' proposals on Morada Co's forecast after-tax earnings and forecast financial position for the coming year; and**

(7 marks)

(iii) **Discusses the impact on Morada Co of the changes proposed by the first and second directors and recommends whether or not either proposal should be accepted. The discussion should include an explanation of any assumptions made in the estimates in (b)(i) and (b)(ii) above.**

(9 marks)

Professional marks will be awarded in part (b) for the format, structure and presentation of the report.

(4 marks)

(c) **Discuss the possible reasons for the third director's proposal that a risk management system should consider each risk, before taking appropriate action.**

(7 marks)

(Total: 50 marks)

18 CHRYSOS CO (MAR/JUN 17)

The eight-member board of executive directors (BoD) of Chrysos Co, a large private, unlisted company, is considering the company's long-term business and financial future. The BoD is considering whether or not to undertake a restructuring programme. This will be followed a few years later by undertaking a reverse takeover to obtain a listing on the stock exchange in order to raise new finance. However, a few members of the BoD have raised doubts about the restructuring programme and the reverse takeover, not least the impact upon the company's stakeholders. Some directors are of the opinion that an initial public offering (IPO) would be a better option when obtaining a listing compared to a reverse takeover.

Chrysos Co was formed about 15 years ago by a team of five senior equity holders who are part of the BoD and own 40% of the equity share capital in total; 30 other equity holders own a further 40% of the equity share capital but are not part of the BoD; and a consortium of venture capital organisations (VCOs) own the remaining 20% of the equity share capital and have three representatives on the BoD. The VCOs have also lent Chrysos Co substantial debt finance in the form of unsecured bonds due to be redeemed in 10 years' time. In addition to the BoD, Chrysos Co also has a non-executive supervisory board consisting of members of Chrysos Co's key stakeholder groups. Details of the supervisory board are given below.

Chrysos Co has two business units: a mining and shipping business unit, and a machinery parts manufacturing business unit. The mining and shipping business unit accounts for around 80% of Chrysos Co's business in terms of sales revenue, non-current and current assets, and payables. However, it is estimated that this business unit accounts for around 75% of the company's operating costs. The smaller machinery parts manufacturing business unit accounts for the remaining 20% of sales revenue, non-current and current assets, and payables; and around 25% of the company's operating costs.

The following figures have been extracted from Chrysos Co's most recent financial statements:

Profit before depreciation, interest and tax for the year to 28 February 20X7

	$m
Sales revenue	16,800
Operating costs	(10,080)
Profit before depreciation, interest and tax	6,720

Financial position as at 28 February 20X7

	$m
Non-current assets	
Land and buildings	7,500
Equipment	5,400
Current assets	
Inventory	1,800
Receivables	900
Total assets	15,600
Equity	
Share capital ($1 par value per share)	1,800
Reserves	5,400
Non-current liabilities	
4.50% unsecured bonds 20Y6 (from the VCOs)	4,800
Other debt	1,050
Current liabilities	
Payables	750
Bank overdraft	1,800
Total equity and liabilities	15,600

Corporate restructuring programme

The purpose of the restructuring programme is to simplify the company's gearing structure and to obtain extra funding to expand the mining and shipping business in the future. At present, Chrysos Co is having difficulty obtaining additional funding without having to pay high interest rates.

Machinery parts manufacturing business unit

The smaller machinery parts manufacturing business unit will be unbundled either by having its assets sold to a local supplier for $3,102 million after its share of payables have been paid; or

The smaller machinery parts manufacturing business unit will be unbundled through a management buy-out by four managers. In this case, it is estimated that its after-tax net cash flows will increase by 8% in the first year only and then stay fixed at this level for the foreseeable future. The cost of capital related to the smaller business unit is estimated to be 10%. The management buy-out team will pay Chrysos Co 70% of the estimated market value of the smaller machinery parts manufacturing business unit.

Mining and shipping business unit

Following the unbundling of the smaller machinery parts manufacturing business unit, Chrysos Co will focus solely on the mining and shipping business unit, prior to undertaking the reverse takeover some years into the future.

As part of the restructuring programme, the existing unsecured bonds lent by the VCOs will be cancelled and replaced by an additional 600 million $1 shares for the VCOs. The VCOs will pay $400 million for these shares. The bank overdraft will be converted into a 15-year loan on which Chrysos Co will pay a fixed annual interest of 4.50%. The other debt under non-current liabilities will be repaid. In addition to this, Chrysos Co will invest $1,200 million into equipment for its mining and shipping business unit and this will result in its profits and cash flows growing by 4% per year in perpetuity.

Additional financial information

Chrysos Co aims to maintain a long-term capital structure of 20% debt and 80% equity in market value terms. Chrysos Co's finance director has assessed that the 4.50% annual interest it will pay on its bank loan is a reasonable estimate of its long-term cost of debt, based on the long-term capital structure above.

Although Chrysos Co does not know what its cost of capital is for the mining and shipping business unit, its finance director has determined that the current ungeared cost of equity of Sidero Co, a large quoted mining and shipping company, is 12.46%. Chrysos Co's finance director wants to use Sidero Co's ungeared cost of equity to calculate its cost of capital for the mining and shipping business unit.

The annual corporation tax rate on profits applicable to all companies is 18% and it can be assumed that tax is payable in the year incurred. All the non-current assets are eligible for tax allowable depreciation of 12% annually on the book values. The annual reinvestment needed to keep operations at their current levels is equivalent to the tax allowable depreciation.

Details of the supervisory board

The non-executive supervisory board provides an extra layer of governance over the BoD. It consists of representatives from the company's internal stakeholder groups including the finance providers, employees and the company's management. It ensures that the actions taken by the BoD are for the benefit of all the stakeholder groups and to the company as a whole. Any issues raised in board meetings are resolved through negotiation until an agreed position is reached.

Required:

(a) **Explain what a reverse takeover involves and discuss the relative advantages and disadvantages to a company, such as Chrysos Co, of obtaining a listing through a reverse takeover as opposed to an initial public offering (IPO).** (9 marks)

(b) **Prepare a report for the board of directors of Chrysos Co which includes:**

   (i) **An extract of the financial position and an estimate of Chrysos Co's value to the equity holders, after undertaking the restructuring programme.**

   (18 marks)

   (ii) **An explanation of the approach taken and assumptions made in estimating Chrysos Co's value to the equity holders, after undertaking the restructuring programme.** (5 marks)

   (iii) **A discussion of the impact of the restructuring programme on Chrysos Co and on the venture capital organisations.** (10 marks)

   Professional marks will be awarded in part (b) for the format, structure and presentation of the report. (4 marks)

(c) **Discuss why the attention Chrysos Co pays to its stakeholders represented on the supervisory board may change once it has obtained a listing.** (4 marks)

(Total: 50 marks)

19 CONEJO CO (SEP/DEC 17)

Conejo Co is a listed company based in Ardilla and uses the $ as its currency. The company was formed around 20 years ago and was initially involved in cybernetics, robotics and artificial intelligence within the information technology industry. At that time due to the risky ventures Conejo Co undertook, its cash flows and profits were very varied and unstable. Around 10 years ago, it started an information systems consultancy business and a business developing cyber security systems. Both these businesses have been successful and have been growing consistently. This in turn has resulted in a stable growth in revenues, profits and cash flows. The company continues its research and product development in artificial intelligence and robotics, but this business unit has shrunk proportionally to the other two units.

Just under eight years ago, Conejo Co was successfully listed on Ardilla's national stock exchange, offering 60% of its share capital to external equity holders, whilst the original founding members retained the remaining 40% of the equity capital. The company remains financed largely by equity capital and reserves, with only a small amount of debt capital. Due to this, and its steadily growing sales revenue, profits and cash flows, it has attracted a credit rating of A from the credit rating agencies.

At a recent board of directors (BoD) meeting, the company's chief financial officer (CFO) argued that it was time for Conejo Co to change its capital structure by undertaking a financial reconstruction, and be financed by higher levels of debt. As part of her explanation, the CFO said that Conejo Co is now better able to bear the increased risk resulting from higher levels of debt finance; would be better protected from predatory acquisition bids if it was financed by higher levels of debt; and could take advantage of the tax benefits offered by increased debt finance. She also suggested that the expected credit migration from a credit rating of A to a credit rating of BBB, if the financial reconstruction detailed below took place, would not weaken Conejo Co financially.

Financial reconstruction

The BoD decided to consider the financial reconstruction plan further before making a final decision. The financial reconstruction plan would involve raising $1,320 million ($1.32 billion) new debt finance consisting of bonds issued at their face value of $100. The bonds would be redeemed in five years' time at their face value of $100 each. The funds raised from the issue of the new bonds would be used to implement one of the following two proposals:

(i)   Proposal 1: Either buy back equity shares at their current share price, which would be cancelled after they have been repurchased; or

(ii)   Proposal 2: Invest in additional assets in new business ventures.

Conejo Co, Financial information

Extract from the forecast financial position for next year

	$m
Non-current assets	1,735
Current assets	530
Total assets	**2,265**
Equity and liabilities	
Share capital ($1 per share par value)	400
Reserves	1,700
Total equity	**2,100**
Non-current liabilities	120
Current liabilities	45
Total liabilities	**165**
Total liabilities and capital	**2,265**

Conejo Co's forecast after-tax profit for next year is $350 million and its current share price is $11 per share.

The non-current liabilities consist solely of 5.2% coupon bonds with a face value of $100 each, which are redeemable at their face value in three years' time. These bonds are currently trading at $107.80 per $100. The bond's covenant stipulates that should Conejo Co's borrowing increase, the coupon payable on these bonds will increase by 37 basis points.

Conejo Co pays tax at a rate of 15% per year and its after-tax return on the new investment is estimated at 12%.

Other financial information

Current government bond yield curve

Year	1	2	3	4	5
	1.5%	1.7%	1.9%	2.2%	2.5%

Yield spreads (in basis points)

	1 year	2 years	3 years	4 years	5 years
A	40	49	59	68	75
BBB	70	81	94	105	112
BB	148	167	185	202	218

The finance director wants to determine the percentage change in the value of Conejo Co's current bonds, if the credit rating changes from A to BBB. Furthermore, she wants to determine the coupon rate at which the new bonds would need to be issued, based on the current yield curve and appropriate yield spreads given above.

Conejo Co's chief executive officer (CEO) suggested that if Conejo Co paid back the capital and interest of the new bond in fixed annual repayments of capital and interest through the five-year life of the bond, then the risk associated with the extra debt finance would be largely mitigated. In this case, it was possible that credit migration, by credit rating companies, from A rating to BBB rating may not happen. He suggested that comparing the duration of the new bond based on the interest payable annually and the face value in five years' time with the duration of the new bond where the borrowing is paid in fixed annual repayments of interest and capital could be used to demonstrate this risk mitigation.

Required:

(a) Discuss the possible reasons for the finance director's suggestions that Conejo Co could benefit from higher levels of debt with respect to risk, from protection against acquisition bids, and from tax benefits. **(7 marks)**

(b) Prepare a report for the board of directors of Conejo Co which:

(i) Estimates, and briefly comments on, the change in value of the current bond and the coupon rate required for the new bond, as requested by the CFO;
(6 marks)

(ii) Estimates the Macaulay duration of the new bond based on the interest payable annually and face value repayment, and the Macaulay duration based on the fixed annual repayment of the interest and capital, as suggested by the CEO; **(6 marks)**

(iii) Estimates the impact of the two proposals on how the funds may be used on next year's forecast earnings, forecast financial position, forecast earnings per share and on forecast gearing; **(11 marks)**

(iv) Using the estimates from (b)(i), (b)(ii) and (b)(iii), discusses the impact of the proposed financial reconstruction and the proposals on the use of funds on:

- Conejo Co;

- Possible reaction(s) of credit rating companies and on the expected credit migration, including the suggestion made by the CEO;

- Conejo Co's equity holders;

- Conejo Co's current and new debt holders. **(16 marks)**

Professional marks will be awarded in part (b) for the format, structure and presentation of the report. **(4 marks)**

(Total: 50 marks)

TREASURY AND ADVANCED RISK MANAGEMENT TECHNIQUES

20 LAMMER PLC (JUN 06 ADAPTED) *Walk in the footsteps of a top tutor*

Lammer plc is a UK-based company that regularly trades with companies in the USA. Several large transactions are due in five months' time. These are shown below. The transactions are in '000' units of the currencies shown.

Assume that it is now 1 June and that futures and options contracts mature at the relevant month end.

	Exports to:	Imports from:
Company 1	$490	£150
Company 2	–	$890
Company 3	£110	$750
Exchange rates:	$US/£	
Spot	1.9156–1.9210	
3 months forward	1.9066–1.9120	
1 year forward	1.8901–1.8945	

Annual interest rates available to Lammer plc

	Borrowing	Investing
Sterling up to 6 months	5.5%	4.2%
Dollar up to 6 months	4.0%	2.0%

CME $/£ Currency futures (£62,500)

September 1.9045

December 1.8986

CME currency options prices, $/£ options £31,250 (cents per pound)

	CALLS		PUTS	
	Sept	Dec	Sept	Dec
1.8800	4.76	5.95	1.60	2.96
1.9000	3.53	4.70	2.36	4.34
1.9200	2.28	3.56	3.40	6.55

Required:

(a)   Discuss the relative advantages and disadvantages of the use of a money market hedge compared with using exchange traded derivatives for hedging a foreign exchange exposure. **(8 marks)**

(b)   Prepare a report for the managers of Lammer plc on how the five-month currency risk should be hedged. Include in your report all relevant calculations relating to the alternative types of hedge. **(24 marks)**

16 marks are available for calculations and 8 marks for discussion.

Professional marks for format, structure and presentation of the report for part (b)
(4 marks)

(c)   In a typical financial year Lammer plc has net dollar imports of $4.2 million. This is expected to continue for five years.

The company's cost of capital is estimated to be 11% per year. Taxation may be ignored, and cash flows may be assumed to occur at the year end.

Required:

Assuming that there is no change in the physical volume or dollar price of imports, estimate the impact on the expected market value of Lammer plc if the market expects the dollar to strengthen by 3% per year against the pound. **(8 marks)**

(d)   Briefly discuss how Lammer plc might manage the economic exposure of any foreign subsidiaries in the USA. **(6 marks)**

(Total: 50 marks)

21   CASASOPHIA CO (JUN 11 ADAPTED)

Casasophia Co, based in a European country that uses the Euro (€), constructs and maintains advanced energy efficient commercial properties around the world. It has just completed a major project in the USA and is due to receive the final payment of US$20 million in four months.

Casasophia Co is planning to commence a major construction and maintenance project in Mazabia, a small African country, in six months' time. This government-owned project is expected to last for three years during which time Casasophia Co will complete the construction of state-of-the-art energy efficient properties and provide training to a local Mazabian company in maintaining the properties. The carbon-neutral status of the building project has attracted some grant funding from the European Union and these funds will be provided to the Mazabian government in Mazabian Shillings (MShs).

Casasophia Co intends to finance the project using the US$20 million it is due to receive and borrow the rest through a € loan. It is intended that the US$ receipts will be converted into € and invested in short-dated treasury bills until they are required. These funds plus the loan will be converted into MShs on the date required, at the spot rate at that time.

Mazabia's government requires Casasophia Co to deposit the MShs2.64 billion it needs for the project, with Mazabia's central bank, at the commencement of the project. In return, Casasophia Co will receive a fixed sum of MShs1.5 billion after tax, at the end of each year for a period of three years. Neither of these amounts is subject to inflationary increases. The relevant risk adjusted discount rate for the project is assumed to be 12%.

Exchange Rates available to Casasophia

	Per €1	Per €1
Spot	US$1.3585–US$1.3618	MShs116–MShs128
4-month forward	US$1.3588–US$1.3623	Not available

Currency Futures (Contract size €125,000, Quotation: US$ per €1)

2-month expiry	1.3633
5-month expiry	1.3698

Currency Options
(Contract size €125,000, Exercise price quotation: US$ per €1, cents per Euro)

	Calls		Puts	
Exercise price	2-month expiry	5-month expiry	2-month expiry	5-month expiry
1.36	2.35	2.80	2.47	2.98
1.38	1.88	2.23	4.23	4.64

Casasophia Co Local Government Base Rate	2.20%
Mazabia Government Base Rate	10.80%
Yield on short-dated Euro Treasury Bills (assume 360-day year)	1.80%

Mazabia's current annual inflation rate is 9·7% and is expected to remain at this level for the next six months. However, after that, there is considerable uncertainty about the future and the annual level of inflation could be anywhere between 5% and 15% for the next few years. The country where Casasophia Co is based is expected to have a stable level of inflation at 1·2% per year for the foreseeable future. A local bank in Mazabia has offered Casasophia Co the opportunity to swap the annual income of MShs1.5 billion receivable in each of the next three years for Euros, at the estimated annual MShs/€ forward rates based on the current government base rates.

Required:

(a) Explain the role of the International Monetary Fund (IMF) and its significance to the activities of multinational companies. **(8 marks)**

(b) Warren Buffett, the stock market investor, views derivatives as a 'time bomb', but many corporate treasurers clearly perceive them as very useful tools for reducing risk. Explain and discuss the reasons for such divergent viewpoints. **(8 marks)**

(c) Prepare a report to advise Casasophia Co on, and recommend, an appropriate hedging strategy for the US$ income it is due to receive in four months. Include all relevant calculations. **(15 marks)**

Professional marks will be awarded in part (c) for the format, structure and presentation of the report. **(4 marks)**

(d) Provide a reasoned estimate of the additional amount of loan finance Casasophia Co needs to obtain to undertake the project in Mazabia in six months. **(5 marks)**

(e) Given that Casasophia Co agrees to the local bank's offer of the swap, calculate the net present value of the project, in six months' time, in €. Discuss whether the swap would be beneficial to Casasophia Co. **(10 marks)**

(Total: 50 marks)

22 CMC CO (SPECIMEN PAPER 2018)

Cocoa-Mocha-Chai (CMC) Co is a large listed company based in Switzerland and uses Swiss Francs as its currency. It imports tea, coffee and cocoa from countries around the world, and sells its blended products to supermarkets and large retailers worldwide. The company has production facilities located in two European ports where raw materials are brought for processing, and from where finished products are shipped out. All raw material purchases are paid for in US dollars (US$), while all sales are invoiced in Swiss Francs (CHF).

Until recently CMC Co had no intention of hedging its foreign currency exposures, interest rate exposures or commodity price fluctuations, and stated this intent in its annual report. However, after consultations with senior and middle managers, the company's new board of directors (BoD) has been reviewing its risk management and operations strategies.

You are a financial consultant hired by CMC Co to work on the following two proposals which have been put forward by the BoD for further consideration:

Proposal one

Setting up a treasury function to manage the foreign currency and interest rate exposures (but not commodity price fluctuations) using derivative products. The treasury function would be headed by the finance director. The purchasing director, who initiated the idea of having a treasury function, was of the opinion that this would enable her management team to make better decisions. The finance director also supported the idea as he felt this would increase his influence on the BoD and strengthen his case for an increase in his remuneration.

In order to assist in the further consideration of this proposal, the BoD wants you to use the following upcoming foreign currency and interest rate exposures to demonstrate how they would be managed by the treasury function:

(i)   a payment of US$5,060,000 which is due in four months' time; and

(ii)   a four-year CHF60,000,000 loan taken out to part-fund the setting up of four branches (see proposal two below). Interest will be payable on the loan at a fixed annual rate of 2.2% or a floating annual rate based on the yield curve rate plus 0.40%. The loan's principal amount will be repayable in full at the end of the fourth year.

Additional information relating to proposal one

The current spot rate is US$1.0635 per CHF1. The current annual inflation rate in the USA is three times higher than Switzerland.

The following derivative products are available to CMC Co to manage the exposures of the US$ payment and the interest on the loan:

Exchange-traded currency futures

Contract size CHF125,000 price quotation: US$ per CHF1

3-month expiry   1.0647

6-month expiry   1.0659

Exchange-traded currency options

Contract size CHF125,000, exercise price quotation: US$ per CHF1, premium: cents per CHF1

	Call Options		Put Options	
Exercise price	3-month expiry	6-month expiry	3-month expiry	6-month expiry
1.06	1.87	2.75	1.41	2.16
1.07	1.34	2.22	1.88	2.63

It can be assumed that futures and option contracts expire at the end of the month and transaction costs related to these can be ignored.

Over-the-counter products

In addition to the exchange-traded products, Pecunia Bank is willing to offer the following over-the-counter derivative products to CMC Co:

(i) A forward rate between the US$ and the CHF of US$ 1.0677 per CHF1.

(ii) An interest rate swap contract with a counterparty, where the counterparty can borrow at an annual floating rate based on the yield curve rate plus 0.8% or an annual fixed rate of 3.8%. Pecunia Bank would charge a fee of 20 basis points each to act as the intermediary of the swap. Both parties will benefit equally from the swap contract.

Alternative loan repayment proposal

As an alternative to paying the principal on the loan as one lump sum at the end of the fourth year, CMC Co could pay off the loan in equal annual amounts over the four years similar to an annuity. In this case, an annual interest rate of 2% would be payable, which is the same as the loan's gross redemption yield (yield to maturity).

Proposal two

This proposal suggested setting up four new branches in four different countries. Each branch would have its own production facilities and sales teams. As a consequence of this, one of the two European-based production facilities will be closed. Initial cost-benefit analysis indicated that this would reduce costs related to production, distribution and logistics, as these branches would be closer to the sources of raw materials and also to the customers. The operations and sales directors supported the proposal, as in addition to above, this would enable sales and marketing teams in the branches to respond to any changes in nearby markets more quickly. The branches would be controlled and staffed by the local population in those countries. However, some members of the BoD expressed concern that such a move would create agency issues between CMC Co's central management and the management controlling the branches. They suggested mitigation strategies would need to be established to minimise these issues.

Response from the non-executive directors

When the proposals were put to the non-executive directors, they indicated that they were broadly supportive of the second proposal if the financial benefits outweigh the costs of setting up and running the four branches. However, they felt that they could not support the first proposal, as this would reduce shareholder value because the costs related to undertaking the proposal are likely to outweigh the benefits.

Required:

(a) Advise CMC Co on an appropriate hedging strategy to manage the foreign exchange exposure of the US$ payment in four months' time. Show all relevant calculations, including the number of contracts bought or sold in the exchange-traded derivative markets. **(15 marks)**

(b) Demonstrate how CMC Co could benefit from the swap offered by Pecunia Bank. **(6 marks)**

(c) Calculate the modified duration of the loan if it is repaid in equal amounts and explain how duration can be used to measure the sensitivity of the loan to changes in interest rates. **(7 marks)**

(d) Prepare a memorandum for the board of directors (BoD) of CMC Co which:

(i) Discusses proposal one in light of the concerns raised by the non-executive directors; and **(9 marks)**

(ii) Discusses the agency issues related to proposal two and how these can be mitigated. **(9 marks)**

Professional marks will be awarded in part (d) for the presentation, structure, logical flow and clarity of the memorandum. **(4 marks)**

(Total: 50 marks)

23 LIRIO CO (MAR/JUN 16)

Lirio Co is an engineering company which is involved in projects around the world. It has been growing steadily for several years and has maintained a stable dividend growth policy for a number of years now. The board of directors (BoD) is considering bidding for a large project which requires a substantial investment of $40 million. It can be assumed that the date today is 1 March 20X6.

The BoD is proposing that Lirio Co should not raise the finance for the project through additional debt or equity. Instead, it proposes that the required finance is obtained from a combination of funds received from the sale of its equity investment in a European company and from cash flows generated from its normal business activity in the coming two years. As a result, Lirio Co's current capital structure of 80 million $1 equity shares and $70 million 5% bonds is not expected to change in the foreseeable future.

The BoD has asked the company's treasury department to prepare a discussion paper on the implications of this proposal. The following information on Lirio Co has been provided to assist in the preparation of the discussion paper.

Expected income and cash flow commitments prior to undertaking the large project for the year to the end of February 20X7

Lirio Co's sales revenue is forecast to grow by 8% next year from its current level of $300 million, and the operating profit margin on this is expected to be 15%. It is expected that Lirio Co will have the following capital investment requirements for the coming year, before the impact of the large project is considered:

1 A $0.10 investment in working capital for every $1 increase in sales revenue

2 An investment equivalent to the amount of depreciation to keep its non-current asset base at the present productive capacity. The current depreciation charge already included in the operating profit margin is 25% of the non-current assets of $50 million

3   A $0.20 investment in additional non-current assets for every $1 increase in sales revenue

4   $8 million additional investment in other small projects.

In addition to the above sales revenue and profits, Lirio Co has one overseas subsidiary – Pontac Co, from which it receives dividends of 80% on profits. Pontac Co produces a specialist tool which it sells locally for $60 each. It is expected that it will produce and sell 400,000 units of this specialist tool next year. Each tool will incur variable costs of $36 per unit and total annual fixed costs of $4 million to produce and sell.

Lirio Co pays corporation tax at 25% and Pontac Co pays corporation tax at 20%. In addition to this, a withholding tax of 8% is deducted from any dividends remitted from Pontac Co. A bi-lateral tax treaty exists between the countries where Lirio Co is based and where Pontac Co is based. Therefore corporation tax is payable on profits made by subsidiary companies, but full credit is given for corporation tax already paid.

It can be assumed that receipts from Pontac Co are in $ equivalent amounts and exchange rate fluctuations on these can be ignored.

Sale of equity investment in the European country

It is expected that Lirio Co will receive Euro (€) 20 million in three months' time from the sale of its investment. The € has continued to remain weak, while the $ has continued to remain strong through 20X5 and the start of 20X6. The financial press has also reported that there may be a permanent shift in the €/$ exchange rate, with firms facing economic exposure. Lirio Co has decided to hedge the € receipt using one of currency forward contracts, currency futures contracts or currency options contracts.

The following exchange contracts and rates are available to Lirio Co.

	Per €1
Spot rates	$1.1585–$1.1618
Three-month forward rates	$1.1559–$1.1601

Currency futures (contract size $125,000, quotation: € per $1)

March futures	€0.8638
June futures	€0.8656

Currency options
(contract size $125,000, exercise price quotation € per $1, premium € per $1)

	Calls		Puts	
Exercise price	March	June	March	June
0.8600	0.0255	0.0290	0.0267	0.0319

It can be assumed that futures and options contracts expire at the end of their respective months.

Dividend history, expected dividends and cost of capital, Lirio Co

Year to end of February	20X3	20X4	20X5	20X6
Number of $1 equity shares in issue (000)	60,000	60,000	80,000	80,000
Total dividends paid ($ 000)	12,832	13,602	19,224	20,377

It is expected that dividends will grow at the historic rate, if the large project is not undertaken.

Expected dividends and dividend growth rates if the large project is undertaken.

Year to end of February 20X7	Remaining cash flows after the investment in the $40 million project will be paid as dividends.
Year to end of February 20X8	The dividends paid will be the same amount as the previous year.
Year to end of February 20X9	Dividends paid will be $0.31 per share.
In future years from February 20X9	Dividends will grow at an annual rate of 7%.

Lirio Co's cost of equity capital is estimated to be 12%.

Required:

(a)   With reference to purchasing power parity, explain how exchange rate fluctuations may lead to economic exposure.   **(6 marks)**

(b)   Prepare a discussion paper, including all relevant calculations, for the board of directors (BoD) of Lirio Co which:

    (i)   Estimates Lirio Co's dividend capacity as at 28 February 20X7, prior to investing in the large project   **(9 marks)**

    (ii)   Advises Lirio Co on, and recommends, an appropriate hedging strategy for the Euro (€) receipt it is due to receive in three months' time from the sale of the equity investment   **(14 marks)**

    (iii)   Using the information on dividends provided in the question, and from (b) (i) and (b) (ii) above, assesses whether or not the project would add value to Lirio Co   **(8 marks)**

    (iv)   Discusses the issues of proposed methods of financing the project which need to be considered further.   **(9 marks)**

Professional marks will be awarded in part (b) for the format, structure and presentation of the discussion paper.   **(4 marks)**

(Total: 50 marks)

Section 2

PRACTICE QUESTIONS – SECTION B

ROLE OF SENIOR FINANCIAL ADVISER IN THE MULTINATIONAL ORGANISATION

24 MOOSE CO (DEC 09 ADAPTED)

You are the Chief Financial Officer of Moose Co. Moose Co is a manufacturer of cleaning equipment and has an international market for its products. Your company places a strong emphasis on innovation and design with patent protection across all its product range.

The company has two principal manufacturing centres, one in Europe which has been reduced in size in recent years because of high labour costs and the other in South East Asia. However, Moose Co's development has relied upon ready access to the debt market both in Europe and in South East Asia and the company is planning significant expansion with a new manufacturing and distribution centre in South America. Your company is highly profitable with strong cash flows although in the last two quarters there has been a downturn in sales in all markets as the global recession has begun to take effect.

Since August 20X7, credit conditions have deteriorated across all of the major economies as banks have curtailed their lending following the down rating of US asset-backed securities. In 20X8 and 20X9 many banks recorded significant multibillion dollar losses as they attempted to sell off what had become known as 'toxic debt', leading to a further collapse in their value. In response many banks also attempted to repair their balance sheets by rights and other equity issues.

The founder and executive chairman of the company, Alan Bison, is planning a round of meetings with a number of investment banks in leading financial centres around the world to explore raising a $350 million dollar loan for the new development.

It has already been suggested that a loan of this size would need to be syndicated or alternatively raised through a bond issue, and that the company would be well advised to hedge against interest rate risk.

In preparation for those meetings he has asked you to provide him with some briefing notes.

Required:

(a) Explain why Moose Co should manage its exposure to interest rate risk.   **(5 marks)**

(b) Given conditions in the global debt market as described above, advise on the likely factors banks will consider in offering a loan of this size.   **(7 marks)**

(c) Assess the relative advantages of loan syndication versus a bond issue to Moose Co.   **(7 marks)**

(d) Assess the relative advantages and disadvantages of entering into a capital investment of this scale at this stage of the global economic cycle.   **(6 marks)**

(Total: 25 marks)

25 LAMRI CO (DEC 10 ADAPTED)

Lamri Co (Lamri), a listed company, is expecting sales revenue to grow to $80 million next year, which is an increase of 20% from the current year. The operating profit margin for next year is forecast to be the same as this year at 30% of sales revenue. In addition to these profits, Lamri receives 75% of the after-tax profits from one of its wholly owned foreign subsidiaries – Magnolia Co (Magnolia), as dividends. However, its second wholly owned foreign subsidiary – Strymon Co (Strymon) does not pay dividends.

Lamri is due to pay dividends of $7.5 million shortly and has maintained a steady 8% annual growth rate in dividends over the past few years. The company has grown rapidly in the last few years as a result of investment in key projects and this is likely to continue.

For the coming year it is expected that Lamri will require the following capital investment.

1   An investment equivalent to the amount of depreciation to keep its non-current asset base at the present productive capacity. Lamri charges depreciation of 25% on a straight-line basis on its non-current assets of $15 million. This charge has been included when calculating the operating profit amount.

2   A 25% investment in additional non-current assets for every $1 increase in sales revenue.

3    $4.5 million additional investment in non-current assets for a new project.

Lamri also requires a 15% investment in working capital for every $1 increase in sales revenue.

Strymon produces specialist components solely for Magnolia to assemble into finished goods. Strymon will produce 300,000 specialist components at $12 variable cost per unit and will incur fixed costs of $2.1 million for the coming year. It will then transfer the components to Magnolia at full cost price, where they will be assembled at a cost of $8 per unit and sold for $50 per unit. Magnolia will incur additional fixed costs of $1.5 million in the assembly process.

Tax-Ethic (TE) is a charitable organisation devoted to reducing tax avoidance schemes by companies operating in poor countries around the world. TE has petitioned Lamri's Board of Directors to reconsider Strymon's policy of transferring goods at full cost. TE suggests that the policy could be changed to cost plus 40% mark-up. If Lamri changes Strymon's policy, it is expected that Strymon would be asked to remit 75% of its after-tax profits as dividends to Lamri.

Other Information

1   Lamri's outstanding non-current liabilities of $35 million, on which it pays interest of 8% per year, and its 30 million $1 issued equity capital will not change for the coming year.

2   Lamri's, Magnolia's and Strymon's profits are taxed at 28%, 22% and 42% respectively. A withholding tax of 10% is deducted from any dividends remitted from Strymon.

3   The tax authorities where Lamri is based charge tax on profits made by subsidiary companies but give full credit for tax already paid by overseas subsidiaries.

4   All costs and revenues are in $ equivalent amounts and exchange rate fluctuations can be ignored.

Required:

(a)   **Calculate Lamri's dividend capacity for the coming year prior to implementing TE's proposal and after implementing the proposal.**   **(14 marks)**

(b)   **Comment on the impact of implementing TE's proposal and suggest possible actions Lamri may take as a result.**   **(6 marks)**

(c)   Money laundering is a process in which assets obtained or generated by criminal activity are moved or concealed to obscure their link with the crime.

Required:

Explain what steps have been taken by global governments and other bodies to prevent international money laundering and terrorist financing.   **(5 marks)**

(Total: 25 marks)

26   STROM CO (DEC 12 ADAPTED)

Assume that it is now December 2012.

Strom Co is a clothing retailer, with stores selling mid-price clothes and clothing accessories throughout Europe. It sells its own-brand items, which are produced by small manufacturers located in Africa, who work solely for Strom Co. The recent European sovereign debt crisis has affected a number of countries in the European Union (EU). Consequently, Strom Co has found trading conditions to be extremely difficult, putting pressure on profits and sales revenue.

The sovereign debt crisis in Europe resulted in countries finding it increasingly difficult and expensive to issue government bonds to raise funds. Two main reasons have been put forward to explain why the crisis took place: firstly, a number of countries continued to borrow excessive funds, because their expenditure exceeded taxation revenues; and secondly, a number of countries allocated significant sums of money to support their banks following the 'credit crunch' and the banking crisis.

In order to prevent countries defaulting on their debt obligations and being downgraded, the countries in the EU and the International Monetary Fund (IMF) established a fund to provide financial support to member states threatened by the risk of default, credit downgrades and excessive borrowing yields. Strict economic conditions known as austerity measures were imposed on these countries in exchange for receiving financial support.

The austerity measures have affected Strom Co negatively, and the years 2011 and 2012 have been particularly bad, with sales revenue declining by 15% and profits by 25% in 2011, and remaining at 2011 levels in 2012. On investigation, Strom Co noted that clothing retailers selling clothes at low prices and at high prices were not affected as badly as Strom Co or other mid-price retailers. Indeed, the retailers selling low-priced clothes had increased their profits, and retailers selling luxury, expensive clothes had maintained their profits over the last two to three years.

In order to improve profitability, Strom Co's board of directors expects to cut costs where possible. A significant fixed cost relates to quality control, which includes monitoring the working conditions of employees of Strom Co's clothing manufacturers, as part of its ethical commitment.

Required:

(a) Explain the role and aims of the International Monetary Fund (IMF) and discuss possible reasons why the austerity measures imposed on European Union (EU) countries might have affected Strom Co negatively. **(10 marks)**

(b) Suggest, giving reasons, why the austerity measures might not have affected clothing retailers at the high and low price range, as much as the mid-price range retailers like Strom Co. **(4 marks)**

(c) Discuss the risks to Strom Co of reducing the costs relating to quality control and how the detrimental impact of such reductions in costs could be decreased.

(6 marks)

(d) Explain what is meant by the term 'money laundering', and explain the steps taken internationally to prevent it. **(5 marks)**

(Total: 25 marks)

27 ENNEA CO (JUN 12)

Three proposals were put forward for further consideration after a meeting of the executive directors of Ennea Co to discuss the future investment and financing strategy of the business. Ennea Co is a listed company operating in the haulage and shipping industry.

Proposal 1

To increase the company's level of debt by borrowing a further $20 million and use the funds raised to buy back share capital.

Proposal 2

To increase the company's level of debt by borrowing a further $20 million and use these funds to invest in additional non-current assets in the haulage strategic business unit.

Proposal 3

To sell excess non-current haulage assets with a net book value of $25 million for $27 million and focus on offering more services to the shipping strategic business unit. This business unit will require no additional investment in non-current assets. All the funds raised from the sale of the non-current assets will be used to reduce the company's debt.

Ennea Co financial information

Extracts from the forecast financial position for the coming year

	$m
Non-current assets	282
Current assets	66
Total assets	**348**

Equity and liabilities

	$m
Share capital (40c per share par value)	48
Retained earnings	123
Total equity	**171**
Non-current liabilities	140
Current liabilities	37
Total liabilities	**177**
Total liabilities and capital	**348**

Ennea Co's forecast after tax profit for the coming year is expected to be $26 million and its current share price is $3.20 per share. The non-current liabilities consist solely of a 6% medium term loan redeemable within seven years. The terms of the loan contract stipulates that an increase in borrowing will result in an increase in the coupon payable of 25 basis points on the total amount borrowed, while a reduction in borrowing will lower the coupon payable by 15 basis points on the total amount borrowed.

Ennea Co's effective tax rate is 20%. The company's estimated after tax rate of return on investment is expected to be 15% on any new investment. It is expected that any reduction in investment would suffer the same rate of return.

Required:

(a) Estimate and discuss the impact of each of the three proposals on the forecast statement of financial position, the earnings and earnings per share, and gearing of Ennea Co. **(20 marks)**

(b) An alternative suggestion to proposal three was made where the non-current assets could be leased to other companies instead of being sold. The lease receipts would then be converted into an asset through securitisation. The proceeds from the sale of the securitised lease receipts asset would be used to reduce the outstanding loan borrowings.

Required:

Explain what the securitisation process would involve and what would be the key barriers to Ennea Co undertaking the process. **(5 marks)**

(Total: 25 marks)

28   LIMNI CO (JUN 13)

Limni Co is a large company manufacturing hand-held electronic devices such as mobile phones and tablet computers. The company has been growing rapidly over the last few years, but it also has high research and development expenditure. It is involved in a number of projects worldwide, developing new and innovative products and systems in a rapidly changing industry. Due to the nature of the industry, this significant growth in earnings has never been stable, but has depended largely on the success of the new innovations and competitor actions. However, in the last two years it seems that the rapid period of growth is slowing, with fewer products coming to market compared to previous years.

Limni Co has never paid dividends and has financed projects through internally generated funds and with occasional rights issues of new share capital. It currently has insignificant levels of debt. The retained cash reserves have recently grown because of a drop in the level of investment in new projects.

The company has an active treasury division which invests spare funds in traded equities, bonds and other financial instruments; and releases the funds when required for new projects. The division also manages cash flow risk using money and derivative markets. The treasury division is currently considering investing in three companies with the following profit after tax (PAT) and dividend history:

Year	Company Theta		Company Omega		Company Kappa	
	PAT	Dividends	PAT	Dividends	PAT	Dividends
	$000	$000	$000	$000	$000	$000
20X3	57,100	22,840	93,300	60,560	162,400	44,100
20X2	54,400	21,760	90,600	57,680	141,500	34,200
20X1	52,800	21,120	88,000	54,840	108,900	26,300
20X0	48,200	19,280	85,400	52,230	105,700	20,250
20W9	45,500	18,200	82,900	49,740	78,300	15,700

All of the three companies' share capital has remained largely unchanged since 20W9.

Recently, Limni Co's Board of Directors (BoD) came under pressure from the company's larger shareholders to start returning some of the funds, currently retained by the company, back to the shareholders. The BoD thinks that the shareholders have a strong case to ask for repayments. However, it is unsure whether to pay a special, one-off large dividend from its dividend capacity and retained funds, followed by small annual dividend payments; or to undertake a periodic share buyback scheme over the next few years.

Limni Co is due to prepare its statement of profit or loss shortly and estimates that the annual sales revenue will be $600 million, on which its profit before tax is expected to be 23% of sales revenue. It charges depreciation of 25% on a straight-line basis on its non-current assets of $220 million. It estimates that $67 million investment in current and non-current assets was spent during the year. It is due to receive $15 million in dividends from its subsidiary companies, on which annual tax of 20% on average has been paid. Limni Co itself pays annual tax at 26%, and the tax authorities where Limni Co is based charge tax on dividend remittances made by overseas subsidiary companies, but give full credit on tax already paid on those remittances. In order to fund the new policy of returning funds to shareholders, Limni Co's BoD wants to increase the current estimated dividend capacity by 10%, by asking the overseas subsidiary companies for higher repatriations.

Required:

(a) Discuss Limni Co's current dividend, financing and risk management policies, and suggest how the decision to return retained funds back to the shareholders will affect these policies. **(8 marks)**

(b) Evaluate the dividend policies of each of the three companies that Limni Co is considering investing in, and discuss which company Limni Co might select. **(8 marks)**

(c) Calculate, and briefly comment on, how much the dividends from overseas companies need to increase by, to increase Limni Co's dividend capacity by 10%. **(6 marks)**

(d) Discuss the benefits to Limni Co's shareholders of receiving repayments through a share buyback scheme as opposed to the dividend scheme described above. **(3 marks)**

(Total: 25 marks)

29   CHAWAN CO (JUN 15)

 Online question assistance

The treasury department of Chawan Co, a listed company, aims to maintain a portfolio of around $360 million consisting of equity shares, corporate bonds and government bonds, which it can turn into cash quickly for investment projects. Chawan Co is considering disposing 27 million shares, valued at $2.15 each, which it has invested in Oden Co. The head of Chawan Co's treasury department is of the opinion that, should the decision be made to dispose of its equity stake in Oden Co, this should be sold through a dark pool network and not sold on the stock exchange where Oden Co's shares are listed. In the last few weeks, there have also been rumours that Oden Co may become subject to a takeover bid.

Oden Co operates in the travel and leisure (T&L) sector, and the poor weather conditions in recent years, coupled with a continuing recession, has meant that the T&L sector is under-performing. Over the past three years, sales revenue fell by an average of 8% per year in the T&L sector. However, there are signs that the economy is starting to recover, but this is by no means certain.

Given below are extracts from the recent financial statements and other financial information for Oden Co and the T&L sector.

Oden Co

Year ending 31 May (all amounts in $m)

	20X3	20X4	20X5
Total non-current assets	972	990	980
Total current assets	128	142	126
Total assets	1,100	1,132	1,106

	20X3	*20X4*	*20X5*
Equity			
Ordinary shares ($0.50)	300	300	300
Reserves	305	329	311
Total equity	605	629	611
Non-current liabilities			
Bank loans	115	118	100
Bonds	250	250	260
Total non-current liabilities	365	368	360
Current liabilities			
Trade and other payables	42	45	37
Bank overdraft	88	90	98
Total current liabilities	130	135	135
Total equity and liabilities	1,100	1,132	1,106

Oden Co

Year ending 31 May (all amounts in $m)

	20X3	*20X4*	*20X5*
Sales revenue	1,342	1,335	1,185
Operating profit	218	203	123
Finance costs	(23)	(27)	(35)
Profit before tax	195	176	88
Taxation	(35)	(32)	(16)
Profit for the year	160	144	72

Other financial information (Based on annual figures till 31 May of each year)

	20X2	20X3	20X4	20X5
Oden Co average share price ($)	2.10	2.50	2.40	2.20
Oden Co dividend per share ($)	0.15	0.18	0.20	0.15
T&L sector average share price ($)	3.80	4.40	4.30	4.82
T&L sector average earnings per share ($)	0.32	0.36	0.33	0.35
T&L sector average dividend per share ($)	0.25	0.29	0.29	0.31
Oden Co's equity beta	1.5	1.5	1.6	2.0
T&L sector average equity beta	1.5	1.4	1.5	1.6

The risk-free rate and the market return have remained fairly constant over the last ten years at 4% and 10% respectively.

Required:

(a) **Explain what a dark pool network is and why Chawan Co may want to dispose of its equity stake in Oden Co through one, instead of through the stock exchange where Oden Co's shares are listed.** **(5 marks)**

(b) **Discuss whether or not Chawan Co should dispose of its equity stake in Oden Co. Provide relevant calculations to support the discussion.**

Note: Up to 10 marks are available for the calculations. **(20 marks)**

(Total: 25 marks)

30 CHITHURST CO (SEP/DEC 16)

Chithurst Co gained a stock exchange listing five years ago. At the time of the listing, members of the family who founded the company owned 75% of the shares, but now they only hold just over 50%. The number of shares in issue has remained unchanged since Chithurst Co was listed. Chithurst Co's directors have continued the policy of paying a constant dividend per share each year which the company had before it was listed. However, investors who are not family members have become increasingly critical of this policy, saying that there is no clear rationale for it. They would prefer to see steady dividend growth, reflecting the increase in profitability of Chithurst Co since its listing.

The finance director of Chithurst Co has provided its board with details of Chithurst Co's dividends and investment expenditure, compared with two other similar-sized companies in the same sector, Eartham Co and Iping Co. Each company has a 31 December year end.

	Chithurst Co			Eartham Co			Iping Co		
	Profit for year after interest and tax	Dividend paid	New investment expenditure	Profit for year after interest and tax	Dividend paid	New investment expenditure	Profit for year after interest and tax	Dividend paid	New investment expenditure
	$m	$m	$m	$m	$m	$m	$m	$m	$m
20X2	77	33	18	95	38	30	75	35	37
20X3	80	33	29	(10)	15	15	88	17	64
20X4	94	33	23	110	44	42	118	39	75
20X5	97	33	21	120	48	29	132	42	84

Other financial information relating to the three companies is as follows:

	Chithurst Co	Eartham Co	Iping Co
Cost of equity	11%	14%	12%
Market capitalisation $m	608	1,042	1,164
Increase in share price in last 12 months	1%	5%	10%

Chithurst Co's finance director has estimated the costs of equity for all three companies. None of the three companies has taken out significant new debt finance since 20X1.

Required:

(a)   Discuss the benefits and drawbacks of the dividend policies which the three companies appear to have adopted. Provide relevant calculations to support your discussion.

Note: Up to 5 marks are available for the calculations.   **(15 marks)**

(b)   Discuss how the market capitalisation of the three companies compares with your valuations calculated using the dividend valuation model. Use the data provided to calculate valuations based on growth rates for the most recent year and for the last three years.

Note: Up to 5 marks are available for the calculations.   **(10 marks)**

(Total: 25 marks)

31   BOURNELORTH CO (MAR/JUN 17)

Bournelorth Co is an IT company which was established by three friends ten years ago. It was listed on a local stock exchange for smaller companies nine months ago.

Bournelorth Co originally provided support to businesses in the financial services sector. It has been able to expand into other sectors over time due to the excellent services it has provided and the high quality staff whom its founders recruited. The founders have been happy with the level of profits which the IT services have generated. Over time they have increasingly left the supervision of the IT services in the hands of experienced managers and focused on developing diagnostic applications (apps). The founders have worked fairly independently of each other on development work. Each has a small team of staff and all three want their teams to work in an informal environment which they believe enhances creativity.

Two apps which Bournelorth Co developed were very successful and generated significant profits. The founders wanted the company to invest much more in developing diagnostic apps. Previously they had preferred to use internal funding, because they were worried that external finance providers would want a lot of information about how Bournelorth Co is performing. However, the amount of finance required meant that funding had to be obtained from external sources and they decided to seek a listing, as two of Bournelorth Co's principal competitors had recently been successfully listed.

25% of Bournelorth Co's equity shares were made available on the stock exchange for external investors, which was the minimum allowed by the rules of the exchange. The founders have continued to own the remaining 75% of Bournelorth Co's equity share capital. Although the listing was fully subscribed, the price which new investors paid was lower than the directors had originally hoped.

The board now consists of the three founders, who are the executive directors, and two independent non-executive directors, who were appointed when the company was listed. The non-executive directors have expressed concerns about the lack of frequency of formal board meetings and the limited time spent by the executive directors overseeing the company's activities, compared with the time they spend leading development work. The non-executive directors would also like Bournelorth Co's external auditors to carry out a thorough review of its risk management and control systems.

The funds obtained from the listing have helped Bournelorth Co expand its development activities. Bournelorth Co's competitors have recently launched some very successful diagnostic apps and its executive directors are now afraid that Bournelorth Co will fall behind its competitors unless there is further investment in development. However, they disagree about how this investment should be funded. One executive director believes that Bournelorth Co should consider selling off its IT support and consultancy services business. The second executive director favours a rights issue and the third executive director would prefer to seek debt finance. At present Bournelorth Co has low gearing and the director who is in favour of debt finance believes that there is too much uncertainty associated with obtaining further equity finance, as investors do not always act rationally.

Required:

(a) **Discuss the factors which will determine whether the sources of finance suggested by the executive directors are used to finance further investment in diagnostic applications (apps).** **(8 marks)**

(b) **(i)** **Identify the risks associated with investing in the development of apps and describe the controls which Bournelorth Co should have over its investment in development.** **(6 marks)**

(ii) **Discuss the issues which determine the information Bournelorth Co communicates to external finance providers.** **(3 marks)**

(c) **(i)** **Explain the insights which behavioural finance provides about investor behaviour.** **(3 marks)**

(ii) **Assess how behavioural factors may affect the share price of Bournelorth Co.** **(5 marks)**

(Total: 25 marks)

32 HIGH K CO (SEP/DEC 17)

High K Co is one of the three largest supermarket chains in the country of Townia. Its two principal competitors, Dely Co and Leminster Co, are of similar size to High K Co. In common with its competitors (but see below), High K Co operates three main types of store:

- Town centre stores – these sell food and drink and a range of small household items. High K Co's initial growth was based on its town centre stores, but it has been shutting them over the last decade, although the rate of closure has slowed in the last couple of years.

- Convenience stores – these are smaller and sell food and drink and very few other items. Between 20X3 and 20Y3, High K Co greatly expanded the number of convenience stores it operated. Their performance has varied, however, and since 20Y3, High K Co has not opened any new stores and closed a number of the worst-performing stores.

- Out-of-town stores – these sell food and drink and a full range of household items, including large electrical goods and furniture. The number of out-of-town stores which High K Co operated increased significantly until 20Y0, but has only increased slightly since.

The majority of town centre and out-of-town stores premises are owned by High K Co, but 85% of convenience stores premises are currently leased.

High K Co also sells most of its range of products online, either offering customers home delivery or 'click and collect' (where the customer orders the goods online and picks them up from a collection point in one of the stores).

High K Co's year end is 31 December. When its 20Y6 results were published in April 20Y7, High K Co's chief executive emphasised that the group was focusing on:

- Increasing total shareholder return by improvements in operating efficiency and enhancement of responsiveness to customer needs

- Ensuring competitive position by maintaining flexibility to respond to new strategic challenges

- Maintaining financial strength by using diverse sources of funding, including making use in future of revolving credit facilities

Since April 20Y7, Dely Co and Leminster Co have both announced that they will be making significant investments to boost online sales. Dely Co intends to fund its investments by closing all its town centre and convenience stores, although it also intends to open more out-of-town stores in popular locations.

The government of Townia was re-elected in May 20Y7. In the 18 months prior to the election, it eased fiscal policy and consumer spending significantly increased. However, it has tightened fiscal policy since the election to avoid the economy overheating. It has also announced an investigation into whether the country's large retail chains treat their suppliers unfairly.

Extracts from High K Co's 20Y6 financial statements and other information about it are given below:

High K Co statement of profit or loss extracts

Year ending 31 December (all amounts in $m)

	20Y4	20Y5	20Y6
Sales revenue	23,508	23,905	24,463
Gross profit	1,018	1,211	1,514
Operating profit	204	407	712
Finance costs	(125)	(115)	(100)
Profit after tax	52	220	468
Dividends	150	170	274

High K Co statement of financial position extracts

Year ending 31 December (all amounts in $m)

	20Y4	20Y5	20Y6
Non-current assets	10,056	9,577	8,869
Cash and cash equivalents	24	709	1,215
Other current assets	497	618	747
Total non-current and current assets	10,577	10,904	10,831

Equity

	20Y4	20Y5	20Y6
Ordinary shares ($1)	800	800	800
Reserves	7,448	7.519	7,627
Total equity	8,248	8,319	8,427
Non-current liabilities	1,706	1,556	1,246
Current liabilities	623	1,029	1,158

Other information

	20Y4	20Y5	20Y6
Market price per share	3.54	3.34	3.23
(in $, $3.89 at end of 20Y3, $3.17 currently)			
Staff working in shops ('000)	78	75	72

Segment information

Revenue ($m)	20Y4	20Y5	20Y6
Town centre stores	5,265	5,189	5,192
Convenience stores	3,786	3,792	3,833
Out-of-town stores	10,220	10,340	10,547
Store revenue	19,271	19,321	19,572
Online sales	4,237	4,584	4,891
Number of stores			
Town centre stores	165	157	153
Convenience stores	700	670	640
Out-of-town stores	220	224	227

Required:

(a) Evaluate High K Co's financial performance. You should indicate in your discussion areas where further information about High K Co would be helpful. Provide relevant calculations for ratios and trends to support your evaluation.

Note: Up to 10 marks are available for calculations. **(21 marks)**

(b) Discuss how High K Co may seek to finance an investment programme. **(4 marks)**

(Total: 25 marks)

ADVANCED INVESTMENT APPRAISAL

33 STRAYER INC (JUN 02 ADAPTED) *Walk in the footsteps of a top tutor*

The managers of Strayer Inc are investigating a potential $25 million investment. The investment would be a diversification away from existing mainstream activities and into the printing industry. $6 million of the investment would be financed by internal funds, $10 million by a rights issue and $9 million by long-term loans. The investment is expected to generate pre-tax net cash flows of approximately $5 million per year, for a period of ten years. The residual value at the end of Year 10 is forecast to be $5 million after tax. As the investment is in an area that the government wishes to develop, a subsidised loan of $4 million out of the total $9 million is available. This will cost 2% below the company's normal cost of long-term debt finance, which is 8%.

Strayer's equity beta is 0.85, and its financial gearing is 60% equity, 40% debt by market value. The average equity beta in the printing industry is 1.2, and average gearing 50% equity, 50% debt by market value. The risk-free rate is 5.5% per annum and the market return 12% per annum. Issue costs are estimated to be 1% for debt financing (excluding the subsidised loan), and 4% for equity financing. These costs are not tax allowable.

The corporate tax rate is 30%.

Required:

(a) Estimate the Adjusted Present Value (APV) of the proposed investment. **(12 marks)**

(b) Explain the difference between APV and NPV as methods of investment appraisal and comment upon the circumstances under which APV might be a better method of evaluating a capital investment than NPV. **(5 marks)**

(c) Explain the major differences between Islamic finance and other conventional forms of finance such as those being considered by Strayer. Identify, and briefly discuss, two Islamic financial instruments that could be of use to Strayer in the above situation. **(8 marks)**

(Total: 25 marks)

34 DIGUNDER (DEC 07 ADAPTED)

Digunder, a property development company, has gained planning permission for the development of a housing complex at Newtown which will be developed over a three year period. The resulting property sales less land purchase and building costs would have an expected net present value of $4 million if the investment was made immediately (at a cost of capital of 10% per annum).

Immediate building of the housing complex would be risky as the project has a volatility attaching to its net present value of 40%.

Digunder has an option to purchase a plot of land in Newtown, at an agreed price of $24 million, which must be exercised within the next two years.

One source of risk is the potential for development of Newtown as a regional commercial centre for the large number of professional firms leaving the capital, Bigcity, because of high rents and local business taxes. Within the next two years, an announcement by the government will be made about the development of transport links into Newtown from outlying districts including the area where Digunder hold the land option concerned.

The risk free rate of interest is 6% per annum.

Required:

(a) **Estimate the value of the option to delay the start of the project for two years using the Black Scholes option pricing model. Assume that the government will make its announcement about the potential transport link at the end of the two-year period.** **(12 marks)**

(b) **On the basis of your valuation of the option to delay, estimate the overall value of the project, giving a concise rationale for the valuation method you have used.**

(4 marks)

(c) **Describe the limitations of the valuation method you used in (a) above and describe how you would value the option if the government were to make the announcement at ANY time over the next two years.** **(4 marks)**

(d) Digunder's finance director is considering introducing a system of integrated reporting in the next accounting period.

Required:

Explain the objectives of integrated reporting. **(5 marks)**

(Total: 25 marks)

35 KENAND CO

(a) Kenand Co has a cash surplus of $1m, which the financial manager is keen to invest in corporate bonds. He has identified two potential investment opportunities, in two different companies which are both rated A by the major credit rating agencies:

Option 1:

AB Co has $100m of bonds already in issue. The bonds carry a coupon rate of 5% per annum, and the financial press is reporting that the bonds have a bid yield of 6.2% per annum. The bonds are redeemable at a 10% premium to nominal value in 4 years.

Option 2:

XY Co is about to issue $50m of 3 year bonds with a coupon rate of 4% per annum. The bonds will be redeemable at par in 3 years. The annual spot yield curve for government bonds is:

1 year 3.54%

2 year 4.01%

3 year 4.70%

4 year 5.60%

Extract from a major credit rating agency's website:

Table of spreads (in basis points)

Rating	1 year	2 year	3 year	4 year
AAA	5	18	29	40
AA	16	30	42	50
A	26	39	50	60

Required:

(i) Calculate the theoretical market value of a $100 bond in AB Co, and the theoretical issue price of a $100 bond in XY Co. Calculate how many bonds Kenand Co will be able to buy with its $1m. **(6 marks)**

(ii) Estimate the Macaulay duration of the AB Co bonds and the XY Co bonds, and interpret your results. **(8 marks)**

(b) XY Co (details presented in part (a) above) is keen to hedge against interest rate risk on the new bonds which are being issued. The company treasurer expects interest rates to be flat for the coming year, but he is keen to arrange a Forward Rate Agreement (FRA) which will fix the company's borrowing rate for the following year.

Required:

Calculate the forward rate which the bank will quote for a 12 v 24 FRA. **(3 marks)**

(c) XY Co already has $20m of borrowings in the form of variable rate loans, where the interest rate is based on the given A rated company's yield curve figures. Because of the long-term threat of interest rate rises, the company treasurer has approached the bank to discuss the possibility of entering into a 4 year interest rate swap, whereby XY Co would pay the bank a fixed rate of interest for 4 years, in exchange for receiving a variable rate of return from the bank of the given yield rates less 30 basis points.

Required:

Calculate the fixed rate of interest payable by XY Co to the bank in such a swap arrangement. **(8 marks)**

(Total: 25 marks)

36 FUBUKI CO (DEC 10)

Fubuki Co, an unlisted company based in Megaera, has been manufacturing electrical parts used in mobility vehicles for people with disabilities and the elderly, for many years. These parts are exported to various manufacturers worldwide but at present there are no local manufacturers of mobility vehicles in Megaera. Retailers in Megaera normally import mobility vehicles and sell them at an average price of $4,000 each. Fubuki Co wants to manufacture mobility vehicles locally and believes that it can sell vehicles of equivalent quality locally at a discount of 37.5% to the current average retail price.

Although this is a completely new venture for Fubuki Co, it will be in addition to the company's core business. Fubuki Co's directors expect to develop the project for a period of four years and then sell it for $16 million to a private equity firm. Megaera's government has been positive about the venture and has offered Fubuki Co a subsidised loan of up to 80% of the investment funds required, at a rate of 200 basis points below Fubuki Co's borrowing rate. Currently Fubuki Co can borrow at 300 basis points above the five-year government debt yield rate.

A feasibility study commissioned by the directors, at a cost of $250,000, has produced the following information.

1   Initial cost of acquiring suitable premises will be $11 million, and plant and machinery used in the manufacture will cost $3 million. Acquiring the premises and installing the machinery is a quick process and manufacturing can commence almost immediately.

2   It is expected that in the first year 1,300 units will be manufactured and sold. Unit sales will grow by 40% in each of the next two years before falling to an annual growth rate of 5% for the final year. After the first year the selling price per unit is expected to increase by 3% per year.

3   In the first year, it is estimated that the total direct material, labour and variable overheads costs will be $1,200 per unit produced. After the first year, the direct costs are expected to increase by an annual inflation rate of 8%.

4   Annual fixed overhead costs would be $2.5 million of which 60% are centrally allocated overheads. The fixed overhead costs will increase by 5% per year after the first year.

5   Fubuki Co will need to make working capital available of 15% of the anticipated sales revenue for the year, at the beginning of each year. The working capital is expected to be released at the end of the fourth year when the project is sold.

Fubuki Co's tax rate is 25% per year on taxable profits. Tax is payable in the same year as when the profits are earned. Tax allowable depreciation is available on the plant and machinery on a straight-line basis. It is anticipated that the value attributable to the plant and machinery after four years is $400,000 of the price at which the project is sold. No tax allowable depreciation is available on the premises.

Fubuki Co uses 8% as its discount rate for new projects but feels that this rate may not be appropriate for this new type of investment. It intends to raise the full amount of funds through debt finance and take advantage of the government's offer of a subsidised loan. Issue costs are 4% of the gross finance required. It can be assumed that the debt capacity available to the company is equivalent to the actual amount of debt finance raised for the project.

Although no other companies produce mobility vehicles in Megaera, Haizum Co, a listed company, produces electrical-powered vehicles using similar technology to that required for the mobility vehicles. Haizum Co's cost of equity is estimated to be 14% and it pays tax at 28%. Haizum Co has 15 million shares in issue trading at $2.53 each and $40 million bonds trading at $94.88 per $100. The five-year government debt yield is currently estimated at 4.5% and the market risk premium at 4%.

Required:

(a)   **Evaluate, on financial grounds, whether Fubuki Co should proceed with the project.**
                                                                                                        (17 marks)

(b)   **Discuss the appropriateness of the evaluation method used and explain any assumptions made in part (a) above.**   **(8 marks)**

                                                                                                        (Total: 25 marks)

37   INVESTMENT PROJECT REVIEW (JUN 09 ADAPTED)

You have been conducting a detailed review of an investment project proposed by one of the divisions of your business. Your review has two aims: first to correct the proposal for any errors of principle and second, to recommend a financial measure to replace payback as one of the criteria for acceptability when a project is presented to the company's board of directors for approval. The company's current weighted average cost of capital is 10% per annum.

The initial capital investment is for $150 million followed by $50 million one year later. The post-tax cash flows, for this project, in $million, including the estimated tax benefit from tax allowable depreciation, are as follows:

Year	0	1	2	3	4	5	6
Capital investment (plant and machinery):							
First phase	−127.50						
Second phase		−36.88					
Project post tax cash flow ($ millions)			44.00	68.00	60.00	35.00	20.00

Company tax is charged at 30% and is paid/recovered in the year in which the liability is incurred. The company has sufficient profits elsewhere to recover tax allowable depreciation on this project, in full, in the year they are incurred. All the capital investment is eligible for a first year allowance for tax purposes of 50% followed by tax allowable depreciation of 25% per annum on a reducing balance basis.

You notice the following points when conducting your review:

1   An interest charge of 8% per annum on a proposed $50 million loan has been included in the project's post tax cash flow before tax has been calculated.

2   Depreciation for the use of company shared assets of $4 million per annum has been charged in calculating the project post tax cash flow.

3   Activity based allocations of company indirect costs of $8 million have been included in the project's post tax cash flow. However, additional corporate infrastructure costs of $4 million per annum have been ignored which you discover would only be incurred if the project proceeds.

4   It is expected that the capital equipment will be written off and disposed of at the end of year six. The proceeds of the sale of the capital equipment are expected to be $7 million which have been included in the forecast of the project's post tax cash flow. You also notice that an estimate for site clearance of $5 million has not been included nor any tax saving recognised on the unclaimed tax allowable depreciation on the disposal of the capital equipment.

Required:

(a)   Prepare a corrected project evaluation using the net present value technique supported by a separate assessment of the sensitivity of the project to a $1 million change in the initial capital expenditure.   (14 marks)

(b)   Estimate the discounted payback period and the duration for this project commenting on the relative advantages and disadvantages of each method.

(5 marks)

(c)   Draft a brief report for presentation to the board of directors with a recommendation on the acceptability of this project and on the techniques that the board should consider when reviewing capital investment projects in future.   (6 marks)

(Total: 25 marks)

38 MMC (JUN 11 ADAPTED)

MesmerMagic Co (MMC) is considering whether to undertake the development of a new computer game based on an adventure film due to be released in 22 months. It is expected that the game will be available to buy two months after the film's release, by which time it will be possible to judge the popularity of the film with a high degree of certainty. However, at present, there is considerable uncertainty about whether the film, and therefore the game, is likely to be successful. Although MMC would pay for the exclusive rights to develop and sell the game now, the directors are of the opinion that they should delay the decision to produce and market the game until the film has been released and the game is available for sale.

MMC has forecast the following end of year cash flows for the four-year sales period of the game.

Year	1	2	3	4
Cash flows ($ million)	25	18	10	5

MMC will spend $12 million immediately to develop the game, the gaming platform, and to pay for the exclusive rights to develop and sell the game. Following this, the company will require $35 million for production, distribution and marketing costs at the start of the four-year sales period of the game.

It can be assumed that all the costs and revenues include inflation. The relevant cost of capital for this project is 11% and the risk free rate is 5%. MMC has estimated the likely volatility of the cash flows at a standard deviation of 50%.

Required:

(a) **Estimate the financial impact of the directors' decision to delay the production and marketing of the game. The Black-Scholes Option Pricing model may be used, where appropriate. All relevant calculations should be shown.** (13 marks)

(b) **Briefly discuss the implications of the answer obtained in part (a) above.** (6 marks)

(c) MMC is funded partly by equity and partly by debt. The yield on its five year debt is 5.2% and the yield on its ten year debt is 5.4% i.e. MMC faces an upward sloping yield curve.

Required:

Explain the possible reasons for an upward sloping yield curve. (6 marks)

(Total: 25 marks)

39 TISA CO (JUN 12 ADAPTED)

 *Question debrief*

Tisa Co is considering an opportunity to produce an innovative component which, when fitted into motor vehicle engines, will enable them to utilise fuel more efficiently. The component can be manufactured using either process Omega or process Zeta. Although this is an entirely new line of business for Tisa Co, it is of the opinion that developing either process over a period of four years and then selling the productions rights at the end of four years to another company may prove lucrative.

The annual after-tax cash flows for each process are as follows:

Process Omega

Year	0	1	2	3	4
After-tax cash flows ($000)	(3,800)	1,220	1,153	1,386	3,829

Process Zeta

Year	0	1	2	3	4
After-tax cash flows ($000)	(3,800)	643	546	1,055	5,990

Tisa Co has 10 million 50c shares trading at 180c each. Its loans have a current value of $3.6 million and an average after-tax cost of debt of 4.50%. Tisa Co's capital structure is unlikely to change significantly following the investment in either process.

Elfu Co manufactures electronic parts for cars including the production of a component similar to the one being considered by Tisa Co. Elfu Co's equity beta is 1.40, and it is estimated that the equivalent equity beta for its other activities, excluding the component production, is 1.25. Elfu Co has 400 million 25c shares in issue trading at 120c each. Its debt finance consists of variable rate loans redeemable in seven years. The loans paying interest at base rate plus 120 basis points have a current value of $96 million. It can be assumed that 80% of Elfu Co's debt finance and 75% of Elfu Co's equity finance can be attributed to other activities excluding the component production. Both companies pay annual corporation tax at a rate of 25%. The current base rate is 3.5% and the market risk premium is estimated at 5.8%.

Required:

(a) Provide a reasoned estimate of the cost of capital that Tisa Co should use to calculate the net present value of the two processes. Include all relevant calculations.

(8 marks)

(b) Calculate the net present value (NPV), the internal rate of return (IRR) and the modified internal rate of return (MIRR) for Process Omega. Given that the NPV, IRR and MIRR of Process Zeta are $1.64 million, 26.6% and 23.3% respectively, recommend which process, if any, Tisa Co should proceed with and explain your recommendation. (12 marks)

(c) Elfu Co has estimated an annual standard deviation of $800,000 on one of its other projects, based on a normal distribution of returns. The average annual return on this project is $2,200,000.

Required:

Estimate the project's Value at Risk (VAR) at a 99% confidence level for one year and over the project's life of five years. Explain what is meant by the answers obtained. (5 marks)

(Total: 25 marks)

 Calculate your allowed time and allocate the time to the separate parts

40   COEDEN CO (DEC 12 ADAPTED)

Coeden Co is a listed company operating in the hospitality and leisure industry. Coeden Co's board of directors met recently to discuss a new strategy for the business. The proposal put forward was to sell all the hotel properties that Coeden Co owns and rent them back on a long-term rental agreement. Coeden Co would then focus solely on the provision of hotel services at these properties under its popular brand name. The proposal stated that the funds raised from the sale of the hotel properties would be used to pay off 70% of the outstanding non-current liabilities and the remaining funds would be retained for future investments.

The board of directors are of the opinion that reducing the level of debt in Coeden Co will reduce the company's risk and therefore its cost of capital. If the proposal is undertaken and Coeden Co focuses exclusively on the provision of hotel services, it can be assumed that the current market value of equity will remain unchanged after implementing the proposal.

Coeden Co: Extract from the most recent Statement of Financial Position

	$000
Non-current assets (re-valued recently)	42,560
Current assets	26,840
	———
Total assets	69,400
	———
Share capital (25c per share par value)	3,250
Reserves	21,780
Non-current liabilities (5.2% redeemable bonds)	42,000
Current liabilities	2,370
	———
Total capital and liabilities	69,400
	———

Coeden Co's latest free cash flow to equity of $2,600,000 was estimated after taking into account taxation, interest and reinvestment in assets to continue with the current level of business. It can be assumed that the annual reinvestment in assets required to continue with the current level of business is equivalent to the annual amount of depreciation. Over the past few years, Coeden Co has consistently used 40% of its free cash flow to equity on new investments while distributing the remaining 60%. The market value of equity calculated on the basis of the free cash flow to equity model provides a reasonable estimate of the current market value of Coeden Co.

The bonds are redeemable at par in three years and pay the coupon on an annual basis. Although the bonds are not traded, it is estimated that Coeden Co's current debt credit rating is BBB but would improve to A+ if the non-current liabilities are reduced by 70%.

Other Information

Coeden Co's current equity beta is 1.1 and it can be assumed that debt beta is 0. The risk free rate is estimated to be 4% and the market risk premium is estimated to be 6%.

There is no beta available for companies offering just hotel services, since most companies own their own buildings. The average asset beta for property companies has been estimated at 0.4. It has been estimated that the hotel services business accounts for approximately 60% of the current value of Coeden Co and the property company business accounts for the remaining 40%.

Coeden Co's corporation tax rate is 20%. The three-year borrowing credit spread on A+ rated bonds is 60 basis points and 90 basis points on BBB rated bonds, over the risk free rate of interest.

Required:

(a) Calculate, and comment on, Coeden Co's cost of equity and weighted average cost of capital before and after implementing the proposal. Briefly explain any assumptions made. **(20 marks)**

(b) Discuss the validity of the assumption that the market value of equity will remain unchanged after the implementation of the proposal. **(5 marks)**

(Total: 25 marks)

41 ARBORE CO (DEC 12 ADAPTED)

(a) Explain the different methods of dealing with a capital rationing problem, in the circumstances where

(i) capital is rationed in a single period, and

(ii) capital is rationed in several periods. **(5 marks)**

(b) Arbore Co is a large listed company with many autonomous departments operating as investment centres. It sets investment limits for each department based on a three-year cycle. Projects selected by departments would have to fall within the investment limits set for each of the three years. All departments would be required to maintain a capital investment monitoring system, and report on their findings annually to Arbore Co's board of directors.

The Durvo department is considering the following five investment projects with three years of initial investment expenditure, followed by several years of positive cash inflows. The department's initial investment expenditure limits are $9,000,000, $6,000,000 and $5,000,000 for years one, two and three respectively. None of the projects can be deferred and all projects can be scaled down but not scaled up.

Investment required at start of year

Project	Year one (Immediately)	Year two	Year three	Project net present value
PDur01	$4,000,000	$1,100,000	$2,400,000	$464,000
PDur02	$800,000	$2,800,000	$3,200,000	$244,000
PDur03	$3,200,000	$3,562,000	$0	$352,000
PDur04	$3,900,000	$0	$200,000	$320,000
PDur05	$2,500,000	$1,200,000	$1,400,000	Not provided

PDur05 project's annual operating cash flows commence at the end of year four and last for a period of 15 years. The project generates annual sales of 300,000 units at a selling price of $14 per unit and incurs total annual relevant costs of $3,230,000. Although the costs and units sold of the project can be predicted with a fair degree of certainty, there is considerable uncertainty about the unit selling price. The department uses a required rate of return of 11% for its projects, and inflation can be ignored.

The Durvo department's managing director is of the opinion that all projects which return a positive net present value should be accepted and does not understand the reason(s) why Arbore Co imposes capital rationing on its departments. Furthermore, she is not sure why maintaining a capital investment monitoring system would be beneficial to the company.

Required:

(i) Calculate the net present value of project PDur05. Calculate and comment on what percentage fall in the selling price would need to occur before the net present value falls to zero. **(6 marks)**

(ii) Formulate an appropriate capital rationing model, based on the above investment limits, that maximises the net present value for department Durvo. Finding a solution for the model is not required. **(3 marks)**

(c) Assume the following output is produced when the capital rationing model in part (b) above is solved:

Category 1: Total Final Value
$1,184,409

Category 2: Adjustable Final Values
Project PDur01: 0.958
Project PDur02: 0.407
Project PDur03: 0.732
Project PDur04: 0.000
Project PDur05: 1.000

Category 3:

Constraints Utilised	*Slack*
Year one: $9,000,000	Year one: $0
Year two: $6,000,000	Year two: $0
Year three: $5,000,000	Year three: $0

Required:

Explain the figures produced in each of the three output categories. **(5 marks)**

(d) Provide a brief response to the managing director's opinions by:

(i) Explaining why Arbore Co may want to impose capital rationing on its departments; **(2 marks)**

(ii) Explaining the features of a capital investment monitoring system and discussing the benefits of maintaining such a system. **(4 marks)**

(Total: 25 marks)

42 BURUNG CO (SPECIMEN PAPER 2018)

You have recently commenced working for Burung Co and are reviewing a four-year project which the company is considering for investment. The project is in a business activity which is very different from Burung Co's current line of business.

The following net present value estimate has been made for the project:

All figures are in $ million

Year	0	1	2	3	4
Sales revenue		23.03	36.60	49.07	27.14
Direct project costs		(13.82)	(21.96)	(29.44)	(16.28)
Interest		(1.20)	(1.20)	(1.20)	(1.20)
Profit		8.01	13.44	18.43	9.66
Tax (20%)		(1.60)	(2.69)	(3.69)	(1.93)
Investment/sale	(38.00)				4.00
Cash flows	(38.00)	6.41	10.75	14.74	11.73
Discount factors (7%)	1	0.935	0.873	0.816	0.763
Present values	(38.00)	5.99	9.38	12.03	8.95

Net present value is negative $1.65 million, and therefore the recommendation is that the project should not be accepted.

Notes to NPV appraisal

In calculating the net present value of the project, the following notes were made:

(i) Since the real cost of capital is used to discount cash flows, neither the sales revenue nor the direct project costs have been inflated. It is estimated that the inflation rate applicable to sales revenue is 8% per year and to the direct project costs is 4% per year.

(ii) The project will require an initial investment of $38 million. Of this, $16 million relates to plant and machinery, which is expected to be sold for $4 million when the project ceases, after taking any taxation and inflation impact into account.

(iii) Tax allowable depreciation is available on the plant and machinery at 50% in the first year, followed by 25% per year thereafter on a reducing balance basis. A balancing adjustment is available in the year the plant and machinery is sold. Burung Co pays 20% tax on its annual taxable profits. No tax allowable depreciation is available on the remaining investment assets and they will have a nil value at the end of the project.

(iv) Burung Co uses either a nominal cost of capital of 11% or a real cost of capital of 7% to discount all projects, given that the rate of inflation has been stable at 4% for a number of years.

(v) Interest is based on Burung Co's normal borrowing rate of 150 basis points over the 10-year government yield rate.

(vi) At the beginning of each year, Burung Co will need to provide working capital of 20% of the anticipated sales revenue for the year. Any remaining working capital will be released at the end of the project.

(vii) Working capital and depreciation have not been taken into account in the net present value calculation above, since depreciation is not a cash flow and all the working capital is returned at the end of the project.

Further financial information

It is anticipated that the project will be financed entirely by debt, 60% of which will be obtained from a subsidised loan scheme run by the government, which lends money at a rate of 100 basis points below the 10-year government debt yield rate of 2.5%. Issue costs related to raising the finance are 2% of the gross finance required. The remaining 40% will be funded from Burung Co's normal borrowing sources. It can be assumed that the debt capacity available to Burung Co is equal to the actual amount of debt finance raised for the project.

Burung Co has identified a company, Lintu Co, which operates in the same line of business as that of the project it is considering. Lintu Co is financed by 40 million shares trading at $3.20 each and $34 million debt trading at $94 per $100. Lintu Co's equity beta is estimated at 1.5. The current yield on government treasury bills is 2% and it is estimated that the market risk premium is 8%. Lintu Co pays tax at an annual rate of 20%.

Both Burung Co and Lintu Co pay tax in the same year as when profits are earned.

Required:

(a) Calculate the adjusted present value (APV) for the project, correcting any errors made in the net present value estimate above, and conclude whether the project should be accepted or not. Show all relevant calculations. **(15 marks)**

(b) Comment on the corrections made to the original net present value estimate and explain the APV approach taken in part (a), including any assumptions made.

(10 marks)

(Total: 25 marks)

43 RIVIERE CO (DEC 14)

Riviere Co is a small company based in the European Union (EU). It produces high quality frozen food which it exports to a small number of supermarket chains located within the EU as well. The EU is a free trade area for trade between its member countries.

Riviere Co finds it difficult to obtain bank finance and relies on a long-term strategy of using internally generated funds for new investment projects. This constraint means that it cannot accept every profitable project and often has to choose between them.

Riviere Co is currently considering investment in one of two mutually exclusive food production projects: Privi and Drugi. Privi will produce and sell a new range of frozen desserts exclusively within the EU. Drugi will produce and sell a new range of frozen desserts and savoury foods to supermarket chains based in countries outside the EU. Each project will last for five years and the following financial information refers to both projects.

Project Drugi, annual after-tax cash flows expected at the end of each year (€000s)

Year	Current	1	2	3	4	5
Cash flows (€000s)	(11,840)	1,230	1,680	4,350	10,240	2,200

	Privi	Drugi
Net present value	€2,054,000	€2,293,000
Internal rate of return	17.6%	Not provided
Modified internal rate of return	13.4%	Not provided
Value at risk (over the project's life)		
95% confidence level	€1,103,500	Not provided
90% confidence level	€860,000	Not provided

Both projects' net present values have been calculated based on Riviere Co's nominal cost of capital of 10%. It can be assumed that both projects' cash flow returns are normally distributed and the annual standard deviation of project Drugi's present value of after-tax cash flows is estimated to be €400,000. It can also be assumed that all sales are made in € (Euro) and therefore the company is not exposed to any foreign exchange exposure.

Notwithstanding how profitable project Drugi may appear to be, Riviere Co's board of directors is concerned about the possible legal risks if it invests in the project because they have never dealt with companies outside the EU before.

Required:

(a)   Discuss the aims of a free trade area, such as the European Union (EU), and the possible benefits to Riviere Co of operating within the EU.   **(5 marks)**

(b)   Calculate the figures which have not been provided for project Drugi and recommend which project should be accepted. Provide a justification for the recommendation and explain what the value at risk measures.   **(13 marks)**

(c)   Discuss the possible legal risks of investing in project Drugi which Riviere Co may be concerned about and how these may be mitigated.   **(7 marks)**

(Total: 25 marks)

44   FURLION CO (MAR/JUN 16)

Furlion Co manufactures heavy agricultural equipment and machinery which can be used in difficult farming conditions. Furlion Co's chief executive has been investigating a significant opportunity in the country of Naswa, where Furlion Co has not previously sold any products. The government of Naswa has been undertaking a major land reclamation programme and Furlion Co's equipment is particularly suitable for use on the reclaimed land. Because of the costs and other problems involved in transporting its products, Furlion Co's chief executive proposes that Furlion Co should establish a plant for manufacturing machinery in Naswa. He knows that the Naswan government is keen to encourage the development of sustainable businesses within the country.

Initial calculations suggest that the proposed investment in Naswa would have a negative net present value of $1.01 million. However, Furlion Co's chief executive believes that there may be opportunities for greater cash flows in future if the Naswan government expands its land reclamation programme. The government at present is struggling to fund expansion of the programme out of its own resources and is looking for other funding. If the Naswan government obtains this funding, the chief executive has forecast that the increased demand for Furlion Co's products would justify $15 million additional expenditure at the site of the factory in three years' time. The expected net present value for this expansion is currently estimated to be $0.

It can be assumed that all costs and revenues include inflation. The relevant cost of capital is 12% and the risk free rate is 4%. The chief executive has estimated the likely volatility of cash flows at a standard deviation of 30%.

One of Furlion Co's non-executive directors has read about possible changes in interest rates and wonders how these might affect the investment appraisal.

Required:

(a) **Assess, showing all relevant calculations, whether Furlion Co should proceed with the significant opportunity. Discuss the assumptions made and other factors which will affect the decision of whether to establish a plant in Naswa. The Black Scholes pricing model may be used, where appropriate.** **(16 marks)**

(b) **Explain what is meant by an option's rho and discuss the impact of changes in interest rates on the appraisal of the investment.** **(5 marks)**

(c) **Discuss the possibility of the Naswan government obtaining funding for further land reclamation from the World Bank, referring specifically to the International Development Association.** **(4 marks)**

(Total: 25 marks)

45 FERNHURST CO (SEP/DEC 16)

Fernhurst Co is a manufacturer of mobile communications technology. It is about to launch a new communications device, the Milland, which its directors believe is both more technologically advanced and easier to use than devices currently offered by its rivals.

Investment in the Milland

The Milland will require a major investment in facilities. Fernhurst Co's directors believe that this can take place very quickly and production be started almost immediately.

Fernhurst Co expects to sell 132,500 units of the Milland in its first year. Sales volume is expected to increase by 20% in Year 2 and 30% in Year 3, and then be the same in Year 4 as Year 3, as the product reaches the end of its useful life. The initial selling price in Year 1 is expected to be $100 per unit, before increasing with the rate of inflation annually.

The variable cost of each unit is expected to be $43.68 in year 1, rising by the rate of inflation in subsequent years annually. Fixed costs are expected to be $900,000 in Year 1, rising by the rate of inflation in subsequent years annually.

The initial investment in non-current assets is expected to be $16,000,000. Fernhurst Co will also need to make an immediate investment of $1,025,000 in working capital. The working capital will be increased annually at the start of each of Years 2 to 4 by the inflation rate and is fully recoverable at the end of the project's life. Fernhurst Co will also incur one-off marketing expenditure of $1,500,000 post inflation after the launch of the Milland. The marketing expenditure can be assumed to be made at the end of Year 1 and be a tax allowable expense.

Fernhurst Co pays company tax on profits at an annual rate of 25%. Tax is payable in the year that the tax liability arises. Tax allowable depreciation is available at 20% on the investment in non-current assets on a reducing balance basis. A balancing adjustment will be available in Year 4. The realisable value of the investment at the end of Year 4 is expected to be zero.

The expected annual rate of inflation in the country in which Fernhurst Co is located is 4% in Year 1 and 5% in Years 2 to 4.

The applicable cost of capital for this investment appraisal is 11 %.

Other calculations

Fernhurst Co's finance director has indicated that besides needing a net present value calculation based on this data for the next board meeting, he also needs to know the figure for the project's duration, to indicate to the board how returns from the project will be spread over time.

Failure of launch of the Milland

The finance director would also like some simple analysis based on the possibility that the marketing expenditure is not effective and the launch fails, as he feels that the product's price may be too high. He has suggested that there is a 15% chance that the Milland will have negative net cash flows for Year 1 of $1,000,000 or more. He would like to know by what percentage the selling price could be reduced or increased to result in the investment having a zero net present value, assuming demand remained the same.

Assessment of new products

Fernhurst Co's last board meeting discussed another possible new product, the Racton, and the finance director presented a range of financial data relating to this product, including the results of net present value and payback evaluations. One of the non-executive directors, who is not a qualified accountant, stated that he found it difficult to see the significance of the different items of financial data. His understanding was that Fernhurst Co merely had to ensure that the investment had a positive net present value and shareholders were bound to be satisfied with it, as it would maximise their wealth in the long term. The finance director commented that, in reality, some shareholders looked at the performance of the investments which Fernhurst Co made over the short term, whereas some were more concerned with the longer term. The financial data he presented to board meetings included both short and long-term measures.

Required:

(a)   Evaluate the financial acceptability of the investment in the Milland and, calculate and comment on the investment's duration.   **(15 marks)**

(b)   Calculate the % change in the selling price required for the investment to have a zero net present value, and discuss the significance of your results.   **(5 marks)**

(c)   Discuss the non-executive director's understanding of net present value and explain the importance of other measures in providing data about an investment's short and long-term performance.   **(5 marks)**

(Total: 25 marks)

46 MOONSTAR CO (SEP/DEC 15)

Moonstar Co is a property development company which is planning to undertake a $200 million commercial property development. Moonstar Co has had some difficulties over the last few years, with some developments not generating the expected returns and the company has at times struggled to pay its finance costs. As a result Moonstar Co's credit rating has been lowered, affecting the terms it can obtain for bank finance. Although Moonstar Co is listed on its local stock exchange, 75% of the share capital is held by members of the family who founded the company. The family members who are shareholders do not wish to subscribe for a rights issue and are unwilling to dilute their control over the company by authorising a new issue of equity shares. Moonstar Co's board is therefore considering other methods of financing the development, which the directors believe will generate higher returns than other recent investments, as the country where Moonstar Co is based appears to be emerging from recession.

Securitisation proposals

One of the non-executive directors of Moonstar Co has proposed that it should raise funds by means of a securitisation process, transferring the rights to the rental income from the commercial property development to a special purpose vehicle. Her proposals assume that the leases will generate an income of 11% per annum to Moonstar Co over a ten-year period. She proposes that Moonstar Co should use 90% of the value of the investment for a collateralised loan obligation which should be structured as follows:

- 60% of the collateral value to support a tranche of A-rated floating rate loan notes offering investors LIBOR plus 150 basis points

- 15% of the collateral value to support a tranche of B-rated fixed rate loan notes offering investors 12%

- 15% of the collateral value to support a tranche of C-rated fixed rate loan notes offering investors 13%

- 10% of the collateral value to support a tranche as subordinated certificates, with the return being the excess of receipts over payments from the securitisation process

The non-executive director believes that there will be sufficient demand for all tranches of the loan notes from investors. Investors will expect that the income stream from the development to be low risk, as they will expect the property market to improve with the recession coming to an end and enough potential lessees to be attracted by the new development.

The non-executive director predicts that there would be annual costs of $200,000 in administering the loan. She acknowledges that there would be interest rate risks associated with the proposal, and proposes a fixed for variable interest rate swap on the A-rated floating rate notes, exchanging LIBOR for 9.5%.

However the finance director believes that the prediction of the income from the development that the non-executive director has made is over-optimistic. He believes that it is most likely that the total value of the rental income will be 5% lower than the non-executive director has forecast. He believes that there is some risk that the returns could be so low as to jeopardise the income for the C-rated fixed rate loan note holders.

Islamic finance

Moonstar Co's chief executive has wondered whether Sukuk finance would be a better way of funding the development than the securitisation.

Moonstar Co's chairman has pointed out that a major bank in the country where Moonstar Co is located has begun to offer a range of Islamic financial products. The chairman has suggested that a Mudaraba contract would be the most appropriate method of providing the funds required for the investment.

Required:

(a)   Calculate the amounts in $ which each of the tranches can expect to receive from the securitisation arrangement proposed by the non-executive director and discuss how the variability in rental income affects the returns from the securitisation.

(11 marks)

(b)   Discuss the benefits and risks for Moonstar Co associated with the securitisation arrangement that the non-executive director has proposed.   (6 marks)

(c)   (i)   Discuss the suitability of Sukuk finance to fund the investment, including an assessment of its appeal to potential investors.   (4 marks)

(ii)   Discuss whether a Mudaraba contract would be an appropriate method of financing the investment and discuss why the bank may have concerns about providing finance by this method.   (4 marks)

(Total: 25 marks)

47   GNT CO (PILOT 12)

GNT Co is considering an investment in one of two corporate bonds. Both bonds have a par value of $1,000 and pay coupon interest on an annual basis. The market price of the first bond is $1,079·68. Its coupon rate is 6% and it is due to be redeemed at par in five years. The second bond is about to be issued with a coupon rate of 4% and will also be redeemable at par in five years. Both bonds are expected to have the same gross redemption yields (yields to maturity).

GNT Co considers duration of the bond to be a key factor when making decisions on which bond to invest.

Required:

(a)   Estimate the Macaulay duration of the two bonds GNT Co is considering for investment.   (9 marks)

(b)   Discuss how useful duration is as a measure of the sensitivity of a bond price to changes in interest rates.   (8 marks)

(c)   Among the criteria used by credit agencies for establishing a company's credit rating are the following: industry risk, earnings protection, financial flexibility and evaluation of the company's management.

Briefly explain each criterion and suggest factors that could be used to assess it.

(8 marks)

(Total: 25 marks)

48 TOLTUCK CO (MAR/JUN 17)

Toltuck Co is a listed company in the building industry which specialises in the construction of large commercial and residential developments. Toltuck Co had been profitable for many years, but has just incurred major losses on the last two developments which it has completed in its home country of Arumland. These developments were an out-of-town retail centre and a major residential development. Toltuck Co's directors have blamed the poor results primarily on the recent recession in Arumland, although demand for the residential development also appears to have been adversely affected by it being located in an area which has suffered serious flooding over the last two years.

As a result of returns from these two major developments being much lower than expected, Toltuck Co has had to finance current work-in-progress by a significantly greater amount of debt finance, giving it higher gearing than most other construction companies operating in Arumland. Toltuck Co's directors have recently been alarmed by a major credit agency's decision to downgrade Toltuck Co's credit rating from AA to BBB. The directors are very concerned about the impact this will have on the valuation of Toltuck Co's bonds and the future cost of debt.

The following information can be used to assess the consequences of the change in Toltuck Co's credit rating.

Toltuck Co has issued an 8% bond, which has a face or nominal value of $100 and a premium of 2% on redemption in three years' time. The coupon on the bond is payable on an annual basis.

The government of Arumland has three bonds in issue. They all have a face or nominal value of $100 and are all redeemable at par. Taxation can be ignored on government bonds. They are of the same risk class and the coupon on each is payable on an annual basis. Details of the bonds are as follows:

Bond	Redeemable	Coupon	Current market value $
1	1 year	9%	104
2	2 years	7%	102
3	3 years	6%	98

Credit spreads, published by the credit agency, are as follows (shown in basis points):

Rating	1 year	2 years	3 years
AA	18	31	45
BBB	54	69	86

Toltuck Co's shareholder base can be divided broadly into two groups. The majority of shareholders are comfortable with investing in a company where dividends in some years will be high, but there will be low or no dividends in other years because of the cash demands facing the business. However, a minority of shareholders would like Toltuck Co to achieve at least a minimum dividend each year and are concerned about the company undertaking investments which they regard as very speculative. Shareholders from both groups have expressed some concerns to the board about the impact of the fall in credit rating on their investment.

Required:

(a) Calculate the valuation and yield to maturity of Toltuck Co's $100 bond under its old and new credit ratings. **(10 marks)**

(b) Discuss the factors which may have affected the credit rating of Toltuck Co published by the credit agency. **(8 marks)**

(c) Discuss the impact of the fall in Toltuck Co's credit rating on its ability to raise financial capital and on its shareholders' return. **(7 marks)**

(Total: 25 marks)

ACQUISITIONS AND MERGERS

49   KODIAK COMPANY (DEC 09 ADAPTED)

Kodiak Company is a small software design business established four years ago. The company is owned by three directors who have relied upon external accounting services in the past. The company has grown quickly and the directors have appointed you as a financial consultant to advise on the value of the business under their ownership.

The directors have limited liability and the bank loan is secured against the general assets of the business. The directors have no outstanding guarantees on the company's debt.

The company's latest statement of profit or loss and the extracted balances from the latest statement of financial position are as follows:

	$000	Financial Position	$000
Revenue	5,000	Opening non-current assets	1,200
Cost of Sales	3,000	Additions	66
	___		___
Gross profit	2,000	Non-current assets (gross)	1,266
Other operating costs	1,877	Accumulated depreciation	367
	___		___
Operating profit	123	Net book value	899
Interest on loan	74	Net current assets	270
	___		
Profit before tax	49	Loan	(990)
			___
Income tax expense	15	Net Assets Employed	179
	___		___
Profit for the period	34		
	___		

During the current year:

1   Depreciation is charged at 10% per annum on the year end non-current asset balance before accumulated depreciation, and is included in other operating costs in the statement of profit or loss.

2   The investment in net working capital is expected to increase in line with the growth in gross profit.

3   Other operating costs consisted of:

	$000
Variable component at 15% of sales	750
Fixed costs	1,000
Depreciation on non-current assets	127

4   Revenue and variable costs are projected to grow at 9% per annum and fixed costs are projected to grow at 6% per annum.

5   The company pays interest on its outstanding loan of 7.5% per annum and incurs tax on its profits at 30%, payable in the following year. The company does not pay dividends.

6   The net current assets reported in the statement of financial position contain $50,000 of cash.

One of your first tasks is to prepare for the directors a forward cash flow projection for three years and to value the firm on the basis of its expected free cash flow to equity. In discussion with them you note the following:

- The company will not dispose of any of its non-current assets but will increase its investment in new non-current assets by 20% per annum. The company's depreciation policy matches the currently available tax allowable depreciation. This straight-line write off policy is not likely to change.

- The directors will not take a dividend for the next three years but will then review the position taking into account the company's sustainable cash flow at that time.

- The level of the loan will be maintained at $990,000 and, on the basis of the forward yield curve, interest rates are not expected to change.

- The directors have set a target rate of return on their equity of 10% per annum which they believe fairly represents the opportunity cost of their invested funds.

Required:

(a)   **Prepare a three-year cash flow forecast for the business on the basis described above highlighting the free cash flow to equity in each year.   (13 marks)**

(b)   **Estimate the value of the business based upon the expected free cash flow to equity and a terminal value based upon a sustainable growth rate of 3% per annum thereafter.   (6 marks)**

(c)   **Advise the directors on the assumptions and the uncertainties within your valuation.**
          (6 marks)

          (Total: 25 marks)

50 KILENC CO (JUN 12 ADAPTED)

Kilenc Co, a large listed company based in the UK, produces pharmaceutical products which are exported around the world. It is reviewing a proposal to set up a subsidiary company to manufacture a range of body and facial creams in Lanosia. These products will be sold to local retailers and to retailers in nearby countries.

Lanosia has a small but growing manufacturing industry in pharmaceutical products, although it remains largely reliant on imports. The Lanosian government has been keen to promote the pharmaceutical manufacturing industry through purchasing local pharmaceutical products, providing government grants and reducing the industry's corporate tax rate. It also imposes large duties on imported pharmaceutical products which compete with the ones produced locally.

Although politically stable, the recent worldwide financial crisis has had a significant negative impact on Lanosia. The country's national debt has grown substantially following a bailout of its banks and it has had to introduce economic measures which are hampering the country's ability to recover from a deep recession. Growth in real wages has been negative over the past three years, the economy has shrunk in the past year and inflation has remained higher than normal during this time.

On the other hand, corporate investment in capital assets, research and development, and education and training, has grown recently and interest rates remain low. This has led some economists to suggest that the economy should start to recover soon. Employment levels remain high in spite of low nominal wage growth.

Lanosian corporate governance regulations stipulate that at least 40% of equity share capital must be held by the local population. In addition at least 50% of members on the Board of Directors, including the Chairman, must be from Lanosia. Kilenc Co wants to finance the subsidiary company using a mixture of debt and equity. It wants to raise additional equity and debt finance in Lanosia in order to minimise exchange rate exposure. The small size of the subsidiary will have minimal impact on Kilenc Co's capital structure. Kilenc Co intends to raise the 40% equity through an initial public offering (IPO) in Lanosia and provide the remaining 60% of the equity funds from its own cash funds.

Required:

(a) Discuss the key risks and issues that Kilenc Co should consider when setting up a subsidiary company in Lanosia, and suggest how these may be mitigated.

(15 marks)

(b) Discuss whether Kilenc Co should use the Net Present Value method or the Adjusted Present Value method to appraise the investment in Lanosia. (5 marks)

(c) The directors of Kilenc Co have learnt that a sizeable number of equity trades in Lanosia are conducted using dark pool trading systems.

Required:

Explain what dark pool trading systems are and how Kilenc Co's proposed Initial Public Offering (IPO) may be affected by these. (5 marks)

(Total: 25 marks)

51   SIGRA CO (DEC 12 ADAPTED)

Sigra Co is a listed company producing confectionary products which it sells around the world. It wants to acquire Dentro Co, an unlisted company producing high quality, luxury chocolates. Sigra Co proposes to pay for the acquisition using one of the following three methods:

Method 1

A cash offer of $5.00 per Dentro Co share; or

Method 2

An offer of three of its shares for two of Dentro Co's shares; or

Method 3

An offer of a 2% coupon bond in exchange for 16 Dentro Co's shares. The bond will be redeemed in three years at its par value of $100.

Extracts from the latest financial statements of both companies are as follows:

	Sigra Co	Dentro Co
	$000	$000
Sales revenue	44,210	4,680
Profit before tax	6,190	780
Taxation	(1,240)	(155)
Profit after tax	4,950	625
Dividends	(2,700)	(275)
Retained earnings for the year	2,250	350
Non-current assets	22,450	3,350
Current assets	3,450	247
Non-current liabilities	9,700	873
Current liabilities	3,600	436
Share capital (40c per share)	4,400	500
Reserves	8,200	1,788

Sigra Co's current share price is $3.60 per share and it has estimated that Dentro Co's price to earnings ratio is 12.5% higher than Sigra Co's current price to earnings ratio. Sigra Co's non-current liabilities include a 6% bond redeemable in three years at par which is currently trading at $104 per $100 par value. Sigra Co estimates that it could achieve synergy savings of 30% of Dentro Co's estimated equity value by eliminating duplicated administrative functions, selling excess non-current assets and through reducing the workforce numbers, if the acquisition were successful.

Required:

(a)   Explain briefly, in general terms, why many acquisitions in the real world are not successful. **(5 marks)**

(b)   Estimate the percentage gain on a Dentro Co share under each of the above three payment methods. Comment on the answers obtained. **(16 marks)**

(c)   In relation to the acquisition, the board of directors of Sigra Co are considering the following two proposals:

Proposal 1

Once Sigra Co has obtained agreement from a significant majority of the shareholders, it will enforce the remaining minority shareholders to sell their shares.

Proposal 2

Sigra Co will offer an extra 3 cents per share, in addition to the bid price, to 30% of the shareholders of Dentro Co on a first-come, first-serve basis, as an added incentive to make the acquisition proceed more quickly.

Required:

With reference to the key aspects of the global regulatory framework for mergers and acquisitions, briefly discuss the above proposals.   (4 marks)

(Total: 25 marks)

52   MAKONIS CO (DEC 13)

Makonis Co, a listed company producing motor cars, wants to acquire Nuvola Co, an engineering company involved in producing innovative devices for cars. Makonis Co is keen to incorporate some of Nuvola Co's innovative devices into its cars and thereby boosting sales revenue.

The following financial information is provided for the two companies:

	Makonis Co	Nuvola Co
Current share price	$5.80	$2.40
Number of issued shares	210 million	200 million
Equity beta	1.2	1.2
Asset beta	0.9	1.2

It is thought that combining the two companies will result in several benefits. Free cash flows to firm of the combined company will be $216 million in current value terms, but these will increase by an annual growth rate of 5% for the next four years, before reverting to an annual growth rate of 2.25% in perpetuity. In addition to this, combining the companies will result in cash synergy benefits of $20 million per year, for the next four years. These synergy benefits are not subject to any inflationary increase and no synergy benefits will occur after the fourth year. The debt-to-equity ratio of the combined company will be 40:60 in market value terms and it is expected that the combined company's cost of debt will be 4.55%.

The corporation tax rate is 20%, the current risk free rate of return is 2% and the market risk premium is 7%. It can be assumed that the combined company's asset beta is the weighted average of Makonis Co's and Nuvola Co's asset betas, weighted by their current market values.

Makonis Co has offered to acquire Nuvola Co through a mixed offer of one of its shares for two Nuvola Co shares plus a cash payment, such that a 30% premium is paid for the acquisition. Nuvola Co's equity holders feel that a 50% premium would be more acceptable. Makonis Co has sufficient cash reserves if the premium is 30%, but not if it is 50%.

Required:

(a)   Estimate the additional equity value created by combining Nuvola Co and Makonis Co, based on the free cash flows to firm method. Comment on the results obtained and briefly discuss the assumptions made.   (13 marks)

(b)   Estimate the impact on Makonis Co's equity holders if the premium paid is increased to 50% from 30%.   (5 marks)

(c)   Estimate the additional funds required if a premium of 50% is paid instead of 30% and discuss how this premium could be financed.   (7 marks)

(Total: 25 marks)

53   VOGEL CO (JUN 14)

Vogel Co, a listed engineering company, manufactures large scale plant and machinery for industrial companies. Until ten years ago, Vogel Co pursued a strategy of organic growth. Since then, it has followed an aggressive policy of acquiring smaller engineering companies, which it feels have developed new technologies and methods, which could be used in its manufacturing processes. However, it is estimated that only between 30% and 40% of the acquisitions made in the last ten years have successfully increased the company's shareholder value.

Vogel Co is currently considering acquiring Tori Co, an unlisted company, which has three departments. Department A manufactures machinery for industrial companies, Department B produces electrical goods for the retail market, and the smaller Department C operates in the construction industry. Upon acquisition, Department A will become part of Vogel Co, as it contains the new technologies which Vogel Co is seeking, but Departments B and C will be unbundled, with the assets attached to Department C sold and Department B being spun off into a new company called Ndege Co.

Given below are extracts of financial information for the two companies for the year ended 30 April 20X4.

	Vogel Co $ million	Tori Co $ million
Sales revenue	790.2	124.6
Profit before depreciation, interest and tax (PBDIT)	244.4	37.4
Interest	13.8	4.3
Depreciation	72.4	10.1
Pre-tax profit	158.2	23.0
Non-current assets	723.9	98.2
Current assets	142.6	46.5
7% unsecured bond	–	40.0
Other non-current and current liabilities	212.4	20.2
Share capital (50c/share)	190.0	20.0
Reserves	464.1	64.5

Share of current and non-current assets and profit of Tori Co's three departments:

	Department A	Department B	Department C
Share of current and non-current assets	40%	40%	20%
Share of PBDIT and pre-tax profit	50%	40%	10%

Other information

(i)   It is estimated that for Department C, the realisable value of its non-current assets is 100% of their book value, but its current assets' realisable value is only 90% of their book value. The costs related to closing Department C are estimated to be $3 million.

(ii)   The funds raised from the disposal of Department C will be used to pay off Tori Co's other non-current and current liabilities.

(iii)   The 7% unsecured bond will be taken over by Ndege Co. It can be assumed that the current market value of the bond is equal to its book value.

(iv)   At present, around 10% of Department B's PBDIT come from sales made to Department C.

(v)   Ndege Co's cost of capital is estimated to be 10%. It is estimated that in the first year of operation Ndege Co's free cash flows to firm will grow by 20%, and then by 5.2% annually thereafter.

(vi)   The tax rate applicable to all the companies is 20%, and Ndege Co can claim 10% tax allowable depreciation on its non-current assets. It can be assumed that the amount of tax allowable depreciation is the same as the investment needed to maintain Ndege Co's operations.

(vii)   Vogel Co's current share price is $3 per share and it is estimated that Tori Co's price-to-earnings (PE) ratio is 25% higher than Vogel Co's PE ratio. After the acquisition, when Department A becomes part of Vogel Co, it is estimated that Vogel Co's PE ratio will increase by 15%.

(viii) It is estimated that the combined company's annual after-tax earnings will increase by $7 million due to the synergy benefits resulting from combining Vogel Co and Department A.

Required:

(a)   **Discuss the possible reasons why Vogel Co may have switched its strategy of organic growth to one of growing by acquiring companies.**   **(4 marks)**

(b)   **Discuss the possible actions Vogel Co could take to reduce the risk that the acquisition of Tori Co fails to increase shareholder value.**   **(7 marks)**

(c)   **Estimate, showing all relevant calculations, the maximum premium Vogel Co could pay to acquire Tori Co, explaining the approach taken and any assumptions made.**
          (14 marks)

          (Total: 25 marks)

54   LOUIEED CO (MAR/JUN 16)

Louieed Co, a listed company, is a major supplier of educational material, selling its products in many countries. It supplies schools and colleges and also produces learning material for business and professional exams. Louieed Co has exclusive contracts to produce material for some examining bodies. Louieed Co has a well-defined management structure with formal processes for making major decisions.

Although Louieed Co produces online learning material, most of its profits are still derived from sales of traditional textbooks. Louieed Co's growth in profits over the last few years has been slow and its directors are currently reviewing its long-term strategy. One area in which they feel that Louieed Co must become much more involved is the production of online testing materials for exams and to validate course and textbook learning.

Bid for Tidded Co

Louieed Co has recently made a bid for Tidded Co, a smaller listed company. Tidded Co also supplies a range of educational material, but has been one of the leaders in the development of online testing and has shown strong profit growth over recent years. All of Tidded Co's initial five founders remain on its board and still hold 45% of its issued share capital between them. From the start, Tidded Co's directors have been used to making quick decisions in their areas of responsibility. Although listing has imposed some formalities, Tidded Co has remained focused on acting quickly to gain competitive advantage, with the five founders continuing to give strong leadership.

Louieed Co's initial bid of five shares in Louieed Co for three shares in Tidded Co was rejected by Tidded Co's board. There has been further discussion between the two boards since the initial offer was rejected and Louieed Co's board is now considering a proposal to offer Tidded Co's shareholders two shares in Louieed Co for one share in Tidded Co or a cash alternative of $22.75 per Tidded Co share.

It is expected that Tidded Co's shareholders will choose one of the following options:

(i)   To accept the two-shares-for-one-share offer for all the Tidded Co shares; or,

(ii)   To accept the cash offer for all the Tidded Co shares; or,

(iii)   60% of the shareholders will take up the two-shares-for-one-share offer and the remaining 40% will take the cash offer.

In case of the third option being accepted, it is thought that three of the company's founders, holding 20% of the share capital in total, will take the cash offer and not join the combined company. The remaining two founders will probably continue to be involved in the business and be members of the combined company's board.

Louieed Co's finance director has estimated that the merger will produce annual post-tax synergies of $20 million. He expects Louieed Co's current price-earnings (P/E) ratio to remain unchanged after the acquisition.

Extracts from the two companies' most recent accounts are shown below:

	Louieed	Tidded
	$m	$m
Profit before finance cost and tax	446	182
Finance costs	(74)	(24)
Profit before tax	372	158
Tax	(76)	(30)
Profit after tax	296	128
Issued $1 nominal shares	340 million	90 million
P/E ratios, based on most recent accounts	14	15.9
Long-term liabilities (market value) ($m)	540	193
Cash and cash equivalents ($m)	220	64

The tax rate applicable to both companies is 20%.

Assume that Louieed Co can obtain further debt funding at a pre-tax cost of 7.5% and that the return on cash surpluses is 5% pre-tax.

Assume also that any debt funding needed to complete the acquisition will be reduced instantly by the balances of cash and cash equivalents held by Louieed Co and Tidded Co.

Required:

(a) **Discuss the advantages and disadvantages of the acquisition of Tidded Co from the viewpoint of Louieed Co.** **(6 marks)**

(b) **Calculate the P/E ratios of Tidded Co implied by the terms of Louieed Co's initial and proposed offers, for all three of the above options.** **(5 marks)**

(c) **Calculate, and comment on, the funding required for the acquisition of Tidded Co and the impact on Louieed Co's earnings per share and gearing, for each of the three options given above.**

Note: Up to 10 marks are available for the calculations. **(14 marks)**

(Total: 25 marks)

55 HAV CO (SPECIMEN PAPER 2018)

Hav Co is a publicly listed company involved in the production of highly technical and sophisticated electronic components for complex machinery. It has a number of diverse and popular products, an active research and development department, significant cash reserves and a highly talented management who are very good in getting products to market quickly.

A new industry which Hav Co is looking to venture into is biotechnology, which has been expanding rapidly and there are strong indications that this recent growth is set to continue. However, Hav Co has limited experience in this industry. Therefore it believes that the best and quickest way to expand would be through acquiring a company already operating in this industry sector.

Strand Co

Strand Co is a private company operating in the biotechnology industry and is owned by a consortium of business angels and company managers. The owner-managers are highly skilled scientists who have developed a number of technically complex products, but have found it difficult to commercialise them. They have also been increasingly constrained by the lack of funds to develop their innovative products further.

Discussions have taken place about the possibility of Strand Co being acquired by Hav Co. Strand Co's managers have indicated that the consortium of owners is happy for the negotiations to proceed. If Strand Co is acquired, it is expected that its managers would continue to run the Strand Co part of the larger combined company.

Strand Co is of the opinion that most of its value is in its intangible assets, comprising intellectual capital. Therefore, the premium payable on acquisition should be based on the present value to infinity of the after tax excess earnings the company has generated in the past three years, over the average return on capital employed of the biotechnological industry. However, Hav Co is of the opinion that the premium should be assessed on synergy benefits created by the acquisition and the changes in value, due to the changes in the price-to-earnings (PE) ratio before and after the acquisition.

Financial information

Given below are extracts of financial information for Hav Co for 20X3 and Strand Co for 20X1, 20X2 and 20X3:

	Hav Co		Strand Co	
Year ended 30 April	20X3	20X3	20X2	20X1
	$ million	$ million	$ million	$ million
Earnings before tax	1,980	397	370	352
Non-current assets	3,965	882	838	801
Current assets	968	210	208	198
Share capital ($0.25/share)	600	300	300	300
Reserves	2,479	183	166	159
Non-current liabilities	1,500	400	400	400
Current liabilities	354	209	180	140

The current average PE ratio of the biotechnology industry is 16.4 times and it has been estimated that Strand Co's PE ratio is 10% higher than this. However, it is thought that the PE ratio of the combined company would fall to 14.5 times after the acquisition. The annual after tax earnings will increase by $140 million due to synergy benefits resulting from combining the two companies.

Both companies pay tax at 20% per annum and Strand Co's annual cost of capital is estimated at 7%. Hav Co's current share price is $9.24 per share. The biotechnology industry's pre-tax return on capital employed is currently estimated to be 20% per annum.

Acquisition proposals

Hav Co has proposed to pay for the acquisition using one of the following three methods:

(i) A cash offer of $5.72 for each Strand Co share; or

(ii) A cash offer of $1.33 for each Strand Co share plus one Hav Co share for every two Strand Co shares; or

(iii) A cash offer of $1.25 for each Strand Co share plus one $100 3% convertible bond for every $5 nominal value of Strand Co shares. In six years, the bond can be converted into 12 Hav Co shares or redeemed at par.

Required:

(a) Distinguish between the different types of synergy and discuss possible sources of synergy based on the above scenario. **(9 marks)**

(b) Based on the two different opinions expressed by Hav Co and Strand Co, calculate the maximum acquisition premium payable in each case. **(6 marks)**

(c) Calculate the percentage premium per share which Strand Co's shareholders will receive under each acquisition payment method and justify, with explanations, which payment method would be most acceptable to them. **(10 marks)**

(Total: 25 marks)

CORPORATE RECONSTRUCTION AND REORGANISATION

56 ALASKA SALVAGE (DEC 09 ADAPTED)

Alaska Salvage is in discussion with potential lenders about financing an ambitious five-year project searching for lost gold in the central Atlantic. The company has had great success in the past with its various salvage operations and is now quoted on the London Alternative Investment Market. The company is currently financed by 120,000 equity shares trading at $85 per share. It needs to borrow $1.6 million and is concerned about the level of the fixed rates being suggested by the lenders. After lengthy discussions the lenders are prepared to offer finance against a mezzanine issue of fixed rate five-year notes with warrants attached. Each $10,000 note, repayable at par, would carry a warrant for 100 equity shares at an exercise price of $90 per share. The estimated volatility of the returns on the company's equity is 20% and the risk free rate of interest is 5%. The company does not pay dividends to its equity investors.

You may assume that the issue of these loan notes will not influence the current value of the firm's equity. The issue will be made at par.

Required:

(a) Estimate, using Black-Scholes Option Pricing Model as appropriate, the current value of each warrant to the lender noting the assumptions that you have made in your valuation. **(10 marks)**

(b) Estimate the coupon rate that would be required by the lenders if they wanted a 13% rate of return on their investment. **(4 marks)**

(c) Discuss the advantages and disadvantages of issuing mezzanine debt in the situation outlined in the case. **(6 marks)**

(d) Explain how sukuk bonds could be used (instead of more conventional loan notes) to fund the project being considered by Alaska Salvage. **(5 marks)**

(Total: 25 marks)

57   PROTEUS CO (DEC 11 ADAPTED)

Proteus Co, a large listed company, has a number of subsidiaries in different industries but its main line of business is developing surveillance systems and intruder alarms. It has decided to sell a number of companies that it considers are peripheral to its core activities. One of these subsidiary companies is Tyche Co, a company involved in managing the congestion monitoring and charging systems that have been developed by Proteus Co. Tyche Co is a profitable business and it is anticipated that its revenues and costs will continue to increase at their current rate of 8% per year for the foreseeable future.

Tyche Co's managers and some employees want to buy the company through a leveraged management buy-out. An independent assessment estimates Tyche Co's market value at $81 million if Proteus Co agrees to cancel its current loan to Tyche Co. The managers and employees involved in the buy-out will invest $12 million for 75% of the equity in the company, with another $4 million coming from a venture capitalist for the remaining 25% equity.

Palaemon Bank has agreed to lend the balance of the required funds in the form of a 9% loan. The interest is payable at the end of the year, on the loan amount outstanding at the start of each year. A covenant on the loan states that the following debt-equity ratios should not be exceeded at the end of each year for the next five years:

Year	1	2	3	4	5
Debt/Equity (%)	350%	250%	200%	150%	125%

Shown below is an extract of the latest annual statement of profit or loss for Tyche Co:

	$000
Sales Revenue	60,000
Materials and consumables	12,000
Labour costs	22,000
Other costs	4,000
Allocated overhead charge payable to Proteus Co	14,000
Interest paid	2,000
Taxable Profit	6,000
Taxation	1,500
Retained Earnings	4,500

As part of the management buy-out agreement, it is expected that Proteus Co will provide management services costing $12 million for the first year of the management buy-out, increasing by 8% per year thereafter.

The current tax rate is 25% on profits and it is expected that 25% of the after-tax profits will be payable as dividends every year. The remaining profits will be allocated to reserves. It is expected that Tyche Co will repay $3 million of the outstanding loan at the end of each of the next five years from the cash flows generated from its business activity.

Required:

(a)   **Briefly discuss the possible benefits to Proteus Co of disposing Tyche Co through a management buy-out.** **(4 marks)**

(b)   **Calculate whether the debt-equity covenant imposed by Palaemon Bank on Tyche Co will be breached over the five-year period.** **(9 marks)**

(c) Discuss briefly the implications of the results obtained in part (b) and outline two possible actions Tyche Co may take if the covenant is in danger of being breached.

(5 marks)

(d) Explain (in general terms and without presenting any calculations) how the Black Scholes option pricing model can be used to value the equity and the debt of a company. (7 marks)

(Total: 25 marks)

58 DORIC CO (PILOT 12)

 Question debrief

Doric Co has two manufacturing divisions: parts and fridges. Although the parts division is profitable, the fridges division is not, and as a result its share price has declined to $0.50 per share from a high of $2.83 per share around three years ago. Assume it is now 1 January 20X3.

The board of directors are considering two proposals:

(i) To cease trading and close down the company entirely, or

(ii) To close the fridges division and continue the parts division through a leveraged management buyout. The new company will continue with manufacturing parts only, but will make an additional investment of $50 million in order to grow the parts division after-tax cash flows by 3.5% in perpetuity. The proceeds from the sale of the fridges division will be used to pay the outstanding liabilities. The finance raised from the management buy-out will pay for any remaining liabilities, the funds required for the additional investment, and to purchase the current equity shares at a premium of 20%. The fridges division is twice the size of the parts division in terms of its assets attributable to it.

Extracts from the most recent financial statements:

Financial position as at 31 December 20X2

	$m
Non-current Assets	110
Current Assets	220
Share capital ($0.40 per share par value)	40
Reserves	10
Liabilities (Non-current and current)	280

Statement of profit or loss for the year ended 31 December 20X2

Sales revenue:	Parts division	170
	Fridges division	340
Costs prior to depreciation, interest payments and tax:	Parts division	(120)
	Fridges division	(370)
Depreciation, tax and interest		(34)
Loss		(14)

If the entire company's assets are sold, the estimated realisable values of assets are as follows:

	$m
Non-current assets	100
Current assets	110

The following additional information has been provided:

Redundancy and other costs will be approximately $54 million if the whole company is closed, and pro rata for individual divisions that are closed. These costs have priority for payment before any other liabilities in case of closure. The taxation effects relating to this may be ignored.

Corporation tax on profits is 20% and it can be assumed that tax is payable in the year incurred. Annual depreciation on non-current assets is 10% and this is the amount of investment needed to maintain the current level of activity. The new company's cost of capital is expected to be 11%.

Required:

(a) Briefly discuss the possible benefits of Doric Co's parts division being divested through a management buy-out. **(4 marks)**

(b) Estimate the return the liability holders and the shareholders would receive in the event that Doric Co is closed and all its assets sold. **(3 marks)**

(c) Estimate the additional amount of finance needed and the value of the new company, if only the assets of fridges division are sold and the parts division is divested through a management buy-out. Briefly discuss whether or not the management buy-out would be beneficial. **(10 marks)**

(d) Doric Co's directors are of the opinion that they could receive a better price if the fridges division is sold as a going concern instead of its assets sold separately. They have been told that they need to consider two aspects when selling a company or part of a company:

(i) seeking potential buyers and negotiating the sale price; and

(ii) due diligence.

Discuss the issues that should be taken into consideration with each aspect. **(8 marks)**

(Total: 25 marks)

 Calculate your allowed time and allocate the time to the separate parts

---

59   NUBO CO (DEC 13)

Nubo Co has divisions operating in two diverse sectors: production of aircraft parts and supermarkets. Whereas the aircraft parts production division has been growing rapidly, the supermarkets division's growth has been slower. The company is considering selling the supermarkets division and focusing solely on the aircraft parts production division.

Extracts from Nubo Co's most recent financial statements are as follows:

Year ended 30 November	20X3
	$m
Profit after tax	166
Non-current assets	550
Current assets	122
Non-current liabilities	387
Current liabilities	95

About 70% of Nubo Co's non-current assets and current assets are attributable to the supermarkets division and the remainder to the aircraft parts production division. Each of the two divisions generates roughly half of the total profit after tax. The market value of the two divisions is thought to be equivalent to the price-to-earnings (PE) ratios of the two divisions' industries. The supermarket industry's PE ratio is 7 and the aircraft parts production industry's PE ratio is 12.

Nubo Co can either sell the supermarkets division as a going concern or sell the assets of the supermarkets division separately. If the assets are sold separately, Nubo Co believes that it can sell the non-current assets for 115% of the book value and the current assets for 80% of the book value. The funds raised from the sale of the supermarkets division will be used to pay for all the company's current and non-current liabilities.

Following the sale of the supermarkets division and paying off the liabilities, Nubo Co will raise additional finance for new projects in the form of debt. It will be able to borrow up to a maximum of 100% of the total asset value of the new downsized company.

One of the new projects which Nubo Co is considering is a joint venture with Pilvi Co to produce an innovative type of machinery which will be used in the production of light aircraft and private jets. Both companies will provide the expertise and funding required for the project equally. Representatives from both companies will make up the senior management team and decisions will be made jointly. Legal contracts will be drawn up once profit-sharing and other areas have been discussed by the companies and agreed on.

Pilvi Co has approached Ulap Bank for the finance it requires for the venture, based on Islamic finance principles. Ulap Bank has agreed to consider the request from Pilvi Co, but because the financing requirement will be for a long period of time and because of uncertainties surrounding the project, Ulap Bank wants to provide the finance based on the principles of a Musharaka contract, with Ulap Bank requiring representation on the venture's senior management team. Normally Ulap Bank provides funds based on the principles of a Mudaraba contract, which the bank provides for short-term, low-risk projects, where the responsibility for running a project rests solely with the borrower.

Required:

(a)   Advise Nubo Co whether it should sell the supermarkets division as a going concern or sell the assets separately and estimate the additional cash and debt funds which could be available to the new, downsized company. Show all relevant calculations.

(7 marks)

KAPLAN PUBLISHING

(b) An alternative to selling the supermarkets division would be to demerge both the divisions. In this case, all of Nubo Co's liabilities would be taken over by the demerged supermarkets division. Also, either of the demerged companies can borrow up to 100% of their respective total asset values.

Required:

Discuss whether a demerger of the supermarkets division may be more appropriate than a sale. **(6 marks)**

(c) **Discuss why Ulap Bank may want to consider providing the finance based on a Musharaka contract instead of a Mudaraba contract, and the key concerns Nubo Co may have from the arrangement between Pilvi Co and Ulap Bank.** **(12 marks)**

(Total: 25 marks)

60   BENTO CO (JUN 15)

In order to raise funds for future projects, the management of Bento Co, a large manufacturing company, is considering disposing of one of its subsidiary companies, Okazu Co, which is involved in manufacturing rubber tubing. They are considering undertaking the disposal through a management buy-out (MBO) or a management buy-in (MBI). Bento Co wants $60 million from the sale of Okazu Co.

Given below are extracts from the most recent financial statements for Okazu Co:

Year ending 30 April (all amounts in $000)

	20X5
Total non-current assets	40,800
Total current assets	12,300
Total assets	53,100
Equity	24,600
Non-current liabilities	16,600
Current liabilities	
Trade and other payables	7,900
Bank overdraft	4,000
Total current liabilities	11,900
Total equity and liabilities	53,100

Year ending 30 April (all amounts in $000)

	20X5
Sales revenue	54,900
Operating profit	12,200
Finance costs	1,600
Profit before tax	10,600
Taxation	2,120
Profit for the year	8,480

Notes relating to the financial statements above:

(i)   Current assets, non-current assets and the trade and other payables will be transferred to the new company when Okazu Co is sold. The bank overdraft will be repaid by Bento Co prior to the sale of Okazu Co.

(ii)   With the exception of the bank overdraft, Bento Co has provided all the financing to Okazu Co. No liabilities, except the trade and other payables specified above, will be transferred to the new company when Okazu Co is sold.

(iii)   It is estimated that the market value of the non-current assets is 30% higher than the book value and the market value of the current assets is equivalent to the book value.

(iv)   The group finance costs and taxation are allocated by Bento Co to all its subsidiaries in pre-agreed proportions.

Okazu Co's senior management team has approached Dofu Co, a venture capital company, about the proposed MBO. Dofu Co has agreed to provide leveraged finance for a 50% equity stake in the new company on the following basis:

(i) $30 million loan in the form of an 8% bond on which interest is payable annually, based on the loan amount outstanding at the start of each year. The bond will be repaid on the basis of fixed equal annual payments (constituting of interest and principal) over the next four years

(ii) $20 million loan in the form of a 6% convertible bond on which interest is payable annually. Conversion may be undertaken on the basis of 50 equity shares for every $100 from the beginning of year five onwards

(iii)   5,000,000 $1 equity shares for $5,000,000.

Okazu Co's senior management will contribute $5,000,000 for 5,000,000 $1 equity shares and own the remaining 50% of the equity stake.

As a condition for providing the finance, Dofu Co will impose a restrictive covenant that the new company's gearing ratio will be no higher than 75% at the end of its first year of operations, and then fall to no higher than 60%, 50% and 40% at the end of year two to year four respectively. The gearing ratio is determined by the book value of debt divided by the combined book values of debt and equity.

After the MBO, it is expected that earnings before interest and tax will increase by 11% per year and annual dividends of 25% on the available earnings will be paid for the next four years. It is expected that the annual growth rate of dividends will reduce by 60% from year five onwards following the MBO. The new company will pay tax at a rate of 20% per year. The new company's cost of equity has been estimated at 12%.

Required:

(a) **Distinguish between a management buy-out (MBO) and a management buy-in (MBI). Discuss the relative benefits and drawbacks to Okazu Co if it is disposed through a MBO instead of a MBI.** **(5 marks)**

(b) **Estimate, showing all relevant calculations, whether the restrictive covenant imposed by Dofu Co is likely to be met.** **(12 marks)**

(c) **Discuss, with supporting calculations, whether or not an MBO would be beneficial for Dofu Co and Okazu Co's senior management team.** **(8 marks)**

(Total: 25 marks)

61 FLUFFTORT CO (SEP/DEC 15)

Five years ago the Patel family invested in a new business, Flufftort Co, which manufactures furniture. Some family members became directors of Flufftort Co; others have not been actively involved in management. A venture capital firm, Gupte VC, also made a 20% investment in Flufftort Co. A representative of Gupte VC was appointed to Flufftort Co's board. Flufftort Co also took out a long-term 8.5% bank loan.

Sales have generally been disappointing. As a result, members of the Patel family have been reluctant to invest further in Flufftort Co. Over the last year Gupte VC has taken a tougher attitude towards Flufftort Co. Gupte VC pressurised Flufftort Co to pay a dividend of $2 million for the year ended 30 June 20X5. Gupte VC has also said that if Flufftort Co's financial results do not improve, Gupte VC may exercise its right to compel Flufftort Co to buy back its shares at par on 30 June 20X6.

However, Flufftort Co's most recent product, the Easicushion chair, has been a much bigger success than expected. In order to produce enough Easicushion chairs to affect its results substantially, Flufftort Co will need to make significant expenditure on manufacturing facilities and additional working capital.

Extracts from the statement of profit or loss for year ended 30 June 20X5, and the forecast statement of profit or loss for year ended 30 June 20X6 are presented below:

	20X5	20X6
		Forecast
	$m	$m
Operating profit	8.0	6.0
Finance cost	(3.0)	(3.0)
Profit before tax	5.0	3.0
Tax on profits (20%)	(1.0)	(0.6)
Profit for the period	4.0	2.4
Dividends	(2.0)	–
Retained earnings	2.0	2.4

Note: The forecast statement of profit or loss for the year ended 30 June 20X6 is not affected by the proposed investment. This can be assumed only to affect results after 30 June 20X6. The figure shown for retained earnings in the 20X6 forecast can be assumed to be the net increase in cash for the year ended 30 June 20X6.

Summarised statement of financial position as at 30 June 20X5

Assets	$m
Non-current assets	69.0
Current assets excluding cash	18.0
Cash	7.6
	———
Total assets	94.6
	———

Equity and liabilities	
Share capital ($1 shares)	50.0
Retained earnings	2.6
	———
Total equity	52.6
	———

Long-term liabilities	
8.5% Bank loan	30.0
9% Loan note	5.0
	———
Total long-term liabilities	35.0
Current liabilities	7.0
	———
Total liabilities	42.0
	———
Total equity and liabilities	94.6
	———

Notes:

1 55% of shares are owned by the members of the Patel family who are directors, 25% by other members of the Patel family and 20% by Gupte VC.

2 The bank loan is secured on the non-current assets of Flufftort and is due for repayment on 31 December 20X9. The loan is subject to a covenant that the ratio of equity to non-current liabilities should be greater than 1.3 on a book value basis. Flufftort has also been granted an overdraft facility of up to $5 million by its bank.

3 The loan note is held by Rajiv Patel, a member of the Patel family who is not a director. The loan note is unsecured, is subordinated to the bank loan and has no fixed date for repayment.

4 If no finance is available for investment in manufacturing facilities, non-current assets, current assets excluding cash, the bank loan, loan note and current liabilities can be assumed to be the same at 30 June 20X6 as at 30 June 20X5.

However, the chief executive and finance director of Flufftort Co intend to propose that the company should be refinanced to fund the expanded production of the Easicushion chair. They have not yet consulted anyone else about their proposals.

Details of the proposed refinancing are as follows:

1   The members of the Patel family who are directors would subscribe to an additional 15 million $1 shares at par.

2   Gupte VC would subscribe to an additional 20 million $1 shares at par.

3   The 8.5% bank loan would be renegotiated with the bank and the borrowing increased to $65 million, to be repaid on 30 June 2022. The expected finance cost of the loan would be 10% per annum.

4   Rajiv Patel's loan note would be replaced by 5 million $1 shares.

5   The refinancing would mean non-current assets would increase to $125 million, current assets other than cash would increase to $42 million and current liabilities would increase to $12 million.

6   Operating profits would be expected to increase to $20 million in the first full year after the facilities are constructed (year ended 30 June 20X7) and $25 million in the second year (year ended 30 June 20X8). No dividends would be paid for these two years, as cash surpluses would be used for further investment as required. Tax on company profits can be assumed to remain at 20%.

Required:

(a)   (i)   Prepare a projected statement of financial position as at 30 June 20X6, on the assumption that Gupte VC exercises its rights and Gupte VC's shares are repurchased and cancelled by Flufftort Co.   (4 marks)

(ii)   Prepare a projected statement of financial position as at 30 June 20X6 on the assumption that the proposed refinancing and investment take place.

(4 marks)

(iii)   Prepare projected statements of profit or loss for the years ended 30 June 20X7 and 30 June 20X8 on the basis that the profit forecasts are correct.

(4 marks)

(b)   Evaluate whether the suggested refinancing scheme is likely to be agreed by all finance providers. State clearly any assumptions which you make.   (13 marks)

(Total: 25 marks)

62   STAPLE GROUP (MAR/JUN 16)

Staple Group is one of Barland's biggest media groups. It consists of four divisions, organised as follows:

- **Staple National** – the national newspaper, the Daily Staple. This division's revenues and operating profits have decreased for the last two years.

- **Staple Local** – a portfolio of 18 local and regional newspapers. This division's operating profits have fallen for the last five years and operating profits and cash flows are forecast to be negative in the next financial year. Other newspaper groups with local titles have also reported significant falls in profitability recently.

- **Staple View** – a package of digital channels showing sporting events and programmes for a family audience. Staple Group's board has been pleased with this division's recent performance, but it believes that the division will only be able to sustain a growth rate of 4% in operating profits and cash flows unless it can buy the rights to show more major sporting events. Over the last year, Staple View's biggest competitor in this sector has acquired two smaller digital broadcasters.

- **Staple Investor** – established from a business which was acquired three years ago, this division offers services for investors including research, publications, training events and conferences. The division gained a number of new clients over the last year and has thus shown good growth in revenues and operating profits.

Some of Staple Group's institutional investors have expressed concern about the fall in profitability of the two newspaper divisions.

The following summarised data relates to the group's last accounting year. The % changes in pre-tax profits and revenues are changes in the most recent figures compared with the previous year.

	Division				
	Total	*National*	*Local*	*View*	*Investor*
Revenues ($m)	1,371.7	602.4	151.7	496.5	121.1
Increase/(decrease) in revenues (%)		(5.1)	(14.7)	8.2	16.5
Pre-tax profits ($m)	177.3	75.6	4.5	73.3	23.9
Increase/(decrease) in pre-tax profits (%)		(4.1)	(12.6)	7.4	19.1
Post-tax cash flows ($m)	120.2	50.7	0.3	53.5	15.7
Share of group net assets ($m)	635.8	267.0	66.6	251.2	51.0
Share of group long-term liabilities ($m)	230.9	104.4	23.1	93.4	10.0

Staple Group's board regards the *Daily Staple* as a central element of the group's future. The directors are currently considering a number of investment plans, including the development of digital platforms for the *Daily Staple*. The finance director has costed the investment programme at $150 million. The board would prefer to fund the investment programme by disposing parts or all of one of the other divisions. The following information is available to help assess the value of each division:

- One of Staple Group's competitors, Postway Co, has contacted Staple Group's directors asking if they would be interested in selling 15 of the local and regional newspapers for $60 million. Staple Group's finance director believes this offer is low and wishes to use the net assets valuation method to evaluate a minimum price for the Staple Local division.

- Staple Group's finance director believes that a valuation using free cash flows would provide a fair estimate of the value of the Staple View division. Over the last year, investment in additional non-current assets for the Staple View division has been $12.5 million and the incremental working capital investment has been $6.2 million. These investment levels will have to increase at 4% annually in order to support the expected sustainable increases in operating profit and cash flow.

- Staple Group's finance director believes that the valuation of the Staple Investor division needs to reflect the potential it derives from the expertise and experience of its staff. The finance director has calculated a value of $118.5 million for this division, based on the earnings made last year but also allowing for the additional earnings which he believes that the expert staff in the division will be able to generate in future years.

Assume a risk-adjusted, all-equity financed, cost of capital of 12% and a tax rate of 30%. Goodwill should be ignored in any calculations.

Staple Group's finance and human resources directors are looking at the staffing of the two newspaper divisions. The finance director proposes dismissing most staff who have worked for the group for less than two years, two years' employment being when staff would be entitled to enhanced statutory employment protection. The finance director also proposes a redundancy programme for longer-serving staff, selecting for redundancy employees who have complained particularly strongly about recent changes in working conditions. There is a commitment in Staple Group's annual report to treat employees fairly, communicate with them regularly and enhance employees' performance by structured development.

Required:

(a)   **Evaluate the options for disposing of parts of Staple Group, using the financial information to assess possible disposal prices. The evaluation should include a discussion of the benefits and drawbacks to Staple Group from disposing of parts of the Staple Group.** **(19 marks)**

(b)   **Discuss the significance of the finance director's proposals for reduction in staff costs for Staple Group's relationships with its shareholders and employees and discuss the ethical implications of the proposals.** **(6 marks)**

(Total: 25 marks)

63   EVIEW CINEMAS CO (SEP/DEC 17)

Eview Cinemas Co is a long-established chain of cinemas in the country of Taria. Twenty years ago Eview Cinemas Co's board decided to convert some of its cinemas into sports gyms, known as the EV clubs. The number of EV clubs has expanded since then. Eview Cinemas Co's board brought in outside managers to run the EV clubs, but over the years there have been disagreements between the clubs' managers and the board. The managers have felt that the board has wrongly prioritised investment in, and refurbishment of, the cinemas at the expense of the EV clubs.

Five years ago, Eview Cinemas Co undertook a major refurbishment of its cinemas, financing this work with various types of debt, including loan notes at a high coupon rate of 10%. Shortly after the work was undertaken, Taria entered into a recession which adversely affected profitability. The finance cost burden was high and Eview Cinemas Co was not able to pay a dividend for two years.

The recession is now over and Eview Cinemas Co has emerged in a good financial position, as two of its competitors went into insolvency during the recession. Eview Cinemas Co's board wishes to expand its chain of cinemas and open new, multiscreen cinemas in locations which are available because businesses were closed down during the recession.

In two years' time Taria is due to host a major sports festival. This has encouraged interest in sport and exercise in the country. As a result, some gym chains are looking to expand and have contacted Eview Cinemas Co's board to ask if it would be interested in selling the EV clubs. Most of the directors regard the cinemas as the main business and so are receptive to selling the EV clubs.

The finance director has recommended that the sales price of the EV clubs be based on predicted free cash flows as follows:

1   The predicted free cash flow figures in $millions for EV clubs are as follows:

Year	1	2	3	4
	390	419	455	490

2   After Year 4, free cash flows should be assumed to increase at 5.2% per annum.

3   The discount rate to be used should be the current weighted average cost of capital, which is 12%.

4   The finance director believes that the result of the free cash flow valuation will represent a fair value of the EV clubs' business, but Eview Cinemas Co is looking to obtain a 25% premium on the fair value as the expected sales price.

Other information supplied by the finance director is as follows:

1   The predicted after-tax profits of the EV clubs are $454 million in Year 1. This can be assumed to be 40% of total after-tax profits of EV Cinemas Co.

2   The expected proceeds which Eview Cinemas Co receives from selling the EV clubs will be used firstly to pay off the 10% loan notes. Part of the remaining amount from the sales proceeds will then be used to enhance liquidity by being held as part of current assets, so that the current ratio increases to 1.5. The rest of the remaining amount will be invested in property, plant and equipment. The current net book value of the non-current assets of the EV clubs to be sold can be assumed to be $3,790 million. The profit on the sale of the EV clubs should be taken directly to reserves.

3   Eview Cinemas Co's asset beta for the cinemas can be assumed to be 0.952.

4   Eview Cinemas Co currently has 1,000 million $1 shares in issue. These are currently trading at $15.75 per share. The finance director expects the share price to rise by 10% once the sale has been completed, as he thinks that the stock market will perceive it to be a good deal.

5   Tradeable debt is currently quoted at $96 per $100 for the 10% loan notes and $93 per $100 for the other loan notes. The value of the other loan notes is not expected to change once the sale has been completed. The overall pre-tax cost of debt is currently 9% and can be assumed to fall to 8% when the 10% loan notes are redeemed.

6   The current tax rate on profits is 20%.

7   Additional investment in current assets is expected to earn a 7% pre-tax return and additional investment in property, plant and equipment is expected to earn a 12% pre-tax return.

8   The current risk-free rate is 4% and the return on the market portfolio is 10%.

Eview Cinemas Co's current summarised statement of financial position is shown below. The CEO wants to know the impact the sale of the EV clubs would have immediately on the statement of financial position, the impact on the Year 1 forecast earnings per share and on the weighted average cost of capital.

Assets	$m
Non-current assets	15,621
Current assets	2,347
Total assets	17,968
Equity and liabilities	
Called up share capital	1,000
Retained earnings	7,917
Total equity	8,917
Non-current liabilities	
10% loan notes	3,200
Other loan notes	2,700
Bank loans	985
Total non-current liabilities	6,885
Current liabilities	2,166
Total liabilities	9,051
Total equity and liabilities	17,968

Required:

(a)   Calculate the expected sales price of the EV clubs and demonstrate its impact on Eview Cinemas Co's statement of financial position, forecast earnings per share and weighted average cost of capital.   (17 marks)

(b)   Evaluate the decision to sell the EV clubs.   (8 marks)

(Total: 25 marks)

TREASURY AND ADVANCED RISK MANAGEMENT TECHNIQUES

64 FAOILEAN CO (JUN 14)

The chief executive officer (CEO) of Faoilean Co has just returned from a discussion at a leading university on the 'application of options to investment decisions and corporate value'. She wants to understand how some of the ideas which were discussed can be applied to decisions made at Faoilean Co. She is still a little unclear about some of the discussion on options and their application, and wants further clarification on the following:

(i) Faoilean Co is involved in the exploration and extraction of oil and gas. Recently there have been indications that there could be significant deposits of oil and gas just off the shores of Ireland. The government of Ireland has invited companies to submit bids for the rights to commence the initial exploration of the area to assess the likelihood and amount of oil and gas deposits, with further extraction rights to follow. Faoilean Co is considering putting in a bid for the rights. The speaker leading the discussion suggested that using options as an investment assessment tool would be particularly useful to Faoilean Co in this respect.

(ii) The speaker further suggested that options were useful in determining the value of equity and default risk, and suggested that this was why companies facing severe financial distress could still have a positive equity value.

(iii) Towards the end of the discussion, the speaker suggested that changes in the values of options can be measured in terms of a number of risk factors known as the 'Greeks', such as the 'vega'. The CEO is unclear why option values are affected by so many different risk factors.

Required:

(a) **With regard to (i) above, discuss how Faoilean Co may use the idea of options to help with the investment decision in bidding for the exploration rights, and explain the assumptions made when using the idea of options in making investment decisions.**

(11 marks)

(b) **With regard to (ii) above, discuss how options could be useful in determining the value of equity and default risk, and why companies facing severe financial distress still have positive equity values.** **(9 marks)**

(c) **With regard to (iii) above, explain why changes in option values are determined by numerous different risk factors and what 'vega' determines.** **(5 marks)**

(Total: 25 marks)

65 LEVANTE CO (DEC 11 ADAPTED)

Levante Co has identified a new project for which it will need to increase its long-term borrowings from $250 million to $400 million. This amount will cover a significant proportion of the total cost of the project and the rest of the funds will come from cash held by the company.

The current $250 million borrowing is in the form of a 4% bond which is trading at $98.71 per $100 and is due to be redeemed at par in three years. The issued bond has a credit rating of AA. The new borrowing will also be raised in the form of a traded bond with a par value of $100 per unit. It is anticipated that the new project will generate sufficient cash flows to be able to redeem the new bond at $100 par value per unit in five years. It can be assumed that coupons on both bonds are paid annually.

Both bonds would be ranked equally for payment in the event of default and the directors expect that as a result of the new issue, the credit rating for both bonds will fall to A. The directors are considering the following two alternative options when issuing the new bond:

(i)   Issue the new bond at a fixed coupon of 5% but at a premium or discount, whichever is appropriate to ensure full take up of the bond; or

(ii)   Issue the new bond at a coupon rate where the issue price of the new bond will be $100 per unit and equal to its par value.

The following extracts are provided on the current government bond yield curve and yield spreads for the sector in which Levante Co operates:

Current Government Bond Yield Curve

Years	1	2	3	4	5
	3.2%	3.7%	4.2%	4.8%	5.0%

Yield spreads (in basis points)

Bond Rating	1 year	2 years	3 years	4 years	5 years
AAA	5	9	14	19	25
AA	16	22	30	40	47
A	65	76	87	100	112
BBB	102	121	142	167	193

Required:

(a)   **Calculate the expected percentage fall in the market value of the existing bond if Levante Co's bond credit rating falls from AA to A.**   **(3 marks)**

(b)   **Advise the directors on the financial implications of choosing each of the two options when issuing the new bond. Support the advice with appropriate calculations.**

(7 marks)

(c)   **Among the criteria used by credit agencies for establishing a company's credit rating are the following: industry risk, earnings protection, financial flexibility and evaluation of the company's management.**

Briefly explain each criterion and suggest factors that could be used to assess it.

(8 marks)

(d)   **Discuss the importance to a company of recognising all of its stakeholders when making a new project investment decision.**   **(7 marks)**

(Total: 25 marks)

66   SEMBILAN CO (JUN 12 ADAPTED)

Sembilan Co, a listed company, recently issued debt finance to acquire assets in order to increase its activity levels. This debt finance is in the form of a floating rate bond, with a face value of $320 million, redeemable in four years. The bond interest, payable annually, is based on the spot yield curve plus 60 basis points. The next annual payment is due at the end of year one.

Sembilan Co is concerned that the expected rise in interest rates over the coming few years would make it increasingly difficult to pay the interest due. It is therefore proposing to either swap the floating rate interest payment to a fixed rate payment, or to raise new equity capital and use that to pay off the floating rate bond. The new equity capital would either be issued as rights to the existing shareholders or as shares to new shareholders.

Ratus Bank has offered Sembilan Co an interest rate swap, whereby Sembilan Co would pay Ratus Bank interest based on an equivalent fixed annual rate of 3.76¼% in exchange for receiving a variable amount based on the current yield curve rate. Payments and receipts will be made at the end of each year, for the next four years. Ratus Bank will charge an annual fee of 20 basis points if the swap is agreed.

The current annual spot yield curve rates are as follows:

Year	One	Two	Three	Four
Rate	2.5%	3.1%	3.5%	3.8%

The current annual forward rates for years two, three and four are as follows:

Year	Two	Three	Four
Rate	3.7%	4.3%	4.7%

Required:

(a) Based on the above information, calculate the amounts Sembilan Co expects to pay or receive every year on the swap (excluding the fee of 20 basis points). Explain why the fixed annual rate of interest of 3.76¼% is less than the four-year yield curve rate of 3.8%.

(6 marks)

(b) Demonstrate that Sembilan Co's interest payment liability does not change, after it has undertaken the swap, whether the interest rates increase or decrease.

(5 marks)

(c) Discuss the advantages of hedging with interest rate caps and collars. (6 marks)

(d) Discuss the factors that Sembilan Co should consider when deciding whether it should raise equity capital to pay off the floating rate debt. (8 marks)

(Total: 25 marks)

67 PAULT CO (SEP/DEC 16)

Pault Co is currently undertaking a major programme of product development. Pault Co has made a significant investment in plant and machinery for this programme. Over the next couple of years, Pault Co has also budgeted for significant development and launch costs for a number of new products, although its finance director believes there is some uncertainty with these budgeted figures, as they will depend upon competitor activity amongst other matters.

Pault Co issued floating rate loan notes, with a face value of $400 million, to fund the investment in plant and machinery. The loan notes are redeemable in ten years' time. The interest on the loan notes is payable annually and is based on the spot yield curve, plus 50 basis points.

Pault Co's finance director has recently completed a review of the company's overall financing strategy. His review has highlighted expectations that interest rates will increase over the next few years, although the predictions of financial experts in the media differ significantly.

The finance director is concerned about the exposure Pault Co has to increases in interest rates through the loan notes. He has therefore discussed with Millbridge Bank the possibility of taking out a four-year interest rate swap. The proposed terms are that Pault Co would pay Millbridge Bank interest based on an equivalent fixed annual rate of 4.847%. In return, Pault Co would receive from Millbridge Bank a variable amount based on the forward rates calculated from the annual spot yield curve rate at the time of payment minus 20 basis points. Payments and receipts would be made annually, with the first one in a year's time. Millbridge Bank would charge an annual fee of 25 basis points if Pault Co enters the swap.

The current annual spot yield curve rates are as follows:

Year	One	Two	Three	Four
Rate	3.70%	4.25%	4.70%	5.10%

A number of concerns were raised at the recent board meeting when the swap arrangement was discussed.

- Pault Co's chairman wondered what the value of the swap arrangement to Pault Co was, and whether the value would change over time.

- One of Pault Co's non-executive directors objected to the arrangement, saying that in his opinion the interest rate which Pault Co would pay and the bank charges were too high. Pault Co ought to stick with its floating rate commitment. Investors would be critical if, at the end of four years, Pault Co had paid higher costs under the swap than it would have done had it left the loan unhedged.

Required:

(a) (i) Using the current annual spot yield curve rates as the basis for estimating forward rates, calculate the amounts Pault Co expects to pay or receive each year under the swap (excluding the fee of 25 basis points). **(6 marks)**

(ii) Calculate Pault Co's interest payment liability for Year 1 if the yield curve rate is 4.5% or 2.9%, and comment on your results. **(6 marks)**

(b) Advise the chairman on the current value of the swap to Pault Co and the factors which would change the value of the swap. **(4 marks)**

(c) Discuss the disadvantages and advantages to Pault Co of not undertaking a swap and being liable to pay interest at floating rates. **(9 marks)**

(Total: 25 marks)

68 INTEREST RATE HEDGES (JUN 05 ADAPTED) *Walk in the footsteps of a top tutor*

Assume that it is now 1 June. Your company expects to receive £7.1 million from a large order in five months' time. This will then be invested in high-quality commercial paper for a period of four months, after that it will be used to pay part of the company's dividend. The company's treasurer wishes to protect the short-term investment from adverse movements in interest rates, by using futures or forward rate agreements (FRAs).

The current yield on high-quality commercial paper is LIBOR + 0.60%.

LIFFE £500,000 three month sterling futures. £12.50 tick size.

September	96.25
December	96.60

Futures contracts mature at the month end. LIBOR is currently 4%.

FRA prices (%)

4 v 5	3.85 – 3.80
4 v 9	3.58 – 3.53
5 v 9	3.50 – 3.45

Required:

(a)   Devise a futures hedge to protect the interest yield of the short-term investment, and estimate the expected lock-in interest rate as a result of the hedge.   **(4 marks)**

(b)   Ignoring transactions costs, explain whether the futures or FRA hedge would provide the higher expected interest rate from the short-term investment.

(2 marks)

(c)   If LIBOR fell by 0.5% during the next five months, show the expected outcomes of each hedge in the cash market, futures market and FRA market as appropriate.

(6 marks)

(d)   Explain why the futures market outcome might differ from the outcome in (c) above.   **(3 marks)**

(e)   Discuss how interest rate swaps and currency swaps might be of value to the corporate financial manager.   **(10 marks)**

(Total: 25 marks)

69   ARNBROOK PLC (JUN 06 ADAPTED)

Arnbrook plc is considering a £50 million three-year interest rate swap. The company wishes to expand and to have use of floating rate funds, but because of its AA credit rating has a comparative advantage over lower-rated companies when borrowing in the domestic fixed-rate market. Arnbrook can borrow fixed rate at 6.25% or floating rate at LIBOR plus 0.75%.

LIBOR is currently 5.25%, but parliamentary elections are due in six months' time and future interest rates are uncertain. A swap could be arranged using a bank as an intermediary. The bank would offset the swap risk with a counterparty BBB-rated company that could borrow fixed rate at 7.25% and floating rate at LIBOR plus 1.25%. The bank would charge a fee of £90,000 per year to each party in the swap. Arnbrook would require 60% of any arbitrage savings (before the payment of fees) from the swap because of its higher credit rating.

Ignore tax.

Required:

(a)   Discuss the risks that Arnbrook and a participating bank might face when undertaking an interest rate swap.   **(3 marks)**

(b)   Evaluate whether or not the proposed swap might be beneficial to all parties.

(6 marks)

(c)   If LIBOR was to increase immediately after the forthcoming election to 5.75% and then stay constant for the period of the swap, estimate the present value of the savings from the swap for Arnbrook plc. Interest payments are made semi-annually in arrears. Comment upon whether the swap would have been beneficial to Arnbrook plc.

The money market may be assumed to be an efficient market.   **(6 marks)**

(d)   Discuss the advantages and disadvantages of arranging a swap through a bank rather than negotiating directly with a counterparty.   **(5 marks)**

(e)   Explain the nature of a *mudaraba* contract and discuss briefly how this form of Islamic finance could be used to finance the planned expansion.   **(5 marks)**

(Total: 25 marks)

70   PONDHILLS (JUN 01 ADAPTED)

(a)   Discuss the significance to a multinational company of translation exposure and economic exposure.   **(7 marks)**

(b)   Pondhills Inc is a US multinational company with subsidiaries in the UK and Africa. The currency of the African country is pegged against the dollar, with a current exchange rate of 246.3 dinars/$US1. In recent months political unrest and an increasing inflation rate has led the finance director of Pondhills to become concerned about a possible devaluation of the dinar. He believes that the dinar could devalue by up to 15% relative to the dollar during the next few months.

Summarised financial data for the African subsidiary, Ponda SA are shown below:

	Million dinars
Revenue	2,300
Non-current assets	510
Current assets	
Cash	86
Receivables	410
Inventory	380
	876
Short-term payables	(296)
Long-term loans	(500)
	590
Shareholders' equity	590

Current exchange rates are:

$US/£1	1.5780
Dinar/$US1	246.3

Notes:

(i)   All sales from the African subsidiary are denominated in US dollars, and all receivables are therefore payable in dollars.

(ii)   50% of payables are debts owned in sterling to the UK subsidiary by Ponda SA.

(iii)   Long-term loans are in dinars from an African bank, at an interest rate of 12% per annum.

(iv)   The cost of goods sold and other operating expenses (excluding interest) for Ponda SA are 70% of revenue. 40% of this is payable in dollars or sterling and 60% in dinars.

(v)   No significant changes in exchange rates are expected between the dollar and other major currencies.

Required:

(i)   Calculate the statement of financial position translation exposure of Pondhills Inc, AND the potential profit or loss on translation of the statement of financial position using the current or closing rate method where all EXPOSED assets and liabilities are translated at the current exchange rate;

(9 marks)

(ii)   Calculate the expected impact on the dollar value of Ponda SA's annual cash flow in the first full year after devaluation. The time value of money may be ignored. (6 marks)

(c)   Comment upon whether or not Pondhills Inc should hedge against the exposures estimated in (b)(i) and (b)(ii). (3 marks)

(Total: 25 marks)

71   CURRENCY SWAPS (DEC 04 ADAPTED)

(a)   From the perspective of a corporate financial manager, discuss the advantages and potential problems of using currency swaps. (10 marks)

(b)   Galeplus plc, a UK-based company, has been invited to purchase and operate a new telecommunications centre in the republic of Perdia. The purchase price is 2,000 million rubbits. The Perdian government has built the centre in order to improve the country's infrastructure, but has currently not got enough funds to pay money owed to the local constructors. Galeplus would purchase the centre for a period of three years, after which it would be sold back to the Perdian government for an agreed price of 4,000 million rubbits. Galeplus would supply three years of technical expertise and training for local staff, for an annual fee of 40 million rubbits, after Perdian taxation. Other after-tax net cash flows from the investment in Perdia are expected to be negligible during the three-year period.

Perdia has only recently become a democracy, and in the last five years has experienced inflation rates of between 25% and 500%. The managers of Galeplus are concerned about the foreign exchange risk of the investment. Perdia has recently adopted economic stability measures suggested by the IMF, and inflation during the next three years is expected to be between 15% per year and 50% per year. Galeplus's bankers have suggested using a currency swap for the purchase price of the factory, with a swap of principal immediately and in three years' time, both swaps at today's spot rate. The bank would charge a fee of 0.75% per year (in sterling) for arranging the swap. Galeplus would take 75% of any net arbitrage benefit from the swap, after deducting bank fees. Relevant borrowing rates are:

	UK	Perdia
Galeplus	6.25%	PIBOR + 2.0%
Perdian counterparty	8.3%	PIBOR + 1.5%

NB: PIBOR is the Perdian interbank offered rate, which has tended to be set at approximately the current inflation level. Inflation in the UK is expected to be negligible.

	Exchange rates
Spot	85.4 rubbits/£
3-year forward rate	Not available

Required:

(i)   Estimate the potential annual percentage interest saving that Galeplus might make from using a currency swap relative to borrowing directly in Perdia.

(6 marks)

(ii)   Assuming the swap takes place as described, provide a reasoned analysis, including relevant calculations, as to whether or not Galeplus should purchase the communications centre. The relevant risk adjusted discount rate may be assumed to be 15% per year.   (9 marks)

(Total: 25 marks)

72   FNDC PLC (DEC 06 ADAPTED)

Several months ago FNDC plc, a UK television manufacturer, agreed to offer financial support to a major sporting event. The event will take place in seven months' time, but an expenditure of £45 million for temporary facilities will be necessary in five months' time. FNDC has agreed to lend the £45 million, and expects the loan to be repaid at the time of the event. At the time the support was offered, FNDC expected to have sufficient cash to lend the £45 million from its own resources, but new commitments mean that the cash will have to be borrowed. Interest rates have been showing a rising trend, and FNDC wishes to protect itself against further interest rate rises when it takes out the loan. The company is considering using either interest rate futures or options on interest rate futures.

Assume that it is now 1 December and that futures and options contracts mature at the relevant month end.

LIBOR is currently 4%. FNDC can borrow at LIBOR plus 1.25%

Euronext.LIFFE STIR £500,000 three-month sterling futures. Tick size 0.01%, tick value £12.50

December	96.04
March	95.77
June	95.55

Euronext.LIFFE options on three month £500,000 sterling futures. Tick size 0.005%, tick value £6.25. Option premiums are in annual %.

	CALLS			PUTS		
	December	*March*	*June*	*December*	*March*	*June*
9400	1.505	1.630	1.670	–	–	–
9450	1.002	1.130	1.170	–	–	–
9500	0.502	0.630	0.685	–	–	0.015
9550	0.252	0.205	0.285	0.060	0.115	0.165
9600	0.002	0.025	0.070	0.200	0.450	0.710

Required:

(a)   Discuss the relative merits of using short-term interest rate futures and market-traded options on short-term interest rates futures to hedge short-term interest rate risk.   (5 marks)

(b) If LIBOR interest rates were to increase by 0.5% or to decrease by 0.5%, estimate the expected outcomes from hedging using:

(i) an interest rate futures hedge; and

(ii) options on interest rate futures.

Briefly discuss your findings.

Note: In the futures hedge, the expected basis at the close-out date should be estimated, but basis risk may be ignored. **(15 marks)**

(c) Calculate and discuss the outcome of a collar hedge which would limit the maximum interest rate paid by the company to 5.75%, and the minimum to 5.25%. (These interest rates do not include any option premium.) **(5 marks)**

(Total: 25 marks)

73 LIGNUM CO (DEC 12 ADAPTED)

Lignum Co, a large listed company, manufactures agricultural machines and equipment for different markets around the world. Although its main manufacturing base is in France and it uses the Euro (€) as its base currency, it also has a few subsidiary companies around the world. Lignum Co's treasury division is considering how to approach the following three cases of foreign exchange exposure that it faces.

Case One

Lignum Co regularly trades with companies based in Zuhait, a small country in South America whose currency is the Zupesos (ZP). It recently sold machinery for ZP140 million, which it is about to deliver to a company based there. It is expecting full payment for the machinery in four months. Although there are no exchange traded derivative products available for the Zupesos, Medes Bank has offered Lignum Co a choice of two over-the-counter derivative products.

The first derivative product is an over-the-counter forward rate determined on the basis of the Zuhait base rate of 8.5% plus 25 basis points and the French base rate of 2.2% less 30 basis points.

Alternatively, with the second derivative product Lignum Co can purchase either Euro call or put options from Medes Bank at an exercise price equivalent to the current spot exchange rate of ZP142 per €1. The option premiums offered are: ZP7 per €1 for the call option or ZP5 per €1 for the put option.

The premium cost is payable in full at the commencement of the option contract. Lignum Co can borrow money at the base rate plus 150 basis points and invest money at the base rate minus 100 basis points in France.

Case Two

Namel Co is Lignum Co's subsidiary company based in Maram, a small country in Asia, whose currency is the Maram Ringit (MR). The current pegged exchange rate between the Maram Ringit and the Euro is MR35 per €1. Due to economic difficulties in Maram over the last couple of years, it is very likely that the Maram Ringit will devalue by 20% imminently. Namel Co is concerned about the impact of the devaluation on its Statement of Financial Position.

Given below is an extract from the current Statement of Financial Position of Namel Co.

	MR '000
Non-current assets	179,574
Current assets	146,622
Total assets	326,196
Share capital and reserves	102,788
Non-current liabilities	132,237
Current liabilities	91,171
Total capital and liabilities	326,196

The current assets consist of inventories, receivables and cash. Receivables account for 40% of the current assets. All the receivables relate to sales made to Lignum Co in Euro. About 70% of the current liabilities consist of payables relating to raw material inventory purchased from Lignum Co and payable in Euro. 80% of the non-current liabilities consist of a Euro loan and the balance are borrowings sourced from financial institutions in Maram.

Case Three

Lignum Co manufactures a range of farming vehicles in France which it sells within the European Union to countries which use the Euro. Over the previous few years, it has found that its sales revenue from these products has been declining and the sales director is of the opinion that this is entirely due to the strength of the Euro. Lignum Co's biggest competitor in these products is based in the USA and US$ rate has changed from almost parity with the Euro three years ago, to the current value of US$1.47 for €1. The agreed opinion is that the US$ will probably continue to depreciate against the Euro, but possibly at a slower rate, for the foreseeable future.

Required:

Prepare a report for Lignum Co's treasury division that:

(i)   Briefly explains the type of currency exposure Lignum Co faces for each of the above cases;   (3 marks)

(ii) Recommends which of the two derivative products Lignum Co should use to manage its exposure in case one and advises on alternative hedging strategies that could be used. Show all relevant calculations;   (9 marks)

(iii) Computes the gain or loss on Namel Co's Statement of Financial Position, due to the devaluation of the Maram Ringit in case two, and discusses whether and how this exposure should be managed;   (8 marks)

(iv) Discusses how the exposure in case three can be managed.   (3 marks)

Professional marks will be awarded in this question for the structure and presentation of the report.   (2 marks)

(Total: 25 marks)

74   ALECTO CO (PILOT 12)

Alecto Co, a large listed company based in Europe, is expecting to borrow €22,000,000 in four months' time on 1 May 20X2. It expects to make a full repayment of the borrowed amount nine months from now. Currently there is some uncertainty in the markets, with higher than normal rates of inflation, but an expectation that the inflation level may soon come down. This has led some economists to predict a rise in interest rates and others suggesting an unchanged outlook or maybe even a small fall in interest rates over the next six months.

Although Alecto Co is of the opinion that it is equally likely that interest rates could increase or fall by 0.5% in four months, it wishes to protect itself from interest rate fluctuations by using derivatives. The company can borrow at LIBOR plus 80 basis points and LIBOR is currently 3.3%. The company is considering using interest rate futures, options on interest rate futures or interest rate collars as possible hedging choices.

The following information and quotes from an appropriate exchange are provided on Euro futures and options. Margin requirements may be ignored.

Three month Euro futures, €1,000,000 contract, tick size 0.01% and tick value €25.

March 96.27

June 96.16

September 95.90

Options on three month Euro futures, €1,000,000 contract, tick size 0.01% and tick value €25. Option premiums are in annual %.

	Calls		Strike	Puts		
March	*June*	*September*		*March*	*June*	*September*
0.279	0.391	0.446	96.00	0.006	0.163	0.276
0.012	0.090	0.263	96.50	0.196	0.581	0.754

It can be assumed that settlement for both the futures and options contracts is at the end of the month. It can also be assumed that basis diminishes to zero at contract maturity at a constant rate and that time intervals can be counted in months.

Required:

(a)   Briefly discuss the main advantage and disadvantage of hedging interest rate risk using an interest rate collar instead of options.   **(4 marks)**

(b)   Based on the three hedging choices Alecto Co is considering and assuming that the company does not face any basis risk, recommend a hedging strategy for the €22,000,000 loan. Support your recommendation with appropriate comments and relevant calculations in €.   **(17 marks)**

(c)   Explain what is meant by basis risk and how it would affect the recommendation made in part (b) above.   **(4 marks)**

(Total: 25 marks)

75 KENDURI CO (JUN 13)

Kenduri Co is a large multinational company based in the UK with a number of subsidiary companies around the world. Currently, foreign exchange exposure as a result of transactions between Kenduri Co and its subsidiary companies is managed by each company individually. Kenduri Co is considering whether or not to manage the foreign exchange exposure using multilateral netting from the UK, with the Sterling Pound (£) as the base currency. If multilateral netting is undertaken, spot mid-rates would be used.

The following cash flows are due in three months between Kenduri Co and three of its subsidiary companies. The subsidiary companies are Lakama Co, based in the United States (currency US$), Jaia Co, based in Canada (currency CAD) and Gochiso Co, based in Japan (currency JPY).

Owed by	Owed to	Amount
Kenduri Co	Lakama Co	US$ 4.5 million
Kenduri Co	Jaia Co	CAD 1.1 million
Gochiso Co	Jaia Co	CAD 3.2 million
Gochiso Co	Lakama Co	US$ 1.4 million
Jaia Co	Lakama Co	US$ 1.5 million
Jaia Co	Kenduri Co	CAD 3.4 million
Lakama Co	Gochiso Co	JPY 320 million
Lakama Co	Kenduri Co	US$ 2.1 million

Exchange rates available to Kenduri Co

	US$/£1	CAD/£1	JPY/£1
Spot	1.5938–1.5962	1.5690–1.5710	131.91–133.59
3-month forward	1.5996–1.6037	1.5652–1.5678	129.15–131.05

Currency options available to Kenduri Co Contract size £62,500, Exercise price quotation: US$/£1, Premium: cents per £1

	Call Options		Put Options	
Exercise price	*3-month expiry*	*6-month expiry*	*3-month expiry*	*6-month expiry*
1.60	1.55	2.25	2.08	2.23
1.62	0.98	1.58	3.42	3.73

It can be assumed that option contracts expire at the end of the relevant month

Annual interest rates available to Kenduri Co and subsidiaries

Borrowing rate Investing rate

	Borrowing rate	*Investing rate*
UK	4.0%	2.8%
United States	4.8%	3.1%
Canada	3.4%	2.1%
Japan	2.2%	0.5%

Required:

(a) Advise Kenduri Co on, and recommend, an appropriate hedging strategy for the US$ cash flows it is due to receive or pay in three months, from Lakama Co. Show all relevant calculations to support the advice given. **(12 marks)**

(b) Calculate, using a tabular format (transactions matrix), the impact of undertaking multilateral netting by Kenduri Co and its three subsidiary companies for the cash flows due in three months. Briefly discuss why some governments allow companies to undertake multilateral netting, while others do not. **(10 marks)**

(c) When examining different currency options and their risk factors, it was noticed that a long call option had a high gamma value. Explain the possible characteristics of a long call option with a high gamma value. **(3 marks)**

(Total: 25 marks)

76 AWAN CO (DEC 13)

 Online question assistance

Awan Co is expecting to receive $48,000,000 on 1 February 20X4, which will be invested until it is required for a large project on 1 June 20X4. Due to uncertainty in the markets, the company is of the opinion that it is likely that interest rates will fluctuate significantly over the coming months, although it is difficult to predict whether they will increase or decrease.

Awan Co's treasury team want to hedge the company against adverse movements in interest rates using one of the following derivative products:

- Forward rate agreements (FRAs);

- Interest rate futures; or

- Options on interest rate futures.

Awan Co can invest funds at the relevant inter-bank rate less 20 basis points. The current inter-bank rate is 4.09%. However, Awan Co is of the opinion that interest rates could increase or decrease by as much as 0.9% over the coming months.

The following information and quotes are provided from an appropriate exchange on $ futures and options. Margin requirements can be ignored.

Three-month $ futures, $2,000,000 contract size

Prices are quoted in basis points at 100 – annual % yield

December 20X3:	94.80
March 20X4:	94.76
June 20X4:	94.69

Options on three-month $ futures, $2,000,000 contract size, option premiums are in annual %

Calls			Strike	Puts		
December	March	June		December	March	June
0.342	0.432	0.523	94.50	0.090	0.119	0.271
0.097	0.121	0.289	95.00	0.312	0.417	0.520

Voblaka Bank has offered the following FRA rates to Awan Co:

1–7: 4.37%

3–4: 4.78%

3–7: 4.82%

4–7: 4.87%

It can be assumed that settlement for the futures and options contracts is at the end of the month and that basis diminishes to zero at contract maturity at a constant rate, based on monthly time intervals. Assume that it is 1 November 20X3 now and that there is no basis risk.

Required:

(a) **Based on the three hedging choices Awan Co is considering, recommend a hedging strategy for the $48,000,000 investment, if interest rates increase or decrease by 0.9%. Support your answer with appropriate calculations and discussion.**

(19 marks)

(b) A member of Awan Co's treasury team has suggested that if option contracts are purchased to hedge against the interest rate movements, then the number of contracts purchased should be determined by a hedge ratio based on the delta value of the option.

Required:

Discuss how the delta value of an option could be used in determining the number of contracts purchased.
(6 marks)

(Total: 25 marks)

77 KESHI CO (DEC 14)

Keshi Co is a large multinational company with a number of international subsidiary companies. A centralised treasury department manages Keshi Co and its subsidiaries' borrowing requirements, cash surplus investment and financial risk management. Financial risk is normally managed using conventional derivative products such as forwards, futures, options and swaps.

Assume it is 1 December 20X4 today and Keshi Co is expecting to borrow $18,000,000 on 1 February 20X5 for a period of seven months. It can either borrow the funds at a variable rate of LIBOR plus 40 basis points or a fixed rate of 5.5%. LIBOR is currently 3.8% but Keshi Co feels that this could increase or decrease by 0.5% over the coming months due to increasing uncertainty in the markets.

The treasury department is considering whether or not to hedge the $18,000,000, using either exchange-traded March options or over-the-counter swaps offered by Rozu Bank.

The following information and quotes for $ March options are provided from an appropriate exchange. The options are based on three-month $ futures, $1,000,000 contract size and option premiums are in annual %.

March calls	Strike price	March puts
0.882	95.50	0.662
0.648	96.00	0.902

Option prices are quoted in basis points at 100 minus the annual % yield and settlement of the options contracts is at the end of March 20X5. The current basis on the March futures price is 44 points; and it is expected to be 33 points on 1 January 20X5, 22 points on 1 February 20X5 and 11 points on 1 March 20X5.

Rozu Bank has offered Keshi Co a swap on a counterparty variable rate of LIBOR plus 30 basis points or a fixed rate of 4.6%, where Keshi Co receives 70% of any benefits accruing from undertaking the swap, prior to any bank charges. Rozu Bank will charge Keshi Co 10 basis points for the swap.

Keshi Co's chief executive officer believes that a centralised treasury department is necessary in order to increase shareholder value, but Keshi Co's new chief financial officer (CFO) thinks that having decentralised treasury departments operating across the subsidiary companies could be more beneficial. The CFO thinks that this is particularly relevant to the situation which Suisen Co, a company owned by Keshi Co, is facing.

Suisen Co-operates in a country where most companies conduct business activities based on Islamic finance principles. It produces confectionery products including chocolates. It wants to use Salam contracts instead of commodity futures contracts to hedge its exposure to price fluctuations of cocoa. Salam contracts involve a commodity which is sold based on currently agreed prices, quantity and quality. Full payment is received by the seller immediately, for an agreed delivery to be made in the future.

Required:

(a) Based on the two hedging choices Keshi Co is considering, recommend a hedging strategy for the $18,000,000 borrowing. Support your answer with appropriate calculations and discussion. **(15 marks)**

(b) Discuss how a centralised treasury department may increase value for Keshi Co and the possible reasons for decentralising the treasury department. **(6 marks)**

(c) Discuss the key differences between a Salam contract, under Islamic finance principles, and futures contracts. **(4 marks)**

(Total: 25 marks)

78 DAIKON CO (JUN 15)

For a number of years Daikon Co has been using forward rate agreements to manage its exposure to interest rate fluctuations. Recently its chief executive officer (CEO) attended a talk on using exchange-traded derivative products to manage risks. She wants to find out by how much the extra cost of the borrowing detailed below can be reduced, when using interest rate futures, options on interest rate futures, and a collar on the options, to manage the interest rate risk. She asks that detailed calculations for each of the three derivative products be provided and a reasoned recommendation to be made.

Daikon Co is expecting to borrow $34,000,000 in five months' time. It expects to make a full repayment of the borrowed amount in 11 months' time. Assume it is 1 June 20X5 today. Daikon Co can borrow funds at LIBOR plus 70 basis points. LIBOR is currently 3.6%, but Daikon Co expects that interest rates may increase by as much as 80 basis points in five months' time.

The following information and quotes from an appropriate exchange are provided on LIBOR-based $ futures and options.

Three-month $ December futures are currently quoted at 95.84. The contract size is $1,000,000, the tick size is 0.01% and the tick value is $25.

Options on three-month $ futures, $1,000,000 contract, tick size 0.01% and tick value $25. Option premiums are in annual %.

December calls	Strike price	December puts
0.541	95.50	0.304
0.223	96.00	0.508

Initial assumptions

It can be assumed that settlement for both the futures and options contracts is at the end of the month; that basis diminishes to zero at a constant rate until the contract matures and time intervals can be counted in months; that margin requirements may be ignored; and that if the options are in-the-money, they will exercised at the end of the hedge instead of being sold.

Further issues

In the talk, the CEO was informed of the following issues:

(i) Futures contracts will be marked-to-market daily. The CEO wondered what the impact of this would be if 50 futures contracts were bought at 95.84 on 1 June and 30 futures contracts were sold at 95.61 on 3 June, based on the $ December futures contract given above. The closing settlement prices are given below for four days:

Date	Settlement price
1 June	95.84
2 June	95.76
3 June	95.66
4 June	95.74

(ii) Daikon Co will need to deposit funds into a margin account with a broker for each contract they have opened, and this margin will need to be adjusted when the contracts are marked-to-market daily.

(iii) It is unlikely that option contracts will be exercised at the end of the hedge period unless they have reached expiry. Instead, they more likely to be sold and the positions closed.

Required:

(a) Based on the three hedging choices available to Daikon Co and the initial assumptions given above, draft a response to the chief executive officer's (CEO) request made in the first paragraph of the question. **(15 marks)**

(b) Discuss the impact on Daikon Co of each of the three further issues given above. As part of the discussion, include the calculations of the daily impact of the mark-to-market closing prices on the transactions specified by the CEO. **(10 marks)**

(Total: 25 marks)

79 THE ARMSTRONG GROUP (SEP/DEC 15)

The Armstrong Group is a multinational group of companies. Today is 1 September. The treasury manager at Massie Co, one of Armstrong Group's subsidiaries based in Europe, has just received notification from the group's head office that it intends to introduce a system of netting to settle balances owed within the group every six months. Previously inter-group indebtedness was settled between the two companies concerned.

The predicted balances owing to, and owed by, the group companies at the end of February are as follows:

Owed by	Owed to	Local currency million (m)
Armstrong (USA)	Horan (South Africa)	US $12.17
Horan (South Africa)	Massie (Europe)	SA R42.65
Giffen (Denmark)	Armstrong (USA)	D Kr21.29
Massie (Europe)	Armstrong (USA)	US $19.78
Armstrong (USA)	Massie (Europe)	€1.57
Horan (South Africa)	Giffen (Denmark)	D Kr16.35
Giffen (Denmark)	Massie (Europe)	€1.55

The predicted exchange rates, used in the calculations of the balances to be settled, are as follows:

	D Kr	US$	SAR	€
1 D Kr =	1.0000	0.1823	1.9554	0.1341
1 US $ =	5.4855	1.0000	10.7296	0.7358
1 SA R =	0.5114	0.0932	1.0000	0.0686
1 € =	7.4571	1.3591	14.5773	1.0000

Settlement will be made in dollars, the currency of Armstrong Group, the parent company. Settlement will be made in the order that the company owing the largest net amount in dollars will first settle with the company owed the smallest net amount in dollars.

Note: D Kr is Danish Krone, SA R is South African Rand, US $ is United States dollar and € is Euro.

Required:

(a) (i) Calculate the inter-group transfers which are forecast to occur for the next period.   (8 marks)

     (ii) Discuss the problems which may arise with the new arrangement.   (3 marks)

The most significant transaction which Massie Co is due to undertake with a company outside the Armstrong Group in the next six months is that it is due to receive €25 million from Bardsley Co on 30 November. Massie Co's treasury manager intends to invest this money for the six months until 31 May, when it will be used to fund some major capital expenditure. However, the treasury manager is concerned about changes in interest rates. Predictions in the media range from a 0.5% rise in interest rates to a 0.5% fall.

Because of the uncertainty, the treasury manager has decided to protect Massie Co by using derivatives. The treasury manager wishes to take advantage of favourable interest rate movements. Therefore she is considering options on interest rate futures or interest rate collars as possible methods of hedging, but not interest rate futures. Massie Co can invest at LIBOR minus 40 basis points and LIBOR is currently 3.6%.

The treasury manager has obtained the following information on Euro futures and options. She is ignoring margin requirements.

Three-month Euro futures, €1,000,000 contract, tick size 0.01% and tick value €25.

September	95.94
December	95.76
March	95.44

Options on three-month Euro futures, €1,000,000 contract, tick size 0.01% and tick value €25. Option premiums are in annual %.

Calls			Strike	Puts		
September	December	March		September	December	March
0.113	0.182	0.245	96.50	0.002	0.123	0.198
0.017	0.032	0.141	97.00	0.139	0.347	0.481

It can be assumed that settlement for the contracts is at the end of the month. It can also be assumed that basis diminishes to zero at contract maturity at a constant rate and that time intervals can be counted in months.

Required:

(b)   Based on the choice of options on futures or collars which Massie Co is considering and assuming the company does not face any basis risk, recommend a hedging strategy for the €25 million receipt. Support your recommendations with appropriate comments and relevant calculations. (14 marks)

(Total: 25 marks)

80   BURYECS CO (MAR/JUN 17)

Buryecs Co is an international transport operator based in the Eurozone which has been invited to take over a rail operating franchise in Wirtonia, where the local currency is the dollar ($). Previously this franchise was run by a local operator in Wirtonia but its performance was unsatisfactory and the government in Wirtonia withdrew the franchise.

Buryecs Co will pay $5,000 million for the rail franchise immediately. The government has stated that Buryecs Co should make an annual income from the franchise of $600 million in each of the next three years. At the end of the three years the government in Wirtonia has offered to buy the franchise back for $7,500 million if no other operator can be found to take over the franchise.

Today's spot exchange rate between the Euro and Wirtonia $ is €0.1430 = $1. The predicted inflation rates are as follows:

Year	1	2	3
Eurozone	6%	4%	3%
Wirtonia	3%	8%	11%

Buryecs Co's finance director (FD) has contacted its bankers with a view to arranging a currency swap, since he believes that this will be the best way to manage financial risks associated with the franchise. The swap would be for the initial fee paid for the franchise, with a swap of principal immediately and in three years' time, both these swaps being at today's spot rate. Buryecs Co's bank would charge an annual fee of 0.5% in € for arranging the swap. Buryecs Co would take 60% of any benefit of the swap before deducting bank fees, but would then have to pay 60% of the bank fees.

Relevant borrowing rates are:

	Buryecs Co	Counterparty
Eurozone	4.0%	5.8%
Wirtonia	Wirtonia bank rate +0.6%	Wirtonia bank rate +0.4%

In order to provide Buryecs Co's board with an alternative hedging method to consider, the FD has obtained the following information about over-the-counter options in Wirtonia $ from the company's bank.

The exercise price quotation is in Wirtonia $ per €1, premium is % of amount hedged, translated at today's spot rate.

Exercise price	Call options	Put options
7.75	2.8%	1.6%
7.25	1.8%	2.7%

Assume a discount rate of 14%.

Required:

(a) Discuss the advantages and drawbacks of using the currency swap to manage financial risks associated with the franchise in Wirtonia. **(6 marks)**

(b) **(i)** Calculate the annual percentage interest saving which Buryecs Co could make from using a currency swap, compared with borrowing directly in Wirtonia, demonstrating how the currency swap will work. **(4 marks)**

(ii) Evaluate, using net present value, the financial acceptability of Buryecs Co operating the rail franchise under the terms suggested by the government of Wirtonia and calculate the gain or loss in € from using the swap arrangement. **(8 marks)**

(c) Calculate the results of hedging the receipt of $7,500 million using the currency options and discuss whether currency options would be a better method of hedging this receipt than a currency swap. **(7 marks)**

(Total: 25 marks)

81 WARDEGUL CO (SEP/DEC 17)

Wardegul Co, a company based in the Eurozone, has expanded very rapidly over recent years by a combination of acquiring subsidiaries in foreign countries and setting up its own operations abroad. Wardegul Co's board has found it increasingly difficult to monitor its activities and Wardegul Co's support functions, including its treasury function, have struggled to cope with a greatly increased workload. Wardegul Co's board has decided to restructure the company on a regional basis, with regional boards and appropriate support functions. Managers in some of the larger countries in which Wardegul Co operates are unhappy with reorganisation on a regional basis, and believe that operations in their countries should be given a large amount of autonomy and be supported by internal functions organised on a national basis.

Assume it is now 1 October 20X7. The central treasury function has just received information about a future transaction by a newly-acquired subsidiary in Euria, where the local currency is the dinar (D). The subsidiary expects to receive D27,000,000 on 31 January 20X8. It wants this money to be invested locally in Euria, most probably for five months until 30 June 20X8.

Wardegul Co's treasury team is aware that economic conditions in Euria are currently uncertain. The central bank base rate in Euria is currently 4.2% and the treasury team believes that it can invest funds in Euria at the central bank base rate less 30 basis points. However, treasury staff have seen predictions that the central bank base rate could increase by up to 1.1% or fall by up to 0.6% between now and 31 January 20X8.

Wardegul Co's treasury staff normally hedge interest rate exposure by using whichever of the following products is most appropriate:

- Forward rate agreements (FRAs)

- Interest rate futures

- Options on interest rate futures

Treasury function guidelines emphasise the importance of mitigating the impact of adverse movements in interest rates. However, they also allow staff to take into consideration upside risks associated with interest rate exposure when deciding which instrument to use.

A local bank in Euria, with which Wardegul Co has not dealt before, has offered the following FRA rates:

4–9:   5.02%

5–10:   5.10%

The treasury team has also obtained the following information about exchange traded Dinar futures and options:

Three-month D futures, D500,000 contract size

Prices are quoted in basis points at 100 – annual % yield:

December 2017: 94.84

March 20X8: 94.78

June 20X8: 94.66

Options on three-month D futures

D500,000 contract size, option premiums are in annual %

	Calls		Strike price	Put		
December	March	June		December	March	June
0.417	0.545	0.678	94.25	0.071	0.094	0.155
0.078	0.098	0.160	95.25	0.393	0.529	0.664

It can be assumed that futures and options contracts are settled at the end of each month. Basis can be assumed to diminish to zero at contract maturity at a constant rate, based on monthly time intervals. It can also be assumed that there is no basis risk and there are no margin requirements.

Required:

(a) Recommend a hedging strategy for the D27,000,000 investment, based on the hedging choices which treasury staff are considering, if interest rates increase by 1.1% or decrease by 0.6%. Support your answer with appropriate calculations and discussion. **(18 marks)**

(b) Discuss the advantages of operating treasury activities through regional treasury functions compared with:

- Each country having a separate treasury function.

- Operating activities through a single global treasury function. **(7 marks)**

(Total: 25 marks)

Section 3

ANSWERS TO PRACTICE QUESTIONS – SECTION A

ROLE OF SENIOR FINANCIAL ADVISER IN THE MULTINATIONAL ORGANISATION

1   VADENER PLC (JUN 06 ADAPTED)

Key answer tips

Requirement (a) is a standard corporate appraisal. To achieve a good answer ensure that you discuss all ratios calculated and conclude by commenting on the firm's resource allocation plans.

Part (b) is easier if you think of issues as you approach part (a), rather than as a separate exercise.

In part (c) the key issue is that translation losses are unrealised unless the division or asset concerned is sold.

Part (d) covers the problem of using options for speculation rather than hedging.

(a) Group performance may be analysed by using financial ratios, growth trends and comparative market data. Alternative definitions exist for some ratios, and other ratios are equally valid.

Operating and profitability ratios:

		20X3	20X4	20X5
Return on capital employed:	$\dfrac{\text{EBIT}}{\text{Capital employed}}$	$\dfrac{410}{1,486} = 27.6\%$	$\dfrac{540}{1,665} = 32.4\%$	$\dfrac{560}{1,876} = 29.9\%$
Asset turnover:	$\dfrac{\text{Sales}}{\text{Capital employed}}$	$\dfrac{1,120}{1,486} = 0.81$	$\dfrac{1,410}{1,665} = 0.85$	$\dfrac{1,490}{1,876} = 0.79$
Profit margin:	$\dfrac{\text{EBIT}}{\text{Sales}}$	$\dfrac{410}{1,210} = 33.9\%$	$\dfrac{540}{1,410} = 38.3\%$	$\dfrac{560}{1,490} = 37.6\%$

Liquidity ratios:

Current ratio:	$\dfrac{\text{Current assets}}{\text{Current liabilities}}$	$\dfrac{728}{565} = 1.29$	$\dfrac{863}{728} = 1.19$	$\dfrac{1{,}015}{799} = 1.27$
Acid test:	$\dfrac{\text{Current assets} - \text{Inventory}}{\text{Current liabilities}}$	$\dfrac{388}{565} = 0.69$	$\dfrac{453}{728} = 0.62$	$\dfrac{525}{799} = 0.66$

Market ratios:

Dividend yield:	$\dfrac{\text{Dividend per share}}{\text{Market price}}$	$\dfrac{48.7}{1{,}220} = 4.0\%$	$\dfrac{56.7}{1{,}417} = 4.0\%$	$\dfrac{61.7}{1{,}542} = 4.0\%$
Earnings per share (pence):	$\dfrac{\text{Earnings after tax}}{\text{Number of shares}}$	$\dfrac{259}{300} = 86.3$	$\dfrac{339}{300} = 113.0$	$\dfrac{346}{300} = 115.3$
PE ratio	$\dfrac{\text{Market price}}{\text{Earnings per share}}$	$\dfrac{1{,}220}{86.3} = 14.1$	$\dfrac{1{,}417}{113} = 12.5$	$\dfrac{1{,}542}{115.3} = 13.4$
Gearing:	$\dfrac{\text{Total borrowing}}{\text{Borrowing} + \text{Equity}}$	$\dfrac{535}{1{,}621} = 33\%$	$\dfrac{580}{1{,}835} = 32\%$	$\dfrac{671}{2{,}077} = 32\%$

It is difficult to reach conclusions about the performance of Vadener without more comparative data from similar companies.

Return on capital at around 30% is dominated by the effect of high profit margins, but the split between divisions is not provided. Asset utilisation is well below 1, which implies relatively inefficient utilisation of assets. Vadener might investigate whether this could be improved.

Liquidity has improved during the last year, and although below some commonly used benchmarks might be satisfactory for the sectors that Vadener is involved with. However, some aspects of working capital require attention. Stock levels have increased from 28% of revenue in 20X3 to 33% in 20X5, and the collection period for debtors has similarly increased from 114 days to 125 days. Creditors have also increased more than proportionately to revenue. Vadener should take action to improve the efficiency of its working capital management.

In contrast operating costs have fallen over the three years from 66% to 62% of revenue, indicating greater efficiency. Gearing appears to be relatively low at around 32%, but comparative data is needed, and interest cover is high at more than eight times in 20X5.

Investors do not appear to be entirely satisfied with group performance. The FT market index has increased by 34% between 20X3 and 20X5, whereas Vadener's share price has only increased by 26%. With an equity beta of 1.1 Vadener's share price would be expected to increase by more than the market index. Vadener's PE ratios are also lower than those of similar companies, suggesting that investors do not value the company's future prospects as highly as those of its competitors.

The required return from Vadener's shares may be estimated using the capital asset pricing model (CAPM).

Required return = 5% + (12% − 5%) 1.1 = 12.7%

An approximation of the actual return from Vadener's shares is the 12% average annual increase in share price plus 4% annual dividend yield, or 16%. The total return is higher than expected for the systematic risk. Given this, Vadener should investigate the reasons why its share price has performed relatively poorly. One possibility is the company's dividend policy.

Dividends have consistently been more than 50% of available after tax earnings, which might not be popular with investors.

Divisional performance

The information on the individual divisions is very sparse. All divisions are profitable, but the return from the pharmaceutical division is relatively low for its systematic risk.

Using CAPM to approximate required returns:

	Required return	Actual return
Construction	5% + (12% – 5%) 0.75 = 10.25%	13%
Leisure	5% + (12% – 5%) 1.1 = 12.7%	16%
Pharmaceuticals	5% + (12% – 5%) 1.40 = 14.8%[1]	14%

[1] It is assumed that the same market parameters are valid for the US based division.

The construction and leisure divisions appear to have greater than expected returns (a positive alpha) and the pharmaceutical division slightly less than expected for the risk of the division. The pharmaceutical division has recently suffered a translation loss due to the weakness of the US dollar, and the potential economic exposure from changes in the value of the dollar should be investigated.

From a financial perspective it would appear that the company should not devote equal resources to the divisions, and should focus its efforts on construction and leisure. However, the future prospects of the sectors are not known, nor the long term strategy of Vadener, which might be to expand international operations in the USA or elsewhere. The strategic use of resources should not be decided on the basis of the limited financial information that is available.

(b) Other information that would be useful includes:

(i) Cash flow forecasts for the group and the individual divisions.

(ii) Full product and market information for each of the divisions.

(iii) Details of recent investments in each of the divisions and the expected impact of such investment on future performance.

(iv) Detailed historic performance data of the divisions over at least three years, and similar data for companies in the relevant sectors.

(v) Competitors and potential growth rates in each of the sectors.

(vi) The economic exposure of the US division

(vii) The future strategic plans of Vadener. Are there any other proposed initiatives?

(viii) How the company's equal resource strategy will be viewed by investors. The company has performed worse than the market in recent years despite having a higher beta than the market.

(c) A translation loss of £10 million is not necessarily a problem for Vadener plc.

Translation exposure, sometimes known as accounting exposure, often does not reflect any real cash flow changes. It is changes in cash flow that, in an efficient market, will impact on the share price and value of a company. For example, a translation loss might in part reflect a lower home currency value of an overseas factory, but the factory will still be the same and will still be producing goods. It is the impact on the home currency cash flows from the continuing operations of the factory that will affect share price.

However, if the market is not efficient, investors might not understand that there are no real cash flow implications from the exposure, and might be worried about the effect of the translation loss on Vadener, and possibly sell their shares. If this is the case Vadener might consider internal hedges to reduce translation exposure. In most cases this would not be recommended, and companies must also be careful that hedges to manage translation exposure do not adversely affect the efficient operations of the business, or be contrary to hedges that are being undertaken to protect against other forms of currency exposure such as transaction exposure.

(d) Income may be increased by writing (selling) options, as the writer of the option receives the option premium.

However, unless the option is hedged, writing options exposes the writer to a theoretically unlimited loss.

Uncovered writing of options is effectively speculating, involves very high risk, and is not normally recommended as a strategy to companies such as Vadener.

ADVANCED INVESTMENT APPRAISAL

2 WURRALL INC (JUN 04 ADAPTED)

Key answer tips

This is an extremely time-pressured question so a logical approach is vital. Lay out a proforma for all four years before you start, and put figures in for all four years as you go along. For example, when looking at sales revenue, it is quite easy to forecast the figures for all four years at the same time by applying the relevant growth forecast to the number in your calculator.

(a) **Appendix to the report: Proforma accounts**

Proforma statements of profit or loss for the years ended March 20X5–8

	$ million			
	20X5	*20X6*	*20X7*	*20X8*
Sales revenue	1,787	1,929	2,064	2,188
Operating costs before depreciation	(1,215)	(1,312)	(1,404)	(1,488)
EBITDA	572	617	660	700
Tax-allowable depreciation	(165)	(179)	(191)	(203)
EBIT	407	438	469	497
Net interest payable	(63)	(65)	(66)	(70)
Profit on ordinary activities before tax	344	373	403	427
Tax on ordinary activities	(103)	(112)	(121)	(128)
Profit after tax	241	261	282	299
Dividends	135	146	158	167

Proforma statements of financial position 20X5–8

	$ million			
	20X5	*20X6*	*20X7*	*20X8*
Non-current assets				
Land and buildings	310	310	350	350
Plant and machinery (net)	1,103	1,191	1,275	1,351
Investments	32	32	32	32
	1,445	1,533	1,657	1,733
Current assets				
Inventory	488	527	564	598
Receivables	615	664	710	753
Cash in hand and short-term deposits	22	24	25	27
	2,570	2,748	2,956	3,111
Equity and liabilities				
Called-up share capital (10 cents par)	240	240	240	240
Reserves	970	1,085	1,209	1,341
	1,210	1,325	1,449	1,581
Non-current liabilities:				
Borrowings[1]	580	580	580	580
Current liabilities				
Short-term loans and overdrafts (balancing fig)	266	287	332	320
Other payables	514	556	595	630
	2,570	2,748	2,956	3,111

[1]Refinanced with a similar type of loan in 20X6

Tutorial note

This is a fairly straightforward forecast of proforma accounts and should be a good opportunity to score marks. However, ensure that presentation is both clear and appropriate.

(b)   **Report to the Board of Directors**

Prepared by A.N. Accountant

Problems with the assumptions

The proforma accounts (see Appendix – part (a)) are based primarily upon the percentage of sales method of forecasting. This provides a simple approach to forecasting, but is based upon assumptions of existing or planned relationships between variables remaining constant, which are highly unlikely. It also does not allow for improvements in efficiency over time.

(i)   Accurate forecasts of sales growth are very difficult. Sensitivity or simulation analysis is recommended to investigate the implications of sales differing from the forecast levels. A constant growth rate of 6% forever after four years is most unlikely.

(ii)   Cash operating costs are unlikely to increase in direct proportion with sales. The variable elements (wages, materials, distribution costs, etc) could all move at a higher or lower rate than sales, while the fixed elements will not change with the value of sales at all in the short run. If the company becomes more efficient then costs as a proportion of sales should reduce.

(iii)   Unless tax-allowable depreciation from new asset purchases exactly offsets the diminishing allowances on older assets, and effect of the increase in assets with sales growth, this relationship is unlikely to be precise. The government might also change the rates of tax-allowable depreciation.

(iv)   Assuming a direct relationship between inventories, receivables, cash and other payables to sales could promote inefficiency. Although a strong correlation between such variables exists, there should be no need to increase inventories, receivables and payables in direct proportion to sales.

(v)   Paying dividends as a constant percentage of earnings could lead to quite volatile dividend pay-outs. Most investors are believed to prefer reasonably constant dividends (allowing for inflation) and might not value a company with volatile dividends as highly as one with relatively stable dividends.

(c)   Free cash flow analysis

Free cash flow will be estimated by EBIT(1–T) plus depreciation less adjustments for changes in working capital and expenditure on non-current assets. (**NB**: Other definitions of free cash flow exist)

	$ million			
	20X5	*20X6*	*20X7*	*20X8*
Change in land and buildings	–	–	40	–
Change in plant and machinery	91	88	84	76
Change in working capital	15	27	–	56
Change in assets	106	115	124	132
EBIT (1–T)	285	307	328	348
Depreciation	165	179	191	203
Change in assets	(106)	(115)	(124)	(132)
Free cash flow	344	371	395	419

The present value of free cash flow for the company after 20X8 may be estimated by

$$\frac{FCF20X8(1+g)}{WACC-g} \text{ or } \frac{419(1.06)}{0.11-0.06} = 8,883$$

The estimated value of the company at the end of 20X8 is $8,883 million. From this must be deducted the value of any loans in order to find the value accruing to shareholders. From the proforma accounts, loans are expected to total $900 million, leaving a net value of $7,983 million. If the number of issued shares has not changed, the estimated market value per share is $\frac{7,983}{2,400}$ = 333 cents per share, an increase of 58% on the current share price.

Based upon this data, the managing director's claim that the share price will double in four years is not likely to occur. However, the impact of the performance of the economy, and unforeseen significant changes affecting Wurrall Inc mean that such estimates are subject to a considerable margin of error.

(d)   Ratio analysis

	20X5	*20X6*	*20X7*	*20X8*
Gearing (%)	41.1	39.6	38.6	36.3
Current ratio	1.44	1.44	1.40	1.45
Quick ratio	0.82	0.82	0.79	0.82
Return on capital employed[1] (%)	22.7	23.0	23.1	23.0
Asset turnover	1.00	1.01	1.02	1.01
EBIT/Sales (%)	22.8	22.7	22.7	22.7
Debtor collection period (days)	126	126	126	126

[1]EBIT/(shareholders equity plus long term debt). Other definitions are possible

Tutorial note

You have a wide choice of ratios in this question. Do not produce a long list of ratios illustrating similar trends. Choose carefully and produce a few key ratios that provide a valuable insight into the business. Equally, there are ratios other than those above that could be used alternatively to provide this insight.

It is difficult to comment upon ratios without comparative data for companies in the same industry. The current gearing level, at 42.3%, breaches the covenant limit of 40%, and it is expected to continue to do so in 20X5. Whether or not this breaches the one-year covenant is not clear, but would need to be investigated by the company and action taken to reduce gearing if the covenant was to be breached for too long a period. The debtor collection period appears high at 126 days. It is unlikely that credit would be given for such a long period, and the company might consider improving its credit control procedures to reduce the collection period. If this is successful it could also reduce the overdraft and help reduce the gearing level.

Another ratio that would need investigating is the asset turnover. At around one this is relatively low. Unless the industry is very capital intensive, management should consider if assets could be utilised more efficiently to improve this ratio, and with it the return on capital employed.

As previously mentioned, managers might also review the company's dividend policy. Paying a constant level of earnings could lead to volatile dividend payments which might not be popular with investors, including financial institutions, that rely upon dividends for part of their annual cash flow.

Wurrall proposes to finance any new capital needs with increases in the overdraft. Overdraft finance is not normally considered to be appropriate for long term financing, and the company should consider longer term borrowing or equity issues for its long-term financing requirements.

3   DARON (DEC 95 ADAPTED)

Key answer tips

The question clearly states that 12 of the marks for part (a) are for the discussion – make sure you pay sufficient attention to the written aspects as opposed to getting bogged down in the computational aspects of the problem.

(a) **Report for the managers of Daron**

Offer to purchase the company

Any recommendation regarding the sale of the company to a competitor for $20 million should be made in the best interests of the shareholders. An offer of $20 million is an 8.7% premium over the current share price (which is quite low).

Estimates of the present values of future cash flows from internal data suggest that no matter which party wins the election, the company's value will be in excess of $20 million; $21 million if party B wins, and $30.3 million if party A wins.

However, these estimates are by no means precise. Inaccuracy could exist due to:

(i)   Incorrect inflation estimates.

(ii)   Errors in sales volume and cost projections.

(iii)   Inaccurate discount rate estimates.

(iv)   The assumption of a constant 30% corporate tax rate.

Sensitivity analysis is recommended to analyse the significance of changes in key variables. The cash flow estimates do not incorporate any value for options relating to opportunities that might exist between now and 20Y3 if operations continue. Nor is there data on the expected realisable value of the company in 20Y3 (that is the last year for which cash flow data is available). Even if further investment was not undertaken at that time, the present value of the realisable value of land, buildings and cash flow released from working capital needs to be considered. This would increase the above present-value estimates. On financial grounds the informal offer of $20 million is not high enough to be recommended. Additionally, selling to a competitor might have other implications such as redundancies, closure of part of the existing operations and a detrimental impact on the local community.

Investing in the purchase of a hotel

Appendix 2 shows the financial estimates of the hotel purchase. An APV of $0.56 million suggests that the hotel investment is financially viable. However, this estimate is also subject to many of the possible inaccuracies noted above. The base case NPV is heavily influenced by the realisable value of $10 million in 20X8. Future hotel values could vary substantially from this estimate.

Investment in the hotel industry is a strategic departure from the company's core competence. If the objective is primarily to diversify activities to reduce risk, this may not be in the shareholders' best interest as they can easily achieve diversification of their investment portfolios, through unit trusts or similar investments. As the company is in a declining industry, in the long term diversification may be essential for survival. A medium- to long-term strategic plan should be formulated examining alternative strategies, and alternative investments that may offer better financial returns than the hotel investment, and/or be closer to the company's existing core competence.

Appendix 1

Valuation of business cash flows

Present value estimates:

Political party A wins the election

				$ million		
	20X4	*20X5*	*20X6*	*20X7*	*20X8*	*20X9 – Y3*
Sales	28.0	29.0	26.0	22.0	19.0	19.0
Variable costs	17.0	18.0	16.0	14.0	12.0	12.0
Fixed costs	3.0	3.0	3.0	3.0	3.0	3.0
Depreciation	4.0	3.0	3.0	2.0	1.0	–
	24.0	24.0	22.0	19.0	16.0	15.0
Taxable profit	4.0	5.0	4.0	3.0	3.0	4.0
Taxation (30%)	1.2	1.5	1.2	0.9	0.9	1.2
	2.8	3.5	2.8	2.1	2.1	2.8
Add back depreciation	4.0	3.0	3.0	2.0	1.0	–
Working capital	–	1.0	2.0	3.0	3.0	–
Net cash flow	6.8	7.5	7.8	7.1	6.1	2.8
Discount factors at 13%	0.885	0.783	0.693	0.613	0.543	1.910
Present values	6.0	5.9	5.4	4.4	3.3	5.3

Expected total present value, up to year 20Y3 = $30.3 million.

Tutorial note

The discount factor for years 20X9–Y3, which are Years 6–10 (five years) is calculated by taking the cumulative discount factor at 13% for Years 1–5. This (from tables) is 3.517. However, applying this discount factor to the annual cash flows would give a value as at the end of Year 5. To obtain a present value (Year 0 value) we must discount further by the Year 5 factor at 13%, which is 0.543, giving 3.517 × 0.543 = 1.910.

Political party B wins the election

	$ million					
	20X4	*20X5*	*20X6*	*20X7*	*20X8*	*20X9–Y3*
Sales	30.0	26.0	24.0	20.0	16.0	16.0
Variable costs	18.0	16.0	15.0	12.0	11.0	11.0
Fixed costs	3.0	3.0	4.0	4.0	4.0	4.0
Depreciation	4.0	3.0	3.0	2.0	1.0	–
	25.0	22.0	22.0	18.0	16.0	15.0
Taxable profit	5.0	4.0	2.0	2.0	0.0	1.0
Taxation (30%)	1.5	1.2	0.6	0.6	–	0.3
	3.5	2.8	1.4	1.4	0.0	0.7
Add back depreciation	4.0	3.0	3.0	2.0	1.0	–
Working capital	(1.0)	2.0	2.0	3.0	3.0	–
Net cash flow	6.5	7.8	6.4	6.4	4.0	0.7
Discount factors at 18%	0.847	0.718	0.609	0.516	0.437	1.366
Present values	5.5	5.6	3.9	3.3	1.7	1.0

Expected total present value, up to year 20Y3 = $21 million.

Tutorial note

The discount factor for years 20X9–Y3, is calculated the same way as before, giving 3.127 × 0.437 = 1.366.

Notes:

1   The use of expected values is not recommended as it does not reflect a situation that is likely to occur in reality.

2   **Discount rate, political party A wins**

	$m
Market value of equity 20m shares at 92c =	18.4
Debt	14.0
	32.4

The risk-free rate *including inflation*, given expected inflation of 5% each year, is:

(1.04) (1.05) = 1.092 or 9.2%

The market return including inflation at 5% per annum is:

(1.10) (1.05) = 1.155 or 15.5%

Using CAPM, the cost of equity $K_e = E(r_i) = R_f + \beta_i(E(r_m) - R_f)$

$K_e = 9.2\% + 1.25\ (15.5\% - 9.2\%) = 17.075\%$

$$\text{WACC} = 17.075\% \times \frac{18.4}{32.4} + 10\%\ (1 - 0.3)\ \frac{14}{32.4}$$

$= 12.72\%$ or approximately 13%.

3 **Discount rate, political party B wins**

The risk-free rate including inflation, given expected inflation of 10% each year, is:

$(1.04)\ (1.10) = 1.144$ or 14.4%

The market return including inflation at 10% per annum is:

$(1.10)\ (1.10) = 1.21$ or 21%

Using CAPM, the cost of equity $K_e = 14.4\% + 1.25\ (21\% - 14.4\%) = 22.65\%$

$$\text{WACC} = 22.65\% \times \frac{18.4}{32.4} + 15.5\%\ (1 - 0.3)\ \frac{14}{32.4} = 17.6\%\ \text{or approximately 18\%.}$$

Note: This is only a rough estimate of the cost of capital, as the share price is likely to fall with higher inflation, leading to higher gearing and a change in risk for the providers of the debt finance.

Both K_e and K_d could alter because of these factors.

The use of the current share price in both WACC estimates is problematic. In an efficient market this price will reflect the present uncertainty about the forthcoming election. Once this uncertainty is resolved the share price is likely to change, leading to new market weighted gearing levels. Fortunately the investment decision is not highly sensitive to marginal changes in the discount rate.

Appendix 2

Base case NPV

For APV the base case NPV is required, which is estimated from the ungeared cost of equity.

Assuming corporate debt is risk free:

$$\beta_a = \left[\frac{V_e}{(V_e + V_d(1-T))} \beta_e \right] = 1.25 \times \frac{18.4}{18.4 + 14(1 - 0.3)} = 0.82$$

Ke ungeared $= 9.2\% + (15.5\% - 9.2\%)\ 0.82 = 14.4\%$ or approximately 14%.

A discount rate of 14% has therefore been used to calculate the base case NPV.

Cash flows, possible hotel purchase

	$ million				
	20X4	*20X5*	*20X6*	*20X7*	*20X8*
Revenue	9.0	10.0	11.0	12.0	13.0
Variable costs	6.0	6.0	7.0	7.0	8.0
Fixed costs	2.0	2.0	2.0	2.0	2.0
	8.0	8.0	9.0	9.0	10.0
Taxable profit	1.0	2.0	2.0	3.0	3.0
Taxation (30%)	0.3	0.6	0.6	0.9	0.9
	0.7	1.4	1.4	2.1	2.1
Realisable value					10.0
Working capital	(1.0)	–	–	(1.0)	–
Net cash flows	(0.3)	1.4	1.4	1.1	12.1
Discount factors at 14%	0.877	0.769	0.675	0.592	0.519
Present values	(0.3)	1.1	0.9	0.7	6.3

Base case NPV = ($9.0)m + $8.7m = $(0.3)m

Financing side effects for the five-year period:

Including issue costs, the gross sum of finance to be raised will be $\dfrac{9m}{0.98}$ = $9,184,000.

Issue costs are therefore $184,000.

Interest is at 10%, so this will give **annual tax savings** of:

$9.18m × 10% × 30% = $275,520 per year.

Discounted at 10%, this gives a present value of 3.791 × $275,520 = $1,044,000

Note: This assumes that an extra $9.184 million debt capacity is created by the hotel investment. If less debt capacity is created, the present value of the tax shield attributable to the investment will be reduced.

The 10% coupon is assumed to reflect correctly the risk of the convertible, and is used as the discount rate for the tax savings.

The estimated APV is the base case NPV plus the financing side effects.

	$m
Base case NPV	(0.30)
Issue costs	(0.18)
PV of tax saving	1.04
APV	0.56

(b) Daron's current gearing, measured by the *book value* of medium and long term loans to the *book value* of equity is: 14/22 or 63.6%

No information is provided about short-term loans which would increase this gearing figure further. A $9 million convertible debenture issue would initially increase gearing to 23/22 = 104.5%.

Such a high level of gearing involves 'high' financial risk, especially for a company in a declining industry. The coupon rate of 10%, or $918,400 interest per year would have to be paid for five years or more. Convertible debentures normally carry lower coupon rates than straight debt. Daron can borrow long term from its bank at 10% per year, and the 10% coupon on the convertible appears to be expensive. However, this could be explained by the market seeking a relatively high return because of the size of the loan.

If conversion takes place the gearing level will fall, but this is will not occur for at least five years. At the $100 issue price the effective conversion price is $100/60 or 167 centos per share

This represents an average share price increase of 12.7% per year over five years, which is possible if market prices in general increase, but is by no means guaranteed.

The existence of the call and put options has potentially significant implications for Daron plc. The call option allows the company to limit the potential gains made by debenture holders. If the share price reaches 200 centos between 1 January 20X9 and 31 December 20Y1 the company can force the debenture holders to convert, giving maximum capital gains on conversion of 33 centos per share (relative to the $100 issue price). This is a small gain and may not be popular with investors. If the share price falls below 100 centos between the same dates, the debenture holders can ask the company to redeem the debentures at par, forcing the company to find $9 million for repayment of the debentures. If the market price of the shares has only moved by a maximum of eight centos over five years, the company might experience difficulty refinancing the $9 million, leading to severe problems in finding the cash for redemption.

(c) The regulation of takeovers usually includes the following factors:

- At the most important time in the company's life – when it is subject to a takeover bid – its directors should act in the best interest of their shareholders, and should disregard their personal interests.

- All shareholders must be treated equally

- Shareholders must be given all the relevant information to make an informed judgement.

- The board of the target company must not take action without the approval of shareholders, which could result in the offer being defeated.

- All information supplied to shareholders must be prepared to the highest standards of care and accuracy.

- The assumptions on which profit forecasts are based and the accounting polices used should be examined and reported on by accountants.

- An independent valuer should support valuations of assets

4   SLEEPON HOTELS INC (DEC 05 ADAPTED) *Walk in the footsteps of a top tutor*

Walkthrough question – key answer tips

This is an excellent investment appraisal question, which covers all the examiner's favourite tricks in this syllabus area. It also contains a fully written part (b), which comprises little more than bookwork, so should yield plenty of easy marks.

A clear answer layout and systematic approach that gets the easier numerical marks first will help tremendously.

Also, it is important to note that the question contains 10 marks for discussion points in part (a), specifically for "...a discussion of what other information would be useful..." and for stating assumptions (stated in the requirement). As you go through the numbers, keep thinking about these written elements at the same time, and jot ideas down as you go along, to save you having to rush things at the end.

Calculations: The main tricks to look out for in the calculations are:

- You need to calculate a cost of capital that reflects the risks and finance of the project – the existing WACC of the company is no use. You need to de-gear and re-gear the beta of Thrillall.

- You need to make assumptions about the timing of asset purchases, as this will affect the timing of tax allowable depreciation.

- Only $250 million of the investment will attract tax allowable depreciation – this is assumed to be split equally between the two payments.

- Be careful identifying relevant cash flows, particularly with respect to interest, overheads and the 'savings' in advertising costs.

- Incorporating inflation – most (but not all!) figures are in current terms. The question is not clear regarding the working capital as strictly speaking the outflow at t=1 is not a cost. The examiner's answer inflates the working capital requirement and hence has annual increments.

- Ensure all working capital is released at the end of the project.

- Use a worst-case estimate for the realisable value of assets.

If you set up your pro forma answer neatly and slot in numbers as you calculate them, it doesn't really matter if you don't complete the full question in the time available, you will still score plenty of method marks for the work you have done.

Make sure you leave time for the easier part (b), and structure your answer to part (a) professionally to ensure you pick up the 4 professional skills marks.

(a)   Report on the proposed theme park investment

The decision to invest in a major project must be evaluated using both financial and non-financial information. From a financial perspective the estimated net present value of the investment will provide an indicator of whether or not the project will create wealth. Non-financial considerations will include the strategic fit of the investment with the company and its future plans.

Financial evaluation

Cash flow forecasts ($ million)

Year	0	1	2	3	4	5	6
Cash receipts:							
Adult admission			41.25	42.49	43.76	45.07	
Child admission			34.37	35.40	36.47	37.56	
Food (incremental cash flow)			13.75	14.16	14.59	15.02	
Gifts (incremental cash flow)			11.46	11.80	12.16	12.52	
Total receipts			100.83	103.85	106.98	110.17	
Expenses:							
Labour			42.44	43.70	45.02	46.37	
Maintenance			15.00	19.00	23.00	27.00	
Insurance			2.12	2.19	2.25	2.32	
Tax allowable depreciation			62.50	46.88	35.16	26.37	
Total expenses			122.06	111.77	105.43	102.06	
Taxable			(21.23)	(7.92)	1.55	8.11	
Taxation (30%)			6.37	2.38	(0.47)	(2.43)	
			(14.86)	(5.54)	1.08	5.68	
Add back tax allowable depreciation			62.50	46.88	35.16	26.37	
Initial cost	(200)	(200)					
Realisable value						250.00	
Working capital		(51.5)	(1.55)	(1.59)	(1.64)	(1.69)	57.97
Net cash flow	(200)	(251.50)	46.09	39.75	34.60	280.36	57.97
Discount factors (11%)		0.901	0.812	0.731	0.659	0.593	0.535
Present values	(200)	(226.60)	37.43	29.06	22.80	166.25	31.01

The estimated net present value is ($140.05 million).

Even if the higher realisable value estimate is used, the expected net present value is still significantly negative.

Notes:

(i) *Receipts Year 2:*

Adult admission (6,000) (360) (18) $(1.03)^2$ = 41.25 million

Child admission (9,000) (360) (10) $(1.03)^2$ = 34.37 million

Food (15,000) (360) (8) (0.3) $(1.03)^2$ = 13.75 million

Gifts (15,000) (360) (5) (0.4) $(1.03)^2$ = 11.46 million

(ii) *Tax allowable depreciation:*

It is assumed that allowances are available with a one-year lag.

Year	Written down value	Tax allowable depreciation (25%)	Year available
0 + 1	250	62.50	2
2	187.50	46.88	3
3	140.62	35.16	4
4	105.47	26.37	5

No balancing allowances or charges have been estimated as the Year 5 realisable value of non-current assets has been estimated on an after-tax basis.

As the hotel business is successful, it is assumed that allowances may be used as soon as they are available against other taxable cash flows of Sleepon.

(iii) Interest is not a relevant cash flow. All financing costs are included in the discount rate.

(iv) The market research is a sunk cost.

(v) Apportioned overhead is not a relevant cash flow.

(vi) Although the company will save money by advertising in its existing hotels, this is not a change in cash flow as a result of the project and is not included in cash flows. (In effect the benefit from the savings is present as there is no cash outflow for advertising.)

(vii) Discount rate

The current weighted average cost of capital should not be used. The discount rate should reflect the risk of the investment being undertaken; theme parks are likely to have very different risks to hotels. The cost of capital will be estimated using the risk (beta) of Thrillall, as Thrillall operates in the theme park sector.

The market weighted capital gearing of Thrillall is:

Equity 400 × 3.86   = $1,544 m (78.3%)

Debt 460 × 0.93   = $428 m (21.7%)

As the gearing of Thrillall is much less than that of Sleepon, the beta used to estimate the relevant cost of equity will need to be adjusted to reflect this difference in gearing.

Assuming corporate debt is virtually risk free:

Ungearing Thrillall's equity beta:

$$\beta_a = \left[\frac{V_e}{(V_e + V_d(1-T))}\beta_e\right] = 1.45 \times \frac{1,544}{1,544 + 428(1-0.3)} = 1.214$$

Regearing to take into account the gearing of Sleepon:

$$\beta_e = \beta_a \times \frac{V_e + V_d(1-T)}{V_e} = 1.214 \times \frac{61.4 + 38.6(1-0.3)}{61.4} = 1.748$$

The cost of equity may be estimated using the capital asset pricing model.

$$E(r_i) = R_f + \beta_i(E(r_m) - R_f)$$

Ke = 3.5% + 1.748 (10% – 3.5%) = 14.86%

Kd is 7.5%, the cost of the new debt used for the project.

The weighted average cost of capital relevant to the new investment is estimated to be:

14.86% (0.614) + 7.5% (1 – 0.3) (0.386) = 11.15%

11% will be used as the discount rate for the investment.

Other relevant information

The financial projections used in the estimated net present value are the subject of considerable inaccuracy. It would be useful to know:

(i)   The accuracy of estimates of attendance levels and spending in the theme park.

(ii)   The accuracy of price and cost changes.

(iii)   Whether or not tax rates are subject to change.

(iv)   The accuracy of the estimate of realisable value in Year 4.

(v)   The accuracy of the discount rate estimate. The activities of Thrillall are not likely to be of exactly the same risk as the theme park project.

For a major investment it is unwise to rely on a single estimate of expected net present value. Sensitivity analysis or simulation analysis should be used in order to ascertain the impact on the expected NPV of changes in attendance and other key cash flows. It would be better to undertake simulation analysis, based upon different possible attendance levels, costs, risk, tax rates, etc, in order to estimate a range of possible net present values, rather than use a single point value.

A crucial question is what happens to cash flows beyond the company's four-year planning horizon. The Year 5 realisable values are asset values, not the value of the theme park as a going concern. The value as a going concern could be very different from the asset values, and have a major influence on the investment decision.

Will the theme park investment lead to future opportunities/investments (real options), for example in other theme parks or leisure activities? If so, the value of such options should be estimated, and should form part of the investment decision.

Strategic and other issues

The strategic importance of the venture to Sleepon must also be investigated, as this may heavily influence the final decision. Sleepon currently runs a successful hotel chain. It might be better to keep to its core competence in hotels rather than diversify into another sector. If new investments are sought, are there better opportunities within the hotel sector?

Any final decision must encompass all relevant non-financial factors of which little detail has been provided. Sleepon must be satisfied that it can recruit an appropriately skilled labour force for the theme park, and should thoroughly investigate the competition in the theme park sector, and the likely reaction of competitors if it enters this new market.

(b)   Briefing notes on capital structure strategy

From a corporate perspective there are two vital questions:

Can the value of a company, and hence shareholder wealth, be increased by varying the capital structure?

What effect will capital structure have on risk?

If value can be created by a sensible choice of capital structure, then companies should try to achieve an optimal, or almost optimal, capital mix, as long as this mix does not have detrimental effects on other aspects of the company's activities.

Evidence on the importance of capital structure to a company's value is not conclusive. There is general agreement that, as long as a company is in a tax-paying position, the use of debt can reduce the overall cost of capital due to the interest on debt being a tax-allowable expense in almost all countries. This was suggested by two Nobel prize-winning economists, Miller and Modigliani. However, high levels of debt also bring problems, and companies with very high gearing are susceptible to various forms of risk, sometimes known as the costs of financial distress. This might include the loss of cash flows because customers and suppliers are worried about the financial stability and viability of the company and move business elsewhere or impose less-favourable trading terms, or even extra costs that would exist (payments to receivers, etc) if the company was to go out of business.

A common perception about capital structure is that as capital gearing is increased, the weighted average cost of capital falls at first. However, beyond a certain level of gearing the risk to both providers of debt and equity finance increases, and the return demanded by them to compensate for this risk also increases, leading to an increase in the weighted average cost of capital. There is a trade-off between the value created by additional tax relief on debt and the costs of financial distress. Overall, there is therefore an optimal capital structure, which will vary between companies and will depend upon factors such as the nature of the company's activities, realisable value of assets, business risk, etc. According to the theory, companies with many tangible assets should have relatively high gearing, companies with high growth, or that are heavily dependent on R & D or advertising would have relatively low gearing.

The impact of personal taxation on the capital structure decision is less clear, although investors are undoubtedly interested in after-tax returns. If personal tax treatment differs on different types of capital, then investors may have a preference for the most tax-efficient type of capital.

Not all companies behave as if there is an optimal capital structure, and on average, in countries such as the UK and USA, the average capital gearing is lower than might be expected if companies were trying to achieve an optimal structure. It must, however, be remembered that moving from one capital structure to another cannot take place overnight. The cost of debt, via interest rates, and the cost of equity, can change quite quickly. It is no surprise that companies do not appear to be at an optimal level.

Where no optimal level appears to be sought by a company, there are several suggested strategies with respect to capital structure. Among the most popular is the pecking order theory, which is based upon information asymmetry, the fact that managers have better information about their company than the company's shareholders. This leads to a company preferring internal finance to external finance, and only using external finance in order to undertake wealth-creating (positive NPV) investments. Companies use the safest sources of finance first.

1   Internal funds (including selling marketable securities)

2   Debt

3   Equity

The amount of external finance used depends upon the amount of investment compared with the amount of internal funds, and the resultant capital structure reflects the relative balance of investment and available internal funds.

Another view is that capital structure is strongly influenced by managerial behaviour. There are potential conflicts of objectives between owners and managers (agency problems). Capital structure will be influenced by senior managers' personal objectives, attitudes to risk, compensation schemes and availability of alternative employment. A risk-averse manager seeking security may use relatively little debt. Free cash flow (cash flow available after replacement investment) is sometimes perceived to be used by managers for unwise acquisitions/investments that satisfy their personal objectives, rather than returning it to shareholders. Many such managerial/agency aspects may influence capital structure, and this does not give clear guidance as to capital structure strategy.

No matter what the conclusion about the impact of capital structure on cash flows, it is likely that some financing packages may be more highly regarded by investors than others. For example, securities designed to meet the needs of certain types of investor (zero coupon bonds, etc), securities that are more liquid, securities with lower transactions costs, and securities that reduce conflict between parties concerned with the company, especially shareholders, managers and the providers of debt.

Conclusion

It is likely that the choice of capital structure can directly affect cash flows and shareholder wealth, but too high a level of gearing will increase risk. The impact on cash flows and corporate value of the capital structure decision is far less than the impact of capital investment decisions.

5 BLIPTON INTERNATIONAL (DEC 08 ADAPTED)

Key answer tips

This is a good example of an advanced investment appraisal question. A neat and systematic layout for the NPV part of the question is critical to ensure you pick up all the marks you deserve.

Note that there are plenty of easy marks to be gained even if you struggle to understand all the numbers: part (c) is independent of the numbers, and there are 4 marks available for presenting a professional report.

Management Report: **Blipton International Entertainment Group**

400 bed Olympic Hotel, London

Completion: 31 December 20X9

(a)   **Projection of $value cash flows for both the project investment and the project return.**

In projecting the cash flow for this project we have created a forecast of the capital requirement, the six year operating cash flow and the residual value of the property net of repairs and renewals at the end of the project. On the basis of the specified occupancy rates and a target nightly rental of £60 we have projected the revenues for the hotel and the expected costs. These are converted to nominal cash flows at the UK rate of inflation. Tax is calculated both in terms of the offset available against the construction costs but also at 30% of the operating surplus from the project.

Finally, using purchasing power parity, future spot rates are estimated.

We have separated the calculation of the present value of the investment phase from that of the return phase.

Investment phase cash flows:

Assuming that the 'investment phase' comprises just the initial capital investment, the only investment phase cash flow is an amount of £6.2 million in one year's time (on 31 December 20X9).

i.e. £6.2 million × 1.5260 (see exchange rate workings below) = $9.461 million.

Tutorial note

This answer assumes that the investment phase comprises only the upfront capital investment. Alternatively, it could be argued that the benefit of the tax allowable depreciation will be recovered irrespective of the success of the operating phase of the project, so the tax relief should be incorporated as part of the investment phase.

Either approach would have been marked as correct.

Return phase cash flows:

£000	T₀	T₁	T₂	T₃	T₄	T₅	T₆
Revenue **(W1)**			3,681	4,717	8,702	5,947	6,095
Variable costs			(1,841)	(2,359)	(4,351)	(2,974)	(3,048)
Fixed costs			(1,786)	(1,831)	(1,876)	(1,923)	(1,971)
TAD		(3,100)	(1,033)	(1,033)	(1,033)		
		———	———	———	———	———	———
Taxable profit		(3,100)	(979)	(506)	1,442	1,050	1,076
Tax (30%)		930	294	152	(433)	(315)	(323)
Add back TAD		3,100	1,033	1,033	1,033		
Disposal proceeds **(W2)**							8,915
		———	———	———	———	———	———
Net cash flow in £000		930	348	679	2,042	735	9,668
X rate (×1.048/1.025 throughout)	1.4925	1.5260	1.5602	1.5952	1.6310	1.6676	1.7051
		———	———	———	———	———	———
Net cash flow in $000		1,419	542	1,083	3,331	1,226	16,485

(W1) Revenue working:

Year 2 revenue = 400 rooms × 40% occupancy × 365 days × £60 room rate (i.e. £30 + 100%) = £3,504,000 in current terms.

Adjusting for inflation gives a nominal figure of £3,504,000 × 1.025² = £3,681,390.

(W2) The terminal value of the property is £8,915,309, which is the difference between:

- the forecast open market value, being £6.2m × $(1.08 \times 1.025)^5$ = £10,306,941

- the charge for repairs and renewals, being £1.2m × 1.025^6 = £1,391,632

(b)   Project evaluation

Net present value

Given that the US rate of inflation is 4.8% per annum and the company's real cost of capital is 4.2% per annum the nominal cost of capital is estimated using the Fisher formula:

$i_{nom} = (1 + inf)(1 + i_{real}) - 1$

$i_{nom} = (1.048)(1.042) - 1 = 9.2016\%$ (say 9.2%)

Discounting the project cash flows (investment plus return) at this nominal cost of capital gives a project net present value as follows:

$000	T_0	T_1	T_2	T_3	T_4	T_5	T_6
Investment (from (a))		(9,461)					
DF at 9.2%	1.000	0.916	0.839	0.768	0.703	0.644	0.590
Present value	–	(8,666)	–	–	–	–	–

Present value of investment phase = –$8.666 million

Return phase (from (a))		1,419	542	1,083	3,331	1,226	16,485
	1.000	0.916	0.839	0.768	0.703	0.644	0.590
Present value	–	1,300	455	832	2,343	789	9,722

Present value of return phase = $15.441 million

NPV = $15.441 million – $8.666 million = $6.775 million

A net present value of $6.775 million strongly suggests that this project is viable and will add to shareholder value.

Modified internal rate of return

$$MIRR = \left[\frac{PV_R}{PV_I} \right]^{\frac{1}{n}} (1 + r_e) - 1$$

Where PV_R is the present value of the return phase of the project, PV_I is the present value of the investment phase and r_e is the firm's cost of capital.

The calculation of the MIRR is therefore as follows:

$$MIRR = \left[\frac{15.441}{8.666} \right]^{\frac{1}{6}} (1.092) - 1 = 20.2\%$$

(c)   **Recommendation and discussion of method**

I have examined the project plan for the proposed project and referring to the appendices (see above) report that this project is expected to deliver an increase in shareholder value of $6.775 million, at the firm's current cost of finance. I have estimated the increase in shareholder value using the net present value (NPV) method. Net present value focuses on the current equivalent monetary value associated with capital expenditure leading to future cash flows arising from investment. The conversion to present value is achieved by discounting the future cash flows at the firm's cost of capital – a rate designed to reflect the scarcity of capital finance, inflation and risk.

Although the net present value technique is subject to a number of assumptions about the perfection and efficiency of the capital market it does generate an absolute measure of increase in shareholder value and as such avoids scale and other effects associated with percentage performance measures. Given the magnitude of the net present value of the project it is safe to assume that it is value-adding assuming that the underlying cash projections can be relied upon.

However, in certain circumstances it can be useful to have a 'headroom' percentage which reliably measures the rate of return on an investment such as this. In this case the modified internal rate of return of 20.2% is much greater than the firm's cost of capital of 9.2%. MIRR measures the economic yield of the investment (i.e. the discount rate which delivers a zero net present value) under the assumption that any cash surpluses are reinvested at the firm's current cost of capital. The standard IRR assumes that reinvestment will occur at the IRR which may not, in practice, be achievable.

Although MIRR, like IRR, cannot replace net present value as the principle evaluation technique it does give a measure of the maximum cost of finance that the firm could sustain and allow the project to remain worthwhile. For this reason it gives a useful insight into the margin of error, or room for negotiation, when considering the financing of particular investment projects.

(d)   **Using the Black-Scholes model for European-style call options:**

A dividend payment is due during the option period. The share price, Pa, should therefore be reduced by the present value of this expected dividend. The dividend per share has remained constant for three years. It is assumed that it will be constant in the next year.

The present value of the dividend (discounted at the risk-free rate) is:

$$\frac{25}{1.06} = 23.58 \text{ cents}$$

The share price, Pa, is therefore estimated to be $610 - 23.58 = 586.42$ cents.

Using the Black-Scholes model, the call price $= c = P_a N(d_1) - P_e N(d_2)e^{-rt}$

$$d_1 = \frac{\ln(P_a/P_e) + (r + 0.5s^2)t}{s\sqrt{t}} = \frac{\ln(586.42/500) + (0.06 + 0.5(0.38)^2)(1)}{0.38\sqrt{1}}$$

$= 0.7674$. (Round this to 0.77.)

$d_2 = d_1 - s\sqrt{t} = 0.7674 - 0.38 = 0.3874$ (Round this to 0.39.)

The next step is to calculate $N(d_1)$ and $N(d_2)$. For 0.77 standard deviations, the probability is 0.2794. For 0.39 standard deviations, the probability is 0.1517. The values of d_1 and d_2 are both positive, so we add 0.5.

From normal distribution tables:

$N(d_1) = 0.5 + 0.2794 = 0.7794$

$N(d_2) = 0.5 + 0.1517 = 0.6517$

Inputting this data into the call option price formula = $c = P_aN(d_1) - P_eN(d_2)e^{-rt}$

$$\text{Call price} = 586.42(0.7794) - \frac{500(0.6517)}{e^{(0.06)(1)}}$$

$$= 457.06 - (325.85/1.062)$$

$$= 457.06 - 306.83 = 150.23 \text{ cents}$$

The expected option call price is 150.23 cents per share, giving a current option value of 5,000 × 150.23 cents = $7,511.

Tutorial note

Your answer may differ slightly due to rounding differences in the calculations.

Conclusion

The options are currently in the money and are likely to be attractive to managers as they have an expected value in excess of the bonuses that are currently paid. However, the risk to managers of the two schemes differs and this might influence managerial preferences, depending upon individual managers' attitudes to risk. The Black-Scholes model assumes that the volatility of the share price over the past year will continue for the coming year. This is very unlikely. A different volatility will greatly influence the value of the option at the expiry date.

(e) (i) Blipton should not agree to grant the manager put options. The holder of a put option, which allows a share to be sold at a fixed price, would benefit its holder more the further the price of the share fell below the exercise price of the option. As far as the options are concerned it would be in the manager's interest to take decisions that reduced the company's share price, rather than increase it!

(ii) The put option price may be found from the put-call parity equation.

$p = c - P_a + P_ee^{-rt}$

$e^{-rt} = 1/1.062$ (calculated earlier in this solution)

$p = 150.23 - 586.42 + 500/1.062$

$= 34.62 \text{ cents}$

The manager is incorrect. Put options are not more valuable than call options in this situation.

6   TRAMONT CO (PILOT 12)

Key answer tips

This was the first 50 mark question published by the examiner when the format of the exam changed. It is important to note that the examiner's 50 mark questions are always split into several different parts, so don't allow yourself to get bogged down in any one part. The key to success is to attempt the easier parts of the question first and to leave sufficient time to attempt all parts of the question.

REPORT TO THE BOARD OF DIRECTORS, TRAMONT CO

EVALUATION OF WHETHER THE PRODUCTION OF X-IT SHOULD MOVE TO GAMALA

This report evaluates the possibility of moving the production of the X-IT to Gamala from the USA. Following the initial evaluation the report discusses the key assumptions made, the possible impact of a change in the government in Gamala after the elections due to take place shortly and other business factors that should be considered before a final decision is made.

Initially a base case net present value calculation is conducted to assess the impact of the production in Gamala. This is then adjusted to show the impact of cash flows in the USA as a result of the move, the immediate impact of ceasing production and the impact of the subsidy and the tax shield benefits from the loan borrowing.

Based on the calculations presented in the appendix, the move will result in a positive adjusted present value of just over $2.4 million. On this basis, the initial recommendation is that the production of X-IT should cease in the USA and the production moved to Gamala instead.

Assumptions

It is assumed that the borrowing rate of 5% is used to calculate the benefits from the tax shield. It could be argued that the risk free rate of 3% could be used as the discount rate instead of 5% to calculate the present value of benefits from the tax shields and the subsidies.

In adjusted present value calculations, the tax shield benefit is normally related to the debt capacity of the investment, not the actual amount of debt finance used. Since this is not given, it is assumed that the increase in debt capacity is equal to the debt finance used.

It has been assumed that many of the input variables, such as for example the tax and tax allowable depreciation rates, the various costs and prices, units produced and sold, the rate of inflation and the prediction of future exchange rates based on the purchasing power parity, are accurate and will change as stated over the four-year period of the project. In reality any of these estimates could be subject to change to a greater or lesser degree and it would appropriate for Tramont Co to conduct uncertainty assessments like sensitivity analysis to assess the impact of the changes to the initial predictions.

Government change

From the facts of the case it would seem that a change of government could have a significant impact on whether or not the project is beneficial to Tramont Co. The threat to raise taxes may not be too significant as the tax rates would need to increase to more than 30% before Tramont Co would lose money. However, the threat by the opposition party to review 'commercial benefits' may be more significant.

Just over 40% of the present value comes from the tax shield and subsidy benefits. If these were reneged then Tramont Co would lose a significant of the value attached to the project. Also the new government may not allow remittances every year, as is assumed in part (i). However this may not be significant since the largest present value amount comes from the final year of operation.

Other business factors

Tramont Co should consider the possibility of becoming established in Gamala, and this may lead to follow-on projects. The real options linked to this should be included in the analysis.

Tramont Co's overall corporate strategy should be considered. Does the project fit within this strategy? Even if the decision is made to close the operation in the USA, there may be other alternatives and these need to be assessed.

The amount of experience Tramont Co has in international ventures needs to be considered. For example, will it be able to match its systems to the Gamalan culture? It will need to develop strategies to deal with cultural differences. This may include additional costs such as training which may not have been taken into account.

Tramont Co needs to consider if the project can be delayed at all. From part (i), it can be seen that a large proportion of the opportunity cost relates to lost contribution in years 1 and 2. A delay in the commencement of the project may increase the overall value of the project.

Tramont Co needs to consider the impact on its reputation due to possible redundancies. Since the production of X-IT is probably going to be stopped in any case, Tramont Co needs to communicate its strategy to the employees and possibly other stakeholders clearly so as to retain its reputation. This may make the need to consider alternatives even more important.

Conclusion

Following from a detailed sensitivity analysis, analysis of a possible change in the government and an evaluation of the financial benefits accruing from the other business factors discussed above, the BoD can make a decision of whether to move the production to Gamala or not. This initial evaluation suggests that moving the production of the X-IT to Gamala would be beneficial.

Appendix

Gamalan Project Operating Cash Flows

(All amounts in GR/$000s)

Year	Now	1	2	3	4
Sales revenue (w2)		48,888	94,849	214,442	289,716
Local variable costs (w3)		(16,200)	(32,373)	(75,385)	(104,897)
Imported component (w4)		(4,889)	(9,769)	(22,750)	(31,658)
Fixed costs		(30,000)	(32,700)	(35,643)	(38,851)
Profits before tax		(2,201)	20,007	80,664	114,310
Taxation (w5)		0	0	(7,694)	(18,862)
Investment	(230,000)				450,000
Working capital	(40,000)	(3,600)	(3,924)	(4,277)	51,801
Cash flows (GR)	(270,000)	(5,801)	16,083	68,693	597,249
Exchange rate (w1)	55.00	58.20	61.59	65.18	68.98
Cash flows ($)	(4,909)	(100)	261	1,054	8,658
Discount factor for 9.6% (w6)		0.912	0.832	0.760	0.693
(Full credit given if 10% is used as the discount rate)					
Present values ($)	(4,909)	(91)	217	801	6,000

Net present value (NPV) of the cash flows from the project is approx. $2,018,000.

Adjusted present value (APV)	$000
NPV of cash flows	2,018
Additional USA tax, opportunity cost (revenues foregone from current operations) and additional contribution from component exported to project (net of tax) (w7)	(1,237)
Closure revenues and costs ($2,300,000 – $1,700,000)	600
Tax shield and benefit of subsidy (w8)	1,033
Total APV	2,414

Workings:

(W1) Exchange rates

Year	1	2	3	4
GR/$1	55 × 1.09/1.03 = 58.20	58.20 × 1.09/ 1.03 = 61.59	61.59 × 1.09/ 1.03 = 65.18	65.18 × 1.09/ 1.03 = 68.98

(W2) Sales revenue (GR 000s)

Year	1	2	3	4
Price × units × exchange rate	70 × 12,000 × 58.20 = 48,888	70 × 22,000 × 61.59 = 94,849	70 × 47,000 × 65.18 = 214,442	70 × 60,000 × 68.98 = 289,716

(W3) Local variable costs (GR 000s)

Year	1	2	3	4
Cost × units × inflation after yr 1	$1,350 \times 12,000 = 16,200$	$1,350 \times 22,000 \times 1.09 = 32,373$	$1,350 \times 47,000 \times 1.09^2 = 75,385$	$1,350 \times 60,000 \times 1.09^3 = 104,897$

(W4) Imported component (GR 000s)

Year	1	2	3	4
Price × units × inflation after year 1 × exchange rate	$7 \times 12,000 \times 58.20 = 4,889$	$7 \times 22,000 \times 1.03 \times 61.59 = 9,769$	$7 \times 47,000 \times 1.03^2 \times 65.18 = 22,750$	$70 \times 60,000 \times 1.03^3 \times 68.98 = 31,658$

(W5) Local variable costs (GR 000s)

Year	1	2	3	4
Profits before tax	(2,201)	20,007	80,664	114,310
Tax allowable depreciation	(20,000)	(20,000)	(20,000)	(20,000)
Profit/(loss) after depreciation	(22,201)	7	60,664	94,310
Taxable profits	0	0	38,470	94,310
Taxation (20%)	0	0	(7,694)	(18,862)

(W6) Gamala project all-equity financed discount

Tramont Co equity beta = 1.17

MVe = $2.40 × 25m shares = $60m

MVd = $40m × $1,428/$1,000 = $57.12m

Tramont Co asset beta (assuming debt is rate risk free)

1.17 × 60m/(60m + 57.12m × 0.7) = 0.70

Project asset beta = 0.70 + 0.40 = 1.10

Project all-equity financed discount rate = 3% + 6% × 1.1 = 9.6%

(W7) Additional tax, additional contribution and opportunity cost ($000s)

Year	1	2	3	4
Additional tax				
Taxable profits × 1/exchange rate × 10%	0	0	$38,470 \times 1/65.18 \times 10\% = (59)$	$94,310 \times 1/68.98 \times 10\% = (137)$

Opportunity cost

Units × contribution × (1 – tax)	40 × \$20 × 0.7 = (560)	32 × \$20 × 0.7 = (448)	25.6 × \$20 × 0.7 = (358)	20.48 × \$20 × 0.7 = (287)

Additional Contribution

Units × contribution × inflation × (1 – tax)	12 × \$4 × 0.7 = 34	22 × \$4 × 1.03 × 0.7 = 63	47 × \$4 × 1.032 × 0.7= 140	60 × \$4 × 1.033 × 0.7 = 184
Total cash flows	(526)	(385)	(277)	(240)
PV of cash flows Discount at 7%	(492)	(336)	(226)	(183)

NPV is approx.
\$(1,237,000)

(W8) Tax shield and subsidy benefits (\$/GR 000s)

Year	1	2	3	4
Interest × loan × tax rate	6% × 270m × 20% = 3,240	3,240	3,240	3,240

Annual subsidy benefit (GR)

Interest gain × loan × (1 – tax rate)	7% × 270m × 0.8 = 15,120	15,120	15,120	15,120
Total tax shield + subsidy benefits (GR)	18,360	18,360	18,360	18,360
Exchange rate (GR/\$1)	58.20	61.59	65.18	68.98
Cash flows (\$)	**315**	**298**	**282**	**266**
PV of cash flows **Discount at 5%**	**300**	**270**	**244**	**219**

NPV of tax shield and subsidy benefit is approx. \$1,033,000

(b) A triple bottom line (TBL) report provides a quantitative summary of performance in terms of economic or financial impact, impact on the environment and impact on social performance. TBL provides the measurement tool to assess a corporation's or project's performance against its objectives.

The principle of TBL reporting is that true performance should be measured in terms of a balance between economic (profits), environmental (planet) and social (people) factors; with no one factor growing at the expense of the others. The contention is that a corporation that accommodates the pressures of all the three factors in its strategic investment decisions will enhance shareholder value, as long as the benefits that accrue from producing such a report exceeds the costs of producing it.

For example, in the case of the X-IT, reporting on the impact of moving the production to Gamala, in terms of the impact on the employees and environment in the USA and in Gamala will highlight Tramont Co as a good corporate citizen, and thereby increase its reputation and enable it to attract and retain high performing, high calibre employees. It can also judge the impact on the other business factors mentioned in the report above.

(**Note:** Credit will be given for alternative relevant answers)

(c) Portfolio theory suggests that shareholders holding well-diversified portfolios will have diversified away unsystematic or company specific risk, and will only face risk systematic risk, i.e. risk that cannot be diversified away. Therefore a company cannot reduce risk further by undertaking diversification within the same system or market. However, further risk reduction may occur if the diversification is undertaken by the company, on behalf of the shareholders, into a system or market where they themselves do not invest. Some studies indicate that even shareholders holding well-diversified portfolios may benefit from risk diversification where companies invest in emerging markets.

In the case of Tramont Co and the X-IT, it is not clear whether diversification benefits will result in the investment in Gamala. The benefits are dependent on the size of the investment, and on the nature of the business operations undertaken in Gamala by Tramont Co. And whether these operations mirror an investment in a significantly different system or market. If the investment is large, the operations are similar to undertaking a Gamalan company. Tramont Co's shareholders who do not hold similar companies' shares in their portfolios may then gain risk diversification benefits from the Gamalan investment.

7 CHMURA CO (DEC 13)

 Online question assistance

Key answer tips

Investment appraisal and option pricing are very commonly tested syllabus areas. Note that in this question there were lots of easy discussion marks (e.g. assumptions, role of WTO) as well as the many complex calculations. In order to guarantee success, you must attempt all parts of the question, both calculations and discussion.

(a) The World Trade Organisation (WTO) was set up to continue to implement the General Agreement on Tariffs and Trade (GATT), and its main aims are to reduce the barriers to international trade. It does this by seeking to prevent protectionist measures such as tariffs, quotas and other import restrictions. It also acts as a forum for negotiation and offering settlement processes to resolve disputes between countries.

The WTO encourages free trade by applying the most favoured nation principle between its members, where reduction in tariffs offered to one country by another should be offered to all members.

Whereas the WTO has had notable success, some protectionist measures between groups of countries are nevertheless allowed and some protectionist measures, especially non-tariff based ones, have been harder to identify and control.

Mehgam could benefit from reducing protectionist measures because its actions would make other nations reduce their protectionist measures against it. Normally countries retaliate against each other when they impose protectionist measures. A reduction in these may allow Mehgam to benefit from increased trade and economic growth. Such a policy may also allow Mehgam to specialise and gain competitive advantage in certain products and services, and compete more effectively globally. Its actions may also gain political capital and more influence worldwide.

Possible drawbacks of reducing protectionist policies mainly revolve around the need to protect certain industries. It may be that these industries are developing and in time would be competitive on a global scale. However, inaction to protect them now would damage their development irreparably. Protection could also be given to old, declining industries, which, if not protected, would fail too quickly due to international competition, and would create large scale unemployment making such inaction politically unacceptable. Certain protectionist policies are designed to prevent 'dumping' of goods at a very cheap price, which hurt local producers.

(**Note:** Credit will be given for alternative relevant discussion)

(b) **Report to the Board of Directors (BoD), Chmura Co**

This report recommends whether or not Chmura Co should invest in a food packaging project in Mehgam, following Mehgam reducing its protectionist measures. It initially considers the value of the project without taking into account the offer made by Bulud Co to purchase the project after two years. Following this, Bulud Co's offer is considered. The report concludes by recommending a course of action for the BoD to consider further.

Estimated value of the Mehgam project and initial recommendation

The initial net present value of the project is negative at approximately $(451,000) [see Appendix 1]. This would suggest that Chmura Co should not undertake the project.

Bulud Co's offer is considered to be a real option for Mehgam Co. Since it is an offer to sell the project as an abandonment option, a put option value is calculated based on the finance director's assessment of the standard deviation and using the Black-Scholes option pricing (BSOP) model. The value of the put option is added to the initial net present value of the project without the option, to give the value of the project. Although Chmura Co will not actually obtain any immediate cash flow from Bulud Co's offer, the real option computation indicates that the project is worth pursuing because the volatility may result in increases in future cash flows.

After taking account of Bulud Co's offer and the finance director's assessment, the net present value of the project is positive at approximately $2,993,000 [see Appendix 2]. This would suggest that Chmura Co should undertake the project.

Assumptions

It is assumed that all the figures relating to variables such as revenues, costs, taxation, initial investments and their recovery, inflation figures and cost of capital are accurate. There is considerable uncertainty surrounding the accuracy of these, and in addition to the assessments of value conducted in appendices one and two, sensitivity analysis and scenario analysis are probably needed to assess the impact of these uncertainties.

It is assumed that future exchange rates will reflect the differential in inflation rates between the two countries. It is, however, unlikely that exchange rates will move fully in line with the inflation rate differentials.

It is assumed that the value of the land and buildings at the end of the project is a relevant cost, as it is equivalent to an opportunity benefit, even if the land and buildings are retained by Chmura Co.

It is assumed that Chmura Co will be given and will utilise the full benefit of the bi-lateral tax treaty and therefore will not pay any additional tax in the country where it is based.

It is assumed that the short-dated $ treasury bills are equivalent to the risk-free rate of return required for the BSOP model.

And it is assumed that the finance director's assessment of the 35% standard deviation of cash flows is accurate.

It is assumed that Bulud Co will fulfil its offer to buy the project in two years' time and there is no uncertainty surrounding this. Chmura Co may want to consider making the offer more binding through a legal contract.

The BSOP model makes several assumptions such as perfect markets, constant interest rates and lognormal distribution of asset prices. It also assumes that volatility can be assessed and stays constant throughout the life of the project, and that the underlying asset can be traded. Neither of these assumptions would necessarily apply to real options. Therefore the BoD needs to treat the value obtained as indicative rather than definitive.

Additional business risks

Before taking the final decision on whether or not to proceed with the project, Chmura Co needs to take into consideration additional risks, including business risks, and where possible mitigate these as much as possible. The main business risks are as follows:

Investing in Mehgam may result in political risks. For example, the current government may be unstable and if there is a change of government, the new government may impose restrictions, such as limiting the amount of remittances which can be made to the parent company. Chmura Co needs to assess the likelihood of such restrictions being imposed in the future and consider alternative ways of limiting the negative impact of such restrictions.

Chmura Co will want to gain assurance that the countries to which it will sell the packaged food batches remain economically stable and that the physical infrastructure such as railways, roads and shipping channels are maintained in good repair. Chmura Co will want to ensure that it will be able to export the special packaging material into Mehgam. Finally, it will need to assess the likelihood of substantial protectionist measures being lifted and not re-imposed in the future.

As much as possible, Chmura Co will want to ensure that fiscal risks such as imposition of new taxes and limits on expenses allowable for taxation purposes do not change. Currently, the taxes paid in Mehgam are higher than in Chmura Co's host country, and even though the bi-lateral tax treaty exists between the countries, Chmura Co will be keen to ensure that the tax rate does not change disadvantageously.

Chmura Co will also want to protect itself, as much as possible, against adverse changes in regulations. It will want to form the best business structure, such as a subsidiary company, joint venture or branch, to undertake the project. Also, it will want to familiarise itself on regulations such as employee health and safety law, employment law and any legal restrictions around land ownership.

Risks related to the differences in cultures between the host country, Mehgam, and the countries where the batches will be exported to would be a major concern to Chmura Co. For example, the product mix in the batches which are suitable for the home market may not be suitable for Mehgam or where the batches are exported. It may contain foods which would not be saleable in different countries and therefore standard batches may not be acceptable to the customers. Chmura Co will also need to consider the cultural differences and needs of employees and suppliers.

The risk of the loss of reputation through operational errors would need to be assessed and mitigated. For example, in setting up sound internal controls, segregation of duties is necessary. However, personal relationships between employees in Mehgam may mean that what would be acceptable in another country may not be satisfactory in Mehgam. Other areas where Chmura Co will need to focus on are the quality control procedures to ensure that the quality of the food batches is similar to the quality in the host country.

Recommendation

With Bulud Co's offer, it is recommended that the BoD proceed with the project, as long as the BoD is satisfied that the offer is reliable, the sensitivity analysis/scenario analysis indicates that any negative impact of uncertainty is acceptable and the business risks have been considered and mitigated as much as possible.

If Bulud Co's offer is not considered, then the project gives a marginal negative net present value, although the results of the sensitivity analysis need to be considered. It is recommended that, if only these results are taken into consideration, the BoD should not proceed with the project. However, this decision is marginal and there may be other valid reasons for progressing with the project such as possibilities of follow-on projects in Mehgam.

Report compiled by:

Date:

APPENDICES

Appendix 1: Estimated value of the Mehgam project excluding the Bulud Co offer

(Cash flows in MP, millions)

Year	1	2	3	4	5
Sales revenue (w2)	1,209.6	1,905.1	4,000.8	3,640.7	2,205.4
Production and selling costs (w3)	(511.5)	(844.0)	(1,856.7)	(1,770.1)	(1,123.3)
Special packaging costs (w4)	(160.1)	(267.0)	(593.7)	(572.0)	(366.9)
Training and development costs	(409.2)	(168.8)	0	0	0
Tax allowable depreciation	(125)	(125)	(125)	(125)	(125)
Balancing allowance					(125)
Taxable profits/(loss)	3.8	500.3	1,425.4	1,173.6	465.2
Taxation (25%)	(1.0)	(125.1)	(356.4)	(293.4)	(116.3)
Add back depreciation	125	125	125	125	250
Cash flows (MP, millions)	127.8	500.2	1,194.0	1,005.2	598.9

(All amounts in $, 000s)

Year	1	2	3	4	5
Exchange rate (w1)	76.24	80.72	85.47	90.50	95.82
Cash flows ($ 000s)	1,676.3	6,196.7	13,969.8	11,107.2	6,250.3
Discount factor for 12%	0.893	0.797	0.712	0.636	0.567
Present values ($ 000s)	1,496.9	4,938.8	9,946.5	7,064.2	3,543.9

Present value of cash flows approx. = $26,990,000

PV of value of land, buildings and machinery in year 5 = (80% × MP1,250m + MP500m)/95.82 × 0.567 approx. = $8,876,000

PV of working capital = MP200m/95.82 × 0.567 approx. = $1,183,000

Cost of initial investment in $ = (MP2,500 million + MP200 million)/72 = $37,500,000

NPV of project = $26,990,000 + $8,876,000 + $1,183,000 − $37,500,000 = $(451,000)

Workings:

(W1) Exchange rates

Year	1	2	3	4	5
MP/$1	72 × 1.08/1.02 = 76.24	76.24 × 1.08/1.02 = 80.72	80.72 × 1.08/1.02 = 85.47	85.47 × 1.08/1.02 = 90.50	90.50 × 1.08/1.02 = 95.82

(W2) Sales revenue (MP million)

Year	1	2	3	4	5
	$10,000 \times 115,200 \times 1.05 =$ 1,209.6	$15,000 \times 115,200 \times 1.05^2 =$ 1,905.1	$30,000 \times 115,200 \times 1.05^3 =$ 4,000.8	$26,000 \times 115,200 \times 1.05^4 =$ 3,640.7	$15,000 \times 115,200 \times 1.05^5 =$ 2,205.4

(W3) Production and selling (MP million)

Year	1	2	3	4	5
	$10,000 \times 46,500 \times 1.1$ = 511.5	$15,000 \times 46,500 \times 1.1^2 = 844.0$	$30,000 \times 46,500 \times 1.1^3 =$ 1,856.7	$26,000 \times 46,500 \times 1.1^4 =$ 1,770.1	$15,000 \times 46,500 \times 1.1^5 =$ 1,123.3

(W4) Special packaging (MP million)

Year	1	2	3	4	5
	$10,000 \times 200 \times 76.24 \times 1.05 = 160.1$	$15,000 \times 200 \times 80.72 \times 1.05^2 =$ 267.0	$30,000 \times 200 \times 85.47 \times 1.05^3 =$ 593.7	$26,000 \times 200 \times 90.50 \times 1.05^4 =$ 572.0	$15,000 \times 200 \times 95.82 \times 1.05^5 =$ 366.9

Appendix 2: Estimated value of the Mehgam project including the Bulud Co offer

Present value of underlying asset (Pa) = $30,613,600 (approximately)

(This is the sum of the present values of the cash flows foregone in years 3, 4 and 5)

Price offered by Bulud Co (Pe) = $28,000,000

Risk free rate of interest (r) = 4% (assume government treasury bills are valid approximation of the risk free rate of return) Volatility of underlying asset (s) = 35%

Time to expiry of option (t) = 2 years

$d_1 = [\ln(30{,}613.6/28{,}000) + (0.04 + 0.5 \times 0.35^2) \times 2]/[0.35 \times 2^{1/2}] = 0.589$

$d_2 = 0.589 - 0.35 \times 2^{1/2} = 0.094$

$N(d_1) = 0.5 + 0.2220 = 0.7220$

$N(d_2) = 0.5 + 0.0375 = 0.5375$

Call value = $\$30{,}613{,}600 \times 0.7220 - \$28{,}000{,}000 \times 0.5375 \times e^{-0.04 \times 2}$ = approx. $8,210,000

Put value = $\$8{,}210{,}000 - \$30{,}613{,}600 + \$28{,}000{,}000 \times e^{-0.04 \times 2}$ = approx. $3,444,000

Net present value of the project with put option = $3,444,000 – $451,000 = approx. $2,993,000

Marking scheme		
		Marks
(a)	Role of the World Trade Organisation	4–5
	Benefits of reducing protectionist measures	2–3
	Drawbacks of reducing protectionist measures	2–3
		———
	Maximum	**9**
		———
(b) (i)	Future exchange rates predicted on inflation rate differential	1
	Sales revenue	1
	Production and selling costs	1
	Special packaging costs	2
	Training and development costs	1
	Correct treatment of tax and tax allowable depreciation	2
	Years 1 to 5 cash flows in $ and present values of cash flows	2
	Ignoring initial investigation cost and additional taxation in Chmura Co host country	1
	Correct treatment of land, buildings, machinery and working capital	2
	Net present value of the project	1
		———
	Maximum	**14**
		———
(ii)	Inputting correct values for the variables	2
	Calculation of d_1 and d_2	2
	Establishing $N(d_1)$ and $N(d_2)$	2
	Call value	1
	Put value	1
	Value of the project	1
		———
		9
		———
(iii)	Estimated value and initial recommendation	2–3
	Up to 2 marks per assumption discussed	5–6
	Up to 2 marks per additional business risk discussed	5–6
	Overarching recommendation(s)	1–2
		———
	Maximum	**14**
		———
	Professional marks	
	Report format	1
	Structure and presentation of the report	3
		———
	Maximum	**4**
		———
Total		**50**
		———

8 YILANDWE (JUN 15)

 *Question debrief*

Key answer tips

Investment appraisal, with foreign currencies, is a commonly tested topic.

It is critical to lay out your numerical answer clearly, keeping cash flows in different currencies separate.

Also, leave plenty of time for the written parts. More than half the marks here were for discussion/written points, but many students will have spent the vast majority of their time attacking the numbers.

(a)   **Benefits of own investment as opposed to licensing**

Imoni Co may be able to benefit from setting up its own plant as opposed to licensing in a number of ways. Yilandwe wants to attract foreign investment and is willing to offer a number of financial concessions to foreign investors which may not be available to local companies. The company may be able to control the quality of the components more easily, and offer better and targeted training facilities if it has direct control of the labour resources. The company may also be able to maintain the confidentiality of its products, whereas assigning the assembly rights to another company may allow that company to imitate the products more easily. Investing internationally may provide opportunities for risk diversification, especially if Imoni Co's shareholders are not well-diversified internationally themselves. Finally, direct investment may provide Imoni Co with new opportunities in the future, such as follow-on options.

Drawbacks of own investment as opposed to licensing

Direct investment in a new plant will probably require higher, upfront costs from Imoni Co compared to licensing the assembly rights to a local manufacturer. It may be able to utilise these saved costs on other projects. Imoni Co will most likely be exposed to higher risks involved with international investment such as political risks, cultural risks and legal risks. With licensing these risks may be reduced somewhat. The licensee, because it would be a local company, may understand the operational systems of doing business in Yilandwe better. It will therefore be able to get off-the-ground quicker. Imoni Co, on the other hand, will need to become familiar with the local systems and culture, which may take time and make it less efficient initially. Similarly, investing directly in Yilandwe may mean that it costs Imoni Co more to train the staff and possibly require a steeper learning curve from them. However, the scenario does say that the country has a motivated and well-educated labour force and this may mitigate this issue somewhat.

(**Note:** Credit will be given for alternative, relevant suggestions)

(b) **Report on the proposed assembly plant in Yilandwe**

This report considers whether or not it would be beneficial for Imoni Co to set up a parts assembly plant in Yilandwe. It takes account of the financial projections, presented in detail in appendices 1 and 2, discusses the assumptions made in arriving at the projections and discusses other non-financial issues which should be considered. The report concludes by giving a reasoned recommendation on the acceptability of the project.

Assumptions made in producing the financial projections

It is assumed that all the estimates such as sales revenue, costs, royalties, initial investment costs, working capital, and costs of capital and inflation figures are accurate. There is considerable uncertainty surrounding the accuracy of these and a small change in them could change the forecasts of the project quite considerably. A number of projections using sensitivity and scenario analysis may aid in the decision making process.

It is assumed that no additional tax is payable in the USA for the profits made during the first two years of the project's life when the company will not pay tax in Yilandwe either. This is especially relevant to year 2 of the project.

No details are provided on whether or not the project ends after four years. This is an assumption which is made, but the project may last beyond four years and therefore may yield a positive net present value. Additionally, even if the project ceases after four years, no details are given about the sale of the land, buildings and machinery. The residual value of these non-current assets could have a considerable bearing on the outcome of the project.

It is assumed that the increase in the transfer price of the parts sent from the USA directly increases the contribution which Imoni Co earns from the transfer. This is probably not an unreasonable assumption. However, it is also assumed that the negotiations with Yilandwe's government will be successful with respect to increasing the transfer price and the royalty fee. Imoni Co needs to assess whether or not this assumption is realistic.

The basis for using a cost of capital of 12% is not clear and an explanation is not provided about whether or not this is an accurate or reasonable figure. The underpinning basis for how it is determined may need further investigation.

Although the scenario states that the project can start almost immediately, in reality this may not be possible and Imoni Co may need to factor in possible delays.

It is assumed that future exchange rates will reflect the differential in inflation rates between the respective countries. However, it is unlikely that the exchange rates will move fully in line with the inflation rate differentials.

Other risks and issues

Investing in Yilandwe may result in significant political risks. The scenario states that the current political party is not very popular in rural areas and that the population remains generally poor. Imoni Co needs to assess how likely it is that the government may change during the time it is operating in Yilandwe and the impact of the change. For example, a new government may renege on the current government's offers and/or bring in new restrictions. Imoni Co will need to decide what to do if this happens.

Imoni Co needs to assess the likelihood that it will be allowed to increase the transfer price of the parts and the royalty fee. Whilst it may be of the opinion that currently Yilandwe may be open to such suggestions, this may depend on the interest the government may get from other companies to invest in Yilandwe. It may consider that agreeing to such demands from Imoni Co may make it obligated to other companies as well.

The financial projections are prepared on the basis that positive cash flows from Yilandwe can be remitted back to the USA. Imoni Co needs to establish that this is indeed the case and that it is likely to continue in the future.

Imoni Co needs to be careful about its ethical stance and its values, and the impact on its reputation, given that a school is being closed in order to provide it with the production facilities needed. Whilst the government is funding some of the transport costs for the children, the disruption this will cause to the children and the fact that after six months the transport costs become the parents' responsibility, may have a large, negative impact on the company's image and may be contrary to the ethical values which the company holds. The possibility of alternative venues should be explored.

Imoni Co needs to take account of cultural risks associated with setting up a business in Yilandwe. The way of doing business in Yilandwe may be very different and the employees may need substantial training to adapt to Imoni Co's way of doing business. On the other hand, the fact that the population is well educated, motivated and keen may make this process easier to achieve.

Imoni Co also needs to consider fiscal and regulatory risks. The company will need to assess the likelihood of changes in tax rates, laws and regulations, and set up strategies to mitigate eventualities which can be predicted. In addition to these, Imoni Co should also consider and mitigate as far as possible, operational risks such as the quality of the components and maintenance of transport links.

Imoni Co should assess and value alternative real options which it may have. For example, it could consider whether licensing the production of the components to a local company may be more financially viable; it could consider alternative countries to Yilandwe, which may offer more benefits; it could consider whether the project can be abandoned if circumstances change against the company; entry into Yilandwe may provide Imoni Co with other business opportunities.

Recommendation

The result from the financial projections is that the project should be accepted because it results in a positive net present value. It is recommended that the financial projections should be considered in conjunction with the assumptions, the issues and risks, and the implications of these, before a final decision is made.

There is considerable scope for further investigation and analysis. It is recommended that sensitivity and scenario analysis be undertaken to take into consideration continuing the project beyond four years and so on. The value of any alternative real options should also be considered and incorporated into the decision.

Consideration must also be given to the issues, risks and factors beyond financial considerations, such as the impact on the ethical stance of the company and the impact on its image, if the school affected is closed to accommodate it.

Report compiled by: AN Accountant

Date:XX/XX/XXXX

APPENDICES

Appendix 1

(all amounts in YR, millions)

Year	0	1	2	3	4
Sales revenue (w2)		18,191	66,775	111,493	60,360
Parts costs (w2)		(5,188)	(19,060)	(31,832)	(17,225)
Variable costs (w2)		(2,921)	(10,720)	(17,901)	(9,693)
Fixed costs		(5,612)	(6,437)	(7,068)	(7,760)
Royalty fee (w3)		(4,324)	(4,813)	(5,130)	(5,468)
Tax allowable depreciation		(4,500)	(4,500)	(4,500)	(4,500)
Taxable profits/(loss)		(4,354)	21,245	45,062	15,714
Tax loss carried forward				(4,354)	
				40,708	
Taxation (40%)		0	0	(16,283)	(6,286)
Add back loss carried fwd				4,354	
Add back depreciation		4,500	4,500	4,500	4,500
Cash flows after tax		146	25,745	33,279	13,928
Working capital	(9,600)	(2,112)	(1,722)	(1,316)	14,750
Land, buildings and machinery	(39,000)				
Cash flows (YR, millions)	(48,600)	(1,966)	24,023	31,963	28,678

(All amounts in $, 000s)

Year	0	1	2	3	4
Exchange rate	101.4	120.1	133.7	142.5	151.9
Remittable flows	(479,290)	(16,370)	179,678	224,302	188,795
Contribution (parts sales) ($120 + inflation per unit)		18,540	61,108	95,723	48,622
Royalty (w3)		36,000	36,000	36,000	36,000
Tax on contribution and royalty (20%)		(10,908)	(19,422)	(26,345)	(16,924)
Cash flows	(479,290)	27,262	257,364	329,680	256,493
Discount factors (12%)	1	0.893	0.797	0.712	0.636
Present values	(479,290)	24,345	205,119	234,732	163,130

Net present value project before considering the impact of the lost contribution and redundancy is approximately $148.0 million.

Lost contribution and redundancy cost

The lost contribution and redundancy costs are small compared to the net present value and would therefore have a minimal impact of reducing the net present value by $0.1 million approximately.

(**Note:** Full credit will be given if the assumption is made that the amounts are in $000s instead of $.)

Appendix 2: Workings

(W1) Unit prices and costs including inflation

Year	1	2	3	4
Selling price (€)	735	772	803	835
Parts ($)	288	297	306	315
Variable costs (YR)	19,471	22,333	24,522	26,925

(W2) Sales revenue and costs

In YR millions Year

Year	1	2	3	4
Sales revenue	$150 \times 735 \times 165$ = 18,191	$480 \times 772 \times 180.2$ = 66,775	$730 \times 803 \times 190.2$ = 111,493	$360 \times 835 \times 200.8$ = 60,360
Parts costs	$150 \times 288 \times 120.1$ = 5,188	$480 \times 297 \times 133.7$ = 19,060	$730 \times 306 \times 142.5$ = 31,832	$360 \times 315 \times 151.9$ = 17,225
Variable costs	$150 \times 19,471$ = 2,921	$480 \times 22,333$ = 10,720	$730 \times 24,522$ = 17,901	$360 \times 26,925$ = 9,693

(W3) Royalty fee

$20 million × 1.8 = $36 million

This is then converted into YR at the YR/$ rate for each year: 120.1, 133.7, 142.5 and 151.9 for years 1 to 4 respectively.

(**Note:** Credit will be given for alternative, relevant approaches to the calculations, and to the discussion of the assumptions, risks and issues)

Marking scheme			Marks
(ii)	Up to 2 marks per assumption discussed		9
	2–3 marks per issue/risk discussed		11
			——
		Maximum	17
			——
	Note: For (b)(ii), where points can be made either as assumptions or as issues, marks will be allocated to either area as relevant.		
(iii)	Reasoned recommendation		3
			——
	Professional marks for part (b)		
	Report format		1
	Structure and presentation of the report		3
			——
		Maximum	4
			——
Total			50
			——

ACQUISITIONS AND MERGERS

9   STANZIAL INC (DEC 06 ADAPTED)

Key answer tips

This is a very good question on business valuation, one of the most important syllabus topics.

Notice that in part (a) you are expected to calculate the value using four different valuation methods, but also to comment on the methods and state your assumptions. Unless you attempt all these different elements, you'll struggle to score a pass mark here.

(a)   REPORT

The valuation of private companies involves considerable subjectivity. Many alternative solutions to the one presented below are possible and equally valid.

As Stanzial is considering the purchase of Besserlot, this will involve gaining ownership through the purchase of Stanzial's shares, hence an equity valuation is required.

Before undertaking any valuations it is advisable to recalculate the earnings for 20X6 without the exceptional item. It is assumed that this is a one-off expense, which was not fully tax allowable.

The revised statement of profit or loss is:

	20X6
	$000
Sales revenue	22,480
Operating profit before exceptional items	1,302
Interest paid (net)	280
Profit before taxation	1,022
Taxation (30%)	307
Profit after tax	715
Dividend	200
Change in equity	515

Asset-based valuation

An asset valuation might be regarded as the absolute minimum value of the company. Asset-based valuations are most useful when the company is being liquidated and the assets disposed of. In an acquisition, where the company is a going concern, asset-based values do not fully value future cash flows, or items such as the value of human capital, market position, etc.

Asset values may be estimated using book values, which are of little use, replacement cost values, or disposal values. The information provided does not permit a full disposal value, although some adjustments to book value are possible. In this case an asset valuation might be:

	$000
Net assets	6,286
Patent	10,000
Inventory adjustment	(1,020)
	15,266 or $15,266,000

This value is not likely to be accurate as it assumes the economic value of non-current assets is the same as the book value, which is very unlikely. The same argument may also be related to current assets and liabilities other than inventory.

P/E ratios

P/E ratios of competitors are sometimes used in order to value unlisted companies. This is problematic as the characteristics of all companies differ, and a P/E ratio valid for one company might not be relevant to another.

There is also a question of whether or not the P/E ratio should be adjusted downwards for an unlisted company, and how different expected growth rates should be allowed for.

Expected earnings growth for Besserlot is much higher than the average for the industry, especially during this next three years. In view of this it might be reasonable to apply a P/E ratio of at least the industry average when attempting to value Besserlot.

The after-tax earnings of Besserlot, based upon the revised statement of profit or loss, are:

$$1,022 - 307 = 715$$

Using a P/E ratio of 30:1, this gives an estimated value of $715 \times 30 = \$21,450,000$.

This is a very subjective estimate, and it might be wise to use a range of P/E ratio values, for example from 25:1 to 35:1, which would result in a range of values from $17,875,000 to $25,025,000.

It could also be argued that the value should be based upon the anticipated next earnings rather than the past earnings several months ago.

This is estimated to be:

	20X7
	$000
Sales revenue	28,100
Operating profit before exceptional items	2,248
Interest paid (net)	350
Profit before taxation	1,898
Taxation	569
	1,329

$1,329 \times 30$ gives a much higher estimate of $39,870,000

PE-based valuation might also be criticised as it is based upon profits rather than cash flows.

Dividend-based valuation

Dividend-based valuation assumes that the value of the company may be estimated from the present value of future dividends paid. In this case the expected dividend growth rates are different during the next three years and the subsequent period.

The estimated dividend valuation is:

Year	1	2	3	After Year 3	
Expected dividend	250	313	391	$\dfrac{391\,(1.1)}{0.14-0.10}$	Using $P_o = \dfrac{D_o(1+g)}{(r_e-g)}$
Discount factors (14%)	0.877	0.769	0.675	0.675	
Present values	219	241	264	7,258	

The estimated value is $7,982,000.

This is a rather low estimated value and might be the result of Besserlot having a relatively low dividend pay-out ratio, and no value being available for a final liquidating dividend.

The present value of expected future cash flows

The present value of future cash flows will be estimated using the expected free cash flow to equity. In theory, this is probably the best valuation method, but in reality it is impossible for an acquiring company to make accurate estimates of these cash flows. The data below relies upon many assumptions about future growth rates and relationships between variables.

	20X7	20X8	20X9	After 20X9
Sales revenue	28,100	35,125	43,906	
Operating profit	2,248	2,810	3,512	
Interest paid (net)	350	438	547	
Profit before taxation	1,898	2,372	2,965	
Taxation	569	712	890	
	1,329	1,660	2,075	
Add back non-cash expenses	1,025	1,281	1,602	
Less increase in working capital	(172)	(214)	(268)	
Less capital investment	(1,250)	(1,562)	(1,953)	
Free cash flow to equity	932	1,165	1,456	40,040
Discount factors (14%)	0.877	0.769	0.675	0.675
Present values	817	896	983	27,027

The estimated present value of free cash flows to equity is $29,723,000

Note: Free cash flow after 20X9 is estimated by $\dfrac{1.456\,(1.1)}{0.14-0.10} = 40{,}040$

This valuation also ignores any real options that arise as a result of the acquisition.

Recommended valuation

It is impossible to produce an accurate valuation. The valuation using the dividend growth model is out of line with all others and will be ignored.

On the basis of this data, the minimum value should be the adjusted asset value, a little over $15,000,000, and the maximum approximately $30,000,000.

All of the above valuations may be criticised as they are based upon the value of Besserlot as a separate entity, not the valuation as part of Stanzial Inc. There might be synergies, such as economies of scale, savings in duplicated facilities, processes, etc, as a result of the purchase, which would increase the above estimates.

(b) The success of the purchase would depend upon enticing the existing shareholders to sell their shares. The most important shareholders are the senior managers, the venture capital company, and the single shareholder holding 25% of the shares. If any two of these types of shareholder can be persuaded to sell, Stanzial can gain control of Besserlot.

If the shareholders of a private company do not want to sell, there is little Stanzial can do. However, most shareholders will sell if the price or other conditions are attractive enough.

The venture capital company will probably have invested in Besserlot with a view to making a large capital gain, possibly if Besserlot was itself to seek a listing on a stock market. Stanzial will have to offer a sum large enough to satisfy the venture capital company relative to possible alternatives such as the listing.

Similarly, the managers and major shareholder would need to be satisfied. In the case of the managers it might also be necessary to provide some guarantee that they would continue to have managerial positions with attractive contracts within Stanzial, and the large single shareholder might insist on continued representation on the Board of Directors.

The nature of payment might also be important. The managers and single investor could be liable to immediate capital gains tax if payment was to be made in cash. They might have a preference for shares in Stanzial. The venture capital company might prefer cash rather than maintain an equity stake in a different company.

(c) Factors that might influence the medium-term success of the acquisition include:

(i) The thoroughness of the planning of the acquisition. This would include establishing key reporting relationships and control of key factors.

(ii) Corporate objectives and plans should be harmonised. Effective integration will require mutual respect for the different cultures and systems of the two companies.

(iii) Human resource issues are important, such as how any redundancies are dealt with, and the role of the managers of the acquired company in the new organisation.

(iv) Effective post-acquisition audit. Monitoring of whether or not the post-acquisition performance is as expected, and implementation of any necessary action to remedy problems and under-performance.

(v) The reaction of competitors; in particular, can they produce alternative wireless links that would adversely affect Stanzial's market share?

(vi) Maintenance of the pension rights of existing employees post-acquisition.

(d) There are several advantages that are common to both a sell-off and a demerger. Both offer a way to restructure a company. Restructuring may be to dismantle a conglomerate enterprise in order to focus upon a core competence, to react to a change in the strategic focus of the company, or to sell off unwanted assets.

Both forms of restructuring may result in 'reverse synergy', where the separated elements of the business are worth more than the value of the old combined business.

The main difference between a sell-off and a demerger is that the sell-off involves the sale of part of the company to a third party, for cash or some other consideration. Thus control of these assets is lost. However, funds are raised which can be used to develop other parts of the business, or to make acquisitions.

A demerger need not involve a change in ownership. One or more new companies are created and the assets of the old company are transferred to these new companies.

The key question for Stanzial is whether or not it wishes to maintain control of all of its assets. If it does then a demerger is a more appropriate form of restructuring than a sell-off.

10 BURCOLENE (DEC 07 ADAPTED) *Walk in the footsteps of a top tutor*

Walkthrough question – key answer tips

Very quickly at the start of the exam, you should aim to identify which part of the syllabus is being tested by each question.

This question is a 50-mark compulsory question which focuses on business valuation and a foreign investment.

Part (a) is 16 marks of calculations and Part (b) is fully written for 16 marks. In questions like this, you should be looking at Part (b) to establish to what extent it relies on the calculations in Part (a). In many questions, there are easy marks available in Part (b) even if you have struggled to make much headway with the numbers in Part (a). This is one such question – most of the marks in Part (b) are totally unrelated to the specific calculations in Part (a), so you must leave plenty of time to attempt Part (b).

Note also that part (c) is totally unrelated to either part (a) or part (b). This means that you can start this question with whichever is your preferred part.

Part (a) calculations:

First, you are asked to derive a weighted average cost of capital (WACC) for each business. Don't panic when you see lots of financial information quoted in the question. On the formula sheet you are given a formula for WACC which contains 4 inputs – the cost of equity and the market value of equity, and the cost of debt and the market value of debt. Write the formula down first and then pick out the relevant figures from the mass of information provided. Even if you don't manage to pick out all the figures correctly, you will score method marks for your approach.

Next, you are asked to estimate the value of each of the businesses. Typically, you are not told which business valuation method to use, but you must pick up on the clues scattered around in the question. For example, in this question you are not given any P/E ratio information so don't start trying to present a P/E based valuation. However, you are asked to compute a WACC, and then to comment on the Free Cash Flow method in Part (b), so you should try to use the WACC to discount Free Cash Flows here.

You are asked to take account of the impact of the share option scheme and pension fund deficit, which may be something you've not encountered before. Don't panic when you come across requirements like this. You'll see from the model answer that these two issues only come in AFTER the standard calculations have been presented.

If you're not sure how to deal with unusual points like these, the best advice is to ignore them and make sure you get the basic marks first. This question's marking key showed that you could have scored 11 of the 16 marks before starting to worry about these two unusual issues.

> Part (b) written elements:
>
> Leave plenty of time to attempt Part (b). There are plenty of easy marks here.
>
> Present your answer neatly and professionally to ensure you pick up the 4 professional marks on offer.
>
> Use subheadings to show the examiner that you have addressed all three parts of the requirement specifically.
>
> Part (c) foreign subsidiary:
>
> The calculations in part (i) are tricky. However, even if you are not particularly mathematically gifted, a trial and error approach can be used successfully. Part (ii) is much easier though, so leave enough time to attempt it fully.

(a) The first step in the valuation is to calculate each company's weighted average cost of capital. The cost of capital is calculated post tax and using the relevant market values to calculate the market gearing ratio.

	Burcolene	*PetroFrancais*
Cost of equity (using the CAPM, 3% risk free and 4% equity risk premium)	$= 0.03 + 1.85 \times 0.04$ $= 0.104$	$= 0.03 + 0.95 \times 0.04$ $= 0.068$
Market gearing	$= 3.3/(3.3 + 9.9) = 0.25$	$5.8/(5.8 + 6.7) = 0.464$
Cost of debt	$= 0.03 + 0.016 = 0.046$	$= 0.03 + 0.03 = 0.06$
WACC	$= (0.75 \times .104) + (0.25 \times 0.046 \times 0.7) = 0.0861$	$= (0.536 \times .068) + (0.464 \times .06 \times 0.75) = 0.0573$

> **Examiner's note**
>
> There may be rounding differences.

The core valuation formula is:

$$V_0 = \frac{FCF_1}{WACC - g}$$

As free cash flow is NOPAT – net reinvestment then:

$$V_0 = \frac{FCF_1}{WACC - g} = \frac{(NOPAT - \text{net reinvestment}}{WACC - g}$$

The figures quoted are for NOPAT – reinvestment for the current year. For the two companies the value before either pension or share option scheme adjustments is therefore (in $):

$$V_B = \frac{450 \times (1.05)}{0.08606 - 0.05} = \$13.107 \text{ bn}$$

and

$$V_P = \frac{205 \times (1.04)}{0.0573 - 0.04} = \$12.303 \text{ bn}$$

However, both company values will need to be reduced by the relevant charge for the outstanding options and the pension deficit. Using the fair value approach the value of each option outstanding is given by:

Option value = intrinsic value + time value

Option value = (actual price – exercise price) + time value

Option value = 29.12 – 22.00 + 7.31 = $14.43

(the actual price is given by the total value of equity $9.9 billion/340 million = $29.12 per share)

The number of options likely to be exercised:

options = 25.4m × (1 –0.05)^3 × 0.8 = 17.42 million

Which gives a value of options outstanding = $251.4m

And an estimated market valuation of Burcolene of:

V_B = $13.107 bn – $251.35m = $12.855 bn

The value of PetroFrancais is much more straightforward being:

V_P = $12.303 bn – $430m = $11.873 bn

(b) **Burcolene**

Report to management

Subject: Valuation and Financial Implications of an Acquisition of PetroFrancais

This is potentially a type of acquisition where both the firm's exposure to business risk and financial risk change. As a consequence the value of the combined entity will depend upon the post-acquisition values of the component cash streams: (i) the cash flow from the existing business; (ii) the cash flow from the acquired business and (iii) any synergistic cash flows less the cost of acquisition. However, estimating the value of these cash flows relies upon an estimate of the post-acquisition required rate of return – which cannot be estimated until we know the value of the component cash flows. This problem requires an iterative solution and which can be solved using a spreadsheet package.

Validity of the Free Cash Flow to Equity Model

Our estimates of the value using NOPAT as a proxy for free cash flow produces values that are reasonably close to the current market valuation of both companies. The models value Burcolene at $12.855 billion and PetroFrancais at $11.873 billion compared with current market valuations of $13.1 billion and $12.5 billion respectively. The estimation error is 1.9% and 5.3% respectively. Although minor the differences can be explained by any of the following:

- The model used may mis-specify the market valuation process. In either case NOPAT may not be a sufficiently close approximation to each firm's free cash flow.

- The underpinning models in the cost of capital calculations may not be valid. The capital asset pricing model, for examples, does not capture fully all the risk elements that are priced in competitive markets.

- The estimates of growth may be overoptimistic (both valuations are highly sensitive to variation in the implied level of growth).

- The markets may have reacted positively to rumours of an acquisition.

- The capital markets may be inefficient.

However, on the basis of this preliminary analysis, the low levels of modelling error suggest that the NOPAT based model should form the basis for valuing a combined business.

Deriving a bid price:

In preparation of an offer, a due diligence process should, as part of its brief, consider the likely growth of each cash stream within the context of the combined business and the variability associated with the future growth rates of each cash stream. This information could then be used to estimate the firm's future cash flows (i) to (iii) above using a cost of capital derived from the current required rates of return and market values. An iterative procedure can then be employed to bring the derived values into agreement with those used to estimate the firm's cost of capital. This valuation less the cost of acquisition and the firm's current debt gives the post-acquisition equity value. The maximum price that should be paid for PetroFrancais is that which leaves the equity value of Burcolene unchanged. This estimation process whilst procedurally complex does reinforce a key point with type III acquisitions that the sum of the equity valuation of both parties is not a good indication of the value of the combined business.

Providing the management of Burcolene can come to a reliable valuation of the combined business then, providing they remain within the bid-price parameters, the acquisition should increase shareholder value. Good valuation methods should capture the benefits and the consequential costs of combined operation. It is important that management recognises this point and do not double count strategic opportunities when negotiating a bid price. In this case, improving equity value for the Burcolene investors depends upon a number of factors. A simulation of the most important parameters in the valuation model: forward growth, the cost of equity, default premiums and the cost of debt should allow Burcolene to estimate the likely equity value at risk given any chosen bid price. A simulation would also provide an estimate of the probability of a loss of equity value for Burcolene's investors at the chosen bid price.

Implications for gearing and cost of capital:

Financing an acquisition of this magnitude through debt will raise the book gearing of the business although its impact upon the market gearing of the firm is less easy to predict. Much depends on the magnitude of any surplus shareholder value generated by the combination and how it is distributed. An acquisition such as this will increase market gearing if the benefits accrue to the target shareholders. The reverse may occur if the bulk of the acquisition value accrues to the Burcolene investors. Similarly the impact upon the firm's overall cost of capital, the impact of the tax shield and the exposure to default risk again all depend upon the agreed bid price and the distribution of acquisition value between the two groups of investors.

(c) **(i)** The presumption in this question is that if dividend payments out of the country are blocked for three years, the peso income will be invested locally to earn interest, and at the end of the three years, the pesos plus interest will be converted into $ at the spot rate and remitted to Europe.

If there are no blocked funds, the present value in $ expected from dividend remittances is:

Year	1	2	3
Peso remittance (million pesos)	180	180	180
Exchange rate	22/$1	24.2/$1	26.62/$1
$ million	8.182	7.438	6.762
Discount factors (at 20%)	0.833	694	0.579
Present values ($ million)	6.816	5.162	3.915

Total present value is $15.893 million.

If the investment is no longer to be financially viable, the NPV of the investment would have to fall by at least $2 million (its expected NPV), or the present value of cash flows from remittances would have to fall to less than $13.893 million.

If dividend remittances are blocked, and peso income is invested at x%, the cash flows will be as follows.

Year	Income	Interest rate	Income plus interest, end of Year 3
	million pesos		million pesos
1	180	×	$180(1+x)^2$
2	180	×	$180(1+x)$
3	180	×	180

The interest rate that will yield at least $13.893 million may be estimated by solving for x, where × is the interest rate in decimal format:

$$\frac{0.579(180(1+x)^2 + 180(1+x) + 180)}{26.62} = \$13.893 \text{ million}$$

This may be solved using mathematical formulae, but can be estimated by trial and error.

If x = 0.15

$$\frac{0.579(180(1.15)^2 + 180(1.15) + 180)}{26.62} = \$13.595 \text{ million}$$

15% is too low

If x = 0.18

$$\frac{0.579(180(1.18)^2 + 180(1.18) + 180)}{26.62} = \$13.986 \text{ million}$$

At an 18% interest rate the investment will just remain financially viable.

(ii)   Blocked remittances might be avoided by means of:

(i)   Increasing transfer prices paid by the foreign subsidiary to the parent company.

(ii)   Lending the equivalent of the dividend to the parent company.

(iii)   Making payments to the parent company in the form of royalties, payment for patents, or management fees.

(iv)   Charging the subsidiary additional head office overhead.

(v)   Parallel loans, whereby the subsidiary of Burcolene in the South American country lends cash to the subsidiary of another company requiring funds in the South American country. In return Burcolene would receive the loan of an equivalent amount of cash in Europe from the other subsidiary's parent company.

The government of the South American country might try to prevent many of these measures being used.

11   PURSUIT CO (JUN 11 ADAPTED)

Key answer tips

Business valuation, especially using free cash flows, is very commonly tested. Lay out your forecast free cash flows neatly, and leave time to also attempt all the discussion parts of the question.

(a)   Organic growth permits an organisation to carefully plan its strategic growth in line with specified objectives.

However, when entering new markets there may be a substantial cost involved with researching markets and/or buying-in expertise.

Lead-times in establishing production facilities are relatively long in comparison with growth by acquisition, which may be a significant factor when trying to establish or to consolidate market share.

Growth by acquisition is often not as carefully planned, and may be a rapid reaction to a perceived market opportunity.

It permits quick access to new markets or new technology, or the elimination of a competitor.

Information about the financial and other attributes of a potential acquisition target is inevitably less complete than a company's own internal management information.

This makes the valuation of a potential acquisition target difficult, and projections of future cash flows less precise.

The potential for significant savings is often not fully known until after the acquisition, when attempts are made to rationalise and integrate the operations of the two companies.

Growth by acquisition may be the only way to achieve very rapid growth.

(b)   The Euromarkets can be used for very large borrowings, but if a company wants to borrow a large amount of money from domestic banks it might find that some banks are unwilling or unable to offer such large loans. Syndication might have to be used to spread the risk between several banks.

Domestic banking systems are normally subject to more regulation and reserve requirements than the Euromarkets, leading to wider spreads between borrowing and lending rates.

The cost of borrowing on domestic markets is often slightly more expensive than the Euromarkets, and may involve fixed or floating charges on corporate assets as security for loans.

Few Euromarket loans require security. Domestic market loans may be either fixed or floating rate, but bank loans are more likely to be at a floating rate.

An argument in favour of using the domestic banking system is that banks are specialists in analysing and monitoring debts. If large loans are agreed by banks this is a sign of good credit standing, and may facilitate access to cheaper funds on other capital markets.

(c) **REPORT**

Prepared by AN Accountant

(i) The calculations and estimations for part (i) are given in the appendix. To assess whether or not the acquisition would be beneficial to Pursuit's shareholders, the additional synergy benefits after the acquisition has been paid for need to be ascertained.

The estimated synergy benefit from the acquisition is approximately $9,074,000 (see Appendix), which is the post-acquisition value of the combined company less the values of the individual companies. However, once Fodder Co's debt obligations and the equity shareholders have been paid, the benefit to Pursuit Co's shareholders reduces to approximately $52,000 (see Appendix), which is minimal. Even a small change in the variables and assumptions could negate it. It is therefore doubtful that the shareholders would view the acquisition as beneficial to themselves or the company.

(ii) The limitations of the estimates stem from the fact that although the model used is theoretically sound, it is difficult to apply it in practice for the following reasons.

The calculations in part (i) are based on a number of assumptions such as the growth rate in the next four years, the perpetual growth rate after the four years, additional investment in assets, stable tax rates, discount rates and profit margins, assumption that debt is risk free when computing the asset beta. All these assumptions would be subject to varying margins of error.

It may be difficult for Pursuit Co to assess the variables of the combined company to any degree of accuracy, and therefore the synergy benefits may be hard to predict.

No information is provided about the pre-acquisition and post-acquisition costs.

Although it may be possible to estimate the equity beta of Pursuit Co, being a listed company, to a high level of accuracy, estimating Fodder Co's equity beta may be more problematic, because it is a private company.

Given the above, it is probably more accurate to present a range of possible values for the combined company depending on different scenarios and the likelihood of their occurrence, before a decision is made.

(iii) The current value of Pursuit Co is $140,000,000, of which the market value of equity and debt are $70,000,000 each. The value of the combined company before paying Fodder Co shareholders is approximately $189,169,000, and if the capital structure is maintained, the market values of debt and equity will be approximately $94,584,500 each. This is an increase of approximately $24,584,500 in the debt capacity.

The amount payable for Fodder Co's debt obligations and to the shareholders including the premium is approximately $49,116,500 [4,009 + 36,086 × 1.25]. If $24,584,500 is paid using the extra debt capacity and $20,000,000 using cash reserves, an additional amount of approximately $4,532,000 will need to be raised. Hence, if only debt finance and cash reserves are used, the capital structure cannot be maintained.

(iv) If Pursuit Co aims to acquire Fodder Co using debt finance and cash reserves, then the capital structure of the combined company will change. It will also change if they adopt the Chief Financial Officer's recommendation and acquire Fodder Co using only debt finance.

Both these options will cause the cost of capital of the combined company to change. This in turn will cause the value of the company to change. This will cause the proportion of market value of equity to market value of debt to change, and thus change the cost of capital. Therefore the changes in the market value of the company and the cost of capital are interrelated.

To resolve this problem, an iterative procedure needs to be adopted where the beta and the cost of capital are recalculated to take account of the changes in the capital structure, and then the company is re-valued. This procedure is repeated until the assumed capital structure is closely aligned to the capital structure that has been re-calculated. This process is normally done using a spreadsheet package such as Excel. This method is used when both the business risk and the financial risk of the acquiring company change as a result of an acquisition (referred to as a type III acquisition).

Alternatively an adjusted present value approach may be undertaken.

(v) The Chief Financial Officer's suggestion appears to be a disposal of 'crown jewels'. Without the cash reserves, Pursuit Co may become less valuable to SGF Co. Also, the reason for the depressed share price may be because Pursuit Co's shareholders do not agree with the policy to retain large cash reserves. Therefore returning the cash reserves to the shareholders may lead to an increase in the share price and make a bid from SGF Co more unlikely. This would not initially contravene the regulatory framework as no formal bid has been made. However, Pursuit Co must investigate further whether the reason for a possible bid from SGF Co might be to gain access to the large amount of cash or it might have other reasons. Pursuit Co should also try to establish whether remitting the cash to the shareholders would be viewed positively by them.

Whether this is a viable option for Pursuit Co depends on the bid for Fodder Co. In part (iii) it was established that more than the expected debt finance would be needed even if the cash reserves are used to pay for some of the acquisition cost. If the cash is remitted, a further $20,000,000 would be needed, and if this was all raised by debt finance then a significant proportion of the value of the combined company would be debt financed. The increased gearing may have significant implications on Pursuit Co's future investment plans and may result in increased restrictive covenants. Ultimately gearing might have to increase to such a level that this method of financing might not be possible. Pursuit Co should investigate the full implications further and assess whether the acquisition is worthwhile given the marginal value it provides for the shareholders (see part (i)).

Tutorial note

Up to 4 professional marks are available for the presentation of the answer, which should be in a report style.

APPENDIX

Part (i)

Interest is ignored as its impact is included in the companies' discount rates

Fodder cost of capital

K_e = 4.5% + 1.53 × 6% = 13.68%

Cost of capital = 13.68% × 0.9 + 9% × (1 − 0.28) × 0.1 = 12.96% assume 13%

Fodder

Sales revenue growth rate = (16,146/13,559)1/3 − 1 × 100% = 5.99% assume 6%
Operating profit margin = approx. 32% of sales revenue

Fodder Co cash flow and value computation ($000)

Year	1	2	3	4
Sales revenue	17,115	18,142	19,231	20,385
Operating profit	5,477	5,805	6,154	6,523
Less tax (28%)	(1,534)	(1,625)	(1,723)	(1,826)
Less additional investment (22c/$1 of sales revenue increase)	(213)	(226)	(240)	(254)
Free cash flows	3,730	3,954	4,191	4,443
PV (13%)	3,301	3,097	2,905	2,725

	$(000)
PV (first 4 years)	12,028
PV (after 4 years) [4,443 × 1.03/(0.13 − 0.03)] × 1.13^{-4}	28,067
Firm value	40,095

Combined Company: Cost of capital calculation

Asset beta (Pursuit Co) = 1.18 × 0.5/(0.5 + 0.5 × 0.72) = 0.686

Asset beta (Fodder Co) = 1.53 × 0.9/(0.9 + 0.1 × 0.72) = 1.417

Asset beta of combined co. = (0.686 × 140,000 + 1.417 × 40,095)/(140,000 + 40,095) = 0.849

Equity beta of combined company = 0.849 × (0.5 + 0.5 × 0.72)/0.5 = 1.46

K_e = 4.5% + 1.46 × 6% = 13.26%

Cost of capital = 13.26% × 0.5 + 6.4% × 0.5 × 0.72 = 8.93%, assume 9%

Combined Co cash flow and value computation ($000)

Sales revenue growth rate = 5.8%, operating profit margin = 30% of sales revenue

Year	1	2	3	4
Sales revenue	51,952	54,965	58,153	61,526
Operating profit	15,586	16,490	17,446	18,458
Less tax (28%)	(4,364)	(4,617)	(4,885)	(5,168)
Less additional investment (18c/$1 of sales revenue increase)	(513)	(542)	(574)	(607)
Free cash flows	10,709	11,331	11,987	12,683
PV (9%)	9,825	9,537	9,256	8,985

	$(000)
PV (first 4 years)	37,603
PV (after 4 years) [12,683 × 1.029/(0.09 – 0.029)] × 1.09^{-4}	151,566
Firm value	189,169

Synergy benefits = 189,169,000 – (140,000,000 + 40,095,000) = $9,074,000

Estimated premium required to acquire Fodder Co = 0.25 × 36,086,000 = $9,022,000

Net benefit to Pursuit Co shareholders = $52,000

12 NENTE CO (JUN 12 ADAPTED)

Key answer tips

Always make sure that you use a report format in the Section A question. Presenting your answer professionally will enable you to score 4 'professional marks' – the easiest marks on the whole paper.

(a) Synergy might exist for several reasons, including:

Economic efficiency gains

Gains might relate to economies of scale or scope.

Economies of scale occur through such factors as fixed operating costs being spread over a larger production volume, equipment being used more efficiently with higher volumes of production, or bulk purchasing reducing costs.

Economies of scope may arise from reduced advertising and distribution costs when companies have complementary resources. Economies of scale and scope relate mainly to horizontal acquisitions and mergers. Economic efficiency gains may also occur with backward or forward vertical integration which might reduce production costs as the 'middle man' is eliminated, improve control of essential raw materials or other resources that are needed for production, or avoid disputes with what were previously suppliers or customers.

Economic efficiency gains might also result from replacing inefficient management as the result of a merger/takeover.

Financial synergy

Financial synergy might involve a reduction in the cost of capital and risk.

The variability (standard deviation) of returns of a combined entity is usually less than the weighted average of the risk of the individual companies. This is a reduction in total risk, but does not affect systematic risk, and hence might not be regarded as a form of synergy by shareholders. However, reduced variability of returns might improve a company's credit rating making it easier and/or cheaper to obtain a loan.

Another possible financial synergy exists when one company in an acquisition or merger is able to use tax shields, or accumulated tax losses, which would otherwise have been unavailable to the other company.

Market power

A large organisation, particularly one which has acquired competitors, might have sufficient market power to increase its profits through price leadership or other monopolistic or oligopolistic means.

(b)   REPORT TO THE BOARD OF DIRECTORS, NENTE CO

IMPACT OF THE TAKEOVER PROPOSAL FROM MIJE CO AND PRODUCTION RIGHTS OF THE FOLLOW-ON PRODUCT

The report considers the value of the takeover to Nente Co and Mije Co shareholders based on a cash offer and on a share-for-share offer. It discusses the possible reaction of each group of shareholders to the two offers and how best to utilise the follow-on product opportunity. The significant assumptions made in compiling the report are also explained.

The appendices to the report show the detailed calculations in estimating the equity value of Nente Co, the value to Nente Co and Mije Co shareholders of acquiring Nente Co by cash and by a share-for-share exchange, and the value to Nente Co of the exclusive rights to the follow-on product. The results of the calculation are summarised below:

Estimated price of a Nente Co share before the takeover offer and follow-on product is £2.90/share (Appendix i)

Estimated increase in share price	*Nente Co*	*Mije Co*
Cash offer (Appendix ii)	1.7%	9.4%
Share-for-share offer (Appendix ii)	17.9%	6.9%

Estimate of the value per share of the follow-on product to Nente Co is 8.7% (Appendix iii)

It is unlikely that Nente Co shareholders would accept the cash offer because it is little more than the estimated price of a Nente Co share before the takeover offer. However, the share-for-share offer gives a larger increase in value of a share of 17.9%. Given that the normal premium on acquisitions ranges from 20% to 40%, this is closer to what Nente Co shareholders would find acceptable. It is also greater than the additional value from the follow-on product. Therefore, based on the financial figures, Nente Co's shareholders would find the offer of a takeover on a share-for-share exchange basis the most attractive option. The other options considered here yield lower expected percentage increase in share price.

Mije Co shareholders would prefer the cash offer so that they can maximise the price of their shares and also not dilute their shareholding, but they would probably accept either option because the price of their shares increases. However, Mije Co shareholders would probably assess whether or not to accept the acquisition proposal by comparing it with other opportunities that the company has available to it and whether this is the best way to utilise its spare cash flows.

The calculations and analysis in each case is made on a number of assumptions. For example, in order to calculate the estimated price of a Nente Co share, the free cash flow valuation model is used. For this, the growth rate, the cost of capital and effective time period when the growth rate will occur (perpetuity in this instance) are all estimates or based on assumptions. For the takeover offer, the synergy savings and P/E ratio value are both assumptions. For the value of the follow-on product and the related option, the option variables are estimates and it is assumed that they would not change during the period before the decision. The value of the option is based on the possibility that the option will only be exercised at the end of the two years, although it seems that the decision can be made any time within the two years.

The follow-on product is initially treated separately from the takeover, but Nente Co may ask Mije Co to take the value of the follow-on product into consideration in its offer. The value of the rights that allow Nente Co to delay making a decision are themselves worth $603,592 (Appendix iii) and add just over 25c or 8.7% to the value of a Nente Co share. If Mije Co can be convinced to increase their offer to match this or the rights could be sold before the takeover, then the return for Nente Co's shareholders would be much higher at 26.6% (17.9% + 8.7%).

In conclusion, the most favourable outcome for Nente Co shareholders would be to accept the share-for-share offer, and try to convince Mije Co to take the value of the follow-on product into consideration. Prior to accepting the offer Nente Co shareholders would need to be assured of the accuracy of the results produced by the computations in the appendices.

Report compiled by: XXX

Date: XXX

(Note: Credit will be given for alternative relevant discussion and suggestions)

APPENDICES

Appendix i: Estimate of Nente Co Equity Value Based on Free Cash Flows

Company value = Free cash flows (FCF) × (1 + growth rate (g))/(cost of capital (k) – g)

k = 11%

Past g = (latest profit before interest and tax (PBIT)/earliest PBIT)$^{1/\text{no. of years of growth}}$ – 1

Past g = $(1,230/970)^{1/3}$ – 1 = 0.0824

Future g = ¼ × 0.0824 = 0.0206

FCF Calculation

FCF = PBIT + non-cash flows – cash investment – tax

FCF = $1,230,000 + $1,206,000 – $1,010,000 – ($1,230,000 × 20%) = $1,180,000

Company value = $1,180,000 × 1.0206/(0.11 – 0.0206) = $13,471,000

Equity value = $13,471,000 – $6,500,000 = $6,971,000

Per share = $6,971,000/2,400,000 shares = $2.90

Appendix ii: Estimated Returns to Nente Co and Mije Co Shareholders

Cash Offer

Gain in value to a Nente Co share = ($2.95 – $2.90)/$2.90 = 1.7%

Additional earnings after acquisition = $620,000 + $150,000 = $770,000

Additional EPS created from acquisition = $770,000/10,000,000 = 7.7c/share

Increase in share price based on P/E of 15 = 7.7c × 15 = $1.16

Additional value created = $1.16 × 10,000,000 =	$11,600,000
Less: paid for Nente Co acquisition = ($2.95 × 2.4m shares)	$(7,080,000)
Value added for Mije shareholders =	$4,520,000

Gain in value to a Mije Co share = $4,520,000/10,000,000	=	45.2c
or 45.2c/480c	=	9.4%

Share-for-share Offer

Earnings combined company = $620,000 + $150,000 + $3,200,000 = $3,970,000

Shares in combined company = 10,000,000 + 2,400,000 × 2/3 = 11,600,000

EPS = 34.2c/share [$3,970,000/11,600,000]

Expected share price = 34.2c × 15 = 513c or $5.13/share

Three Nente Co shares = $2.90 × 3 = $8.70

Gain in value to a Mije Co share = ($5.13 – $4.80)/$4.80	=	6.9%
Gain in value to a Nente Co share = ($10.26 – $8.70)/$8.70	=	17.9%

Appendix iii: Increase in Value of Follow-On Product

Present value of the positive cash flows	=	$2,434,000
Present value of the cash outflow	=	$(2,029,000)
Net present value of the new product	=	$405,000

Based on conventional NPV, without considering the value of the option to delay the decision, the project would increase the value of the company by $405,000.

Considering the value of the option to delay the decision

Price of asset (PV of future positive cash flows)	=	$2,434,000
Exercise price (initial cost of project, not discounted)	=	$2,500,000
Time to expiry of option	=	2 years
Risk free rate (estimate)	=	3.2%
Volatility	=	42%

$d_1 = [\ln(2,434/2,500) + (0.032 + 0.5 \times 0.42^2) \times 2]/(0.42 \times 2^{1/2}) = 0.359$

$d_2 = 0.359 - (0.42 \times 2^{1/2}) = -0.235$

$N(d_1) = 0.5 + (0.1368 + 0.9 \times (0.1406 - 0.1368)) = 0.6402$

$N(d_2) = 0.5 - (0.0910 + 0.5 \times (0.0948 - 0.0910)) = 0.4071$

Value of option to delay the decision

$= 2,434,000 \times 0.6402 - 2,500,000 \times 0.4071 \times e^{-(0.032 \times 2)}$

$= \$1,558,247 - \$954,655 = \$603,592$

The project increases the value of the company by $603,592 or 25.1c per share ($603,592/2,400,000 shares). In percentage terms this is an increase of about 8.7% (25.1c/290c).

(c) Using the BSOP model in company valuation rests upon the idea that equity is a call option, written by the lenders, on the underlying assets of the business. If the value of the company declines substantially then the shareholders can simply walk away, losing the maximum of their investment. On the other hand, the upside potential is unlimited once the interest on debt has been paid.

The BSOP model can be helpful in circumstances where the conventional methods of valuation do not reflect the risks fully or where they cannot be used. For example if we are trying to value an unlisted company with unpredictable future growth.

There are five variables which are input into the BSOP model to determine the value of the option. Proxies need to be established for each variable when using the BSOP model to value a company. The five variables are: the value of the underlying asset, the exercise price, the time to expiry, the volatility of the underlying asset value and the risk free rate of return.

For the exercise price, the debt of the company is taken. In its simplest form, the assumption is that the borrowing is in the form of zero coupon debt, i.e., a discount bond. In practice such debt is not used as a primary source of company finance and so we calculate the value of an equivalent bond with the same yield and term to maturity as the company's existing debt. The exercise price in valuing the business as a call option is the value of the outstanding debt calculated as the present value of a zero coupon bond offering the same yield as the current debt.

The proxy for the value of the underlying asset is the fair value of the company's assets less current liabilities on the basis that if the company is broken up and sold, then that is what the assets would be worth to the long-term debt holders and the equity holders.

The time to expiry is the period of time before the debt is due for redemption. The owners of the company have that time before the option needs to be exercised, that is when the debt holders need to be repaid.

The proxy for the volatility of the underlying asset is the volatility of the business' assets.

The risk-free rate is usually the rate on a riskless investment such as a short-term government bond.

13 MLIMA CO (JUN 13)

Key answer tips

Notice that part (b) of this question is totally independent of part (a). Feel free to attempt part (b) first if you feel that it is easier than part (a).

(a) **Report to the Board of Directors, Mlima Co Initial public listing: price range and implications**

This report considers a range of values of Mlima Co and possible share price, based on 100 million issued shares in preparation of the initial public listing. The assumptions made in determining the value range and the likelihood of the unsecured bond holders accepting the 10% equity-for-debt swap offer are discussed. Alternative reasons for the listing and reasons for issuing the share at a discount are evaluated.

Mlima Co cost of capital explanation

Ziwa Co's ungeared cost of equity represents the return Ziwa Co's shareholders would require if Ziwa Co was financed entirely by equity and had no debt. The return would compensate them for the business risk undertaken by the company.

This required rate of return would compensate Mlima Co's shareholders as well because, since both companies are in the same industry, they face the same business risk. This rate is then used as Mlima Co's cost of capital because of the assumption that Mlima Co will not issue any debt and faces no financial risk. Therefore its cost of equity (ungeared) is its cost of capital.

Mlima Co Estimated Value

Based on a cost of capital of 11% (Appendix 1), the value of Mlima Co is estimated at $564.3m (Appendix 2), prior to considering the impact of the Bahari project. The value of the Bahari project, without taking into account the benefits of the tax shield and the subsidies, does not exceed the initial investment. With the benefits of the tax shield and subsidies, it is estimated that the project will generate a positive net present value of $21.5m (Appendix 3). Taking the Bahari project into account gives a value for Mlima Co at just under $586m.

Possible share price (100m shares)	Without the Bahari project	With the Bahari project
At full value	$5.64/share	$5.86/share
With 20% discount	$4.51/share	$4.69/share

Unsecured bond holders (equity-for-debt swap)

The current value of the unsecured bond is estimated at $56.8m (Appendix 4) and if the unsecured bond holders are to be offered a 10% equity stake in Mlima Co post-listing, then only the share price at $5.86 would be acceptable to them. If the listing is made at the lowest price of $4.51/share, then they would need to be offered around a 12.6% equity stake ($56.8m/$4.51 = 12.594m).

The value of the bond is based on a flat yield curve (or yield to maturity) of 7%, which is the rate at which Mlima Co can borrow funds and therefore its current yield. A more accurate method would be to assess the yield curve based on future risk-free rates and credit spreads for the company.

Assumptions

The main assumptions made are around the accuracy of the information used in estimating the values of the company and the project. For example, the value of the company is based on assumptions of future growth rates, profit margins, future tax rates and capital investment. The basis for estimating the future growth rates and profit margins on past performance may not be accurate. With the Bahari project, for example, projections of future cash flows are made for 15 years and the variability of these has been estimated. Again, the reasonableness of these estimates needs to be assessed. Are they, for example, based on past experience and/or have professional experts judged the values?

The cost of capital is estimated based on a competitor's ungeared cost of equity, on the basis that Mlima Co is in a similar line of business and therefore faces similar business risk. The financial risk element has been removed since it has been stated that Mlima Co is not looking to raise extra debt finance. However, it is possible that the business risks faced by Mlima Co and that faced by Ziwa Co, the competitor, are not the same. Accepting the Bahari project would also change the risk profile of Mlima Co and therefore its discount rate.

The values are based on the Bahari government fulfilling the subsidised loan concession it has offered. Mlima Co needs to consider the likelihood of this concession continuing for the entire 15 years and whether a change of government may jeopardise the agreement. The political and other risks need to be assessed and their impact assessed.

It has been assumed that the underwriting and other costs involved with the new listing are not significant or have been catered for, before the assessment of the cash flows. This assumption needs to be reviewed and its accuracy assessed.

Reasons for the public listing

The main reason given for the public listing is to use the funds raised to eliminate the debt in the company. There are other reasons why a company may undertake a public listing. These include: gaining a higher reputation by being listed on a recognised stock exchange and therefore reducing the costs of contracting with stakeholders; being able to raise funds more easily in the future to undertake new projects; the listing will provide the current owners with a value for their equity stake; and the listing may enable the current owners to sell their equity stakes and gain from the value in the organisation.

Issuing shares at a discount

Issuing only 20% of the share capital to the public at the initial listing would make them minority shareholders effectively. As such, their ability to influence the decision-making process in the company would be severely curtailed, since even if all the new investors voted as a bloc against a decision, they would not be able to overturn it. The discounted share price would reflect the additional risk of investing in a company as a minority shareholder. In this case, the position of the unsecured bond holders is important. If the unsecured bond holders, holding between 10% and 12.6% of the share capital in an equity-for-debt swap, are included with the new investors, then the equity stake rises to 30%–32.6%. In such a case, shareholders, as a bloc, would have a significant influence on the company's decisions. The question that should be asked is whether the current unsecured bond holders are more closely aligned to the interests of the current owners or to the interests of the new investors.

The second reason for issuing shares at a discount is to ensure that they do all get sold and as a reward for the underwriters. Research suggests that, normally, for new listings, shares are issued at a discount and the price of such shares rises immediately after launch.

Conclusion

The report and the calculations in the appendices suggest a price range for the listing of between $4.51 and $5.86 per share, depending on whether or not the Bahari project is undertaken, the discount at which the shares are issued and the assumptions made. It is recommended that Mlima Co should consult its underwriters and potential investors about the possible price they would be willing to pay before making a final decision (known as book-building).

If 20 million shares are offered to the public for $4.51 each, this will result in total funds raised of just over $90 million. If the $80 million are spent in paying for the secured bond, just over $10 million liquid funds remain. Therefore, Mlima Co needs to consider whether issuing the shares at a discount would ensure sufficient liquid funds are available for it to continue its normal business. In addition to this, the Bahari investment may result in a change in the desired capital structure of the company and have an impact on the cost of capital. Finally, being listed will result in additional listing costs and annual costs related to additional reporting requirements.

These factors should be balanced against the benefits of undertaking the new listing before a final decision is made.

Report compiled by: XXX

Date: XXX

APPENDICES

Appendix 1: Mlima Co, cost of capital

Ziwa Co

MV debt = $1,700m × 1.05 = $1,785m MV equity = 200m × $7 = $1,400m

Ziwa Co, ungeared Ke

$Ke_g = Ke_u + (1 - t)(Ke_u - K_d) D/E$

$16.83\% = Ke_u + 0.75 \times (Ke_u - 4.76\%) \times 1,785/1,400$

$16.83\% + 4.55\% = 1.9563 \times Ke_u$

$Ke_u = 10.93\%$ (say 11%)

Appendix 2: Mlima Co, estimate of value prior to Bahari project

Value based on future free cash flows

Historic mean sales revenue growth = $(389.1/344.7)^{1/2} - 1 = 0.625$ or 6.25%

Next four years annual growth rate of sales revenue = 120% of 6.25% = 7.5%

Thereafter 3.5% of cash flows per annum

Operating profit margin (approx) = 58.4/389.1 = 54.9/366.3 = 51.7/344.7 = 15%

Year (in $ millions)	1	2	3	4
Sales revenue	418.3	449.7	483.4	519.7
Operating profit	62.7	67.5	72.5	78.0
Less taxation (25%)	(15.7)	(16.9)	(18.1)	(19.5)
Less additional capital investment (30c per $1 change in sales revenue)	(8.8)	(9.4)	(10.1)	(10.9)
Free cash flows	38.2	41.2	44.3	47.6
PV of free cash flows (11%)	34.4	33.4	32.4	31.4

PV first four years	$131.6m
PV after four years $(47.6 \times 1.035)/(0.11 - 0.035) \times 1.11^{-4}$	$432.7m
Value of company	$564.3m

Appendix 3: Value of the Bahari project Base case present value

Year	Free Cash flows (in $ millions)	PV (11%) (in $ millions)
1	4.0	3.6
2	8.0	6.5
3	16.0	11.7
4	18.4	12.1
5	21.2	12.6
6 to 15	21.2	**74.0
Total		120.5

** The free cash flows in years 6 to 15 are an annuity for 10 years at 11%, then discounted back for five years: 21.2 × 5.889 × 0.593 = 74.0

PV of the tax shield and subsidy

Annuity factor (7%, 15 years) = 9.108

Annual tax shield benefit interest paid = 3% × $150m × 25% = $1.1m Subsidy benefit = 4% × $150m × (1 − 25%) = $4.5m PV of tax shield and subsidy benefit = 5.6 × 9.108 = $51.0m

Adjusted present value = $120.5m + $51.0m − $150.0m = $21.5m

Appendix 4: Estimated value of the unsecured bond

Assume a flat yield or yield to maturity of 7%

Annual coupon interest = $5.2m (13% × $40m)

10-year annuity at 7% = 7.024; Discount factor (10 years, 7%) = 0.508

Bond value = $5.2m × 7.024 + $40m × 0.508 = $56.8m

(b) It is likely that Mlima Co's actions will be scrutinised more closely in the run up to the listing and once it has been listed. In both the situations, the company should consider the action it should take based on its ethical and accountability code. Most major corporations now publicise such codes of behaviour and would consult these in cases of ethical and/or accountability difficulties.

With the first situation concerning the relocation of the farmers, Mlima Co would consult its ethical code to judge how far its responsibility lay. It may take the view that the matter is between the farmers and the government, and it is not directly or indirectly responsible for the situation. In any case, it is likely that the mining rights will be assigned to another company, should Mlima Co decide to walk away from the deal. It is unlikely that, even if Mlima Co did not agree to the offer, the plight of the farmers would cease.

Instead, Mlima Co may decide to try to influence the government with respect to the farmers by urging the government to keep the community together and offer the farmers better land. Mlima Co may also decide to offer jobs and training to farmers who decide not to leave.

With the second situation concerning the Bahari president and Mlima Co's CEO, whilst it would make good business sense to forge strong relationships as a means of competitive advantage, Mlima Co should ensure that the negotiation was transparent and did not involve any bribery or illegal practice. If both the company and Bahari government can demonstrate that they acted in the best interests of the company and the country respectively, and individuals did not benefit as a result, then this should not be seen in a negative light.

Mlima Co needs to establish a clear strategy of how it would respond to public scrutiny of either issue. This may include actions such as demonstrating that it is acting according to its ethical code, pre-empting media scrutiny by releasing press statements, and using its influence to ensure the best and correct outcome in each case for the stakeholders concerned.

Tutorial note (from the examiner's model answer)

Credit will be given for alternative, relevant approaches to the calculations, comments and suggestions/recommendations.

Marking scheme

			Marks
(a)	(i)	Explanation of Mlima Co's cost of capital based on Ziwa Co's ungeared cost of equity	3
		Ziwa Co, cost of ungeared equity	4
		Maximum	**7**
	(ii)	Sales revenue growth rates	1
		Operating profit rate	1
		Estimate of free cash flows and PV of free cash flows for years 1 to 4	4
		PV of free cash flows after year 4	2
		Base case Bahari project value	2
		Annual tax shield benefit	1
		Annual subsidy benefit	1
		PV of the tax shield and subsidy benefits	1
		Value of the Bahari project	1
		Maximum	**14**
	(iii)	Calculation of unsecured bond value	2
		Comment	2
		Limitation	1
		Maximum	**5**
	(iv)	Comments on the range of values/prices with and without the project, and concluding statement	4–5
		Discussion of assumptions	3–4
		Explanation for additional reasons for listing	2–3
		Assessment of reasons for discounted share price	2–3
		Maximum	**12**
		Professional marks	
		Report format	1
		Structure and presentation of the report	3
		Maximum	**4**
(b)		Discussion of relocation of farmers	4–5
		Discussion of relationship between Bahari president and Mlima Co CEO	4–5
		Maximum	**8**
Total			**50**

14   NAHARA CO AND FUGAE CO (DEC 14)

Online question assistance

Key answer tips

All the Section A questions are very time pressured, with lots of parts to complete in the time.

It is therefore critically important to attempt the easier parts of the question first and leave the more difficult parts until the end.

(a)   Risk diversification, especially into diverse business sectors, has often been stated as a reason for undertaking mergers and acquisitions (M&As). Like individuals holding well-diversified portfolios, a company with a number of subsidiaries in different sectors could reduce its exposure to unsystematic risk. Another possible benefit of diversification is sometimes argued to be a reduction in the volatility of cash flows, which may lead to a better credit rating and a lower cost of capital.

The argument against this states that since individual investors can undertake this level of risk diversification both quickly and cheaply themselves, there is little reason for companies to do so. Indeed, research suggests that markets do not reward this risk diversification.

Nevertheless, for Nahara Co, undertaking M&As may have beneficial outcomes, especially if the sovereign fund has its entire investment in the holding company and is not well-diversified itself. In such a situation unsystematic risk reduction can be beneficial. The case study does not state whether or not the sovereign funds are invested elsewhere and therefore a definitive conclusion cannot be reached.

If Nahara Co is able to identify undervalued companies and after purchasing the company can increase the value for the holding company overall, by increasing the value of the undervalued companies, then such M&As activity would have a beneficial impact on the funds invested. However, for this strategy to work, Nahara Co must:

(i)   Possess a superior capability or knowledge in identifying bargain buys ahead of its competitor companies. To achieve this, it must have access to better information, which it can tap into quicker, and/or have superior analytical tools. Nahara Co should assess whether or not it does possess such capabilities, otherwise its claim is not valid.

(ii)   Ensure that it has quick access to the necessary funds to pursue an undervalued acquisition. Even if Nahara Co possesses superior knowledge, it is unlikely that this will last for a long time before its competitors find out; therefore it needs to have the funds ready, to move quickly. Given that it has access to sovereign funds from a wealthy source, access to funds is probably not a problem.

(iii)   Set a maximum ceiling for the price it is willing to pay and should not go over this amount, or the potential value created will be reduced.

If, in its assessment, Nahara Co is able to show that it meets all the above conditions, then the strategy of identifying and pursuing undervalued companies may be valid.

(b) In a similar manner to the Competition and Markets Authority in the UK, the European Union (EU) will assess significant mergers and acquisitions' (M&As) impact on competition within a country's market. It will, for example, use tests such as worldwide turnover and European turnover of the group after the M&A. It may block the M&A, if it feels that the M&A will give the company monopolistic powers or enable it to carve out a dominant position in the market so as to negatively affect consumer choice and prices.

Sometimes the EU may ask for the company to sell some of its assets to reduce its dominant position rather than not allow an M&A to proceed. It would appear that this may be the case behind the EU's concern and the reason for its suggested action.

(c) **Report to the Board of Directors, Avem Co**

Proposed acquisition of Fugae Co

This report evaluates whether or not it is beneficial for Avem Co to acquire Fugae Co. Initially the value of the two companies is determined separately and as a combined entity, to assess the additional value created from bringing the two companies together. Following this, the report considers how much Nahara Co and Avem Co will gain from the value created. The assumptions made to arrive at the additional value are also considered. The report concludes by considering whether or not the acquisition will be beneficial to Avem Co and to Nahara Co.

Appendix 1 shows that the additional value created from combining the two companies is approximately $451.5 million, of which $276.8 million will go to Nahara Co, as the owner of Fugae Co. This represents a premium of about 30% which is the minimum acceptable to Nahara Co. The balance of the additional value will go to Avem Co which is about $174.7 million, representing an increase in value of 1.46% [$174.7m/$12,000m].

Appendix 2 shows that accepting the project would increase Fugae Co's value as the expected net present value is positive. After taking into account Lumi Co's offer, the expected net present value is higher. Therefore, it would be beneficial for Fugae Co to take on the project and accept Lumi Co's offer, if the tourism industry does not grow as expected, as this will increase Fugae Co's value.

Assumptions

It is assumed that all the figures relating to synergy benefits, betas, growth rates, multipliers, risk adjusted cost of capital and the probabilities are accurate. There is considerable uncertainty surrounding the accuracy of these, and in addition to the probability analysis conducted in Appendix 2 and the assessments of value conducted in Appendix 1, a sensitivity analysis is probably needed to assess the impact of these uncertainties.

It is assumed that the rb model provides a reasonably good estimate of the growth rate, and that perpetuity is not an unreasonable assumption when assessing the value of Fugae Co.

It is assumed that the capital structure would not change substantially when the new project is taken on. Since the project is significantly smaller than the value of Fugae Co itself, this is not an unreasonable assumption.

When assessing the value of the project, the outcomes are given as occurring with discrete probabilities and the resulting cash flows from the outcomes are given with certainty. There may be more outcomes in practice than the ones given and financial impact of the outcomes may not be known with such certainty. The Black-Scholes

Option Pricing model may provide an alternative and more accurate way of assessing the value of the project.

It is assumed that Fugae Co can rely on Lumi Co paying the $50m at the beginning of year two with certainty. Fugae Co may want to assess the reliability of Lumi Co's offer and whether formal contracts should be drawn up between the two companies. Furthermore, Lumi Co may be reluctant to pay the full amount of money once Fugae Co becomes a part of Avem Co.

Concluding comments

Although Nahara Co would gain more than Avem Co from the acquisition both in percentage terms and in monetary terms, both companies benefit from the acquisition. If Fugae Co were to take on the project, although it is value-neutral to the acquisition, Nahara Co could ask for an additional 30% of $12.3 million value to be transferred to it, which is about $3.7 million. Hence the return to Avem Co would reduce by a small amount, but not significantly.

As long as all the parties are satisfied that the value is reasonable despite the assumptions highlighted above, it would appear that the acquisition should proceed.

Report compiled by: AN Accountant

Date: XX/XX/XXXX

APPENDICES

Appendix 1: Additional value created from combining Avem Co and Fugae Co

Avem Co, current value = $7.5/share × 1,600 million shares = $12,000m

Avem Co, free cash flow to equity = $12,000 million/7.2 = $1,666.7m

The growth rate is calculated on the basis of the rb model.

Fugae Co, estimate of growth rate = 0.227 × 0.11 = 0.025 = 2.5%

Fugae Co, current value estimate = $76.5 million × 1.025/(0.11 − 0.025) = $922.5m

Combined company, estimated additional value created =

([$1,666.7m + $76.5m + $40m] × 7.5) − ($12,000m + $922.5m) = $451.5m

Gain to Nahara for selling Fugae Co, 30% × $922.5m = $276.8m

Avem Co will gain $174.7 million of the additional value created, $451.5m − $276.8m = $174.7m

Appendix 2: Value of project to Fugae Co

Appendix 2.1

Estimate of risk-adjusted cost of capital to be used to discount the project's cash flows

The project value is calculated based on its cash flows which are discounted at the project's risk adjusted cost of capital, to reflect the business risk of the project.

Reka Co's asset beta

Reka Co equity value = $4.50 × 80 million shares = $360m

Reka Co debt value = 1.05 × $340 million = $357m

Asset beta = 1.6 × $360m/($360m + $357m × 0.8) = 0.89

Project's asset beta (PAB)

$0.89 = PAB \times 0.15 + 0.80 \times 0.85$

$PAB = 1.4$

Fugae Co

MVe = $922.5m

MVd

Cost of debt = Risk free rate of return plus the credit spread

$= 4\% + 0.80\% = 4.80\%$

Current value of a $100 bond: $\$5.4 \times 1.048^{-1} + \$5.4 \times 1.048^{-2} + \$5.4 \times 1.048^{-3} + \$105.4 \times 1.048^{-4} = \$102.14$ per $100

MVd = $1.0214 \times \$380m = \$388.1$ m

Project's risk adjusted equity beta

$1.4 \times (\$922.5m + \$388.1m \times 0.8)/\$922.5m = 1.87$

Project's risk adjusted cost of equity

$4\% + 1.87 \times 6\% = 15.2\%$

Project's risk adjusted cost of capital

$(15.2\% \times \$922.5m + 4.8\% \times 0.8 \times \$388.1m)/(\$922.5m + \$388.1m) = 11.84\%$, say 12%

Appendix 2.2

Estimate of expected value of the project without the offer from Lumi Co

(All amounts in $000s)

Year	1	2	3	4
Cash flows	3,277.6	16,134.3	36,504.7	35,683.6
Discount factor for 12%	0.893	0.797	0.712	0.636
Present values	2,926.9	12,859.0	25,991.3	22,694.8

Probabilities are assigned to possible outcomes based on whether or not the tourism market will grow. The expected net present value (PV) is computed on this basis.

PV year 1: $2,926,900

50% of PV years 1 to 4: $32,236,000

PV years 2 to 4: $61,545,100

40% PV years 2 to 4: $24,618,040

Expected present value of cash flows

$= [0.75 \times (2,926,900 + (0.8 \times 61,545,100 + 0.2 \times 24,618,040))] + [0.25 \times 32,236,000]$

$= [0.75 \times (2,926,900 + 54,159,688)] + [0.25 \times 32,236,000] = 42,814,941 + 8,059,000$

$= \$50,873,941$

Expected NPV of project = $50,873,941 – $42,000,000 = $8,873,941

Estimate of expected value of the project with the offer from Lumi Co

PV of $50m = $50,000,000 × 0.893 = $44,650,000

If the tourism industry does not grow as expected in the first year, then it is more beneficial for Fugae Co to exercise the offer made by Lumi Co, given that Lumi Co's offer of $44.65 million (PV of $50 million) is greater than the PV of the years two to four cash flows ($30.8 million approximately) for that outcome. This figure is then incorporated into the expected net present value calculations.

50% of year 1 PV: $1,463,450

Expected present value of project

= [0.75 × (2,926,900 + 54,159,688)] + [0.25 × (1,463,450 + 44,650,000)]

= 42,814,941 + 11,528,363 = $54,343,304

Expected NPV of project = $54,343,304 – $42,000,000 = $12,343,304

				Marks
Marking scheme				
(a)	Risk diversification			2–3
	Purchasing undervalued companies			4–5
			Maximum	**7**
(b)	1–2 marks per point		**Maximum**	**4**
(c)	(i)	Avem Co, current value		1
		Avem Co, free cash flows to equity		1
		Fugae Co, estimate of growth rate		2
		Fugae Co, current value estimate		2
		Combined company, estimated additional value created		2
		Gain to Nahara Co when selling Fugae Co		1
		Gain to Avem Co		1
			Maximum	**10**
	(ii)	Reka Co asset beta		2
		Project asset beta		1
		Fugae Co's market value of debt		2
		Project's risk adjusted equity beta		1
		Project's risk adjusted cost of equity		1
		Project's risk adjusted cost of capital		1
		Annual PVs of project		1
		Different outcomes PVs (year 1, years 2 to 4, 50% and 40%)		2
		Expected NPV of project before Lumi Co offer		3
		PV of Lumi Co offer		1
		Expected NPV of project with Lumi Co's offer		3
			Maximum	**18**
	(iii)	Presentation of benefits to each group of equity holders		
		With and without the project		2–3
		Assumptions made		3–4
		Concluding comments		1–2
			Maximum	**7**
		Note: Maximum 6 marks if no concluding comments given		
		Professional marks		
		Report format		1
		Structure and presentation of the report		3
			Maximum	**4**
Total				**50**

CORPORATE RECONSTRUCTION AND REORGANISATION

15 BBS STORES (JUN 09 ADAPTED)

Key answer tips

Corporate reconstruction and weighted average cost of capital are commonly tested topics, but this question was very time pressured, with lots of parts to complete in the time.

Notice the efficient way which the answer has dealt with part (a) – laying out the original statement of financial position together with the necessary adjustments helped to show the impact of the unbundling clearly.

(a) **Report to Management**

From: Financial Consultant

(i) **Impact of Property Unbundling on the Statement of Financial Position and the Reported Earnings per Share**

The unbundling of the buildings component entails a sale value of 50% of the land and buildings and 50% of the assets under construction to yield a sale value of $1,231 million. Under option 1 $360 million would be used to repay the outstanding medium-term loan notes and the balance as reinvestment within the business of $871 million. Option 2 would entail repayment of the loan and a share buyback. The value released would buy back $871 million/$4 = 217.75 million shares with a nominal value of $54.44 million and a charge to reserves of $817 million. The comparative statements of financial position under each option are as follows:

	As at year end 20X8	Sale proceeds	Reinvestment option 1		Share buyback option 2		As at year end 20X7
	$m	$m	$m	$m	$m	$m	$m
ASSETS							
Non-current assets							
Intangible assets	190			190		190	160
Property, plant and equipment	4,050	−1,231	871	3,690	−1,231	2,819	3,600
Other assets	500			500		500	530
	4,740			4,380		3,509	4,290
Current assets	840	1,231	−1,231	840		840	1,160
Total assets	5,580			5,220		4,349	5,450

EQUITY						
Called up share capital – equity	425		425	–54	371	420
Retained earnings	1,535		1,535	–817	718	980
Total equity	1,960		1,960		1,089	1,400
LIABILITIES						
Current liabilities	1,600		1,600		1,600	2,020
Non-current liabilities						
Borrowings and other financial liabilities	1,130	–360	770	–360	770	1,130
Other liabilities	890		890		890	900
	2,020		1,660		1,660	2,030
Total liabilities	3,620		3,260		3,260	4,050
Total equity and liabilities	5,580		5,220		4,349	5,450

The first option has the effect of reducing the company's book gearing from 36.6% (borrowing and other financial liabilities to total capital employed) to 28.2% with option 1 or increasing it to 41.4% with option 2. The net impact upon the earnings of the business is less straightforward. Under options 1 and 2 the company would benefit from a reduction in interest payable but would be required to pay an open market rent at 8% per annum on the property released. In addition, under option 1, the reduction in gearing would lead to a 30 basis points saving in interest on the variable component of the swap. Under option 1 the company would be able to earn a rate of return of 13% on the funds reinvested. The adjustment to earnings to show these effects is:

Earnings for the year

	Current $m	Option 1 $m	Option 2 $m
Earnings for the year	670.00	670.00	670.00
add back interest saved (net of tax) $360 million × 6.2% × 0.65		14.51	14.51
reduction in credit spread on six-year debt $770 million × 0.003 × 0.65		1.50	
deduct additional property rent (net of tax) $1,231 × 8% × 0.65		–64.01	–64.01
add additional return on equity $871 million × 13% × 0.65		74.00	
Revised earnings	670.00	696.00	620.50
Number of shares in issue	1,700	1,700	1,484
Revised EPS (c per share)	39.41	40.94	41.81

Given that the company has swapped out its variable rate liability there will be no change in the interest charge to earnings for the six-year debt from the current 5.5% per annum unless the lender has the ability to vary the variable rate on current borrowing for changes in credit rating. Because the fixed rate and the floating rate are the same at 6.2% (given the current credit spread is 70 basis points over LIBOR, or in addition to the swap rate of 5.5%) the nominal value of the company's debt is equal to its current market value.

(ii)   Impact of unbundling on the firm's overall cost of finance

Because the current firm is a combination of both retail and property it is necessary to estimate the asset beta for the retail business alone. Once this is achieved it is then straightforward to estimate the asset beta of a firm with a given element of property removed.

The current equity cost of capital is given as follows:

$$E(r_e) = R_F + \beta_i \times ERP$$

$$E(r_e) = 5\% + 1.824 \times 3\% = 10.47\%$$

The current weighted average cost of capital is:

$$WACC = \left[\frac{V_e}{V_e + V_d}\right]k_e + \left[\frac{V_d}{V_e + V_d}\right]k_d(1-T)$$

$$WACC = \frac{6,800}{6,800+1,130} \times 10.47\% + \frac{1,130}{6,800+1,130} \times 6.2\% \times 0.65 = 9.56\%$$

To calculate the unbundled cost of equity capital we first ungear the current company beta as follows (assuming debt beta is zero):

$$\beta_a = \left[\frac{V_e}{(V_e + V_d(1-T))}\beta_e\right]$$

so

$$\beta_a = \left[\frac{6,800}{(6,800 + 1,130(1 - 0.35))}1.824\right]$$

$$= 1.646$$

The retail asset beta can then be calculated from the weighted average of the component betas as:

$$\beta_a = \frac{V_{retail}}{V_{total}}\beta_{retail} + \frac{V_{property}}{V_{total}}\beta_{property}$$

$$1.646 = \frac{4,338}{6,800}\beta_{retail} + \frac{2,462}{6,800} \times 0.625$$

$$\beta_{retail} = \left[1.646 - \frac{2,462}{6,800} \times 0.625\right] \times \frac{6,800}{4,338} = 2.225$$

However, the beta of the continuing firm will be a combination of this retail beta and the property beta of the remaining firm. On the assumption that the share price does not change under either option the cost of equity capital is estimated as follows:

Option 1

Value of the equity $= 425 \times 4 \times 4 = \$6,800$ million

Asset beta of reconstructed firm $\beta_a = \dfrac{V_{retail}}{V_{total}}\beta_{retail} + \dfrac{V_{property}}{V_{total}}\beta_{property}$

$$\beta_a = \frac{5,569}{6,800} \times 2.225 + \frac{1,231}{6,800} \times 0.625 = 1.935$$

Equity beta of reconstructed firm $\beta_a = \left[\dfrac{V_e}{(V_e + V_d(1-T))}\beta_e\right]$

So $1.935 = \left[\dfrac{6,800}{(6,800 + 770(1-0.35))}\beta_e\right]$

$\beta_e = 2.0775$

Cost of equity = 5% + 2.0775 × 3% = 11.23%

Option 2

Value of the equity $= 371 \times 4 \times 4 = \$5,936$ million

Asset beta of reconstructed firm $\beta_a = \dfrac{V_{retail}}{V_{total}}\beta_{retail} + \dfrac{V_{property}}{V_{total}}\beta_{property}$

$$\beta_a = \frac{4,705}{5,936} \times 2.225 + \frac{1,231}{5,936} \times 0.625 = 1.893$$

Equity beta of reconstructed firm $\beta_a = \left[\dfrac{V_e}{(V_e + V_d(1-T))}\beta_e\right]$

So $1.893 = \left[\dfrac{5,936}{(5,936 + 770(1-0.35))}\beta_e\right]$

$\beta_e = 2.053$

Cost of equity = 5% + 2.053 × 3% = 11.16%

$$\text{WACC(1)} = \frac{6,800}{(6,800+770)} \times 11.23\% + \frac{770}{(6,800+770)} \times 5.9\% \times 0.65 = 10.48\%$$

And

$$\text{WACC(2)} = \frac{5,936}{(5,936+770)} \times 11.16\% + \frac{770}{(5,936+770)} \times 6.2\% \times 0.65 = 10.34\%$$

Note that under option 1, the variable component of the swap would be reduced by 30 basis points. However, the market value of the debt would remain unchanged because given LIBOR and the fixed component of the swap are the same at 5.5%, the reduction in basis points will reduce the effective coupon and the yield to 5.9%.

Both options will significantly increase the cost of capital for the company from 9.56% to 10.48% in the case of option 1 and 10.34% in the case of option 2.

(iii)   The potential impact upon the value of the firm

The value of the firm for a low geared business such as this is represented by the present value of the firm's future earnings discounted at the company's cost of capital. The ownership of property does not add value to the business providing that the company can enjoy a continuing and unencumbered use of the asset concerned.

On the assumption that an independent property company can be established and an arm's length rental agreement concluded then it is possible that the ownership of the property assets could be taken off balance sheet. However, the ease with which this can be done depends upon the local accounting regulations and accounting standards.

As it stands option 1 appears to increase the potential earnings more than currently or than option 2. However option 2 offers the highest EPS. With an unbundling exercise such as this it is difficult to predict with precision the likely impact upon the value of the firm. The removal of part of the firm's property portfolio will increase the equity beta but this will be offset by the reduction in the firm's gearing. Much also depends upon the ability of the business to generate a return of 13% on the reinvested proceeds of the property sale. If this is not achieved then a significant loss in shareholder value would result. For this reason the shareholders might prefer the lower risk option of a repurchase of their equity at 400c leaving the firm's EPS largely unchanged.

The analysis of the impact upon the firm's equity cost of capital assumes that the value of the firm's equity at 400c per share will remain unchanged. In practice that is unrealistic and a model of the firm's value would have to be constructed to test the full impact of either option on shareholder value. Given the problem is recursive in that the output value determines the estimation of the equity beta, which is also an input variable in the calculation, computer modelling would be required.

(b)   Differing views exist about the effect of dividends on a company's share price. Several authors, including Modigliani and Miller (M&M) have argued that dividend policy is irrelevant to the value of a company. Such arguments are formulated under very restrictive assumptions. If such conditions existed then shareholders would not value an increase in dividend payments. However, there are several real world factors that are likely to influence the preference of shareholders towards dividends or retentions (and hence expected capital gains). These include:

(i)   Taxation. In some countries dividends and capital gains are subject to different marginal rates of taxation, usually with capital gains being subject to a lower level of taxation than dividends.

(ii)   Brokerage fees. If shareholders have a preference for some current income and are paid no or low dividends their wealth will be reduced if they have to sell some of their shares and incur brokerage fees in order to create current income. Shareholders, especially institutional shareholders, often rely on dividends to meet their cash flow needs.

(iii)   The corporate tax treatment of dividends may favour a higher level of retention.

(iv)   If the company needs to finance new investment it is usually cheaper to use retained earnings. This is because most forms of external finance involve issue costs, which, in the case of equity finance can be three percent or more or the funds raised.

(v)   Information asymmetry may exist between shareholders and directors. If the market is not strong form efficient shareholders may have less complete knowledge of the likely future prospects of the company than directors, which may influence the shareholders' desire for dividends or capital gains.

The implications of an increase in dividends need to be considered by the company. Dividends are often regarded as an unbiased signal of a company's future prospects, an increase in dividends signalling higher expected earnings. A company should be careful to inform its shareholders of the reason for any increase in dividends.

A further factor is the use that the company can make of funds. If the company has a number of possible positive NPV investments then shareholders will normally favour undertaking these investments (at least on financial grounds), as they will lead to an increase in shareholder wealth. As previously mentioned internal finance is cheaper than external finance and, ceteris paribus, would lead to a preference for retentions. If, however, the company has relatively few projects and can only invest surplus cash in money market or other financial investments at an expected zero NPV, relative high dividends or share repurchase might be preferred.

(c)   Pioneers in the field of behavioural finance have identified the following factors as some of the key factors that contribute to irrational and potentially detrimental financial decision making.

Anchoring

Investors have a tendency to attach or 'anchor' their thoughts to a reference point even though it may have no logical relevance to the decision at hand e.g. investors are often attracted to buy shares whose price has fallen considerably because they compare the current price to the previous high (but now irrelevant) price.

Gambler's fallacy

Investors have a tendency to believe that the probability of a future outcome changes because of the occurrence of various past outcomes e.g. if the value of a share has risen for seven consecutive days, some investors might sell the shares, believing that the share price is more likely to fall on the next day. This is not necessarily the case.

Herd behaviour

This is the tendency for individuals to mimic the actions (rational or irrational) of a larger group. There are a couple of reasons why herd behaviour happens. The first is the social pressure of conformity most people are very sociable and have a natural desire to be accepted by a group. The second is the common rationale that it's unlikely that such a large group could be wrong. This is especially prevalent in situations in which an individual has very little experience.

Overreaction and availability bias

According to the EMH, new information should more or less be reflected instantly in a security's price. For example, good news should raise a business' share price accordingly. Reality, however, tends to contradict this theory. Often, participants in the stock market predictably overreact to new information, creating a larger than appropriate effect on a security's price.

16   CIGNO CO (SEP/DEC 15)

Question debrief

Key answer tips

This question contained lots of loosely connected parts.

Many students are drawn to the numbers first, but notice that parts (a), (b)(iii), (c) and (d) can be answered independently of the numerical section.

To make sure that you don't over-run on time in a question like this, attack these independent written bits first before starting on the numbers.

(a)   Both forms of unbundling involve disposing the non-core parts of the company.

The divestment through a sell-off normally involves selling part of a company as an entity or as separate assets to a third party for an agreed amount of funds or value. This value may comprise of cash and non-cash based assets. The company can then utilise the funds gained in alternative, value-enhancing activities.

The management buy-in is a particular type of sell-off which involves selling a division or part of a company to an external management team, who will take up the running of the new business and have an equity stake in the business. A management buy-in is normally undertaken when it is thought that the division or part of the company can probably be run better by a different management team compared to the current one.

(b)   Report to the board of directors (BoD), CIGNO CO

This report assesses the potential value of acquiring Anatra Co for the equity holders of Cigno Co, both with and without considering the benefits of the reduction in taxation and in employee costs. The possible issues raised by reduction in taxation and in employee costs are discussed in more detail below. The assessment also discusses the estimates made and the methods used.

Assessment of value created

Cigno Co estimates that the premium payable to acquire Anatra Co largely accounts for the benefits created from the acquisition and the divestment, before considering the benefits from the tax and employee costs' saving. As a result, before these savings are considered, the estimated benefit to Cigno Co's shareholders of $128 million (see Appendix 3) is marginal. Given that there are numerous estimations made and the methods used make various assumptions, as discussed below, this benefit could be smaller or larger. It would appear that without considering the additional benefits of cost and tax reductions, the acquisition is probably too risky and would probably be of limited value to Cigno Co's shareholders.

If the benefits of the taxation and employee costs saved are taken into account, the value created for the shareholders is $5,609 million (see Appendix 4), and therefore significant. This would make the acquisition much more financially beneficial. It should be noted that no details are provided on the additional pre-acquisition and post-acquisition costs or on any synergy benefits that Cigno Co may derive in addition to the cost savings discussed. These should be determined and incorporated into the calculations.

Basing corporate value on the price-earnings (PE) method for the sell-off, and on the free cash flow valuation method for the absorbed business, is theoretically sound. The PE method estimates the value of the company based on its earnings and on competitor performance. With the free cash flow method, the cost of capital takes account of the risk the investors want to be compensated for and the non-committed cash flows are the funds which the business can afford to return to the investors, as long as they are estimated accurately.

However, in practice, the input factors used to calculate the organisation's value may not be accurate or it may be difficult to assess their accuracy. For example, for the free cash flow method, it is assumed that the sales growth rate, operating profit margin, the taxation rate and incremental capital investment can be determined accurately and remain constant. It is assumed that the cost of capital will remain unchanged and it is assumed that the asset beta, the cost of equity and cost of debt can be determined accurately. It is also assumed that the length of the period of growth is accurate and that the company operates in perpetuity thereafter. With the PE model, the basis for using the average competitor figures needs to be assessed, for example, have outliers been ignored; and the basis for the company's higher PE ratio needs to be justified as well. The uncertainties surrounding these estimates would suggest that the value is indicative, rather than definitive, and it would be more prudent to undertake sensitivity analysis and obtain a range of values.

Key factors to consider in relation to the redundancies and potential tax savings

It is suggested that the BoD should consider the impact of the cost-savings from redundancies and from the tax payable in relation to corporate reputation and ethical considerations.

At present, Cigno Co enjoys a good reputation and it is suggested that this may be because it has managed to avoid large scale redundancies. This reputation may now be under threat and its loss could affect Cigno Co negatively in terms of long-term loss in revenues, profits and value; and it may be difficult to measure the impact of this loss accurately.

Whilst minimising tax may be financially prudent, it may not be considered fair. For example, currently there is ongoing discussion and debate from a number of governments and other interested parties that companies should pay tax in the countries they operate and derive their profits, rather than where they are based. Whilst global political consensus in this area seems some way off, it is likely that the debate in this area will increase in the future. Companies that are seen to be operating unethically with regard to this, may damage their reputation and therefore their profits and value.

Nonetheless, given that Cigno Co is likely to derive substantial value from the acquisition, because of these savings, it should not merely disregard the potential savings. Instead it should consider public relations exercises it could undertake to minimise the loss of reputation, and perhaps meet with the government to discuss ways forward in terms of tax payments.

Conclusion

The potential value gained from acquiring and unbundling Anatra Co can be substantial if the potential cost savings are taken into account. However, given the assumptions that are made in computing the value, it is recommended that sensitivity analysis is undertaken and a range of values obtained. It is also recommended that Cigno Co should undertake public relations exercises to minimise the loss of reputation, but it should probably proceed with the acquisition, and undertake the cost saving exercise because it is likely that this will result in substantial additional value.

Report compiled by: AN Accountant

Date: XX/XX/XXXX

Appendix 1: Estimate of value created from the sell-off of the equipment manufacturing business

Average industry PE ratio = $2.40/$0.30 = 8

Anatra Co's equipment manufacturing business PE ratio = 8 × 1.2 = 9.6

Value from sell-off of equipment manufacturing business

Share of pre-tax profit = 30% × $2,490 million = $747m

After tax profit = $747 million × (1 − 0.22) = $582.7m

Value from sell-off = $582.7 million × 9.6 = $5,594m (approximately)

Appendix 2: Estimate of the combined company cost of capital

Anatra Co, asset beta = 0.68

Cigno Co, asset beta:

Equity beta =1.10

Proportion of market value of debt = 40%; Proportion of market value of equity = 60%

Asset beta = 1.10 × 0.60/(0.60 + 0.40 × 0.78) = 0.72

Combined company, asset beta

Market value of equity, Anatra Co = $3 × 7,000 million shares = $21,000m

Market value of equity, Cigno Co = 60% × $60,000 million = $36,000m

Asset beta = (0.68 × 21,000 + 0.72 × 36,000)/(21,000 + 36,000) = 0.71 (approximately)

Combined company equity beta = 0.71 × (0.6 + 0.4 × 0.78)/0.6 = 1.08

Combined company, cost of equity = 4.3% + 1.08 × 7% = 11.86%

Combined company, cost of capital = 11.86% × 0.6 + 6.00% × 0.78 × 0.4 = 8.99, say 9%

Appendix 3: Estimate of the value created for Cigno Co's equity holders from the acquisition

Anatra Co, Medical R&D value estimate:

Sales revenue growth rate = 5%

Operating profit margin = 17.25%

Tax rate = 22%

Additional capital investment = 40% of the change in sales revenue Cost of capital = 9% (Appendix 2)

Free cash flow growth rate after four years = 3%

Current sales revenue = 70% × $21,400m = $14,980m

Cash flows, years 1 to 4 ($ millions)

Year	1	2	3	4
Sales revenue	15,729	16,515	17,341	18,208
Profit before interest and tax	2,713	2,849	2,991	3,141
Tax	597	627	658	691
Additional capital investment	300	314	330	347
Free cash flows	1,816	1,908	2,003	2,103
Present value of cash flows (9% discount)	1,666	1,606	1,547	1,490

Value, years 1 to 4: $6,309m

Value, year 5 onwards: [$2,103 × 1.03/(0.09 – 0.03)] × 1.09 – 4 = $25,575m

Total value of Anatra Co's medical R&D business area = $31,884m

Total value of Anatra Co following unbundling of equipment manufacturing business and absorbing medical R&D business: $5,594m (Appendix 1) + $31,884m = $37,478m (approximately)

Anatra Co, current market value of equity = $21,000m Anatra Co, current market value of debt = $9,000m Premium payable = $21,000m × 35% = $7,350m

Total value attributable to Anatra Co's investors = $37,350m

Value attributable to Cigno Co's shareholders from the acquisition of Anatra Co before taking into account the cash benefits of potential tax savings and redundancies = $128m

Appendix 4: Estimate of the value created from savings in tax and employment costs following possible redundancies

Cash flows, years 1 to 4 ($ millions)

Year	1	2	3	4
Cash flows (4% increase p.a.)	1,600	1,664	1,731	1,800
Present value of cash flows (9%)	1,468	1,401	1,337	1,275

Total value = $5,481m

Value attributable to Cigno Co's shareholders from the acquisition of Anatra Co after taking into account the cash benefits of potential tax savings and redundancies = $5,609m

(c) The feasibility of disposing of assets as a defence tool against a possible acquisition depends upon the type of assets sold and how the funds generated from the sale are utilised.

If the type of assets are fundamental to the continuing business then this may be viewed as disposing of the corporation's 'crown-jewels'. Such action may be construed as being against protecting the rights of shareholders (similar to the conditions discussed in part (d) below). In order for key assets to be disposed of, the takeover regulatory framework may insist on the corporation obtaining permission from the shareholders first before carrying it out.

On the other hand, the assets may be viewed as not being fundamental to the core business and may be disposed of to generate extra funds through a sell-off (see part (a) above). This may make sense if the corporation is undertaking a programme of restructuring and re-organisation.

In addition to this, the company needs to consider what it intends to do with the funds raised from the sale of assets. If the funds are used to grow the core business and therefore enhancing value, then the shareholders would see this positively and the value of the corporation will probably increase. Alternatively, if there are no profitable alternatives, the funds could be returned to the shareholders through special dividends or share buy-backs. In these circumstances, disposing of assets may be a feasible defence tactic.

However, if the funds are retained but not put to value-enhancing use or returned to shareholders, then the share price may continue to be depressed. And the corporation may still be an attractive takeover target for corporations which are in need of liquid funds. In these circumstances, disposing of assets would not be a feasible defence tactic.

(d) Each of the three conditions aims to ensure that shareholders are treated fairly and equitably.

The mandatory-bid condition through sell out rights allows remaining shareholders to exit the company at a fair price once the bidder has accumulated a certain number of shares. The amount of shares accumulated before the rule applies varies between countries. The bidder must offer the shares at the highest share price, as a minimum, which had been paid by the bidder previously. The main purpose for this condition is to ensure that the acquirer does not exploit their position of power at the expense of minority shareholders.

The principle of equal treatment condition stipulates that all shareholder groups must be offered the same terms, and that no shareholder group's terms are more or less favourable than another group's terms. The main purpose of this condition is to ensure that minority shareholders are offered the same level of benefits, as the previous shareholders from whom the controlling stake in the target company was obtained.

The squeeze-out rights condition allows the bidder to force minority shareholders to sell their stake, at a fair price, once the bidder has acquired a specific percentage of the target company's equity. The percentage varies between countries but typically ranges between 80% and 95%. The main purpose of this condition is to enable the acquirer to gain 100% stake of the target company and prevent problems arising from minority shareholders at a later date.

Note: Credit will be given for alternative, relevant approaches to the calculations, comments and suggestions/recommendations.

			Marking scheme	Marks
(a)			Up to 2 marks for distinguishing the two forms of unbundling	**4**
(b)	(i)		Appendix 1	
			Anatra Co, Manufacturing business, PE ratio	1
			Estimate of the value created from sell-off	3
			Appendix 2	
			Cigno Co asset beta	1
			Combined company asset beta	1
			Combined company equity beta	1
			Combined company cost of capital	1
			Appendix 3	
			Sales revenue, years 1 to 4	1
			Operating profit, years 1 to 4	1
			Taxation, years 1 to 4	1
			Capital investment, years 1 to 4	1
			Value from years 1 to 4	1
			Value from year 5 onwards	1
			Value for Cigno Co shareholders before impact of savings from tax and employee cost reduction	2
			Appendix 4	
			Value created from tax and employee cost savings	1
			Value for Cigno Co shareholders after impact of savings from tax and employee cost reduction	1
			Maximum	**18**
	(ii)		Discussion of values for the equity holders, additional costs/benefits not given	3–4
			Methods used and assumptions made	4–5
			Maximum	**8**
	(iii)		Reputation factors	1–2
			Ethical factors	1–2
			Comment on value	1–2
			Maximum	**4**
			Professional marks for part (b)	
			Report format	1
			Structure and presentation of the report	3
			Maximum	**4**
(c)			1 to 2 marks per point	
			Maximum	**6**
(d)			Up to 2 marks for explaining the purpose of each condition	**6**
Total				**50**

17   MORADA CO (SEP/DEC 16)

Key answer tips

There are lots of marks here for calculating the company's cost of equity and cost of capital in different scenarios.

However, note that there are also lots of marks available for (easier?) discussion points, such as parts (a) and (c). These two parts can be answered independently of the tricky cost of capital calculations, so always try to answer these parts first to build up confidence at the start of the question.

(a)   The owners or shareholders of a business will accept that it needs to engage in some risky activities in order to generate returns in excess of the risk free rate of return. A business will be exposed to differing amounts of business and financial risk depending on the decisions it makes. Business risk depends on the decisions a business makes with respect to the services and products it offers and consists of the variability in its profits. For example, it could be related to the demand for its products, the rate of innovation, actions of competitors, etc. Financial risk relates to the volatility of earnings due to the financial structure of the business and could be related to its gearing, the exchange rate risk it is exposed to, its credit risk, its liquidity risk, etc. A business exposed to high levels of business risk may not be able to take excessive financial risk, and vice versa, as the shareholders or owners may not want to bear risk beyond an acceptable level.

Risk management involves the process of risk identification, of assessing and measuring the risk through the process of predicting, analysing and quantifying it, and then making decisions on which risks to assume, which to avoid, which to retain and which to transfer. As stated above, a business will not aim to avoid all risks, as it will want to generate excess returns. Dependent on factors such as controllability, frequency and severity of the risk, it may decide to eliminate or reduce some risks from the business through risk transfer. Risk mitigation is the process of transferring risks out of a business through, for example, hedging or insurance, or avoiding certain risks altogether. Risk diversification is a process of risk reduction through spreading business activity into different products and services, different geographical areas and/or different industries to minimise being excessively exposed by focusing exclusively on one product/service.

(b)   **Report to the board of directors (BoD), Morada Co**

This report provides a discussion on the estimates of the cost of equity and the cost of capital and the impact on the financial position and the earnings after tax, as a result of the proposals put forward by the first director and the second director. The main assumptions made in drawing up the estimates will also be explained. The report concludes by recommending which of the two directors' proposals, if any, should be adopted.

Discussion

The table below shows the revised figures of the cost of equity and the cost of capital (Appendix 1), and the forecast earnings after tax for the coming year (Appendix 2), following each proposal from the first and second directors. For comparison purposes, figures before any changes are given as well.

	Cost of equity	Cost of capital	Earnings after tax
	Appendix 1	Appendix 1	Appendix 2
Current position	12.2%	10.0%	$28.0 million
Following first director's proposal	11.6%	11.1%	$37.8 million
Following second director's proposal	12.3%	9.8%	$30.8 million

Under the first director's proposal, although the cost of equity falls due to the lower financial risk in Morada Co because of less debt, the cost of capital actually increases. This is because, even though the cost of debt has decreased, the benefit of the tax shield is reduced significantly due to the lower amount of debt borrowing. Added to this is the higher business risk, reflected by the asset beta, of Morada Co just operating in the travel services sector. This higher business risk and reduced tax shield more than override the lower cost of debt resulting in a higher cost of capital.

Under the second director's proposal, the cost of equity is almost unchanged. There has been a significant increase in the cost of debt from 4.7% to 6.2%. However, the cost of capital has not reduced significantly because the benefit of the tax shield is also almost eroded by the increase in the cost of debt.

If no changes are made, then the forecast earnings after tax as a percentage of non-current assets is 10% ($28m/$280m). Under the first director's proposal, this figure almost doubles to 19.3% ($37.8m/$196m), and even if the one-off profit from the sale of non-current assets is excluded, this figure is still higher at 12.9% ($25.2m/$196m). Under the second director's proposal, this figure falls to 8.8% ($30.8m/$350m).

Assumptions

1   It is assumed that the asset beta of Morada Co is a weighted average of the asset betas of the travel services and the maintenance services business units, using non-current assets invested in each business unit as a fair representation of the size of each business unit and therefore the proportion of the business risk which business unit represents within the company.

2   The assumption of the share price not changing after either proposal is not reasonable. It is likely that due to changes in the business and financial risk from implementing either proposal, the risk profile of the company will change. The changes in the risk profile will influence the cost of equity, which in turn will influence the share price.

3   In determining the financial position of Morada Co, it is assumed that the current assets will change due to changes in the profit after tax figure; therefore this is used as the balancing figure for each proposal.

Recommendation

It is recommended that neither the first director's proposal nor the second director's proposal should be adopted. The second director's proposal results in a lower return on investment and a virtually unchanged cost of capital. So there will not be a meaningful benefit for Morada Co. The first director's proposal does increase the return on investment but results in a higher cost of capital. If the reason for adopting either proposal is to reduce risk, then this is not achieved. The main caveat here is that where the assumptions made in the calculations are not reasonable, they will reduce the usefulness of the analysis.

Report compiled by:

Date:

(Note: Credit will be given for alternative and relevant points)

Appendix 1: Estimates of cost of equity and cost of capital

Before either proposal is implemented

Cost of equity (K_e) = 3.8% + 1.2 × 7% = 12.2%
Cost of debt (K_d) = 3.8% + 0.9% = 4.7%

Market value of equity (MV_e) = $2.88 × 125 million shares = $360m

Market value of debt (MV_d)
Per $100 $6.20 × 1.047^{-1} + $6.20 × 1.047^{-2} + $6.20 × 1.047^{-3} + $106.20 × 1.047^{-4}
= $105.36
Total MV_d = $105.36/$100 × $120m = $126.4m

Cost of capital = (12.2% × $360m + 4.7% × 0.8 × $126.4m)/$486.4m = 10.0%

If the first director's proposal is implemented

MV_e = $360m
BV_d = $120m × 0.2 = $24m
K_d = 4.4%

MV_d per $100 $6.20 × 1.044^{-1} + $6.20 × 1.044^{-2} + $6.20 × 1.044^{-3} + $106.20 × 1.044^{-4}
= $106.47
Total MV_d = 106.47/$100 × $24 = $25.6m

Morada Co, asset beta
1.2 × $360m/($360m + $126.4m × 0.8) = 0.94
Asset beta of travel services = [0.94 − (0.65 × 30%)]/70% = 1.06
Equity beta of travel services = 1.06 × ($360m + $25.6m × 0.8)/$360m = 1.12

K_e = 3.8% + 1.12 × 7% = 11.6%
Cost of capital = (11.6% × $360m + 4.4% × 0.8 × $25.6m)/$385.6 = 11.1%

If the second director's proposal is implemented

MV_e = $360m
The basis points for the Ca3 rated bond is 240 basis points higher than the risk free-free rate of interest, giving a cost of debt of 6.2%, therefore:
MV_d = BV_d = $190m

Equity beta of the new, larger company = 1.21

K_e = 3.8% + 1.21 × 7% = 12.3%
Cost of capital = (12.3% × $360m + 6.2% × 0.8 × $190m)/$550m = 9.8%

Appendix 2: Estimates of forecast after-tax earnings and forecast financial position

Morada Co, extracts from the forecast after-tax earnings for the coming year (Amounts in $000)

	Current forecast	Forecast: first director proposal	Forecast: second director proposal
Current forecast after-tax earnings	28,000	28,000	28,000
Interest saved due to lower borrowing ($96m × 6.2% × 0.8)		4,762	
Interest payable on additional borrowing ($70m × 6.2% × 0.8)			(3,472)
Reduction in earnings due to lower investment (9% × $84m)		(7,560)	
Additional earnings due to higher investment (9% × $70m)			6,300
Profit on sale of non-current assets (15% × $84m)		12,600	
Revised forecast after-tax earnings	28,000	37,802	30,828
Increase in after-tax earnings		9,802	2,828

Morada Co, extracts from the forecast financial position for the coming year (Amounts in $000)

	Current forecast	Forecast: first director proposal	Forecast: second director proposal
Non-current assets	280,000	196,000	350,000
Current assets (balancing figure)	48,000	43,702	57,828
Total assets	328,000	239,702	407,828
Equity and liabilities			
Share capital (40c/share)	50,000	50,000	50,000
Retained earnings**	137,000	146,802	139,828
Total equity	187,000	196,802	189,828
Non-current liabilities (6.2% redeemable bonds)	120,000	24,000	190,000
Current liabilities	21,000	18,900	28,000
Total liabilities	141,000	42,900	218,000
Total liabilities and capital	328,000	239,702	407,828

** **Note:** With the two directors' proposals, the retained earnings amount is adjusted to reflect the revised forecast after-tax earnings.

(c) [**Note:** This is an open-ended question and a variety of relevant answers can be given by candidates depending on how the question requirement is interpreted. The following answer is just one possible approach which could be taken. Credit will be given for alternative, but valid, interpretations and answers therein.]

According to the third director, risk management involves more than just risk mitigation or risk diversification as proposed by the first and second directors. The proposals suggested by the first and the second directors are likely to change the makeup of the company, and cause uncertainty amongst the company's owners or clientele. This in turn may cause unnecessary fluctuations in the share price. She suggests that these changes are fundamental and more than just risk management tools.

Instead, it seems that she is suggesting that Morada Co should follow the risk management process suggested in part (a) above, where risks should be identified, assessed and then mitigated according to the company's risk appetite.

The risk management process should be undertaken with a view to increasing shareholder wealth, and therefore the company should consider what drives this value and what are the risks associated with these drivers of value. Morada Co may assess that some of these risks are controllable and some not controllable. It may assess that some are severe and others less so, and it may assess some are likely to occur more frequently than others.

Morada Co may take the view that the non-controllable, severe and/or frequent risks should be eliminated (or not accepted). On the other hand, where Morada Co is of the opinion that it has a comparative advantage or superior knowledge of risks, and therefore is better able to manage them, it may come to the conclusion that it should accept these. For example, it may take the view that it is able to manage events such as flight delays or hotel standards, but would hedge against currency fluctuations and insure against natural disasters due to their severity or non-controllability.

Theory suggests that undertaking risk management may increase the value of a company if the benefits accruing from the risk management activity are more than the costs involved in managing the risks. For example, smoothing the volatility of profits may make it easier for Morada Co to plan and match long-term funding with future projects, it may make it easier for Morada Co to take advantage of market imperfections by reducing the amount of taxation payable, or it may reduce the costs involved with incidences of financial distress. In each case though, the benefits accrued should be assessed against the costs involved.

Therefore, a risk management process is more than just mitigating risk through reducing financial risk as the first director is suggesting or risk diversification as the second director is suggesting. Instead it is a process of risk analysis and then about judgement of which risks to hedge or mitigate, and finally, which risk-reduction mechanisms to employ, depending on the type of risk, the cost of the risk analysis and mitigation, and the benefits accruing from the mitigation.

		Marking scheme		
				Marks
(a)		Relationship between business and financial risk		3
		Risk mitigation and risk diversification as part of a company's risk management strategy		3
				6
(b)	(i)	**[Appendix 1]**		
		Prior to implementation of any proposal		
		Cost of equity		1
		Cost of debt		1
		Market value of equity		1
		Market value of debt		2
		Cost of capital		1
		After implementing the first director's proposal		
		Market value of debt		2
		Morada Co, asset beta		1
		Asset beta of travel services only		1
		Equity beta of travel services only		1
		Cost of equity		1
		Cost of capital		1
		After implementing the second director's proposal		
		Market value of debt		2
		Cost of equity		1
		Cost of capital		1
				17
	(ii)	**[Appendix 2]**		
		Adjusted earnings, first director's proposal		2
		Financial position, first director's proposal		2
		Adjusted earnings, second director's proposal		2
		Financial position, second director's proposal		1
				7
	(iii)	Discussion		5–6
		Assumptions		2–3
		Reasoned recommendation		1–2
		(**Note:** Maximum 8 marks if no recommendation given)		
			Maximum	9
		Professional marks for part (b)		
		Report format		1
		Structure and presentation of the report		3
				4
(c)		1–2 marks per point	Maximum	7
Total				50

18 CHRYSOS CO (MAR/JUN 17)

Key answer tips

There was a lot to do in this question, but students would have been pleased to see that the question was split up into several smaller sub-requirements to help with time management.

A good exam technique would have been critical – the calculations in part (i) of the report were quite tricky (preparing a statement of financial position after the reconstruction, and two business valuations using the FCF method) and it would have been easy to spend too much time on them.

The discussion points in the question were more straightforward though, and the requirements were very clear.

A well prepared student, who presented the answer in a report format and left enough time to answer to both calculations and discussions, should have been able to pass this question.

(a) A reverse takeover enables a private, unlisted company, like Chrysos Co, to gain a listing on the stock exchange without needing to go through the process of an initial public offering (IPO). The private company merges with a listed 'shell' company. The private company initially purchases equity shares in the listed company and takes control of its board of directors. The listed company then issues new equity shares and these are exchanged for equity shares in the unlisted company, thereby the original private company's equity shares gain a listing on the stock exchange. Often the name of the listed company is also changed to that of the original unlisted company.

Advantages relative to an IPO

1   An IPO can take a long time, typically between one and two years, because it involves preparing a prospectus and creating an interest among potential investors. The equity shares need to be valued and the issue process needs to be administered. Since with the reverse takeover shares in the private company are exchanged for shares in the listed company and no new capital is being raised, the process can be completed much quicker.

2   An IPO is an expensive process and can cost between 3% and 5% of the capital being raised due to involvement of various parties, such as investment banks, law firms, etc, and the need to make the IPO attractive through issuing a prospectus and marketing the issue. A reverse takeover does not require such costs to be incurred and therefore is considerably cheaper.

3   In periods of economic downturn, recessions and periods of uncertainty, an IPO may not be successful. A lot of senior managerial time and effort will be spent, as well as expenditure, with nothing to show for it. On the other hand, a reverse takeover would not face this problem as it does not need external investors and it is not raising external finance, but is being used to gain from the potential benefits of going public by getting a listing.

Disadvantages relative to an IPO

1   The 'shell' listed company being used in the reverse takeover may have hidden liabilities and may be facing potential litigation, which may not be obvious at the outset. Proper and full due diligence is necessary before the process is started. A company undertaking an IPO would not face such difficulties.

2   The original shareholders of the listed company may want to sell their shares immediately after the reverse takeover process has taken place and this may affect the share price negatively. A lock-up period during which shares cannot be sold may be necessary to prevent this. [NB: An IPO may need a lock-up period as well, but this is not usually the case.]

3   The senior management of an unlisted company may not have the expertise and/or understanding of the rules and regulations which a listed company needs to comply with. The IPO process normally takes longer and is more involved, when compared to a reverse takeover. It also involves a greater involvement from external experts. These factors will provide the senior management involved in an IPO, with opportunities to develop the necessary expertise and knowledge of listing rules and regulations, which the reverse takeover process may not provide.

4   One of the main reasons for gaining a listing is to gain access to new investor capital. However, a smaller, private company which has become public through a reverse takeover may not obtain a sufficient analyst coverage and investor following, and it may have difficulty in raising new finance in future. A well-advertised IPO will probably not face these issues and find raising new funding to be easier.

(b)   Report to the board of directors (BoD), Chrysos Co

This report provides extracts from the financial position and an estimate of the value of Chrysos Co after it has undertaken a restructuring programme. It also contains an explanation of the process used in estimating the value and of the assumptions made. Finally, the report discusses the impact of the restructuring programme on the company and on venture capital organisations.

It is recommended that the manufacturing business unit is unbundled through a management buy-out, rather than the assets being sold separately, and it is estimated that Chrysos Co will receive $3,289m from the unbundling of the manufacturing business unit (Appendix one). This amount is recorded as a cash receipt in the extract of the financial position given below.

Extract of Chrysos Co's financial position following the restructuring programme

	$m
Non-current assets	
Land and buildings (80% × $7,500m)	6,000
Equipment ((80% × $5,400m) + $1,200m)	5,520
Current assets	
Inventory (80% × $1,800m)	1,440
Receivables (80% × $900m)	720
Cash ($3,289m + $400m – $1,200m – $1,050m)	1,439
	———
Total assets	15,119
	———

	$m
Equity	
Share capital ($1,600m + $800m)	2,400
Reserves **	10,319
Non-current liabilities: Bank loan	1,800
Current liabilities: Payables (80% × $750m)	600
	———
Total equity and liabilities	15,119
	———

** Balancing figure

Estimate of Chrysos Co's equity value following the restructuring programme

It is estimated that Chrysos Co's equity value after the restructuring programme has taken place will be just over $46 billion (Appendix three).

Process undertaken in determining Chrysos Co's equity value

The corporate value is based on a growth rate of 4% on cash flows in perpetuity, which are discounted at Chrysos Co's cost of capital (Appendix two). The cash flows are estimated by calculating the profit before depreciation and tax of the unbundled firm consisting of just the mining and shipping business unit and then deducting the depreciation and taxation amounts from this.

The bank loan debt is then deducted from the corporate value to estimate the value of the firm which is attributable to the equity holders (Appendix three).

Assumptions made in determining Chrysos Co's equity value

It is assumed that Sidero Co's ungeared cost of equity is equivalent to Chrysos Co's ungeared cost of equity, given that they are both in the same industry and therefore face the same business risk. Modigliani and Miller's proposition 2 is used to estimate Chrysos Cos's restructured cost of equity and cost of capital.

It is assumed that deducting depreciation and tax from the profit before depreciation, interest and tax provides a reasonably accurate estimate of the free cash flows (Appendix three). Other adjustments such as changes in working capital are reckoned to be immaterial and therefore not considered. Depreciation is not added back because it is assumed to be the same as the capital needed for reinvestment purposes.

It is assumed that the cash flows will grow in perpetuity. The assumption of growth in perpetuity may be over-optimistic and may give a higher than accurate estimate of Chrysos Co's equity value.

(**Note:** Credit will be given for alternative and relevant assumptions)

Impact of the restructuring programme on Chrysos Co and on the venture capital organisations (VCOs)

By acquiring an extra 600 million equity shares, the proportion of the VCOs' equity share capital will increase to 40% ((600m + 20% × 1,800)/(1,800 + 600)) from 20%. Therefore, the share of the equity value the VCOs will hold in Chrysos Co will increase by $9,229m, which is 77.5% more than the total of the value of bonds cancelled and extra payment made (Appendix four). As long as the VCOs are satisfied that the equity value of Chrysos Co after the restructuring programme has been undertaken is accurate, the value of their investment has increased substantially.

The VCOs may want undertake a feasibility study on the annual growth rate in cash flows of 4% and the assumption of growth in perpetuity. However, the extent of additional value created seems to indicate that the impact for the VCOs is positive.

By cancelling the VCOs' unsecured bonds and repaying the other debt in non-current liabilities, an opportunity has been created for Chrysos Co to raise extra debt finance for future projects. Based on a long-term capital structure ratio of 80% equity and 20% debt, and a corporate value of $47,944m (Appendix three), this equates to just under $9,600m of possible debt finance which could be accessed. Since the bank loan has a current value of $1,800m, Chrysos Co could raise just under an extra $7,800m debt funding and it would also have $1,439 million in net cash available from the sale of the machinery parts manufacturing business unit.

Chrysos Co's current value has not been given and therefore it is not possible to determine the financial impact of the equity value after the restructuring has taken place on the company as a whole. Nevertheless, given that the company has access to an extra $7,800m debt funding to expand its investment into new value-creating projects, it is likely that the restructuring programme will be beneficial. However, it is recommended that the company tries to determine its current equity value and compares this with the proposed new value. A concern may be that both the five senior equity holders' group and the 30 other equity holders group's proportion of equity shares will reduce to 30% from 40% each, as a result of the VCOs acquiring an additional 600 million shares. Both these shareholder groups need to be satisfied about the potential negative impact of these situations against the potential additional benefits accruing from the restructuring programme, before the company proceeds with the programme.

Conclusion

The restructuring programme creates an opportunity for Chrysos Co to have access to extra funding and additional cash for investment in projects in the future. The VCOs are likely to benefit financially from the restructuring programme as long as they are satisfied about the assumptions made when assessing the value created. However, Chrysos Co will need to ensure that all equity holder groups are satisfied with the change in their respective equity holdings.

Report compiled by:

Date:

(**Note:** Credit will be given for alternative and relevant points)

APPENDICES

Appendix One: Unbundling the manufacturing business unit

Option 1: Sale of assets

Net proceeds to Chrysos Co from net sale of assets of the manufacturing business unit are $3,102 million.

Option 2: Management buy-out

	$m
Sales revenue (20% × $16,800m)	3,360
Operating costs (25% × 10,080m)	(2,520)
Profit before depreciation, interest and tax	840
Depreciation (12% × 20% × ($7,500m + $5,400m))	(310)
	530
Tax (18% × $530m)	(95)
Cash flows	435

Estimated value = ($435m × 1.08)/0.10 = $4,698m

Amount payable to Chrysos Co = 70% × $4,698m = $3,289m

The option to unbundle through a management buy-out (option 2) is marginally better for Chrysos Co and it will opt for this.

Appendix Two: Calculation of cost of equity and cost of capital

Chrysos Co, estimate of cost of equity (Ke) and cost of capital (CoC)

Ke = 12.46% + [0.82 × (12.46% – 4.5%) × (0.2/0.8)]

Ke = 14.09%

CoC = 0.8 × 14.09% + 0.2 × 4.5% × 0.82 = 12.01, say 12%

Appendix Three: Estimate of value

	$m
Sales revenue (80% × $16,800m)	13,440
Costs prior to depreciation, interest and tax (75% × 10,080m)	(7,560)
Profit before depreciation and tax	5,880
Depreciation (12% × ($6,000m + $5,520m))	(1,382)
	4,498
Tax (18% × $4,498m)	(810)
Cash flows	3,688

Cost of capital to be used in estimating Chrysos Co's value is 12% (Appendix two) Estimated corporate value = ($3,688m × 1.04)/(0.12 – 0.04) = $47,944m

Estimated equity value = $47,944m – $1,800m = $46,144m

(**Note:** It is also acceptable to calculate cash flows after interest payment and use the cost of equity to estimate the equity value based on cash flows to equity instead of cash flows to firm.)

Appendix Four: Value created for VCOs

Value attributable to the VCOs = 40% × $46,144m = $18,458m

Value from increased equity ownership (this has doubled from 20% to 40%)

50% × $18,458m = $9,229m

Value of unsecured bonds foregone by the VCOs = $4,800m

Additional capital invested by the VCOs = $400m

Total of additional capital invested and value of bonds forgone = $5,200m

Additional value = ($9,229m – $5,200m)/$5,200m = 77.5% (or $4,029m)

(c)   As a private company, Chrysos Co is able to ensure that the needs of its primary stakeholder groups – finance providers, managers and employees – are taken into account through the supervisory board. The supervisory board has representatives from each of these groups and each group member has a voice on the board. Each stakeholder group should be able to present its position to the board through its representatives, and decisions will be made after agreement from all group representatives. In this way, no single stakeholder group holds primacy over any other group.

    Once Chrysos Co is listed and raises new capital, it is likely that it will have a large and diverse range of equity shareholders, who will likely be holding equity shares in many other companies. Therefore there is likely to be pressure on Chrysos Co to engage in value creating activity aimed at keeping its share price buoyant and thereby satisfying the equity shareholders. It is, therefore, likely that the equity shareholders' needs will hold primacy over the other stakeholder groups and quite possibly the power of the supervisory board will diminish as a result of this.

19   CONEJO CO (SEP/DEC 17)

Key answer tips

A good exam technique would have been critical here – the calculations in part (i) and (ii) of the report were quite tricky and related specifically to a technical article written by the examiner in 2011, and then the calculations in part (iii) (preparing a statement of financial position etc after the reconstruction) could have been very time consuming. It would have been easy to spend too much time on these calculations.

The discussion points in the question were more straightforward though, and the requirements were very clear.

Students understand how important it is to read the examiner's *recent* articles before they attempt the AFM exam, but this question demonstrates how important it is to read all the previous technical articles.

(a)   Increasing the debt finance of a company relative to equity finance increases its financial risk, and therefore the company will need to be able to bear the consequences of this increased risk. However, companies face both financial risk, which increases as the debt levels in the capital structure increase, and business risk, which is present in a company due to the nature of its business.

In the case of Conejo Co, it could be argued that as its profits and cash flows have stabilised, the company's business risk has reduced, in contrast to early in its life, when its business risk would have been much higher due to unstable profits and cash flows. Therefore, whereas previously Conejo Co was not able to bear high levels of financial risk, it is able to do so now without having a detrimental impact on the overall risk profile of the company. It could therefore change its capital structure and have higher levels of debt finance relative to equity finance.

The predatory acquisition of one company by another could be undertaken for a number of reasons. One possible reason may be to gain access to cash resources, where a company which needs cash resources may want to take over another company which has significant cash resources or cash generative capability. Another reason may be to increase the debt capacity of the acquirer by using the assets of the target company. Where the relative level of debt finance is increased in the capital structure of a company through a financial reconstruction, like in the case of Conejo Co, these reasons for acquiring a company may be diminished. This is because the increased levels of debt would probably be secured against the assets of the company and therefore the acquirer cannot use them to raise additional debt finance, and cash resources would be needed to fund the higher interest payments.

Many tax jurisdictions worldwide allow debt interest to be deducted from profits before the amount of tax payable is calculated on the profits. Increasing the amount of debt finance will increase the amount of interest paid, reducing the taxable profits and therefore the tax paid. Modigliani and Miller referred to this as the benefit of the tax shield in their research into capital structure, where their amended capital proposition demonstrated the reduction in the cost of capital and increase in the value of the firm, as the proportion of debt in the capital structure increases.

(b) **Report to the board of directors (BoD), Conejo Co**

Introduction

This report discusses whether the proposed financial reconstruction scheme which increases the amount of debt finance in Conejo Co would be beneficial or not to the company and the main parties affected by the change in the funding, namely the equity holders, the debt holders and the credit rating companies. Financial estimates provided in the appendices are used to support the discussion.

Impact on Conejo Co

Benefits to Conejo Co include the areas discussed in part (a) above and as suggested by the CFO. The estimate in Appendix 3 assumes that the interest payable on the new bonds and the extra interest payable on the existing bonds are net of the 15% tax. Therefore, the tax shield reduces the extra amount of interest paid. Further, it is likely that because of the large amount of debt finance which will be raised, the company's assets would have been used as collateral. This will help protect the company against hostile takeover bids. Additionally, proposal 2 (Appendix 3) appears to be better than proposal 1, with a lower gearing figure and a higher earnings per share figure. However, this is dependent on the extra investment being able to generate an after-tax return of 12% immediately. The feasibility of this should be assessed further.

Conejo Co may also feel that this is the right time to raise debt finance as interest rates are lower and therefore it does not have to offer large coupons, compared to previous years. Appendix 1 estimates that the new bond will need to offer a coupon of 3.57%, whereas the existing bond is paying a coupon of 5.57%.

The benefits above need to be compared with potential negative aspects of raising such a substantial amount of debt finance. Conejo Co needs to ensure that it will be able to finance the interest payable on the bonds and it should ensure it is able to repay the capital amount borrowed (or be able to re-finance the loan) in the future. The extra interest payable (Appendix 3) will probably not pose a significant issue given that the profit after tax is substantially more than the interest payment. However, the repayment of the capital amount will need careful thought because it is significant.

The substantial increase in gearing, especially with respect to proposal 1 (Appendix 3), may worry some stakeholders because of the extra financial risk. However, based on market values, the level of gearing may not appear so high. The expected credit migration from A to BBB seems to indicate some increase in risk, but it is probably not substantial.

The BoD should also be aware of, and take account of, the fact that going to the capital markets to raise finance will require Conejo Co to disclose information, which may be considered strategically important and could impact negatively on areas where Conejo Co has a competitive advantage.

Reaction of credit rating companies

Credit ratings assigned to companies and to borrowings made by companies by credit rating companies depend on the probability of default and recovery rate. A credit migration from A to BBB means that Conejo Co has become riskier in that it is more likely to default and bondholders will find it more difficult to recover their entire loan if default does happen. Nevertheless, the relatively lower increase in yield spreads from A to BBB, compared to BBB to BB, indicates that BBB can still be considered a relatively safe investment.

Duration indicates the time it takes to recover half the repayments of interest and capital of a bond, in present value terms. Duration measures the sensitivity of bond prices to changes in interest rates. A bond with a higher duration would see a greater fluctuation in its value when interest rates change, compared to a bond with a lower duration. Appendix 2 shows that a bond which pays interest (coupon) and capital in equal annual instalments will have a lower duration. This is because a greater proportion of income is received earlier and income due to be received earlier is less risky. Therefore, when interest rates change, this bond's value will change by less than the bond with the higher duration. The CEO is correct that the bond with equal annual payments of interest and capital is less sensitive to interest rate changes, but it is not likely that this will be a significant factor for a credit rating company when assigning a credit rating.

A credit rating company will consider a number of criteria when assigning a credit rating, as these would give a more appropriate assessment of the probability of default and the recovery rate. These criteria include, for example, the industry within which the company operates, the company's position within that industry, the company's ability to generate profits in proportion to the capital invested, the amount of gearing, the quality of management and the amount of financial flexibility the company possesses. A credit rating company will be much less concerned about the manner in which a bond's value fluctuates when interest rates change.

Impact on equity holders

The purpose of the financial reconstruction would be of interest to the equity holders. If, for example, Conejo Co selects proposal 1 (Appendix 3), it may give equity holders an opportunity to liquidate some of their invested capital. At present, the original members of the company hold 40% of the equity capital and proposal 1 provides them with the opportunity to realise a substantial capital without unnecessary fluctuations in the share price. Selling large quantities of equity shares in the stock exchange may move the price of the shares down and cause unnecessary fluctuations in the share price.

If, on the other hand, proposal 2 (Appendix 3) is selected, any additional profits after the payment of interest will benefit the equity holders directly. In effect, debt capital is being used for the benefit of the equity holders.

It may be true that equity holders may be concerned about the increased risk which higher gearing will bring, and because of this, they may need higher returns to compensate for the higher risk. However, in terms of market values, the increased gearing may be of less concern to equity holders. Conejo Co should consider the capital structure of its competitors to assess what should be an appropriate level of gearing.

Equity holders will probably be more concerned about the additional restrictive covenants which will result from the extra debt finance, and the extent to which these covenants will restrict the financial flexibility of Conejo Co when undertaking future business opportunities.

Equity holders may also be concerned that because Conejo Co has to pay extra interest to debt holders, its ability to pay increasing amounts of dividends in the future could be affected. However, Appendix 3 shows that the proportion of interest relative to after-tax profits is not too high and any concern from the equity holders is probably unfounded.

Impact on debt holders

Although the current debt holders may be concerned about the extra gearing which the new bonds would introduce to Conejo Co, Appendix 1 shows that the higher coupon payments which the current debt holders will receive would negate any fall in the value of their bonds due to the credit migration to BBB rating from an A rating. Given that currently Conejo Co is subject to low financial risk, and probably lower business risk, it is unlikely that the current and new debt holders would be overly concerned about the extra gearing. The earnings figures in Appendix 3 also show that the after-tax profit figures provide a substantial interest cover and therefore additional annual interest payment should not cause the debt holders undue concern either.

The current and new debt holders would be more concerned about Conejo Co's ability to pay back the large capital sum in five years' time. However, a convincing explanation of how this can be achieved or a plan to roll over the debt should allay these concerns.

The current and new debt holders may be concerned that Conejo Co is not tempted to take unnecessary risks with the additional investment finance, but sensible use of restrictive covenants and the requirement to make extra disclosures to the markets when raising the debt finance should help mitigate these concerns.

Conclusion

Overall, it seems that the proposed financial reconstruction will be beneficial, as it will provide opportunities for Conejo Co to make additional investments and/or an opportunity to reduce equity capital, and thereby increasing the earnings per share. The increased gearing may not look large when considered in terms of market values. It may also be advantageous to undertake the reconstruction scheme in a period when interest rates are low and the credit migration is not disadvantageous. However, Conejo Co needs to be mindful of how it intends to repay the capital amount in five years' time, the information it will disclose to the capital markets and the impact of any negative restrictive covenants.

Report compiled by:

Date:

APPENDICES

Appendix 1: Change in the value of the current bond from credit migration and coupon rate required from the new bond (Question (b) (i))

Spot yield rates (yield curve) based on BBB rating

1 year: 2.20%

2 year: 2.51%

3 year: 2.84%

4 year: 3.25%

5 year: 3.62%

Bond value based on BBB rating

$\$5.57 \times 1.0220^{-1} + \$5.57 \times 1.0251^{-2} + \$105.57 \times 1.0284^{-3} = \$107.81$

Current bond value = $107.80

Although the credit rating of Conejo Co declines from A to BBB, resulting in higher spot yield rates, the value of the bond does not change very much at all. This is because the increase in the coupons and the resultant increase in value almost exactly matches the fall in value from the higher spot yield rates.

Coupon rate required from the new bond

Take R as the coupon rate, such that:

$(\$R \times 1.0220^{-1}) + (\$R \times 1.0251^{-2}) + (\$R \times 1.0284^{-3}) + (\$R \times 1.0325^{-4}) + (\$R \times 1.0362^{-5}) + (\$100 \times 1.0362^{-5}) = \$100$

4.5665R + 83.71 = 100

R = $3.57

Coupon rate for the new bond is 3.57%.

If the coupon payments on the bond are at a rate of 3.57% on the face value, it ensures that the present values of the coupons and the redemption of the bond at face value exactly equals the bond's current face value, based on Conejo Co's yield curve.

Appendix 2: Macaulay durations (Question (b) (ii))

Macaulay duration based on annual coupon of $3.57 and redemption value of $100 in year 5:

$[(\$3.57 \times 1.0220^{-1} \times 1 \text{ year}) + (\$3.57 \times 1.0251^{-2} \times 2 \text{ years}) + (\$3.57 \times 1.0284^{-3} \times 3 \text{ years}) + (\$3.57 \times 1.0325^{-4} \times 4 \text{ years}) + (\$103.57 \times 1.0362^{-5} \times 5 \text{ years})]/\$100$

$= [3.49 + 6.79 + 9.85 + 12.57 + 433.50]/100 = 4.7 \text{ years}$

Macaulay duration based on fixed annual repayments of interest and capital:

Annuity factor: $(3.57\%, 5 \text{ years}) = (1 - 1.0357^{-5})/0.0357 = 4.51$ approximately

Annual payments of capital and interest required to pay back new bond issue = $100/4.51 = $22.17 per $100 bond approximately

$[(\$22.17 \times 1.0220^{-1} \times 1 \text{ year}) + (\$22.17 \times 1.0251^{-2} \times 2 \text{ years}) + (\$22.17 \times 1.0284^{-3} \times 3 \text{ years}) + (\$22.17 \times 1.0325^{-4} \times 4 \text{ years}) + (\$22.17 \times 1.0362^{-5} \times 5 \text{ years})]/\$100$

$= [21.69 + 42.20 + 61.15 + 78.03 + 92.79]/100 = 3.0 \text{ years}$

Appendix 3: Forecast earnings, financial position, earnings per share and gearing (Question (b) (iii))

Adjustments to forecast earnings (Amounts in $ millions)

	Current	Proposal 1	Proposal 2
Forecast after-tax profit	350.00	350.00	350.00
Interest payable on additional borrowing (based on a coupon rate of 3.57%) 3.57% × $1,320m × (1 − 0.15)		(40.06)	(40.06)
Additional interest payable due to higher coupon 0.37% × $120m × (1 − 0.15)		(0.38)	(0.38)
Return on additional investment (after tax) 12% × $1,320m			158.40
Revised forecast after-tax earnings	350.00	309.56	467.96

Forecast financial position (Amounts in $ millions)

	Current	Proposal 1	Proposal 2
Non-current assets	1,735.00	1,735.00	3,055.00
Current assets	530.00	489.56	647.96
Total assets	2,265.00	2,224.56	3,702.96

	Current	Proposal 1	Proposal 2
Equity and liabilities			
Share capital ($1 per share par)	400.00	280.00	400.00
Reserves	1,700.00	459.56	1,817.96
Total equity	2,100.00	739.56	2,217.96
Non-current liabilities	120.00	1,440.00	1,440.00
Current liabilities	45.00	45.00	45.00
Total liabilities	165.00	1,485.00	1,485.00
Total liabilities and capital	2,265.00	2,224.56	3,702.96

	Current	Proposal 1	Proposal 2
Gearing % (non-current liabilities/equity)	5.7%	194.7%	64.9%
Earnings per share (in cents)			
(adj profit after tax/no. of shares)	87.5c	110.6c	117.0c

Notes:

If gearing is calculated based on non-current liabilities/(non-current liabilities + equity) and/or using market value of equity, instead of as above, then this is acceptable as well.

Proposal 1

Additional interest payable is deducted from current assets, assuming it is paid in cash and this is part of current assets. Reserves are also reduced by this amount.

Shares repurchased as follows: $1 × 120m shares deducted from share capital and $10 × 120m shares deducted from reserves. $1,320m, consisting of $11 × 120m shares, added to non-current liabilities.

Proposal 2

Treatment of additional interest payable is as per proposal 1.

Additional debt finance raised, $1,320 million, is added to non-current liabilities and to non-current assets, assuming that all this amount is invested in non-current assets to generate extra income.

It is assumed that this additional investment generates returns at 12%, which is added to current assets and to profits (and therefore to reserves).

(Explanations given in notes are not required for full marks, but are included to explain how the figures given in Appendix 3 are derived)

(**Note:** Credit will be given for alternative relevant presentation of financial positions and discussion)

TREASURY AND ADVANCED RISK MANAGEMENT TECHNIQUES

20   LAMMER PLC (JUN 06 ADAPTED) *Walk in the footsteps of a top tutor*

Walkthrough question – key answer tips

Risk management questions like this one can be very time pressured, especially when you are not told which hedging methods to look at. It is important to adopt a systematic approach.

Part (b) is a very typical risk management question. The first job is to identify which transaction(s) will need to be hedged. Five transactions are presented here, but two of them are in sterling (the home currency) so they can immediately be ignored. Furthermore, the other three transactions are all in dollars and they all arise in five months' time, so they can be netted off. As a consequence, only one transaction (a net dollar payment of $1,150,000) needs covering. Had you not spotted this, you could have wasted a lot of time trying to cover all five transactions separately.

The next problem is to identify which hedging methods are available. Forward rates, futures prices and options prices are quoted explicitly, but notice also that you are given interest rates, so you will be able to set up a money market hedge too.

As you go through and present calculations on all these methods, make sure you keep explaining your methods too. The marking key shows that 8 of the 24 marks in Part (b) were awarded for discussion points.

Parts (a), (c) and (d) between them account for nearly half of the total marks on the question. You must therefore make sure that you leave enough time to attempt them properly. Note that these parts are totally unrelated to the calculations in Part (b), so have a go at them even if you have struggled to finish Part (b).

Parts (a) and (d) in particular contain some very easy marks, arguably the easiest marks on the whole question. If you want to be certain that you'll get the marks in Part (d), answer this part first, before you even start the more detailed work in the other parts of the question.

(a)   **The relative advantages and disadvantages of the use of a money market hedge versus exchange traded derivatives**

A money market hedge is a mechanism for the delivery of foreign currency, at a future date, at a specified rate without recourse to the forward FOREX market. If a company is able to achieve preferential access to the short term money markets in the base and counter currency zones then it can be a cost effective substitute for a forward agreement. However, it is difficult to reverse quickly and is cumbersome to establish as it requires borrowing/lending agreements to be established denominated in the two currencies.

Exchange traded derivatives such as futures and foreign exchange options offer a rapid way of creating a hedge and are easily closed out. For example, currency futures are normally closed out and the profit/loss on the derivative position used to offset the gain or loss in the underlying. The fixed contract sizes for exchange traded products mean that it is often impossible to achieve a perfect hedge and some gain or loss on the unhedged element of the underlying or the derivative will be carried. Also, given that exchange traded derivatives are priced in a separate market to the underlying there may be discrepancies in the movements of each and the observed delta may not equal one. This basis risk is minimised by choosing short maturity derivatives but cannot be completely eliminated unless maturity coincides exactly with the end of the exposure. Furthermore less than perfectly hedged positions require disclosure under IFRS 39. Although rapid to establish, currency hedging using the derivatives market may also involve significant cash flows in meeting and maintaining the margin requirements of the exchange. Unlike futures, currency options will entail the payment of a premium which may be an expensive way of eliminating the risk of an adverse currency movement.

With relatively small amounts, the OTC market represents the most convenient means of locking in exchange rates. Where cross border flows are common and business is well diversified across different currency areas then currency hedging is of questionable benefit. Where, as in this case, relatively infrequent flows occur then the simplest solution is to engage in the forward market for hedging risk. The use of a money market hedge as described may generate a more favourable forward rate than direct recourse to the forex market. However the administrative and management costs in setting up the necessary loans and deposits are a significant consideration.

(b) **Report on possible hedging strategies for the foreign exchange exposure in five months' time.**

Only relevant net dollar exposures should be hedged. Net dollar imports in five months' time are $1,150,000. This is the amount to be hedged. The transactions in sterling are not exposed and should not be hedged. The exposure may be hedged using the forward foreign exchange market, a money market hedge, currency futures hedge or currency options hedge. A combination of these hedges is also possible, or alternatively a partial hedge may be selected that protects only part of the exposure.

Forward market hedge:

No five-month forward rate is given. The rate may be interpolated from the three-month and one-year rates for buying dollars.

The estimated five-month forward rate is:

$$1.9066 \times \frac{7}{9} + 1.8901 \times \frac{2}{9} = 1.9029$$

Hedging with a forward contact will fix the £ payment at:

$$\frac{\$1,150,000}{1.9029} = £604,341$$

Money market hedge:

In order to protect against any future strengthening of the dollar, Lammer could borrow £ now and convert £ into dollars to ensure that the company is not exposed if there are changes in the $/£ exchange rate.

Borrow £595,373 at 5.5% per annum for five months, total cost £609,017

Convert into dollars at the spot rate of $1.9156/£ to yield $1,140,496

Invest in the USA at 2.0% per annum to yield a total of $1,150,000, which will be used to make payment for the imports.

($1,140,496 × 1.008333 = $1,150,000)

A money market hedge is more expensive than the forward hedge.

Currency futures hedge:

The currency exposure is in five months' time. To protect against the risk of the dollar strengthening, December futures should be sold.

The basis is 1.9156 − 1.8986 = 1.7 cents. This relates to a futures contract maturing in seven months' time.

The expected basis in five months' time is $1.7 \times \dfrac{1}{7} \times 2 = 0.486$ cents

The expected lock-in futures rate may be estimated by:

1.8986 + 0.00486 = 1.9035

This is slightly more favourable than the forward market rate, but there are a number of possible disadvantages of using currency futures:

(i)   Basis risk might exist. The actual basis at the close-out date in five months' time might be different from the expected basis of 0.486 cents.

(ii)   Currency futures will involve either underhedging or overhedging as an exact number of contracts for the risk is not available.

$$\frac{\$1,150,000}{1.9035} = £604,150 \qquad \frac{£604,150}{£62,500} = 9.67 \text{ contracts}$$

(iii)   Currency futures involve the upfront payment of a margin (security deposit). If daily losses are made on the futures contracts additional margin will need to be provided to keep the futures contracts open.

Currency options hedge:

As dollars need to be purchased, Lammer will need to buy December put options on £.

Exercise price	$	£	No. of contracts
1.8800	1,150,000	611,702	19.57
1.9000	1,150,000	605,263	19.37
1.9200	1,150,000	598,958	19.17

It is assumed that Lammer will underhedge using 19 contracts and will purchase the remaining dollars in the forward market (in reality it would probably wait and use the spot market in five months' time); 19 contracts is £593,750.

Exercise price	$	Premium $	Premium £ at spot	Underhedge $
1.8800	1,116,250	17,575	9,175	33,750
1.9000	1,128,125	25,769	13,452	21,875
1.9200	1,140,000	38,891	20,302	10,000

Worst-case outcomes if the options are exercised:

Exercise price	Basic cost (£)	Premium	Underhedged £ at forward	Total
1.8800	593,750	9,175	17,736	620,661
1.9000	593,750	13,452	11,496	618,698
1.9200	593,750	20,302	5,255	619,307

Tutorial note

This lengthy calculation has shown that the exercise price of 1.9000 is likely to be most attractive to Lammer (it has the lowest overall cost of £618,698. To reduce the amount of time spent on this calculation, you could have identified the cheapest exercise price right at the start as follows:

Exercise Price (A)	Premium($) (B)	(A)–(B)
1.8800	0.0296	1.8504
1.9000	0.0434	1.8566
1.9200	0.0655	1.8545

The (A)–(B) column shows the net amount of $ receivable, after paying the premium, for each £1 covered. The 1.9000 exercise price corresponds to the highest net $ receipt, so is the preferred option. Once you have identified the preferred exercise price, just present calculations for that one to save time

As is normal, the currency options worst-case outcomes are much more expensive than alternative hedges. However, if the dollar weakens relative to the pound, option contracts allow the company to purchase the required dollars in five months' time in the spot market and let the options lapse (or alternatively sell the options to take advantage of any remaining time value). In this situation the dollar would have to weaken to about 1.98/£ before the currency options became more favourable than the forward contract or futures hedge. This is possible, but unlikely, especially as the forward market expects the dollar to strengthen rather than weaken.

Forward contracts or futures contracts appear to be the best form of hedge.

(c) Estimated effect on value:

	Exchange rate $/£	£ equivalent of $4.2m	£ difference to spot	DF (11%)	PV
Spot	1.9156	2,192,525	–	1	–
1 year	1.8581	2,260,374	67,849	0.901	61,132
2 years	1.8024	2,330,226	137,701	0.812	111,813
3 years	1.7483	2,402,334	209,809	0.731	153,370
4 years	1.6959	2,476,561	284,036	0.659	187,180
5 years	1.6450	2,553,191	360,666	0.593	213,875
					727,370

The strengthening of the dollar is expected to reduce the present value of cash flows, and, if the market is efficient, the market value of Lammer, by £727,370.

(d) Economic exposure relates to the change in the value of a company as a result of unexpected changes in exchange rates.

Unless there are known contractual future cash flows it is difficult to hedge economic exposure using options, swaps, or other financial hedges, as the amount of the exposure is unknown.

Economic exposure is normally managed by internationally diversifying activities, and organising activities to allow flexibility to vary the location of production, the supply sources of raw materials and components, and international financing, in response to changes in exchange rates.

To some extent multinational companies may offset economic exposure by arranging natural hedges, for example by borrowing funds in the USA, and then servicing the interest payments and the repayment of principal on the borrowing with cash flows generated by subsidiaries in the USA.

Marketing strategies may also be used to offset the effects of economic exposure. For example, if UK products were to become relatively expensive in the USA due to a fall in the value of the dollar, a UK company might adopt an intensive marketing campaign to create a better brand or quality image for its products.

21 CASASOPHIA CO (JUN 11 ADAPTED)

Key answer tips

This question covers the three most commonly tested currency hedging methods: forward contracts, futures and traded options. In any hedging question like this you should show how to set up the hedge and then demonstrate what the likely result of the hedge will be.

(a) The International Monetary Fund (IMF) was established at the Bretton Wood Conference of 1945. Its initial tasks were to promote world trade and to help support the fixed exchange rate system that existed at that time. Support was mainly in the form of temporary loans to member countries which experienced balance of payments difficulties.

Such loans were financed by member countries' quota subscriptions. Although floating exchange rates and exchange rate agreements between blocs of countries have replaced the fixed exchange rate system, the IMF still provides loans to many of its members, particularly developing countries. Today loans are also granted to help countries repay large commercial debts that they have built up from the international banking system.

An important feature of most IMF loans is the conditions attached to the loans. Countries receiving IMF loans are required to take strong economic measures to try to improve or eliminate the economic problems that made the loans necessary, and to stimulate medium to long-term economic development. These conditions typically include currency devaluation, controls over inflation via the money supply, public expenditure cuts to reduce government budget deficits and local tax increases.

Loans of up to 25% of a member country's quotas are given without condition. A further 25% is available to countries that 'demonstrate reasonable efforts' to overcome balance of payments difficulties. Upper credit tranches of up to a further 75% of quota, normally in the form of standby facilities, are available subject to conditionality agreements. Most loans are for a period of up to five years.

The IMF has undoubtedly been successful in helping to reduce volatility in international exchange rates, and in facilitating world trade. This has beneficial effects on the trading activities of multinational companies. However, the strong influence of the IMF on the macro-economic policies of developing nations often leads to short term deflation and reductions in the size of markets for multinational companies' products.

Conflicts may exist between multinationals, who wish to freely move capital internationally, and governments trying to control the money supply and inflation. Tax increases often accompany economic austerity measures, import tariff quotas may make operations more difficult and increases in interest rates raise the cost of finance. In the medium to long term it is hoped that the structural adjustments will stimulate economic growth and will increase the size of markets for multinational companies, but IMF economic conditions may cause significant short to medium term difficulties for subsidiaries of multinationals in the countries concerned.

(b) There is no inconsistency between the views of Warren Buffett and the views of many corporate treasurers. Derivatives such as futures contracts, swaps and options enable the holder to manage the risk associated with an underlying position. Thus they can be used to reduce the risk of a position (e.g. if you are due to receive a certain amount of foreign currency on a known date in the future, you can sell it forward and thus fix the amount of the receipt in your own home currency to eliminate the currency risk) or to speculate to increase the risk of a position (e.g. you can buy a financial futures contract for trading purposes, hoping that you can sell it in the future for more than you paid for it). Buffett is concerned about speculators who buy derivatives for trading purposes with no underlying need for them. Corporate treasurers see the value in using derivatives to hedge their risk away, thus reducing their overall risk exposure.

Let us consider Buffett's views in more detail. He has been a long-term investor in the US stock market. As an investor, he would like relevant and reliable financial information on the companies that he is thinking of investing in. In the past, the financial accounting for derivatives has been inadequate throughout the world. Favouring the historical cost convention meant that derivatives were stated at cost in the SOFP, with any profit or loss only being recognised when the derivative was sold. However the initial cost of a derivative is small or even zero, while its market value at a SOFP date might be large. It is in this sense that Buffett is correct in having described derivatives as a 'time-bomb', waiting for their profit or loss to be recognised in the future, at a time to be decided by the company holding the speculative position. However, this problem has now been mitigated somewhat by improved standards on financial accounting for derivatives. International Standard IAS 39 now requires all derivatives to be measured at their fair values in each SOFP. This certainly improves the relevance of the SOFP, but the volatility of derivative values means that the description of a 'time-bomb' is still appropriate. Things can go wrong very quickly with derivatives, so the fact that they were measured at fair value in the previous SOFP is of little comfort to the investor who has seen his company suddenly lose a huge sum of money through losing control (e.g. Procter and Gamble lost $150m in 1994 when speculating on the spread between the German mark and the US dollar).

The opposite view is generally held by corporate treasurers who see derivatives as a means of reducing risk, whether currency risk, interest rate risk or other market risk. Many treasury departments are set up as cost centres and instructed not to engage in speculation. One often sees the statement in companies' Annual Reports that the company does not engage in speculation with derivative instruments. The situation is less clear-cut where the treasury is set up as a profit centre which may choose to take speculative positions within established limits. It is often in these circumstances that the distinction between hedging and speculation becomes blurred in the department's pursuit of profits, and once again the time-bomb can blow up with devastating consequences.

(c)   REPORT

The following report calculates the likely outcomes of various currency hedges. The information provided enables Casasophia Co to hedge its US$ income using forward contracts, future contracts or option contracts.

Forward contracts

Since it is a dollar receipt, the 1.3623 rate will be used.

Locked in receipt = US$20,000,000/1.3623 = €14,681,054

The hedge fixes the rate at 1.3623 and is legally binding.

Futures contracts

This hedging strategy needs to show a gain when the Dollar exchange rate depreciates against the Euro and the underlying market shows a loss. Hence, for a US$ receipt, the five-month futures contracts (two-month is too short for the required hedge period) need be bought, that is a long position needs to be adopted. It is assumed that the basis differential will narrow proportionally to the time expired. However, when the contract is closed out before expiry, this may not be the case due to basis risk, and a better or worse outcome may result.

Predicted futures rate = 1.3698 − (1/3 × (1.3698 − 1.3633)) = 1.3676 (when the five-month contract is closed out in four months' time)

Expected receipt = US$20,000,000/1.3676 = €14,624,159

Number of contracts to be bought = €14,624,159/€125,000 = 117 contracts

[OR: Futures lock-in rate may be estimated from the spot and five-month futures rate:

1.3698 + (1/5 × (1.3618 − 1.3698)) = 1.3682

US$20,000,000/1.3682 = €14,617,746

€14,617,746/€125,000 = 116.9 or 117 contracts (a slight over-hedge)]

This is worse than the forward rate. In addition to this, futures contracts require margin payments and are marked-to-market on a daily basis, although any gain is not realised until the contracts are closed out.

Like the forward contracts, futures contracts fix the rate and are legally binding.

Option contracts

Options have an advantage over forwards and futures because the prices are not fixed and the option buyer can let the option lapse if the rates move favourably. Hence options have an unlimited upside but a limited downside. However, a premium is payable for this benefit.

Casasophia Co would purchase Euro call options to protect itself against a weakening Dollar to the Euro.

Exercise Price: $1.36/€1

€ receipts = 20,000,000/1.36 = 14,705,882 or 117.6 contracts

117 call options purchased

€ receipts = 117 × 125,000 = €14,625,000

Premium payable = 117 × 0.0280 × 125,000 = US$409,500

Premium in € = 409,500/1.3585 = €301,435

Amount not hedged = US$20,000,000 – (117 × €125,000 × 1.36) = US$110,000

Use forwards to hedge amount not hedged = US$110,000/1.3623 = €80,746

Total receipts = 14,625,000 – 301,435 + 80,746 = €14,404,311

Exercise Price: $1.38/€1

€ receipts = 20,000,000/1.38 = 14,492,754 or 115.9 contracts

115 call options purchased

€ receipts = 115 × 125,000 = €14,375,000

Premium payable = 115 × 0.0223 × 125,000 = US$320,563

Premium in € = 320,563/1.3585 = €235,968

Amount not hedged = US$20,000,000 – (115 × €125,000 × 1.38) = US$162,500

Use forwards to hedge amount not hedged = US$162,500/1.3623 = €119,284

Total receipts = 14,375,000 – 235,968 + 119,284 = €14,258,316

Both these hedges are significantly worse than the forward or futures contracts hedges. This is due to the high premiums payable to let the option lapse if the prices move in Casasophia Co's favour. With futures and forwards, Casasophia Co cannot take advantage of the Dollar strengthening against the Euro. However, this needs to be significant before the cost of the premium is covered.

Conclusion

It is recommended that Casasophia Co use the forward markets to hedge against the Dollar depreciating in four months' time against the Euro in order to maximise receipts. However, Casasophia Co needs to be aware that forward contracts are not traded on a formal exchange and therefore default risk exists. And the exchange rate is fixed once the contract is agreed.

(d) Amount expected from US$ receipts is €14,681,054 assuming that forward contracts used.

Invested for two months = €14,681,054 × (1 + (60/360 × 0.0180)) = €14,725,097 say €14,725,000 approximately.

Expected spot rate (E(s)) in 12 months (using purchasing power parity) =

E(s) = 116 × 1.097/1.012 = 125.7

Expected spot rate in 6 months

116 + (125.7 − 116)/2 = 120.9

Investment amount required = MShs 2,640,000,000/120.9 = €21.84m

Loan finance required = 21.84 − 14.73 = €7.11m

Casasophia Co will need to raise just over €7 million in loans in addition to the receipts from the USA to finance the project in Mazabia. This is on the assumption that the future spot rate follows the purchasing power parity conditions.

Tutorial note

Casasophia Co could also consider whether it may be more beneficial to transfer funds directly from the USA to Mazabia instead of converting them into Euros first. This would save transaction costs of converting first into Euros and then into MShs, and also the costs related to using the forward markets. The rates for investing the funds in the USA for two months and the exchange rate between US$ and MShs are not given, but if these were available a comparative analysis could be conducted. In these circumstances the amount of loan finance required would possibly be lower.

(e) Calculate expected forward rates

Interest Rate Parity

Year	Forward rate [MShs/1€]
½ year	128 × 1.108/1.022 = 138.77
	128 + (138.77 − 128)/2 = 133.4
1.5 years	133.4 × 1.108/1.022 = 144.6
2.5 years	144.6 × 1.108/1.022 = 156.8
3.5 years	156.8 × 1.108/1.022 = 170.0

Present Value calculations (Present values in six months)

	Year 1	Year 2	Year 3	Total
Income (MShs, million)	1,500	1,500	1,500	
Income (€ million, based on forward rates)	10.37	9.57	8.82	
Discounted Income (€ million at 12%)	9.26	7.63	6.28	23.17

Net present value = €23.17m − €21.84m = €1.33m

The calculation of the forward rates based on the interest rate parity indicates that the MShs rates are depreciating against the Euro because the Mazabia base rates at 10.8% are higher than the European country's local base rates at 2.2%. However, even where the forward rates are fixed, based on interest rate parity, the project is worthwhile for Casasophia Co.

According to the purchasing power parity, future spot currency rates will change in proportion to the inflation level differentials between two countries. Hence if Mazabia's inflation level is higher than the European Union, its currency will depreciate against the Euro.

Given that the inflation level in Mazabia is expected to range from 5% to 15% over the next few years, there is uncertainty over the NPV of the project in Euros if the swap is not accepted. The swap fixes the future exchange rates, although Casasophia Co will lose out if the inflation rate is lower than 9.7%, since the future spot rate will depreciate by less than what is predicted by the forward rates. The situation will be opposite if the level of inflation is higher than 9.7%.

Casasophia Co will also need to consider the risk of default by the local bank. Casasophia Co may ask Mazabia's government to act as guarantor to reduce this risk. Overall, if such an agreement could be reached, it would probably be beneficial to agree to the swap to ensure a certain level of income.

Casasophia Co may also want to explore whether it is possible for the grant funding from the European Union being paid to it directly, to reduce its exposure to the likely depreciation of MShs.

22 CMC CO (SPECIMEN PAPER 2018)

Key answer tips

All the Section A questions are very time pressured, with lots of parts to complete in the time.

It is therefore critically important to attempt the easier parts of the question first and leave the more difficult parts until the end.

(a) The foreign exchange exposure of the dollar payment due in four months can be hedged using the following derivative products:

- Forward rate offered by Pecunia Bank

- Exchange-traded futures contracts; and

- Exchange-traded options contracts

Using the forward rate

Payment in Swiss Francs = US$5,060,000/1.0677 = CHF4,739,159

Using futures contract

Since a dollar payment needs to be made in four months' time, CMC Co needs to hedge against Swiss Francs weakening.

Hence, the company should go short and the six-month futures contract is undertaken. It is assumed that the basis differential will narrow in proportion to time.

Predicted futures rate = 1.0647 + [(1.0659 — 1.0647) × 1/3] = 1.0651

[Alternatively, can predict futures rate based on spot rate: 1.0635 + [(1.0659 — 1.0635) × 4/6] = 1.0651]

Expected payment = US$5,060,000/1.0651 = CHF4,750,728

No. of contracts sold = CHF4,750,728/CHF125,000 = approx. 38 contracts

Using options contracts

Since a dollar payment needs to be made in four months' time, CMC Co needs to hedge against Swiss Francs weakening. Hence, the company should purchase six-month put options.

Exercise price US$1.06/CHF1

Payment = US$5,060,000/1.06 = CHF4,773,585

Buy 4,773,585/125,000 = 38.19 put contracts, say 38 contracts

CHF payment = CHF4,750,000

Premium payable = 38 × 125,000 × 0.0216 = US$102,600

In CHF = 102,600/1.0635 = CHF96,474

Amount not hedged = US$5,060,000 — (38 × 125,000 × 1.06) = US$25,000

Use forward contracts to hedge this = US$25,000/1.0677 = CHF23,415

Total payment = CHF4,750,000 + CHF96,474 + CHF23,415 = CHF4,869,889

Exercise price US$1.07/CHF1

Payment = US$5,060,000/1.07 = CHF4,728,972

Buy 4,728,972/125,000 = 37.83 put contracts, say 38 contracts (but this is an over-hedge)

CHF payment = CHF4,750,000

Premium payable = 38 × 125,000 × 0.0263 = US$124,925

In CHF = 124,925/1.0635 = CHF117,466

Amount over-hedged = US$5,060,000 — (38 × 125,000 × 1.07) = US$22,500

Using forward contracts to show benefit of this = US$22,500/1.0677 = CHF21,073

Total payment = CHF4,750,000 + CHF117,466 — CHF21,073 = CHF4,846,393

Advice

Forward contracts minimise the payment and option contracts would maximise the payment, with the payment arising from the futures contracts in between these two. With the option contracts, the exercise price of US$1.07/CHF1 gives the lower cost. Although transaction costs are ignored, it should be noted that with exchange-traded futures contracts, margins are required and the contracts are marked-to-market daily.

It would therefore seem that the futures contracts and the option contract with an exercise price of US$1.06/CHF1 should be rejected. The choice between forward contracts and the 1.07 options depends on CMC Co's attitude to risk. The forward rate is binding, whereas option contracts give the company the choice to let the option contract lapse if the CHF strengthens against the US$. Observing the rates of inflation between the two countries and the exchange-traded derivatives this is likely to be the case, but it is not definite. Moreover, the option rates need to move in favour considerably before the option is beneficial to CMC Co, due to the high premium payable.

It would therefore seem that forward markets should be selected to minimise the amount of payment, but CMC Co should also bear in mind that the risk of default is higher with forward contracts compared with exchange-traded contracts.

(b)

	CMC Co	Counterparty	Interest rate differential
Fixed rate	2.2%	3.8%	1.6%
Floating rate	Yield rate + 0.4%	Yield rate + 0.8%	0.4%

CMC Co has a comparative advantage in borrowing at the fixed rate and the counterparty has a comparative advantage in borrowing at the floating rate. Total possible benefit before Pecunia Bank's fee is 1.2%, which if shared equally results in a benefit of 0.6% each, for both CMC Co and the counterparty.

	CMC Co	Counterparty
CMC Co borrows at	2.2%	
Counterparty borrows at		Yield rate + 0.8%
Advantage	60 basis points	60 basis points
Net result	Yield rate – 0.2%	3.2%
SWAP		
Counterparty receives		Yield rate
CMC Co pays	Yield rate	
Counterparty pays		2.4%
CMC Co receives	2.4%	

After paying the 20 basis point fee, CMC Co will effectively pay interest at the yield curve rate and benefit by 40 basis points or 0.4%, and the counterparty will pay interest at 3.4% and benefit by 40 basis points or 0.4% as well.

> **Examiner's note**
>
> Full marks will be given where the question is answered by estimating the arbitrage gain of 1.2% and deducting the fees of 0.4%, without constructing the above table.

(c) Annuity factor, 4 years, 2% = 3.808 Equal annual amounts repayable per year = CHF60,000,000/3.808 = CHF15,756,303

Macaulay duration

(15,756,303 × 0.980 × 1 year +
15,756,303 × 0.961 × 2 years +
15,756,303 × 0.942 × 3 years +
15,756,303 × 0.924 × 4 years)/60,000,000
= 2.47 years

Modified duration = 2.47/1.02 = 2.42 years

The equation linking modified duration (D), and the relationship between the change in interest rates (Ai) and change in price or value of a bond or loan (AP) is given as follows:

$$\Delta P = [-D \times \Delta i \times P]$$

(P is the current value of a loan or bond and is a constant)

The size of the modified duration will determine how much the value of a bond or loan will change when there is a change in interest rates. A higher modified duration means that the fluctuations in the value of a bond or loan will be greater, hence the value of 2.42 means that the value of the loan or bond will change by 2.42 times the change in interest rates multiplied by the original value of the bond or loan.

The relationship is only an approximation because duration assumes that the relationship between the change in interest rates and the corresponding change in the value of the bond or loan is linear. In fact, the relationship between interest rates and bond price is in the form of a curve which is convex to the origin (i.e. non-linear). Therefore duration can only provide a reasonable estimation of the change in the value of a bond or loan due to changes in interest rates, when those interest rate changes are small.

(d) **MEMORANDUM**

From:

To: **The Board of Directors, CMC Co**

Date: **xx/xx/xxxx**

Subject: Discussion of the proposal to manage foreign exchange and interest rate exposures, and the proposal to move operations to four branches and consequential agency issues

This memo discusses the proposal of whether or not CMC Co should undertake the management of foreign exchange and interest rate exposure, and the agency issues resulting from the proposal to locate branches internationally and how these issues may be mitigated. Each proposal will be considered in turn.

(i) **Proposal one: Management of foreign exchange and interest rate exposure**

The non-executive directors are correct if CMC Co is in a situation where markets are perfect and efficient, where information is freely available and where securities are priced correctly. In this circumstance, risk management or hedging would not add value and if shareholders hold well diversified portfolios, unsystematic risk will be largely eliminated. The position against hedging states that in such cases companies would not increase shareholder value by hedging or eliminating risk because there will be no further reduction in unsystematic risk. Furthermore, the cost of reducing any systematic risk will equal or be greater than the benefit derived from such risk reduction. Shareholders would not gain from risk management or hedging; in fact, if the costs exceed the benefits, then hedging may result in a reduction in shareholder value.

Risk management or hedging may result in increasing corporate (and therefore shareholder) value if market imperfections exist, and in these situations, reducing the volatility of a company's earnings will result in higher cash inflows. Proponents of hedging cite three main situations where reduction in volatility or risk may increase cash flows – in situations: where the rate of tax is increasing;

where a firm could face significant financial distress costs due to high volatility in earnings; and where stable earnings increases certainty and the ability to plan for the future, thus resulting in stable investment policies by the firm.

Active hedging may also reduce agency costs. For example, unlike shareholders, managers and employees of the company may not hold diversified portfolios. Hedging allows the risks faced by managers and employees to be reduced. Additionally, hedging may allow managers to be less concerned about market movements which are not within their control and instead allow them to focus on business issues over which they can exercise control. This seems to be what the purchasing director is contending. On the other hand, the finance director seems to be more interested in increasing his personal benefits and not necessarily in increasing the value of CMC Co.

A consistent hedging strategy or policy may be used as a signalling tool to reduce the conflict of interest between bondholders and shareholders, and thus reduce restrictive covenants.

It is also suggested that until recently CMC Co had no intention of hedging and communicated this in its annual report. It is likely that shareholders will therefore have created their own risk management policies. A strategic change in the policy may have a negative impact on the shareholders and the clientele impact of this will need to be taken into account.

The case of whether to hedge or not is not clear cut and CMC Co should consider all the above factors and be clear about why it is intending to change its strategy before coming to a conclusion. Any intended change in policy should be communicated to the shareholders. Shareholders can also benefit from risk management because the risk profile of the company may change, resulting in a reduced cost of capital.

(ii) **Proposal two: International branches, agency issues and their mitigation**

Principal–agent relationships can be observed within an organisation between different stakeholder groups. With the proposed branches located in different countries, the principal–agent relationship will be between the directors and senior management at CMC Co in Switzerland, and the managers of the individual branches. Agency issues can arise where the motivations of the branch managers, who are interested in the performance of their individual branches, diverge from the management at CMC Co headquarters, who are interested in the performance of the whole organisation.

These issues may arise because branch managers are not aware of, or appreciate the importance of, the key factors at corporate level. They may also arise because of differences in cultures and divergent backgrounds.

Mitigation mechanisms involve monitoring, compensation and communication policies. All of these mechanisms need to work in a complementary fashion in order to achieve goal congruence, much like the mechanisms in any principal–agent relationship.

Monitoring policies would involve ensuring that key aims and strategies are agreed between all parties before implementation, and results monitored to ensure adherence with the original agreements. Where there are differences, for example, due to external factors, new targets need to be agreed. Where deviations are noticed, these should be communicated quickly.

Compensation packages should ensure that reward is based on achievement of organisational value and therefore there is every incentive for the branch managers to act in the best interests of the corporation as a whole.

Communication should be two-way, in that branch managers should be made fully aware of the organisational objectives, and any changes to these, and how the branch contributes to these, in order to ensure their acceptance of the objectives. Furthermore, the management at CMC Co headquarters should be fully aware of cultural and educational differences in the countries where the branches are to be set up and fully plan for how organisational objectives may nevertheless be achieved within these differences.

(**Note:** Credit will be given for alternative, relevant approaches to the calculations, comments and suggestions/recommendations).

		Marking scheme	Marks
(a)		Calculation of payment using the forward rate	1
		Going short on futures and purchasing put options	2
		Predicted futures rate based on basis reduction	1
		Futures: expected payment and number of contracts	2
		Options calculation using either 1.06 or 1.07 rate	3
		Options calculation using the second rate (or explanation)	2
		Advice (1 to 2 marks per point)	4
			──
			15
			──
(b)		Comparative advantage and recognition of benefit as a result	2
		Initial decision to borrow fixed by CMC Co and floating by counterparty	1
		Swap impact	2
		Net benefit after bank charges	1
			──
			6
			──
(c)		Calculation of annual annuity amount	1
		Calculation of Macaulay duration	2
		Calculation of modified duration	1
		Explanation	3
			──
			7
			──
(d)	(i)	Discussion of efficient markets	2
		Discussion of inefficient markets and volatility	2
		Discussion of consistent strategy/impact of change	2
		Other relevant discussion or additional detail	3
			──
			9
			──
	(ii)	Discussion of the agency issues	4
		Discussion of mitigation strategies and policies	4
		Other relevant discussion or additional detail	1
			──
			9
			──
		Professional marks	
		Memorandum format	1
		Structure and presentation of the memorandum	3
			──
			4
			──
	Total		50
			──

23 LIRIO CO (MAR/JUN 16)

Key answer tips

This Section A question was a wide ranging question that covered several diverse areas of the syllabus (dividend capacity, foreign currency hedging, discounted cash flow techniques, financing options).

In questions like this it is important to manage time carefully, to avoid running over time on one part and not leaving enough time for the other parts.

Note that there is no requirement to answer the question in the order it is set. So for example if you feel confident with foreign currency hedging, you could start with part (b)(ii) (as long as you label your answer clearly in your answer booklet, to avoid confusing the marker).

(a) Purchasing power parity (PPP) predicts that the exchange rates between two currencies depend on the relative differences in the rates of inflation in each country. Therefore, if one country has a higher rate of inflation compared to another, then its currency is expected to depreciate over time. However, according to PPP the 'law of one price' holds because any weakness in one currency will be compensated by the rate of inflation in the currency's country (or group of countries in the case of the euro).

Economic exposure refers to the degree by which a company's cash flows are affected by fluctuations in exchange rates. It may also affect companies which are not exposed to foreign exchange transactions, due to actions by international competitors.

If PPP holds, then companies may not be affected by exchange rate fluctuations, as lower currency value can be compensated by the ability to raise prices due to higher inflation levels. This depends on markets being efficient.

However, a permanent shift in exchange rates may occur, not because of relative inflation rate differentials, but because a country (or group of countries) lose their competitive positions. In this case the 'law of one price' will not hold, and prices readjust to a new and long-term or even permanent rate. For example, the UK £ to USA $ rate declined in the 20th century, as the USA grew stronger economically and the UK grew weaker. The rate almost reached parity in 1985 before recovering. Since the financial crisis in 2009, it has fluctuated between roughly $1.5 to £1 and $1.7 to £1.

In such cases, where a company receives substantial amounts of revenue from companies based in countries with relatively weak economies, it may find that it is facing economic exposure and its cash flows decline over a long period of time.

(b) **Discussion paper to the board of directors (BoD), Lirio Co**

Discussion paper compiled by

Date

Purpose of the discussion paper

The purpose of this discussion paper is:

(i) To consider the implications of the BoD's proposal to use funds from the sale of its equity investment in the European company and from its cash flows generated from normal business activity over the next two years to finance a large project, instead of raising funds through equity and/or debt;

(ii) To assess whether or not the project adds value for Lirio Co or not.

Background information

The funds needed for the project are estimated at $40,000,000 at the start of the project. $23,118,000 of this amount is estimated to be received from the sale of the equity investment (appendices 2 and 3). This leaves a balance of $16,882,000 (Appendix 3), which will be obtained from the free cash flows to equity (the dividend capacity) of $21,642,000 (Appendix 1) expected to be generated in the first year. However, this would leave only $4,760,000 available for dividend payments in the first year, meaning a cut in expected dividends from $0.27/share to $0.0595/share (Appendix 3). The same level of dividends will be paid in the second year as well.

Project assessment

Based on the dividend valuation model, Lirio Co's market capitalisation, and therefore its value, is expected to increase from approximately $360 million to approximately $403 million, or by just under 12% (Appendix 3). This would suggest that it would be beneficial for the project to be undertaken.

Possible issues

1 The dividend valuation model is based on a number of factors such as: an accurate estimation of the dividend growth rate, a non-changing cost of equity and a predictable future dividend stream growing in perpetuity. In addition to this, it is expected that the sale of the investment will yield €20,000,000 but this amount could increase or reduce in the next three months. The dividend valuation model assumes that dividends and their growth rate are the sole drivers of corporate value, which is probably not accurate.

2 Although the dividend irrelevancy theory proposed by Modigliani and Miller suggests that corporate value should not be affected by a corporation's dividend policy, in practice changes in dividends do matter for two main reasons. First, dividends are used as a signalling device to the markets and unexpected changes in dividends paid and/or dividend growth rates are not generally viewed positively by them. Changes in dividends may signal that the company is not doing well and this may affect the share price negatively.

3 Second, corporate dividend policy attracts certain groups of shareholders or clientele. In the main this is due to personal tax reasons. For example, higher rate taxpayers may prefer low dividend pay-outs and lower rate taxpayers may prefer higher dividend pay-outs. A change in dividends may result in the clientele changing and this changeover may result in excessive and possibly negative share price volatility.

4   It is not clear why the BoD would rather not raise the required finance through equity and/or debt. The BoD may have considered increasing debt to be risky. However, given that the current level of debt is $70 million compared to an estimated market capitalisation of $360 million (Appendix 3), raising another $40 million through debt finance will probably not result in a significantly higher level of financial risk. The BoD may have been concerned that going into the markets to raise extra finance may result in negative agency type issues, such as having to make proprietary information public; or being forced to give extra value to new equity owners; or sending out negative signals to the markets.

Areas for further discussion by the BoD

Each of these issues should be considered and discussed further by the BoD. With reference to point 1, the BoD needs to discuss whether the estimates and the model used are reasonable in estimating corporate value or market capitalisation. With reference to points 2 and 3, the BoD needs to discuss the implications of such a significant change in the dividend policy and how to communicate Lirio Co's intention to the market so that any negative reaction is minimised. With reference to point 4, the BoD should discuss the reasons for any reluctance to raise finance through the markets and whether any negative impact of this is perhaps less than the negative impact of points 2 and 3.

Appendix 1: Expected dividend capacity prior to large project investment

	$000
Operating profit (15% × (1.08 × $300 million)	48,600
Less interest (5% of $70 million)	(3,500)
Less taxation (25% × ($48.6 million − 3.5 million))	(11,275)
Less investment in working capital ($0.10 × (0.08 × $300 million)	(2,400)
Less investment in additional non-current assets ($0.20 × (0.08 × $300 million)	(4,800)
Less investment in projects	(8,000)
	———
Cash flows from domestic operations	18,625
Cash flows from Pontac Co's dividend remittances (see Appendix 1.1)	3,297
Additional tax payable on Pontac Co's profits (5% × $5.6 million)	(280)
	———
Dividend capacity	21,642

Appendix 1.1: Dividend remittances expected from Pontac Co

	$000
Total contribution $24 × 400,000 units	9,600
Less fixed costs	(4,000)
Less taxation (20% × $5.6 million)	(1,120)
	———
Profit after tax	4,480
	———
Remitted to Lirio Co (80% × $4.48 million × 92%)	3,297
	———

Appendix 2: Euro (€) investment sale receipt hedge

Lirio Co can use one of forward contracts, futures contracts or option contracts to hedge the € receipt.

Forward contract

Since it is a € receipt, the 1.1559 rate will be used.

€20,000,000 × 1.1559 = $23,118,000

Futures contracts

Go long to protect against a weakening € and use the June contracts to hedge as the receipt is expected at the end of May 20X6 or beginning of June 20X6 (in three months' time).

June contracts will be closed out one month before expiry, therefore expected futures price (based on a linear narrowing of basis) is:

0.8638 + (2/3 × (0.8656 − 0.8638)) = 0.8650 [This can also be done using the spot rates or forward rates] Expected receipt = €20,000,000/0.8650 = $23,121,387

Number of contracts bought = $23,121,387/$125,000 = approximately 185 contracts (resulting in a very small over-hedge and therefore not material)

[Full credit will be given where the calculations are used to show the correction of the over-hedge using forwards]

Option contracts

Purchase the June call option to protect against a weakening € and because receipt is expected at the end of May 20X6 or beginning of June 20X6.

Exercise price is 0.86, therefore expected receipt is €20,000,000/0.8600 = $23,255,814
Contracts purchased = $23,255,814/$125,000 = 186.05, say 186

Amount hedged = $125,000 × 186 = $23,250,000

Premium payable = 186 × 125,000 × 0.0290 = €674,250

Premium in $ = €674,250 × 1.1618 = $783,344

Amount not hedged = €20,000,000 − (186 × 125,000 × 0.8600) = €5,000

Use forward contracts to hedge €5,000 not hedged. €5,000 × 1.1559 = $5,780

[Full credit will be given if a comment on the under-hedge being immaterial and therefore not hedged is made, instead of calculating the correction of the under-hedge]

Total receipts = $23,250,000 + $5,780 − $783,344 = $22,472,436

Advice and recommendation

Hedging using options will give the lowest receipt at $22,472,436 from the sale of the investment, while hedging using futures will give the highest receipt at $23,127,387, with the forward contracts giving a receipt of $23,118,000.

The lower receipt from the option contracts is due to the premium payable, which allows the option buyer to let the option lapse should the € strengthen. In this case, the option would be allowed to lapse and Lirio Co would convert the € into $ at the prevailing spot rate in three months' time. However, the € would need to strengthen significantly before the cost of the option is covered. Given market expectation of the weakness in the € continuing, this is not likely to be the case.

Although futures and forward contracts are legally binding and do not have the flexibility of option contracts, they both give higher receipts. Hedging using futures gives the higher receipt, but futures require margin payments to be made upfront and contracts are marked-to-market daily. In addition to this, the basis may not narrow in a linear fashion and therefore the amount received is not guaranteed. All these factors create uncertainty in terms of the exact amounts of receipts and payments resulting on a daily basis and the final receipt.

On the other hand, when using forward contracts to hedge the receipt exposure, Lirio Co knows the exact amount it will receive. It is therefore recommended that Lirio Co use the forward markets to hedge the expected receipt.

[**Note:** It could be argued that in spite of the issues when hedging with futures, the higher receipt obtained from using futures markets to hedge mean that they should be used. This is acceptable as well.]

Appendix 3: Estimate of Lirio Co's value based on the dividend valuation model

If the large project is not undertaken and dividend growth rate is maintained at the historic level

Dividend history

Year to end of February	20X3	20X4	20X5	20X6
Number of $1 equity shares in issue (000)	60,000	60,000	80,000	80,000
Total dividends paid ($000)	12,832	13,602	19,224	20,377
Dividend per share	$0.214	$0.227	$0.240	$0.255

Average dividend growth rate = $(0.255/0.214)^{1/3} - 1 = 1.0602$ (or say 6%) Expected dividend in February 20X7 = $0.255 × 1.06 = $0.270

Lirio Co, estimate of value if large project is not undertaken =

$0.270/(0.12 – 0.06) = $4.50 per share or $360 million market capitalisation

If the large project is undertaken

Funds required for project	$40,000,000
Funds from sale of investment (Appendix 2)	$23,118,000
Funds required from dividend capacity cash flows	$16,882,000
Dividend capacity funds before transfer to project (Appendix 1)	$21,642,000
Dividend capacity funds left after transfer	$4,760,000
Annual dividend per share after transfer	$0.0595
Annual dividend paid (end of February 20X7 and February 20X8)	$0.0595
Dividend paid (end of February 20X9)	$0.3100
New growth rate	7%

Lirio Co, estimate of value if large project is undertaken =

$0.0595 × 1.12^{-1} + $0.0595 × 1.12^{-2} + $0.3100 × 1.12^{-3}

+ [$0.3100 × 1.07/(0.12 – 0.07)] × 1.12^{-3} = $5.04 per share or $403 million market capitalisation

Tutorial note

A discussion paper can take many formats. The answer provides one possible format. Credit will be given for alternative and sensible formats; and for relevant approaches to the calculations and commentary.)

				Marks
		Marking scheme		*Marks*
(a)		Up to 2 marks per well-explained point		
			Maximum	6
(b)	(i)	**Appendices 1 and 1.1**		
		Operating profit		1
		Interest paid		1
		Tax paid for normal activities		1
		Investment in working capital		1
		Investment in additional non-current assets		1
		Correct treatment of depreciation		1
		Cash flows remitted from Pontac Co		2
		Additional tax payable		1
			Maximum	9
	(ii)	**Appendix 2**		
		Amount received based on forward contracts		1
		Correctly identifying long contracts and purchasing call options		1
		Expected futures price based on linear narrowing of basis		1
		Amount received based on futures contracts		1
		Recognition of small over-hedge when using futures contracts		1
		Option contracts or futures contracts purchased		1
		Premium paid in dollars		1
		Amount received based on options contracts		2
		1–2 marks for each well-discussed point		4
		Reasonable recommendation		1
			Maximum	14
	(iii)	**Appendix 3 and project assessment**		
		Estimate of dividend growth rate (prior to project undertaken)		2
		Estimate of corporate value (prior to project undertaken)		1
		Annual dividend per share after transfer of funds to project		2
		Estimate of value after project is undertaken		2
		Concluding comments on project assessment		1
			Maximum	8

	Marking scheme		*Marks*
(iv)	**Discussion of issues**		
	Limitations of method used		1–2
	Signalling impact of change in dividend policy		1–2
	Clientele impact of change in dividend policy		2–3
	Rationale for not considering debt or equity		3–4
	Other relevant discussion points		2–3
		Maximum	9
	Professional marks for part (b)		
	Structure and presentation of the discussion paper		3
	Clearly highlighting/emphasising areas for further discussion/detailed summary		1
		Maximum	4
Total			50

Section 4

ANSWERS TO PRACTICE QUESTIONS – SECTION B

ROLE OF SENIOR FINANCIAL ADVISER IN THE MULTINATIONAL ORGANISATION

24 MOOSE CO (DEC 09 ADAPTED)

Key answer tips

The examiner has stated his intention to make the AFM exam a contemporary test of current real world issues. This question is a good example of how real world issues in financial management can be tested.

Note that this past exam question contains no calculations. The new AFM syllabus states that in future "there will not be any wholly narrative questions" i.e. the topics covered here may well be covered, but in questions that contain a mixture of calculation and narrative parts.

(a) Companies that borrow (or deposit) will be exposed to the risk that interest rate changes impact the value of their payments or receipts of interest.

The impact of interest rate changes can impact either positively or negatively, but the key issue is that any uncertainty created by interest rate risk can reduce the attractiveness of the company to its investors and potential investors.

Investors don't like nasty surprises, so they prefer companies to hedge against risks to reduce the potential variability of returns.

Hence, companies that effectively manage their exposure to interest rate risk are more likely to be appealing to investors, so there could be a positive impact on shareholder wealth if a company can reduce the risk created by interest rate movements.

(b) The credit crunch has led to an unwillingness by the banks to lend, particularly to one another, resulting in a drain in the liquidity across the capital markets. Interest rates are now low as central banks attempt to stimulate their economies. The business of banks is to earn profits by borrowing short and lending long and they are still willing to lend to high class corporate customers. And probably at competitive interest rates.

The banks will be concerned about the following:

The risk of default: although there has been a slackening of demand for the company's product our relatively high credit rating would still make us an attractive prospect for lenders. They will need to undertake a credit risk assessment which will include a thorough examination of our asset strength, existing capitalisation, operating strength and income gearing. An important measure will be the firm's current cash flow/debt obligations ratio.

Recovery: the assessment of our asset strength will form a part of their assessment of the potential recoverability of the debt in the event of default.

(c)   Syndication is where a group of banks combine with one bank taking the lead in the arrangement. Syndication allows banks to offer much larger loans in combination than would be feasible singly, and given the range of banks involved can tailor loans (perhaps across different currencies) to more exactly match our requirements. The management of the syndicate lies with the arranging bank but the effective cost will be somewhat higher than with a conventional loan but usually much lower than the cost of raising the necessary finance through a bond issue.

A bond issue is where the debt is securitised and floated onto the capital market normally with a fixed interest coupon and a set redemption date. Initial set up costs can be high especially if the issue is underwritten. A loan of the size envisaged is towards the low end of what would normally be raised through this means. Some bond issues can be syndicated in that a number of borrowers of similar risk are combined by the investment bank chosen to manage the issue.

The advantage of syndication is that it reduces the costs of issue. However, it may be that the best offer would entail accepting a variable rate based on LIBOR which would have to be swapped out if we wished to minimise interest rate risk.

(d)   In assessing this capital investment we have to make some assumptions about the immediate future in terms of the general economic conditions and to what extent we have a delay option on the project concerned. Where there is a positive delay option then from a financial perspective the best advice may be to delay investment dependent on the likely actions by the competitors and how markets for the product develop. Where there are significant competitive reasons for proceeding we should only proceed if the net present value of the project is worthwhile. Given the magnitudes of the uncertainties involved at this stage of the economic cycle the decision to proceed should only be made when we are sure that we have estimated the potential magnitude of the risks and taken them into account in our analysis.

Examiner's note

For all parts to this question, credit will be given for alternative and relevant points.

---

25 LAMRI CO (DEC 10 ADAPTED)

Key answer tips

When asked to calculate dividend capacity, you should try to estimate the amount of cash that the company will generate, after paying any operating expenses and interest, and investing in assets. This is commonly known as the free cash flow to equity.

(a) **Dividend Capacity Prior to TE Proposal Implementation**

	$000
Operating profit (30% × $80,000,000)	24,000
Less interest (8% × $35,000,000)	(2,800)
Less taxation (28% × (24,000 – 2,800))	(5,936)
Less investment in working capital (15% × (20/120 × 80,000))	(2,000)
Less investment in additional non-current assets (25% × (20/120 × 80,000))	(3,333)
Less investment in project	(4,500)
Cash flows from domestic operations	5,431
Cash flows from overseas subsidiary dividend remittances (W1)	3,159
Additional tax payable on Magnolia profits (6% × 5,400)	(324)
Dividend capacity	8,266

Dividend Capacity After TE Proposal Implementation	
Cash flows from domestic operations (as above)	5,431
Cash flows from overseas subsidiaries dividend remittances (W2)	2,718
Additional tax payable on Magnolia profits (6% × 3,120)	(187)
Dividend capacity	7,962

Estimate of actual dividend for coming year (7,500 × 1.08)	8,100

Note: The impact of depreciation is neutral, as this amount will be spent to retain assets at their current productive capability.

Workings:

(W1) Prior to Implementation of TE Proposal

	$000 Strymon	$000 Magnolia
Sales revenue	5,700	15,000
Cost		
Variable	(3,600)	(2,400)
Fixed	(2,100)	(1,500)
Transfer		(5,700)
Profit before tax	Nil	5,400
Tax	Nil	1,188
Profit after tax	Nil	4,212
Remitted	Nil	3,159
Retained	Nil	1,053

(W2) After Implementation of TE Proposal

	$000 Strymon	$000 Magnolia
Sales revenue	7,980	15,000
Cost		
Variable	(3,600)	(2,400)
Fixed	(2,100)	(1,500)
Transfer		(7,980)
Profit before tax	2,280	3,120
Tax (42%, 22%)	958	686
Profit after tax	1,322	2,434
Remitted (75% × 1,322 × 90%)	892	
Remitted		1,826
Retained	331	608
Total remitted	2,718	

(b) Lamri's dividend capacity before implementing TE's proposal ($8,266,000) is more than the dividend required for next year ($8,100,000). If the recommendation from TE is implemented as policy for next year then there is a possibility that Lamri will not have sufficient dividend capacity to make the required dividend payments. It requires $8,100,000 but will have $7,962,000 available. The reason is due to the additional tax that will be paid in the country in which Strymon operates, for which credit cannot be obtained. Effectively 14% additional tax and 10% withholding tax will be paid. Some of this amount is recovered because lower additional tax is paid on Magnolia's profits but not enough.

The difference between what is required and available is small and possible ways of making up the shortfall are as follows. Lamri could lower its growth rate in dividends to approximately 6.2% (7962/7500 – 1 × 100%) and have enough capacity to make the payment. However, if the reasons for the lower growth rate are not explained to the shareholders and accepted by them, the share price may fall.

An alternative could be to borrow the small amount needed possibly through increased overdraft facilities. However, Lamri may not want to increase its borrowings and may be reluctant to take this option. In addition to this, there is a possibility that because of the change of policy this shortfall may occur more often than just one off, and Lamri may not want to increase borrowing regularly.

Lamri may consider postponing the project or part of the project, if that option were available. However, this must be considered in the context of the business. From the question narrative, the suggestion is that Lamri have a number of projects in the pipeline for the future. The option to delay may not be possible or feasible.

Perhaps the most obvious way to get the extra funds required is to ask the subsidiary companies (most probably Strymon) to remit a higher proportion of their profits as dividends. In the past Strymon did not make profits and none were retained hence there may be a case for a higher level of remittance from there. However, this may have a negative impact on the possible benefits, especially manager morale.

(Note: Credit will be given for alternative relevant suggestions)

(c)   The free movement of goods, services and capital across national barriers has long been considered a key factor in establishing stable and independent world economies. However, removing barriers to the free movement of capital also increases the opportunities for international money laundering and terrorist financing.

Bodies such as the international monetary fund (IMF) work in conjunction with national governments to establish a multilateral framework for trade and finance, but they are also aware of the possible opportunities this creates for criminals.

International efforts to combat money laundering and terrorist financing have resulted in:

- the establishment of an international task force on money laundering

- the issue of specific recommendations to be adopted by nation states

- the enactment of legislation by many countries on matters covering:

    - the criminal justice system and law enforcement

    - the financial system and its regulation

    - international cooperation.

26   STROM CO (DEC 12 ADAPTED)

Key answer tips

The examiner often sets questions to test that students have an awareness of real world financial management issues (such as the IMF and the banking/debt crisis here).

As well as studying your text book to prepare for the AFM exam, you should regularly read a good quality business newspaper to keep up to date with current issues.

Note that the examiner's model answer was accompanied by the following statement: 'The following answer is indicative. Credit will be given for alternative, valid points.'

Also note that this past exam question contains no calculations. The new AFM syllabus states that in future "there will not be any wholly narrative questions" i.e. the topics covered here may well be covered, but in questions that contain a mixture of calculation and narrative parts.

(a)   The role of the IMF is to oversee the global financial systems, in particular to stabilise international exchange rates, help countries to achieve balance of payments and facilitate in the country's development through influencing the economic policies of the country in question. Where necessary, it offers temporary loans, from member states' deposits, to countries facing severe financial and economic difficulties. These temporary loans are often offered with different levels of conditions or austerity measures.

The IMF believes that in order to regain control of the balance of payments, the country should take action to reduce the level of demand for goods and services. To achieve this, the IMF often requires countries to adopt strict austerity measures such as reducing public spending and increased taxation, as conditions of the loan.

It believes these conditions will help control the inflationary pressures on the economy, and reduce the demand for goods and services. As a result, this will help the country to move away from a position of a trade deficit and achieve control of its balance of payments.

However, these deflationary pressures may cause standards of living to fall and unemployment to rise. The IMF regards these as short-term hardships necessary to help countries sort out their balance of payment difficulties and international debt problems. The IMF has faced a number of criticisms for the conditions it has imposed, including the accusation that its policies impact more negatively on people with lower or mid-range incomes, hinder long-term development and growth, and possibly result in a continuous downward spiral of economic activity.

Strom Co trades throughout Europe and economic activity in these countries has been curtailed in the last few years due, initially, to the banking crisis, and then due to the austerity measures that governments have adopted. For retailers, this could pose two possible problems. First, with limited growth and higher taxes, people would have less money to spend. Secondly, increasing levels of unemployment would also limit disposable incomes. It is possible that customers may have curtailed their expenditure on clothes and clothing accessories in order to meet other needs.

Some companies may have to spend proportionally more on marketing and possibly offer more discounts and other customer incentives in order to stay competitive and to maintain market share. This additional cost would hit their profit levels negatively.

From the details in the question, it is evident that in 2011 profits have reduced by more than the fall in sales revenue. This could be due to Strom Co being forced to spend more on activities such as marketing or it could be because it has found it difficult to reduce its cost base. More analysis is needed to determine the exact cause.

It seems that Strom Co is trying to address the problem of declining profitability by trimming its costs. In circumstances where sales revenues are declining, and it is not possible to stabilise or increase these, then cost structures may need to be altered in order to make reasonable profits.

(b) The low-price clothing retailers might have benefited from the austerity measures because of a switch by customers from mid-price clothes to low-price clothes. If, due to the austerity measures, people have less money to spend, and if, as stated above, austerity measures impact the mid-income and low-income earners more negatively, then it is possible that their buying preferences change from mid-price to low-price clothes. This would be especially true if there is limited brand loyalty and customers perceive that the low-price items are of a similar quality or provide a better value-for-money.

On the other hand, it is possible that brand loyalty is more significant with high-price clothes, making switching to mid-price clothes difficult. Customers who buy these clothes may prefer not to switch and would rather spend less elsewhere. It is also possible that the austerity measures did not affect the population who buy high-price clothes to the same extent as other groups of the population. Or it may be that this population group is more resilient to the austerity measures imposed by the government, especially if the assertion is true that the IMF conditions affect people who are in the low or mid income categories more than the people in the high income category.

(c) The obvious risk in reducing resources allocated to the quality control functions would be that some inspections would be reduced. This may result in defective goods being sold. The costs related to processing returns of defective goods may outweigh the savings made. Reduction in monitoring the working conditions of employees of the clothing suppliers may encourage them to retain their questionable employment practices. This may compromise the company's ethical stance and standards.

The less obvious, but more significant, risk is the impact that unethical labour practices and working conditions may have on the reputation of the company and its products. Potentially, lower quality and defective clothes could seriously harm the company's reputation and result in lower sales revenue over a long period of time. Once damaged, such reputation would be hard to rebuild. The damage in reputation of the company regarding its ethical stance could also be potentially disastrous. Different stakeholder groups could react in negative ways, for example, customers may switch their custom, investors may sell their shares and the press may run negative campaigns against the company. The consequences of such damage could be long term and sometimes permanent.

Strom Co will need to review where and how resources are allocated in order to decrease or minimise the detrimental impact of a reduction in the quality control costs. For example, savings could be made by eliminating duplicated quality control processes or eliminating processes that are not necessary. Strom Co should also evaluate whether alternative, less resource intensive processes and procedures can be implemented without compromising the quality control and monitoring of working conditions. Experts should be used to undertake the assessment. Critical processes and procedures should be retained even if they require significant resources.

The risk of making errors in the assessment should be evaluated and discussed at a senior level to ensure that Strom Co is comfortable with undertaking the likely risk.

(d) Money laundering is a process in which assets obtained or generated by criminal activity are moved or concealed to obscure their link with the crime.

Terrorist activities are sometimes funded from the proceeds of illegal activities, and perpetrators must find ways to launder the funds in order to use them without drawing the attention of authorities.

The international community has made the fight against money laundering and terrorist financing a priority.

International efforts to combat money laundering have resulted in:

- the establishment of an international task force on money laundering

- the issue of specific recommendations to be adopted by nation states

- the enactment of legislation by many countries on matters covering:

    - the criminal justice system and law enforcement

    - the financial system and its regulation

    - international cooperation.

Marking scheme		Marks
(a)	Explanation of the role and aims of the IMF	5–6
	Reasons for austerity measures affecting Strom Co negatively	4–5
	Maximum	**10**
(b)	Suggestion(s) for not affecting low-price retailers	2
	Suggestion(s) for not affecting high-price retailers	2
	Maximum	**4**
(c)	Discussion of the risks	3–4
	Reduction of the detrimental impact	2–3
	Maximum	**6**
(d)	Definition of money laundering	1-2
	Explanation of steps taken	3-4
	Maximum	**5**
Total		**25**

27 ENNEA CO (JUN 12)

Key answer tips

Notice how this model answer is presented in a very efficient way. The use of columns to show the current position and then the three proposals side by side makes it easy to identify the differences and similarities between the proposals.

(a) **Forecast financial position**

Amounts in $000	Current	Proposal 1	Proposal 2	Proposal 3
Non-current assets	282,000	282,000	302,000	257,000
Current assets	66,000	64,720	67,720	63,682
Total assets	348,000	346,720	369,720	320,682
Current liabilities	37,000	37,000	37,000	37,000
Non-current liabilities	140,000	160,000	160,000	113,000
Total liabilities	177,000	197,000	197,000	150,000
Share capital (40c/share)	48,000	45,500	48,000	48,000
Retained earnings	123,000	104,220	124,720	122,682
Total equity	171,000	149,720	172,720	170,682
Total liabilities and capital	348,000	346,720	369,720	320,682

Adjustments to forecast earnings

Amounts in $000	Current	Proposal 1	Proposal 2	Proposal 3
Initial profit after tax	26,000	26,000	26,000	26,000
Interest payable on additional borrowing ($20m × 6% × (1 – 0.2))		(960)	(960)	
Additional interest payable on extra coupon ($160m × 0.25% × (1 – 0.2))		(320)	(320)	
Interest saved on less borrowing ($27m × 6% × (1 – 0.2))				1,296
Interest saved on lower coupon ($113m × 0.15% × (1 – 0.2))				136
Return on additional investment ($20m × 15%)			3,000	
Return lost on less investment ($25m × 15%)				(3,750)
Profit on sale of non-current assets				2,000
Adjusted profit after tax	26,000	24,720	27,720	25,682

	Current	Proposal 1	Proposal 2	Proposal 3
Gearing % (non-current liabilities/equity)	81.9%	106.9%	92.6%	66.2%
Number of shares ('000)	120,000	113,750	120,000	120,000
Earnings per share (adjusted profit after tax/number of shares)	21.67c	21.73c	23.10c	21.40c

Note: Gearing defined as non-current liabilities/(non-current liabilities + equity) and/or using market value of equity is acceptable as well.

Tutorial note

Explanations are not required for the answer but are included to explain the approach taken.

Explanations of the financial position based on the three proposals

Proposal 1

Debt is increased by $20m and share capital reduced by the same amount as follows: from par value = $20m × 40c/320c = $2.5m; from retained earnings = $20m × 280c/320c = $17.5m.

Additional interest payable totalling $1,280,000 ($960,000 + $320,000) is taken off retained earnings due to reduction in profit after tax and taken off current assets because presumably it is paid from cash. Note that an alternative answer would be to add the additional interest payable to current liabilities.

Proposal 2

Debt and non-current assets are increased by $20m.

Additional interest payable as above, plus the additional investment of $20 million will generate a rate of return of 15%, which is $3,000,000 income. Net impact is $1,720,000 income which is added to retained earnings as an addition to profit after tax and added to current assets as a cash income (presumably).

Proposal 3

Net non-current assets are reduced by the $25 million, their value at disposal. Since they were sold for $27 million, this is how much the non-current liabilities are reduced by and the profit of $2 million is included in the retained earnings.

Interest saved totals $1,432,000 ($1,296,000 + $136,000). The reduction in investment of $25 million will lose $3,750,000, at a rate of return of 15%. Net impact is $2,318,000 loss which is subtracted from earnings as a reduction from profit after tax and deducted from current assets as a cash expense (presumably).

Discussion

Proposals 1 and 3 appear to produce opposite results to each other. Proposal 1 would lead to a small increase in the earnings per share (EPS) due to a reduction in the number of shares although profits would decrease by approximately 5%, due to the increase in the amount of interest payable as a result of increased borrowings. However, the level of gearing would increase substantially (by about 30%).

With proposal 3, although the overall profits would fall, because of the lost earnings due to downsizing being larger than the gain in interest saved and profit made on the sale of assets, this is less than proposal 1 (1.2%). Gearing would reduce substantially (19.2%).

Proposal 2 would give a significant boost in the EPS from 21.67c/share to 23.10c/share, which the other two proposals do not. This is mainly due to increase in earnings through extra investment. However, the amount of gearing would increase by more than 13%.

Overall proposal 1 appears to be the least attractive option. The choice between proposals 2 and 3 would be between whether the company would prefer larger EPS or less gearing. This would depend on factors such as the capital structure of the competitors, the reaction of the equity market to the proposals, the implications of the change in the risk profile of the company and the resultant impact on the cost of capital. Ennea Co should also bear in mind that the above are estimates and the actual results will probably differ from the forecasts.

(**Note:** Credit will be given for alternative relevant comments and suggestions)

(b)   Asset securitisation in this case would involve taking the future incomes from the leases that Ennea Co makes and converting them into assets. These assets are sold as bonds now and the future income from lease interest will be used to pay coupons on the bonds. Effectively Ennea Co foregoes the future lease income and receives money from sale of the assets today.

The income from the various leases would be aggregated and pooled, and new securities (bonds) issued based on these. The tangible benefit from securitisation occurs when the pooled assets are divided into tranches and tranches are credit rated. The higher rated tranches would carry less risk and have less return, compared to lower rated tranches. If default occurs, the income of the lower tranches is reduced first, before the impact of increasing defaults move to the higher rated tranches. This allows an asset of low liquidity to be converted into securities which carry higher liquidity.

Ennea Co would face a number of barriers in undertaking such a process. Securitisation is an expensive process due to management costs, legal fees and ongoing administrative costs. The value of assets that Ennea Co wants to sell is small and therefore these costs would take up a significant proportion of the income. High cost implications mean that securitisation is not feasible for small asset pools.

Normally asset pools would not offer the full value of the asset as securities. For example, only 90% of the asset value would be converted into securities, leaving the remaining 10% as a buffer against possible default. This method of credit enhancement would help to credit-rate the tranches at higher levels and help their marketability. However, Ennea Co would not be able to take advantage of the full asset value if it proceeds with the asset securitisation.

(**Note:** Credit will be given for alternative relevant comments and suggestions)

Marking scheme		
		Marks
(a)	Financial position calculations: proposal 1	3
	Financial position calculations: proposal 2	2
	Financial position calculations: proposal 3	3
	Adjustments to forecast earnings	
	Interest payable on additional borrowing and higher coupon	2
	Interest saved lower borrowing and lower coupon	1
	Return on additional investment	1
	Return lost on less investment and profit on sale of non-current assets	1
	Gearing and EPS calculations	2
	Discussion of the results of the proposals	2–3
	Discussion of the implications (e.g. risk, market reaction, etc.)	2–3
		────
	Maximum	**20**
		────
(b)	Explanation of the process	2–3
	Key barriers in undertaking the process	2–3
		────
	Maximum	**5**
		────
Total		**25**
		────

28   LIMNI CO (JUN 13)

Key answer tips

This was a very wide-ranging question, covering risk management, dividend policy and financing. Use these three subheadings in your answer to make sure that you are addressing all the necessary issues.

(a) As a high growth company, Limni Co probably requires the cash flows it generates annually for investing in new projects and has therefore not paid any dividends. This is a common practice amongst high-growth companies, many of which declare that they have no intention of paying any dividends. The shareholder clientele in such companies expects to be rewarded by growth in equity value as a result of the investment policy of the company.

Capital structure theory would suggest that because of the benefit of the tax shield on interest payments, companies should have a mix of equity and debt in their capital structure. Furthermore, the pecking order proposition would suggest that companies tend to use internally generated funds before going to markets to raise debt capital initially and finally equity capital. The agency effects of having to provide extra information to the markets and where one investor group benefits at the expense of another have been cited as the main deterrents to companies seeking external sources of finance. To a certain extent, this seems to be the case with Limni Co in using internal finance first, but the pecking order proposition seems to be contradicted in that it seeks to go straight to the equity market and undertake rights issues thereafter. Perhaps the explanation for this can be gained from looking at the balance of business and financial risk. Since Limni Co operates in a rapidly changing industry, it probably faces significant business risk and therefore cannot afford to undertake high financial risk, which a capital structure containing significant levels of debt would entail.

This, together with agency costs related to restrictive covenants, may have determined Limni Co's financing policy.

Risk management theory suggests that managing the volatility of cash flows enables a company to plan its investment strategy better. Since Limni Co uses internally generated funds to finance its projects, it needs to be certain that funds will be available when needed for the future projects, and therefore managing its cash flows will enable this. Moreover, because Limni Co faces high business risk, managing the risk that the company's managers cannot control through their actions, may be even more necessary.

The change to making dividend payments or undertaking share buybacks will affect all three policies. The company's clientele may change and this may cause share price fluctuations. However, since the recommendation for the change is being led by the shareholders, significant share price fluctuations may not happen. Limni Co's financing policy may change because having reduced internal funds means it may have to access debt markets and therefore have to look at its balance between business and financial risk. The change to Limni Co's financial structure may result in a change in its risk management policy, because it may be necessary to manage interest rate risk as well.

(Note: Credit will be given for alternative relevant comments)

(b)   In the case of company Theta, dividends are growing but not at a stable rate. In fact company Theta is paying out $0.40 in dividends for every $1 in earnings, and has a fixed dividend cover ratio of 2.50. This would be confusing for the shareholders, as they would not know how much dividend they would receive from year to year. Although profits have risen over the past five years, if profits do fall, company Theta may reduce dividends and therefore send the wrong signals to shareholders and investors. This may cause unnecessary fluctuations of the share price or result in a depressed share price.

In the case of company Omega, annual dividends are growing at a stable rate of approximately 5% per year, while the company's earnings are growing steadily at around 3% per year, resulting in an increasing pay-out ratio. Also a high proportion of earnings are paid out as dividends, increasing from 60% in 20W9 to almost 65% in 20X3. This would indicate a company operating in a mature industry, signalling that there are few new projects to invest in and therefore reducing the retention rate. Such an investment would be attractive to investors requiring high levels of dividend returns from their investments.

In the case of company Kappa, although a lower proportion of earnings is paid out as dividends (from about 20% in 20W9 to about 27% in 20X3), they are growing at a higher but stable rate of 29%–30% per year. The company's earnings are growing rapidly but erratically, ranging between 3% and 35% between 20W9 and 20X3. This probably indicates a growing company, possibly similar to Limni Co itself, where perhaps returns to investors having been coming from share price growth, but one where dividends are becoming more prominent. Such an investment would be attractive to investors requiring lower levels of dividend returns, but higher capital returns from their investments.

Due to company Theta's confusing dividend policy, which may lead to erratic dividend pay-outs and a depressed share price, Limni Co would probably not want to invest in that company. The choice between company Omega and company Kappa would depend on how Limni Co wants to receive its return from the investment, maybe taking into account factors such as taxation implications, and the period of time it wishes to invest for, in terms of when the returns from an investment will be maximised and when it will need the funds for future projects.

(Note: Credit will be given for alternative relevant comments)

(c)   Limni Co, current dividend capacity

	$000
Profit before tax (23% × $600,000,000)	138,000
Tax (26% × $138,000,000)	(35,880)
Profit after tax	102,120
Add back depreciation (25% × $220,000,000)	55,000
Less investment in assets	(67,000)
Remittances from overseas subsidiaries	15,000
Additional tax on remittances (6% × $15,000,000)	(900)
Dividend capacity	104,220

Increase in dividend capacity = 10% × $104,220,000 = $10,422,000

Gross up for tax = $10,422,000/0.94 = $11,087,234

Percentage increase in remittances from overseas subsidiaries = 73.9% [$11,087,234/$15,000,000]

Dividend repatriations need to increase by 73.9% from Limni Co's international subsidiaries in order to increase the dividend capacity by 10%. Limni Co would need to consider whether or not it is feasible for its subsidiaries to increase their repatriations to such an extent, and the impact this will have on the motivation of the subsidiaries' managers and on the subsidiaries' ability to operate as normal.

(d)   The main benefit of a share buyback scheme to investors is that it helps to control transaction costs and manage tax liabilities. With the share buyback scheme, the shareholders can choose whether or not to sell their shares back to the company. In this way they can manage the amount of cash they receive. On the other hand, with dividend payments, and especially large special dividends, this choice is lost, and may result in a high tax bill. If the shareholder chooses to re-invest the funds, it will result in transaction costs. An added benefit is that, as the share capital is reduced, the earnings per share and the share price may increase. Finally, share buybacks are normally viewed as positive signals by markets and may result in an even higher share price.

(Note: Credit will be given for alternative relevant comments)

Marking scheme		
		Marks
(a)	Discussion of dividend policy	1–2
	Discussion of financing policy	3–4
	Discussion of risk management policy	1–2
	Effect of dividends and share buybacks on the policies	2–3
	Maximum	**8**
(b)	2 marks per evaluation of each of the three companies	6
	Discussion of which company to invest in	2
	Maximum	**8**

	Marking scheme		
(c)	Calculation of initial dividend capacity		3
	Calculation of new repatriation amount		2
	Comment		1–2
		Maximum	6
(d)	1 mark per relevant point		3
Total			25

29 CHAWAN CO (JUN 15)

 Online question assistance

Key answer tips

This is a very difficult question, because part (b) is so open-ended.

To assess whether Chawan Co should dispose of its equity stake in Oden Co, you should first assess the performance of Oden Co using ratio analysis.

In order to make your ratio analysis useful, make sure you incorporate trends over time and comparisons with the rest of the industry.

(a)   A dark pool network allows shares to be traded anonymously, away from public scrutiny. No information on the trade order is revealed prior to it taking place. The price and size of the order are only revealed once the trade has taken place. Two main reasons are given for dark pool networks: first they prevent the risk of other traders moving the share price up or down; and second they often result in reduced costs because trades normally take place at the mid-price between the bid and offer; and because broker-dealers try and use their own private pools, and thereby saving exchange fees.

Chawan Co's holding in Oden Co is 27 million shares out of a total of 600 million shares, or 4.5%. If Chawan Co sold such a large holding all at once, the price of Oden Co shares may fall temporarily and significantly, and Chawan Co may not receive the value based on the current price. By utilising a dark pool network, Chawan Co may be able to keep the price of the share largely intact, and possibly save transaction costs.

Although the criticism against dark pool systems is that they prevent market efficiency by not revealing bid-offer prices before the trade, proponents argue that in fact market efficiency is maintained because a large sale of shares will not move the price down artificially and temporarily.

(b)   Ratio calculations

Focus on investor and profitability ratios

Oden Co	20X2	20X3	20X4	20X5
Operating profit/sales revenue		16.2%	15.2%	10.4%
Operating profit/capital employed		22.5%	20.4%	12.7%
Earnings per share		$0.27	$0.24	$0.12
Price to earnings ratio		9.3	10.0	18.3
Gearing ratio (debt/(debt + equity))		37.6%	36.9%	37.1%
Interest cover (operating profit/finance costs)		9.5	7.5	3.5
Dividend yield	7.1%	7.2%	8.3%	6.8%

Travel and leisure (T&L) sector

Price to earnings ratio	11.9	12.2	13.0	13.8
Dividend yield	6.6%	6.6%	6.7%	6.4%

Other calculations

Oden Co, sales revenue annual growth rate average between 20X3 and 20X5 = $(1,185/1,342)1/2 - 1 = - 6.0\%$.

Between 20X4 and 20X5 = $(1,185 - 1,335)/1,335 = - 11.2\%$.

Oden Co, average financing cost

20X3:	$23/(365 + 88) = 5.1\%$
20X4:	$27/(368 + 90) = 5.9\%$
20X5:	$35/(360 + 98) = 7.6\%$

Share price changes	20X2–20X3	20X3–20X4	20X4–20X5
Oden Co	19.0%	- 4.0%	- 8.3%
T&L sector	15.8%	- 2.3%	12.1%

Oden Co

Return to shareholders (RTS)	20X3	20X4	20X5
Dividend yield	7.2%	8.3%	6.8%
Share price gain	19.0%	- 4.0%	- 8.3%
Total	26.2%	4.3%	- 1.5%
Average: 9.7%			
Required return (based on capital asset pricing model (CAPM))	13.0%	13.6%	16.0%
Average: 14.2%			

T&L sector (RTS)	20X3	20X4	20X5
Dividend yield	6.6%	6.7%	6.4%
Share price gain	15.8%	- 2.3%	12.1%
Total	22.4%	4.4%	18.5%
Average: 15.1%			
Required return (based on CAPM)	12.4%	13.0%	13.6%
Average: 13.0%			

(**Note:** The averages for Oden Co, RTS and for the T&L sector, RTS are the simple averages of the three years: 20X3 to 20X5)

Discussion

The following discussion compares the performance of Oden Co over time, to the T&L sector and against expectations, in terms of it being a sound investment. It also considers the wider aspects which Chawan Co should take account of and the further information which the company should consider before coming to a final decision.

In terms of Oden Co's performance between 20X3 and 20X5, it is clear from the calculations above, that the company is experiencing considerable financial difficulties. Profit margins have fallen and so has the earnings per share (EPS). Whereas the amount of gearing appears fairly stable, the interest cover has deteriorated. The reason for this is that borrowing costs have increased from an average of 5.1% to an average of 7.6% over the three years. The share price has decreased over the three years as well and in the last year so has the dividend yield. This would indicate that the company is unable to maintain adequate returns for its investors (please also see below).

Although Oden Co has tried to maintain a dividend yield which is higher than the sector average, its price to earnings (PE) ratio has been lower than the sector average between 20X3 and 20X4. It does increase significantly in 20X5, but this is because of the large fall in the EPS, rather than an increase in the share price. This could be an indication that there is less confidence in the future prospects of Oden Co, compared to the rest of the T&L sector. This is further corroborated by the higher dividend yield which may indicate that the company has fewer value-creating projects planned in the future. Finally, whereas the T&L sector's average share price seems to have recovered strongly in 20X5, following a small fall in 20X4, Oden Co's share price has not followed suit and the decline has gathered pace in 20X5. It would seem that Oden Co is a poor performer within its sector.

This view is further strengthened by comparing the actual returns to the required returns based on the capital asset pricing model (CAPM). Both the company and the T&L sector produced returns exceeding the required return in 20X3 and Oden Co experienced a similar decline to the sector in 20X4. However, in 20X5, the T&L sector appears to have recovered but Oden Co's performance has worsened. This has resulted in Oden Co's actual average returns being significantly below the required returns between 20X2 and 20X5.

Taking the above into account, the initial recommendation is for Chawan Co to dispose of its investment in Oden Co. However, there are three important caveats which should be considered before the final decision is made.

The first caveat is that Chawan Co should look at the balance of its portfolio of investments. A sale of $58 million worth of equity shares within a portfolio total of $360 million may cause the portfolio to become unbalanced, and for unsystematic risk to be introduced into the portfolio. Presumably, the purpose of maintaining a balanced portfolio is to virtually eliminate unsystematic risk by ensuring that it is well diversified. Chawan Co may want to re-invest the proceeds from the sale of Oden Co (if it decides to proceed with the disposal) in other equity shares within the same sector to ensure that the portfolio remains balanced and diversified.

The second caveat is that Chawan Co may want to look into the rumours of a takeover bid of Oden Co and assess how realistic it is that this will happen. If there is a realistic chance that such a bid may happen soon, Chawan Co may want to hold onto its investment in Oden Co for the present time. This is because takeover bids are made at a premium and the return to Chawan Co may increase if Oden Co is sold during the takeover.

The third caveat is that Chawan Co may want to consider Oden Co's future prospects. The calculations above are based on past performance between 20X2 and 20X5 and indicate an increasingly poor performance. However, the economy is beginning to recover, albeit slowly and erratically. Chawan Co may want to consider how well placed Oden Co is to take advantage of the improving conditions compared to other companies in the same industrial sector.

If Chawan Co decides that none of the caveats materially affect Oden Co's poor performance and position, then it should dispose of its investment in Oden Co.

Marking scheme				Marks
(a)	Explanation of a dark pool network			3–4
	Explanation of why Chawan Co may want to use one			1–2
			Maximum	**5**
(b)	Profitability ratios			1–2
	Investor ratios			3–4
	Other ratios			1–2
	Trends and other calculations			3–4
			Maximum	**10**
	Note: Maximum 7 marks if only ratio calculations provided			
	Discussion of company performance over time			2–3
	Discussion of company performance against competitors			2–3
	Discussion of actual returns against expected returns			1–2
	Discussion of need to maintain portfolio and alternative investments			1–2
	Discussion of future trends and expectations			1–2
	Discussion of takeover rumour and action as a result			1–2
	Other relevant discussion/commentary			1–2
			Maximum	**10**
Total				**25**

30 CHITHURST CO (SEP/DEC 16)

Key answer tips

Parts (a) and (b) in this question cover dividend policy and business valuation respectively – but note that they can be answered independently of each other.

In any question like this, start with the part that you feel most confident about, to build up confidence at the start of the question.

(a)   Dividend pay-out ratio

	Chithurst Co	Eartham Co	Iping Co
	%	%	%
20X2	42.9	40.0	46.7
20X3	41.3	(150.0)	19.3
20X4	35.1	40.0	33.1
20X5	34.0	40.0	31.8

Residual profit (after-tax profit for the year – dividend – new investment)

	Chithurst Co	Eartham Co	Iping Co
	£m	£m	£m
20X2	26	27	3
20X3	18	(40)	7
20X4	38	24	4
20X5	43	43	6

Chithurst Co's policy

Benefits

Chithurst Co's policy provides shareholders with a stable, predictable income each year. As profits have grown consistently, dividend cover has increased, which suggests that, for now, dividend levels are sustainable. These are positive signals to the stock market.

Drawbacks

Chithurst Co's dividend policy is unpopular with some of its shareholders. They have indicated a preference for dividend levels to bear a greater relation to profit levels. Although they are still in a minority and cannot force the directors to pay more dividends, they are now possibly a significant minority. Ultimately, Chithurst Co's share price could fall significantly if enough shareholders sell their shares because they dislike the dividend policy.

The dividend policy may also have been established to meet the financial needs of the shareholders when Chithurst Co was unquoted. However, it is now difficult to see how it fits into Chithurst Co's overall financial strategy. The greater proportion of funds retained does not appear to be linked to the levels of investment Chithurst Co is undertaking. Chithurst Co's shareholders may be concerned that best use is not being made of the funds available. If there are profitable investments which Chithurst Co could be making but is not doing so, then Chithurst Co may find it more difficult in future to sustain the levels of profit growth. Alternatively, if profitable investments do not exist, some shareholders may prefer to have funds returned in the form of a special dividend or share repurchase.

Eartham Co

Benefits

For three out of four years, Eartham Co has been paying out dividends at a stable pay-out ratio. This may be attractive to some investors, who have expectations that the company's profits will keep increasing in the longer term and wish to share directly in increases in profitability.

The year when Eartham Co's dividend pay-out ratio differed from the others was 20X3, when Eartham Co made a loss. A dividend of $15 million was paid in 20X3, which may be a guaranteed minimum. This limits the downside risk of the dividend pay-out policy to shareholders, as they know they will receive this minimum amount in such a year.

Drawbacks

Although shareholders are guaranteed a minimum dividend each year, dividends have been variable. Eartham Co's shareholders may prefer dividends to increase at a steady rate which is sustainable over time, even if this rate is lower than the rate of increase in some years under the current policy.

If Eartham Co had another poor year of trading like 20X3, shareholders' expectations that they will be paid a minimum dividend may mean that cash has to be earmarked to pay the minimum dividend, rather than for other, maybe better, uses in the business.

Having a 'normal' dividend policy results in expectations about what the level of dividend will be. Over time Eartham Co's managers may be reluctant to change to a lower pay-out ratio because they fear that this will give shareholders an adverse signal. Even if its directors maintain a constant ratio normally, shareholders may question whether the proportion of funds being retained is appropriate or whether a higher proportion could be paid out as dividends.

Eartham Co appears to be linking investment and dividend policy by its normal policy of allocating a constant proportion of funds for dividends and therefore a constant proportion of funds to invest. However, the actual level of new investments does not seem to bear much relation to the proportion of funds put aside for investment. When deciding on investments, the directors would also take into account the need to take advantage of opportunities as they arise and the overall amount of surplus funds built up over the years, together with the other sources of external finance available.

Iping Co

Benefits

Iping Co seems to have adopted a residual dividend policy, which links investment and dividend decisions. The strategy appears to be to make investments if they offer sufficient return to increase long-term company value and only pay dividends if there are no more profitable investments. They are assuming that internal funds are cheaper than external funds, or maybe Iping Co cannot raise the funds required from external sources.

The policy is likely to appeal to shareholders who are more concerned with capital growth than short-term income.

Drawbacks

Dividend payments are totally unpredictable, as they depend on the investment choices. Shareholders cannot rely on having any dividend income in a particular year.

Many shareholders may be prepared to sacrifice dividends for a while in order for funds to be available for investment for growth. However, at some point they may consider that Iping Co is well established enough to be able to maintain a consistent dividend policy as well as invest sufficiently for future growth.

(b) **Use of dividend valuation model**

Chithurst Co

Valuation = 33/0.11 = $300m

Chithurst Co's market capitalisation of $608m is considerably in excess of the valuation suggested by the dividend valuation model. This may suggest that investors have some positive expectations about the company and the lower cost of equity compared with the other two companies suggests it is regarded as a more stable investment. Investors could also be valuing the company using earnings growth rather than dividend growth. However, the lower market capitalisation compared with the other two companies and the smaller increase in share price suggest that investors have higher expectations of long-term growth from Eartham Co and Iping Co.

Eartham Co

One-year growth rate = (48/44) – 1 = 9.1 %

Valuation using one-year growth rate = 48 (1 + 0.091)/(0.14 – 0.091) = $1,068.7m

Three-year growth rate = $^3\sqrt{(48/38)}$ – 1 = 8.1%

Valuation using three-year growth rate = 48 (1 + 0.081)/(0.14 – 0.081) = $879m

Eartham Co's market capitalisation is closer to the valuation suggested by the dividend growth model using the one-year growth rate between 20X4 and 20X5 rather than the three-year growth rate between 20X2 and 20X5. This, together with the recent increase in share price, suggests that Eartham Co's shareholders have an optimistic view of its ability to sustain the profit growth and hence the dividend growth of the last two years, although its higher cost of equity than the other companies suggests that they are more wary about the risks of investing in Eartham Co. It indicates confidence in the directors' strategy, including the investments they have made.

Iping Co

One-year growth rate = (42/39) – 1 = 7.7%

Valuation using one-year growth rate = 42 (1 + 0.077)/(0.12 – 0.077) = $1,052.0m

Three-year growth rate = $^3\sqrt{(42/35)}$ – 1 = 6.3%

Valuation using three-year growth rate = 42 (1 + 0.063)/(0.12 – 0.063) = $783.3m

The market capitalisation of Iping Co is higher than is suggested by the dividend valuation model, but the dividend valuation model may not provide a realistic valuation because dividends payable are dependent on investment opportunities.

The larger increase in share price compared with the other two companies suggests that Iping Co's investors expect its investments to produce high long-term returns and hence are presumably satisfied with its dividend policy.

Marking scheme			
			Marks
(a)	Benefits of dividend policy – 1–2 marks for each company	Maximum	5
	Drawbacks of dividend policy – 2–3 marks for each company	Maximum	7
	Calculations – Dividend pay-out ratios – 1 mark per company		3
	Other calculations		2
			___
		Maximum	15
			___
(b)	Comments on valuation of each company, max 4 marks per company (max 5 marks for valuation calculation(s))		
			___
		Maximum	10
			___
Total			25
			___

31 BOURNELORTH CO (MAR/JUN 17)

Key answer tips

The requirements to this question were clear and mainly covered familiar topics. Part (c) required a knowledge of behavioural finance, a new topic in the syllabus, but any student who had read the recent technical article should have been able to answer this easily.

A well prepared student should have been able to score extremely good marks on this question.

Note that this past exam question contains no calculations. The new AFM syllabus states that in future "there will not be any wholly narrative questions" i.e. the topics covered here may well be covered, but in questions that contain a mixture of calculation and narrative parts.

(a) According to traditional finance theory, Bournelorth Co's directors will wish to strive for long-term shareholder wealth maximisation. The directors may not have been fully committed to long-term wealth maximisation, as they seemed to have focused on the development aspects which interested them most and left the original business mostly to others. However, now they are likely to come under pressure from the new external shareholders to maximise shareholder wealth and pay an acceptable level of dividend. To achieve this, it seems that Bournelorth Co will have to commit further large sums to investment in development of diagnostic applications (apps) in order to keep up with competitors.

Selling off the IT services business

At present the IT services business seems to be a reliable generator of significant profits. Selling it off would very likely produce a significant cash boost now, when needed. However, it would remove the safety net of reasonably certain income and mean that Bournelorth Co followed a much riskier business model. The IT services business also offers a possible gateway to reach customers who may be interested in the apps which Bournelorth Co develops.

Rights issue

If the executive directors wish to maintain their current percentage holdings, they would have to subscribe to 75% of the shares issued under the rights issue. Even though the shares would be issued at a discount, the directors might well not have the personal wealth available to subscribe fully. Previously they had to seek a listing to obtain enough funds for expansion, even though they were reluctant to bring in external investors, and this suggests their personal financial resources are limited.

However, the directors may need to take up the rights issue in order to ensure its success. If they do not, it may send out a message to external investors that the directors are unwilling to make a further commitment themselves because of the risks involved. There are also other factors which indicate that the rights issue may not be successful. The directors did not achieve the initial market price which they originally hoped for when Bournelorth Co was listed and shareholders may question the need for a rights issue soon after listing.

If the executive directors do not take up all of their rights, and the rights issue is still successful, this may have consequences for the operation of the business. The external shareholders would own a greater percentage of Bournelorth Co's equity share capital and may be in a position to reinforce the wishes of non-executive directors for improved governance and control systems and change of behaviour by the executive directors. Possibly they may also demand additional executive and non-executive directors, which would change the balance of power on the board.

The level of dividend demanded by shareholders may be less predictable than the interest on debt. One of the directors is also concerned whether the stock market is efficient or whether the share price may be subject to behavioural factors (discussed in (c) below).

Debt finance

Debt providers will demand Bournelorth Co commits to paying interest and ultimately repaying debt. This may worry the directors because of the significant uncertainties surrounding returns from new apps. Significant debt may have restrictive covenants built in, particularly if Bournelorth Co cannot provide much security. The directors may be faced with restrictions on dividends, for example, which may upset external shareholders.

Uncertainties surrounding funding may also influence directors' decisions. Loan finance may be difficult to obtain, but the amount and repayments would be fixed and could be budgeted, whereas the success of a rights issue is uncertain.

(b)   (i) The main risks connected with development work are that time and resources are wasted on projects which do not generate sales or are not in line with corporate strategy. Directors may choose apps which interest them rather than apps which are best for the business. There is also the risk that projects do not deliver benefits, take too long or are too costly.

Bournelorth Co's directors' heavy involvement in development activities may have made it easier to monitor them. However, the dangers with this are that the directors focus too much on their own individual projects, do not consider their projects objectively and do not step back to consider the overall picture.

The board must decide on a clear strategy for investment in development and needs to approve major initiatives before they are undertaken. There must be proper planning and budgeting of all initiatives and a structured approach to development. The board must regularly review projects, comparing planned and actual expenditure and resource usage. The board must be prepared to halt projects which are unlikely to deliver benefits. One director should be given responsibility for monitoring overall development activity without being directly involved in any of the work. Post-completion reviews should be carried out when development projects have been completed.

(ii) Communication with shareholders and other important stakeholders, such as potential customers, may be problematic. Bournelorth Co faces the general corporate governance requirement of transparency and has to comply with the specific disclosure requirements of its local stock market.

However, governance best practice also acknowledges that companies need to be allowed to preserve commercial confidentiality if appropriate, and clearly it will be relevant for Bournelorth Co. However, the less that it discloses, the less information finance providers will have on which to base their decisions.

Another issue with disclosure is that product failures may be more visible now that Bournelorth Co has obtained a listing and may have to include a business review in its accounts.

(c) (i) Sewell defines behavioural finance as the influence of psychology on the behaviour of financial practitioners and the subsequent effect on markets. Behavioural finance suggests that individual decision-making is complex and will deviate from rational decision-making. Under rational decision-making, individual preferences will be clear and remain stable. Individuals will make choices with the aim of maximising utility, and adopt a rational approach for assessing outcomes.

Under behavioural finance, individuals may be more optimistic or conservative than appears to be warranted by rational analysis. They will try to simplify complex decisions and may make different decisions based on the same facts at different times.

(ii) Bournelorth Co's share price may be significantly influenced by the impact of behavioural factors, as it is a newly listed company operating in a sector where returns have traditionally been variable and unpredictable. The impact of behavioural factors may be complex, and they may exert both upward and downward pressures on Bournelorth Co's share price. Investors may, for example, compensate for not knowing much about Bournelorth Co by anchoring, which means using information which is irrelevant, but which they do have, to judge investment in Bournelorth Co.

The possibility of very high returns may add to the appeal of Bournelorth Co's shares. Some investors may want the opportunity of obtaining high returns even if it is not very likely that they will. The IT sector has also been subject to herd behaviour, notably in the dotcom boom. The herd effect is when a large number of investors have taken the same decision, for example to invest in a particular sector, and this influences others to conform and take the same decision.

However, even if Bournelorth Co produces high returns for some time, the fact that it is in a volatile sector may lead to investors selling shares before it appears to be warranted on the evidence, on the grounds that by the laws of chance Bournelorth Co will make a loss eventually (known as the gambler's fallacy).

Under behavioural finance, the possible volatility of Bournelorth Co's results may lead to downward pressure on its share price for various reasons. First some investors have regret aversion, a general bias against making a loss anyway. This, it is claimed, means that the level of returns on equity is rather higher than the returns on debt than is warranted by a rational view of the risk of equity.

Similarly under prospect theory, investors are more likely to choose a net outcome which consists entirely of small gains, rather than an identical net outcome which consists of a combination of larger gains and some losses. At present also, Bournelorth Co does not have much of a history of results for the market to analyse. Even when it has been listed for some time, however, another aspect of behavioural finance is investors placing excessive weight on the most recent results.

If the market reacts very well or badly to news about Bournelorth Co, the large rise or fall in the share price which results may also not be sustainable, but may revert back over time.

32 HIGH K CO (SEP/DEC 17)

Key answer tips

Part (a) of this question (worth 21 marks) was quite unusual. Previous exam questions had sometimes required students to appraise the performance of a company, to identify whether the company is likely to fail, but rarely for so many marks (only once before – in June 2015). Also, the open-ended nature of this requirement may have caused problems.

Given that 10 marks were available for calculations and 11 marks for discussion, it would have been important not to spend too long calculating ratios, and to leave plenty of time for commentary.

Part (b) was a very straightforward discussion of financing options.

(a) Profitability

Revenues from the different types of store and online sales have all increased this year, despite a drop in store numbers. The increase in revenue this year may be largely due, however, to the government-induced pre-election boom in consumer expenditure, which appears unlikely to be sustained. Because the split of profits is not given, it is impossible to tell what has been the biggest contributor to increased profit. Profit as well as revenue details for different types of store would be helpful, also profit details for major product lines.

Improvements in return on capital employed derive from increases in profit margins and asset turnover.

The improvements in gross margins may be due to increased pressure being put on suppliers, in which case they may not be sustainable because of government pressure. The increased sales per store employee figures certainly reflects a fall in staff numbers, improving operating profit, although it could also be due to staff being better utilised or increased sales of higher value items in larger stores. If staff numbers continue to be cut, however, this could result in poorer service to customers, leading ultimately to decreased sales, so again it is questionable how much further High K Co can go.

The asset turnover shows an improvement which partly reflects the increase in sales. There have been only limited movements in the portfolio of the larger stores last year. The fall in non-current assets suggests an older, more depreciated, asset base. If there is no significant investment, this will mean a continued fall in capital employed and improved asset turnover. However, in order to maintain their appeal to customers, older stores will need to be refurbished and there is no information about refurbishment plans. Information about recent impairments in asset values would also be helpful, as these may indicate future trading problems and issues with realising values of assets sold.

Liquidity

The current ratio has improved, although the higher cash balances have been partly reflected by higher current liabilities. The increase in current liabilities may be due to a deliberate policy of taking more credit from suppliers, which the government may take measures to prevent. Being forced to pay suppliers sooner will reduce cash available for short-term opportunities.

Gearing

The gearing level in 20Y6 is below the 20Y4 level, but it would have fallen further had a fall in debt not been partly matched by a fall in High K Co's share price. It seems surprising that High K Co's debt levels fell during 20Y6 at a time of lower interest rates. Possibly lenders were (rightly) sceptical about whether the cut in central bank lending rate would be sustained and limited their fixed rate lending. Interest cover improved in 20Y6 and will improve further if High K Co makes use of revolving credit facilities. However, when High K Co's loans come up for renewal, terms available may not be as favourable as those High K Co has currently.

Investors

The increase in after-tax profits in 20Y5 and 20Y6 has not been matched by an increase in share price, which has continued to fall. The price/earnings ratio has been falling from an admittedly artificially high level, and the current level seems low despite earnings and dividends being higher. The stock market does not appear convinced by High K Co's current strategy. Return to shareholders in 20Y6 has continued to rise, but this has been caused by a significant % increase in dividend and hence increase in dividend yield. The continued fall in share price after the year end suggests that investors are sceptical about whether this increase can be maintained.

Revenue analysis

Town centre stores

High K Co has continued to close town centre stores, but closures have slowed recently and revenue increased in 20Y6. This suggests High K Co may have selected wisely in choosing which stores to keep open, although Dely Co believes there is no future for this type of store. Arguably though, town centre stores appeal to some customers who cannot easily get to out-of-town stores. Town centre stores may also be convenient collection points for customers using online click and collect facilities.

Convenience stores

High K Co has invested heavily in these since 20X3. The figures in 20Y4 suggest it may have over-extended itself or possibly suffered from competitive pressures and saturation of the market. The 20Y6 results show an improvement despite closures of what may have been the worst-performing stores. The figures suggest Dely Co's decision to close its convenience stores may be premature, possibly offering High K Co the opportunity to take over some of its outlets. Maintaining its convenience store presence would also seem to be in line with High K Co's commitment to be responsive to customer needs. Profitability figures would be particularly helpful here, to assess the impact of rental commitments under leases.

Out-of-town stores

Although the revenue per store for out-of-town stores has shown limited improvement in 20Y6, this is less than might have been expected. The recent consumer boom would have been expected to benefit the out-of-town stores particularly, because expenditure on the larger items which they sell is more likely to be discretionary expenditure by consumers which will vary with the business cycle. Where Dely Co sites its new out-of-town stores will also be a major issue for High K Co, as it may find some of its best-performing stores face more competition. High K Co again may need to consider significant refurbishment expenditure to improve the look of these stores and customer experience in them.

Online sales

Online sales have shown steady growth over the last few years, but it is difficult to say how impressive High K Co's performance is. Comparisons with competitors would be particularly important here, looking at how results have changed over the years compared with the level of investment made. It is also impossible to tell from the figures how much increases in online sales have been at the expense of store sales.

Conclusion

If High K Co's share price is to improve, investors need it to make some sort of definite decision about strategy the way its competitors have since its last year end. What the chief executive has been saying about flexibility and keeping a varied portfolio has not convinced investors. If High K Co is to maintain its competitive position, it may well have no choice but to make a significant further investment in online operations. Possibly as well it could review where its competitor is closing convenience stores, as it may be able to open, with limited investment, new stores in locations with potential.

However, it also must decide what to do about the large out-of-town stores, as their performance is already stagnating and they are about to face enhanced competition. High K Co will also need to determine its dividend policy, with maybe a level of dividend which is considered the minimum acceptable to shareholders allowed for in planning cash outflows.

Appendix

	20Y4	20Y5	20Y6
Profitability			
Gross profit %	4.33	5.07	6.19
Operating profit %	0.87	1.70	2.91
Asset turnover (sales revenue/(total assets – current liabilities))	2.36	2.42	2.53
Return on capital employed % (operating profit % × asset turnover)	2.05	4.11	7.36
Liquidity			
Current ratio	0.84	1.29	1.69
Solvency			
Gearing (non-current liabilities/ non-current liabilities + share capital) (Market values of share capital) %	37.6	36.8	32.5
Interest cover	1.63	3.54	7.12
Investors			
Dividend cover	0.35	1.29	1.71
Price/earnings ratio	54.46	12.15	5.52
Return to shareholders			
Dividend yield %	5.30	6.36	10.60
Share price gain/(loss) %	(9.00)	(5.65)	(3.29)
Total	(3.70)	0.71	7.31
Revenue/store ($m)			
Town centre	31.91	33.05	33.93
Convenience	5.41	5.66	5.99
Out-of-town	46.45	46.16	46.46
Store revenue per store staff member ($000)	247	258	272

(**Note:** Credit will be given for alternative relevant calculations and discussion. Candidates are not expected to complete all of the calculations or evaluation above to obtain the available marks.)

(b) High K Co has not raised any equity finance over the last five years. Its falling share price means that a new share issue may not be successful. It may not only need debt finance to be renewed, but additional funding to be obtained.

High K Co intends to make more use of revolving credit facilities, which it need not draw on fully, rather than loans, which will mean that its finance costs are lower than on ordinary debt. However, these facilities are likely to be at floating rates, so if the government increases the central bank rate significantly, they could come at significant cost if High K Co decides to utilise them fully.

Finance costs on new debt, whatever form it takes, may therefore be significant and lower interest cover. High K Co may have to investigate selling some of the stores it owns either outright or on a sale or leaseback basis.

ADVANCED INVESTMENT APPRAISAL

33 STRAYER INC (JUN 02 ADAPTED) *Walk in the footsteps of a top tutor*

Walkthrough question – key answer tips

This is an excellent APV question, which covers all the examiner's favourite tricks in this syllabus area.

Before you start by attempting the numbers in part (a), notice that the discussion in parts (b) and (c) is general bookwork which does not depend on the calculations. A good approach might be to do parts (b) and (c) first – as long as you label things clearly in your answer book, this will not cause a problem for the marker, but it will enable you to pick up the easy marks in the question.

When you attempt the numbers, lay your answer out clearly so that the marker can understand your workings. APV is a topic which is easy to confuse!

Start by identifying project cash flows – ignore any financing information for now. When you have picked up all the project cash flows (don't forget the tax impact), you need to discount them using an ungeared cost of equity. This is not given directly, but the method of degearing the industry equity beta and then using CAPM is extremely commonly tested, so make sure you are happy with that.

Next, move on to the financing costs and benefits. The main benefit is the tax relief to be received on the debt interest, but don't forget to include the value of the subsidised loan too. In order to work out the present value of these costs and benefits, use the risk free rate (5.5%), or the pre-tax cost of debt (8%) as a discount rate. In theory, since APV was developed from the theories of Modigliani and Miller, the risk free rate and the pre-tax cost of debt should be one and the same thing, but if they aren't in a question, you will get credit for using either figure as a discount rate.

(a)   **Step 1: Base case NPV**

Assuming the risk of companies in the printing industry is similar to that of Strayer's new investment, the beta of the printing industry will be used to estimate the discount rate for the base case NPV.

Assuming that debt used in the printing industry is typically risk-free (i.e. has a beta of zero), then we can ungear the equity beta of the printing industry as follows:

$$\beta_a = \left[\frac{V_e}{(V_e + V_d(1-T))} \beta_e \right] = \left[\frac{50}{50+50(1-0.30)} \times 1.2 \right] = 0.706$$

Using the capital asset pricing model: $E(r_i) = R_f + \beta_i(E(r_m) - R_f)$

K_e ungeared = 5.5% + (12% – 5.5%) 0.706 = 10.09% or approximately 10%.

Annual after-tax cash flows = $5 million (1 – 0.3) = $3,500,000.

From annuity tables with a 10% discount rate:

			$
Present value of annual cash flows	3,500,000 × 6.145	=	21,507,500
Present value of the residual value	5,000,000 × 0.386	=	1,930,000
			23,437,500
Less initial investment			25,000,000
Base case NPV			(1,562,500)

Step 2: Financing side effects

Financing side effects relate to the tax shield on interest payments, the subsidised loan, and issue costs associated with external financing.

Tax relief:

- $5 million 8% loan.

  Interest payable is $400,000 per year, tax relief is $400,000 × 0.3 = $120,000 per year.

- $4 million subsidised loan.

  Interest is $240,000 per year, tax relief $72,000 per year.

- Total annual tax relief $192,000 per year. The present value of this tax relief, discounted at the risk-free rate of 5.5% per year, is: $192,000 × 7.541 = $1,447,872.

(The tax relief on interest payments allowed by government is assumed to be risk free. The mid-point between 5% and 6% in annuity tables is used. **NB:** Discounting at a rate higher than the risk-free rate could be argued, especially if the company might be in a non-taxpaying position in some years.)

Subsidy:

- The company saves 2% per year on $4,000,000 equal to interest saved of $80,000

- After tax, this equates to $80,000 × (1 − 0.30) = $56,000.

- As this is a government subsidy, it is assumed to be risk free and will be discounted at 5.5% per year.

- Present value = $56,000 × 7.541 = $422,296.

Issue costs:

		$
Debt: $5 million × 1%	=	50,000
Equity: $10 million × 4%	=	400,000
		450,000

Step 3: APV = base case NPV + PV of financing side effects

	$
Base case NPV	(1,562,500)
PV of tax relief	1,447,872
PV of subsidy	422,296
Issue costs	(450,000)
APV	(142,332)

Based upon these estimates the project is not financially viable. The benefits of the finance are insufficient to outweigh the inherent problems with the proposed project.

(b) Both APV and NPV are discounted cash flow techniques but differ in the way project finance is incorporated into the process. With NPV, finance is usually incorporated into the discount rate which is then applied to project-only (i.e. excluding finance) cash flows. The clearest example of this is when a project (or company) WACC is used to discount project cash flows.

APV involves a two stage process dealing with project and financing flows separately. Project cash flows are discounted at an ungeared cost of equity to calculate a base case NPV. Financing side effects are then discounted at an appropriate rate – usually the pre-tax risk free rate.

APV may be a better technique to use than NPV when:

(i) There is a significant change in capital structure as a result of the investment.

(ii) The investment involves complex tax payments and tax allowances, and/or has periods when taxation is not paid.

(iii) Subsidised loans, grants or issue costs exist.

(iv) Financing side effects exist (e.g. the subsidised loan), which require discounting at a different rate than that applied to the mainstream project.

(c) **Islamic finance**

Islamic finance rests on the application of Islamic, or Shariah, law.

The main principles of Islamic finance are that:

- Wealth must be generated from legitimate trade and asset-based investment. The use of money for the purposes of making money is forbidden.

- Investment should also have a social and an ethical benefit to wider society beyond pure return.

- Risk should be shared.

- Harmful activities (such as gambling, alcohol and the sale of certain foods) should be avoided.

The raising of term loan debt finance as proposed by Strayer (where the lender would make a straight interest charge, irrespective of how the underlying assets fare) would violate the principle of sharing risk and of not using money for the purposes of making money. Under Islamic finance, the charging and receiving of interest (riba) is strictly prohibited. This is in stark contrast to more conventional, Western forms of finance.

One alternative form of finance would be Murabaha, a form of trade credit for asset acquisition. Here the provider of finance would buy the item and then sell it on to Strayer at a price that includes an agreed mark-up for profit. The mark-up is fixed in advance and cannot be increased and the payment is made by instalments.

Another form of finance would be Islamic bonds, known as sukuk. To be Shariah-compliant, the sukuk holders must have a proprietary interest in the assets which are being financed. The sukuk holders' return for providing finance is a share of the income generated by the assets. The key distinction between sukuk and murabaha is that sukuk holders have ownership of the cash flows but not the assets themselves.

34   DIGUNDER (DEC 07 ADAPTED)

Key answer tips

In any Black Scholes question, start by writing out the five key input factors. This will ensure that you focus on picking out the key information from the question before you start using the formulae.

(a)   **Five input factors for the Black Scholes model.**

Exercise date (t) = 2 years

Risk free rate (r) = 6%

Volatility (s) = 40%

Exercise price (P_e) = capital expenditure required = $24 million

Current price (P_a) = Present Value of the Project's cash inflows = $23.13 million (see working below)

Working for P_a: If the project were started immediately, its NPV would be $4 million at a cost of capital of 10%.

Given that the land purchase cost is $24 million, this means that the present value of the future cash flows from the project must be $28 million.

If the option to delay for two years is exercised, these future cash flows will arise two years later, so the present value (at a cost of capital of 10%) will reduce to

$28 million × 0.826 (2 year discount factor) = $23.13 million.

This is the value of P_a that should be used in the Black Scholes formula.

Using the Black Scholes formula as specified:

$$d_1 = \frac{\ln\left(\frac{23.13}{24}\right) + (0.06 + 0.5 \times 0.40^2)}{0.40 \times \sqrt{2}} = 0.4297 \text{ (i.e. 0.43)}$$

$d_2 = 0.4297 - 0.40 \times \sqrt{2} = -0.1360 \text{ (i.e. } -0.14)$

The areas under the normal curves for these two values are $N(d_1) = 0.6664$ and $N(d_2) = 0.4443$.

Using the derived values for N(d$_1$) and N(d$_2$) the value of the call option on the value represented by this project is as follows:

c = 0.6664 × 23.13 –0.4443 × 24 × e$^{-.06 \times 2}$ = $5.95 million

Tutorial note

Note that the value of $5.95 million here is made up of an intrinsic value of $4m (the project's NPV) plus the time value of the option of $1.95m.

(b)   **Digunder**

Housing Development at Newtown

This project has a net present value of $4 million on a capital expenditure of $24 million which whilst significant has a volatility estimate of 40% of the present value per annum. This volatility is brought about by uncertainties about Government's intentions with respect to the Bigcity–Newtown transport link and the consequential impact upon property values. Currently, the project presents substantial value at risk and there is a high likelihood that the project will not be value generating. To surmount this, an estimate is provided of the value of the option to delay construction for two years until the Government's transport plans will be made known.

The option to delay

The option to delay construction is particularly valuable in this case. It eliminates much of the downside risk that the project does not generate the cash flows expected and it gives us the ability to proceed at a point in time most favourable to us. The nature of the delay option is that it is more valuable the greater the volatility of the underlying cash flows and the greater the time period before we are required to exercise.

The valuation of the option to delay has been under taken using the Black and Scholes model. The model has some limiting assumptions relating to the underlying nature of the cash flows and our ability to adjust our exposure to risk as time passes. In reality, the use of this type of modelling is more appropriate for financial securities that are actively traded. Our use of the model is an approximation of the value of the flexibility inherent in this project and although the model will not have the precision found in its security market applications it does indicate the order of magnitude of the real option available. A positive value of $5.95 million is suggested by the model underlying the considerable benefit in delay.

In interpreting this valuation it is important to note that the actual project present value at commencement could be significantly larger than currently estimated and will certainly not be less than zero (otherwise we will not exercise the option to build). The additional value reflects the fact that downside risk is eliminated by our ability to delay the decision to proceed.

On the basis of our valuation the option to delay commencement of the project should be taken and investment delayed until the Government's intention with respect to transport links becomes clearer. On this basis we would place a value of $5.95 million on the project including the delay option.

(c) The Black and Scholes model makes a number of assumptions about the underlying nature of the pricing and return distributions which may not be valid with this type of project. More problematically it assumes that continuous adjustment of the hedged position is possible and that the option is European style. Where the option to delay can be exercised over any set period of time up to the exercise date the Black and Scholes model will cease to be accurate. For a call option, such as the option to delay, then the level of inaccuracy is likely to be quite low especially for options that are close to the money. Given that an option always has time value it will invariably be in the option holder's interest to wait until exercise date before exercising his or her option. However, in those situations where the level of accuracy is particularly important, or where it is suspected that the Black and Scholes assumptions do not hold, then the binomial option pricing approach is necessary.

(d) The objectives of integrated reporting include:

- To improve the quality of information available to providers of financial capital to enable a more efficient and productive allocation of capital.

- To provide a more cohesive and efficient approach to corporate reporting that draws on different reporting strands and communicates the full range of factors that materially affect the ability of an organisation to create value over time.

- To enhance accountability and stewardship for the broad base of capitals (financial, manufactured, intellectual, human, social and relationship, and natural) and promote understanding of their interdependencies.

- To support integrated thinking, decision making and actions that focus on the creation of value over the short, medium and long term.

Marking scheme		
		Marks
(a)	Identification of inputs into BS model	5
	Calculation of d1 and d2	4
	Calculation of real option value	2
	Conclusion on the value of the option to delay	1
	Maximum	**12**
(b)	1–2 marks per sensible point	**4**
(c)	Outline of the limitations of the BS model	2
	Identification of the American style real option in the given circumstances	1
	Note on the appropriate technique for solving the American style option	1
	Maximum	**4**
(d)	1–2 marks per sensible point	**5**
Total		**25**

35 KENAND CO

Key answer tips

In autumn 2011, the examiner wrote two articles for Student Accountant magazine about bonds, FRAs and swaps. The contents of the articles are tested in this question.

The contents of the articles were also tested in the December 2011 and June 2012 exams.

This shows how important it is to keep an eye on Student Accountant and to fully understand any articles presented there.

Note that this question covers just the calculations. Real AFM exam questions will always contain a mixture of calculation and narrative parts.

(a) (i) AB Co bond value

'Bid yield' = yield to maturity (YTM) = 6.2% i.e. the value of the bond should be the present value of the future receipts to an investor, discounted at 6.2%.

	Year 1	Year 2	Year 3	Year 4
Receipts (for a $100 nominal bond)	5	5	5	110 + 5
DF at 6.2%	$\dfrac{1}{1.062}$	$\dfrac{1}{1.062^2}$	$\dfrac{1}{1.062^3}$	$\dfrac{1}{1.062^4}$
PV	4.71	4.43	4.17	90.41

NPV (i.e. bond value, per $100 nominal) = $103.72

So with $1m, Kenand Co will be able to buy $1m/$103.72 = 9,641 bonds on the market.

XY Co bond value

These bonds have not yet been issued, so we need to compute the likely issue price based on the spot yield curve for an A rated company.

	1 year	2 year	3 year	4 year
Govt bond annual spot yield curve (%)	3.54	4.01	4.70	5.60
A rated credit spread (%)	0.26	0.39	0.50	0.60
Total = A rated company's annual spot yield curve (%)	3.80	4.40	5.20	6.20

XY Co's new 3 year bonds can be separated into three separate bonds with the following payment structures (for a $100 nominal bond):

	Year 1	Year 2	Year 3
Bond 1	4		
Bond 2		4	
Bond 3			104

The sum of the present values of these amounts (when each is discounted at the relevant rate from the A rated company's yield curve table above) is then the likely issue price of the bond.

i.e. issue price (bond value) =

$$\left(4 \times \frac{1}{1.0380}\right) + \left(4 \times \frac{1}{1.0440^2}\right) + \left(104 \times \frac{1}{1.0520^3}\right) = \$96.85$$

So with $1m, Kenand Co will be able to buy $1m/$96.85 = 10,325 bonds on issue.

(ii) To find the Macaulay duration, we first need to calculate the yield to maturity (YTM), or gross redemption yield, of the bonds, which will be used to discount the cash flows to the investor.

YTM calculations

AB Co bonds

The bid yield of the bonds quoted in the question is the same as the bond's YTM. Therefore, 6.2% will be used to discount AB Co's bond cash flows.

XY Co bonds

The YTM is the IRR of the current bond value, the interest receipts and the redemption amount.

Tutorial note

The YTM will be very similar to the 5.20% rate calculated in part (a) above, which was the spot yield for a 3 year A rated bond. In the exam, using the 5.20% as a discount rate in the Macaulay duration calculation would not be completely accurate, but it would save time.

	$	DF 4%	PV @ 4%	DF 6%	PV @ 6%
t_0	MV (96.85)	1	(96.85)	1	(96.85)
t_1-t_3	Interest 4	2.775	11.10	2.673	10.69
t_3	Redemption 100	0.889	88.90	0.840	84.00
			3.15		(2.16)

So, IRR = 4% + $\left[\left(\dfrac{3.15}{3.15 + 2.16}\right)(6\% - 4\%)\right]$ = 5.19%

Duration calculations

AB Co bonds

PV of cash flows (years 1–4) = $\dfrac{5}{1.062} + \dfrac{5}{1.062^2} + \dfrac{5}{1.062^3} + \dfrac{115}{1.062^4}$

= 4.708 + 4.433 + 4.174 + 90.407

So Macaulay duration =

[(4.708 × 1) + (4.433 × 2) + (4.174 × 3) + (90.407 × 4)]/103.72 = 3.74 years

XY Co bonds

PV of cash flows (years 1–3) = $\dfrac{4}{1.0519} + \dfrac{4}{1.0519^2} + \dfrac{104}{1.0519^3}$

= 3.803 + 3.615 + 89.353

So Macaulay duration =

[(3.803 × 1) + (3.615 × 2) + (89.353 × 3)]/96.85 = 2.88 years

Interpretation

Macaulay duration is a measure of risk associated with a bond, or specifically a measure of the sensitivity of the bond value to changes in interest rates. Generally, the prices of shorter dated bonds are less sensitive to interest rate changes. This is proved by the Macaulay duration calculations here, which show that AB Co's longer dated bonds have a higher duration, so the price of these bonds is more sensitive to interest changes.

Given that both companies have an A credit rating, it is perhaps initially surprising that there is such a large difference between the duration of the bonds. However, the greater risk attached to the longer dated bond is consistent with the spot yield and credit spreads information provided, which shows that the yield curve is upward sloping i.e. yields are higher on longer dated bonds in a particular risk class.

Tutorial note

There is a quicker way to derive the Macaulay duration of the XY bonds, which avoids the need to first work out the YTM using the IRR method.

	Year 1	Year 2	Year 3
Receipts (for a $100 nominal bond)	4	4	104
DF at relevant spot yield rates	$\dfrac{1}{1.038}$	$\dfrac{1}{1.044^2}$	$\dfrac{1}{1.052^3}$
PV	3.854	3.670	89.328

So Macaulay duration = [(3.854 × 1) + (3.670 × 2) + (89.328 × 3)]/96.85 = 2.88 years, as before.

(b) XY Co is an A rated company, so the annual spot yield curve for its bonds is:

1 year 3.54% + 0.26% = 3.80%

2 year 4.01% + 0.39% = 4.40%

3 year 4.70% + 0.50% = 5.20%

4 year 5.60% + 0.60% = 6.20%

(based on the spot yield for government bonds adjusted for the A rated company's credit spread – all information taken from the scenario of part (a)).

Therefore, the rate quoted on a 12 v 24 FRA will be (1.0440²/1.0380) – 1 = 5.00%.

Tutorial note 1

This calculation is explained as follows:

XY Co could borrow money for 2 years, without incurring interest rate risk, in two ways. It could issue a 2 year fixed rate bond and pay 4.40% per annum for each of the two years.

Alternatively it could issue a 1 year bond at 3.80%, redeem this and issue a 1 year bond again for the second year. In the latter case it could hedge the risk for the second year by using an FRA. The total interest cost has to be the same either way and therefore if R is the 12 v 24 FRA rate then:

$$(1.0440^2) = (1.0380) \times (1+R)$$

Tutorial note 2

Note that the forward rates on other FRAs could also be calculated as follows:

24 v 36 FRA $\quad (1.0520^3/1.0440^2) - 1 = 6.81\%$

36 v 48 FRA $\quad (1.0620^4/1.0520^3) - 1 = 9.26\%$

(c) The bank will calculate the fixed interest rate to make sure that the present value of the fixed payments made by XY Co is equal to the present value of the variable payments made by the bank to XY Co when both are discounted at the spot yield.

Variable payments made by the bank to XY Co each year will be

$20m × expected interest rate for each year less 30 basis points.

In year 1 the expected interest rate is 3.80% (spot yield), so the expected payment will be $20m × (3.80% – 0.30%) = $0.7m.

In years 2–4 the expected interest rate is the forward rate calculated in part (b) above, hence the expected payments will be:

Year 2	$20m × (5.00% – 0.30%)	$0.94m
Year 3	$20m × (6.81% – 0.30%)	$1.302m
Year 4	$20m × (9.26% – 0.30%)	$1.792m

So, each year XY Co will pay a fixed amount (say X) to the bank in exchange for these variable amounts. In order for the present values of the fixed payments to be equal to the present values of the variable payments,

$$\frac{0.7}{1.0380} + \frac{0.94}{1.0440^2} + \frac{1.302}{1.0520^3} + \frac{1.792}{1.0620^4} = \frac{X}{1.0380} + \frac{X}{1.0440^2} + \frac{X}{1.0520^3} + \frac{X}{1.0620^4}$$

or, by simplifying the equation:

$$\frac{0.7}{1.0380} + \frac{0.94}{1.0440^2} + \frac{1.302}{1.0520^3} + \frac{1.792}{1.0620^4} = \left\| \frac{1}{1.0380} + \frac{1}{1.0440^2} + \frac{1}{1.0520^3} + \frac{1}{1.0620^4} \right\| X$$

so

4.064 = 3.526X

i.e. X = $1.153m

which (as a percentage of the $20m loan) is a rate of (1.153/20) = 5.77%.

Tutorial note

Whilst the present value of the fixed interest payments will equal the present value of the variable interest payments on the date that the swap is created, over time, as interest rates change, this will not be the case.

If, for example, interest rates, and the spot yields, rise, the present value of the fixed payments will fall (remember the higher the discount rate the lower the present value). This will not be the case with the variable payments because the payment itself will rise as the discount rate rises. This is why a swap will, in due course, become either a financial asset, or a financial liability.

36 FUBUKI CO (DEC 10)

Key answer tips

APV is very commonly tested. As long as you remember to use the ungeared cost of equity for discounting, the project appraisal is almost identical to a standard NPV question.

(a) Base Case Net Present Value

Fubuki Co: Project Evaluation

Base Case

	$000 Unit price/cost	Inflation	Now	Year 1	Year 2	Year 3	Year 4
Units Produced and sold				1,300	1,820	2,548	2,675
Sales revenue	2.5	3%		3,250	4,687	6,758	7,308
Direct costs	1.2	8%		1,560	2,359	3,566	4,044
Attributable fixed costs	1,000	5%		1,000	1,050	1,103	1,158
Profits				690	1,278	2,089	2,106
Working capital	15%		(488)	(215)	(311)	(82)	1,096
Taxation (W1)				(10)	(157)	(360)	(364)
Incremental cash flows							
Investment/sale			(14,000)				16,000
Net cash flows			(14,488)	465	810	1,647	18,838
Present Value (10%) (W2)			(14,488)	422	670	1,237	12,867
Base case NPV			708				

Workings:

(W1)

Profits	690	1,278	2,089	2,106
Less: allowances	650	650	650	650
Taxable profits	40	628	1,439	1,456
Tax	10	157	360	364

(W2) Discount rate (Haizum's ungeared Ke)

$ke(g) = ke(u) + (1 - t)(ke(u) - kd)Vd/Ve$

$Ve = 2.53 \times 15 = 37.95$

$Vd = 40 \times 0.9488 = 37.952$

Assume $Vd/Ve = 1$

$14 = ke(u) + 0.72 \times (ke(u) - 4.5) \times 1$

$14 = 1.72ke(u) - 3.24$

$ke(u) = 10.02$ assume 10%

Tutorial note

In calculating the ungeared cost of equity, this model answer has used the Modigliani and Miller formula from the formula sheet. The same answer could have been derived using the asset beta formula and the CAPM as follows:

CAPM: $E(r_i) = R_f + \beta_i(E(r_m) - R_f)$

So 14% = 4.5% + ($\beta_i \times 4\%$)

Hence $\beta_i = 2.375$ (this is the equity beta)

Therefore (since there is no debt beta in this question), the asset beta is:

$$2.375 \times \frac{1}{1 + 1(1 - 0.28)} = 1.381$$

Then CAPM can be used again to give the ungeared cost of equity as:

4.5% + (1.381 × 4) = 10.02%

The base case net present value is calculated as approximately $708,000. This is positive but marginal.

The following financing side effects apply

	$000
Issue costs 4/96 × $14,488	(604)

Tax Shield

Annual tax relief = (14,488 × 80% × 0.055 × 25%)

$$+ (14{,}488 × 20\% × 0.075 × 25\%)$$

$$= 159.4 + 54.3 = 213.7$$

213.7 × 3.588	766

Subsidy benefit

14,488 × 80% × 0.02 × 75% × 3.588	624
Total benefit of financing side effects	786
Adjusted present value (708 + 786)	1,494

The addition of the financing side effects gives an increased present value and probably the project would not be considered marginal. Once these are taken into account Fubuki Co would probably undertake the project.

Tutorial note (extracted from the examiner's comments)

In calculating the present values of the tax shield and subsidy benefits, the annuity factor used is based on 4.5% debt yield rate for four years.

It could be argued that 7.5% may also be used as this reflects the normal borrowing/default risk of the company. Full credit was given where this assumption was made to estimate the annuity factor.

(b) The adjusted present value can be used where the impact of using debt financing is significant. Here the impact of each of financing side effects from debt is shown separately rather than being imputed into the weighted average cost of capital. The project is initially evaluated by only taking into account the business risk element of the new venture. This shows that although the project results in a positive net present value, it is fairly marginal and volatility in the input factors could turn the project. Sensitivity analysis can be used to examine the sensitivity of the factors. The financing side effects show that almost 110% value is added when the positive impact of the tax shields and subsidy benefits are taken into account even after the issue costs.

Assumptions (Credit given for alternative, valid assumptions)

1   Haizum Co's ungeared cost of equity is used because it is assumed that this represents the business risk attributable to the new line of business.

2   The ungeared cost of equity is calculated on the assumption that Modigliani and Miller's (MM) proposition 2 applies.

3   It is assumed that initial working capital requirement will form part of the funds borrowed but the subsequent requirements will be available from the funds generated from the project.

4   The feasibility study is ignored as a past cost.

5   It is assumed that the five-year debt yield is equivalent to the risk-free rate,

6 It is assumed that the annual reinvestment needed on plant and machinery is equivalent to the tax allowable depreciation.

7 It is assumed that all cash flows occur at the end of the year unless specified otherwise.

8 All amounts are given in $'000 to the nearest $'000. When calculating the units produced and sold, the nearest approximation for each year is taken.

Assumptions 4, 5, 6, 7 and 8 are standard assumptions made for a question of this nature. Assumptions 1, 2 and 3 warrant further discussion. Taking assumption 3 first, it is reasonable to assume that before the project starts, the company would need to borrow the initial working capital as it may not have access to the working capital needed. In subsequent years, the cash flows generated from the operation of the project may be sufficient to fund the extra working capital required. In the case of Fubuki Co, because of an expected rapid growth in sales in years 2 and 3, the working capital requirement remains high and the management need to assess how to make sufficient funds available.

Considering assumptions 1 and 2, the adjusted present values methodology assumes that MM proposition 2 applies and the equivalent ungeared cost of equity does not take into account the cost of financial distress. This may be an unreasonable assumption. The ungeared cost of equity is based on another company which is in a similar line of business to the new project, but it is not exactly the same. It can be difficult to determine an accurate ungeared cost of equity in practice. However, generally the discount rate (cost of funds) tends to be the least sensitive factor in investment appraisal and therefore some latitude can be allowed.

Marking scheme		
		Marks
(a)	Sales revenue, direct costs and additional fixed costs	4
	Incremental working capital	1
	Taxation	2
	Estimation of Ke (ungeared)	2
	Net cash flows, present value and base case NPV	2
	Issue costs	1
	Calculation of tax shield impact	2
	Calculation of subsidy impact	1
	Adjusted present value and conclusion	2
		–––
	Maximum	**17**
		–––
(b)	Discussion of using APV	2–3
	Assumption about Haizum as proxy and MM proposition 2	3–4
	Other assumptions	2–3
		–––
	Maximum	**8**
		–––
Total		**25**
		–––

37   INVESTMENT PROJECT REVIEW (JUN 09 ADAPTED)

Key answer tips

This is a clever way of testing investment appraisal. There are many errors in the original computation, but there are also some points which have been dealt with correctly.

List out the errors, to show the examiner clearly what adjustments need to be made, and then make any necessary adjustments to the given figures.

(a) The project cash flow contains a number of errors of principle which should be corrected. As the project cash flows are shown after tax, the corrections should be made net of tax by either adding back or deducting the change required.

- Interest has been deducted and should be added back as this finance charge is properly charged through the application of the discount rate.

- Depreciation should be added back as this is not a cash flow.

- The indirect cost charge should be added back as this does not appear to be a decision relevant cost.

- Infrastructure costs should be deducted as these have not been included in the original projection.

- Site clearance and reinstatement costs of $5 million have been included net of tax.

- The unclaimed tax allowable depreciation (TAD) is calculated as follows:

	0	1	2	3	4	5	6
Capital investment	150.00	50.00					
Deduct FYA at 50%	−75.00	−25.00					
Deduct TAD at 25% of residual		−18.75	−20.31	−15.23	−11.43	−8.57	−6.43
Pool	75.00	81.25	60.94	45.71	34.28	25.71	19.28
Proceeds of sale							7.00
Unclaimed TAD							12.28

This will generate a positive tax benefit in year six of $3.68 million at the tax rate of 30%.

The adjusted project cash flow and net present value calculation for this project are as follows:

	0	1	2	3	4	5	6
Project after tax cash flow	−127.50	−36.88	44.00	68.00	60.00	35.00	20.00
Add back net interest			2.80	2.80	2.80	2.80	2.80
Add back depreciation (net of tax)			2.80	2.80	2.80	2.80	2.80
Add back ABC charge (net of tax)			5.60	5.60	5.60	5.60	5.60
Less corporate infrastructure costs			−2.80	−2.80	−2.80	−2.80	−2.80
Estimate for site clearance							−3.50
Tax benefit of unrecovered TAD							3.68
Adjusted project cash flow	−127.50	−36.88	52.40	76.40	68.40	43.40	28.58
Discount factor	1.0000	0.9091	0.8264	0.7513	0.6830	0.6209	0.5645
Discounted cash flow at 10%	−127.50	−33.52	43.31	57.40	46.72	26.95	16.14
Net present value	29.48						

The sensitivity of the project to a 1% increase in capital expenditure is as follows:

Sensitivity to a $1 million increase in CAPEX at year 0

	0	1	2	3	4	5	6
Equipment purchase/written down value	1	0.50	0.37	0.28	0.21	0.16	0.12
FYA	−0.5						
TAD		−0.13	−0.09	−0.07	−0.05	−0.04	−0.03
Balance	0.5	0.37	0.28	0.21	0.16	0.12	0.09
Impact upon CAPEX	−1						
Tax saving due to TAD and FYA	0.15	0.039	0.028	0.021	0.015	0.012	0.009
Unrecovered allowance							0.027
Net impact	−0.85	0.039	0.028	0.021	0.015	0.012	0.036
Discount factor	1.0000	0.9091	0.8264	0.7513	0.6830	0.6209	0.5645
Discounted cash flow	−0.85	0.0355	0.0223	0.0158	0.0102	0.0075	0.0203
Net present value	−0.63						

Thus an increase in CAPEX by $1 million results in a loss of NPV of $0.63 million due to the benefit of the tax allowable depreciation available discounted over the life of the project.

(b) The discounted payback is estimated as follows:

	1	1	2	3	4	5	6
Discounted cash flows from project	−127.50	−33.52	43.31	57.40	46.72	26.95	16.14
Cumulative discounted cash flow	−127.50	−161.02	−117.72	−60.32	−13.60	13.35	29.48
Payback (discounted)	4.50						

The duration of a project is the average number of years required to recover the present value of the project.

Duration	0	1	2	3	4	5	6
DCF at 10%			43.31	57.40	46.72	26.95	16.14
PV of return phase	190.52						
Proportion of present value in each year			0.2273	0.3013	0.2452	0.1415	0.0847
Weighted years			0.4546	0.9039	0.9809	0.7073	0.5082
Duration (= sum of the weighted years)	3.55						

Tutorial note

Duration is a relatively simple calculation once you have calculated NPV, so review this answer carefully.

Payback, discounted payback and duration are three techniques that measure the return to liquidity offered by a capital project. In theory, a firm that has ready access to the capital markets should not be concerned about the time taken to recapture the investment in a project. However, in practice managers prefer projects to appear to be successful as quickly as possible. Payback as a technique fails to take into account the time value of money and any cash flows beyond the project date. It is used by many firms as a coarse filter of projects and it has been suggested to be a proxy for the redeployment real option. Discounted payback does surmount the first difficulty but not the second in that it is still possible for projects with highly negative terminal cash flows to appear attractive because of their initial favourable cash flows. Conversely, discounted payback may lead a project to be discarded that has highly favourable cash flows after the payback date.

Duration measures either the average time to recover the initial investment (if discounted at the project's internal rate of return) of a project, or to recover the present value of the project if discounted at the cost of capital as is the case in this question. Duration captures both the time value of money and the whole of the cash flows of a project. It is also a measure which can be used across projects to indicate when the bulk of the project value will be captured. Its disadvantage is that it is more difficult to conceptualise than payback and may not be employed for that reason.

(c)   **Report to Management Prepared by: AN Accountant, ACCA**

Project acceptance and criteria for acceptability

I have reviewed the proposed capital investment and after making a number of adjustments have estimated that the project will increase the value of the firm by approximately $29.48 million. The project is highly sensitive to changes in the level of capital investment. Increases in immediate capital spending on this project will lead to a concomitant loss in the overall project value less the tax saving resulting from the increased tax allowable depreciation. However, given the size of the net present value of the project, it is unlikely that an adverse movement in this variable would lead to a significant reduction in the value of the firm.

The analysis of the payback on this project using discounted cash flows suggests that the value of the capital invested will be wholly recovered within four years of commencement. The bulk of the cash flow recovery occurs early within the life cycle of the project with an average recovery of the total present value occurring 3.55 years from commencement.

On the basis of the figures presented and the sensitivity analysis conducted, I recommend the Board approves this project for investment.

For many years the Board has used payback as one technique for evaluating investment projects. The Board has noted concerns that (i) the method chosen does not reflect the cost of finance either in the cash flows or in the discount rate applied and (ii) it fails to reflect cash flows beyond the payback date. Discounted payback surmounts the first but not the second difficulty. I would recommend that the Board considers the use of 'duration' which measures the time to recover either half the value invested in a project or, by alternative measurement, half the project net present value. Because this measure captures both the full value and the time value of a project it is recommended as a superior measure to either payback or discounted payback when comparing the time taken by different projects to recover the investment involved.

As part of its review process the Board has asked for sensitivities of the project to key variables. Sensitivity analysis demonstrates the likely gain or loss of project value as a result of small changes in the value of the variables chosen. Unfortunately, some variables such as, for example, price changes and the cost of finance, are highly correlated with one another and focusing upon the movement in a single variable may well ignore significant changes in another variable. To deal with this and given our background information about the volatility of input variables and their correlation, I would recommend that a simulation is conducted taking these component risks into account. Simulation works by randomly drawing a possible value for each variable on a repeated basis until a distribution of net present value outcomes can be established and the priority of each variable in determining the overall net present value obtained. Furthermore, the Board will be in a position to review the potential 'value at risk' in a given project.

I recommend that the Board reviews a simulation of project net present values in future and that this forms part of its continuing review process.

38   MMC (JUN 11 ADAPTED)

Key answer tips

Before calculating the value of the real option, it is important to do a basic NPV calculation for the project, in order to identify the value of Pa for the Black-Scholes formula.

(a)   The $12 million initial cost will be incurred whether the option to delay is exercised or not. Therefore, since it is common to both scenarios, it can be ignored in the calculations for the moment.

Net Present Value if the project was undertaken immediately (i.e. without the option to delay the decision)

Time	0	1	2	3	4
Cash flows ($)	(35m)	25m	18m	10m	5m
PV (11%) ($)	(35m)	22.52m	14.61m	7.31m	3.29m

Net Present Value = $47.73 million – $35 million = $12.73 million

(or $0.73 million after taking account of the initial $12 million investment).

If the project were to be delayed for 2 years, the cash inflows would now run from year 3 to year 6 inclusive (rather than year 1 to year 4 as above). Therefore, the present value of the cash flows would become:

Time	3	4	5	6
Cash flows ($)	25m	18m	10m	5m
PV (11%) ($)	18.28m	11.86m	5.93m	2.68m

Present value of cash inflows = $38.75 million. This becomes P_a in the Black Scholes Option Pricing model formula.

Tutorial note

The present value of cash inflows could alternatively have been found by simply applying a 2 year discount factor (0.812 at 11%) to the existing figures.

i.e. the present value of cash inflows was $47.73 million in the original calculation, so this becomes $47.73 million × 0.812 = $38.75 million after the 2 year delay.

Value of option to delay the decision until the film is released and its popularity established. Black-Scholes Option Pricing model is used to value the call option.

Variables:

Current price (P_a) = $38.75m (see calculations above)

Exercise price (P_e) = $35m

Exercise date = 2 years

Risk free rate = 5%

Volatility = 50%

$d_1 = [\ln(38.75/35) + (0.05 + 0.5 \times 0.50^2) \times 2]/(0.50 \times 2^{1/2}) = 0.6389$ (i.e. 0.64)

$d_2 = 0.6389 - (0.50 \times 2^{1/2}) = -0.0682$ (i.e. -0.07)

Using the Normal Distribution Table provided

$N(d_1) = 0.5 + 0.2389 = 0.7389$

$N(d_2) = 0.5 - 0.0279 = 0.4721$

Value of option to delay the decision = $38.75 \times 0.7389 - 35 \times 0.4721 \times e^{-0.05 \times 2}$

= 28.63 - 14.95 = $13.68 million (positive value)

(b)   The option to delay the decision has given MMC's managers the opportunity to monitor and respond to changing circumstances before committing to the project, such as a rise in popularity of this type of genre of films in the next two years or increased competition from similar new releases or a sustained marketing campaign launched by the film's producers before its launch.

Without taking account of the option to delay, the project has an NPV of $12.73 million, which reduces to $0.73 million when the initial $12 million investment is brought in to consideration. Although this is a positive NPV, it is quite a small positive figure, so the project is very sensitive to changes in the cash flows.

By taking account of the option to delay the project, the value of the project increases to $13.68 million (or $1.68 million after bringing in the unavoidable $12 million initial investment).

This shows that the existence of the option to delay makes the project more attractive.

Unfortunately, the option pricing formula requires numerous assumptions to be made about the variables, the primary one being the assumption of volatility. It therefore does not provide a definitive correct value but an indication of the value of the option to delay the decision.

Hence it indicates that the management should consider the project further and not dismiss it, even though current conventional net present value is quite small.

The option to delay the decision may not be the only option within the project. For example, the gaming platform that the company needs to develop for this game may have general programmes which may be used in future projects and MMC should take account of these (options to redeploy). Or if the film is successful, it may lead to follow-on projects involving games based on film sequels.

(**Note:** Credit will be given for alternative relevant comments)

(c)   A yield curve may be upward-sloping because of:

   (i)   **Future expectations**. If future short-term interest rates are expected to increase then the yield curve will be upward sloping.

          The greater the expected future rise in interest rates, the steeper the upward-slope of the yield curve will be.

   (ii)   **Liquidity preference**. It is argued that investors seek extra return for giving up a degree of liquidity with longer-term investments.

          Other things being equal, the longer the maturity of the investment, the higher the required return, leading to an upward-sloping yield curve.

   (iii) **Preferred habitat/market segmentation**. Different investors are more active in different segments of the yield curve.

For example banks would tend to focus on the short-term end of the curve, whilst pension funds are likely to be more concerned with medium- and long-term segments.

An upward-sloping curve could in part be the result of a fall in demand in the longer-term segment of the yield curve leading to lower bond prices and higher yields.

39   TISA CO (JUN 12 ADAPTED)

 *Question debrief*

Key answer tips

Don't waste time here calculating NPV, IRR and MIRR for project Zeta. You are given the figures for Zeta to compare with your figures for Omega in part (b).

(a)   Use Elfu Co's information to estimate the component project's asset beta. Then based on Tisa Co's capital structure, estimate the component project's equity beta and weighted average cost of capital. Assume that the beta of debt is zero.

Elfu Co MVe = $1.20 × 400m shares = $480m

Elfu Co MVd = $96m

Elfu Co portfolio asset beta =

1.40 × $480m/($480m + $96m × (1 – 0.25)) = 1.217

Elfu Co asset beta of other activities =

1.25 × $360m/($360m + $76.8m × (1 – 0.25)) = 1.078

1.217 = component asset beta × 0.25 + 1.078 × 0.75

Component asset beta = [1.217 – (1.078 × 0.75)]/0.25 = 1.634

Component equity beta based on Tisa Co capital structure =

1.634 × [($18m + $3.6m × 0.75)/$18m] = 1.879

Using CAPM, component Ke = 3.5% + 1.879 × 5.8% = 14.40%

Component WACC = (14.40% × $18m + 4.5% × $3.6m)/($18m + $3.6m) = 12.75%

(b)   **Process Omega**

Year	0	1	2	3	4
Net cash flows ($000)	(3,800)	1,220	1,153	1,386	3,829
PV 12.75% ($000)	(3,800)	1,082	907	967	2,369
NPV ($000)	1,525				
PV 30%	(3,800)	938	682	631	1,341
NPV ($000)	(208)				

Internal rate of return is approximately 27.3%

Modified internal rate of return (MIRR) is approximately 22.7%

$([(5,325/3,800)^{1/4} \times (1.1275)] - 1)$

Alternatively:

MIRR can be calculated as follows:

Year	Cash flows ($000)	Multiplier	Re-invested amount ($000)
1	1,220	1.1275^3	1,749
2	1,153	1.1275^2	1,466
3	1,386	1.1275	1,563
4	3,829	1	3,829

Total re-invested amount ($000) = 8,607

MIRR = $(8,607/3,800)^{1/4} - 1 = 22.7\%$

Process Zeta has a higher NPV at Tisa's cost of capital, showing that it generates more wealth for the shareholders than process Omega. This is the over-riding objective of most companies.

The internal rate of return (IRR) assumes that positive cash flows in earlier years are reinvested at the IRR and therefore process Omega, which has higher initial cash flows when compared to process Zeta, gives a slightly higher IRR.

The modified internal rate of return (MIRR) assumes that positive cash flows are reinvested at the cost of capital. This is a more reasonable assumption and produces a result consistent with the net present value.

Overall, process Zeta should be adopted (although the difference is not significant).

[**Note:** Using 13% instead of 12.75% as the cost of capital is acceptable]

(c) 99% confidence level requires the value at risk (VAR) to be within 2.33 standard deviations from the mean, based on a single tail measure.

Annual VAR = 2.33 × $800,000 = $1,864,000

Five year VAR = $1,864,000 × $5^{1/2}$ approx. = $4,168,000

The figures mean that Elfu Co can be 99% confident that the cash flows will not fall by more than $1,864,000 in any one year and $4,168,000 in total over five years from the average returns. Therefore the company can be 99% certain that the returns will be $336,000 or more every year [$2,200,000 − $1,864,000]. And it can be 99% certain that the returns will be $6,832,000 or more in total over the five-year period [$11,000,000 − $4,168,000]. There is a 1% chance that the returns will be less than $336,000 each year or $6,832,000 over the five-year period.

Marking scheme			
			Marks
(a)	Reasoning behind cost of capital calculation		2
	Calculation of component asset beta		3
	Calculation of component equity beta, and Ke and WACC		3
		Maximum	**8**
(b)	Calculation of NPV for Process Omega		2
	Calculation of IRR for Process Omega		2
	Calculation of MIRR for Process Omega		2
	Recommendation and explanation of the recommendation		6
		Maximum	**12**
(c)	Annual and five-year VAR		2
	Explanation		3
		Maximum	**5**
Total			**25**

40 COEDEN CO (DEC 12 ADAPTED)

Key answer tips

Weighted average cost of capital is a key syllabus area. Invariably, the calculation of cost of capital will involve degearing and/or regearing given beta factors and using the CAPM equation. It is vital that you have practised the calculations so that you are able to manipulate the beta factors quickly.

(a) Before implementing the proposal

Cost of equity = 4% + 1.1 × 6% = 10.6%

Cost of debt = 4% + 0.9% = 4.9%

Market value of debt (MV_d):

Per \$100: \$5.2 × 1.049^{-1} + \$5.2 × 1.049^{-2} + \$105.2 × 1.049^{-3} = \$100.82

Total value = \$42,000,000 × \$100.82/\$100 = \$42,344,400

Market value of equity (MV_e):

As share price is not given, use the free cash flow growth model to estimate this. The question states that the free cash flow to equity model provides a reasonable estimate of the current market value of the company.

Assumption 1: *Estimate growth rate using the rb model. The assumption here is that free cash flows to equity which are retained will be invested to yield at least at the rate of return required by the* company's *shareholders. This is the estimate of how much the free cash* flows *to equity will grow by each year.*

r = 10.6% and b = 0.4, therefore g is estimated at 10.6% × 0.4 = 4.24%

MV_e = 2,600 × 1.0424/(0.106 – 0.0424) approximately = \$42,614,000

The proportion of MV_e to MV_d is approximately 50:50

Therefore, cost of capital:

$10.6\% \times 0.5 + 4.9\% \times 0.5 \times 0.8 = 7.3\%$

After implementing the proposal

Coeden Co, asset beta estimate

$1.1 \times 0.5/(0.5 + 0.5 \times 0.8) = 0.61$

Asset beta, hotel services only

Assumption 2: *The question does not provide an asset beta for hotel services only, which is the approximate measure of Coeden Co's business risk once the properties are sold. Assume that Coeden Co's asset beta is a weighted average of the property companies' average beta and hotel services beta.*

Asset beta of hotel services only:

0.61 = Asset beta (hotel services) $\times 60\% + 0.4 \times 40\%$ Asset beta (hotel services only) approximately $= 0.75$

Coeden Co, hotel services only, estimate of equity beta:

$MV_e = \$42,614,000$ (Based on the assumption stated in the question)

MV_d = Per $100: $5.2 \times 1.046^{-1} + \$5.2 \times 1.046^{-2} + \$105.2 \times 1.046^{-3} = \$101.65$

Total value = $12,600,000 \times \$101.65/\$100 = \$12,807,900$ say $12,808,000

0.75 = equity beta $\times 42,614/(42,614 + 12,808 \times 0.8)$

0.75 = equity beta $\times 0.806$

Equity beta $= 0.93$

Coeden Co, hotel services only, weighted average cost of capital

Cost of equity $= 4\% + 0.93 \times 6\% = 9.6\%$

Cost of capital $= 9.6\% \times 0.769 + 4.6\% \times 0.231 \times 0.8 = 8.2\%$

Comment:

	Before proposal implementation	*After proposal implementation*
Cost of equity	10.6%	9.6%
WACC	7.3%	8.2%

Implementing the proposal would increase the asset beta of Coeden Co because the hotel services industry on its own has a higher business risk than a business which owns its own hotels as well. However, the equity beta and cost of equity both decrease because of the fall in the level of debt and the consequent reduction in the company's financial risk. The company's cost of capital increases because the lower debt level reduces the extent to which the weighted average cost of capital can be reduced due to the lower cost of debt. Hence the board of directors is not correct in assuming that the lower level of debt will reduce the company's cost of capital.

(b) It is unlikely that the market value of equity would remain unchanged because of the change in the growth rate of free cash flows and sales revenue, and the change in the risk situation due to the changes in the business and financial risks of the new business.

In estimating the asset beta of Coeden Co as offering hotel services only, no account is taken of the changes in business risk due to renting rather than owning the hotels. A revised asset beta may need to be estimated due to changes in the business risk.

The market value of equity is used to estimate the equity beta and the cost of equity of the business after the implementation of the proposal. But the market value of equity is dependent on the cost of equity, which is, in turn, dependent on the equity beta. Therefore, neither the cost of equity nor the market value of equity is independent of each other and they both will change as a result of the change in business strategy.

41 ARBORE CO (DEC 12 ADAPTED)

Key answer tips

This question shows how important it is to revise the whole syllabus in preparation for the exam. Capital rationing is a small topic in the syllabus but it was tested in detail here. You will never be expected to solve the capital rationing linear programming model, but it is important that you can interpret the results.

(a) Shareholder wealth is maximised if a company undertakes all possible positive NPV projects.

Capital rationing is where there are insufficient funds to do so.

This shortage of funds may be for a single period only, or for more than one period.

A single period capital rationing problem is solved by ranking competing projects according to profitability index i.e. the NPV of the project divided by the capital investment needed in the restricted period.

The limited amount of capital available is then allocated to the project(s) with the highest profitability index, in order to generate the highest possible NPV per unit of investment.

A solution to a multi period capital rationing problem cannot be found using profitability indices. This method can only deal with one limiting factor (i.e. one period of shortage). Where there are a number of limiting factors (i.e. a number of periods of shortage) a linear programming model has to be formulated.

The solution to the linear programming model will give the combination of projects to maximise the NPV generated.

(b) **(i)** **PDur05**

Annual sales revenue = $14 × 300,000 units = $4,200,000

Annual costs = $3,230,000

Annual cash flows = $970,000

Net present value of PDur05 =

($2,500,000) + ($1,200,000 × 1.11^{-1}) + ($1,400,000 × 1.11^{-2}) + $970,000 × 7.191 × 1.11^{-3}

= ($2,500,000) + ($1,081,000) + ($1,136,000) + $5,100,000

= $383,000

In order for the net present value to fall to nil, the PV of the project's annual cash flows needs to equal to: $2,500,000 + $1,081,000 + $1,136,000 = $4,717,000

Annual cash flows need to reduce to: $4,717,000/(7.191 × 1.11^{-3}) = $897,110

Sales revenue would reduce to: $897,110 + $3,230,000 = $4,127,110

Selling price would fall to: $4,127,110/300,000 units = $13.76

Percentage fall = ($14.00 − $13.76)/$14 × 100% = 1.7%

[**Note:** The estimate of the annual cash flows will differ if tables are used rather than a calculator. This is acceptable and will be allowed for when marking]

Comment: The net present value of the project is very sensitive to changes in the selling price of the product. A small fall in the selling price would reduce the net present value to nil or negative and make the project not worthwhile.

(ii) A multi-period capital rationing model would use linear programming and is formulated as follows:

If:

Y1 = investment in project PDur01; Y2 = investment in project PDur02; Y3 = investment in project PDur03; Y4 investment in project PDur04; and Y5 = investment in project PDur05

Then the objective is to maximise

464Y1 + 244Y2 + 352Y3 + 320Y4 + 383Y5

Given the following constraints

Year 1: 4,000Y1 + 800Y2 + 3,200Y3 + 3,900Y4 + 2,500Y5 ≤ 9,000

Year 2: 1,100Y1 + 2,800Y2 + 3,562Y3 + 0Y4 + 1,200Y5 ≤ 6,000

Year 3: 2,400Y1 + 3,200Y2 + 0Y3 + 200Y4 + 1,400Y5 ≤ 5,000

And where Y1, Y2, Y3, Y4, Y5 ≥ 0

(c) **Category 1:** Total Final Value. This is the maximum net present value that can be earned within the three-year constraints of capital expenditure, by undertaking whole, part or none of the five projects. This amount is less than the total net present value of all five projects if there were no constraints.

Category 2: Adjustable Final Values. These are the proportions of projects undertaken within the constraints to maximise the net present value. In this case, all of project PDur05, 95.8% of project PDur01, 73.2% of project PDur03 and 40.7% of project PDur02 will be undertaken.

Category 3: Constraints utilised, slack. This indicates to what extent the constraint limits are used and whether any investment funds will remain unused. The figures indicate that, in order to achieve maximum net present value, all the funds in all three years are used up and no funds remain unused.

(d) **(i)** Normally, positive net present value projects should be accepted as they add to the value of the company by generating returns in excess of the required rate of return (the discount rate). However, in this case, Arbore Co seems to be employing soft capital rationing by setting internal limits on capital available for each department, possibly due to capital budget limits placed by the company on the amounts it wants to borrow or can borrow. In the latter case, the company faces limited access to capital from external sources, for example, because of restrictions in bank lending, costs related to the issue of new capital and lending to the company being perceived as too risky. This is known as hard capital rationing and can lead to soft capital rationing.

(ii) A capital investment monitoring system (CIMS) monitors how an investment project is progressing once it has been implemented. Initially the CIMS will set a plan and budget of how the project is to proceed. It sets milestones for what needs to be achieved and by when. It also considers the possible risks, both internal and external, which may affect the project. CIMS then ensures that the project is progressing according to the plan and budget. It also sets up contingency plans for dealing with the identified risks.

The benefits, to Arbore Co, of CIMS are that it tries to ensure, as much as possible, that the project meets what is expected of it in terms of revenues and expenses. Also that the project is completed on time and risk factors that are identified remain valid. A critical path of linked activities which make up the project will be identified. The departments undertaking the projects will be proactive, rather than reactive, towards the management of risk, and therefore possibly be able to reduce costs by having a better plan. CIMS can also be used as a communication device between managers charged with managing the project and the monitoring team. Finally CIMS would be able to re-assess and change the assumptions made of the project, if changes in the external environment warrant it.

42   BURUNG CO (SPECIMEN PAPER 2018)

Key answer tips

This question presented the investment appraisal as part of the question, and asked for the necessary corrections to be made.

This sort of question is an excellent test of whether you really understand the topic. A student with only a vague understanding of APV would have really struggled to pick out the subtle mistakes.

(a)   All figures are in $ million

Year	0	1	2	3	4
Sales revenue (inflated, 8% p.a.)		24.87	42.69	61.81	36.92
Costs (inflated, 4% p.a.)		(14.37)	(23.75)	(33.12)	(19.05)
Incremental profit		10.50	18.94	28.69	17.87
Tax (W1)		(0.50)	(3.39)	(5.44)	(3.47)
Working capital (W2)	(4.97)	(3.57)	(3.82)	4.98	7.38
Investment/sale of machinery	(38.00)				4.00
Cash flows	(42.97)	6.43	11.73	28.23	25.78
Discount factors (12%, W3)	1	0.893	0.797	0.712	0.636
Present values	(42.97)	5.74	9.35	20.10	16.40

Base case net present value is approximately $8.62 million.

(W1) All figures are in $ million

Year	0	1	2	3	4
Incremental profit		10.50	18.94	28.69	17.87
Tax allowable depreciation		8.00	2.00	1.50	0.50
Taxable profit		2.50	16.94	27.19	17.37
Tax (20%)		0.50	3.39	5.44	3.47

(W2) All figures are in $ million

Year	0	1	2	3	4
Working capital (20% of sales revenue)		4.97	8.54	12.36	7.38
Working capital required/(released)	4.97	3.57	3.82	(4.98)	(7.38)

(W3) Lintu Co asset beta = 1.5 × $128m/($128m + $31.96m × 0.8) approx. = 1.25

All-equity financed discount rate = 2% + 1.25 × 8% = 12%

Financing side effects

	$000
Issue costs 2/98 × $42,970,000	(876.94)

Tax shield

Annual tax relief = ($42,970,000 × 60% × 0.015 × 20%)

+ ($42,970,000 × 40% × 0.04 × 20%)

= 77.35 + 137.50 = 214.85

	$000
The present value of the tax relief annuity = 214.85 × 3.63	779.91

Annual subsidy benefit

$42,970,000 × 60% × 0.025 × 80% = 515.64

	$000
The present value of the subsidy benefit annuity = 515.64 × 3.63	1,871.77
Total benefit of financing side effects	1,774.74

Financing the project entirely by debt would add just under $1.78 million to the value of the project, or approximately, an additional 20% to the all-equity financed project.

The adjusted present value (APV) of the project is just under $10.4 million and therefore it should be accepted.

Examiner's note

In calculating the present values of the tax shield and subsidy benefits, the annuity factor used is based on 4% to reflect the normal borrowing/default risk of the company.

Alternatively, 2% or 2.5% could be used depending on the assumptions made. Credit will be given where these are used to estimate the annuity factor, where the assumption is explained.

(b) **Corrections made to the original net present value**

The approach taken to exclude depreciation from the net present value computation is correct, but tax allowable depreciation needs to be taken away from profit estimates before tax is calculated, reducing the profits on which tax is payable.

Interest is not normally included in the net present value calculations. Instead, it is normally imputed within the cost of capital or discount rate. In this case, it is included in the financing side effects.

Cash flows are inflated and the nominal rate based on Lintu Co's all-equity financed rate is used (see below). Where different cash flows are subject to different rates of inflation, applying a real rate to non-inflated amounts would not give an accurate answer.

The impact of the working capital requirement is included in the estimate as, although all the working capital is recovered at the end of the project, the flows of working capital are subject to different discount rates when their present values are calculated.

Approach taken

The value of the project is initially assessed considering only the business risk involved in undertaking the project. The discount rate used is based on Lintu Co's asset beta which measures only the business risk of that company. Since Lintu Co is in the same line of business as the project, it is deemed appropriate to use its discount rate, instead of 11% which Burung Co uses normally.

The impact of debt financing and the subsidy benefit are then considered. In this way, Burung Co can assess the value created from its investment activity and then the additional value created from the manner in which the project is financed.

Assumptions made

It is assumed that all figures used are accurate and any estimates made are reasonable. Burung Co may want to consider undertaking a sensitivity analysis to assess this.

It is assumed that the initial working capital required will form part of the funds borrowed but that the subsequent working capital requirements will be available from the funds generated by the project. The validity of this assumption needs to be assessed since the working capital requirements at the start of years 2 and 3 are substantial.

It is assumed that Lintu Co's asset beta and all-equity financed discount rate represent the business risk of the project. The validity of this assumption also needs to be assessed. For example, Lintu Co's entire business may not be similar to the project, and it may undertake other lines of business. In this case, the asset beta would need to be adjusted so that just the project's business risk is considered.

(Note: Credit will be given for alternative, relevant explanations)

	Marking scheme	Marks
(a)	Inflated incremental profit	2
	Taxation	2
	Working capital	2
	Estimate of discount rate	2
	Net present value	1
	Issue costs	1
	Tax shield benefit	2
	Subsidy benefit	1
	Adjusted present value and conclusion	2
		15
(b)	Corrections made	4
	Approach taken	2
	Assumptions made	3
	Other relevant discussion or additional detail	1
		10
Total		**25**

43 RIVIERE CO (DEC 14)

Key answer tips

Value at Risk is often perceived to be a tricky topic. Remember to multiply by the square root of 5 to extend your calculation from one year to five years.

Don't worry if you find the mathematics involved in Value at Risk complex. There are plenty of easier, discursive marks in this question if you have a good exam technique.

(a) A free trade area like the European Union (EU) aims to remove barriers to trade and allow freedom of movement of production resources such as capital and labour. The EU also has an overarching common legal structure across all member countries and tries to limit any discriminatory practice against companies operating in these countries. Furthermore, the EU erects common external barriers to trade against countries which are not member states.

Riviere Co may benefit from operating within the EU in a number of ways as it currently trades within it. It should find that it is able to compete on equal terms with rival companies within the EU. Companies outside the EU may find it difficult to enter the EU markets due to barriers to trade. A common legal structure should ensure that the standards of food quality and packaging apply equally across all the member countries. Due diligence of logistic networks used to transport the food may be easier to undertake because of common compliance requirements. Having access to capital and labour within the EU may make it easier for the company to set up branches inside the EU, if it wants to. The company may also be able to access any grants which are available to companies based within the EU.

(b) **Project Drugi**

Internal rate of return (IRR)

10% NPV: €2,293,000 approximately

Year	Current	1	2	3	4	5
Cash flows (€000s)	(11,840)	1,230	1,680	4,350	10,240	2,200
Try 20%		0.833	0.694	0.579	0.482	0.402
	(11,840)	1,025	1,166	2,519	4,936	884

NPV = €(1,310,000)

IRR = 10% + 2,293/(2,293 + 1,310) × 10% approximately = 16.4%

Modified internal rate of return (MIRR)

Total PVs years 1 to 5 at 10% discount rate = €11,840,000 + €2,293,000 = €14,133,000

MIRR (using formula) = $[(14,133/11,840)^{1/5} \times 1.10] - 1 = 14\%$

Alternatively:

Year	Cash flows (€000s)	Multiplier	Re-invested amount (€000s)
1	1,230	1.1^4	1,801
2	1,680	1.1^3	2,236
3	4,350	1.1^2	5,264
4	10,240	1.1	11,264
5	2,200	1	2,200

Total re-invested amount approx. = €22,765,000

MIRR = $(€22,765,000/€11,840,000)^{1/5} - 1 = 14\%$

Value at risk (VAR)

Based on a single tail test:

A 95% confidence level requires the annual present value VAR to be within approximately 1.645 standard deviations from the mean.

A 90% confidence level requires annual present value VAR to be within approximately 1.282 standard deviations from the mean.

(**Note:** An approximation of standard deviations to two decimal places is acceptable.)

95%, five-year present value VAR = $400,000 × 1.645 × $5^{0.5}$ = approx. €1,471,000

90%, five-year present value VAR = $400,000 × 1.282 × $5^{0.5}$ = approx. €1,147,000

	Privi	*Drugi*
Net present value (10%)	€2,054,000	€2,293,000
Internal rate of return	17.6%	16.4%
Modified internal rate of return	13.4%	14.0%
VAR (over the project's life)		
95% confidence level	€1,103,500	€1,471,000
90% confidence level	€860,000	€1,147,000

The net present value and the modified internal rate of return both indicate that project Drugi would create more value for Riviere Co. However, the internal rate of return (IRR) for project Privi is higher. Where projects are mutually exclusive, the IRR can give an incorrect answer. This is because the IRR assumes that returns are re-invested at the internal rate of return, whereas net present value and the modified IRR assume that they are re-invested at the cost of capital (discount rate) which in this case is 10%. The cost of capital is a more realistic assumption as this is the minimum return required by investors in a company. Furthermore, the manner in which the cash flows occur will have a bearing on the IRR calculated. For example, with project Drugi, a high proportion of the cash flows occur in year four and these will be discounted by using the higher IRR compared to the cost of capital, thus reducing the value of the project faster. The IRR can give the incorrect answer in these circumstances. Therefore, based purely on cash flows, project Drugi should be accepted due to the higher net present value and modified IRR, as they give the theoretically correct answer of the value created.

The VAR provides an indication of the potential riskiness of a project. For example, if Riviere Co invests in project Drugi then it can be 95% confident that the present value will not fall by more than €1,471,000 over its life. Hence the project will still produce a positive net present value. However, there is a 5% chance that the loss could be greater than €1,471,000. With project Privi, the potential loss in value is smaller and therefore it is less risky. It should be noted that the VAR calculations indicate that the investments involve different risk. However, the cash flows are discounted at the same rate, which they should not be, since the risk differs between them.

Notwithstanding that, when risk is also taken into account, the choice between the projects is not clear cut and depends on Riviere Co's attitude to risk and return. Project Drugi gives the higher potential net present value but is riskier, whereas project Privi is less risky but gives a smaller net present value. This is before taking into account additional uncertainties such as trading in an area in which Riviere Co is not familiar. It is therefore recommended that Riviere Co should only proceed with project Drugi if it is willing to accept the higher risk and uncertainty.

(c) **Possible legal risks**

There are a number of possible legal risks which Riviere Co may face, for example:

- The countries where the product is sold may have different legal regulations on food preparation, quality and packaging.

- The company needs to ensure that the production processes and the transportation of the frozen foods comply with these regulations. It also needs to ensure that the promotional material on the packaging complies with regulations in relation to what is acceptable in each country.

- The legal regulations may be more lax in countries outside the EU but Riviere Co needs to be aware that complying only with the minimum standards may impact its image negatively overall, even if they are acceptable in the countries concerned.

- There may be import quotas in the countries concerned or the governments may give favourable terms and conditions to local companies, which may make it difficult for Riviere Co to compete.

- The legal system in some countries may not recognise the trademarks or production patents which the company holds on its packaging and production processes. This may enable competitors to copy the food and the packaging.

- Different countries may have different regulations regarding product liability from poorly prepared and/or stored food which cause harm to consumers. For example, Riviere Co may use other companies to transport its food and different supermarkets may sell its food. It needs to be aware of the potential legal claims on it and its supplier should the food prove harmful to the customers.

Possible mitigation strategies

- Riviere Co needs to undertake sufficient research of the countries' current laws and regulations to ensure that it complies with the standards required. It may even want to ensure that it exceeds the required standards to ensure that it maintains its reputation.

- Riviere Co needs to ensure that it also keeps abreast of potential changes in the law. It may also want to ensure that it complies with best practice, even if it is not the law yet. Often current best practices become enshrined in future legislation.

- Riviere Co needs to investigate the extent to which it may face difficulty in overcoming quota restrictions, less favourable trading conditions and lack of trademark and patent protection. If necessary, these should be factored into the financial analysis. It could be that Riviere Co has already taken these into account.

- Strict contracts need to be set up between Riviere Co and any agents it uses to transport and sell the food. These could be followed up by regular checks to ensure that the standards required are maintained.

- All the above will add extra costs and if these have not been included in the financial analysis, they need to be. These extra costs may mean that the project is no longer viable.

(**Note:** Credit will be given for alternative, relevant discussion for parts (a) and (c).)

Marking scheme			Marks
(a)	Discussion of the EU as a free trade area		2–3
	Discussion of the possible benefits to Riviere Co		2–3
			―――
		Maximum	5
			―――
(b)	Calculation of internal rate of return		2
	Calculation of modified internal rate of return		2
	Determining the two standard deviations (1.645 and 1.282)		1
	Calculations of the two value at risk figures		2
	Explanation of weakness of internal rate of return and why net present value and modified		
	internal rate of return are better		2–3
	Explanation of value at risk figures and what they indicate		2–3
	Recommendation		1–2
			―――
		Maximum	13
			―――
(c)	Discussion of possible legal risks		3–4
	Discussion of how these may be mitigated		3–4
			―――
		Maximum	7
			―――
	Total		25
			―――

44   FURLION CO (MAR/JUN 16)

Key answer tips

The Black-Scholes option pricing model is regularly tested, especially in the context of real options.

Most of the input factors for the model are easy to pick up from the question text, but take care with the Pa ('value of the underlying asset'). In real options theory, the Pa is the present value of all the expected cash flows from the project, excluding the initial investment.

(a)   Value of option to expand

Variables

Volatility = 30%

Current price (value of project including option exercise price)

= $15m × 0.712 = $10.68m

Exercise price (capital expenditure) = $15m

Exercise date = 3 years

Risk free rate = 4%

$d_1 = [\ln(10.68/15) + (0.04 + 0.5 \times 0.3^2) \times 3]/(0.3 \times \sqrt{3}) = -0.1630$

$d_2 = -0.1630 - 0.3 \times \sqrt{3} = -0.6826$

$N(d_1) = 0.5 — 0.0636 = 0.4364$ (using 0.16 for d_1)

$N(d_2) = 0.5 — 0.2517 = 0.2483$ (using 0.68 for d_2)

Value of call option = $P_a \times N(d_1) - P_e \times N(d_2) \times e^{-rt}$

$= (10.68 \times 0.4364) - (15 \times 0.2483 \times e^{-0.04 \times 3})$

$= 4.66 - 3.30$

$= \$1.36$ million

Overall value = $\$1.36m - \$1.01m = \$0.35m$

The investment has a positive net present value, so should be accepted on those grounds. Furlion Co should also consider the value of an abandonment option if results turn out to be worse than expected or a delay option if it wants to see how the reclamation programme is going to continue.

Assumptions made and other factors

Using real options for decision-making has limitations. Real options are built around uncertainties surrounding future cash flows, but real option theory is only useful if management can respond effectively to these uncertainties as they evolve. The Black-Scholes model for valuing real options has a number of assumptions which may not be true in practice. It assumes that there is a market for the underlying asset and the volatility of returns on the underlying asset follows a normal distribution. The model also assumes perfect markets, a constant risk-free interest rate and constant volatility.

Furlion Co will also consider expectations about the future of the land reclamation programme. Has the programme been as quick and as effective as the Naswan government originally expected? Furlion Co will also want to consider how the programme will be affected by the amount of funding the government obtains and any conditions attached to that funding.

Furlion Co may also wish to consider whether its investment of this type will be looked on favourably by the Naswan government and whether tax or other concessions will be available. These may come with conditions, given the government's commitment to a sustainable economy, such as the way production facilities operate or the treatment of employees.

Given that this is a market which may expand in the future, Furlion Co should also consider the reaction of competitors. This may be a market where establishing a significant presence quickly may provide a significant barrier if competitors try to enter the market later.

As the investment is for the manufacture of specialist equipment, it is possible that there is insufficient skilled labour in the local labour pool in Naswa. As well as training local labour, supervision is likely to be required, at least initially, from staff based in other countries. This may involve cultural issues such as different working practices.

(b) The sensitivity of the valuation of options to interest rate changes can be measured by the option's rho. The option's rho is the amount of change in the option's value for a 1% change in the risk-free interest rate. The rho is positive for calls and so will be positive if the risk-free interest rate does increase.

However, interest rates tend to move quite slowly and the interest rate is often not a significant influence on the option's value, particularly for short-term options. However, many real options are longer term and will have higher rhos than short-term options. A change in interest rates will be more significant the longer the time until expiry of an option.

In addition, there are possible indirect economic effects of interest rate changes, such as on the return demanded by finance providers and hence on the cost of capital.

(c) The World Bank provides loans, often direct to governments, on a commercial basis, for capital projects. Loans are generally for a long-term period, which may suit the Naswan government. However, the terms of the loan may be onerous, not just the finance costs but the other conditions imposed on the scope of the projects.

Given the circumstances of the investment, Naswa may be able to obtain assistance from the International Development Association, which is part of the World Bank. This provides loans on more generous terms to the poorest countries. However, it is designed for countries with very high credit risk which would struggle to obtain funding by other means, and Naswa may not be eligible.

Marking scheme			
			Marks
(a)	Current price variable (Pa) in BSOP formula		1
	Other variables in BSOP formula		1
	Calculation of d1 and d2		3
	Determination of N(d1) and N(d2)		2
	Value of the option to expand decision		1
	Revised value of projects and comments	Max	3
	Assumptions	Max	3
	Other factors	Max	3
			───
		Maximum	**16**
			───
(b)	Explanation of rho		2
	Impact of interest rate movements		3
			───
		Maximum	**5**
			───
(c)	Role of World Bank		1
	Usefulness of World Bank as a source of finance		1–2
	Role of IDA		1
	Usefulness of IDA as a source of finance		1–2
			───
		Maximum	**4**
			───
Total			**25**
			───

45   FERNHURST CO (SEP/DEC 16)

Key answer tips

This is a very standard investment appraisal question.

Note that part (a) requires you to calculate duration as well as NPV, but once you have forecast the free cash flows from the project this should be a simple extra step.

Part (b) was a standard sensitivity calculation. The easiest way to calculate the percentage sensitivity is by using the formula:

(NPV / PV of cash flows affected by the selling price estimate) × 100%

(a)

	0	1	2	3	4
	$000	$000	$000	$000	$000
Sales revenue (W1)		13,250	16,695	22,789	23,928
Variable costs (W2)		(5,788)	(7,292)	(9,954)	(10,452)
		———	———	———	———
Contribution		7,462	9,403	12,835	13,476
Marketing expenditure		(1,500)			
Fixed costs		(900)	(945)	(992)	(1,042)
Tax-allowable depreciation (W3)		(3,200)	(2,560)	(2,048)	(8,192)
		———	———	———	———
Taxable profits/(losses)		1,862	5,898	9,795	4,242
Taxation (25%)		(466)	(1,475)	(2,449)	(1,061)
Add back tax-allowable depreciation		3,200	2,560	2,048	8,192
		———	———	———	———
Cash flows after tax		4,596	6,983	9,394	11,373
Initial investment	(16,000)				
Working capital	(1,025)	(41)	(53)	(56)	1,175
	———	———	———	———	———
Cash flows	(17,025)	4,555	6,930	9,338	12,548
Discount factor	1.000	0.901	0.812	0.731	0.659
	———	———	———	———	———
Present values	(17,025)	4,104	5,627	6,826	8,269
	———	———	———	———	———
Net present value	7,801				

The NPV is positive, which indicates the project should be undertaken.

Workings:

(W1) Sales revenue

Year

		$000
1	132,500 × 100	13,250
2	132,500 × 100 × 1.05 × 1.2	16,695
3	132,500 × 100 × 1.05^2 × 1.2 × 1.3	22,789
4	132,500 × 100 × 1.05^3 × 1.2 × 1.3	23,928

(W2) Variable costs

Year

		$m
1	132,500 × 43.68	5,788
2	132,500 × 43.68 × 1.05 × 1.2	7,292
3	132,500 × 43.68 × 1.05^2 × 1.2 × 1.3	9,954
4	132,500 × 43.68 × 1.05^3 × 1.2 × 1.3	10,452

(W3) Tax allowable depreciation

Year

		$000
		16,000
1	Tax-allowable depreciation	(3,200)
		———
		12,800
2	Tax-allowable depreciation	(2,560)
		———
		10,240
3	Tax-allowable depreciation	(2,048)
		———
		8,192
4	Balancing allowance	(8,192)
		———
		0
		———

Duration

Year	1	2	3	4
Present value $000	4,104	5,627	6,826	8,269
Percentage of total PV	16.5%	22.7%	27.5%	33.3%

Duration = (1 × 0.165) + (2 × 0.227) + (3 × 0.275) + (4 × 0.333) = 2.78 years

The result indicates that it will take approximately 2.78 years to recover half the present value of the project. Duration considers the time value of money and all of the cash flows of a project.

(b)   **Reduction in selling price**

Discounted revenue cash flows = (13,250 × 0.75 × 0.901) + (16,695 × 0.75 × 0.812) + (22,789 × 0.75 × 0.731) + (23,928 × 0.75 × 0.659) = $43,441,000

Reduction in selling price = 7,801/43,441 = 18.0%

Fernhurst Co would appear to have some scope to reduce the price in order to guarantee the success of the product launch. It would be useful to know whether the finance director's views on the success of the product would change if the product was launched at a lower price. There may be scope to launch at a price which is more than 18.0% lower than the planned launch price, and increase the sales price subsequently by more than the rate of inflation if the launch is a success.

If the directors are unwilling to reduce the price, then their decision will depend on whether they are willing to consider other ways of mitigating a failed launch or take a chance that the product will make a loss and be abandoned. They will take into account both the probability (15%) of the loss and the magnitude (at least $1,000,000 but possibly higher).

Presumably the finance director's assessment of the probability of a loss is based more on doubts about the demand level rather than the level of costs, as costs should be controllable. Possibly Fernhurst Co's directors may consider a smaller scale launch to test the market, but then Fernhurst Co would still be left with expensive facilities if the product were abandoned. The decision may therefore depend on what alternative uses could be made of the new facilities.

(c)   The non-executive director has highlighted the importance of long-term maximisation of shareholders' wealth. The net present value is the most important indicator of whether an investment is likely to do that. However, the assessment of investments using net present value has to be modified if the company is undertaking a number of different investments and capital is rationed. It is not necessarily the case that the investments with the highest net present value will be chosen, as account has to be taken of the amount of capital invested as well.

However, investors are not necessarily concerned solely with the long term. They are also concerned about short-term indicators, such as the annual dividend which the company can sustain. They may be concerned if the company's investment portfolio is weighted towards projects which will produce good long-term returns, but limited returns in the near future.

Risk will also influence shareholders' views. They may prefer investments where a higher proportion of returns are made in the shorter term, if they feel that longer term returns are much more uncertain. The NPV calculation itself discounts longer term cash flows more than shorter term cash flows.

The payback method shows how long an investment will take to generate enough returns to pay back its investment. It favours investments which pay back quickly, although it fails to take into account longer term cash flows after the payback period. Duration is a better measure of the distribution of cash flows, although it may be less easy for shareholders to understand.

Marking scheme		Marks
(a)	Sales revenue	2
	Variable costs	2
	Fixed costs	1
	Tax-allowable depreciation	2
	Tax payable	1
	Working capital	2
	NPV of project	1
	Comment on NPV	1
	Duration calculation	2
	Comment on duration	1
		15
(b)	Reduction in selling price	3
	Discussion	2–3
	Maximum	**5**
		5
(c)	Significance of net present value	1–2
	Shareholders' attitude to the longer and shorter term	2–3
	Timeframe measures	1–2
	Maximum	**5**
Total		**25**

46 MOONSTAR CO (SEP/DEC 15)

Key answer tips

In 2014 and 2015, two articles on Islamic Finance and one on securitisation and tranching were published on the ACCA website. Therefore it was no surprise to see these two topics tested here.

Reading the recent articles on the ACCA website is a critical part of preparing properly for the exam.

(a) An annual cash flow account compares the estimated cash flows receivable from the property against the liabilities within the securitisation process. The swap introduces leverage into the arrangement.

Cash flow receivable	$ million	Cash flow payable	$ million
$200 million × 11%	22.00	A-rated loan notes	
	———	Pay $108 million (W1) × 11% (W2)	11.88
Less: Service charge	(0.20)	B-rated loan notes	
		Pay $27 million (W1) × 12%	3.24
		C-rated loan notes	
		Pay $27 million (W1) × 13%	3.51
	———		———
	21.80		18.63
	———		———
		Balance to the subordinated certificates	3.17

Workings:

(W1) Loan notes

		$million
A	$200m × 0.9 × 0.6	108
B	$200m × 0.9 × 0.15	27
C	$200m × 0.9 × 0.15	27

(W2) Swap

Pay fixed rate under swap	9.5%
Pay floating rate	LIBOR + 1.5%
Receive floating rate under swap	(LIBOR)
Net payment	11%

The holders of the certificates are expected to receive $3.17million on $18 million, giving them a return of 17.6%. If the cash flows are 5% lower than the non-executive director has predicted, annual revenue received will fall to $20.90 million, reducing the balance available for the subordinated certificates to $2.07 million, giving a return of 11.5% on the subordinated certificates, which is below the returns offered on the B and C-rated loan notes. The point at which the holders of the certificates will receive nothing and below which the holders of the C-rated loan notes will not receive their full income will be an annual income of $18.83 million (a return of 9.4%), which is 14.4% less than the income that the non-executive director has forecast.

(b)   **Benefits**

The finance costs of the securitisation may be lower than the finance costs of ordinary loan capital. The cash flows from the commercial property development may be regarded as lower risk than Moonstar Co's other revenue streams. This will impact upon the rates that Moonstar Co is able to offer borrowers.

The securitisation matches the assets of the future cash flows to the liabilities to loan note holders. The non-executive director is assuming a steady stream of lease income over the next 10 years, with the development probably being close to being fully occupied over that period.

The securitisation means that Moonstar Co is no longer concerned with the risk that the level of earnings from the properties will be insufficient to pay the finance costs. Risks have effectively been transferred to the loan note holders.

Risks

Not all of the tranches may appeal to investors. The risk-return relationship on the subordinated certificates does not look very appealing, with the return quite likely to be below what is received on the C-rated loan notes. Even the C-rated loan note holders may question the relationship between the risk and return if there is continued uncertainty in the property sector.

If Moonstar Co seeks funding from other sources for other developments, transferring out a lower risk income stream means that the residual risks associated with the rest of Moonstar Co's portfolio will be higher. This may affect the availability and terms of other borrowing.

It appears that the size of the securitisation should be large enough for the costs to be bearable. However Moonstar Co may face unforeseen costs, possibly unexpected management or legal expenses.

(c) **(i)** Sukuk finance could be appropriate for the securitisation of the leasing portfolio. An asset-backed Sukuk would be the same kind of arrangement as the securitisation, where assets are transferred to a special purpose vehicle and the returns and repayments are directly financed by the income from the assets. The Sukuk holders would bear the risks and returns of the relationship.

The other type of Sukuk would be more like a sale and leaseback of the development. Here the Sukuk holders would be guaranteed a rental, so it would seem less appropriate for Moonstar Co if there is significant uncertainty about the returns from the development.

The main issue with the asset-backed Sukuk finance is whether it would be as appealing as certainly the A-tranche of the securitisation arrangement which the non-executive director has proposed. The safer income that the securitisation offers A-tranche investors may be more appealing to investors than a marginally better return from the Sukuk. There will also be costs involved in establishing and gaining approval for the Sukuk, although these costs may be less than for the securitisation arrangement described above.

(ii) A Mudaraba contract would involve the bank providing capital for Moonstar Co to invest in the development. Moonstar Co would manage the investment which the capital funded. Profits from the investment would be shared with the bank, but losses would be solely borne by the bank. A Mudaraba contract is essentially an equity partnership, so Moonstar Co might not face the threat to its credit rating which it would if it obtained ordinary loan finance for the development. A Mudaraba contract would also represent a diversification of sources of finance. It would not require the commitment to pay interest that loan finance would involve.

Moonstar Co would maintain control over the running of the project. A Mudaraba contract would offer a method of obtaining equity funding without the dilution of control which an issue of shares to external shareholders would bring. This is likely to make it appealing to Moonstar Co's directors, given their desire to maintain a dominant influence over the business.

The bank would be concerned about the uncertainties regarding the rental income from the development. Although the lack of involvement by the bank might appeal to Moonstar Co's directors, the bank might not find it so attractive. The bank might be concerned about information asymmetry – that Moonstar Co's management might be reluctant to supply the bank with the information it needs to judge how well its investment is performing.

		Marking scheme		Marks
(a)		Calculation of receivable		1
		Loan note amounts attributable to the A, B and C tranches		1
		Impact of swap		2
		Calculation of interest payable on interest for tranches A, B and C-rated tranches		3
		Estimation of return to subordinated certificates		1
		Comments and calculation relating to sensitivity		3
			Maximum	11
(b)		Benefits of securitisation		3–4
		Risks associated with securitisation		2–3
			Maximum	6
(c)	(i)	Explanation/discussion of suitability of Sukuk finance		2–3
		Discussion of investors' views		1–2
			Maximum	4
	(ii)	Explanation/discussion of suitability of Mudaraba contract		2–3
		Discussion of bank's views		1–2
			Maximum	4
Total				25

47 GNT CO (PILOT 12)

Key answer tips

Historically, duration has been more commonly tested in the context of project appraisal, but note that it can also be usefully applied to bonds, to assess the risk associated with different bonds.

(a) In order to calculate the duration of the two bonds, the present value of the annual cash flows and the price or value at which the bonds are trading at need to be determined. To determine the present value of the annual cash flows, they need to be discounted by the gross redemption yield.

Gross Redemption Yield

Try 5%

$60 \times 1.05^{-1} + 60 \times 1.05^{-2} + 60 \times 1.05^{-3} + 60 \times 1.05^{-4} + 1,060 \times 1.05^{-5} =$

$60 \times 4.3295 + 1,000 \times 0.7835 = 1,043.27$

Try 4%

$60 \times 4.4518 + 1,000 \times 0.8219 = 1,089.01$

$i = 4 + [(1,089.01 - 1,079.68)/(1,089.01 - 1,043.27)] = 4.2\%$

Bond 1 (PV of cash flows)

$60 \times 1.042^{-1} + 60 \times 1.042^{-2} + 60 \times 1.042^{-3} + 60 \times 1.042^{-4} + 1,060 \times 1.042^{-5}$

PV of cash flows (years 1 to 5) = 57.58 + 55.26 + 53.03 + 50.90 + 862.91 = 1,079.68

Market price = $1,079.68

Duration = [57.58 × 1 + 55.26 × 2 + 53.03 × 3 + 50.90 × 4 + 862.91 × 5]/1,079.68 = 4.49 years

Bond 2 (PV of Coupons and Bond Price)

Price = $40 \times 1.042^{-1} + 40 \times 1.042^{-2} + 40 \times 1.042^{-3} + 40 \times 1.042^{-4} + 1,040 \times 1.042^{-5}$

PV of cash flows (years 1 to 5) = 38.39 + 36.84 + 35.36 + 33.93 + 846.63 = 991.15

Market Price = $991.15

Duration = [38.39 × 1 + 36.84 × 2 + 35.36 × 3 + 33.93 × 4 + 846.63 × 5]/991.15 = 4.63 years

(b) The sensitivity of bond prices to changes in interest rates is dependent on their redemption dates. Bonds which are due to be redeemed at a later date are more price-sensitive to interest rate changes, and therefore are riskier.

Duration measures the average time it takes for a bond to pay its coupons and principal and therefore measures the redemption period of a bond. It recognises that bonds which pay higher coupons effectively mature 'sooner' compared to bonds which pay lower coupons, even if the redemption dates of the bonds are the same. This is because a higher proportion of the higher coupon bonds' income is received sooner. Therefore these bonds are less sensitive to interest rate changes and will have a lower duration.

Duration can be used to assess the change in the value of a bond when interest rates change using the following formula: $\Delta P = [-D \times \Delta i \times P][1+i]$, where P is the price of the bond, D is the duration and i is the redemption yield.

However, duration is only useful in assessing small changes in interest rates because of convexity. As interest rates increase, the price of a bond decreases and vice versa, but this decrease is not proportional for coupon paying bonds, the relationship is non-linear. In fact, the relationship between the changes in bond value to changes in interest rates is in the shape of a convex curve to origin, see below.

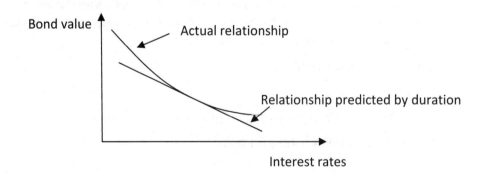

Duration, on the other hand, assumes that the relationship between changes in interest rates and the resultant bond is linear. Therefore duration will predict a lower price than the actual price and for large changes in interest rates this difference can be significant.

Duration can only be applied to measure the approximate change in a bond price due to interest changes, only if changes in interest rates do not lead to a change in the shape of the yield curve. This is because it is an average measure based on the gross redemption yield (yield to maturity). However, if the shape of the yield curve changes, duration can no longer be used to assess the change in bond value due to interest rate changes.

(**Note:** Credit will be given for alternative benefits/limitations of duration)

(c)   Industry risk measures the resilience of the company's industrial sector to changes in the economy. In order to measure or assess this, the following factors could be used:

- Impact of economic changes on the industry in terms how successfully the firms in the industry operate under differing economic outcomes;

- How cyclical the industry is and how large the peaks and troughs are;

- How the demand shifts in the industry as the economy changes.

Earnings protection measures how well the company will be able to maintain or protect its earnings in changing circumstances. In order to assess this, the following factors could be used:

- Differing range of sources of earnings growth;

- Diversity of customer base;

- Profit margins and return on capital.

Financial flexibility measures how easily the company is able to raise the finance it needs to pursue its investment goals. In order to assess this, the following factors could be used:

- Evaluation of plans for financing needs and range of alternatives available;

- Relationships with finance providers, e.g. banks;

- Operating restrictions that currently exist in the form of debt covenants.

Evaluation of the company's management considers how well the managers are managing and planning for the future of the company. In order to assess this, the following factors could be used:

- The company's planning and control policies, and its financial strategies;

- Management succession planning;

- The qualifications and experience of the managers;

- Performance in achieving financial and non-financial targets.

48   TOLTUCK CO (MAR/JUN 17)

Key answer tips

This was a 25 mark optional question from the June 2017 exam paper, covering bond valuations, bond yields and credit ratings.

The question was based on the topics covered in the examiner's technical article from 2011. (Interestingly there was a question on the September 2016 exam paper that also tested the contents of a 2011 technical article!)

Students understand how important it is to read the examiner's recent articles before they attempt the exam, but this demonstrates how important it is to read all the previous technical articles.

If students were familiar with the content of the 2011 technical article, this question would have been very straight forward.

(a)   The government yield curve can be estimated from the data available:

Bond 1: $104 = \$109/(1 + r_1)$

$r_1 = (\$109/\$104) - 1 = 4.81\%$

Bond 2: $102 = \$7/1.0481 + \$107/(1 + r_2)^2$

$r_2 = [107/(102 - 6.68)]^{1/2} - 1 = 5.95\%$

Bond 3: $98 = \$6/1.0481 + \$6/1.05952 + \$106/(1 + r_3)^3$

$r_3 = [106/(98 - 5.72 - 5.35)]^{1/3} - 1 = 6.83\%$

Year	Govt yield curve (%)	Spread old rating (%)	Toltuck Co spot old rating (%)	Spread new rating (%)	Toltuck Co spot new rating (%)
1	4.81	0.18	4.99	0.54	5.35
2	5.95	0.31	6.26	0.69	6.64
3	6.83	0.45	7.28	0.86	7.69

Valuation of bond under old credit rating

Year	Payment ($)	Discount factor	PV
1	8	$1/1.0499$	7.62
2	8	$1/1.0626^2$	7.09
3	110	$1/1.0728^3$	89.09
			———
			103.80
			———

Valuation of bond under new credit rating

Year	Payment ($)	Discount factor	PV
1	8	1/1.0535	7.59
2	8	$1/1.0664^2$	7.03
3	110	$1/1.0769^3$	88.08
			102.70

Yield to maturity under old credit rating

Year	Payment ($)	DF 8%	PV @ 8%	DF 7%	PV @ 7%
1	(103.80)	1	(103.80)	1	(103.80)
1–3	8.00	2.577	20.62	2.624	20.99
3	102.00	0.794	80.99	0.816	83.23
			(2.19)		0.42

Using IRR approach, yield to maturity = 7 + ((0.42/(2.19 + 0.42)) × (8 – 7)) = 7.16%

Yield to maturity under new credit rating

Year	Payment ($)	DF 8%	PV @ 8%	DF 7%	PV @ 7%
1	(102.70)	1	(102.70)	1	(102.70)
1–3	8.00	2.577	20.62	2.624	20.99
3	102.00	0.794	80.99	0.816	83.23
			(1.09)		1.52

Using IRR approach, yield to maturity = 7 + ((1.52/(1.09 + 1.52)) × (8 – 7)) = 7.58%

Market value of $100 bond has fallen by $1.10 and the yield to maturity has risen by 0.42%.

(b) The credit agency will have taken the following criteria into consideration when assessing Toltuck C's credit rating:

Country

Toltuck Co's debt would not normally be rated higher than the credit ratings of its country of origin, Arumland. Therefore the credit rating of Arumland should normally be at least AA. The rating will also have depended on Toltuck Co's standing relative to other companies in Arumland. The credit agency may have reckoned that Toltuck Co's recent poor results have weakened its position.

Industry

The credit agency will have taken account of the impact of the recession on property construction companies generally in Arumland. Toltuck Co's position within the industry compared with competitors will also have been assessed. If similar recent developments by competitors have been more successful, this is likely to have had an adverse impact on Toltuck Co's rating.

Management

The credit agency will have made an overall assessment of management and succession planning at Toltuck Co. It will have looked at business and financing strategies and planning and controls. It will also have assessed how successful the management has been in terms of delivering financial results. The credit agency may have believed the poor returns on recent developments show shortcomings in management decision-making processes and it may have rated the current management team poorly.

Financial

The credit agency will have analysed financial results, using measures such as return on capital employed. The agency will also have assessed possible sources of future earnings growth. It may have been sceptical about prospects, certainly for the short term, given Toltuck Co's recent problems.

The credit agency will also have assessed the financial position of Toltuck Co, looking at its gearing and working capital management, and considering whether Toltuck Co has enough cash to finance its needs. The agency will also have looked at Toltuck Co's relationship with its bankers and its debt covenants, to assess how flexible its sources of finances are if it comes under stress. It may well have been worried about Toltuck Co's gearing being higher than the industry average and concerned about the high levels of cash it needs to finance operations. It will also have assessed returns on developments-in-progress compared with commitments to repay loans. Greater doubt about Toltuck Co's ability to meet its commitments is likely to have been a significant factor in the fall in its rating.

The agency will also have needed reassurance about the quality of the financial information it was using, so it will have looked at the audit report and accounting policies.

(c) Toltuck Co may not have increased problems raising debt finance if debtholders do not react in the same way as the credit rating agency. They may attach different weightings to the criteria which they use. They may also come to different judgements about the quality of management and financial stability. Debtholders may believe that the recent problems Toltuck Co has had generating returns may be due more to external factors which its management could not have controlled.

However, it is probable that the fall in Toltuck Co's credit rating will result in it having more difficulty raising debt finance. Banks may be less willing to provide loans and investors less willing to subscribe for bonds. Even if debt finance is available, it may come with covenants restricting further debt or gearing levels. This will mean that if Toltuck Co requires substantial additional finance, it is more likely to have to make a rights issue or issue new equity on the stock market. Shareholders may be faced with the choice of subscribing large amounts for new capital or having their influence diluted. This may particularly worry the more cautious shareholders.

Even if Toltuck Co can obtain the debt it needs, the predicted increase in yield to maturity may be matched by debtholders demanding a higher coupon rate on debt. This will increase finance costs, and decrease profits and earnings per share, with a possible impact on share price. It will also mean that fewer funds are available for paying dividends. Toltuck Co has been faced with difficult decisions on balancing investment expenditure versus paying dividends and these difficulties may well increase.

Additional debt may have other restrictive covenants. They may restrict Toltuck Co's buying and selling of assets, or its investment strategy. Restrictions on Toltuck Co's decisions about the developments it undertakes may impact adversely on shareholder returns.

Loan finance or bonds will also come with repayment covenants. These may require Toltuck Co to build up a fund over time which will be enough to redeem the debt at the end of its life. Given uncertainties over cash flows, this commitment to retain cash may make it more difficult to undertake major developments or pay an acceptable level of dividend.

The fall in Toltuck Co's credit rating may result in its cost of equity rising as well as its cost of debt. In turn, Toltuck Co's weighted average cost of capital will rise. This will affect its investment choices and hence its ability to generate wealth for shareholders. It may result in Toltuck Co prioritising developments offering better short-term returns. This may suit the more cautious shareholders, but the current majority may worry that Toltuck Co will have to turn down opportunities which offer the possibility of high returns.

ACQUISITIONS AND MERGERS

49   KODIAK COMPANY (DEC 09 ADAPTED)

Key answer tips

Business valuation is commonly tested, especially using the discounted cash flow method. Be careful to lay out your workings carefully. With lots of forecast figures to derive, it is easy to get in a muddle. A neat columnar format, with references to detailed workings, will ensure that you score well.

(a)   Given the details supplied, a forward forecast of the statement of profit or loss and of the statement of financial position is a precursor to the cash flow forecast. On the assumptions (as stated in the question but not reproduced here) the following projection is obtained (all figures in $000):

Projected statement of profit or loss

	Year 1	Year 2	Year 3
Revenue (9% growth)	5,450	5,941	6,475
Cost of sales (9% growth)	3,270	3,564	3,885
Gross Profit	2,180	2,377	2,590
Operating costs (W1)	2,012	2,159	2,317
Operating profit	168	218	273

	Year 1	Year 2	Year 3
Projected cash flows			
Operating profit	168	218	273
Add depreciation (W2)	134	144	155
Less incremental working capital (W3)	(20)	(21)	(24)
Less taxation (W4)	(15)	(28)	(43)
Less interest	(74)	(74)	(74)
	193	239	287
Less investment in non-current assets (W2)	(79)	(95)	(114)
Free cash flow to equity	114	144	173

Workings:

(W1) Operating costs

	Year 1	Year 2	Year 3
Variable costs (9% growth)	818	891	971
Fixed costs (6% growth)	1,060	1,124	1,191
Depreciation (W2)	134	144	155
Total operating costs	2,012	2,159	2,317

(W2) Non-current assets and depreciation

	Year 1	Year 2	Year 3
Non-current assets at beginning	1,266	1,345	1,440
Additions (20% growth)	79	95	114
Non-current assets	1,345	1,440	1,554
Depreciation (10%)	134	144	155

(W3) Working capital

Working capital (9% growth)	240	261	285
Incremental WC	240 − 220 = 20	261 − 240 = 21	285 − 261 = 24

Initial working capital equals net current assets less cash. Alternatively, the full 270 can be used as working capital as well. Credit will be given for either assumption.

(W4) Taxation

One year in arrears (30%)	15 (given)	30% × (168 − 74) = 28	30% × (218 − 74) = 43

(b) Our estimate of the value of this business on a going concern basis assumes that cash will be generated and reinvestment made according to the above projection. The free cash flow after reinvestment which is potentially distributable and the terminal value of the business assuming a constant rate of reinvestment of 3% forward is as follows:

	0	1	2	3
Free cash flow after reinvestment		114	144	173
Terminal value				2,546
Required rate of return	10%			
Present value of cash flows (discounted at 10%)		104	119	2,043
Value of the firm	2,266			

The terminal value is calculated as follows:

$$\text{Value}_3 \frac{\text{FCFE}_3(1.03)}{R_e - 3\%}$$

$$\text{Value}_3(\$000) \frac{173 \times (1.03)}{10\% - 3\%} = 2,546$$

Where R_e is the required rate of return of 10% per annum.

The value of the firm, on the basis of the above projections, is $2,266,000.

(c) This valuation is based upon a number of assumptions which you should consider when reviewing this analysis. We have taken your judgement that 10% fairly reflects the market rate of return required for an investment of this type. This rate should compensate you for the business risk to which your firm is exposed. For an investment held within the context of a widely diversified portfolio the rate of return you should expect will only be conditioned by your exposure to market risk. However, in the context of a sole equity investment then the rate of return you may require could be more than that which would be available from the market for an investment of this type.

In generating our projections we have assumed the estimates are certain and that the firm is a going concern. In considering this investment further you may wish to explicitly consider the variability attaching to the underlying variables in the projection and the possible range of values that may result. Of particular importance is the assumption of a three-year forecast. In practice the period chosen does depend upon the nature of the business and in particular the uncertainties to which it is exposed.

Finally we have assumed a terminal value based upon future cash flows from year three forward growing at a compound rate of 3% into the indefinite future. The resulting value will be particularly sensitive to this figure and it may be that you may wish to consider a different rate depending upon what you regard as sustainable in the long term for a business of this type.

50   KILENC CO (JUN 12 ADAPTED)

Key answer tips

Note that this past exam question contains no calculations. The new AFM syllabus states that in future "there will not be any wholly narrative questions" i.e. the topics covered here may well be covered, but in questions that contain a mixture of calculation and narrative parts.

(a)   Kilenc Co needs to consider a number of risks and issues when making the decision about whether or not to set up a subsidiary company in Lanosia. It should then consider how these may be managed or controlled.

Tutorial note (from the examiner's model answer)

The following answer is indicative. Credit will be given for alternative suggestions of risks and issues, and their management or control.

Key Risks/Issues

Kilenc Co needs to assess the impact on its current exports to Lanosia and the nearby countries if the subsidiary is set up. Presumably, products are currently exported to these countries and if these exports stop, then there may be a negative impact on the employees and facilities currently employed in this area. Related to this may be the risk of loss of reputation if the move results in redundancies. Furthermore, Kilenc Co should consider how the subsidiary and its products would be seen in Lanosia and the nearby countries. For example, would the locally made products be perceived as being of comparative quality as the imported products?

The recession in Lanosia may have a negative impact on the market for the products. The cost of setting up the subsidiary company needs to be compared with the benefits from extra sales revenue and reduced costs. There is a risk that the perceived benefits may be less than predicted or the establishment of a subsidiary may create opportunities in the future once the country recovers from the recession.

Currently the government offers support for companies involved in the pharmaceutical industry. Kilenc Co may find it difficult to set up the subsidiary if it is viewed as impeding the development of the local industry by the government. For example, the government may impose restrictions or increase the taxes the subsidiary may have to pay. On the other hand, the subsidiary may be viewed as supporting the economy and the growth of the pharmaceutical industry, especially since 40% of the shares and 50% of the Board of Directors would be in local hands. The government may even offer the same support as it currently offers the other local companies.

Kilenc Co wants to finance the subsidiary through a mixture of equity and debt. The implications of raising equity finance are discussed in part (b) of the question. However, the risks surrounding debt finance needs further discussion. Raising debt finance in Lanosia would match the income generated in Lanosia with debt interest payments, but the company needs to consider whether or not it would be possible to borrow the money. Given that the government has had to finance the banks may mean that the availability of funds to borrow may be limited. Also interest rates are low at the moment but inflation is high, this may result in pressure on the government to raise interest rates in the future. The consequences of this may be that the borrowing costs increase for Kilenc Co.

The composition of the Board of Directors and the large proportion of the subsidiary's equity held by minority shareholders may create agency issues and risks. Kilenc Co may find that the subsidiary's Board may make decisions which are not in the interests of the parent company, or that the shareholders attempt to move the subsidiary in a direction which is not in the interests of the parent company. On the other hand, the subsidiary's Board may feel that the parent company is imposing too many restrictions on its ability to operate independently and the minority shareholders may feel that their interests are not being considered by the parent company.

Kilenc Co needs to consider the cultural issues when setting up a subsidiary in another country. These may range from cultural issues of different nationalities and doing business in the country to cultural issues within the organisation. Communication of how the company is organised and understanding of cultural issues is very important in this case. The balance between independent autonomy and central control needs to be established and agreed.

Risks such as foreign exchange exposure, product health and safety compliance, employee health and safety regulations and physical risks need to be considered and assessed. For example, foreign exchange exposures arising from exporting the products to nearby countries need to be assessed. The legal requirements around product health and safety and employee health and safety need to be understood and complied with. Risks of physical damage such as from floods or fires on the assets of the business need to be established.

Mitigating the Risks and Issues

A full analysis of the financial costs and benefits should be undertaken to establish the viability of setting up the subsidiary. Sensitivity and probability analysis should be undertaken to assess the impact and possibility of falling revenues and rising costs. Analysis of real options should be undertaken to establish the value of possible follow-on projects.

Effective marketing communication such as media advertising should be conducted on the products produced by the subsidiary to ensure that the customers' perceptions of the new products do not change. This could be supported by retaining the packaging of the products. Internal and external communication should explain the consequences of any negative impact of the move to Lanosia to minimise any reputational damage. Where possible, employees should be redeployed to other divisions, in order to minimise any negative disruption.

Negotiations with the Lanosian government should be undertaken regularly during the process of setting up the subsidiary to minimise any restrictions and to maximise any benefits such as favourable tax rates. Where necessary and possible, these may be augmented with appropriate insurance and legal advice. Continuing lobbying may also be necessary after the subsidiary has been established to reduce the possibility of new rules and regulations which may be detrimental to the subsidiary's business.

An economic analysis may be conducted on the likely movements in inflation and interest rates. Kilenc Co may also want to look into using fixed rate debt for its long-term financing needs, or use swaps to change from variable rates to fixed rates. The costs of such activity need to be taken into account.

Clear corporate governance mechanisms need to be negotiated and agreed on, to strike a balance between central control and subsidiary autonomy. The negotiations should involve the major parties and legal advice may be sought where necessary. These mechanisms should be clearly communicated to the major parties.

The subsidiary organisation should be set up to take account of cultural differences where possible. Induction sessions for employees and staff handbooks can be used to communicate the culture of the organisation and how to work within the organisation.

Foreign exchange exposure, health and safety regulation and risk of physical loss can be managed by a combination of hedging, insurance and legal advice.

(b) Net Present Value (NPV) is used by many companies to appraise investments in both a domestic and an international setting.

In an efficient market a positive NPV, in theory, should lead to a commensurate increase in the value of the company and share price.

However, the use of the existing weighted average cost of capital (WACC) in NPV is only appropriate if there is no significant change in gearing as a result of the investment, the investment is marginal in size, and the operating risk of the company does not change.

In the case of Kilenc Co, it is likely that the operating risk of the new (foreign) investment will be different from Kilenc Co's existing risk, so a risk adjusted WACC, calculated using the beta factor of a proxy company in the CAPM model, would have to be used to appraise the investment in place of the company's existing WACC.

The Adjusted Present Value (APV) method treats the investment as being initially all equity financed and then directly adjusts for the present value of any cash flow effects associated with financing.

It is particularly useful when the gearing of a company is likely to change as a result of a new investment. In the case of Kilenc Co, this is not expected to be the case, so it is unlikely that an APV approach will be required here.

(c) Dark pool trading systems allow share orders to be placed and matched without the traders' interests being declared publicly on the normal stock exchange. Therefore the price of these trades is determined anonymously and the trade is only declared publicly after it has been agreed. Large volume trades which use dark pool trading systems prevent signals reaching the markets in order to minimise large fluctuations in the share price or the markets moving against them.

The main argument put forward in support of dark pool trading systems is that by preventing large movements in the share price due to volume sales, the markets' artificial price volatility would be reduced and the markets maintain their efficiency. The contrary arguments suggest that in fact market efficiency is reduced by dark pool trading systems because such trades do not contribute to the price changes. Furthermore, because most of the individuals who use the markets to trade equity shares are not aware of the trade, transparency is reduced. This, in turn, reduces the liquidity in the markets and therefore may compromise their efficiency. The ultimate danger is that the lack of transparency and liquidity may result in an uncontrolled spread of risks similar to what led to the recent global financial crisis.

It is unlikely that the dark pool trading systems would have an impact on Kilenc Co's subsidiary company because the subsidiary's share price would be based on Kilenc Co's share price and would not be affected by the stock market in Lanosia. Market efficiency in general in Lanosia would probably be much more important.

51 SIGRA CO (DEC 12 ADAPTED)

Key answer tips

Different methods of payment (e.g. cash offer, share for share exchange) have been tested frequently in recent sittings. Valuation using P/E ratios is a critical starting point in this question.

(a) **Common reason why acquisitions are unsuccessful**

Lack of industrial or commercial fit

Failure can result from a takeover where the acquired entity turns out not to have the product range or industrial position that the acquirer anticipated.

Lack of goal congruence

This may apply not only to the acquired entity but, more dangerously, to the acquirer, whereby disputes over the treatment of the acquired entity might well take away the benefits of an otherwise excellent acquisition.

'Cheap' purchases

The 'turn around' costs of an acquisition purchased at what seems to be a bargain price may well turn out to be a high multiple of that price.

Paying too much

The fact that a high premium is paid for an acquisition does not necessarily mean that it will fail. Failure would result only if the price paid is beyond that which the acquirer considers acceptable to increase satisfactorily the long term wealth of its shareholders.

Failure to integrate effectively

An acquirer needs to have a workable and clear plan of the extent to which the acquired company is to be integrated. The plan must address such problems as differences in management styles, incompatibilities in data information systems, and continued opposition to the acquisition by some of the acquired entity's staff.

(b) Number of Sigra Co shares = 4,400,000/0.4 = 11,000,000 shares

Sigra Co earnings per share (EPS) = $4,950,000/11,000,000 shares = 45c/share

Sigra Co price to earnings (PE) ratio = $3.6/$0.45 = 8

Dentro PE ratio = 8 × 1.125 = 9

Dentro Co shares = $500,000/0.4 = 1,250,000 shares

Dentro Co EPS = $625,000/1,250,000 = 50c/share

Estimate of Dentro Co value per share = $0.5 × 9 = $4.50/share

Cash offer

Dentro share percentage gain under cash offer

$0.50/$4.50 × 100% = 11.1%

Share-for-share exchange

Equity value of Sigra Co = 11,000,000 × $3.60 =	$39,600,000
Equity value of Dentro Co = 1,250,000 × $4.50 =	$5,625,000
Synergy savings = 30% × $5,625,000 =	$1,688,000
Total equity value of combined company	$46,913,000
Number of shares for share-for-share exchange	
11,000,000 + [1,250,000 × 3/2] =	12,875,000

Expected share price of combined company $3.644/share

Dentro share percentage gain under share-for-share offer

[($3.644 × 3 − $4.50 × 2)/2]/$4.50 × 100% = 21.5%

Bond offer

Rate of return

$104 = $6 × (1 + r)^{-1} + $6 × (1 + r)^{-2} + $106 × (1 + r)^{-3}$

If r is 5%, price is $102.72 If r is 4%, price is $105.55

r is approximately = 4% + (105.55 − 104)/(105.55 − 102.72) × 1% = 4.55%

Price of new bond =

$2 × 1.0455^{-1} + $2 × 1.0455^{-2} + $102 × 1.0455^{-3} = 93.00

Value per share = $93.00/16 = $5.81/share

Dentro share percentage gain under bond offer

Bond offer: ($5.81 − $4.50)/$4.50 × 100% = 29.1%

Comments

An initial comparison is made between the cash and the share-for-share offers. Although the share-for-share exchange gives a higher return compared to the cash offer, Dentro Co's shareholders may prefer the cash offer as the gains in the share price are dependent on the synergy gains being achieved. However, purchase for cash may mean that the shareholders face an immediate tax burden. Sigra Co's shareholders would probably prefer the cash option because the premium would only take $625,000 of the synergy benefits ($0.50 × 1,250,000 shares), whereas a share-for-share exchange would result in approximately $1,209,000 of the synergy benefits being given to the Dentro Co shareholders (21.5% × $4.50 × 1,250,000 shares).

The bond offer provides an alternative which may be acceptable to both sets of shareholders. Dentro Co's shareholders receive the highest return for this and Sigra Co's shareholders may be pleased that a large proportion of the payment is deferred for three years. In present value terms, however, a very high proportion of the projected synergy benefits are given to Dentro Co's shareholders (29.1% × $4.50 × $1,250,000 = $1,637,000).

(c)   The regulatory framework within the European Union, the EU takeovers directive, will be used to discuss the proposals. However it is acceptable for candidates to refer to other directives and discuss the proposals on that basis.

Proposal 1

With regards to the first proposal, the directive gives the bidder squeeze-out rights, where the bidder can force minority shareholders to sell their shares. However, the limits set for squeeze-out rights are generally high (UK: 90%; Belgium, France, Germany and the Netherlands: 95%; Ireland 80%). It is likely therefore that Sigra Co will need a very large proportion of Dentro Co's shareholders to agree to the acquisition before they can force the rest of Dentro Co's shareholders to sell their shares. Dentro Co's minority shareholders may also require Sigra Co to purchase their shares, known as sell-out rights.

Proposal 2

With regards to the second proposal, the principle of equal treatment in the directive requires that all shareholders should be treated equally. In general terms, the bidder must offer to minority shareholders the same terms as those offered to other shareholders. It could be argued here that the principle of equal treatment is contravened because later shareholders are not offered the extra 3 cents per share, even though the 30% is less than a majority shareholding. It is highly unlikely that Sigra Co will be allowed to offer these terms.

52   MAKONIS CO (DEC 13)

Key answer tips

Valuation using free cash flows is very commonly tested. However, the need to calculate a cost of capital for discounting here made this a very time-pressured question. Allocate time carefully to make sure that you leave enough time to attempt all parts of the question.

(a)   **Combined company, cost of capital**

Asset beta

$(1.2 \times 480 + 0.9 \times 1,218)/(480 + 1,218) = 0.985$

Equity beta

$0.985 \times (60 + 40 \times 0.8)/60 = 1.51$

Cost of equity

$2\% + 1.51 \times 7\% = 12.57\%$

Cost of capital

$12.57\% \times 0.6 + 4.55\% \times 0.8 \times 0.4 = 9.00\%$

Combined company equity value

Years 1 to 4 ($ millions)

Year	1	2	3	4
Free cash flows before synergy (growing at 5%)	226.80	238.14	250.05	262.55
Synergies	20.00	20.00	20.00	20.00
Free cash flows	246.80	258.14	270.05	282.55
PV of free cash flows at 9%	226.42	217.27	208.53	200.17

Tutorial note

The present value (PV) figures are slightly different if discount table factors are used, instead of formulae. Full credit will be given if discount tables are used to calculate PV figures.

Total PV of cash flows (years 1 to 4) = $852.39 million

Total PV of cash flows (years 5 to perpetuity)

$= [262.55 \times 1.0225/(0.09 - 0.0225)] \times 1.09^{-4}$

= $2,817.51 million

Total value to firm = $3,669.90 million

Value attributable to equity holders = $3,669.90 million × 0.6 = $2,201.94 million

Additional value created from the combined company

= $2,201.94 million − ($1,218 million + $480 million)

= $2,201.94 million − $1,698.00 million = $503.94 million (or 29.7%)

Although the equity beta and therefore the risk of the combined company is more than Makonis Co on its own, probably due to Nuvola Co's higher business risk (reflected by the higher asset beta), overall the benefits from growth in excess of the risk free rate and additional synergies have led to an increase in the value of combined company of just under 30% when compared to the individual companies' values.

However, a number of assumptions have been made in obtaining the valuation, for example:

- The assumption of growth of cash flows in perpetuity and whether this is realistic or not;

- Whether the calculation of the combined company's asset beta when based on the weighted average of market values is based on good evidence or not;

- It has been assumed that the figures such as growth rates, tax rates, free cash flows, risk free rate of return, risk premium, and so on are accurate and do not change in the future.

In all these circumstances, it may be appropriate to undertake sensitivity analysis to determine how changes in the variables would impact on the value of the combined company, and whether the large increase in value is justified.

(b)   Value of Nuvola equity = $2.40 × 200m shares = $480m

30% premium: 1.3 × $480m = $624m 50% premium: 1.5 × $480m = $720m

New number of shares = 210m + 1/2 × 200m = 310m

Loss in value per share of combined company, if 50% premium paid instead of 30% premium = ($720m – $624m)/310m shares = $0.31/share. This represents a drop in value of approx. 5.3% on original value of a Makonis Co share ($0.31/$5.80).

(c)   The amount of cash required will increase substantially, by about $96 million, if Makonis Co agrees to the demands made by Nuvola Co's equity holders and pays the 50% premium. Makonis Co needs to determine how it is going to acquire the additional funds and the implications from this. For example, it could borrow the money required for the additional funds, but taking on more debt may affect the cost of capital and therefore the value of the company. It could raise the funds by issuing more equity shares, but this may not be viewed in a positive light by the current equity holders.

Makonis Co may decide to offer a higher proportion of its shares in the share-for-share exchange instead of paying cash for the additional premium. However, this will affect its equity holders and dilute their equity holding further. Even the current proposal to issue 100 million new shares will mean that Nuvola Co's equity holders will own just under 1/3 of the combined company and Makonis Co's shareholders would own just over 2/3 of the combined company.

Makonis Co should also consider what Nuvola Co's equity holders would prefer. They may prefer less cash and more equity due to their personal tax circumstances, but, in most cases, cash is preferred by the target firm's equity holders.

Marking scheme		Marks
(a) Market values of Makonis Co and Nuvola Co		1
Combined company asset beta		1
Combined company equity beta		1
Combined company: cost of capital		1
Combined company value: years 1 to 4		3
Combined company value: years 5 to perpetuity		1
Combined company value: value to equity holders and additional value		2
Comment and discussion of assumptions		3–4
	Maximum	**13**
(b) Payment if 30% premium paid		1
Payment if 50% premium paid		1
Estimate of impact on Makonis Co's equity holders		3
	Maximum	**5**
(c) Additional amount payable if 50% premium paid instead of 30% premium		1
Discussion of how Makonis Co would finance the additional premium		6
	Maximum	**7**
Total		**25**

53 VOGEL CO (JUN 14)

Key answer tips

This was a fairly typical question on acquisitions, with a good mix of calculations and discussion.

When asked to perform a valuation calculation, follow the clues in the question to decide which valuation method to use. In this case the given P/E ratios, costs of capital and growth rates meant that DCF and P/E methods should have been used.

(a) Vogel Co may have switched from a strategy of organic growth to one of growth by acquisition, if it was of the opinion that such a change would result in increasing the value for the shareholders.

Acquiring a company to gain access to new products, markets, technologies and expertise may be quicker and less costly. Horizontal acquisitions may help Vogel Co eliminate key competitors and enable it to take advantage of economies of scale. Vertical acquisitions may help Vogel Co to secure the supply chain and maximise returns from its value chain.

Organic growth may take a long time, can be expensive and may result in little competitive advantage being established due to the time taken. Also organic growth, especially into a new area, would need managers to gain knowledge and expertise of an area or function, which they not currently familiar with. Furthermore, in a saturated market, there may be little opportunity for organic growth.

(**Note:** Credit will be given for alternative relevant comments.)

(b) Vogel Co can take the following actions to reduce the risk that the acquisition of Tori Co fails to increase shareholder value.

Since Vogel Co has pursued an aggressive policy of acquisitions, it needs to determine whether or not this has been too aggressive and detailed assessments have been undertaken. Vogel Co should ensure that the valuation is based on reasonable input figures and that proper due diligence of the perceived benefits is undertaken prior to the offer being made. Often it is difficult to get an accurate picture of the target when looking at it from the outside. Vogel Co needs to ensure that it has sufficient data and information to enable a thorough and sufficient analysis to be undertaken.

The sources of synergy need to be properly assessed to ensure that they are achievable and what actions Vogel Co needs to undertake to ensure their achievement. This is especially so for the revenue-based synergies. An assessment of the impact of the acquisition on the risk of the combined company needs to be undertaken to ensure that the acquisition is not considered in isolation but as part of the whole company.

The Board of Directors of Vogel Co needs to ensure that there are good reasons to undertake the acquisition, and that the acquisition should result in an increase in value for the shareholders. Research studies into mergers and acquisitions have found that often companies are acquired not for the shareholders' benefit, but for the benefit or self-interest of the acquiring company's management. The non-executive directors should play a crucial role in ensuring that acquisitions are made to enhance the value for the shareholders. A post-completion audit may help to identify the reasons behind why so many of Vogel Co's acquisitions have failed to create value. Once these reasons have been identified, strategies need to be put in place to prevent their repetition in future acquisitions.

Procedures need to be established to ensure that the acquisition is not overpaid. Vogel Co should determine the maximum premium it is willing to pay and not go beyond that figure. Research indicates that often too much is paid to acquire a company and the resultant synergy benefits are not sufficient to cover the premium paid. Often this is the result of the management of the acquiring company wanting to complete the deal at any cost, because not completing the deal may be perceived as damaging to both their own, and their company's, reputation. The acquiring company's management may also want to show that the costs related to undertaking due diligence and initial negotiation have not been wasted. Vogel Co and its management need to guard against this and maybe formal procedures need to be established which allow managers to step back without loss of personal reputation.

Vogel Co needs to ensure that it has proper procedures in place to integrate the staff and systems of the target company effectively, and also to recognise that such integration takes time. Vogel Co may decide instead to give the target company a large degree of autonomy and thus make integration less necessary; however, this may result in a reduction in synergy benefits. Vogel Co should also have strategies which allow it sufficient flexibility when undertaking integration so that it is able to respond to changing circumstances or respond to inaccurate information prior to the acquisition. Vogel Co should also be mindful that its own and the acquired company's staff and management need to integrate and ensure a good working relationship between them.

(**Note:** The above answer covers more areas than would be needed to achieve full marks for the part. Credit will be given for alternative relevant comments.)

(c)   **Approach taken**

The maximum premium payable is equal to the maximum additional benefit created from the acquisition of Tori Co, with no increase in value for the shareholders of Vogel Co (although the shareholders of Vogel Co would probably not approve of the acquisition if they do not gain from it).

The additional benefit can be estimated as the sum of the cash gained (or lost) from selling the assets of Department C, spinning off Department B and integrating Department A, less the sum of the values of Vogel Co and Tori Co as separate companies.

Estimation

Cash gained from selling the assets of Department C = (20% × $98.2m) + (20% × $46.5m × 0.9) – ($20.2 + $3m) = $19.64m + $8.37m – $23.2m = $4.81m

Value created from spinning off Department B into Ndege Co

	$ *million*
Free cash flow of Ndege Co	
Current share of PBDIT (0.4 × $37.4m)	14.96
Less: attributable to Department C (10%)	(1.50)
Less: tax allowable depreciation (0.4 × 98.2 × 0.10)	(3.93)
	———
Profits before tax	9.53
Tax (20%)	(1.91)
	———
Free cash flows	7.62
	———

Value of Ndege Co =

Present value of cash flow in year 1: $7.62m × 1.2 × 1.1^{-1} = $8.31m

Add: present value of cash flows from year 2 onwards:

($9.14m × 1.052)/(0.1 – 0.052) × 1.1^{-1} = $182.11m

Less: debt = $40m

Value to shareholders of Ndege Co = $150.42m

Vogel Co's current value = $3 × 380m = $1,140m

Vogel Co, profit after tax = $158.2m × 0.8 = $126.56m

Vogel Co, PE ratio before acquisition = $1,140.0m/$126.56m = 9.01 say 9

Vogel Co, PE ratio after acquisition = 9 × 1.15 = 10.35

Tori Co, PE ratio before acquisition = 9 × 1.25 = 11.25

Tori Co's current value = 11.25 × ($23.0 × 0.8) = $207.0m

Value created from combined company

($126.56m + 0.5 × $23.0m × 0.8 + $7m) × 10.35 = $1,477.57

Maximum premium = ($1,477.57m + $150.42m + $4.81m) – ($1,140m + $207.0m) = $285.80m

Assumptions

Based on the calculations given above, it is estimated that the value created will be 64.9% or $285.80m.

However, Vogel Co needs to assess whether the numbers it has used in the calculations and the assumptions it has made are reasonable. For example, Ndege Co's future cash flows seem to be growing without any additional investment in assets and Vogel Co needs to establish whether or not this is reasonable. It also needs to establish how the increase in its PE ratio was determined after acquisition. Perhaps sensitivity analysis would be useful to show the impact on value changes, if these figures are changed. Given its poor record in generating value previously, Vogel Co needs to pay particular attention to these figures.

	Marking scheme		
			Marks
(a)	1–2 marks per point	**Maximum**	4
(b)	2–3 marks per point	**Maximum**	7
(c)	Cash gained from sales of Department C assets		1
	Calculation of free cash flows for Ndege Co		2
	Calculation of present values of Ndege Co cash flows and value		2
	Vogel Co PE ratios before and after acquisition		2
	Tori Co PE ratio and value		1
	Value created from combining Department A with Vogel Co		1
	Maximum premium payable		1
	Approach taken		1–2
	Assumptions made		2–3
		Maximum	14
Total			25

54 LOUIEED CO (MAR/JUN 16)

Key answer tips

There was a lot to do here in the time available, so strict time management would have been critical.

The calculations in part (b) were quite tricky. In most past valuation questions, the requirement has been to use given P/E ratios to calculate values, but here you were given the values and asked to work back to the P/E ratios.

In part (c) you were asked to calculate and discuss gearing and earnings per share in three alternative scenarios. In questions like this it is very important to present the numbers clearly, so that it is then easy to compare the positions and complete the discussion parts of the question.

(a) **Advantages of the acquisition**

Louieed Co and Tidded Co appear to be a good strategic fit for a number of reasons. Louieed Co appears to have limited potential for further growth. Acquiring Tidded Co, a company with better recent growth, should hopefully give Louieed Co the impetus to grow more quickly.

Acquiring a company which has a specialism in the area of online testing will give Louieed Co capabilities quicker than developing this function in-house. If Louieed Co does not move quickly, it risks losing contracts to its competitors.

Acquiring Tidded Co will give Louieed Co access to the abilities of some of the directors who have led Tidded Co to becoming a successful company. They will provide continuity and hopefully will help integrate Tidded Co's operations successfully into Louieed Co. They may be able to lead the upgrading of Tidded Co's existing products or the development of new products which ensures that Louieed Co retains a competitive advantage.

It appears that Tidded Co's directors now want to either realise their investment or be part of a larger company, possibly because it will have more resources to back further product development. If Louieed Co does not pursue this opportunity, one of Louieed Co's competitors may purchase Tidded Co and acquire a competitive advantage itself.

There may also be other synergistic benefits, including savings in staff costs and other savings, when the two companies merge.

Disadvantages of the acquisition

It is not known what the costs of developing in-house capabilities will be. Although the process may be slower, the costs may be less and the process less disruptive to Louieed Co than suddenly adding on Tidded Co's operations.

It is not possible to tell which of Tidded Co's directors are primarily responsible for its success. Loss of the three directors may well represent a significant loss of its capability. This will be enhanced if the three directors join a competitor of Louieed Co or set up in competition themselves.

There is no guarantee that the directors who remain will fit into Louieed Co's culture. They are used to working in a less formal environment and may resent having Louieed Co's way of operating imposed upon them. This could result in departures after the acquisition, jeopardising the value which Tidded Co has brought.

Possibly Tidded Co's leadership in the online testing market may not last. If competitors do introduce major advances, this could mean that Tidded Co's current growth is not sustainable.

(b)   P/E Ratio calculations

Value of Louieed Co's share = $296m × 14/340m = $12.19

Value of Tidded Co share per original bid = $12.19 × (5/3) = $20.32

Tidded Co earnings per share = $128m/90 = $1.42

Tidded Co P/E ratio implied by original bid = $20.32/$1.42 = 14.3

Tidded Co P/E ratio implied by all Tidded Co's shareholders taking up the share offer = $12.19 × 2/$1.42 = 17.2

Tidded Co P/E ratio implied by mixed cash and share offer

= ($22.75 × 0.4 + $12.19 × 2 × 0.6)/$1.42 = 16.7

Tidded Co P/E ratio implied by all Tidded Co's shareholders taking up the cash offer

= $22.75/$1.42 = 16.0

(c)   Funding of bid

No extra finance will be required if all Tidded Co's shareholders take up the share offer.

All Tidded Co's shareholders take up cash offer

Cash required = 90 million × $22.75 = $2,048m

Extra debt finance required = $2,048m − $220m − $64m = $1,764m

60% share-for-share offer, 40% cash offer

Cash required = 40% × 90m × $22.75 = $819m

Extra debt finance required = $819m − $220m − $64m = $535m

Impact of bid on EPS

Louieed Co's EPS prior to acquisition = $296m/340 = $0.87

All Tidded Co's shareholders take up share offer

Number of shares after acquisition = 340m + (90m × 2) = 520m

EPS after acquisition = ($296m + $128m + $20m)/520m = $0.85

All Tidded Co's shareholders take up cash offer

Number of shares after acquisition = 340m

EPS after acquisition = ($296m + $128m + $20m − $11.36m − $105.84m)/340m = $0.96

$105.84m is the post-tax finance cost on the additional loan finding required of $1,764m. Therefore $1,764m × 7.5% × 80% = $105.84m

$11.36m is the post-tax opportunity cost of interest foregone on the cash and cash equivalents surpluses of the two companies of $220m + $64m = $284m. Therefore $284m × 5% × 80% = $11.36m

60% share-for-share offer, 40% cash offer

Number of shares after acquisition 340m + (90m × 2 × 0.6) = 448m

EPS after acquisition = ($296m + $128m + $20m − $11.36m − $32.1m)/448m = $0.89

$32.1m is the post-tax finance cost on the additional loan funding required of $535m. Therefore $535m × 7.5% × 80% = $32.1 m

Impact of bid on gearing (using market values)

Louieed Co's gearing (debt/(debt + equity)) prior to bid = 540/(540 + (340 × 12.19)) = 11.5%

All Tidded Co's shareholders take up share offer

Debt/(Debt + equity) after bid = (540 + 193)/(540 + 193 + (520 × $0.85 × 14)) = 10.6%

All Tidded Co's shareholders take up cash offer

Debt/(Debt + equity) after anticipated bid

= (540 + 193 + 1,764)/(540 + 193 + 1,764 + (340 × $0.96 × 14)) = 35.3%

60% share-for-share offer, 40% cash offer

Debt/(Debt + equity) after bid

= (540 + 193 + 535)/(540 + 193 + 535 + (448 × $0.89 × 14)) = 18.5%

Comments

The calculations suggest that if Tidded Co's shares are acquired on a share-for-share exchange on the terms required by its shareholders, Louieed Co's shareholders will suffer a fall in earnings per share attributable to them from $0.87 to $0.85. This is because Tidded Co is being bought on a higher price-earnings ratio than Louieed Co and the synergies arising from the acquisition are insufficient to compensate for this.

Use of loan finance to back a cash offer will attract tax relief on interest. The cost of debt will be lower than the cost of equity.

Issuing extra shares will lead to a dilution of the power of Louieed Co's existing shareholders. If all of Tidded Co's shareholders take up the share-for-share offer, they will hold around a third of the shares of the combined company (180m/520m) and this may be unacceptable to Louieed Co's shareholders.

The benefits which Tidded Co's shareholders will gain will be fixed if they take up a cash offer and do not acquire shares in the combined company. If there are significant gains after the acquisition, these will mostly accrue to Louieed Co's existing shareholders if a significant proportion of Tidded Co's shareholders have taken a cash offer.

If the forecast for take up of the offer is correct, even by combining the cash flows of the two companies, the new company will have insufficient funds to be able to pay all the shareholders who are expected to take up the cash offer. Further finance will be required.

The alternative to loan finance is financing the bid by issuing shares. Depending on the method used, this may also result in dilution of existing shareholders' ownership and also there is no guarantee that the issue will be successful.

There is also no guarantee that the forecast of 40% of the shareholders taking up the cash offer is correct. If all five of the major shareholders decide to realise their investment rather than just two, this will increase the cash required by $512 million (25% × $22.75 × 90m), for example.

Gearing will increase if loan finance is needed to finance the cash offer. If the mixed share and cash offer is taken up in the proportions stated, the gearing level of the combined company will increase from 11.5% to 18.5%. Current shareholders may not be particularly concerned about this. However, if all or most of the share capital is bought for cash, the gearing level of the combined company will be significantly greater, at maximum 35.3%, than Louieed Co's current gearing. This may be unacceptable to current shareholders and could mean an increase in the cost of equity, because of the increased risk, and also possibly an increase in the cost of debt, assuming in any case that debt finance at the maximum level required will be available. To guard against this risk, Louieed Co's board may want to limit the cash offer to a certain percentage of share value.

Marking scheme			
			Marks
(a)	Reasons for acquisition		3
	Reasons against acquisition		3
		Maximum	6
(b)	Calculations: 1 mark for EPS, 1 mark each for PE ratio for original offer, and for each of the three options for the proposed offer		
		Maximum	5
(c)	Funding of bid: 1 mark for cash option, 1 mark for mixed option		2
	Earnings per share: 1 mark for share-for-share option, 2 marks for cash option, 2 marks for mixed option		5
	Gearing: 1 mark for each option		3
	Comments		4–5
		Maximum	14
Total			25

55   HAV CO (SPECIMEN PAPER 2018)

Key answer tips

In many valuation questions you will also have to address discursive issues such as synergy. Make sure that you allocate your time carefully to enable you to attempt both the calculations and the discussion parts.

(a)   An acquisition creates synergy benefits when the value of the combined entity is more than the sum of the two companies' values. Synergies can be separated into three types: revenue synergies which result in higher revenues for the combined entity, higher return on equity and a longer period when the company is able to maintain competitive advantage; cost synergies which result mainly from reducing duplication of functions and related costs, and from taking advantage of economies of scale; financial synergies which result from financing aspects such as the transfer of funds between group companies to where it can be utilised best, or from increasing debt capacity.

In this scenario, the following synergy benefits may arise from the two companies coming together. Financial synergies may be available because Strand Co does not have the funds to innovate new products. On the other hand, Hav Co has cash reserves available. It may be possible to identify and quantify this synergy based on the projects which can be undertaken after the acquisition, but would have been rejected before, and their corresponding net present value. Furthermore, as the company increases in size, the debt capacity of the combined company may increase, giving it additional access to finance. Finally, the acquisition may result in a decrease in the cost of capital of the combined company.

Cost synergies may arise from the larger company being able to negotiate better terms and lower costs from their suppliers. And there may be duplication of functional areas such as in research and development and head office which could be reduced and costs saved. These types of synergies are easier to identify and quantify but would be more short-lived. Therefore, if the markets are going to be positive about the acquisition, Hav Co will need to show where more long-term synergies are coming from as well as these.

Revenue synergies are perhaps where the greatest potential for growth comes from but are also more difficult to identify, quantify and enact. Good post-acquisition planning is essential for these synergies to be realised but they can be substantial and long-lasting. In this case, Hav Co's management can help market Strand Co's products more effectively by using their sales and marketing talents resulting in higher revenues and longer competitive advantage. Research and development activity can be combined to create new products using the technologies in place in both companies, and possibly bringing innovative products to market quicker. The services of the scientists from Strand Co will be retained to drive innovation forward, but these need to be nurtured with care since they had complete autonomy when they were the owners of Strand Co.

The main challenge in ensuring long-lasting benefits is not only ensuring accurate identification of potential synergies but putting into place integration processes and systems to gain full benefit from them. This is probably the greater challenge for management, and, when poorly done, can result in failure to realise the full value of the acquisition. Hav Co needs to be aware of this and make adequate provisions for it.

(Note: Credit will be given for alternative relevant comments and suggestions)

(b) **Maximum premium based on excess earnings method**

Average pre-tax earnings: (397 + 370 + 352)/3 = $373.0m

Average capital employed:

[(882 + 210 – 209) + (838 + 208 – 180) + (801 + 198 – 140)]/3 = $869.3m

Excess annual value/annual premium = 373m – (20% × $869.3m) = $199.1m

After-tax annual premium = $199.1m × 0.8 = $159.3m

PV of annual premium (assume perpetuity) = $159.3m/0.07 = $2,275.7m

According to this method, the maximum premium payable is $2,275.7m in total.

Maximum premium based on price-to-earnings (PE) ratio method

Strand Co estimated PE ratio = 16.4 × 1.10 = 18.0

Strand Co profit after tax: $397m × 0.8 = $317.6m

Hav Co profit after tax = $1,980m × 0.8 =$1,584.0m

Hav Co, current value = $9.24 × 2,400 shares = $22,176.0m

Strand Co, current value = $317.6m × 18.0 = $5,716.8m

Combined company value = ($1,584m + $317.6m + $140.0m) × 14.5 = $29,603.2m

Maximum premium = $29,603.2m – ($22,176.0m + $5,716.8) = $1,710.4m

(c) Strand Co, current value per share = $5,716.8m/1,200m shares = $4.76 per share

Maximum premium % based on PE ratio = $1,710.4m/$5,716.8m × 100% = 29.9%

Maximum premium % based on excess earnings
= $2,275.7m/$5,716.8m × 100% = 39.8%

Cash offer: premium (%)

($5.72 – $4.76)/$4.76 × 100% = 20.2%

Cash and share offer: premium (%)

1 Hav Co share for 2 Strand Co shares

Hav Co share price = $9.24

Per Strand Co share = $4.62

Cash payment per share= $1.33

Total return = $1.33 + $4.62 = $5.95

Premium percentage = ($5.95 – $4.76)/$4.76 × 100% = 25.0%

Cash and bond offer: premium (%)

Each share has a nominal value of $0.25, therefore $5 is $5/$0.25 = 20 shares

Bond value = $100/20 shares = $5 per share

Cash payment = $1.25 per share

Total = $6.25 per share

Premium percentage = ($6.25 – $4.76)/$4.76 = 31.3%

On the basis of the calculations, the cash together with bond offer yields the highest return; in addition to the value calculated above, the bonds can be converted to 12 Hav Co shares, giving them a price per share of $8.33 ($100/12). This price is below Hav Co's current share price of $9.24, and therefore the conversion option is already in-the-money. It is probable that the share price will increase in the 10-year period and therefore the value of the convertible bond should increase. A bond also earns a small coupon interest of $3 per $100 a year. The 31.3% return is the closest to the maximum premium based on the excess earnings method and more than the maximum premium based on the PE ratio method. It would seem that this payment option transfers more value to the owners of Strand Co than the value created based on the PE ratio method.

However, with this option Strand Co shareholders only receive an initial cash payment of $1.25 per share compared to $1.33 per share and $5.72 per share for the other methods. This may make it the more attractive option for the Hav Co shareholders as well, and although their shareholding will be diluted most under this option, it will not happen for some time.

The cash and share offer gives a return in between the pure cash and the cash and bonds offers. Although the return is lower, Strand Co's shareholders become owners of Hav Co and have the option to sell their equity immediately. However, the share price may fall between now and when the payment for the acquisition is made. If this happens, then the return to Strand Co's shareholders will be lower.

The pure cash offer gives an immediate and definite return to Strand Co's shareholders, but is also the lowest offer and may also put a significant burden on Hav Co having to fund so much cash, possibly through increased debt.

It is likely that Strand Co's shareholder/managers, who will continue to work within Hav Co, will accept the mixed cash and bond offer. They, therefore, get to maximise their current return and also potentially gain when the bonds are converted into shares. Different impacts on shareholders' personal taxation situations due to the different payment methods might also influence the choice of method.

	Marking scheme	
		Marks
(a)	Distinguish between the different synergies	1
	Discuss possible financial synergy sources	2
	Discuss possible cost synergy sources	1
	Discuss possible revenue synergy sources	3
	Other relevant discussion or additional detail	1
	Concluding comments	1
		9
(b)	Average earnings and capital employed	1
	After-tax annual premium	1
	PV of premium (excess earnings method)	1
	Hav Co and Strand Co values	1
	Combined company value	1
	Value created/premium (PE method)	1
		6
(c)	Strand Co, value per share	1
	Cash offer premium (%)	1
	Cash and share offer premium (%)	2
	Cash and bond offer premium (%)	2
	Explanation and justification	4
		10
Total		25

CORPORATE RECONSTRUCTION AND REORGANISATION

56   ALASKA SALVAGE (DEC 09 ADAPTED)

Key answer tips

The examiner is constantly trying to think of new ways to test the application of the Black-Scholes model. In previous exams, the application of the model to warrants had never been tested, so many students found this a very difficult question.

However, as with any Black-Scholes question, the key thing is to pick out the five key input factors at the start and to list them out. This will ensure that you are awarded all the available method marks even if you make an error with one or more of the input factors.

(a)   A warrant is an option attached to another financial instrument on issue which can be detached and negotiated independently of the underlying issue. Warrants are usually exercised over a longer term than traded options but can be valued in exactly the same way using the Black Scholes Option Pricing Model by inserting into the standard formula.

The calculation has been performed as follows:

$$c = 85N(d_1) - 90N(d_2)e^{-0.05 \times 5}$$

Where:

$$d_1 = \frac{\ln(85/90) + (0.05 + 0.5 \times 0.2^2) \times 5}{0.2 \times \sqrt{5}} = 0.6548$$

$$d_2 = d_1 - 0.2 \times \sqrt{5} = 0.2076$$

From normal tables we calculate the area under the normal curve represented by d_1 and d_2:

$$c = 85 \times 0.7437 - 90 \times 0.5822 \times e^{-0.05 \times 5} = 22.41$$

Given that each warrant represents an option on 100 equity shares the value of each warrant is $2,241.

The Black Scholes model makes a number of restrictive assumptions:

1   The warrant is a 'European' style option.

2   The share price follows a log-normal distribution and is continuously traded.

3   Unrestricted short selling of the underlying security is permitted.

4   There are no market frictions such as taxes or transaction costs.

5   No dividends are paid during the life of the warrant.

These assumptions are less realistic with a company such as Alaska Salvage than with a large enterprise with a full listing. It is unlikely, for example, that the company's shares will be actively traded or that the share market is efficient in its pricing of the equity.

(b)   The coupon rate is derived from the cash flow to the lender as follows:

1   Lay out the cash flow to the lender showing the value of the warrant as a benefit accruing immediately to the lender.

	0	1	2	3	4	5
Coupon	(10,000)	100 × c%	100 × c%	100 × c%	100 × c%	100 × c%
Repayment						10,000
Call value	2,241					
Cash flow to lender	(7,759)	100 × c%	100 × c%	100 × c%	100 × c%	10,000 + 100 × c%

2   Solve the following equation where c% is the coupon rate and A and V are the five-year annuity and discount factors at 13% respectively:

7,759 = 100 × c% × A + 10,000 × V

Therefore:

7,759 = 100 × c% × 3.517 + 10,000 × 0.543

By rearrangement:

$$c\% = \frac{7,759 - 10,000 \times 0.543}{100 \times 3.517}$$

Therefore a 6.62% coupon rate will give an effective rate of return on the investment to the lender of 13%.

(c)   Mezzanine debt such as this is one mechanism by which a small, high growth firm such as Alaska Salvage can raise debt finance where the risk of default is high and/or there is a low level of asset coverage for the loan. In this case raising a loan of $1.6 million would raise the market gearing of the firm from zero (assuming there is no current outstanding debt) to 13.6% (debt to total capitalisation). This increase in borrowing against what might be presumed to be specialised salvaging equipment and the forward cost of operation may not be attractive to the commercial banking sector and may need specialised venture finance. The issue of warrants gives the lender the opportunity to participate in the success of the venture but with a reasonable level of coupon assured. However, the disadvantage for the current equity investors is that the value of their investment will be reduced by the value of the warrants issued. The extent to which this will be worthwhile depends upon the value of the firm on the assumption that the project proceeds and is financed in the way described. This should ultimately decide the maximum value that they would be prepared to pay to finance the new project.

(d)   **Sukuk bonds**

Sukuk bonds are a type of Islamic financing method.

At the moment, Alaska Salvage intends to issue loan notes to raise debt finance. The loan note holder will receive interest (to be paid before dividends).

This is prohibited under Islamic law.

Instead, Islamic bonds (or sukuk) are linked to an underlying asset, such that a sukuk holder is a partial owner in the underlying assets and profit is linked to the performance of the underlying asset. So, for example, a sukuk holder will participate in the ownership of the company issuing the sukuk and has a right to profits (but will equally bear their share of any losses).

There are two types of sukuk bonds:

- Asset based – raising finance where the principal is covered by the capital value of the asset but the returns and repayments to sukuk holders are not directly financed by these assets.

- Asset backed – raising finance where the principal is covered by the capital value of the asset but the returns and repayments to sukuk holders are directly financed by these assets.

Asset backed sukuk bonds are often considered to be more akin to equity finance, so Alaska Salvage would be best advised to issue asset based sukuk bonds here, to provide the investors with an investment more similar to the conventional loan notes.

Marking scheme		Marks
(a) Calculation of:		
d_1		3
d_2		1
value of the warrant		2
assumptions (one each to a maximum of 4)		4
		___
	Maximum	**10**
		___

Marking scheme			
(b)	Estimation of the coupon rate (2 marks for deducting option value from face value of warrant and 2 marks for calculation of coupon using annuity and discount factors)		4
		Maximum	4
(c)	Identification of mezzanine debt as a source of high risk finance		2
	Disadvantage for equity investors (reduction in equity value on exercise)		2
	Advantages: low coupon, additional equity participation		2
		Maximum	6
(d)	1–2 marks per sensible, well-explained point		5
Total			25

57 PROTEUS CO (DEC 11 ADAPTED)

Key answer tips

In order to assess whether the debt/equity covenant will be breached, it is first necessary to forecast the debt level and the equity level over the next five years.

(a) Possible benefits of disposing Tyche Co through a management buy-out may include:

Management buy-out costs may be less for Proteus Co compared with other forms of disposal such as selling the assets of the company or selling the company to a third party.

It may be the quickest method in raising funds for Proteus Co compared to the other methods.

There would be less resistance from the managers and employees, making the process smoother and easier to accomplish.

Proteus Co may retain a better relationship and beneficial links with Tyche Co and may be able to purchase or sell goods and services to it, as seems to have happened with the management service.

It may be able to get a better price for the company. The current management and employees possibly have the best knowledge of the company and are able to make it successful. Therefore they may be willing to pay more for it.

It may increase Proteus Co's reputation among its internal stakeholders such as the management and employees. It may also increase its reputation with external stakeholders and the markets if it manages the disposal successfully and efficiently.

(**Note:** Credit will be given for alternative relevant comments)

(b) In order to calculate whether or not the covenant is breached every year, the proportion of debt to equity needs to be calculated each year. The debt will reduce by $3 million every year and the equity will increase by reserves every year. In order to calculate the increase in reserves every year, the forecast statements of profit or loss need to be determined.

Forecast statement of profit or loss ($000)

Year	1	2	3	4	5
Operating income before mgmt. fee (W1)	23,760	25,661	27,714	29,931	32,325
Management service fee	12,000	12,960	13,997	15,116	16,326
Interest payable (W2)	5,850	5,580	5,310	5,040	4,770
Profit before tax	5,910	7,121	8,407	9,775	11,229
Tax payable (25%)	1,478	1,780	2,102	2,444	2,807
Profit after tax	4,432	5,341	6,305	7,331	8,422
Dividend payable (25%)	1,108	1,335	1,576	1,833	2,106
Balance transferred to reserves	3,324	4,006	4,729	5,498	6,316

Book value of equity

Year	1	2	3	4	5
Opening equity	16,000	19,324	23,330	28,059	33,557
Reserves	3,324	4,006	4,729	5,498	6,316
Closing equity	19,324	23,330	28,059	33,557	39,873

Debt/Equity Computations

Year	1	2	3	4	5
Debt Outstanding at year end ($000s)	62,000	59,000	56,000	53,000	50,000
Equity value at year end	19,324	23,330	28,059	33,557	39,873
Debt/Equity	321%	253%	200%	158%	125%
Restrictive Condition	350%	250%	200%	150%	125%
Restriction Breached?	No	Yes	No	Yes	No

Workings:

(W1)

Current operating profit before management service charge

= $60,000,000 – ($12,000,000 + 22,000,000 + 4,000,000) = $22,000,000.

This amount will grow by 8% every year.

(W2)

Year	1	2	3	4	5
Outstanding loan at the start of the year ($000s)	65,000	62,000	59,000	56,000	53,000
Interest ($000s)	5,850	5,580	5,310	5,040	4,770

(c) **Implications**

Based on the calculations in part (b) above, the restrictive covenant is due to be breached in years two and four. In years three and five, it has just been met, and only in year one will Tyche Co be operating well within the conditions of the restrictive covenant. This raises two main issues: firstly, Tyche Co needs to establish how the bank will react to the conditions not being met and will it put Tyche Co's business in jeopardy? Secondly, because the conditions are nearly breached in years three and five, Tyche Co needs to determine the likelihood of the revenues and costs figures being achieved. A very small deviation from the figures may cause the conditions to be breached. Sensitivity analysis and other forms of risk analysis may need to be undertaken and provisions put into place to deal with unexpected breaches in the covenant.

Possible actions

Tyche Co can consider the following possible actions in the years where it is likely that the covenant may be breached:

(i)   The directors may decide to award themselves and the other shareholders lower or no dividends. This would probably need to be negotiated and agreed.

(ii)   The directors may want to ask the venture capitalist to take a higher equity stake for more funds at the outset. Both parties would need to agree to this.

(iii)   Tyche Co may want to try and negotiate less onerous terms with the bank or ask it for more flexibility when applying the restrictive covenant. Given that the restrictive covenant is not likely to be breached by a significant amount, the bank will probably not want to undertake legal proceedings to close Tyche Co and would probably be open to negotiations.

(iv)   Tyche Co may decide to pay off more of the loan each year from its cash reserves, if it has enough funds, in order to reduce the year-end outstanding debt.

(**Note:** Only two actions needed)

(d) **Use of the Black Scholes model in equity valuation**

The basic idea is that, because of limited liability, shareholders can walk away from a company when the debt exceeds the asset value. However, when the assets exceed the debts, those shareholders will keep running the business, in order to collect the surplus.

Therefore, the value of shares can be seen as a call option owned by shareholders – we can use the Black Scholes model to value such an option.

Of course it is therefore critical that we can correctly identify the five variables to input into the Black Scholes model.

For equity valuation, these are as follows:

t = time until debt is redeemed

r = risk free interest rate

s = standard deviation of the assets' value

Pa = fair value of the firm's assets

Pe = amount owed to bank.

Note that the value of Pe will not just be the redemption value of the debt. The amount owed to the bank incorporates all the interest payments as well as the ultimate capital repayment. In fact, the value of Pe to input into the Black Scholes model should be calculated as the theoretical redemption value of an equivalent zero coupon debt.

Use of the Black Scholes model in debt valuation

The Black Scholes model can also be used in debt valuation. The value of a (risky) bond issued by a company can be calculated as the value of an equivalent risk free bond minus the value of a put option over the company's assets.

Therefore, if the value of equity has already been calculated as a call option over the company's assets (as explained above), the value of debt can then be calculated using the put call parity equation.

58 DORIC CO (PILOT 12)

 Question debrief

Key answer tips

Many past exam questions on reconstruction have focussed on the difference from the stakeholders' point of view between liquidation and a given reconstruction scheme. Read the details of the reconstruction scheme carefully and follow the instructions exactly.

(a) Possible benefits of disposing a division through a management buy-out may include:

Management buy-out costs may be less compared with other forms of disposal such as selling individual assets of the division or selling it to a third party.

It may be the quickest method in raising funds compared to the other methods.

There would be less resistance from the managers and employees making the process smoother and easier to accomplish than if both divisions were to be closed down.

It may offer a better price. The current management and employees possibly have the best knowledge of the division and are able to make it successful. Therefore they may be willing to pay more for it.

(**Note:** Credit will be given for alternative relevant benefits)

(b) Close the company

	$m
Sale of all assets	210
Less redundancy and other costs	(54)
Net proceeds from sale of all assets	156
Total liabilities	280

The liability holders will receive $0.56 per $1 owing to them ($156m/$280m). Shareholders will receive nothing.

(c)

	$m
Value of selling fridges division (2/3 × 210)	140
Redundancy and other costs (2/3 ×54)	(36)
Funds available from sale of division	104
Amount of current and non-current liabilities	280
Amount of management buy-out funds needed to pay current and non-current liabilities (280 – 104)	176
Amount of management buy-out funds needed to pay shareholders	60
Investment needed for new venture	50
Total funds needed for management buy-out	286

Estimating value of new company after buy-out

	$m
Sales revenue	170
Costs	(120)
Profits before depreciation	50
** Depreciation ((1/3 ×£100m + $50m) × 10%)	(8.3)
Tax (20%)	(8.3)
** Cash flows before interest payment	33.4

** It is assumed that the depreciation is available on the re-valued non-current assets plus the new investment. It is assumed that no additional investment in non-current assets or working capital is needed, even though cash flows are increasing.

Estimate of value based on perpetuity = $33.4 (1.035)/(0.11 – 0.035) = $461m

This is about 61% in excess of the funds invested in the new venture, and therefore the buy-out is probably beneficial. However, the amounts are all estimates and a small change in some variables like the growth rate or the cost of capital can have a large impact on the value. Also the assumption of cash flow growth in perpetuity may not be accurate. It is therefore advisable to undertake a sensitivity analysis.

(d) Potential buyers will need to be sought through open tender or through an intermediary. Depending upon the nature of the business being sold a single bidder may be sought or preparations made for an auction of the business. Doric Co's suppliers and distributors may be interested, as may be competitors in the same industry. High levels of discretion are required in the search process to protect the value of the business from adverse competitive action. Otherwise, an interested and dominant competitor may open a price war in order to force down prices and hence the value of the fridges division prior to a bid.

Once a potential buyer has been found, access should be given so that they can conduct their own due diligence. Up-to-date accounts should be made available and all legal documentation relating to assets to be transferred made available. Doric Co should undertake its own due diligence to check the ability of the potential purchaser to complete a transaction of this size. Before proceeding, it would be necessary to establish how the purchaser intends to finance the purchase, the timescale involved in their raising the necessary finance and any other issues that may impede a clean sale. Doric Co's legal team will need to assess any contractual issues on the sale, the transfer of employment rights, the transfer of intellectual property and any residual rights and responsibilities to Doric Co.

A sale price will be negotiated which is expected to maximise the return. The negotiation process should be conducted by professional negotiators who have been thoroughly briefed on the terms of the sale, the conditions attached and all of the legal requirements. The consideration for the sale, the deeds for the assignment of assets and terms for the transfer of staff and their accrued pension rights will also all be subject to agreement.

59 NUBO CO (DEC 13)

Key answer tips

Islamic finance came into the syllabus in 2013 and it was tested here for the first time. Make sure that you understand the different Islamic financing methods and how they differ from the more traditional financing options.

(a) **Current and non-current liabilities = $387m + $95m = $482m**

Sale of assets of supermarkets division

Proportion of assets to supermarkets division

Non-current assets = 70% × $550m = $385m; Current assets = 70% × $122m = $85.4m

Sale of assets = $385m × 1.15 + $85.4m × 0.80 = $511.07m

Sale of supermarkets division as a going concern

Profit after tax attributable to the supermarkets division: $166m/2 = $83m

Estimate of value of supermarkets division based on the PE ratio of supermarket industry: $83 × 7 = $581m

Although both options generate sufficient funds to pay for the liabilities, the sale of the supermarkets division as a going concern would generate higher cash flows and the spare cash of $99m [$581m – $482m] can be used by Nubo Co for future investments. This is based on the assumption that the value based on the industries' PE ratios is accurate.

Proportion of assets remaining within Nubo Co 30% ×

($550m + $122m) = $201.6m

Add extra cash generated from the sale of $99m

Maximum debt capacity = $300.6m

Total additional funds available to Nubo Co for new investments = $300.6m + $99m = $399.6m

(b) A demerger would involve splitting Nubo Co into two separate companies which would then operate independently of each other. The equity holders in Nubo Co would continue to have an equity stake in both companies.

Normally demergers are undertaken to ensure that each company's equity values are fair. For example, the value of the aircraft parts production division based on the PE ratio gives a value of $996m (12 × $83m) and the value of the supermarkets division as $581m. If the current company's value is less than the combined values of $1,577m, then a demerger may be beneficial. However, the management and shareholders of the new supermarkets company may not be keen to take over all the debt.

Nubo Co's equity holders may view the demerger more favourably than the sale of the supermarkets division. At present their equity investment is diversified between the aircraft parts production and supermarkets. If the supermarkets division is sold, then the level of their diversification may be affected. With the demerger, since the equity holders will retain an equity stake in both companies, the benefit of diversification is retained.

However, the extra $99m cash generated from the sale will be lost in the case of a demerger. Furthermore, if the new aircraft parts production company can only borrow 100% of its asset value, then its borrowing capacity and additional funds available to it for new investments will be limited to $201.6m instead of $399.6m.

(c) With a Mudaraba contract, the profits which Pilvi Co makes from the joint venture would be shared according to a pre-agreed arrangement when the contract is constructed between Pilvi Co and Ulap Bank. Losses, however, would be borne solely by Ulap Bank as the provider of the finance, although provisions can be made where losses can be written off against future profits. Ulap Bank would not be involved in the executive decision-making process. In effect, Ulap Bank's role in the relationship would be similar to an equity holder, holding a small number of shares in a large organisation.

With a Musharaka contract, the profits which Pilvi Co makes from the joint venture would still be shared according to a pre-agreed arrangement similar to a Mudaraba contract, but losses would also be shared according to the capital or other assets and services contributed by both the parties involved in the arrangement. Therefore a value could be put to the contribution-in-kind made by Pilvi Co and any losses would be shared by Ulap Bank and Pilvi Co accordingly. Within a Musharaka contract, Ulap Bank can also take the role of an active partner and participate in the executive decision-making process. In effect, the role adopted by Ulap Bank would be similar to that of a venture capitalist.

With the Mudaraba contract, Pilvi Co would essentially be an agent to Ulap Bank, and many of the agency issues facing corporations would apply to the arrangement, where Pilvi Co can maximise its own benefit at the expense of Ulap Bank. Pilvi Co may also have a propensity to undertake excessive risk because it is essentially holding a long call option with an unlimited upside and a limited downside.

Ulap Bank may prefer the Musharaka contract in this case, because it may be of the opinion that it needs to be involved with the project and monitor performance closely due to the inherent risk and uncertainty of the venture, and also to ensure that the revenues, expenditure and time schedules are maintained within initially agreed parameters. In this way, it may be able to monitor and control agency related issues more effectively and control Pilvi Co's risky actions and decisions. Being closely involved with the venture would change both Pilvi Co's and Ulap Bank's roles and make them more like stakeholders rather than principals and agents, with a more equitable distribution of power between the two parties.

Nubo Co's concerns would mainly revolve around whether it can work with Ulap Bank and the extra time and cost which would need to be incurred before the joint venture can start. If Pilvi Co had not approached Ulap Bank for funding, the relationship between Nubo Co and Pilvi Co would be less complex within the joint venture. Although difficulties may arise about percentage ownership and profit sharing, these may be resolved through negotiation and having tight specific contracts. The day-to-day running, management and decision-making process could be resolved through negotiation and consensus. Therefore having a third party involved in all aspects of the joint venture complicates matters.

Nubo Co may feel that it was not properly consulted about the arrangements between Pilvi Co and Ulap Bank, and Pilvi Co would need to discuss the involvement of Ulap Bank with Nubo Co and gets its agreement prior to formalising any arrangements. This is to ensure a high level of trust continues to exist between the parties, otherwise the venture may fail.

Nubo Co may want clear agreements on ownership and profit-sharing. They would want to ensure that the contract clearly distinguishes them as not being part of the Musharaka arrangement which exists between Pilvi Co and Ulap Bank. Hence negotiation and construction of the contracts may need more time and may become more expensive.

Nubo Co may have felt that it could work with Pilvi Co on a day-to-day basis and could resolve tough decisions in a reasonable manner. It may not feel the same about Ulap Bank initially. Clear parameters would need to be set up on how executive decision making will be conducted by the three parties. Therefore, the integration process of bringing a third partner into the joint venture needs to be handled with care and may take time and cost more money.

The above issues would indicate that the relationship between the three parties is closer to that of stakeholders, with different levels of power and influence, at different times, as opposed to a principal–agent relationship. This would create an environment which would need ongoing negotiation and a need for consensus, which may make the joint venture hard work. Additionally, it would possibly be more difficult and time consuming to accomplish the aims of the joint venture.

(Note: Credit will be given for alternative relevant comments and suggestions for parts (b) and (c) of the question)

Marking scheme		
		Marks
(a) Sale of supermarkets division's assets		1
Sale of supermarkets division as going concern		1
Advice		2
Extra cash after liabilities are paid		1
Maximum debt which can be borrowed		1
Additional funds available to Nubo Co		1
	Maximum	7
(b) 1–2 marks per relevant point	**Maximum**	6
(c) Discussion of why Ulap Bank might prefer a Musharaka contract		6–7
Discussion of the key concerns of the joint venture relationship		5–6
	Maximum	12
Total		**25**

60 BENTO CO (JUN 15)

Key answer tips

Achievement of a covenant on a management buyout has been tested several times in recent years.

Make sure you read the specific terms of the covenant carefully before presenting your answer.

(a) A management buy-out (MBO) involves the purchase of a business by the management team running that business. Hence, an MBO of Okazu Co would involve the takeover of that company from Bento Co by Okazu Co's current management team. However, a management buy-in (MBI) involves purchasing a business by a management team brought in from outside the business.

The benefits of a MBO relative to a MBI to Okazu Co are that the existing management is likely to have detailed knowledge of the business and its operations. Therefore they will not need to learn about the business and its operations in a way which a new external management team may need to. It is also possible that a MBO will cause less disruption and resistance from the employees when compared to a MBI. If Bento Co wants to continue doing business with the new company after it has been disposed of, it may find it easier to work with the management team which it is more familiar with.

The internal management team may be more focused and have better knowledge of where costs can be reduced and sales revenue increased, in order to increase the overall value of the company.

The drawbacks of a MBO relative to a MBI to Okazu Co may be that the existing management may lack new ideas to rejuvenate the business. A new management team, through their skills and experience acquired elsewhere, may bring fresh ideas into the business. It may be that the external management team already has the requisite level of finance in place to move quickly and more decisively, whereas the existing management team may not have the financial arrangements in place yet. It is also possible that the management of Bento Co and Okazu Co have had disagreements in the past and the two teams may not be able to work together in the future if they need to. It may be that a MBI is the only way forward for Okazu Co to succeed in the future.

(b) Annuity (8%, 4 years) = 3.312

Annuity payable per year on loan = $30,000,000/3.312 = $9,057,971

Interest payable on convertible loan, per year = $20,000,000 × 6% = $1,200,000

Annual interest on 8% bond

(All amounts in $000s)

Year end	1	2	3	4
Opening loan balance	30,000	23,342	16,151	8,385
Interest at 8%	2,400	1,867	1,292	671
Annuity	(9,058)	(9,058)	(9,058)	(9,058)
Closing loan balance	23,342	16,151	8,385	(2)*

*The loan outstanding in year 4 should be zero. The small negative figure is due to rounding.

Estimate of profit and retained earnings after MBO

(All amounts in $000s)

Year end	1	2	3	4
Operating profit	13,542	15,032	16,686	18,521
Finance costs	3,600	3,067	2,492	1,871
Profit before tax	9,942	11,965	14,194	16,650
Taxation	1,988	2,393	2,839	3,330
Profit for the year	7,954	9,572	11,355	13,320
Dividends	1,989	2,393	2,839	3,330
Retained earnings	5,965	7,179	8,516	9,990

Estimate of gearing

(All amounts in $000s)

Year end	1	2	3	4
Book value of equity	15,965*	23,144	31,660	41,650
Book value of debt	43,342	36,151	28,385	20,000
Gearing	73%	61%	47%	32%
Covenant	75%	60%	50%	40%
Covenant breached?	No	Yes	No	No

*The book value of equity consists of the sum of the 5,000,000 equity shares which Dofu Co and Okazu Co's senior management will each invest in the new company (total 10,000,000), issued at their nominal value of $1 each, and the retained earnings from year 1. In subsequent years the book value of equity is increased by the retained earnings from that year.

The gearing covenant is forecast to be breached in the second year only, and by a marginal amount. It is forecast to be met in all the other years. It is unlikely that Dofu Co will be too concerned about the covenant breach.

(c)   **Net asset valuation**

Based on the net asset valuation method, the value of the new company is approximately: $1.3 \times \$40,800,000 + \$12,300,000 - \$7,900,000$ approx. $= \$57,440,000$

Dividend valuation model

Year	Dividend	DF (12%)	PV
	($000s)		($000s)
1	1,989	0.893	1,776
2	2,393	0.797	1,907
3	2,839	0.712	2,021
4	3,330	0.636	2,118
Total			7,822

Annual dividend growth rate, years 1 to 4 $= (3,330/1,989)^{1/3} - 1 = 18.7\%$

Annual dividend growth rate after year 4 $= 7.5\%$ [40% × 18.7%]

Value of dividends after year 4 $= (\$3,330,000 \times 1.075)/(0.12 - 0.075) \times 0.636 = \$50,594,000$ approximately

Based on the dividend valuation model, the value of new company is approximately:

$\$7,822,000 + \$50,594,000 = \$58,416,000$

The $60 million asked for by Bento Co is higher than the current value of the new company's net assets and the value of the company based on the present value of future dividends based on the dividend valuation model. Although the future potential of the company represented by the dividend valuation model, rather than the current value of the assets, is probably a better estimate of the potential of the company, the price of $60 million seems excessive.

Nevertheless, both the management team and Dofu Co are expected to receive substantial dividends during the first four years and Dofu Co's 8% bond loan will be repaid within four years.

Furthermore, the dividend valuation model can produce a large variation in results if the model's variables are changed by even a small amount. Therefore, the basis for estimating the variables should be examined carefully to judge their reasonableness, and sensitivity analysis applied to the model to demonstrate the impact of the changes in the variables. The value of the future potential of the new company should also be estimated using alternative valuation methods including free cash flows and price-earnings methods.

It is therefore recommended that the MBO should not be rejected at the outset but should be considered further. It is also recommended that the management team and Dofu Co try to negotiate the sale price with Bento Co.

(**Note:** Credit will be given for alternative, relevant discussion for parts (a) and (c).)

	Marking scheme		Marks
(a)	Distinguishing between an MBI and MBO		1–2
	Discussing the relative benefits and drawbacks between the two		3–4
		Maximum	**5**
(b)	Amount of annual annuity of 8% bond		1
	Annual split between interest and capital repayment of 8% bond		2
	Operating profit for first four years		1
	Finance costs		2
	Tax payable for the first four years		1
	Dividend payable for the first four years		1
	Book values of debt and of equity in years 1 to 4		2
	Gearing levels and concluding comment		2
		Maximum	**12**
(c)	Company value based on net asset valuation method		1
	Company value based on the dividend valuation method		3
	Discussion (1 to 2 marks per point)		4
		Maximum	**8**
Total			**25**

61 FLUFFTORT CO (SEP/DEC 15)

Key answer tips

Notice that the discussion of whether the scheme will be acceptable to the various stakeholders accounts for more than 50% of the marks for this question.

It is therefore critical that you don't spend too long on the numerical forecasts in part (a).

(a) (i) **SOFP if Gupfe VC shares are purchased by Flufftort Co and cancelled.**

	$m
Assets	
Non-current assets	69
Current assets excluding cash	18
Cash	–
Total assets	**87**

	$m
Equity and liabilities	
Share capital	40
Retained earnings	5
	───
Total equity	45
	───
Long-term liabilities	
Bank loan	30
Loan note	5
	───
Total long-term liabilities	35
Current liabilities	7
	───
Total liabilities	42
	───
Total equity and liabilities	87
	───

(ii)   **SOFP if full refinancing takes place**

	$m
Assets	
Non-current assets	125
Current assets excluding cash	42
Cash (balancing figure)	5
	───
Total assets	172
	───
Equity and liabilities	
Share capital	90
Retained earnings	5
	───
Total equity	95
	───
Long-term liabilities	
Bank loan	65
Loan note	–
	───
Total long-term liabilities	65
Current liabilities	12
	───
Total liabilities	77
	───
Total equity and liabilities	172
	───

(iii) Projected SOPL

	20X7	20X8
	$m	$m
Operating profit	20.0	25.0
Finance cost	(6.5)	(6.5)
Profit before tax	13.5	18.5
Taxation 20%	(2.7)	(3.7)
Profit after tax	10. 8	14.8
Dividends	–	–
Retained earnings	10.8	14.8

(b) Current situation

Initial product developments have not generated the revenues required to sustain growth. The new Easicushion chair appears to offer Flufftort Co much better prospects of commercial success. At present, however, Flufftort Co does not have the resources to make the investment required.

Purchase of Gupte VC's shares

In the worst case scenario, Gupte VC will demand repayment of its investment in a year's time. The calculations in (a) show the financial position in a year's time, assuming that there is no net investment in non-current assets or working capital, the purchase of shares is financed solely out of cash reserves and the shares are cancelled. Repayment by this method would mean that the limits set out in the covenant would be breached (45/35 = 1.29) and the bank could demand immediate repayment of the loan.

The directors can avoid this by buying some of Gupte VC's shares themselves, but this represents money which is not being put into the business. In addition, the amount of shares which the directors would have to purchase would be greater if results, and therefore reserves, were worse than expected.

Financing the investment

The calculations in (a) show that the cash flows associated with the refinancing would be enough to finance the initial investment. The ratio of equity to non-current liabilities after the refinancing would be 1.46 (95/65), in line with the current limits in the bank's covenant. However, financing for the subsequent investment required would have to come from surplus cash flows.

Shareholdings

The disposition of shareholdings will change as follows:

	Current shareholdings		Shareholdings after refinancing	
	Number in million	%	Number in million	%
Directors	27.5	55.0	42.5	47.2
Other family members	12.5	25.0	12.5	13.9
Gupte VC	10.0	20.0	30.0	33.3
Loan note holder	–	–	5.0	5.6
	50.0	100.0	90.0	100.0

Gupte VC's percentage shareholding will rise from 20% to 33.3%, enough possibly to give it extra rights over the company. The directors' percentage shareholding will fall from 55% to 47.2%, which means that collectively they no longer have control of the company. The percentage of shares held by family members who are not directors falls from 25% to around 19.5%, taking into account the conversion of the loan note. This will mean, however, that the directors can still maintain control if they can obtain the support of some of the rest of the family.

Position of finance providers

The refinancing has been agreed by the chief executive and finance director. At present, it is not clear what the views of the other directors are, or whether the $15 million contributed by directors will be raised from them in proportion to their current shareholdings. Some of the directors may not be able to, or wish to, make a significant additional investment in the company. On the other hand, if they do not, their shareholdings, and perhaps their influence within the company, will diminish. This may be a greater concern than the board collectively losing control over the company, since it may be unlikely that the other shareholders will combine to outvote the board.

The other family shareholders have not been actively involved in Flufftort Co's management out of choice, so a reduction in their percentage shareholdings may not be an issue for them. They may have welcomed the recent dividend payment as generating a return on their investment. However, as they appear to have invested for the longer term, the new investment appears to offer much better prospects in the form of a capital gain on listing or buy-out than an uncertain flow of dividends. The new investment appears only to have an upside for them in the sense that they are not being asked to contribute any extra funding towards it.

Rajiv Patel is unlikely to be happy with the proposed scheme. He is exchanging a guaranteed flow of income for an uncertain flow of future dividends sometime after 20X8. On the other hand, his investment may be jeopardised by the realisation of the worst case scenario, since his debt is subordinated to the bank's debt.

The most important issue from Gupte VC's viewpoint is whether the extra investment required is likely to yield a better outcome than return of its initial investment in a year's time. The plan that no dividends would be paid until after 20X8 is a disadvantage. On the other hand, the additional investment seems to offer the only prospect of realising a substantial gain either by Flufftort Co being listed or sold.

The arrangement will mean that Gupte VC may be able to exercise greater influence over Flufftort Co, which may provide it with a greater sense of reassurance about how Flufftort Co is being run. The fact that Gupte VC has a director on Flufftort Co's board should also give it a clear idea of how successful the investment is likely to be.

The bank will be concerned about the possibility of Flufftort Co breaching the covenant limits and may be concerned whether Flufftort Co is ultimately able to repay the full amount without jeopardising its existence. The bank will be concerned if Flufftort Co tries to replace loan finance with overdraft finance. The refinancing provides reassurance to the bank about gearing levels and a higher rate of interest. The bank will also be pleased that the level of interest cover under the refinancing is higher and increasing (from 2.0 in 20X6 to 3.1 in 20X7 and 3.8 in 20X8). However, it will be concerned about how Flufftort Co finances the additional investment required if cash flows from the new investment are lower than expected. In those circumstances Flufftort Co may seek to draw on its overdraft facility.

Conclusion

The key players in the refinancing are Gupte VC, the bank and the directors other than the chief executive and the finance director. If they can be persuaded, then the scheme has a good chance of being successful. However, Rajiv Patel could well raise objections. He may be pacified if he retains the loan note. This would marginally breach the current covenant limit (90/70 = 1.29), although the bank may be willing to overlook the breach as it is forecast to be temporary. Alternatively, the refinancing would mean that Flufftort Co just had enough spare cash initially to redeem the loan note, although it would be more dependent on cash surpluses after the refinancing to fund the additional investment required.

		Marking scheme		Marks
(a)	(i)	SOFP if shares purchased and cancelled		
		Cash and other assets		2
		Equity		1
		Liabilities		1
			Maximum	4
	(ii)	SOFP if full refinancing takes place		
		Cash and other assets		2
		Equity		1
		Liabilities		1
			Maximum	4
	(iii)	20X7 forecast		2
		20X8 forecast		2
			Maximum	4
(b)		Up to 2 marks for each well discussed point	Maximum	13
Total				25

62   STAPLE GROUP (MAR/JUN 16)

Key answer tips

In all corporate reconstruction questions, it is very important to read the company's plans carefully, and to follow them specifically when presenting the answer.

There were plenty of easy discussion marks in both parts (a) and (b) for students with a good exam technique.

(a)   **Staple Local**

Net assets valuation = 15/18 × $66.6m = $55.5m.

It is assumed that the titles in this division are equal in size.

The division's pre-tax profits are $4.5m and post-tax cash flows $0.3m, with losses forecast for the next year. Therefore any valuation based on current or future expected earnings is likely to be lower than the net assets valuation.

Benefits of selling Staple Local

The local newspapers seem to have the poorest prospects of any part of the group. Further investment may not make a big difference, if the market for local newspapers is in long-term decline.

The offer from Postway Co gives Staple Group the chance to gain cash immediately and to dispose of the papers. The alternative of selling the titles off piecemeal is an uncertain strategy, both in terms of the timescale required and the amounts which can be realised for individual titles. It is very likely that the titles with the best prospects would be sold first, leaving Staple Group with a remaining portfolio which is of very little value.

Drawbacks of selling Staple Local

The offer is not much more than a net asset valuation of the titles. The amount of cash from the sale to Postway Co will be insufficient for the level of investment required in the Daily Staple.

The digital platforms which will be developed for the Daily Staple could also be used to boost the local papers. Staff on the local titles could have an important role to play in providing content for the platforms.

Loss of the local titles may mean loss of economies of size. In particular, printing arrangements may be more economic if both national and local titles are printed at the same locations.

Staple View

Free cash flows to equity = $53.5m – $12.5m – $6.2m = $34.8m

Free cash flow valuation to equity = $34.8m (1.04)/(0.12 – 0.04) = $452.4m

The assumption of constant growth is most important in this valuation. It is possibly fairly conservative, but just as faster growth could be achieved by gaining the rights to broadcast more sporting events, results may be threatened if Staple View loses any of the rights which it currently has.

Benefits of selling Staple View

Present circumstances may be favourable for selling the television channels, given their current profitability. Staple Group may be able to obtain a better offer from a competitor than in the future, given recent acquisition activity in this sector.

Selling Staple View will certainly generate more cash than selling either of the smaller divisions. This will allow investment not only in the Daily Staple, but also investment in the other divisions, and possibly targeted strategic acquisitions.

Drawbacks of selling Staple View

The television channels have become a very important part of the Staple Group. Investors may believe that the group should be focusing on further investment in this division rather than investing in the Daily Staple, which may be in decline.

Selling the television channels removes an important opportunity for cross-selling. Newspaper coverage can be used to publicise important programmes on the television channels and the television channels can be used for advertising the newspaper.

Staple View is a bigger part of the group than the other two divisions and therefore selling it is likely to mean a bigger reduction in the group's borrowing capacity.

Staple Investor

The valuation made by the finance director is questionable as it is based on one year's profits, which may not be sustainable. There is no information about how the additional earnings have been calculated, whether the finance director has used a widely-accepted method of valuation or just used a best estimate. If a premium for additional earnings is justified, there is also no information about whether the benefit from staff's expertise and experience is assumed to be perpetual or just to last for a certain number of years.

Benefits of selling Staple Investor

This division appears to have great potential. Staple Group will be able to sell this division from a position of strength, rather than it being seen as a forced sale like selling the Staple Local division might be.

The division is in a specialist sector which is separate from the other areas in which Staple Group operates. It is not an integral part of the group in terms of the directors' current core strategy.

Drawbacks of selling Staple Investor

The division currently has the highest profit margin at 19.7% compared with Staple National 12.5%, Staple Local 3.0% and Staple View 14.8%. It seems likely to continue to deliver good results over the next few years. Investors may feel that it is the part of the group which offers the safest prospect of satisfactory returns.

Investors may be happy with the structure of the group as it is, as it offers them some diversification. Selling the Staple Investor division and focusing more on the newspaper parts of the group may result in investors seeking diversification by selling some of the shareholding in Staple Group and investing elsewhere.

Although Staple Group's management may believe that the valuation gives a good indication of the division's true value, they may not be able to sell the division for this amount now. If the division remains within the group, they may achieve a higher price in a few years' time. Even if Staple Investor could be sold for the $118.5 million valuation, this is less than the $150 million required for the planned investment.

Conclusion

Selling the Staple View division offers the directors the best chance to obtain the funds they require for their preferred strategy of investment in the Daily Staple. However, the directors are not considering the possibility of selling the Daily Staple, perhaps in conjunction with selling the local newspapers as well. Although this could be seen as selling off the part of the group which has previously been essential to its success, it would allow Staple Group to raise the funds for further investment in the television channels and the Staple Investor division. It could allow the directors to focus on the parts of the group which have been the most successful recently and offer the best prospects for future success.

(b) **Stakeholder conflicts**

If Staple Group takes a simple view of the role of stakeholders, it will prioritise the interest of shareholders over other stakeholders, particularly employees here, and take whatever actions are required to maximise profitability. However, in Staple Group's position, there may be a complication because of the differing requirements of shareholders. Some may want high short-term profits and dividends, which may imply significant cost cutting in under-performing divisions. Other shareholders may wish to see profits maximised over the long term and may worry that short-term cost cutting may result in a reduction of investment and adversely affect staff performance at an important time.

Transformational change of the newspaper business is likely to require the co-operation of at least some current employees. Inevitably redundancy will create uncertainty and perhaps prompt some staff to leave voluntarily. Staple Group's management may want to identify some key current employees who can lead the change and try to retain them.

Also the policy of making employees who have not been with the group very long redundant is likely to make it difficult to recruit good new employees. The group will probably create new roles as a result of its digital investment, but people may be unwilling to join the group if it has a reputation for bad faith and not fulfilling promises to develop its staff.

Ethical issues

The significance of what the firm's annual report says about its treatment of employees may depend on how specific it is. A promise to treat employees fairly is rather vague and may not carry much weight, although it broadly commits the firm to the ethical principle of objectivity. If, however, the policy makes more specific statements about engaging with employees and goes in the statement beyond what is required by law, then Staple Group is arguably showing a lack of honesty if it does not fulfil the commitments it has made.

The suggestion that managers should ensure that employees who are perceived to be 'troublemakers' should be first to be chosen for redundancy is dubious ethically. If managers do this, then they may be breaking the law, and would certainly be acting with a lack of honesty and transparency.

Marking scheme

		Marks
(a)	Sale of Staple Local	
	Calculations/comments on figures	2
	Discussion of benefits/drawbacks	3–4
	Sale of Staple View	
	Calculations/comments on figures	3
	Discussion of benefits/drawbacks	3–4
	Sale of Staple Investor	
	Comments on figures	2
	Discussion of benefits/drawbacks	3–4
	Other points/conclusion	2–3
		──
	Maximum	**19**
		──
(b)	Discussion of importance of different stakeholders and possible conflicts	3–4
	Discussion of other ethical issues	2–3
		──
	Maximum	**6**
		──
Total		**25**
		──

63 EVIEW CINEMAS CO (SEP/DEC 17)

Key answer tips

This question very cleverly integrated lots of separate bits of the syllabus. The free cash flow business valuation was very straight forward, but then the question headed off into an assessment of the impact on financial position, earnings and WACC if the business unit was sold.

The downside of this is that there was an awful lot to do in the time available, but the upside is that a well prepared student with a good exam technique has a wide choice of topics to attempt in order to grab enough marks to ensure a pass.

To be sure of a pass on this question, it would have been vital to leave enough time to attempt the discursive part of the question too, to comment on the figures obtained.

(a) **Proceeds from sales of EV clubs**

Year (all figures $m)	1	2	3	4
Free cash flows	390	419	455	490
Discount factors (12%)	0.893	0.797	0.712	0.636
	──	──	──	──
Present values	348	334	324	312
	──	──	──	──

Present value   1,318

Present value in Year 5 onwards = $490m × 1.052/ (0.12 − 0.052) × 0.636 = $4,821m

Total present value = $1,318m + $4,821m = $6,139m

Desired sales proceeds (25% premium) = $6,139m × 1.25 = $7,674m

Impact on statement of financial position ($m)

Profit on sale = $7,674m – $3,790m = $3,884m

Current assets adjustment = $2,347m + $7,674m – ($2,166m × 1.5) = $6,772m

PPE adjustment = $6,772m – $3,200m = $3,572m

$m	Original	Sale proceeds	Adjust-ments	Final
Non-current assets	15,621	(3,790)	3,572	15,403
Current assets	2,347	7,674	(6,772)	3,249
Total assets	17,968			18,652

Equity and liabilities

Called up share capital	1,000			1,000
Retained earnings	7,917	3,884		11,801
Total equity	8,917			12,801
Non-current liabilities				
10% loan notes	3,200		(3,200)	0
Other loan notes	2,700			2,700
Bank loans	985			985
Current liabilities	2,166			2,166
Total equity and liabilities	17,968			18,652

Impact on EPS ($m)

	Current	Revised
Predicted post-tax profits	1,135	1,135
Less: profits from EV clubs		(454)
Add: interest saved, net of tax ($3,200m × 10% × (1 – 0.2))		256
Add: return on additional non-current assets ($3,572m × 12% × (1 – 0.2))		343
Add: return on additional current assets ($902m × 7% × (1 – 0.2))		51
Adjusted profits	1,135	1,331
Number of shares	1,000m	1,000m
Adjusted EPS	$1.135	$1.331

Impact on WACC

Equity beta

Ve = $15,750m × 1.1 = $17,325m

Vd = ($2,700 × 0.93) + $985m = $3,496m

βe = 0.952 ((17,325 + 3,496 (1 − 0.2))/17,325 = 1.106

Revised cost of equity

ke = 4 + (10 − 4)1.106 = 10.64%

Revised WACC

WACC = 10.64 (17,325/ (17,325 + 3,496)) + 8 (1 − 0.2) (3,496/ (17,325 + 3,496)) = 9.93%

(b)   Shareholders would appear to have grounds for questioning the sale of the EV clubs. It would mean that Eview Cinemas Co was no longer diversified into two sectors. Although shareholders can achieve diversification themselves in theory, in practice transaction costs and other issues may mean they do not want to adjust their portfolio.

The increase in gym membership brought about by the forthcoming sports festival could justify the predicted increases in free cash flows made in the forecasts. Although increased earnings per share are forecast once the EV clubs are sold, these are dependent on Eview Cinemas Co achieving the sales price which it desires for the EV clubs and the predicted returns being achieved on the remaining assets.

The proposed expansion of multiscreen cinemas may be a worthwhile opportunity, but the level of demand for big cinema complexes may be doubtful and there may also be practical problems like negotiating change of use. In Year 1 the EV clubs would be forecast to make a post-tax return on assets of (454/3,790) = 12.0% compared with 9.6% (12% × 0.8) on the additional investment in the cinemas.

Investors may also wonder about the motives of Eview Cinemas Co's board. Selling the EV clubs offers the board a convenient way of resolving the conflict with the management team of the EV clubs and investors may feel that the board is trying to take an easy path by focusing on what they are comfortable with managing.

There may be arguments in favour of the sale, however. The lower WACC will be brought about by a fall in the cost of equity as well as the fall in the cost of debt. A reduction in the complexity of the business may result in a reduction in central management costs.

Eview Cinemas Co may also be selling at a time when the EV clubs chain is at its most attractive as a business, in the period before the sports festival. The premium directors are hoping to obtain (on top of a valuation based on free cash flow figures which may be optimistic) suggest that they may be trying to realise maximum value while they can.

TREASURY AND ADVANCED RISK MANAGEMENT TECHNIQUES

64 FAOILEAN CO (JUN 14)

Key answer tips

Option pricing has often been tested in the exam, but this question was unusual in that it covered just the discursive aspects and no calculations.

This emphasises how important it is to be able to understand the topics in detail at this level, rather than just be able to manipulate the numbers.

Having said that, the new AFM syllabus states that in future "there will not be any wholly narrative questions" i.e. the topics covered here may well be covered, but in questions that contain a mixture of calculation and narrative parts.

(a)   With conventional investment decisions, it is assumed that once a decision is made, it has to be taken immediately and carried to its conclusion. These decisions are normally made through conventional assessments using methods such as net present value. Assessing projects through option pricing may aid the investment decision making process.

Where there is uncertainty with regard to the investment decision and where a company has flexibility in its decision making, valuing projects using options can be particularly useful. For example, situations may exist where a company does not have to make a decision on a now-or-never basis, or where it can abandon a decision, which has been made, at some future point, or where it has an opportunity for further expansion as a result of the original decision. In such situations, using option pricing formulae, which incorporate the uncertainty surrounding a project and the time before a decision has to be made, can determine a value attached to this flexibility. This value can be added to the conventional net present value computation to give a more accurate assessment of the project's value.

In the situation which Faoilean Co is considering, the initial exploration rights may give it the opportunity to delay the decision of whether to undertake the extraction of oil and gas to a later date. In that time, using previous knowledge and experience, it can estimate the quantity of oil and gas which is present more accurately. It can also use its knowledge to assess the variability of the likely quantity. Faoilean Co may be able to negotiate a longer time scale with the government of Ireland for undertaking the initial exploration, before it needs to make a final decision on whether and how much to extract.

Furthermore, Faoilean Co can explore the possibilities of it exiting the extraction project, once started, if it is proving not to be beneficial, or if world prices of oil and gas have moved against it. It could, for example, negotiate a get-out clause which gives it the right to sell the project back to the government at a later date at a pre-agreed price. Alternatively, it could build facilities in such a way that it can redeploy them to other activities, or scale the production up or down more easily and at less cost. These options give the company the opportunity to step out of a project at a future date, if uncertainties today become negative outcomes in the future.

Finally, Faoilean Co can explore whether or not applying for the rights to undertake this exploration project could give it priority in terms of future projects, perhaps due to the new knowledge or technologies it builds during the current project. These opportunities would allow it to gain competitive advantage over rivals, which, in turn, could provide it with greater opportunities in the future, but which are uncertain at present.

Faoilean Co can incorporate these uncertainties and the time before the various decisions need to be made into the option formulae to determine the additional value of the project, on top of the initial net present value calculation.

The option price formula used with investment decisions is based on the Black-Scholes Option Pricing (BSOP) model. The BSOP model makes a number of assumptions as follows:

- The underlying asset operates in perfect markets and therefore the movement of market prices cannot be predicted.

- The BSOP model uses the risk-free rate of interest. It is assumed that this is known and remains constant, which may not be the case where the time it takes for the option to expire may be long.

- The BSOP model assumes that volatility can be assessed and stays constant throughout the life of the project; again with long-term projects these assumptions may not be valid.

- The BSOP model assumes that the underlying asset can be traded freely. This is probably not accurate where the underlying asset is an investment project.

These assumptions mean that the value based around the BSOP model is indicative and not definitive.

(**Note:** Credit will be given for alternative relevant comments.)

(b) Equity can be regarded as purchasing a call option by the equity holders on the value of a company, because they will possess a residual claim on the assets of the company. In this case, the face value of debt is equivalent to the exercise price, and the repayment term of debt as the time to expiry of the option.

If at expiry, the value of the company is greater than the face value of debt, then the option is in-the-money, otherwise if the value of the firm is less than the face value of debt, then the option is out-of-money and equity is worthless.

For example, say V is the market value of the assets in a company, E is the market value of equity, and F is the face value of debt, then...

If at expiry $V > F$ (option is in-the-money), then the option has intrinsic value to the equity holders and $E = V - F$.

Otherwise if $F > V$ (option is out-of-money), then the option has no intrinsic value and no value for the equity holders, and $E = 0$.

Prior to expiry of the debt, the call option (value to holders of equity) will also have a time value attached to it. The BSOP model can be used to assess the value of the option to the equity holders, the value of equity, which can consist of both time value and intrinsic value if the option is in-the-money, or just time value if the option is out-of-money.

Within the BSOP model, $N(d_1)$, the delta value, shows how the value of equity changes when the value of the company's assets change. $N(d_2)$ depicts the probability that the call option will be in-the-money (i.e. have intrinsic value for the equity holders).

Debt can be regarded as the debt holders writing a put option on the company's assets, where the premium is the receipt of interest when it falls due and the capital redemption. If $N(d_2)$ depicts the probability that the call option is in-the-money, then $1 - N(d_2)$ depicts the probability of default.

Therefore the BSOP model and options are useful in determining the value of equity and default risk.

Option pricing can be used to explain why companies facing severe financial distress can still have positive equity values. A company facing severe financial distress would presumably be one where the equity holders' call option is well out-of-money and therefore has no intrinsic value. However, as long as the debt on the option is not at expiry, then that call option will still have a time value attached to it. Therefore, the positive equity value reflects the time value of the option, even where the option is out-of-money, and this will diminish as the debt comes closer to expiry. The time value indicates that even though the option is currently out-of-money, there is a possibility that due to the volatility of asset values, by the time the debt reaches maturity, the company will no longer face financial distress and will be able to meet its debt obligations.

(**Note:** Credit will be given for alternative relevant comments.)

(c)   According to the BSOP model, the value of an option is dependent on five variables: the value of the underlying asset, the exercise price, the risk-free rate of interest, the implied volatility of the underlying asset, and the time to expiry of the option. These five variables are input into the BSOP formula, in order to compute the value of a call option (the value of an equivalent put option can be computed by the BSOP model and put-call parity relationship). The different risk factors determine the impact on the option value of the changes in the five variables.

The 'vega' determines the sensitivity of an option's value to a change in the implied volatility of the underlying asset. Implied volatility is what the market is implying the volatility of the underlying asset will be in the future, based on the price changes in an option. The option price may change independently of whether or not the underlying asset's value changes, due to new information being presented to the markets. Implied volatility is the result of this independent movement in the option's value, and this determines the 'vega'. The 'vega' only impacts the time value of an option and as the 'vega' increases, so will the value of the option.

(**Note:** Credit will be given for alternative relevant comments.)

Marking scheme		Marks
(a) Discussion of the idea of using options in making the project investment decision		7–8
Explanation of the assumptions		3–4
	Maximum	**11**
(b) Discussion of using options to value equity		4–5
Discussion of using options to assess default risk		2–3
Discussion of financial distress and time value of an option		2–3
	Maximum	**9**
(c) Explanation of why option values are determined by different risk factors		2–3
Explanation of what determines 'vega'		2–3
	Maximum	**5**
Total		**25**

65 LEVANTE CO (DEC 11 ADAPTED)

Key answer tips

This question (from the December 2011 exam) tested the contents of an article written by the examiner and published in the September 2011 issue of Student Accountant magazine. It is common for the examiner to test topics covered in recent articles, so keep an eye out for any new articles published.

(a) Spot yield rates applicable to Levante Co (based on A credit rating)

1 year	3.85%
2 year	4.46%
3 year	5.07%
4 year	5.80%
5 year	6.12%

Bond value based on A rating =

$\$4 \times 1.0385^{-1} + \$4 \times 1.0446^{-2} + \$104 \times 1.0507^{-3} = \$97.18$ per $100

Current price based on AA rating = $98.71

Fall in value = (97.18 – 98.71)/98.71 × 100% = 1.55%

(b) Spot rates applicable to Levante Co (based on A credit rating) [from above]

1 year	3.85%
2 year	4.46%
3 year	5.07%
4 year	5.80%
5 year	6.12%

(i) Value of 5% coupon bond

$\$5 \times 1.0385^{-1} + \$5 \times 1.0446^{-2} + \$5 \times 1.0507^{-3} + \$5 \times 1.0580^{-4} + \$105 \times 1.0612^{-5}$
$= \$95.72$

Hence the bond will need to be issued at a discount if only a 5% coupon is offered.

(ii) New coupon rate for bond valued at $100 by the markets

Since the 5% coupon bond is only valued at $95.72, a higher coupon needs to be offered. This coupon amount can be calculated by finding the yield to maturity of the 5% coupon bond discounted at the above yield curve. This yield to maturity will be the coupon amount for the new bond such that its face value will be $100.

Therefore, if the yield to maturity is denoted by YTM then

$\$5 \times (1 + YTM)^{-1} + \$5 \times (1 + YTM)^{-2} + \$5 \times (1 + YTM)^{-3} + \$5 \times (1 + YTM)^{-4} + \$105 \times (1 + YTM)^{-5} = \$95.72$

Solve by trial and error, assume YTM is 5.5%. This gives the bond value as $97.86.

Assume YTM is 6%; this gives the bond value as $95.78, which is close enough to $95.72

$\$5 \times (1.06)^{-1} + \$5 \times (1.06)^{-2} + \$5 \times (1.06)^{-3} + \$5 \times (1.06)^{-4} + \$105 \times (1.06)^{-5} = \$95.78$

Hence if the coupon payment is 6% or $6 per $100 bond unit then the bond market value will equal the par value at $100.

$\$6 \times (1.06)^{-1} + \$6 \times (1.06)^{-2} + \$6 \times (1.06)^{-3} + \$6 \times (1.06)^{-4} + \$106 \times (1.06)^{-5} = \$100$

Alternatively:

Take R as the coupon rate, such that:

$(R \times 1.0385^{-1}) + (R \times 1.0446^{-2}) + (R \times 1.0507^{-3}) + (R \times 1.0580^{-4}) + (R \times 1.0612^{-5}) + (100 \times 1.0612 {-5}) = \$100$

4.2826R + 74.30 = $100

R = 6% or $6 per $100

Advice:

If only a 5% coupon is offered, the bonds will have to be issued at just under a 4.3% discount. To raise the full $150 million, if the bonds are issued at a 4.3% discount, then 1,567,398 $100 bond units need to be issued, as opposed to 1,500,000. This is an extra 67,398 bond units for which Levante Co will need to pay an extra $6,739,800 when the bonds are redeemed in five years.

On the other hand, paying a higher coupon every year of 6% instead of 5% will mean that an extra $1,163,010 is needed for each of the next five years (being 1,500,000 × $100 × 6% compared with 1,567,398 × $100 × 5%).

If the directors feel that the drain in resources of $1,163,010 every year is substantial and that the project's profits will cover the extra $6,739,800 in five years' time, then they should issue the bond at a discount and at a lower coupon rate. On the other hand, if the directors feel that they would like to spread the amount payable then they should opt for the higher coupon alternative.

(c) Industry risk measures the resilience of the company's industrial sector to changes in the economy. In order to measure or assess this, the following factors could be used:

Impact of economic changes on the industry in terms of how successfully the firms in the industry operate under differing economic outcomes;

How cyclical the industry is and how large the peaks and troughs are;

How the demand shifts in the industry as the economy changes.

Earnings protection measures how well the company will be able to maintain or protect its earnings in changing circumstances. In order to assess this, the following factors could be used:

Differing range of sources of earnings growth;

Diversity of customer base;

Profit margins and return on capital.

Financial flexibility measures how easily the company is able to raise the finance it needs to pursue its investment goals. In order to assess this, the following factors could be used:

Evaluation of plans for financing needs and range of alternatives available;

Relationships with finance providers, e.g. banks;

Operating restrictions that currently exist as debt covenants.

Evaluation of the company's management considers how well the managers are managing and planning for the future of the company. In order to assess this, the following factors could be used:

The company's planning and control policies, and its financial strategies;

Management succession planning;

The qualifications and experience of the managers;

Performance in achieving financial and non-financial targets.

(**Note:** Credit will be given for alternative relevant comments and suggestions)

(d) **Importance of recognising stakeholders**

A project investment decision is bound to create 'winners' and 'losers'. In any project appraisal, it is important to identify and recognise the claims of all of the stakeholders for several reasons.

Stakeholder recognition is necessary to gain an understanding of the sources of potential risk and disruption. Environmental pressure groups, for example, could threaten to disrupt any project that is perceived as being environmentally damaging, or could threaten legal action.

Stakeholder recognition is important in terms of assessing the sources of influence over the objectives and outcomes for the project. Stakeholder influence is assessed in terms of each stakeholder's power and interest, with higher power and higher interest combining to generate the highest influence.

Stakeholder recognition is necessary in order to identify potential areas of conflict and tension between stakeholders, especially relevant when it is likely that stakeholders of influence will be in disagreement over the outcomes. A survey of the stakeholders, once mapped in terms of influence, would signal which stakeholders are likely to cause delays to the project and paralysis by disagreement and whose claims can then be studied for ways to reduce disagreement.

There is an ethical and reputational case for knowledge of how decisions affect stakeholders, both inside the organisation or external to it. Society can withdraw its support from organisations that it perceives as unethical or arrogant. This can affect organisational performance by reducing their reputations as employers and suppliers of future services.

A 'deep green' perspective would take an unfavourable view of companies that failed to recognise some stakeholder claims.

(**Note:** Credit will be given for alternative relevant comments and suggestions)

66 SEMBILAN CO (JUN 12 ADAPTED)

Key answer tips

This question (from the June 2012 exam) tested the contents of an article written by the examiner and published in the November 2011 issue of Student Accountant magazine. It is common for the examiner to test topics covered in recent articles, so keep an eye out for any new articles published.

(a) Gross amounts of annual interest receivable by Sembilan Co from Ratus Bank based on year 1 spot rate and years 2, 3 and 4 forward rates:

Year 1	$0.025 \times \$320m = \$8m$
Year 2	$0.037 \times \$320m = \$11.84m$
Year 3	$0.043 \times \$320m = \$13.76m$
Year 4	$0.047 \times \$320m = \$15.04m$

Gross amount of annual interest payable by Sembilan Co to Ratus Bank: $3.76\frac{1}{4}\% \times \$320m = \$12.04m$

At the start of the swap, Sembilan Co will expect to receive or (pay) the following net amounts at the end of each of the next four years:

Year 1:	$\$8m - \$12.04m = \$(4.04m)$ payment
Year 2:	$\$11.84m - \$12.04m = \$(0.20m)$ payment
Year 3:	$\$13.76m - \$12.04m = \$1.72m$ receipt
Year 4:	$\$15.04m - \$12.04m = \$3m$ receipt

Tutorial note

At the commencement of the swap contract the net present value of the net annual flows, discounted at the yield curve rates, is zero.

The reason the equivalent fixed rate of 3.76¼% is less than the 3.8% four-year yield curve rate, is because the 3.8% rate reflects the zero-coupon rate with only one payment made in year four. Here the bond pays coupons at different time periods when the yield curve rates are lower. Therefore the fixed rate is lower.

(b)   After taking the swap, Sembilan Co's net effect is as follows:

	% Impact	Yield Interest 3%	Yield Interest 4%
Borrow at yield interest + 60bp	(Yield + 0.6)%	$(11.52m)	$(14.72m)
Receive yield	Yield	$9.6m	$12.8m
Pay fixed 3.76¼%	(3.76¼)%	$(12.04m)	$(12.04m)
Fee 20bp	(0.2)%	$(0.64m)	$(0.64m)
Net Cost	(4.56¼)%	$(14.6m)	$(14.6m)

The receipt and payment based on the yield curve cancels out interest rate fluctuations, fixing the rate at 3.76¼% + 0.6% + 0.2% = 4.56¼%

(c)   Interest rate caps and collars are available as over the counter (OTC) transactions with a bank, or may be devised using market-based interest rate options (options on interest rate futures). They may be used to hedge current or expected interest receipts or payments.

An **interest rate cap** is a series of call options on a notional amount of principal, exercisable at regular intervals over the term to expiry of the cap. The effect of a cap is to place an upper limit on the interest rate to be paid, and is therefore useful to a borrower of funds who will be paying interest at a future date. By purchasing a cap, a borrower will limit the net interest paid to the agreed cap strike price (less any premium paid for the cap). OTC caps are available for periods of up to ten years and can thus protect against long-term interest rate movements. As with all options, if interest rates were to move in a favourable direction, the buyer of the cap could let the option lapse and take advantage of the more favourable rates in the spot market.

The main disadvantage of options is the premium cost. An **interest rate collar** option reduces the premium cost by limiting the possible benefits of favourable interest rate movements. A collar involves the simultaneous purchase and sale of options, or in the case of OTC collars the equivalent to this. The premium paid for the purchase of one option would be partly or wholly offset by the premium received from the sale of another option. A borrower using an OTC collar would in effect buy a cap at one strike price, to secure a maximum interest cost, and sell a floor at a lower strike rate, which sets a minimum interest cost. The effective interest cost would be somewhere between the exercise price for the floor and the exercise price for the cap. The premium cost would be the cost of the cap less the selling price of the floor. A zero cost collar is a collar for which the cost of the cap is offset exactly by the sales value of the floor.

(d)   Reducing the amount of debt by issuing equity and using the cash raised from this to reduce the amount borrowed changes the capital structure of a company and Sembilan Co needs to consider all the possible implications of this.

As the proportion of debt increases in a company's financial structure, the level of financial distress increases and with it the associated costs. Companies with high levels of financial distress would find it more costly to contract with their stakeholders. For example, they may have to pay higher wages to attract the right calibre of employees, give customers longer credit periods or larger discounts, and may have to accept supplies on more onerous terms. Furthermore, restrictive covenants may make it more difficult to borrow funds (debt and equity) for future projects. On the other hand, because interest is payable before tax, larger amounts of debt will give companies greater taxation benefits, known as the tax shield. Presumably, Sembilan Co has judged the balance between the levels of equity and debt finance, such that the positive and negative effects of gearing result in minimising the required rate of return and maximising the value of the company.

By replacing debt with equity the balance may no longer be optimal and therefore the value of Sembilan Co may not be maximised. However, reducing the amount of debt would result in a higher credit rating for the company and reduce the scale of restrictive covenants. Having greater equity would also increase the company's debt capacity. This may enable the company to raise additional finance and undertake future profitable projects more easily. Less financial distress may also reduce the costs of contracting with stakeholders.

The process of changing the financial structure can be expensive. Sembilan Co needs to determine the costs associated with early redemption of debt. The contractual clauses of the bond should indicate the level and amount of early redemption penalties. Issuing new equity can be expensive especially if the shares are offered to new shareholders, such as costs associated with underwriting the issue and communicating or negotiating the share price. Even raising funds by issuing rights can be expensive.

As well as this, Sembilan Co needs to determine the extent to which the current shareholders will be able to take up the rights and the amount of discount that needs to be given on the rights issue to ensure 100% take up. The impact on the current share price from the issue of rights needs to be considered as well. Studies on rights issues seem to indicate that the markets view the issue of rights as a positive signal and the share price does not reduce to the expected theoretical ex-rights price. However, this is mainly because the markets expect the funds raised to be used on new, profitable projects. Using funds to reduce the debt amount may not be viewed so positively.

Sembilan Co may also have to provide information and justification to the market because both the existing shareholders and any new shareholders will need to be assured that the company is not benefiting one group at the expense of the other. If sufficient information is not provided then either shareholder group may discount the share price due to information asymmetry. However, providing too much information may reduce the competitive position of the company.

(**Note:** Credit will be given for alternative relevant comments and suggestions)

	Marking scheme		Marks
(a)	Gross amount receivable by Sembilan Co		1
	Gross amounts payable by Sembilan Co		1
	Net amounts receivable or payable every year		2
	Explanation of why fixed rate is less than the four-year yield curve rate		2
		Maximum	6
(b)	Demonstration of impact of interest rate changes		4
	Explanation and conclusion		1
		Maximum	5
(c)	1–2 marks per relevant discussion point	Maximum	6
(d)	1–2 marks per relevant discussion point	Maximum	8
Total			25

67 PAULT CO (SEP/DEC 16)

Key answer tips

This was a question from the September 2016 exam paper, covering interest rate swaps. The question was based on the topics covered in an examiner's technical article from 2011.

This shows how important it is to read all the examiner's articles to prepare for the exam, not just the most recent ones.

(a) (i) Gross amount of annual interest paid by Pault Co to Millbridge Bank = 4.847% × $400m = $19.39m.

Gross amounts of annual interest receivable by Pault Co from Millbridge Bank, based on Year 1 spot rates and Years 2–4 forward rates:

Year			
1	0.0350 × $400m	=	$14m
2	0.0460 × $400m	=	$18.4m
3	0.0541 × $400m	=	$21.64m
4	0.0611 × $400m	=	$24.44m

Working:

Year 2 forward rate: $(1.0425^2/1.037) - 1 = 4.80\%$

Year 3 forward rate: $(1.0470^3/1.0425^2) - 1 = 5.61\%$

Year 4 forward rate: $(1.0510^4/1.0470^3) - 1 = 6.31\%$

Rates are reduced by 20 basis points in calculation.

At the start of the swap, Pault will expect to pay or receive the following net amounts at each of the next four years:

Year

1	$14m – $19.39m	=	$(5.39m) payment
2	$18.4m – $19.39m	=	$(0.99m) payment
3	$21.64m – $19.39m	=	$2.25m receipt
4	$24.44m – $19.39m	=	$5.05m receipt

(ii) Interest payment liability

	Impact %	*Yield interest* 2.9% $m	*Yield interest* 4.5% $m
Borrow at yield interest + 50 bp	(Yield + 0.5)	(13.60)	(20.00)
Receive yield – 20 bp	Yield – 0.2	10.80	17.20
Pay fixed 4.847%	(4.847)	(19.39)	(19.39)
Bank fee – 25 bp	(0.25)	(1.00)	(1.00)
	———	———	———
	(5.797)	(23.19)	(23.19)
	———	———	———

The interest payment liability will be $23.19m, whatever the yield interest, as the receipt and payment are based on the yield curve net of interest rate fluctuations.

(b) At the start of the contract, the value of the swap will be zero. The terms offered by Millbridge Bank equate the discounted value of the fixed rate payments by Pault Co with the variable rate payments by Millbridge Bank.

However, the value of the swap will not remain at zero. If interest rates increase more than expected, Pault Co will benefit from having to pay a fixed rate and the value of the swap will increase. The value of the swap will also change as the swap approaches maturity, with fewer receipts and payments left.

(c) Disadvantages of swap arrangement

The swap represents a long-term commitment at a time when interest rates appear uncertain. It may be that interest rates rises are lower than expected. In this case, Pault Co will be committed to a higher interest rate and its finance costs may be higher than if it had not taken out the finance arrangements. Pault Co may not be able to take action to relieve this commitment if it becomes clear that the swap was unnecessary.

On the basis of the expected forward rates, Pault Co will not start benefiting from the swap until Year 3. Particularly during Year 1, the extra commitment to interest payments may be an important burden at a time when Pault Co will have significant development and launch costs.

Pault Co will be liable for an arrangement fee. However, other methods of hedging which could be used will have a cost built into them as well.

Advantages of swap arrangement

The swap means that the annual interest payment liability will be fixed at $23.19m over the next four years. This is a certain figure which can be used in budgeting. Having a fixed figure may help planning, particularly as a number of other costs associated with the investment are uncertain.

The directors will be concerned not just about the probability that floating rates will result in a higher commitment than under the swap, but also be concerned about how high this commitment could be. The directors may feel that rates may possibly rise to a level which would give Pault Co problems in meeting its commitments and regard that as unacceptable.

Any criticism after the end of the loan period will be based on hindsight. What appeared to be the cheapest choice at that stage may not have been what appeared most likely to be the cheapest choice when the loan was taken out. In addition, criticism of the directors for not choosing the cheapest option fails to consider risk. The cheapest option may be the most risky. The directors may reasonably take the view that the saving in cost is not worth the risks incurred.

The swap is for a shorter period than the loan and thus allows Pault Co to reconsider the position in four years' time. It may choose to take out another swap then on different terms, or let the arrangement lapse and pay floating rate interest on the loan, depending on the expectations at that time of future interest rates.

Marking scheme				Marks
(a)	(i)	Gross amount payable by Pault Co		1
		Calculation of forward rates		3
		Basis point reduction		1
		Net amounts receivable or payable each year		1
				___
				6
				___
	(ii)	Yield interest calculations		5
		Comment on interest payment liability		1
				___
				6
				___
(b)		Up to 2 marks per point	**Maximum**	4
				___
(c)		Advantages (up to 2 marks per relevant point) Maximum		5
		Disadvantages (up to 2 marks per relevant point)	Maximum	5
				___
				9
				___
Total				25
				___

68   INTEREST RATE HEDGES (JUN 05 ADAPTED) *Walk in the footsteps of a top tutor*

Walkthrough question – key answer tips

This is a technical, but routine, question on interest rate hedging.

First, you should allocate time carefully between the five different requirements. There is a lot to do here, so it is critical not to spend too long on any part of the question.

Notice that the final two parts (d) and (e) are written questions which are independent of the earlier calculations. It would be advisable to do these parts first, to get the easy marks

With regard to the calculations, try to separate the FRA and the futures information so that you don't muddle things up.

Before you start trying to set up the hedges, identify the transaction carefully first. If you mistakenly interpret the transaction the wrong way round (it is a deposit here) you will lose marks for setting up the hedges incorrectly.

(a)   The company is worried about a fall in interest rates during the next five months. It will need a long futures hedge, with December futures purchased at 96.60. If interest rates fall, the futures price will rise and the contracts may be closed out at a higher price to partially offset the cash market interest rate fall. For a risk of £7.1 million to protect a four-month period the company will need to buy:

$$\frac{£7,100,000}{£500,000} \times \frac{4}{3} = 18.93, \text{ or 19 contracts, a slight over hedge.}$$

Basis is (100 – LIBOR) – futures price,

= (100 – 4.00) – 96.60

= -0.60%.

The time to expiry of the December futures contract is seven months. Remaining time at the close-out date (five months' time) is two months.

The expected basis for two months is $-0.60\% \times \frac{2}{7} = -0.171\%$

The expected LIBOR lock-in rate is

100 – (current futures price + unexpired basis)

= 100 – (96.60 – 0.171)

= 3.571%

The company will invest in commercial paper at LIBOR + 0.60%. The overall expected lock-in rate is 4.171%.

(b)   The relevant FRA rate is 5 v 9. The company would sell the FRA to a bank to fix the interest rate at 3.45%. This is a lower rate than the expected futures LIBOR lock-in rate of 3.571%.

(c)   Cash market:

Expected receipts from the investment on 1 November: £

$$7.1m \times 4.1\% \times \frac{4}{12} = £97,033 \; (4.1\% \text{ is LIBOR of } 3.5\% + 0.6\%)$$

Futures market:

1 June: Buy 19 December contracts at 96.60

1 November: Sell 19 December contracts at 96.671 ((100 − 3.50) + 0.171 unexpired basis)

Profit from futures is 7.1 basis points × £12.50 × 19 = £1,686

Overall receipts are £97,033 + £1,686 = £98,719

(**NB:** $\dfrac{£98,719}{£7,100,000} \times \dfrac{12}{4} = 4.171\%$, the expected lock-in rate).

FRA:

The FRA fixed rate is 3.45%. Actual LIBOR is 3.5%. The company will therefore have to make a payment to the bank.

This will be: $£7.1m \,(3.50\% - 3.45\%) \times \dfrac{4}{12} \times \dfrac{1}{1+(3.5\% \times 4/12)}$ or £1,169.65

This will be deducted from the actual receipts of £97,033 (estimated above) to give a net £95,863, a return of 4.05%. (**NB:** This is the FRA rate of 3.45 plus the 0.6% over LIBOR from the commercial paper.)

(d)   The futures market outcome might differ because:

(i)   The hedge is not exact; 19 contracts is a slight over hedge.

Basis risk might exist. The basis at the futures close-out date might differ from the expected basis of 0.171.

Commercial paper interest rates might not move exactly with LIBOR rates.

(ii)   Any gains or losses on futures contracts would be taken/payable daily when the futures contracts are marked to market. The interest effect of such receipts or payments is ignored in the calculations.

(iii)   The above analysis ignores transactions costs.

(e)   A swap is the exchange of one stream of future cash flows for another stream of future cash flows with different characteristics.

Interest rate and currency swaps offer many potential benefits to companies including:

(i)   The ability to obtain finance cheaper than would be possible by borrowing directly in the relevant market.

As companies with different credit ratings can borrow at different cost differentials in for example the fixed and floating rate markets, a company that borrows in the market where it has a comparative advantage (or least disadvantage) can, through swaps, reduce its borrowing costs. For example a highly rated company might be able to borrow funds 1.5% cheaper in the fixed rate market than a lower rated company, and 0.80% cheaper in the floating rate market. By using swaps an arbitrage gain of 0.70% (1.5% − 0.80%) can be made and split between the participants in the swap.

(ii) Hedging against foreign exchange risk. Swaps can be arranged for up to 10 years which provide protection against exchange rate movements for much longer periods than the forward foreign exchange market. Currency swaps are especially useful when dealing with countries with exchange controls and/or volatile exchange rates.

(iii) The opportunity to effectively restructure a company's capital profile by altering the nature of interest commitments, without physically redeeming old debt or issuing new debt. This can save substantial redemption costs and issue costs. Interest commitments can be altered from fixed to floating rate or vice versa, or from one type of floating rate debt to another, or from one currency to another.

(iv) Access to capital markets in which it is impossible to borrow directly. For example, companies with a relatively low credit rating might not have direct access to some fixed rate markets, but can arrange to pay fixed rate interest by using swaps.

(v) The availability of many different types of swaps developed to meet a company's specific needs. These include amortising swaps, zero coupon swaps, callable, puttable or extendable swaps and swaptions.

69   ARNBROOK PLC (JUN 06 ADAPTED)

Key answer tips

Some students make the error in this question of constructing the swap in detail. This is not necessary to answer all requirements.

In part (a) ensure that you consider the bank's perspective as well as Arnbrook's. Similarly, in part (b) ensure you consider all three parties.

In part (c) an alternative approach to calculating discount rates after 6 months is to incorporate both the 5.7% and 6.2% rates. For example, the discount rate for 2 years = $1/(1.057^{0.5} \times 1.062^{1.5})$.

(a)   The risks faced by Arnbrook and the bank include:

(i) Default risk by the counterparty to the swap. If the counterparty is a bank this risk will normally be very small. A bank would face larger counterparty default risk, especially from counterparties such as the BBB company with a relatively low credit rating.

(ii) Market or position risk. This is the risk that market interest rate will change such that the company undertaking the swap would have been better off, with hindsight, if it had not undertaken the swap.

(iii) Banks often undertake a 'warehousing' function in swap transactions. The size and/or maturity of the transactions desired by each counterparty to the bank often do not match. In such cases, the bank faces gap or mismatch risk, which it will normally hedge in the futures or other markets.

(b)

	Fixed rate	Floating rate
Arnbrook	6.25%	LIBOR + 0.75%
BBB company	7.25%	LIBOR + 1.25%
Difference	1.00%	0.50%

There is a potential 0.50% arbitrage saving from undertaking the swap.

On a £50 million swap this is £250,000 per year.

Arnbrook would require 60% of any saving, or £150,000 annually. The BBB company would receive £100,000 annually.

The bank would charge each party £90,000 per year. This would leave a net saving of only £10,000 for the BBB-rated counterparty company.

The swap is potentially beneficial to all parties, but the counterparty company might press for a larger saving than £10,000.

(c) Arnbrook will pay floating rate interest as a result of the swap. If Arnbrook receives 60% of the arbitrage savings, it will save 0.3% (60% of 0.5%) on its interest rates relative to borrowing directly in the floating-rate market, and effectively pay LIBOR + 0.45%, or 5.70% at current interest rates. If LIBOR moves to 5.75% in six months' time, Arnbrook will then pay 6.20% floating rate interest for the remaining period of the swap.

Interest savings in each six-month period are £50 million × 0.30% × 0.5 = £75,000

If the money market is efficient, the relevant discount rate will be the prevailing interest rate paid by Arnbrook.

Period:	Savings £	Discount factor	Present value (£)
0–6 months	75,000	0.972 (5.7%)	72,900
6 months–1 year	75,000	0.942 (6.2%)	70,650
1 year–18 months	75,000	0.913 (6.2%)	68,475
18 months–2 years	75,000	0.887 (6.2%)	66,525
2 years–30 months	75,000	0.860 (6.2%)	64,500
30 months–3 years	75,000	0.835 (6.2%)	62,625
Total present values			405,675

The interest rate swap is estimated to produce interest rate savings with a present value of £405,675 relative to borrowing floating rate directly. The swap would be beneficial, and, with hindsight, would result in lower interest costs than would have been available by borrowing at 6.25% in the fixed-rate market.

(d) In practice, most swaps are arranged through banks that run a 'swaps book'. There are several advantages in dealing with a bank rather than directly with another company.

1   In dealing with a bank, there is no problem about finding a swaps counterparty with an equal and opposite swapping requirement. The bank will arrange a swap to meet the specific requirements of each individual customer, as to amount and duration of the swap.

2   In dealing with a bank, the credit risk is that the bank might default, whereas in dealing directly with another company, the credit risk is that the other company might default. Banks are usually a much lower credit risk than corporates.

3   Banks are specialists in swaps, and are able to provide standard legal swaps agreements. The operation of the swap is likely to be administratively more straightforward.

The significant drawback to using a bank is that the bank will want to make a profit from its operations. In practice, it will generally do this by charging different swap rates for fixed rate payments and fixed rate receipts on different swaps.

(e)   One central principle of Islamic finance is that making money out of money is not acceptable, i.e. interest is prohibited. A mudaraba contract, in Islamic finance, is a partnership between one party that brings finance or capital into the contract and another party that brings business expertise and personal effort into the contract. The first party is called the owner of capital, while the second party is called the agent, who runs or manages the business. The mudaraba contract specifies how profit from the business is shared proportionately between the two parties. Any loss, however, is borne by the owner of capital, and not by the agent managing the business. It can therefore be seen that three key characteristics of a mudaraba contract are that no interest is paid, that profits are shared, and that losses are not shared.

If Arnbrook were to decide to seek Islamic finance for the planned expansion and if the company were to enter into a mudaraba contract, the company would therefore be entering into a partnership as an agent, managing the business and sharing profits with the Islamic bank that provided the finance and which was acting as the owner of capital. The Islamic bank would not interfere in the management of the business and this is what would be expected if Arnbrook were to finance the business expansion using debt such as a bank loan. However, while interest on debt is likely to be at a fixed rate, the mudaraba contract would require a sharing of profit in the agreed proportions.

70   PONDHILLS (JUN 01 ADAPTED)

(a)   Translation exposure exists because of the need for multinational companies to periodically consolidate the financial statements of overseas subsidiaries with those of the parent company in order to present the financial details and to assess the performance of the entire group. In order to achieve consolidation the subsidiaries™ accounts need to be translated from a foreign currency basis into the currency of the parent company. Translation is not a physical exchange of currencies; it is the change in the monetary expression of the subsidiaries™ activities from one currency to another.

There are several methodologies for translating financial statements. Governments or professional accounting standards bodies will normally specify the preferred or required method(s). Depending on the method used the resulting foreign exchange gain or loss on translation will significantly differ. Translation exposure does not directly measure the cash flow implications of exchange rate changes, or the effect of such changes on the value of a multinational. Because of this many multinational companies do not hedge against translation exposure. However, if the exposure is expected to result in a significant reported loss, which the company believes might, in an inefficient market, have a detrimental effect on share price, some hedging might be undertaken.

Economic exposure results from the fact that a company's economic value will change as a result of changes in foreign exchange rates. It is often categorised into two forms:

(i)   **Transaction exposure**, which focuses on the short-term impact on cash flow, for example through foreign trade activities. Many multinationals hedge against the potential cash flow loss of transaction exposure through forward markets, currency options etc.

(ii)   **Real operating exposure**, which considers the longer term effects on cash flow and NPV after the effect of inflation has been removed.

Economic exposure refers to unexpected changes in exchange rates. As economic exposure has a direct effect on the value of the firm it is important for multinationals to try to manage such exposure. However, as the size and nature of the exposure is unknown it is difficult to hedge against international diversification of sales, production, raw material sources and financing is suggested as this will provide more flexibility to respond to adverse unexpected change in exchange rates.

(b)   (i)   Translation exposure

Analysis is required of the possible foreign exchange exposure of Pondhills Inc the parent company from the operations of its African subsidiary.

The current/closing rate method translates all EXPOSED assets and liabilities at the exchange rate prevailing at the year end. However, from the viewpoint of Pondhills Inc, not all of Ponda SA's assets and liabilities are exposed, as sales are denominated in US dollars, and some payables are payable in sterling. As no change is expected between the dollar and sterling exchange rates, the exposure to Pondhills Inc is only from assets and liabilities that are denominated in dinars.

Current exchange rate is 246.3 dinars/US$1. If a 15% devaluation occurs this will move to 246.3 × 1.15 = 283.2 dinars/US$1.

	Million dinars	Exposed	In US$ at current rate	In US$ post devaluation
Non-current assets	510	Yes	2.071	1.801
Current assets:				
Cash	86	Yes	0.349	0.304
Receivables	410	No	1.665	1.665
Inventory	380	Yes	1.543	1.342
Total current assets	876		3.557	3.311
Short-term payables	(296)	50%	(1.202)	(1.124)
Long–term loans	(500)	Yes	(2.030)	(1.766)
Net assets	590		2.396	2.222
Shareholder's equity	590		2.396	2.222

The balance sheet exposure is (510 + 86 + 380) – ((50% of 296) + 500) or 328 million dinars.

The expected loss on translation exposure:

Exposure in dinars: 328 million	In US$ million
At current exchange rate	1.332
At post-devaluation exchange rate	1.158
Expected loss on translation	0.174

This is the change in shareholders' equity shown in the table above, $US2.396m – $2.222m = $0.174 million.

(ii)   Economic exposure measures the cash flow effects of a change in exchange rates. The data below shows the change over a full year with a 15% devaluation of the dinar.

	Million			
	Current dinars	*Post devaluation dinars*	*Current dollars*	*Post devaluation dollars*
Revenue (all US$)	2,300	2,645	9.338	9.338
COGS and operating expenses:				
Local (dinars)	966	966	3.922	3.411
Overseas (sterling)	644	741	2.615	2.615
Interest (dinars)	60	60	0.244	0.212
Net cash flows	630	878	2.557	3.100

There is an initial annualised gain in cash flow for Pondhills Inc of US$543,000 ($3.100m – $2.557m), resulting from the devaluation of the dinar.

(c)   Unlike the translation exposure estimate where a loss was forecast, the expected impact on economic exposure results in an exposure gain. Translation exposure does not measure the effect of exchange changes on cash flows. Unless a reported translation loss is expected to have a detrimental effect on Pondhills Inc's share price, (which it should not if the market is efficient), no hedging against translation exposure is recommended.

In the light of the expected economic exposure gain there is no need to hedge against the possible devaluation, although it might be advisable to pay any hard currency liabilities to third parties (e.g. sterling creditors) and to reduce dinar cash levels before any devaluation occurred.

71 CURRENCY SWAPS (DEC 04 ADAPTED)

Key answer tips

There are some very easy marks in the discussion parts of this question. Make sure that you leave time to answer the written parts as well as the calculations.

(a) **Advantages of currency swaps include:**

(i) They allow companies to undertake foreign currency hedging, often for longer periods than is possible with forwards.

(ii) They are usually cheaper than long-term forwards, where such products exist.

(iii) Finance may be obtained at a cheaper rate than would be possible by borrowing directly in the relevant market. This occurs by taking advantage of arbitrage if a company has a relative funding advantage in one country.

(iv) They may provide access to finance in currencies that could not be borrowed directly, e.g. due to government restrictions, or lack of a credit rating in the overseas market.

(v) Currency swaps offer the opportunity to restructure the company's debt profile without physically redeeming debt or issuing new debt.

(vi) Currency swaps might be used to avoid a country's exchange control restrictions.

Potential problems include:

(i) If the swap is directly with a corporate counterparty the potential default risk of the counterparty must be considered. Swaps arranged with a bank as the direct counterparty tend to be much less risky.

(ii) Political or sovereign risk; the possibility that a government will introduce restrictions that interfere with the performance of the swap.

(iii) Basis risk. With a floating to floating swap, basis risk might exist if the two floating rates are not pegged to the same index.

(iv) Exchange rate risk. The swap may result in a worse outcome than would have occurred if no swap had been arranged.

(b) **(i)** Interest rate differentials:

	Fixed rate	Floating rate
Galeplus	6.25%	PIBOR + 2%
Counterparty	8.30%	PIBOR + 1.5%
	(2.05%)	0.5%

The overall arbitrage opportunity from using a currency swap is 2.55% per year. Bank fees are 0.75% per year, leaving 1.8%; 75% of 1.8% is 1.35%. That would be the benefit per year to Galeplus in terms of interest saving from using a currency swap.

(ii) Assuming inflation rates in Perdia are between 15% and 50% per year, the best and worst case exchange rates are:

	Rubbits/£	
	Best case	*Worst case*
Spot	85.40	85.40
Year 1	98.21	128.10
Year 2	112.94	192.15
Year 3	129.88	288.23

	Cash flows (million rubbits)			
Year	*0*	*1*	*2*	*3*
Purchase cost	(2,000)			
Fees		40	40	40
Sale price				4,000
	————	————	————	————
	(2,000)	40	40	4,040
Discount factors (15%)	1	0.870	0.756	0.658
Present values	(2,000)	34.8	30.24	2,658.32

With a currency swap, 2,000 million of the Year 3 cash flows will be at the current spot rate of 85.40 rubbits/£, with the remainder at the end of Year 3 spot rate.

	Discounted cash flows (£ million)			
Worst-case rates	(23.42)	0.27	0.16	20.07
Estimated NPV	(£2.92 million)			
Best-case rates	(23.42)	0.35	0.27	25.75
Estimated NPV	£2.95 million			

The financial viability of the investment depends upon exchange rate movements. The greater the depreciation in the value of the rubbit relative to the pound, the worse the outcome of the investment. This is due to the Year 3 price of the telecommunications centre remaining constant no matter what the exchange rate is at the time.

These estimates assume that exchange rates remain in the above range. In reality they could be better or worse. Additionally, non-financial factors such as political risk would influence the decision. For example, given the government's current cash flow position, how likely is the payment of 4,000 million rubbits to be made in three years' time? Other factors such as taxation in the UK would also need to be considered.

Unless there are strong strategic reasons for buying the centre, for example possible future cash flow benefits beyond Year 3, the investment is not recommended. In order for the investment to take place a better hedge against currency risk would need to be found, or the price to be received in Year 3 renegotiated to reflect the impact of adverse exchange rate changes.

72 FNDC PLC (DEC 06 ADAPTED)

(a) Short-term interest rate futures (STIRs) allow a company to hedge an interest rate risk by attempting to create a gain on the futures market to offset a potential loss in the underlying cash market. The futures hedge is expected to protect interest rates at the expected futures price at the time the futures contracts mature or are closed out. However, hedges will rarely be perfect because:

(i) The size of the risk might not correspond to an exact number of futures contracts; the risk might need to be underhedged or overhedged.

(ii) Basis risk might exist, which means that the futures price at the close-out date might be different to that expected.

(iii) The futures contract is based on LIBOR or equivalent. The underlying risk might be based upon a short-term interest rate instrument with different characteristics to LIBOR.

Futures also involve an up-front margin payment, and payments of variation margin if prices move in an adverse direction. They are highly standardised and have a limited number of expiry dates.

Market-traded options on futures share many of the characteristics of the underlying futures contracts. The major differences are that the option contracts involve the payment of an option premium, which is payable whether or not the option is exercised. Additionally, options have the advantage of allowing the buyer to take advantage of favourable movements in interest rates, while still protecting against adverse movements. Options also offer a wider choice of the level of interest rate that may be used to protect against adverse movements.

(b) **Futures hedge**

The period at risk is two months commencing in five months' time, on 1 May. The June futures contract will be used as it has the first maturity date after the period of risk commences. Futures will be sold in order to make a profit if interest rates rise.

As the period at risk is two months, the number of contracts required is:

$$\frac{£45,000,000}{£500,000} \times \frac{2}{3} = 60$$

Sixty June contracts will be sold.

LIBOR is currently 4%, and the June futures price is 95.55 so the basis is

96.00 − 95.55 = 0.45

There are seven months until the futures contract matures. If there is a linear fall in basis (no basis risk) then the expected basis in five months' time when the futures contracts are closed out is:

$$0.45 \times \frac{2}{7} = 0.13$$

The expected lock-in rate for the futures contract is 100 − (95.55 + 0.13) = 4.32%.

FNDC borrows at LIBOR plus 1.25%, therefore the expected lock in interest rate is 5.57%, or £417,750, no matter what rate LIBOR moves to.

Calculations of cash market and futures market profits/losses are not essential, but would be as follows:

0.5% increase in interest rates:

Cash market:

Actual borrowing cost in five months' time

$$(4.5\% + 1.25\%) \times £45,000,000 \times \frac{2}{12} = £431,250$$

Futures market:

1 December sell 60 June contracts at 95.55

1 May buy 60 contracts at the expected futures price of 95.37 (100 – 4.5% – 0.13)

Futures profit is 0.18 or 18 ticks.

18 × 60 × £12.50 = £13,500

The net interest cost is £431,250 – £13,500 = £417,750

$$\frac{£417,750}{£45,000,000} \times \frac{12}{2} = 5.57\%$$

0.5% decrease in interest rates:

Cash market:

Actual borrowing cost in five months' time

$$(3.5\% + 1.25\%) \times £45,000,000 \times \frac{2}{12} = £356,250$$

Futures market:

1 December sell 60 June contracts at 95.55

1 May buy 60 contracts at 96.37 (100 – 3.5% – 0.13)

Futures loss is 0.82 or 82 ticks.

82 × 60 × £12.50 = £61,500

The total interest cost is £356,250 + £61,500 = £417,750 or 5.57%

Interest rate options

Options to sell futures are required, hence June put options will be purchased.

Only three possible exercise prices exist.

Exercise price	Option premium
9500	45,000,000 × 0.015% × 2/12 = 1,125
9550	45,000,000 × 0.165% × 2/12 = 12,375
9600	45,000,000 × 0.710% × 2/12 = 53,250

If interest rates increase by 0.5%, leading to an expected futures price of 95.37 at the close-out date of 1 May.

Exercise price	Exercise option	Profit from exercising options
9500	No	
9550	Yes	(95.50 – 95.37) ÷ 0.005 × 60 × £6.25 = £9,750
9600	Yes	(96.00 – 95.37) ÷ 0.005 × 60 × £6.25 = £47,250

Overall cost if options are used:

	Market borrowing cost +	Option premium –	Option profit	Total
9500	431,250	1,125	–	432,375
9550	431,250	12,375	9,750	433,875
9600	431,250	53,250	47,250	437,250

As expected, all are worse than the expected cost of £417,750 using futures.

If interest rates were to fall by 0.5%, the expected futures close-out price is 96.37

Exercise price	Exercise option
9500	No
9550	No
9600	No

In all cases the option will be allowed to lapse, or sold for any remaining time value.

Overall cost if options are used:

	Market borrowing cost +	Option premium	Total
9500	356,250	1,125	357,375
9550	356,250	12,375	368,625
9600	356,250	53,250	409,500

All of these outcomes are much better than the futures hedge, but would rely on interest rates falling rather than rising. This is not expected to happen by 'the market'. The 9500 exercise price is probably the most attractive of the option contracts as it is relatively low cost and gives a very favourable outcome if interest rates fall. However, it is still £14,625 more expensive than the futures hedge if interest rates rise.

(c) A maximum interest rate to the company of 5.75% implies a LIBOR rate of 4.5%, or 9550. A minimum rate of 5.25% implies LIBOR of 4.0% or 9600.

The collar hedge would be to buy 60 June 9550 put option contracts and to sell 60 June 9600 call option contracts.

The net premium payable would be 0.165 – 0.070 = 0.095, or a cost of:

£45,000,000 × 0.095% × 2/12 = £7,125

If interest rates increase by 0.5%, the 9550 put option will be exercised.

Market borrowing cost +	net option premium –	option profit =	Total
£431,250	£7,125	£9,750	£428,625

If interest falls by 0.5%, the put option will not be exercised, but there will be a loss on the call option as it will be exercised by its buyer.

Market borrowing cost (4.75%) = £356,250

Loss on call option is: (96.00 – 96.37) × 2 × 100 × 60 × 6.25 = £27,750

Total cost is £356,250 + £27,750 + £7,125 = £391,125

The collar hedge saves premium cost and might be attractive to FNDC, although the worst-case outcome is still much more expensive than the futures hedge.

73 LIGNUM CO (DEC 12 ADAPTED)

Key answer tips

Currency risk is most commonly tested in the context of transaction risk. However, this question also covered economic risk and translation risk. Make sure that you understand all three types of risk and how they can be managed.

REPORT TO THE TREASURY DIVISION, LIGNUM CO

Discussion and recommendations for managing the foreign exchange exposure

The report discusses and makes recommendations on how the treasury division may manage the foreign exchange exposure it faces under three unrelated circumstances or cases.

The appendices to the report show the detailed calculations to support the discussion around case one (see Appendix I) and around case two (see Appendix II).

Foreign exchange exposures

With case one, Lignum Co faces a possible exposure due to the receipt it is expecting in four months in a foreign currency, and the possibility that the exchange rates may move against it between now and in four months' time. This is known as transactions exposure. With case two, the exposure is in the form of translation exposure, where a subsidiary's assets are being translated from the subsidiary's local currency into Euro. The local currency is facing an imminent depreciation of 20%. Finally in the third case, the present value of future sales of a locally produced and sold good is being eroded because of overseas products being sold for a relatively cheaper price. The case seems to indicate that because the US$ has depreciated against the Euro, it is possible to sell the goods at the same dollar price but at a lower Euro price. This is known as economic exposure.

Hedging strategies

Case one

Transactions exposure, as faced by Lignum Co in situation one, lasts for a short while and is easier to manage by means of derivative products or more conventional means. Here Lignum Co has access to two derivative products: an OTC forward rate and OTC option. Using the forward rate gives a higher return of €963,988, compared to options where the return is €936,715 (see Appendix I). However, with the forward rate, Lignum Co is locked into a fixed rate (ZP145.23 per €1) whether the foreign exchange rates move in its favour or against it. With the options, the company has a choice and if the rate moves in its favour, that is if the Zupeso appreciates against the Euro, then the option can be allowed to lapse. Lignum Co needs to decide whether it is happy receiving €963,988, no matter what happens to the exchange rate over the four months or whether it is happy to receive at least €936,715 if the ZP weakens against the €, but with a possibility of higher gains if the Zupeso strengthens.

Lignum Co should also explore alternative strategies to derivative hedging. For example, money markets, leading and lagging, and maintaining a Zupeso account may be possibilities. If information on the investment rate in Zupesos could be obtained, then a money market hedge could be considered. Maintaining a Zupeso account may enable Lignum Co to offset any natural hedges and only convert currency periodically to minimise transaction costs.

Case two

Hedging translation risk may not be necessary if the stock market in which Lignum Co's shares are traded is efficient. Translation of currency is an accounting entry where subsidiary accounts are incorporated into the group accounts. No physical cash flows in or out of the company. In such cases, spending money to hedge such risk means that the group loses money overall, reducing the cash flows attributable to shareholders. However, translation losses may be viewed negatively by the equity holders and may impact some analytical trends and ratios negatively. In these circumstances, Lignum Co may decide to hedge the risk.

The most efficient way to hedge translation exposure is to match the assets and liabilities. In Namel Co's case the assets are more exposed to the Maram Ringit compared to the liabilities, hence the weakening of the Maram Ringit from MR35 per €1 to MR42 per €1 would make the assets lose more (accounting) value than the liabilities by €1,018,000 (see Appendix II). If the exposure for the assets and liabilities were matched more closely, for example by converting non-current liabilities from loans in Euro to loans in MR, translation exposure would be reduced.

Case three

Economic exposure, which is not part of transactions exposure, is long-term in nature and therefore more difficult to manage. There are for example, few derivatives which are offered over a long period, with the possible exception of swaps. A further issue is that economic exposure may cause a substantial negative impact to a company's cash flows and value over the long period of time. In this situation, if the US$ continues to remain weak against the Euro, then Lignum Co will find it difficult to maintain a sustained advantage against its American competitor. A strategic, long-term viewpoint needs to be undertaken to manage risk of this nature, such as locating production in countries with favourable exchange rates and cheaper raw material and labour inputs or setting up a subsidiary company in the USA to create a natural hedge for the majority of the US$ cash flows.

In conclusion, the report examined, discussed and made recommendations on managing foreign exchange exposure in each of the three cases.

Report compiled by: XXX

Date: XXX

APPENDICES

Appendix I: Financial impact of derivative products offered by Medes Bank (Case one)

Using forward rate

Forward rate = $142 \times (1 + (0.085 + 0.0025)/3)/(1 + (0.022 - 0.0030)/3) = 145.23$

Income in Euro fixed at ZP145.23 = ZP140,000,000/145.23 = €963,988

Using OTC options

Purchase call options to cover for the ZP rate depreciating

Gross income from option = ZP140,000,000/142 = €985,915

Cost

€985,915 × ZP7 = ZP6,901,405

In € = ZP6,901,405/142 = €48,601

€48,601 × (1 + 0.037/3) = €49,200

(Use borrowing rate on the assumption that extra funds to pay costs need to borrowed initially; investing rate can be used if that is the stated preference)

Net income = €985,915 – €49,200 = €936,715

Appendix II: Financial impact of the devaluation of the Maram Ringit (Case two)

MR devalued rate = MR35 × 1.20 = MR42 per €1

	MR 000	Exposed?	€000 at current rate MR35 per €1	€000 at devalued rate MR42 per €1
Non-current assets	179,574	Yes	5,131	4,276
Current assets	146,622	60%	2,514	2,095
Non-current liabilities	(132,237)	20%	(756)	(630)
Current liabilities	(91,171)	30%	(781)	(651)
Share capital and reserves	102,788		6,108	5,090

Translation loss = €6,108,000 – €5,090,000 = €1,018,000

	Marking scheme		Marks
(a)	**Requirement (i)**		
	1 mark per exposure explained		3
	Requirement (ii)		
	Calculation of forward rate		1
	Calculation of income using the forward rate		1
	Calculation of cash flows using option contracts		3
	Discussion of relative merits of forwards and options		2–3
	Discussion of alternative hedging possibilities and conclusion		1–2
		Maximum	9
	Requirement (iii)		
	Calculation of devalued rate		1
	Calculation of translation loss		3
	Discussion of whether risk of translation loss should be managed		2–3
	Discussion of how risk of translation loss should be managed		1–2
		Maximum	8
	Requirement (iv)		
	1 mark per point		3
	Professional Marks		
	Structure and presentation of report		2
Total			25

74   ALECTO CO (PILOT 12)

Key answer tips

In any interest rate hedging question, be prepared to comment on the advantages and disadvantages of setting up a collar. This question also covers the calculations on the two most commonly tested hedging methods (futures and traded options) in a very typical way.

(a)   The main advantage of using a collar instead of options to hedge interest rate risk is lower cost. A collar involves the simultaneous purchase and sale of both call and put options at different exercise prices. The option purchased has a higher premium when compared to the premium of the option sold, but the lower premium income will reduce the higher premium payable. With a normal uncovered option, the full premium is payable.

However, the main disadvantage is that, whereas with a hedge using options the buyer can get full benefit of any upside movement in the price of the underlying asset, with a collar hedge the benefit of the upside movement is limited or capped as well.

(b)   **Using Futures**

Need to hedge against a rise in interest rates, therefore go short in the futures market. Alecto Co needs June contracts as the loan will be required on 1 May.

No. of contracts needed = €22,000,000/€1,000,000 × 5 months/3 months = 36.67 say 37 contracts.

Basis

Current price (on 1/1) – futures price = total basis

(100 – 3.3) – 96.16 = 0.54

Unexpired basis = 2/6 × 0.54 = 0.18

If interest rates increase by 0.5% to 3.8%

Cost of borrowing funds = 4.6% × 5/12 × €22,000,000 = €421,667

Expected futures price = 100 – 3.8 – 0.18 = 96.02

Gain on the futures market = (9,616 – 9,602) × €25 × 37 = €12,950

Net cost = €408,717

Effective interest rate = 408,717/22,000,000 × 12/5 = 4.46%

If interest rates decrease by 0.5% to 2.8%

Cost of borrowing funds = 3.6% × 5/12 × €22,000,000 = €330,000

Expected futures price = 100 – 2.8 – 0.18 = 97.02

Loss on the futures market = (9,616 – 9,702) × €25 × 37 = €79,550

Net cost = €409,550

Effective interest rate = 409,550/22,000,000 × 12/5 = 4.47%

(**Note:** Net cost should be the same. Difference is due to rounding the number of contracts)

Using Options on Futures

Need to hedge against a rise in interest rates, therefore buy put options. As before, Alecto Co needs 37 June put option contracts (€22,000,000/€1,000,000 × 5 months/ 3 months).

If interest rates increase by 0.5% to 3.8%

Exercise Price	96.00	96.50
Futures Price	96.02	96.02
Exercise ?	No	Yes
Gain in basis points	0	48
Underlying cost of borrowing (from above)	€421,667	€421,667
Gain on options (0 and €25 × 48 × 37)	€0	€44,400
Premium		
16.3 × €25 × 37	€15,078	
58.1 × €25 × 37		€53,743
Net cost	€436,745	€431,010
Effective interest rate	4.76%	4.70%

If interest rates decrease by 0.5% to 2.8%

Exercise Price	96.00	96.50
Futures Price	97.02	97.02
Exercise ?	No	No
Gain in basis points	0	0
Underlying cost of borrowing (from above)	€330,000	€330,000
Gain on options	€0	€0
Premium		
16.3 × €25 × 37	€15,078	
58.1 × €25 × 37		€53,743
Net cost	€345,078	€383,743
Effective interest rate	3.76%	4.19%

Using a collar

Buy June put at 96.00 for 0.163 and sell June call at 96.50 for 0.090.

Premium payable = 0.073

If interest rates increase by 0.5% to 3.8%

	Buy put	Sell Call
Exercise Price	96.00	96.5
Futures Price	96.02	96.02
Exercise ?	No	No
Underlying cost of borrowing (from above)	€421,667	
Premium		
7.3 × €25 × 37	€6,753	
Net cost	€428,420	
Effective interest rate	4.67%	

If interest rates decrease by 0.5% to 2.8%

	Buy put	Sell Call
Exercise Price	96.00	96.50
Futures Price	97.02	97.02
Exercise ?	No	Yes
Underlying cost of borrowing (from above)	€330,000	
Premium		
7.3 × €25 × 37	€6,753	
Loss on exercise (52 × €25 × 37)	€48,100	
Net cost	€384,853	
Effective interest rate	4.20%	

Hedging using the interest rate futures market fixes the rate at 4.47%, whereas with options on futures or a collar hedge, the net cost changes. If interest rates fall in the future then a hedge using options gives the most favourable rate. However, if interest rates increase then a hedge using futures gives the lowest interest payment cost and hedging with options give the highest cost, with the cost of the collar hedge being in between the two. If Alecto Co's aim is to fix its interest rate whatever happens to future rates then the preferred instrument would be futures.

This recommendation is made without considering margin and other transactional costs, and basis risk, which is discussed below. These need to be taken into account before a final decision is made.

(**Note:** Credit will be given for alternative approaches to the calculations in part (b))

(c)   Basis risk occurs when the basis does not diminish at a constant rate. In this case, if a futures contract is held until it matures then there is no basis risk because at maturity the derivative price will equal the underlying asset's price. However, if a contract is closed out before maturity (here the June futures contracts will be closed two months prior to expiry) there is no guarantee that the price of the futures contract will equal the predicted price based on basis at that date. For example, in part (b) above, the predicted futures price in four months assumes that the basis remaining is 0.18, but it could be more or less. Therefore the actual price of the futures contract could be more or less.

This creates a problem in that the effective interest rate for the futures contract above may not be fixed at 4.47%, but may vary and therefore the amount of interest that Alecto Co pays may not be fixed or predictable. On the other hand, it could be argued that the basis risk will probably be smaller than the risk exposure to interest rates without hedging and therefore, although some risk will exist, its impact will be smaller.

Marking scheme		
		Marks
(a)	Discussion of the main advantage	2
	Discussion of the main disadvantage	2
		___
	Maximum	**4**
		___
(b)	Recommendation to go short if futures are used and purchase puts if options are used	1
	Calculation of number of contracts and remaining basis	2
	Futures contracts calculations	4
	Options contracts calculations	4
	Collar approach and calculations	4
	Supporting comments and conclusion	2–3
		___
	Maximum	**17**
		___
(c)	Explanation of basis risk	2–3
	Effect of basis risk on recommendation made	2–3
		___
	Maximum	**4**
		___
Total		**25**
		___

75 KENDURI CO (JUN 13)

(a) Only the transactions resulting in cash flows between Kenduri Co and Lakama Co are considered for hedging. Other transactions are not considered.

Net flow in US$: US$4.5m payment – US$2.1m receipt = US$2.4m payment

Hedge the US$ exposure using the forward market, the money market and options.

Forward market

US$ hedge: 2,400,000/1.5996 = £1,500,375 payment

Money market

US$ hedge

Invest in US$: 2,400,000/(1 + 0.031/4) = US$2,381,543

Convert into £ at spot: US$2,381,543/1.5938 = £1,494,255

Borrow in £: £1,494,255 × (1 + 0.040/4) = £1,509,198

(Note: Full credit will be given to candidates who use the investing rate of 2.8% instead of the borrowing rate of 4%, where this approach has been explained and justified)

The forward market is preferred due to lower payment costs.

Options

Kenduri Co would purchase Sterling three-month put options to protect itself against a strengthening US$ to £.

Exercise price: $1.60/£1

£ payment = 2,400,000/1.60 = 1,500,000 or 24 contracts

24 put options purchased

Premium payable = 24 × 0.0208 × 62,500 = US$31,200

Premium in £ = 31,200/1.5938 = £19,576

Total payments = £1,500,000 + £19,576 = £1,519,576

Exercise price: $1.62/£1

£ payment = 2,400,000/1.62 = 1,481,481 or 23.7 contracts

23 put options purchased

£ payment = 23 × 62,500 = £1,437,500

Premium payable = 23 × 0.0342 × 62,500 = US$49,163

Premium in £ = 49,163/1.5938 = £30,846

Amount not hedged = US$2,400,000 – (23 × 62,500 × 1.62) = US$71,250

Use forwards to hedge amount not hedged = US$71,250/1.5996 = £44,542

Total payments = 1,437,500 + 30,846 + 44,542 = £1,512,888

Both these hedges are worse than the hedge using forward or money markets. This is due to the premiums payable to let the option lapse if the prices move in Kenduri Co's favour. Options have an advantage over forwards and money markets because the prices are not fixed and the option buyer can let the option lapse if the rates move favourably. Hence options have an unlimited upside but a limited downside. With forwards and money markets, Kenduri Co cannot take advantage of the US$ weakening against the £.

Conclusion

The forward market minimises the payment and is therefore recommended over the money market. However, options give Kenduri Co the choice of an unlimited upside, although the cost is higher. Therefore the choice between the forward market and the option market depends on the risk preference of the company.

(b) Based on spot mid-rates: US$1.5950/£1; CAD1.5700/£1; JPY132.75/£1 **In £000**

			Payments from			
		UK	USA	Canada	Japan	Total
Receipts to	UK		1,316.6	2,165.6		3,482.2
	USA	2,821.3		940.4	877.7	4,639.4
	Canada	700.6			2,038.2	2,738.8
	Japan		2,410.5			2,410.5
Total payments		3,521.9	3,727.1	3,106.0	2,915.9	
Total receipts		3,482.2	4,639.4	2,738.8	2,410.5	
Net receipt/(payment)		(39.7)	912.3	(367.2)	(505.4)	

Each of Kenduri Co, Jaia Co and Gochiso Co will make payments of £ equivalent to the amount given above to Lakama Co.

Multilateral netting involves minimising the number of transactions taking place through each country's banks. This would limit the fees that these banks would receive for undertaking the transactions and therefore governments who do not allow multilateral netting want to maximise the fees their local banks receive. On the other hand, some countries allow multilateral netting in the belief that this would make companies more willing to operate from those countries and any banking fees lost would be more than compensated by the extra business these companies and their subsidiaries bring into the country.

(c) Gamma measures the rate of change of the delta of an option. Deltas range from near 0 for a long call option which is deep out-of-money, where the price of the option is insensitive to changes in the price of an underlying asset, to near 1 for a long call option which is deep in-the-money, where the price of the option moves in line and largely to the same extent as the price of the underlying asset. When the long call option is at-the-money, the delta is 0.5 but also changes rapidly. Hence, the gamma is highest for a long call option which is at-the-money. The gamma is also higher when the option is closer to expiry. It would seem, therefore, that the option is probably trading near at-the-money and has a relatively short time period before it expires.

Marking scheme		
		Marks
(a)	Calculation of net US$ amount	1
	Calculation of forward market US$ amount	1
	Calculation of US$ money market amount	2
	Calculation of one put option amount (1.60 or 1.62)	3
	Calculation of the second put option amount or if the preferred exercise price choice is explained	2
	Advice and recommendation	3–4
	Maximum	**12**
(b)	Mid spot rates calculation	1
	Calculation of the £ equivalent amounts of US$, CAD and JPY	4
	Calculation of the net receipt/payment	2
	Explanation of government reaction to multilateral hedging	3
	Maximum	**10**
(c)	1 mark per relevant point	
	Maximum	**3**
Total		**25**

76   AWAN CO (DEC 13)

Online question assistance

Key answer tips

This was a very typical question on interest rate hedging. With any hedging question, make sure that you identify the transaction correctly at the start. In this question, you were asked to hedge the interest receipts on a deposit (rather than the more commonly tested interest payments on a borrowing).

(a)   Using forward rate agreements (FRAs)

FRA rate 4.82% (3–7), since the investment will take place in three months' time for a period of four months.

If interest rates increase by 0.9% to 4.99%

Investment return = 4.79% × 4/12 × $48,000,000 =	$766,400
Payment to Voblaka bank = (4.99% − 4.82%) × $48,000,000 × 4/12 =	$(27,200)
Net receipt =	$739,200
Effective annual interest rate = 739,200/48,000,000 × 12/4 =	4.62%

If interest rates decrease by 0.9% to 3.19%

Investment return = 2.99% × 4/12 × $48,000,000 =	$478,400
Receipt from Voblaka Bank = (4.82% − 3.19%) × $48,000,000 × 4/12 =	$260,800
Net receipt =	$739,200
Effective annual interest rate (as above)	4.62%

Using futures

Need to hedge against a fall in interest rates, therefore go long in the futures market. Awan Co needs March contracts as the investment will be made on 1 February.

No. of contracts needed = $48,000,000/$2,000,000 × 4 months/3 months = 32 contracts.

Basis

Current price (on 1/11) – futures price = total basis

(100 − 4.09) − 94.76 = 1.15

Unexpired basis = 2/5 × 1.15 = 0.46

If interest rates increase by 0.9% to 4.99%

Investment return (from above) =	$766,400
Expected futures price = 100 − 4.99 − 0.46 = 94.55	
Loss on the futures market	
(0.9455 − 0.9476) × $2,000,000 × 3/12 × 32	$(33,600)
Net return =	$732,800
Effective annual interest rate = $732,800/$48,000,000 × 12/4 =	4.58%

If interest rates decrease by 0.9% to 3.19%

Investment return (from above) =	$478,400
Expected futures price = 100 – 3.19 – 0.46 = 96.35	
Gain on the futures market	$254,400
(0.9635 – 0.9476) × $2,000,000 × 3/12 × 32	
Net return =	$732,800
Effective annual interest rate (as above) =	4.58%

Using options on futures

Need to hedge against a fall in interest rates, therefore buy call options. As before, Awan Co needs 32 March call option contracts

($48,000,000/$2,000,000 × 4 months/3 months).

If interest rates increase by 0.9% to 4.99%

Exercise price	94.50	95.00
Futures price	94.55	94.55
Exercise ?	Yes	No
Gain in basis points	5	0
Underlying investment return (from above)	$766,400	$766,400
Gain on options (0.0005 × 2,000,000 × 3/12 × 32, 0)	$8,000	$0
Premium		
0.00432 × $2,000,000 × 3/12 × 32	$(69,120)	
0.00121 × $2,000,000 × 3/12 × 32		$(19,360)
Net return	$705,280	$747,040
Effective interest rate	4.41%	4.67%

If interest rates decrease by 0.9% to 3.19%

Exercise price	94.50	95.00
Futures price	96.35	96.35
Exercise ?	Yes	Yes
Gain in basis points	185	135
Underlying investment return (from above)	$478,400	$478,400
Gain on options		
(0.0185 × 2,000,000 × 3/12 × 32)	$296,000	
(0.0135 × 2,000,000 × 3/12 × 32)		$216,000
Premium		
As above	$(69,120)	
As above		$(19,360)
Net return	$705,280	$675,040
Effective interest rate	4.41%	4.22%

Discussion

The FRA offer from Voblaka Bank gives a slightly higher return compared to the futures market; however, Awan Co faces a credit risk with over-the-counter products like the FRA, where Voblaka Bank may default on any money owing to Awan Co if interest rates should fall. The March call option at the exercise price of 94.50 seems to fix the rate of return at 4.41%, which is lower than the return on the futures market and should therefore be rejected. The March call option at the exercise price of 95.00 gives a higher return compared to the FRA and the futures if interest rates increase, but does not perform as well if the interest rates fall. If Awan Co takes the view that it is more important to be protected against a likely fall in interest rates, then that option should also be rejected. The choice between the FRA and the futures depends on Awan Co's attitude to risk and return, the FRA gives a small, higher return, but carries a credit risk. If the view is that the credit risk is small and it is unlikely that Voblaka Bank will default on its obligation, then the FRA should be chosen as the hedge instrument.

(b) The delta value measures the extent to which the value of a derivative instrument, such as an option, changes as the value of its underlying asset changes. For example, a delta of 0.8 would mean that a company would need to purchase 1.25 option contracts (1/0.8) to hedge against a rise in price of an underlying asset of that contract size, known as the hedge ratio. This is because the delta indicates that when the underlying asset increases in value by $1, the value of the equivalent option contract will increase by only $0.80.

The option delta is equal to $N(d_1)$ from the Black-Scholes Option Pricing (BSOP) formula. This means that the delta is constantly changing when the volatility or time to expiry change. Therefore even when the delta and hedge ratio are used to determine the number of option contracts needed, this number needs to be updated periodically to reflect the new delta.

Marking scheme		Marks
(a)	Calculation of impact of FRA for interest rate increase and decrease	2
	Decision to go long on futures	1
	Selection of March futures and options	1
	Unexpired basis calculation	1
	Impact of interest rates increase/decrease with futures	3
	Decision to buy call options	1
	Impact of interest rates increase/decrease with options	5
	Discussion (up to 2 marks available for general explanation of the products' features)	5–6
	Maximum	19
(b)	1–2 marks per well explained point **Maximum**	6
Total		25

77 KESHI CO (DEC 14)

Key answer tips

More than half the marks in the marking scheme for this question are for the discussion points rather than the calculations. Unfortunately, many students in the real exam focussed on the numbers exclusively so were unable to score a pass mark.

Always make sure that you attempt all parts of all questions in order to maximise your chances of passing the exam.

(a) **Using traded options**

Need to hedge against a rise in interest rates, therefore buy put options.

Keshi Co needs 42 March put option contracts ($18,000,000/$1,000,000 × 7 months/ 3 months).

Expected futures price on 1 February if interest rates increase by 0.5%

= 100 – (3.8 + 0.5) – 0.22 = 95.48

Expected futures price on 1 February if interest rates decrease by 0.5%

= 100 – (3.8 – 0.5) – 0.22 = 96.48

If interest rates increase by 0.5% to 4.3%

Exercise price	95.50	96.00
Futures price	95.48	95.48
Exercise?	Yes	Yes
Gain in basis points	2	52
Underlying cost of borrowing		
4.7% × 7/12 × $18,000,000	$493,500	$493,500
Gain on options		
0.0002 × $1,000,000 × 3/12 × 42	$2,100	
0.0052 × $1,000,000 × 3/12 × 42		$54,600
Premium		
0.00662 × $1,000,000 × 3/12 × 42	$69,510	
0.00902 × $1,000,000 × 3/12 × 42		$94,710
Net cost	$560,910	$533,610
Effective interest rate	5.34%	5.08%

If interest rates decrease by 0.5% to 3.3%

Exercise price	95.50	96.00
Futures price	96.48	96.48
Exercise?	No	No
Gain in basis points	0	0
Underlying cost of borrowing		
3.7% × 7/12 × $18,000,000	$388,500	$388,500
Gain on options	$0	$0
Premium	$69,510	$94,710
Net cost	$458,010	$483,210
Effective interest rate	4.36%	4.60%

Using swaps

	Keshi Co	Rozu Bank offer	Basis differential
Fixed rate	5.5%	4.6%	0.9%
Floating rate	LIBOR + 0.4%	LIBOR + 0.3%	0.1%

Prior to the swap, Keshi will borrow at LIBOR + 0.4% and swaps this rate to a fixed rate. Total possible benefit is 0.8% before Rozu Bank's charges.

Keshi Co borrows at	LIBOR + 0.4%
From swap Keshi Co receives	LIBOR
Keshi Co gets 70% of the benefit	
Advantage (70% × 0.8 – 0.10)	0.46%
Keshi Co's effective borrowing rate (after swap)	5.04%

Alternatively (Swap)

From swap Keshi Co receives	LIBOR
Keshi Co pays	4.54%
Effective borrowing rate (as above)	4.54% + 0.4% + 0.10% = 5.04%

Discussion and recommendation

Under each choice the interest rate cost to Keshi Co will be as follows:

	Doing nothing	95.50 option	96.00 option	Swap
If rates increase by 0.5%	4.7% floating; 5.5% fixed	5.34%	5.08%	5.04%
If rates decrease by 0.5%	3.7% floating; 5.5% fixed	4.36%	4.60%	5.04%

Borrowing at the floating rate and undertaking a swap effectively fixes the rate of interest at 5.04% for the loan, which is significantly lower than the market fixed rate of 5.5%.

On the other hand, doing nothing and borrowing at the floating rate minimises the interest rate at 4.7%, against the next best choice which is the swap at 5.04% if interest rates increase by 0.5%. And should interest rates decrease by 0.5%, then doing nothing and borrowing at a floating rate of 3.7% minimises cost, compared to the next best choice which is the 95.50 option.

On the face of it, doing nothing and borrowing at a floating rate seems to be the better choice if interest rates increase or decrease by a small amount, but if interest rates increase substantially then this choice will no longer result in the lowest cost.

The swap minimises the variability of the borrowing rates, while doing nothing and borrowing at a floating rate maximises the variability. If Keshi Co wants to eliminate the risk of interest rate fluctuations completely, then it should borrow at the floating rate and swap it into a fixed rate.

(b) Free cash flows and therefore shareholder value are increased when corporate costs are reduced and/or income increased. Therefore, consideration should be given to how the centralised treasury department may reduce costs and increase income.

The centralised treasury department should be able to evaluate the financing requirements of Keshi Co's group as a whole and it may be able to negotiate better rates when borrowing in bulk. The department could operate as an internal bank and undertake matching of funds. Therefore it could transfer funds from subsidiaries which have spare cash resources to ones which need them, and thus avoid going into the costly external market to raise funds. The department may be able to undertake multilateral internal netting and thereby reduce costs related to hedging activity. Experts and resources within one location could reduce duplication costs.

The concentration of experts and resources within one central department may result in a more effective decision-making environment and higher quality risk monitoring and control. Further, having access to the Keshi Co group's entire cash funds may give the company access to larger and more diverse investment markets. These factors could result in increasing the company's cash inflows, as long as the benefits from such activity outweigh the costs.

Decentralising Keshi Co's treasury function to its subsidiary companies may be beneficial in several ways. Each subsidiary company may be better placed to take local regulations, custom and practice into consideration. An example of custom and practice is the case of Suisen Co's need to use Salam contracts instead of conventional derivative products which the centralised treasury department may use as a matter of course.

Giving subsidiary companies more autonomy on how they undertake their own fund management may result in increased motivation and effort from the subsidiary's senior management and thereby increase future income. Subsidiary companies which have access to their own funds may be able to respond to opportunities quicker and establish competitive advantage more effectively.

(c) Islamic principles stipulate the need to avoid uncertainty and speculation. In the case of Salam contracts, payment for the commodity is made at the start of the contract. The buyer and seller of the commodity know the price, the quality and the quantity of the commodity and the date of future delivery with certainty. Therefore, uncertainty and speculation are avoided.

On the other hand, futures contracts are marked-to-market daily and this could lead to uncertainty in the amounts received and paid every day. Furthermore, standardised futures contracts have fixed expiry dates and pre-determined contract sizes. This may mean that the underlying position is not hedged or covered completely, leading to limited speculative positions even where the futures contracts are used entirely for hedging purposes. Finally, only a few commodity futures contracts are offered to cover a range of different quality grades for a commodity, and therefore price movement of the futures market may not be completely in line with the price movement in the underlying asset.

(**Note:** Credit will be given for alternative, relevant discussion for parts (b) and (c))

Marking scheme

		Marks
(a)	Buy put options and number of contracts	1
	Futures prices if interest rates increase or decrease	1
	Option contracts calculations: either exercise price	3
	Option contract calculations: second exercise price (or justification for calculations of just one exercise price)	2
	Swap: Keshi Co initially borrows at the floating rate and resulting advantage	2
	Swap impact	2
	Effective borrowing rate	1
	Discussion and recommendation	3–4
	Maximum	15
(b)	Discussion of why a centralised treasury department may increase value	3–4
	Discussion of reasons for decentralisation	2–3
	Maximum	6
(c)	1–2 marks per point **Maximum**	4
Total		25

78 DAIKON CO (JUN 15)

Key answer tips

In 2014, an article published on the ACCA website covered the market terminology associated with foreign exchange derivative products.

Therefore it was no surprise to see the topic tested in part (b) here.

Reading recent articles on the ACCA website is a critical part of preparing properly for the exam.

(a) Borrowing period is 6 months (11 months – 5 months)

Current borrowing cost = $34,000,000 × 6 months/12 months × 4.3% = $731,000

Borrowing cost if interest rates increase by 80 basis points (0.8%)

= $34,000,000 × 6/12 × 5.1% = $867,000

Additional cost = $136,000 [$34,000,000 × 6/12 × 0.8%]

Using futures to hedge

Need to hedge against a rise in interest rates, therefore go short in the futures market.

Borrowing period is 6 months

No. of contracts needed = $34,000,000/ $1,000,000 × 6 months/3 months

= 68 contracts.

Basis

Current price (on 1 June 20X5) – futures price = total basis

$(100 - 3.6) - 95.84 = 0.56$

Unexpired basis (at beginning of November) = $2/7 \times 0.56 = 0.16$

Assume that interest rates increase by 0.8% (80 basis points) to 4.4%

Expected futures price = $100 - 4.4 - 0.16 = 95.44$

Gain on the futures market = $(95.84 - 95.44) \times \$25 \times 68 =$		$68,000
Net additional cost = ($136,000 – $68,000)		$68,000

Using options on futures to hedge

Need to hedge against a rise in interest rates, therefore buy put options. As before, 68 put option contracts are needed ($34,000,000/$1,000,000 × 6 months/3 months).

Assume that interest rates increase by 0.8% (80 basis points) to 4.4%

Exercise price	95.50	96.00
Futures price	95.44	95.44
Exercise ?	Yes	Yes
Gain in basis points	6	56
Gain on options		
6 × $25 × 68	$10,200	
56 × $25 × 68		$95,200
Premium		
30.4 × $25 × 68	$51,680	
50.8 × $25 × 68		$86,360
Option benefit/(cost)	$(41,480)	$8,840
Net additional cost		
($136,000 + $41,480)	$177,480	
($136,000 – $8,840)		$127,160

Using a collar on options to hedge

Buy put options at 95.50 for 0.304 and sell call at 96.00 for 0.223

Net premium payable = 0.081

Assume that interest rates increase by 0.8% (80 basis points) to 4.4%

	Buy put	Sell call
Exercise price	95.50	96.00
Futures price	95.44	95.44
Exercise?*	Yes	No

(*The put option is exercised, since by exercising the option, the option holder has the right to sell the instrument at 95.50 instead of the market price of 95.44 and gain 6 basis points per contract. The call option is not exercised, since by not exercising the option, the option holder can buy the instrument at a lower market price of 95.44 instead of the higher option exercise price of 96.00)

Gain on options

6 × $25 × 68	$10,200

Premium payable

8.1 × $25 × 68	$13,770
Net cost of the collar	$3,570

Net additional cost

($136,000 + $3,570)	$139,570

Based on the assumption that interest rates increase by 80 basis points in the next five months, the futures hedge would lower the additional cost by the greatest amount and is significantly better than either of the options hedge or the collar hedge. In addition to this, futures fix the amount which Daikon Co is likely to pay, assuming that there is no basis risk. The benefits accruing from the options are lower, with the 95.50 option and the collar option actually increasing the overall cost. In each case, this is due to the high premium costs. However, if interest rates do not increase and actually reduce, then the options (and to some extent the collar) provide more flexibility because they do not have to be exercised when interest rates move in the company's favour. But the movement will need to be significant before the cost of the premium is covered.

On that basis, on balance, it is recommended that hedging using futures is the best choice as they will probably provide the most benefit to Daikon Co.

However, it is recommended that the points made in part (b) are also considered before a final conclusion is made.

(b) **Mark-to-market: Daily settlements**

2 June:

8 basis points (95.76 – 95.84) × $25 × 50 contracts = $10,000 loss

3 June:

10 basis points (95.66 – 95.76) × $25 × 50 contracts

+ 5 basis points (95.61 — 95.66) × $25 × 30 contracts = $16,250 loss

[Alternatively: 15 basis points (95.61 – 95.76) × $25 × 30 contracts + 10 basis points (95.66 – 95.76) × $25 × 20 contracts = $16,250 loss]

4 June:

8 basis points (95.74 – 95.66) × $25 × 20 contracts = $4,000 profit

Both mark-to-market and margins are used by markets to reduce (eliminate) the risk of non-payment by purchasers of the derivative products if prices move against them.

Mark-to-market closes all the open deals at the end of each day at that day's settlement price, and opens them again at the start of the following day. The notional profit or loss on the deals is then calculated and the margin account is adjusted accordingly on a daily basis. The impact on Daikon Co is that if losses are made, then the company may have to deposit extra funds with its broker if the margin account falls below the maintenance margin level. This may affect the company's ability to plan adequately and ensure it has enough funds for other activities. On the other hand, extra cash accruing from the notional profits can be withdrawn from the broker account if needed.

Each time a market-traded derivative product is opened, the purchaser needs to deposit a margin (initial margin) with the broker, which consists of funds to be kept with the broker while the position is open. As stated above, this amount may change daily and would affect Daikon Co's ability to plan for its cash requirements, but also open positions require that funds are tied up to support these positions and cannot be used for other purposes by the company.

The value of an option prior to expiry consists of time value, and may also consist of intrinsic value if the option is in-the-money. If an option is exercised prior to expiry, Daikon Co will only receive the intrinsic value attached to the option but not the time value. If the option is sold instead, whether it is in-the-money or out-of-money, Daikon Co will receive a higher value for it due to the time value. Unless options have other features, like dividends, attached to them, which are not reflected in the option value, they would not normally be exercised prior to expiry.

	Marking scheme		Marks
(a)	Additional interest cost		1
	Recommendation to go short if futures are used and purchase puts if options are used		1
	Calculation of number of contracts and remaining basis		2
	Futures contracts calculation		1
	Options contracts calculations		4
	Collar on options calculations		4
	Supporting comments and conclusion		2–3
		Maximum	**15**
(b)	Mark-to-market calculations (1 mark each for 2, 3 and 4 June)		3
	Impact of the daily mark-to-market		2–3
	Impact of the margin requirements		2–3
	Impact of the options sold instead of being exercised		2–3
		Maximum	**10**
	Note: Maximum of 7 marks if no mark-to-market calculations provided		
Total			**25**

79 THE ARMSTRONG GROUP (SEP/DEC 15)

Key answer tips

One of interest rate hedging or foreign currency hedging has been tested on every one of the AFM exams.

In this question, the examiner cleverly worked in both topics.

In order to guarantee success in the AFM exam, you cannot afford to question spot. The examiner tries very hard to avoid setting questions according to any logical pattern.

(a)   (i)

Owed by	Owed to	Local currency	$
		m	m
Armstrong (USA)	Horan (South (Africa)	US $12.17	12.17
Horan (South Africa)	Massie (Europe)	SA R42.65	3.97
Giffen (Denmark)	Armstrong (USA)	D Kr21.29	3.88
Massie (Europe)	Armstrong (USA)	US $19.78	19.78
Armstrong (USA)	Massie (Europe)	€1.57	2.13
Horan (South Africa)	Giffen (Denmark)	D Kr16.35	2.98
Giffen (Denmark)	Massie (Europe)	€1.55	2.11

Owed to			Owed by		
	Giffen (De)	Armtg (US)	Horan (SA)	Massie (Eu)	Total
	$m	$m	$m	$m	$m
Giffen (De)			2.98		2.98
Armtg (US)	3.88			19.78	23.66
Horan (SA)		12.17			12.17
Massie (Eu)	2.11	2.13	3.97		8.21
	———	———	———	———	
Owed by	(5.99)	(14.30)	(6.95)	(19.78)	
Owed to	2.98	23.66	12.17	8.21	
Net	(3.01)	9.36	5.22	(11.57)	

Under the terms of the arrangement, Massie, as the company with the largest debt, will pay Horan $5.22m, as the company with the smallest amount owed. Then Massie will pay Armstrong $6.35m and Giffen will pay Armstrong $3.01 m.

(ii)   The Armstrong Group may have problems if any of the governments of the countries where the subsidiaries are located object to multilateral netting. However, this may be unlikely here.

The new system may not be popular with the management of the subsidiaries because of the length of time before settlement (up to six months). Not only might this cause cash flow issues for the subsidiaries, but the length of time may mean that some of the subsidiaries face significant foreign exchange risks. The system may possibly have to allow for immediate settlement in certain circumstances, for example, if transactions are above a certain size or if a subsidiary will have significant cash problems if amounts are not settled immediately.

(b)   Need to hedge against a fall in interest rate, therefore buy call options. Require 50 contracts (25,000,000/1,000,000) × 6/3. As Massie is looking to invest on 30 November, December contracts are needed.

Basis

Current price (1 September) – futures price = basis

$(100 - 3.6) - 95.76 = 0.64$

Unexpired basis = $1/4 \times 0.64 = 0.16$

Option

Amount received will be (LIBOR − 0.4%) × 25,000,000 × 6/12

If interest rates increase by 0.5% to 4.1%

Expected futures price = (100 − 4.1) − 0.16 = 95.74

Exercise price	97.00	96.50
Futures price	95.74	95.74
Exercise option?	No	No
Gain in basis points	–	–
	€	€
Interest received		
(€25m × 6/12 × (4.1 − 0.4)%)	462,500	462,500
Gain on options	–	–
Premium		
(3.2 × €25 × 50)	(4,000)	
(18.2 × €25 × 50)		(22,750)
	————	————
Net receipt	458,500	439,750
	————	————
Effective interest rates	3.67%	3.52%

If interest rates fall by 0.5% to 3.1%

Expected futures price = (100 − 3.1) − 0.16 = 96.74

Exercise price	97.00	96.50
Futures price	96.74	96.74
Exercise option?	No	Yes
Gain in basis points	–	24
	€	€
Interest received		
(€25m × 6/12 × (3.1 − 0.4)%)	337,500	337,500
Gain on options		
(0 and 24 × €25 × 50)	–	30,000
Premium		
(3.2 × €25 × 50)	(4,000)	
(18.2 × €25 × 50)		(22,750)
	————	————
Net receipt	333,500	344,750
	————	————
Effective interest rates	2.67%	2.76%

Using a collar

Buy December call at 97.00 for 0.032 and sell December put at 96.50 for 0.123. Net premium received = 0.091.

If interest rates increase to 4.1%.

	Buy call	Sell put
Exercise price	97.00	96.50
Futures price	95.74	95.74
Exercise option?	No	Yes
	€	
Interest received	462,500	
Loss on exercise		
(76 × €25 × 50)	(95,000)	
Premium		
(9.1 × €25 × 50)	11,375	
	———	
Net receipt	378,875	
Effective interest rate	3.03%	

If interest rates fall to 3.1%

	Buy call	Sell put
Exercise price	97.00	96.50
Futures price	96.74	96.74
Exercise option?	No	No
	€	
Interest received	337,500	
Loss on exercise	–	
Premium		
(9.1 × €25 × 50)	11,375	
	———	
Net receipt	348,875	
Effective interest rate	2.79%	

Summary

	97.00	96.50	Collar
Interest rates rise to 4.1%	3.67%	3.52%	3.03%
Interest rates fall to 3.1%	2.67%	2.76%	2.79%

The option with the 97.00 exercise price has a higher average figure than the option with the 96.50 exercise price, and can be recommended on that basis, as its worst result is only marginally worse than the 96.50 option. There is not much to choose between them. The collar gives a significantly worse result than either of the options if interest rates rise, because Massie cannot take full advantage of the increase. It is marginally the better choice if interest rates fall. The recommendation would be to choose the option with the 97.00 exercise price, unless interest rates are virtually certain to fall.

		Marking scheme		Marks
(a)	(i)	Dollar amounts owed and owing		2
		Totals owed and owing		3
		Net amounts owed		1
		Payments and receipts		2
				___
			Maximum	8
				___
	(ii)	1–2 marks per problem discussed		
				___
			Maximum	3
				___
(b)		Recommendation to purchase calls		1
		Number and month of contracts		1
		Calculation of basis		1
		Options contracts calculations		4
		Collars approach and calculations		5
		Comments and conclusion		2–3
				___
			Maximum	14
				___
Total				25
				___

80 BURYECS CO (MAR/JUN 17)

Key answer tips

Currency swaps are rarely tested, but well prepared students would have read the recent examiner's technical article and so should have expected this question. It was pleasing to see that the question covered the topic in a very similar way to the article.

The currency options were 'over the counter' options so it would have been important to realise that (unlike with traded options) there was no need to calculate the number of contracts.

As ever, students may have struggled to complete everything in the time available, but there were some easy marks throughout the discussion parts for students with a good exam technique.

(a) The currency swap will involve Buryecs Co taking out a loan in € and making an arrangement with a counterparty in Wirtonia, which takes out a loan in $. Buryecs Co will pay the interest on the counterparty's loan and vice versa.

Advantages

Payment of interest in $ can be used to match the income Buryecs Co will receive from the rail franchise, reducing foreign exchange risk.

Buryecs Co will be able to obtain the swap for the amount it requires and may be able to reverse the swap by exchanging with the other counterparty. Other methods of hedging risk may be less certain. The cost of a swap may also be cheaper than other methods of hedging, such as options.

The swap can be used to change Buryecs Co's debt profile if it is weighted towards fixed-rate debt and its directors want a greater proportion of floating rate debt, to diversify risk and take advantage of probable lower future interest rates.

Drawbacks

The counterparty may default. This would leave Buryecs Co liable to pay interest on the loan in its currency. The risk of default can be reduced by obtaining a bank guarantee for the counterparty.

The swap may not be a worthwhile means of hedging currency risk if the exchange rate is unpredictable. If it is assumed that exchange rates are largely determined by inflation rates, the predicted inflation rate in Wirtonia is not stable, making it more difficult to predict future exchange rates confidently. If the movement in the exchange rate is not as expected, it may turn out to have been better for Buryecs Co not to have hedged.

Buryecs Co is swapping a fixed rate commitment in the Eurozone for a floating rate in Wirtonia. Inflation is increasing in Wirtonia and there is a risk that interest rates will increase as a result, increasing Buryecs Co's finance costs.

The swap does not hedge the whole amount of the receipt in Year 3. Another method will have to be used to hedge the additional receipt from the government in Year 3 and the receipts in the intervening years.

If the government decides to impose exchange controls in Wirtonia, Buryecs Co may not be able to realise the receipt at the end of Year 3, but will still have to fulfil the swap contract.

(b)   (i)

	Buryecs	Counterparty	Interest rate benefit
Eurozone	4.0%	5.8%	1.8%
Wirtonia	Bank rate + 0.6%	Bank rate + 0.4%	0.2%
			———
Gain on swap (60:40)	1.2%	0.8%	2.0%
Bank fee (60:40)	(0.3%)	(0.2%)	(0.5%)
	———	———	———
Gain on swap after fee	0.9%	0.6%	1.5%
	———	———	———

The swap arrangement will work as follows:

	Buryecs	Counterparty
Buryecs borrows at	4.0%	
Counterparty borrows at		Bank rate + 0.4%
Counterparty receives		(Bank rate)
Buryecs pays	Bank rate	
Counterparty pays		4.6%
Buryecs receives	(4.6%)	
Advantage	120 basis points	80 basis points
Net result	Bank rate − 0.6%	5.0%

After paying the 30 point basis fee, Buryecs Co will effectively pay interest at the bank rate – 0.3% and benefit by 90 basis points or 0.9%. The counterparty will effectively pay interest at 5.2% and benefit by 60 basis points or 0.6%.

(ii)   Using the purchasing power parity formula to calculate exchange rates:

$S_1 = S_0 \times (1 + h_c)/(1 + h_b)$

Year	1	2	3
	$0.1430 \times 1.06/1.03$	$0.1472 \times 1.04/1.08$	$0.1417 \times 1.03/1.11$
	= 0.1472	= 0.1417	= 0.1315

At Year 3, $5,000 million will be exchanged at the original spot rate as per the agreement and the remaining inflows will be exchanged at the Year 3 rate.

Year	0	1	2	3
	$m	$m	$m	$m
Initial fee	(5,000)			
Payment at end of franchise				7,500
Annual income		600	600	600
Exchange rates	0.1430	0.1472	0.1417	0.1315
	€m	€m	€m	€m
Swap translated at 0.1430	(715)			715
Amount not covered by swap (7,500 – 5,000) translated at 0.1315				329
Annual income		88	85	79
Cash flows in home currency	(715)	88	85	1,123
Discount factors at 14%	1	0.877	0.769	0.675
Present value	(715)	77	65	758

The net present value of the project is €185 million, indicating that it should go ahead. However, the value is dependent on the exchange rate, which is worsening for the foreign income. If there are also uncertainties about the variability of returns during the three years, the directors may consider the project to be in excess of their risk appetite and decline the opportunity.

As a result of the exchange rates on the initial fee being fixed at the year 0 spot rate, Buryecs Co has gained $5,000 million × (0.1430 – 0.1315) × 0.675 = €39 million.

(c)   Receipt using swap arrangement = €715m + €329m = €1,044m

Receipt if transaction unhedged = $7,500m × 0.1315 = €986m

Predicted exchange rate at year 3 is €0.1315 = $1 or $7.6046 = €1

Options

Buy $ put options as receiving $.

$7.75 exercise price

Do not exercise

Net receipt = €986m – (1.6% × $7,500m × 0.1430) = €969m

$7.25 exercise price

Exercise

Receipt from government = $7,500m/7.25 = €1,034m

Net receipt = €1,034m − (2.7% × $7,500m × 0.1430) = €1,005m

The $7.25 option gives a better result than not hedging, given the current expectations of the exchange rate. However, it gives a worse result than the swap even before the premium is deducted, because of the exchange rate being fixed on the swap back of the original amount paid. These calculations do not take into account possible variability of the finance costs associated with the swap, caused by swapping into floating rate borrowing.

81 WARDEGUL CO (SEP/DEC 17)

Key answer tips

Part (a) covered FRAs, futures, and options over futures in exactly the same way as in many previous exam questions. With any hedging question, it is important to follow a systematic approach to setting the hedges up in the first place, before then going on to show the results of the hedges. There were no unexpected complexities here.

Part (b) covered the issue of centralisation of treasury activities. It would have been important to read the requirement carefully here. Note that you are asked to consider only the advantages of operating a regional treasury compared to the alternatives.

(a)   Forward rate agreement

FRA 5.02% (4–9) since the investment will take place in four months' time for a period of five months.

	D
If interest rates increase by 1.1% to 5.3%	
Investment return = 5.0% × 5/12 × D27,000,000=	562,500
Payment to bank = (5.3% − 5.02%) × 5/12 × D27,000,000=	(31,500)
	———
Net receipt =	531,000
Effective annual interest rate = 531,000/27,000,000 × 12/5=	4.72%
If interest rates fall by 0.6% to 3.6%	
Investment return = 3.3% × 5/12 × D27,000,000=	371,250
Receipt from bank = (5.02% − 3.6%) × 5/12 × D27,000,000=	159,750
	———
Net receipt =	531,000
Effective annual interest rate (as above)	4.72%

Futures

Go long in the futures market, as the hedge is against a fall in interest rates. Use March contracts, as investment will be made on 31 January.

Number of contracts = D27,000,000/D500,000 × 5 months/3 months = 90 contracts

Basis

Current price (1 October) – futures price = basis (100 – 4.20) – 94.78 = 1.02

Unexpired basis on 31 January = 2/6 × 1.02 = 0.34

	D
If interest rates increase by 1.1% to 5.3%	
Investment return (from above) =	562,500
Expected futures price = 100 – 5.3 – 0.34 = 94.36	
Loss on the futures market	
(0.9436 – 0.9478) × D500,000 × 3/12 × 90	(47,250)
	———
Net return =	515,250
Effective annual interest rate = 515,250/27,000,000 × 12/5=	4.58%
If interest rates fall by 0.6% to 3.6%	
Investment return (from above) =	371,250
Expected futures price = 100 – 3.6 – 0.34 = 96.06	
Gain on the futures market	
(0.9606 – 0.9478) × D500,000 × 3/12 × 90	144,000
	———
Net return =	515,250
Effective annual interest rate (as above) =	4.58%

Options on futures

Buy call options as need to hedge against a fall in interest rates. As above, 90 contracts required.

If interest rates increase by 1.1% to 5.3%

Exercise price	94.25	95.25
Futures price as above	94.36	94.36
Exercise ?	Yes	No
Gain in basis points	11	0
	D	D
Underlying investment return (from above)	562,500	562,500
Gain on options (0.0011 × 500,000 × 3/12 × 90)	12,375	$0
Premium		
0.00545 × D500,000 × 3/12 × 90	(61,313)	
0.00098 × D500,000 × 3/12 × 90		(11,025)
	———	———
Net return	513,562	551,475
Effective interest rate	4.56%	4.90%

If interest rates fall by 0.6% to 3.6%

Exercise price	94.25	95.25
Futures price	96.06	96.06
Exercise ?	Yes	Yes
Gain in basis points	181	81
	D	*D*
Underlying investment return (from above)	371,250	371,250
Gain on options		
(0.0181 × D500,000 × 3/12 × 90)	203,625	
(0.0081 × D500,000 × 3/12 × 90)		91,125
Premium		
As above	(61,313)	
As above		(11,025)
	———	———
Net return	513,562	451,350
Effective interest rate	4.56%	4.01%

Discussion

The forward rate agreement gives the highest guaranteed return. If Wardegul Co wishes to have a certain cash flow and is primarily concerned with protecting itself against a fall in interest rates, it will most likely choose the forward rate agreement. The 95.25 option gives a better rate if interest rates rise, but a significantly lower rate if interest rates fall, so if Wardegul Co is at all risk averse, it will choose the forward rate agreement.

This assumes that the bank which Wardegul Co deals with is reliable and there is no risk of default. If Wardegul Co believes that the current economic uncertainty may result in a risk that the bank will default, the choice will be between the futures and the options, as these are guaranteed by the exchange. Again the 95.25 option may be ruled out because it gives a much worse result if interest rates fall to 3.6%. The futures give a marginally better result than the 94.25 option in both scenarios but the difference is small. If Wardegul Co feels there is a possibility that interest rates will be higher than 5.41%, the point at which the 94.25 option would not be exercised, it may choose this option rather than the future.

(b) Regional functions compared with national functions

Organising treasury activities on a regional basis would be consistent with what is happening in the group overall. Other functions will be organised regionally. A regional treasury function may be able to achieve synergies with them and also benefit from information flows being organised based on the regional structure.

If, as part of a reorganisation, some treasury activities were to be devolved outside to a bank or other third party, it would be simpler to arrange for a single provider on a regional basis than arrange for separate providers in each country.

A regional function will avoid duplication of responsibilities over all the countries within a region. A regional function will have more work to do, with maybe a greater range of activities, whereas staff based nationally may be more likely to be under-employed. There may be enough complex work on a regional basis to justify employing specialists in particular treasury areas which will enhance the performance of the function. It may be easier to recruit these specialists if recruitment is done regionally rather than in each country.

Regional centres can carry out some activities on a regional basis which will simplify how funds are managed and mean less cost than managing funds on a national basis. These include pooling cash, borrowing and investing in bulk, and netting of foreign currency income and expenditure.

Regional centres could in theory be located anywhere in the region, rather than having one treasury function based in each country. This means that they could be located in the most important financial centres in each region or in countries which offered significant tax advantages.

From the point of view of Wardegul Co's directors and senior managers, it will be easier to enforce common standards and risk management policies on a few regional functions than on many national functions with differing cultures in individual countries.

Regional functions compared with global function

Wardegul Co is being reorganised on a regional basis because of the demands of its global expansion. As discussed above, reorganising treasury functions regionally will be consistent with the way other functions are organised. Reorganising the treasury function regionally will be one way of dealing with the problem of having a single, overstretched, global function.

A regional function could employ experts with knowledge of the regulations, practices and culture of the major countries within the region. It may be more difficult for a global function to recruit staff with local expertise.

There may be practical issues why individual countries prefer to deal with regional functions rather than a global function, for example, a regional function will be based in the same, or similar, time zone as the countries in its region.

A regional function may have better ideas of local finance and investment opportunities. There may, for example, be better alternatives for investment of the surplus funds than the centralised function has been able to identify.